D1593837

THE HANDBOOK
OF JEWISH THOUGHT

VOLUME 2

The
HANDBOOK
of Jewish Thought

Volume 2

By

Rabbi Aryeh Kaplan *z"l*

1934—1983 / 5695—5743

Edited by

Abraham Sutton

MOZNAIM PUBLISHING CORPORATION
NEW YORK / JERUSALEM 5753 (1992)

This book is dedicated to the memory of
Rabbi Aryeh Kaplan

הרה״ג אריה משה אליהו ז״ל
בן שמואל ופייגא קפלן
נפטר י״ד שבט תשמ״ג
תהא נשמתו צרורה בצרור החיים

לזכר נשמות
רחמים בן שאול
ג׳מילה בת דוד הלוי
שאול בן רחמים
ת.נ.צ.ב.ה.

For information write:

Moznaim Publishing Corporation
4304 12th Avenue
Brooklyn, New York 11219
Tel. (718) 438-7680 853-0525

Printed and bound in Jerusalem, Israel
by Vagshal Ltd.
Typesetting by Vagshal Ltd.
Jerusalem

Printed in Israel

CONTENTS

Editor's Foreword

It is with mixed feelings of gratitude and trepidation that we present these original writings by the late Rabbi Aryeh Kaplan of blessed memory. We are grateful for the privilege of presenting some of the earliest material that the author left behind awaiting final editing and publication. We are also fearful, however, lest the terse, almost notation-like, style of the author's early writings be a barrier to the average reader. Only a patient and careful reading of the material, chapter after chapter, will convince the reader that herein lies a treasure-house of knowledge and wisdom of inestimable value.

The bulk of the present volume is from the author's original 1967-1969 manuscript that consisted of 40 chapters. Thirteen of these chapters were prepared for publication by Rabbi Kaplan himself and published in 1979 as the *Handbook of Jewish Thought — Volume I*. It is clear that the remaining chapters were set aside with the thought of eventually preparing them for publication. Of these remaining chapters, 25 are presented here.

For anyone interested in the development of Rabbi Kaplan's thinking, the present volume preserves important original material not reproduced anywhere else which might otherwise have been lost. It also contains Rabbi Kaplan's original formulation of many of the key ideas which inform his later writings. Thus, even in cases of overlap with other later works, the present volume is to be valued if only because it pre-dates everything else he wrote.

This foreword is not the place for a biographical sketch of the author. Suffice to say that he was an extraordinary man. In order to get an idea of the breadth, depth and power of his mind, the reader is requested to peruse the following list of over 60 original books, translations, booklets, and essays. Even one who has not read all or any of these works, and is therefore unable to fully appreciate the magnitude of such an explosive writing career, will still conclude that Rabbi Kaplan was indeed an extraordinary man. Pay close attention to the dates. [Wherever possible, Rabbi Kaplan's record of the date of completion of a work has been given. If this was not available, the first date of publication appears instead.] Notice that he worked on many books either simultaneously or in such rapid succession as to defy explanation.

1. First Manuscript of the *Handbook of Jewish Thought* (1962)
2. Second Manuscript of the *Handbook of Jewish Thought* (1967-1969)
3. *The God of Israel* (essay, 8 pages, published February, 1972)
4. *On Immortality and the Soul* (essay, 9 pages, published May, 1972)
5. *Rabbi Nachman's Wisdom* (translation, 452 pages, completed May, 1972)
6. *On Extraterrestrial Life* (essay, 4 pages, published December, 1972)
7. *Belief in God* (essay, 12 pages, published 1973)
8. *Free Will and the Purpose of Creation* (essay, 11 pages, published 1973)
9. *The Jew* (essay, 14 pages, published 1973)
10. *Love and the Commandments* (essay, 17 pages, published 1973)
11. *The Structure of Jewish Law* (essay, 14 pages, published 1973)
12. *God, Man and Tefillin* (booklet, 80 pages, published 1973)
13. *Maimonides' Principles* (booklet, 88 pages, completed June, 1973)
14. *The Real Messiah* (7 essays, 50 pages, published 1973)
15. *Rabbi Nachman's Tikun* (translation, published 1973)
16. *Immortality and the Soul* (essay, 9 pages, published 1974)
17. *Paradoxes* (essay, 8 pages, published 1974)
18. *Sabbath — Day of Eternity* (booklet, 51 pages, published 1974)
19. *Love Means Reaching Out* (booklet, 85 pages, completed March, 1974)
20. *Derekh HaShem — The Way of God* (translation and notes, 407 pages, completed June, 1974)
21. *The Light Beyond — Adventures in Chassidic*

Thought (translation and commentary, 372 pages, completed September, 1974)

22. *The Chassidic Masters* (biography and translation, 189 pages, completed January, 1975)

23. *A Call to the Infinite* (translation, 257 pages, completed July, 1975)

24. *Waters of Eden — The Mystery of the Mikvah* (booklet, 91 pages, published 1976)

25. *Jerusalem — The Eye of the Universe* (booklet, 112 pages, published 1976)

26. *Meditation and the Bible* (book, 179 pages, completed March, 1976)

27. *Sefer Yetzirah* (translation and commentary, First Draft begun September 1, 1976 and completed October 3, 1976; Final Draft begun November 24, 1976 and completed December 28, 1976; 406 pages, published posthumously 1990)

28. *The Torah Anthology — Volume I* (translation and notes, 540 pages, completed March, 1977)

29. *The Torah Anthology — Volume II* (translation and notes, 600 pages, completed July 1, 1977)

30. *The Torah Anthology — Volume III* (translation and notes, 708 pages, completed October 13, 1977)

31. *The Torah Anthology — Book of Esther* (translation and notes, 268 pages, completed December 13, 1977)

32. *The Torah Anthology — Passover Haggadah* (translation and notes, 288 pages, completed January 20, 1978)

33. *The Torah Anthology — Volume IV* (translation and notes, 280 pages, completed May 14, 1978)

34. *The Torah Anthology — Volume V* (translation and notes, 425 pages, completed July 12, 1978)

35. *The Handbook of Jewish Thought — Volume I* (315 pages, completed September, 1978)

36. *The Torah Anthology — Pirkey Avoth* (translation and notes, 400 pages, completed February 14, 1979)

37. *The Torah Anthology — Volume VI* (translation and notes, 534 pages, completed June 5, 1979)

38. *The Torah Anthology — Volume VII* (translation and notes, 310 pages, completed August 1, 1979)
39. *Sefer Bahir* (translation and commentary, published 1979)
40. *The Torah Anthology — Volume VIII* (translation and notes, 240 pages, completed November 15, 1979)
41. *The Infinite Light* (booklet, 69 pages, completed November 1979)
42. *Outpouring of the Soul* (translation, 96 pages, completed July 1980)
43. *The Living Torah* (translation, commentary, bibliography, charts, maps, index, 1423 pages, compiled in 9 months, completed August, 1980)
44. *Gems of Rabbi Nachman* (translation, 180 pages, published 1980)
45. *The Torah Anthology — Volume IX* (translation and notes, 403 pages, completed January 8, 1981)
46. *The Torah Anthology — Volume X* (translation and notes, 358 pages, completed February 9, 1981)
47. *The Torah Anthology — Volume XI* (translation and notes, 459 pages, completed March 6, 1981)
48. *The Torah Anthology — Volume XII* (translation and notes, 360 pages, completed March 27, 1981)
49. *The Torah Anthology — Tisha B'Av* (translation, 142 pages, completed in 3 days, May 1981)
50. *The Torah Anthology — Volume XV* (translation and notes, 253 pages, completed June 8, 1982)
51. *The Torah Anthology — Volume XIII* (edited and notes, 448 pages, completed August 19, 1982)
52. *The Torah Anthology — Volume XIV* (edited and notes, 478 pages, completed August 31, 1982)
53. *Meditation and Kabbalah* (book, published 1982)
54. *Made in Heaven — A Jewish Wedding Guide* (book, 234 pages, completed November, 1982)
55. *Rabbi Nachman's Stories* (translation and commentary, 552 pages, completed November, 1982)

56. *Jewish Meditation* (book, 165 pages, completed December, 1982)
57. *The Torah Anthology — Volume XVI* (Rabbi Kaplan died leaving only a rough draft of the translation, 318 pages, published 1984)
58. *If You Were God* (essay, 17 pages, published posthumously 1983)
59. *A World of Love* (essay, 42 pages, published posthumously 1983)
60. *The Aryeh Kaplan Reader* (collected essays, published posthumously 1983)
61. *Tzitzith — A Thread of Light* (booklet, 95 pages, published posthumously 1984)
62. *Until the Messiah — The Life of Rabbi Nachman* (biography and translation, 384 pages, published posthumously 1985)
63. *Innerspace — Introduction to Kabbalah, Meditation and Prophecy* (private classes, 254 pages, edited posthumously 1987-1990)
64. *Encounters* (book, 128 pages, published posthumously 1990)
65. *Moreh Or* (original Hebrew manuscript, 94 pages, published posthumously 1992)
66. *Handbook of Jewish Thought — Volume II* (397 pages, edited posthumously 1991-1992)

ONE

BELIEF IN GOD

1:1   Faith in God is the foundation of Judaism without which all else is worthless.[1] Faith is not just the utterance of words, however, but a firm belief and conviction with one's mind and heart.[2] It is also a commitment to be acted upon, with an earnest adherence to the course prescribed by God.[3] It is for this reason that belief alone without obedience to God is an absurdity. Likewise, good deeds alone without belief in God are worthless.[4]

1:2   Our faith begins with the traditions which have been transmitted to us by our ancestors and in our sacred literature.[5] Through these, we know of God, His works and His teachings. The Torah thus tells us, "Ask your father and he will tell you, your grandfather and he will inform you" (Deuteronomy 32:7). It also declares, "Listen Israel, God is our Lord, God is One" (*ibid.* 6:4), which implies that one is to accept these truths on the basis of hearing and understanding them.[6]

1:3   There are some who maintain that this is only a first step, whereas the highest level of faith comes from the philosophical proof of these truths. According to this opinion, one who has the ability is required to attempt to prove the foundations of our faith. This is alluded to in such passages as "Know that God is the Lord,

---

1.   *Yad, Yesodey HaTorah* 1:6; Ramban on *Sefer HaMitzvoth,* Positive Commandment 1.
2.   *Moreh Nevukhim* 1:50.
3.   *Cf. Kuzari* 1:115, 4:13; *Chinukh* 25.
4.   *Cf.* Ibn Ezra on Proverbs 30:19. See Volume 1, 5:30.
5.   *Moreh Nevukhim* 1:34; Radak on 1 Chronicles 28:29.
6.   *Targum ad. loc. s.v. Kabel; Shiltey Gibborim, Avodah Zarah* (Rif 5b) no. 1. *Cf.* Bachya, Sforno, *ad. loc.*

He made us and we are His" (Psalms 100:3), which indicate that the final goal is knowledge rather than mere tradition.[7]

1:4   There are others, however, who maintain that the highest faith is that derived through tradition alone, in which case metaphysical proof should only be used as a last resort to preclude disbelief.[8] According to this opinion, a well reasoned faith and a deep knowledge of God can be obtained from tradition alone.[9]

1:5   In the final analysis, one should strive to learn the foundations of our faith and acquire a deep understanding of them, since belief based upon mere habit and blind tradition is a weak faith which can be assailed by doubts and overthrown by arguments.[10]

1:6   A strong faith is therefore based upon both reason and tradition, as the prophet taught, "Do you not know? Have you not heard? Was it not told to you from the beginning? Do you not understand how the earth was founded?" (Isaiah 40:21).[11] Similarly, we are taught, "Know the God of your father" (1 Chronicles 28:9). In each case, one is commanded to know and understand rationally that which has been taught and received by tradition.[12]

1:7   If one has the ability, he should use his knowledge to add to what has been derived from tradition. Thus, we read, "This is my God and I will glorify Him, my father's God and I will exalt Him" (Exodus 15:2), which indicates that He is my God through my own understanding, at the same time that He is

7.   *Moreh Nevukhim* 3:51; *Chovoth HaLevavoth* 1:3; Ibn Ezra on Exodus 20:1; *Sefer Mitzvoth Gadol,* Positive Commandment 2; *Amudey Shlomo* (Maharshal) *ad. loc.* Compare *Yad, Yesodey HaTorah* 1:1 and *Sefer HaMitzvoth,* Positive Commandment 1.

8.   *Kuzari* 2:26 (end), 5:1; *Akedath Yitzchak* 36. See *Shiltey Gibborim loc. cit.* who maintains that it is forbidden to engage in secular studies. A detailed discussion of this controversy is brought in *Kol Yehudah* on *Kuzari* 5:21 *s.v. VeNe'ezov.* This may also be related to the controversy between Rabbi Simlai and Rabbi Nachman ben Yitzchak (*Makkoth* 24a) whether the foundation of our faith is "Seek Me and live" (Amos 5:4), or "The righteous lives by his faith" (Habakkuk 2:4).

9.   *Zohar* 2:25a; *Cheredim* 1 (p. 30); *Sefer Chasidim* 14; *B'rith Olam* (Chida) *ad. loc. Cf. Kuzari* 5:21.

10. *Reshith Chokhmah, Shaar HaYirah* 15 (50b); *Sh'nei Luchoth HaB'rith, Mesekheth Rosh HaShanah* 2:156b (note).

11. Ibn Ezra, Radak, *ad. loc.; Emunoth VeDeyoth,* introduction 6.

12. Radak, *Metzudoth David, ad. loc.; Akedath Yitzchak* 16; *Sh'nei Luchoth HaB'rith, BeAsarah Maamaroth* 1:64a.

my father's God through tradition.[13] We similarly pray, "Our
God and God of our fathers"[14] and are called "believers, sons of
believers."[15]

1:8   If one is able, he should learn enough science to be able to
recognize the world as the work of God and comprehend His
greatness, as the prophet declares, "Lift up your eyes to the
stars and see Who has created them" (Isaiah 40:26).[16] If one is a
scholar, he should do this when he cannot otherwise engage in
religious studies.[17]

1:9   At the same time, one should avoid useless metaphysical
speculation[18] as well as the study of philosophy in general, since
they tend to undermine one's faith.[19] If one is in a position where

13. *Sh'nei Luchoth HaB'rith loc. cit.*
14. *Teshuvoth Panim Meiroth* 1:39, quoted in *Taamey HaMinhagim* (p. 43). The Maggid
     of Mezrich (1704-1772) taught, "A person must strongly rely upon the tradition he
     has received from his fathers, but at the same time also arrive at faith through his
     own philosophical endeavors. This is the best and most perfect kind of faith. It is
     for this reason that we say, 'Our God' and then, 'God of our fathers'"; *Likutey
     Yekarim* 199, quoted in Kaplan, *Chasidic Masters* (Moznaim, 1984), p. 47.
15. *Shabbath* 97a.
16. *Cf.* Radak *ad. loc.* and on Isaiah 5:12; *Shabbath* 75a; *Kuzari* 5:21; Ibn Ezra on Exodus
     20:1; *Sefer Chasidim* 14; *Cheredim,* Positive Commandments 1:22.
17. *Cf. Yoreh Deah* 246:4 in *Hagah*; Bertenoro on *Avoth* 5:22 *s.v. U'Minah*; *Tosefoth Yom
     Tov, Sanhedrin* 10:1 *s.v. BeSefarim; Amudey Yerushalayim, Yerushalmi, Sanhedrin* 10:1
     (50b). See, however, *Yad, Yesodey HaTorah* 4:10, 4:13 and *Talmud Torah* 1:12, where
     this may be counted as religious study in itself. See also Maharal, *Tifereth Yisrael* 11.
     The truth is that many great and righteous individuals were expert in the seven
     sciences of antiquity: grammar, rhetoric, logic, arithmetic, music, geometry and
     astronomy. They could accomplish this without spiritual harm only after they had
     spent many years serving God with truth and simplicity, no matter how much sacrifice
     it entailed. Then, when they reached a level where their fear of God came even before
     their Torah wisdom (*cf. Avoth* 3:11), they were able to study secular subjects to benefit
     the world. Even in such cases they did not spend very much time on such studies, but
     learned them quickly and returned to their simple path. Their faith and simplicity were
     so great that these subjects could not harm them. However, if one has not attained
     the path of simplicity, these studies can be very harmful. Regarding secular studies,
     it is written, "Whoever comes to her will not return; he will never attain the paths
     of life" (Proverbs 2:19); see Kaplan, *Rabbi Nachman's Stories,* p. 182.
18. *Chagigah* 2:1; *Emunoth VeDeyoth,* Introduction 6; *Moreh Nevukhim* 1:32; *Sefer
     Mitzvoth Gadol,* Negative Commandment 15.
19. *Teshuvoth HaRosh* 25; *Teshuvoth Rashba* 419; Rabbenu Tam, *Sefer HaYashar* 6:13;
     Rav Hai Gaon on *Chagigah* 14b (in *Eyn Yaakov); Yad, Avodah Zarah* 2:2-3; Rabbi
     Meir Aldebei, *Sheveiley Emunah* 8 (p. 100); *Shiltey Gibborim loc. cit.*; Bertenoro on
     Sanhedrin 10:1 *s.v. Sifrey; Sh'nei Luchoth HaB'rith, Mesekheth Shevuoth* 2:92b; HaGra,
     Yoreh Deah 179:13; *Iggeroth Moshe, Yoreh Deah* 3:53. Regarding the prohibition of
     "Greek wisdom," see *Sotah* 9:14; *Menachoth* 64b, 99b; *Tosefta, Avodah Zarah* 1:3
     (end); *cf. Yerushalmi, Peah* 1:1 (3a); *Yerushalmi, Sotah* 9:15 (46a).

he must engage in such studies, he may do so,[20] but with the utmost caution.[21]

1:10 The path to true faith is through the observance and study of our religious teachings. Even if one feels that his faith is weak, he should continue his observances and studies and they will bring him back to God.[22] We are taught that God said, "If they would have abandoned Me but kept My Torah, its inherent light would have brought them back to Me."[23]

1:11 Conversely, if one does not study our religious teachings, he may find himself not observing the commandments. This will lead him to look down upon those who do observe, and even hate our religious teachers. He may then try to prevent others from observing, for he will have found a way to deny the divine origin of the commandments. In the end, he will be led to deny God Himself. The Torah warns about this type of progression when it says, "[But this is what will happen] if you do not listen to Me, and do not keep all these commandments: You will come to denigrate My decrees and grow tired of My laws. You will not keep all My commandments and you will end up nullifying My covenant" (Leviticus 26:15).[24]

1:12 If one is confronted by questions and doubts concerning our religious fundamentals, he should have faith that these questions are answerable. There is nothing that can stand before absolute faith, as the prophet taught us, "The righteous *lives* by his faith" (Habakkuk 2:4).

---

20. *Tosafoth, Menachoth* 64b *s.v. Arur;* Rash, *Peah* 1:1, from *Sotah* 49b; *Yerushalmi, Shabbath* 6:1 (34a); *Magen Avoth* on *Avoth* 2:14. See also Rambam, Bertenoro, *Sotah* 9:14 who interpret "Greek wisdom" as a sophistic idiom, rather than as philosophy per se. This is supported by the Talmud; *cf.* Rashi, *Sotah* 49b, *Bava Kama* 83a, *s.v. Chokhmath.* Nevertheless, *Menachoth* 99b may be referring to philosophy, as indicated by *Tosefta, Avodah Zarah* above, and this would also answer the question of *Tosafoth, Menachoth* 64b.
21. *Cf.* Rambam on *Avoth* 2:14; *Tosefoth Yom Tov ad. loc. s.v. VeDa.*
22. *Nazir* 23b; *Yad, Teshuvah* 10:5.
23. Reading of *Reshith Chokhmah, Shaar HaTeshuvah* 6 (123c), from *Yerushalmi, Chagigah* 1:7 (6b); *Eikhah Rabbah,* introduction:2; *Pesikta* 15 (121a); *Yalkut Shimoni* 2:282.
24. *Sifra* (111c), Rashi, *ad. loc.; Yalkut Shimoni* 1:673. See Kaplan, *Torah Anthology,* Volume 12, p. 304.

1:13   If one feels that his faith is wavering, he should carefully weigh the possible loss that disbelief will entail against whatever profit it will bring.[25]

1:14   One should trust one's own belief, and not doubt his own motives.[26]

1:15   Some nonbelievers try to explain away our belief psychologically. However, the same argument can be used regarding their disbelief. Furthermore, there is considerable objective evidence for the truth of our religion.

1:16   There are many teachings in our religion that are known only from tradition and cannot be proven at all. There is a limit beyond which rational proof fails and breaks down, and this is where we must rely upon faith and tradition.[27]

1:17   Nevertheless, the Torah does not oblige us to believe absurdities,[28] and one should carefully examine the sources of farfetched common beliefs to determine whether they actually have a basis in tradition. Regarding this it is written, "The fool believes everything, but the prudent man will follow the right path" (Proverbs 14:15).[29]

1:18   Therefore, one must carefully study and trust the words and writings of our prophets and sages. Belief in our great religious leaders, who are the shepherds of our faith, is equated with belief in God Himself. We are thus taught, "Believing in the faithful shepherd is like believing in the One Who spoke and brought the universe into existence."[30] Similarly, it is written, "Believe in God and you will be established; believe in His prophets and you will prosper" (2 Chronicles 20:20).

1:19   The highest level of faith, which is attained only by unique

---

25.   *Cf. Avoth* 2:1; *Bava Bathra* 78b.

26.   *Cf. Avoth* 2:13; *Chagigah* 15a; Maharatz Chajas, *Niddah* 30b.

27.   *Cf. Emunoth VeDeyoth* 3:3; Rambam, *Iggereth Techiyath HaMethim* (Warsaw, 1926), p. 10.

28.   *Ikkarim* 1:2. Rabbi Abraham ben HaRambam, introduction to *Eyn Yaakov;* Ramchal, *Maamar HaAggadah.*

29.   Ralbag *ad. loc.; Moreh Nevukhim* 1:62; *Emunoth VeDeyoth,* Introduction 6.

30.   *Mekhilta* on Exodus 14:31 (33b); *Yalkut Shimoni* 1:240; *Avoth* 6:5; *Machzor Vitri ad. loc. s.v. Emunath. Cf. Bava Kama* 41b; *Pesachim* 22b; *Berakhoth* 64b; *Yoma* 71a; *Kethuvoth* 111b; *Yad, Deyoth* 6:2.

individuals such as our prophets and holy men, is the transcendence of their very physical nature until they actually experience the Divine,[31] and can say "This is my God" (Exodus 15:2).[32] Once a person has experienced this, there can never be a doubt in his mind, as he has surpassed mere faith and belief and has attained the unambiguous cognizance of God.[33] To one who has never experienced this, it is as unimaginable as color is to the blind.

1:20   Belief in God and our religious fundamentals is our most precious possession and must be guarded accordingly. The Bible recognizes the atheist and calls him a fool, as it is written, "The fool says in his heart, there is no God" (Psalms 14:1).

1:21   We are therefore commanded not to let atheistic thoughts or material desires undermine our faith, as the Torah declares, "Do not stray after your heart or after your eyes" (Numbers 15:39).[34] This is a negative commandment, depending upon thought, and can be observed at any time by asserting one's will and refusing to be led astray from our faith.[35]

1:22   One should therefore avoid all thoughts and actions which may undermine his faith. Similarly, one should avoid any speculations regarding the truth of our religious fundamentals. Unless one begins with a firm belief in our religious traditions, such speculation is apt to result in a belief quite different than that preserved through the ages.[36]

1:23   We are commanded to avoid any speculations which might undermine our faith, as the Torah states, "Do not turn aside to idols" (Leviticus 19:4), which also refers to the conceptual idols which are set up to oppose our faith.[37] Included in this is an

31. *Shaarey Kedushah* 1; *Mesilath Yesharim* 26.
32. *Cf.* Rashi *ad. loc.; Mekhilta ad. loc.* (37a) and 20:19 (64a).
33. *Kuzari* 4:5; Rashi on Exodus 20:19; Ramban on Exodus 19:9.
34. *Sifri ad. loc.; Berakhoth* 12b; *Yad, Avodath Kokhavim* 2:3; *Sefer HaMitzvoth,* Negative Commandment 47; *Sefer Mitzvoth Gadol,* Negative Commandment 15.
35. *Chinukh* 387; *Chayay Adam* 1:5 no. 6.
36. *Yad loc. cit.*
37. *Cf. Sifra ad. loc.* (87a); Ramban *ad. loc.; Yerushalmi, Avodah Zarah* 3:1 (18a). *Sefer HaMitzvoth,* Negative Commandment 10; *Sefer Mitzvoth Gadol,* Negative Commandment 14; *Chinukh* 213.

injunction not to read books which preach atheistic ideas,[38] and which lead people away from God.[39]

1:24   One should be familiar enough with the basics of our religion[40] and its rational arguments[41] in order to know how to answer the nonbeliever. However, religious debates can undermine one's faith and should generally be avoided, as scripture warns, "Do not answer a fool according to his folly, lest you become like him yourself" (Proverbs 26:4).[42]

1:25   One should therefore only engage in a religious debate when it is initiated by the nonbeliever and there is danger that he might influence others,[43] and even in such a case one should not debate unless he is thoroughly familiar with the question and skillful in debate.[44] If one has confidence that he can prevail, he may debate, as we are taught, "Answer a fool according to his folly, lest he be wise in his own eyes" (Proverbs 26:5).[45]

1:26   The above only applies to a non-Jewish atheist. However, one should avoid debate with a Jewish nonbeliever entirely, even in the above case,[46] since experience has shown that a Jewish nonbeliever is likely to be more intolerant of a faithful Jew than his non-Jewish counterpart.[47] Worst of all are those who were once religious and have left the path of true belief. Any argument with them is only likely to strengthen their disbelief, as we are taught, "Whoever

---

38. *Yad, Avodath Kokhavim* 2:2; *Orach Chaim* 307:16; *Shiltey Gibborim loc. cit.; cf. Shabbath* 149a.
39. *Sanhedrin* 10:1; Bertenoro *ad. loc.; Sanhedrin* 100b, Rif (19b), Rosh (11:3), *ad. loc.,* that it is counted among the sins for which one loses his portion in the World to Come; *cf. Amudey Yerushalayim loc. cit.; BaMidbar Rabbah* 14:14 (end).
40. *Avoth* 2:14; Rabbenu Yonah *ad. loc.* interprets this that one should study Torah in order to know what to answer an atheist. *Cf.* Rashi, *Sanhedrin* 38b *s.v. K'dey.*
41. Ramban, Meiri, *Magen Avoth, ad. loc.,* interpret the Mishnah to mean that one should specifically study philosophical arguments to answer an atheist; *cf.* Rashi *ad. loc.* The reading of Rabbenu Chananel (*Sanhedrin* 38b) is "be dilligent to know what to answer an atheist"; *cf. Kuzari* 5:16.
42. *Sefer Chasidim* 296; *cf. Avodah Zarah* 27b.
43. Rabbenu Yonah, *Avoth* 2:14.
44. *Sanhedrin* 38b.
45. *Sefer Chasidim loc. cit.; cf.* Rashi, *Shabbath* 30b *s.v. BeDivrey.* Accordingly, we find such debates in *Chagigah* 5b; *Eruvin* 53b, 101a; *Sukkah* 48b; *Sanhedrin* 39a, 99a; *Avodah Zarah* 4a, etc.
46. *Sanhedrin* 38b; *cf. Yad, Avodath Kokhavim* 2:5.
47. *Pesachim* 49b; *Tana DeBei Eliahu Zuta* 16 (24a).

comes to her (atheism) will not return; he will never attain the paths of life" (Proverbs 2:19).[48]

1:27   One should therefore avoid conversing with atheists, and keep away from them as much as possible, as it is written, "Remove your way far from her, and do not come near the door of her house" (Proverbs 5:8).[49] This is particularly true of Jewish atheists, whom one should not even befriend in an attempt to return them to the faith.[50]

1:28   In case of danger, it is preferable to enter a church or house of idolatry than to enter that of a Jew who is an avowed nonbeliever, since the non-Jew is ignorant of our belief, while the Jew knows the truth and denies it.[51]

1:29   Such a Jewish atheist or nonbeliever is considered to be completely outside the Jewish fold and is viewed as a non-Jew as far as all rituals are concerned.[52] One is not even required to mourn his death[53] nor love him as a fellow Jew, as it is written, "Do I not hate those who hate You, O God? Do I not contend with those who rise up against You?" (Psalms 139:21).[54]

1:30   Just as we are warned to keep away from such people, so, conversely, are we commanded to associate with our sages and holy men. The Torah therefore states, "Cling to Him" (Deuteronomy 10:20), which means that one should bring himself close to God by associating with those who emulate His ways.[55]

---

48.   Rambam on *Avoth* 2:14; *Sefer Chasidim loc. cit.; cf. Avodah Zarah* 17a.
49.   *Avodah Zarah* 17a; *Rosh* 1:18; *Yad, Avodath Kokhavim* 2:5; *cf. Avoth* 1:7; *Yad, Deyoth* 6:1; 2 Chronicles 20:37; *Tosafoth, Avodah Zarah* 27b *s.v. Lo.*
50.   *Mekhilta* to 18:1 (57b); *Avoth DeRabbi Nathan* 9:4; *Yalkut Shimoni* 2:3. *Cf. Kesef Mishneh, Lechem Mishneh, Avodath Kokhavim* 2:5.
51.   *Shabbath* 116b. *Cf. Yoreh Deah* 157:3; *Chokhmath Adam* 88:14. See below, Chapter 4, note 9.
52.   *Yad, Avodath Kokhavim* 2:5, *Mamrim* 3:2; Rambam, *Chullin* 1:2; *cf. Chullin* 6a. See *Gittin* 45b; *Orach Chaim* 39:1; *Yoreh Deah* 281:1; *Chullin* 13a; *Yoreh Deah* 2:5; *Yad, Avoth HaTumoth* 9:10; *Shabbath* 116a; *Orach Chaim* 334:21; *Choshen Mishpat* 32:22; *Beer HaGolah ad. loc.; Choshen Mishpat* 266:2.
53.   *Semachoth* 2:10; *Yad, Avel* 1:10; *Yoreh Deah* 345:5.
54.   *Shabbath* 116a; Rambam on *Sanhedrin* 10:1. *Cf. Pesachim* 113a.
55.   *Kethuvoth* 111b; *Yad, Deyoth* 6:2; *Sefer HaMitzvoth,* Positive Commandment 6; *Sefer Mitzvoth Gadol,* Positive Commandment 8; *Chinukh* 434; *cf. Avoth* 1:4. See *Megillath Esther,* Positive Commandment 7; Rabbenu Yonah, *Shaarey Teshuvah* 3:51.

1:31   Faith and trust in God are partners,[56] since one who believes in an omniscient, omnipotent and benevolent God must also believe that He will provide for His faithful.[57] Therefore, one should trust in God and not be overly concerned about the future. It is thus written, "Commit your way to God. Trust in Him and He will do [for you]" (Psalms 37:5), and "Blessed is the man who trusts in God; God will be his trust" (Jeremiah 17:7).[58]

1:32   Therefore, one should not seek to ascertain the future by fortune-telling, astrology[59] or other superstitions.[60] Concerning this, the Torah commands us, "You must remain totally faithful to God your Lord" (Deuteronomy 18:13),[61] which some authorities count as a positive commandment.[62]

1:33   Trusting in God does not mean that one should neglect to make any future plans, nor does it mean that one should sit back and depend upon God to miraculously feed him[63] or neglect one's health and expect God to keep him sound.[64] Regarding these it is written, "A man's foolishness perverts his way; in his heart he ends up blaming [his misfortunes on] God" (Proverbs 19:3).

1:34   One should certainly not place himself in danger and then rely upon a miracle to save him.[65]

1:35   Even in situations where miracles were likely to occur, our sages would not depend upon them,[66] and even refused to benefit from them.[67]

56. *Reshith Chokhmah, Shaar HaAhavah* 12 (100a).
57. *Chovoth HaLevavoth* 4:3.
58. *Sotah* 48b; *Reshith Chokhmah, Shaar HaAhavah* 12 (98b). *Cf.* Rabbi Yosi, *Yerushalmi, Berakhoth* 5:1 (37a). See *Degel Machaneh Ephraim, BeShalach* (33c), quoted in Kaplan, *The Light Beyond* 5:20.
59. *Pesachim* 113b; *Yoreh Deah* 179:1; *Tosafoth, Shabbath* 156b *s.v. Kaldai.*
60. *Sanhedrin* 65b; *Yad, Avodath Kokhavim* 11:4; *Yoreh Deah* 179:3.
61. *Sifri,* Rashi, Ramban, *ad. loc.; Yad, Avodath Kokhavim* 11:16; *Cheredim,* Positive Commandments 1:21.
62. Ramban, additions to *Sefer HaMitzvoth,* Positive Commandment 6.
63. *Chovoth HaLevavoth* 4:4; *cf. Shabbath* 53b.
64. *Cf. Moreh Nevukhim* 3:12.
65. *Shabbath* 32b; *Taanith* 20b; *Yoreh Deah* 116:5 in *Hagah. Cf. Megillah* 7b; *Pesachim* 50b; *Bava Metzia* 106a; *Chovoth HaLevavoth loc. cit.; Kuzari* 5:20 (51b); *Zohar* 1:111b; *Sefer Chasidim* 196; *Chinukh* 546.
66. *Yerushalmi, Shekalim* 6:3 (26b); Rashi, *Shabbath* 124a *s.v. MiShum;* Bertenoro, *Shekalim* 6:4; *Tosefoth Yom Tov, Demai* 1:1 *s.v. VeHaChometz;* Maharatz Chajas, *Yoma* 2a. *Cf. Pesachim* 64b, where this is disputed, and see Rabbi Yechezkel Landau, *Tzion LeNefesh Chayah ad. loc.*
67. *Taanith* 24b; Maharatz Chajas, *Nedarim* 50a.

1:36   If one is engaged in a good deed, he may trust in God and ignore a possible danger. Still, if danger is likely, he is required to take heed.[68]

1:37   We are commanded not to test God by asking for a miracle[69] or demanding an immediate reward for our good deeds,[70] as it is written, "Do not test God your Lord" (Deuteronomy 6:16).[71] The only exception to this is the commandment of charity, regarding which God says, "Bring all the tithes... and with this put Me to the test, says the God of Hosts, to see if I open for you the windows of heaven, and pour out for you an overflowing blessing" (Malachi 3:10).[72]

1:38   Some maintain that one may ask God for a sign to help him make a difficult decision if there is no other logical means available,[73] but this should only be used as a last resort.[74] On the other hand, it is an ancient custom to ask a child his lesson[75] or randomly open a sacred book[76] to help one arrive at a decision.

1:39   Very great is the reward of faith. We thus find that our ancestors were redeemed from Egypt because of their faith and trust in God.[77]

---

68. *Kiddushin* 39b. *Cf. Kuzari* 5:23.
69. *Chovoth HaLevavoth loc. cit.; Kuzari* 5:20.
70. *Sefer Mitzvoth Gadol,* Negative Commandment 4; *Chinukh* 424, from *Taanith* 9a (top).
71. See Ramban *ad. loc.;* Rabbenu Yonah, *Shaarey Teshuvah* 3:30.
72. *Taanith* 9a, *Yoreh Deah* 247:4 in *Hagah,* and *Sefer Chasidim* 144, apply this to charity, but others maintain that it is limited to the tithing of harvests; *cf. Pith'chey Teshuvah, Yoreh Deah* 247:2, from *Teshuvoth Yaabetz* 1:3; *Sh'nei Luchoth HaB'rith, Mesekheth Megillah, Amud HaTzedakah* 2:223a. *Cf. Teshuvoth Chavath Yair* 224; *Teshuvoth Shevuth Yaakov* 2:85-86; *Teshuvoth Peney Yehoshua* 2; Maharshal on *Sefer Mitzvoth Gadol,* Negative Commandment 4. For discussion of monetary tithing, see *Tosafoth, Taanith* 9a *s.v. Asser; Turey Zahav, Yoreh Deah* 331:32.
73. Like Eliezer in Genesis 24:12, Gideon in Judges 6:37-40, Jonathan in 1 Samuel 14:8-10; *Chullin* 95b; Raavad, *Avodath Kokhavim* 11:4; *Tur, Yoreh Deah* 179; Radak on 1 Samuel 14:9; *Yoreh Deah* 179:4 in *Hagah;* HaGra *ad. loc.* 179:11.
74. See Rashi, *Tosafoth, Chullin* 95b; *Yad, Avodath Kokhavim* 11:4; *Sefer Mitzvoth Gadol,* Negative Commandment 51, all of whom forbid it as superstition. See above, 1:32.
75. Rabbi Yochanan, *Chullin* 95b; *Sefer Mitzvoth Gadol loc. cit.* explains that this is because it resembles prophecy; *cf. Bava Bathra* 12b; *Chagigah* 15a-b.
76. Sh'muel, *Chullin* 95b. See *Birkey Yosef, Yoreh Deah* 179; *Teshuvoth Mahari Bruno* 101.
77. *Mekhilta* on Exodus 14:31 (33b); *Yalkut Shimoni* 1:240.

TWO

LOVE OF GOD

2:1   We are commanded to love God, as the Torah states, "Love God your Lord with all your heart, with all your soul, and with all your might" (Deuteronomy 6:5).[1] This is a commandment which depends upon thought and can be fulfilled at any time.[2]

2:2   There are five observances which constantly remind us of our love for God since they involve either a reading or parchment containing the above commandment. They are: the reading of the *Sh'ma* morning and evening, the *Tefillin* on the arm and head, and the *Mezuzah*.[3] Because of its great importance, the love of God is mentioned no less than nine times in the Book of Deuteronomy alone.[4]

2:3   There are two paths to loving God.[5] When a person considers all the good that God does and how He constantly watches and sustains him,[6] he feels obliged to love God just as one would love any other benefactor.[7] Regarding such love, the Psalmist said, "I love God, for He has heard my voice and my plea; because He listened to me on the day I called" (Psalms 116:1).[8] Similarly, we are taught that we should love and praise God for every breath

---

1.   *Yad, Yesodey HaTorah* 2:1; *Sefer HaMitzvoth,* Positive Commandment 3; *Sefer Mitzvoth Gadol,* Positive Commandment 3; *Zohar* 3:263b.
2.   *Chinukh* 418. *Cf.* Ibn Ezra on Exodus 20:1.
3.   *Sefer Mitzvoth Gadol,* Positive Commandment 3; *Reshith Chokhmah, Shaar HaAhavah* 1 (51a).
4.   *Reshith Chokhmah loc. cit.;* Deuteronomy 6:5, 10:12, 11:1, 13:22, 16:20, 19:9, 30:6.
5.   *Zohar* 1:12a; *Chovoth HaLevavoth* 10:2; *Sh'nei Luchoth HaB'rith, BeAsarah Maamaroth* 1:74b; Commentary on *Yad, Yesodey HaTorah* 2:1. *Cf. Avoth* 5:16.
6.   *Reshith Chokhmah, Shaar HaAhavah* 9 (82c); *Sefer Mitzvoth Gadol,* Positive Commandment 3.
7.   *Sefer Chasidim* 31.
8.   See Radak, *Midrash Tehillim, ad. loc.; Yalkut Shimoni* 2:874.

that He allows us to draw.[9] However, this is not the highest level of love, since when one loves God only for the good that he receives, he may abandon his love when things go badly.[10]

2:4   The more a person understands God's true greatness, the more he loves Him for what He is, and for no other reason.[11] In order to achieve this love, one should therefore strive to understand God's greatness from His works.[12] Since such love depends upon nothing other than God Himself, it will prevail even if and when one is beset with troubles. Regarding this it is written, "Many waters cannot quench the love [for God], nor can the floods drown it" (Song of Songs 8:7).

2:5   The study of God's teachings and commandments also brings one to love Him. Our sages thus teach us, "It is written, 'Love God your Lord with all your heart, with all your soul, and with all your might' (Deuteronomy 6:5). But how is such love to be attained? The following verse tells you: 'These words which I am commanding you today must remain on your heart' (*ibid.* 6:6). By immersing yourself in the study of the Torah, you will come to recognize God and cling to His ways."[13]

2:6   True love of God is the desire to understand Him and His teachings[14] and do everything possible to bring oneself close to Him. It is as powerful as the love between man and woman,[15] as the prophet said, "With my soul I have desired You in the night; with my spirit within me I have ardently sought You" (Isaiah 26:9). It is a constant and longing thirst for God, as the Psalmist

---

9. *Devarim Rabbah* 2:26, from Psalms 150:6, "Let everything that has breath (soul and intelligence) praise God, Halleluyah!"; *cf.* Radak *ad. loc.*
10. *Avoth* 5:16. *Cf. Tana DeBei Eliahu Rabbah* 28 (109a); *Zohar* 1:12a; *Sifri, Yalkut Shimoni* (1:837), Rashi, on Deuteronomy 6:5. See *Pele Yo'etz s.v. Ahavah LeHaKadosh Barukh Hu* (1b top).
11. *Emunoth VeDeyoth* 2:13; *Moreh Nevukhim* 3:51. *Cf. Kuzari* 4:5.
12. *Yad, Yesodey HaTorah* 2:2; *Hagahoth Maimonioth ad. loc.; Sefer HaMitzvoth*, Positive Commandment 3; *Kin'ath Sofrim ad. loc.; Chinukh* 418; *Teshuvoth HaRambam (P'er HaDor)* 347; *Sefer Chasidim* 14; *Reshith Chokhmah, Shaar HaAhavah* 5 (63d). See below, note 20.
13. *Sifri*, Rashi, *Yalkut Shimoni* (1:839), *ad. loc.*, also quoted in *Sefer HaMitzvoth, Chinukh, loc. cit.*
14. *Yad, Yesodey HaTorah* 2:2. *Cf. Moreh Nevukhim* 1:30; *Cheredim*, Positive Commandments 1:5.
15. *Sefer Chasidim* 14. *Cf. Cheredim*, Positive Commandments 1:6.

exclaimed, "My soul thirsts for God, for the living God. When will I come and appear before God?" (Psalms 42:3).[16]

2:7 The love of God implies three things in observing His commandments.[17] First, it implies that one will have a strong desire to do God's will, so that one continually seeks out ways to serve Him. A person who loves God will seek to serve Him beyond mere ritual requirements, while one who serves God out of fear or habit alone will do no more than required.[18]

2:8 Second, the love of God implies a strong enthusiasm in obeying His commandments. Even the most difficult observances no longer seem burdensome, while the most trivial practices become highly meaningful. Observance then becomes a great joy, as the Psalmist exclaimed, "Serve God with joy, come before Him with song!" (Psalms 100:2).[19]

2:9 Third, love of God implies a closeness to Him in all walks of life. Such closeness involves knowledge and understanding of God, as well as resembling Him to the greatest possible degree. The Psalmist refers to this when he sings, "For me, the nearness of God is good. I have made God my refuge, that I may tell all His works" (Psalms 73:28). The Psalmist is telling us that his ultimate good is closeness to God. This closeness involves "telling all His works" — that is, a deep knowledge and perception of the Divine.[20]

2:10 A person who truly loves God does not serve Him out of any hope of reward, but for His own sake alone. This is the most perfect way to serve God.[21] However, one who serves God for no

16. *Chovoth HaLevavoth* 10:1; *Reshith Chokhmah, Shaar HaAhavah* 1 (51c).
17. *Cf. Bereshith Rabbah* 80:6; *Reshith Chokhmah, Shaar HaAhavah* 3 (59b); *Mesilath Yesharim* 19.
18. *Cf. Tana DeBei Eliahu Rabbah* 16 (78a), 28 (108b); *Reshith Chokhmah, Shaar HaAhavah* 1 (51b); *Yerushalmi, Berakhoth* 9:5 (67a).
19. *Cf.* Deuteronomy 28:47; *Ikkarim* 3:33; *Reshith Chokhmah, Shaar HaAhavah* 1 (52a), quoting *Rokeach*.
20. Radak *ad. loc.; Moreh Nevukhim* 1:18; *Zohar Chadash, VaYeshev*, quoted in *Mikdash Me'at, Beth HaMidrash ad. loc.; cf.* Ramban on Deuteronomy 11:22; *Cheredim*, Positive Commandments 1:10. *Cf. Yad, Teshuvah* 10:3.
21. *Avoth* 1:3; *Sifri*, Rashi, on Deuteronomy 11:13; *Nedarim* 62a; *Yad, Teshuvah* 10:1-4; *Yoreh Deah* 246:21 in *Hagah; Sefer Chasidim* 63; *Reshith Chokhmah, Shaar HaAhavah* 1 (51b); *Sh'nei Luchoth HaB'rith, BeAsarah Maamaroth* 1:79b; *Pele Yo'etz, Ahavah LeHaKadosh Barukh Hu* (1a-b).

other reason than to receive reward is still considered perfectly righteous,[22] as long as he does not regret it when the reward is not immediately forthcoming.[23] One should have faith that God will reward all good in the end.[24]

2:11   When a person truly loves God, all worldly passions, riches and honors are as nothing compared to this love. The Psalmist thus sang, "Whom have I in heaven but You? And having You, I desire nothing else on earth" (Psalms 73:25).[25] Although love for God exceeds all else, one should avoid asceticism as a way of life. Our sages therefore teach us that it is forbidden to abstain from the pleasures of this world completely.[26] The way of the righteous is to use even worldly things as a means to bring themselves closer to God.[27]

2:12   One who truly loves God, loves Him more than his possessions, his family, and even his very own self. He is therefore willing to sacrifice anything required by God, even life itself.[28]

2:13   Therefore, one who forsakes any religious duty, no matter how minor, because of his love of worldly things, is guilty of violating the commandment to love God.[29]

2:14   Love of God implies the abhorrence of all that runs counter to God's plan and hence all evil. It is thus written, "Those who love God hate evil" (Psalms 97:10).[30]

22.   *Pesachim* 8a; *Rosh HaShanah* 4a; *Bava Bathra* 10b; *Tosefoth Yom Tov, Avoth* 1:3; *Yad, Teshuvah* 10:5.

23.   *Tosafoth, Pesachim* 8b *s.v. SheYizkeh, Rosh HaShanah* 4a *s.v. BiShvil;* Maharsha *ad. loc.; Tosafoth, Avodah Zarah* 19a *s.v. Al Menath; Tikuney Zohar,* p. 76, quoted in *Reshith Chokhmah, Shaar HaAhavah* 1 (51c). *Cf. Chinukh* 428. Also see *Sotah* 14a; Maharatz Chajas, Maharsha, *ad. loc. s.v. Omar Lo.*

24.   *Cf. Avoth DeRabbi Nathan* 5:2; *Sefer Chasidim* 301.

25.   *Sh'nei Luchoth HaB'rith, BeAsarah Maamaroth* 1:79b; *Chovoth HaLevavoth* 9:2.

26.   *Taanith* 22b, 11a; *Tosafoth ad. loc. s.v. Amar; Yerushalmi, Kiddushin* 4:12 (48b); *Tana DeBei Eliahu Rabbah* 14 (72b); *Yad, Deyoth* 1:4; *Kuzari* 2:50; *Emunoth VeDeyoth* 10:4. *Cf. Yerushalmi, Peah* 8:8 (37b); *Yerushalmi, Nedarim* 9:1 (29a). Also see *Orach Chaim* 571:1.

27.   *Mesilath Yesharim* 13; *Likutey Amarim (Tanya), Sefer Shel Benonim* 7 (11a*ff.*). *Cf. Zohar* 3:263b; *Moreh Nevukhim* 3:51; *Yad, Deyoth* 3:1-2.

28.   *Berakhoth* 61b; *Zohar* 1:12a; *Sefer Mitzvoth Gadol,* Positive Commandment 3; *Sefer Chasidim* 14; *Reshith Chokhmah, Shaar HaAhavah* 1 (52b). *Cf.* Genesis 22:12; *Sotah* 31a.

29.   *Chinukh* 418, quoted in *Chayay Adam* 1:5 no. 4.

30.   *Emunoth VeDeyoth* 2:13, from Psalms 139:21; *Sh'nei Luchoth HaB'rith, BeAsarah Maamaroth* 1:79b; *Likutey Amarim, Sefer Shel Benonim* 10 (15a).

2:15 One who loves God seeks to bring others close to Him, both by example[31] and by persuasion.[32]

2:16 One who brings others to God by setting a good example is also considered to have fulfilled the commandment of *Kiddush HaShem* (קִידוּשׁ הַשֵׁם), literally "sanctification of the Name." This is what God meant when when He said, "I shall be sanctified among the children of Israel" (Leviticus 22:32), which means that the Jewish people are to publicize the greatness of God and His Torah.[33]

2:17 Therefore, one who does good without any expectation of reward or recognition, and without any fear of punishment, but simply for the sake of God, thereby demonstrates that God's teachings are a perfect end in themselves, and sanctifies God.[34]

2:18 Similarly, an observant person or religious leader who leads an exemplary life, setting an example that others will desire to follow, sanctifies God by demonstrating how His teachings lead to human perfection. Regarding such a person, it is written, "And He said to me: You, Israel, are My servant, through whom I am honored" (Isaiah 49:3).[35]

2:19 Just as we are commanded to sanctify God, so are we cautioned not to cause *Chillul HaShem* (חִילוּל הַשֵׁם), literally "desecration of the Name." God thus warned, "Do not desecrate My holy name" (Leviticus 22:32). This is a commandment not to do anything which could make people despise God or His teachings.[36] It is one of the most serious sins,[37] for which one is punished even for an accidental transgression,[38] and it is not expiated except by death.[39]

---

31. *Yoma* 86a; *Tana DeBei Eliahu Rabbah* 28 (108b).
32. *Sifri* on Deuteronomy 6:5, quoted in *Yalkut Shimoni* 1:837; *Sefer HaMitzvoth,* Positive Commandment 3; *Chinukh* 418; *Sefer Chasidim* 14; *Cheredim,* Positive Commandments 1:9; *Sh'nei Luchoth HaB'rith, BeAsarah Maamaroth* 1:79b; *Mesilath Yesharim* 19.
33. *Sefer HaMitzvoth,* Positive Commandment 9.
34. *Yad, Yesodey HaTorah* 5:10. *Cf. Sotah* 10b; *Maharatz Chajas ad. loc.*
35. *Yad, Yesodey HaTorah* 5:11, from *Yoma* 86a.
36. *Sefer Mitzvoth Gadol,* Negative Commandment 2; *Sefer HaMitzvoth,* Negative Commandment 63; *Chinukh* 295.
37. *Zohar* 3:231a; *Yerushalmi, Nedarim* 3:9 (12b); Rabbenu Yonah, *Shaarey Teshuvah* 3:158; *Reshith Chokhmah, Shaar HaYirah* 15 (45c).
38. *Avoth* 4:4. See *Tosefoth Yom Tov ad. loc.*
39. *Yoma* 86a; Rashi *ad. loc. s.v. BeOznai; Yad, Teshuvah* 1:4. See next note, and below, 17:4, 17:23-25.

2:20   A person who goes his way, ignoring God completely, is guilty of desecrating His name. Regarding those who say, "Let us eat and drink, for tomorrow we shall die" (Isaiah 22:13), God told His prophet, "Surely they will not be forgiven for this sin until they die" (*ibid.* 22:14).[40]

2:21   Similarly, one who wantonly sins out of spite, without deriving any benefit therefrom, is guilty of desecrating God's name.[41]

2:22   A religious person or scholar can desecrate God's name merely by not being absolutely scrupulous in his business dealings and personal conduct, or by displaying bad manners or weak morality, since he causes people to wonder what benefit there is to religious observance.[42]

2:23   If one has the opportunity to sanctify God's name, he should refuse any money or honor that might detract from it. We learn this from Abraham, who replied to the king of Sodom, "I have lifted my hand [in an oath] to God Most High, Possessor of heaven and earth! Not a thread or a shoelace! I will not take anything that is yours! You should not be able to say, 'It was I who made Abram rich'" (Genesis 14:22-23).[43] Nothing should be more precious in one's eyes than God's honor.[44]

2:24   There is no reward greater than that of one who serves God out of love. We are taught that the reward for a commandment observed with love is twice that of one without love.[45] No accuser on high can speak evil against one who truly loves God.[46] The reward for such love comes directly from God Himself.[47]

40.   *Yoma, Yad, ibid.;* Radak *ad. loc.* See also *Tosafoth, Yoma* 85b *s.v. Chutz.*
41.   *Yad, Yesodey HaTorah* 5:10; Rambam, *Iggereth HaShmad,* p. 13, from swearing falsely where one derives no benefit. *Cf.* Leviticus 19:12; *Sifra ad. loc.* (88c); Rashi on Leviticus 22:32. See *Minchath Chinukh* 296 (end).
42.   *Yad, Yesodey HaTorah* 5:11, from *Yoma* 86a. *Cf. Pesachim* 49a.
43.   *Sefer Chasidim* 14; *B'rith Olam* (Chida) *ad. loc. Cf.* 2 Kings 5:16; Esther 9:15.
44.   *Yerushalmi, Bava Metzia* 2:5 (8a). *Cf. Bava Kama* 113b; *Choshen Mishpat* 266:1.
45.   *Sotah* 31a; *Sifri* on Deuteronomy 6:5; *Yalkut Shimoni* 1:837; *Avoth DeRabbi Nathan* 5:1; *Tana DeBei Eliahu Rabbah* 28 (108b); Rashi on Deuteronomy 7:9.
46.   *Sefer Chasidim* 164 (end). *Cf. Avodah Zarah* 35b; *Zohar* 1:174b.
47.   *Reshith Chokhmah, Shaar HaAhavah* 2 (55a).

THREE

MARTYRDOM

3:1   There are times when one's love for God must be so strong that he or she is ready to be martyred for His sake. We are commanded, "Love God your Lord... with all your soul" (Deuteronomy 6:5), and this is interpreted to mean that one must continue to love God even at the expense of one's life and soul.[1]

3:2   The commandment, "I shall be sanctified among the children of Israel" (Leviticus 22:32), is a specific edict to publicize the greatness of our faith,[2] and we are taught that this must be done even at the expense of one's life.[3] Martyrdom thus establishes the veracity of our faith more dynamically than anything else, since one must accept the Torah as absolute Truth to be martyred for it.

3:3   This commandment applies to all Jews, even children.[4] Non-Jews are not required to martyr themselves for their commandments.[5]

---

1.   *Berakhoth* 9:5 (54a), 61b; *Yerushalmi, Berakhoth* 9:5 (67b); *Yerushalmi, Sotah* 5:5 (25a); *Sifri, Yalkut Shimoni* (1:837), Rashi, on Deuteronomy 6:5; *Mizrachi ad. loc.* Cf. *Mekhilta* to Exodus 20:6 (68b); Ramban *ad. loc.;* *Minchath Chinukh* 296 (p. 224a) maintains that all cases of non-public martyrdom are derived from this commandment, although it applies particularly to idolatry; cf. Rashi, *Sanhedrin* 74a *s.v. VeAhavta*; Maharsha, *Berakhoth* 61b *s.v. Yesh.* See also *Reshith Chokhmah, Shaar HaAhavah* 1 (53b*ff.*), from *Zohar* 1:11b, 3:263b, *Tikuney Zohar* (p. 9). Cf. *Tosafoth, Avodah Zarah* 54a *s.v. Ha.*

2.   See above, 2:16.

3.   *Sifra* on Leviticus 22:32 (99d); Rashi *ad. loc.;* *Yad, Yesodey HaTorah* 5:1, *Hagahoth Maimonioth ad. loc.* 1. Cf. *Sanhedrin* 74a.

4.   *Nimukey Mahari* on *Yad, Yesodey HaTorah* 5:1 (based on *Eikhah Rabbah* 1:53, where a martyred child was young enough to nurse). Cf. *Reshith Chokhmah, Shaar HaAhavah* 1 (52c).

5.   *Yad, Melakhim* 10:2, *Sefer HaMitzvoth*, Positive Commandment 9, from *Sanhedrin* 74b; see *Tosafoth ad. loc. s.v. VeIm; Yerushalmi, Sanhedrin* 3:5 (16a-b); *Shevi'ith* 4:2 (10b). For details, see Volume 1, 4:8-11.

3:4   This commandment specifically[6] requires one to be martyred rather than publicly transgress[7] any religious law[8] where religious persecution is intended. A situation is considered public if it is known to ten Jews, even if they are not present.[9]

3:5   It is considered a desecration of God's name for any power to usurp His absolute authority over us, and we are thus required to choose martyrdom rather than compromise our religious freedom.[10] Therefore, if any government passes an edict forbidding the practice of any religious law,[11] one must be martyred for it, even in private.[12] This is only true, however, if the decree is aimed specifically at the Jewish people,[13] and religious persecution is intended.[14]

3:6   The heritage of our martyrs is apparent, since those commandments for which they died, such as the Passover and Circumcision,[15] are still observed by most of our people, while other precepts are often ignored.[16]

3:7   Even in a time of religious persecution one should not give up hope, as God has promised that no power can destroy our great faith: "No weapon fashioned against you shall prosper, and every tongue that accuses you in judgment you shall indict. This is the heritage of God's servants, and their vindication from Me" (Isaiah 54:17).[17]

6.   *Sefer HaMitzvoth,* Positive Commandment 9. *Cf. Milchamoth HaShem* (Ramban) on Rif, *Sanhedrin* 18a; *Lechem Mishneh, Yesodey HaTorah* 5:4.

7.   *Sanhedrin* 74b; *Yad, Yesodey HaTorah* 5:2; *Yoreh Deah* 157:1.

8.   This is the opinion of Rif, *Sanhedrin* 17b; *Yad, Yesodey HaTorah* 5:2; *cf. Kesef Mishneh ad. loc.;* Rosh, *Sanhedrin* 8:3; *Chinukh* 196; and final decision of *Chayay Adam* 21:13. However, Rashi, *Sanhedrin* 74b (top) *s.v. Arkata D'Mesana* and *Tur, Yoreh Deah* 157, require martyring oneself publicly even to uphold a minor Jewish custom. *Cf. Sifethey Cohen* 157:5; *Turey Zahav* 157:3; *Tosafoth, Shabbath* 49a *s.v. Natlam MeRosho.*

9.   *Sifethey Cohen* 157:4; *Sh'nei Luchoth HaB'rith, Shaar HaOthioth* 1:98a.

10. *Cf.* Rashi, *Sanhedrin* 74a *s.v. VeAfilu;* Ramban on Exodus 20:6.

11. See above, note 8.

12. *Yad, Yesodey HaTorah* 5:2; *Yoreh Deah* 157:1.

13. *Nimukey Yosef, Sanhedrin* (Rif 17b) *s.v. Karka Olam; Sifethey Cohen* 157:6.

14. Rashi, *Sanhedrin* 74b *s.v. Shadee L'Nahara; Nimukey Yosef* (Rif 18a top). This is questioned by *Hagahoth Asheri, Kethuvoth* 3:4 and by *Bayith Chadash, Yoreh Deah* 157. See *Sifethey Cohen* 157:6; *Turey Zahav* 157:3; HaGra 157:7; Rashba, Ramban, *Kethuvoth* 3b.

15. *Mekhilta* on Exodus 20:6 (68b).

16. *Mekhilta* on Exodus 31:17 (104b); *Yalkut Shimoni ad. loc.* 1:391; *Shabbath* 130a.

17. *Cf.* Rambam, *Iggereth Teiman,* p. 7.

3:8   There are three[18] cardinal sins which one may not transgress under any circumstances, even at the expense of one's life. They are: idolatry, murder and sexual crimes.[19] Since these sins outweigh life because of their intrinsic severity,[20] one must be martyred rather than transgress them under all circumstances, even in private and where no religious persecution is intended.[21]

3:9   One must be martyred for idolatry since absolute love of God implies that one not even appear to forsake Him under any conditions.[22]

3:10   One must be martyred rather than kill a fellow Jew, since all life is equally dear to God, and one life may not be destroyed for another.[23]

3:11   One must be martyred for sexual crimes, since they are equated with murder, as the Torah states in the case of rape, "The [rapist] is no different from a man who rises up against his neighbor and murders him" (Deuteronomy 22:26).[24]

3:12   These three cardinal sins require martyrdom because of their intrinsic severity, and not because of the punishment prescribed for them.[25] One must therefore be martyred for any Biblical law associated with them, no matter how minor it may seem.[26] However, one need not be martyred for a rabbinical prohibition.[27]

18. Whether interrupting the Temple service is considered a fourth case, see *Mekhilta* on Exodus 21:14 (80b); *Meir Eyn ad. loc.* 39.
19. *Sanhedrin* 74b; *Yerushalmi, Sanhedrin* 3:5 (16a); *Yerushalmi, Shevi'ith* 4:2 (10b); *Yad, Yesodey HaTorah* 5:2; *Yoreh Deah* 157:1. See below, 13:67.
20. Ramban, *Milchamoth HaShem* on Rif, *Sanhedrin* 18a; *Nimukey Yosef, Sanhedrin* (Rif 17b end); Ran, *Pesachim* (Rif 6a) *s.v. Chutz.*
21. Majority of authorities; *cf.* HaGra 157:12. However, *Meor HaGadol, Sanhedrin* (Rif 17b), requires intent of persecution. *Cf.* Rashi, *Sanhedrin* 74b *s.v. Hani;* HaGra, *Yoreh Deah* 157:7.
22. *Sanhedrin* 74a; Rashi *ad. loc. s.v. VeAhavta.*
23. *Ibid.;* Rashi *ad. loc. s.v. Sevara* and *Mai; cf. Kesef Mishneh, Yesodey HaTorah* 5:5 (end). See below, 3:18.
24. *Ibid.*
25. Since many sins with more serious punishments do not require martyrdom, see below, Tables 13:7, 13:8.
26. Ramban, *Torath HaAdam, "Shaar HaSakanah"* (7b); Ran, *Pesachim* (Rif 5b) *s.v. Bekhol,* from *Yerushalmi, Avodah Zarah* 2:2 (10b); *Nimukey Yosef, Sanhedrin* (Rif 17b) *s.v. Sevara;* Rabbenu Yonah, *Shaarey Teshuvah* 3:137; *Yoreh Deah* 156:1 in *Hagah; Chinukh* 196; *cf. Minchath Chinukh ad. loc.* (p. 224a), who writes that Rambam and Tosafoth, *Avodah Zarah* 25a *s.v. Chutz,* 27b *s.v. Shani,* may dispute this. See Rabbenu Yonah, *Avoth* 3:11.
27. *Sifethey Cohen* 157:10 end. See below, 13:34.

3:13   Martyrdom is only required for the individual involved in the act. One need not give one's life rather than be an accomplice to a cardinal sin.[28]

3:14   Martyrdom is only required for an act. Therefore, one need not be martyred for a passive sin. Similarly, if one is bodily forced to sin, he need not resist at the expense of his life,[29] even in public.[30]

3:15   Martyrdom is only required when one is certain that he can sanctify God, but not where there is any question of his chances for success. Therefore, in the case of a government decree or public display, one need not be martyred for a positive commandment which the government can forcibly prevent one from performing in any case.[31] Nevertheless, during a period of religious persecution, most authorities agree that one should not abandon one's religious observances or studies out of fear of detection.[32]

3:16   In the case of idolatry, one must be martyred rather than profess belief in any idolatrous religion, engage in its religious practices, or even honor its religious images or symbols in any way.[33] These are all included in the commandment, "Do not bow down to [any idol] or worship them. I am God your Lord, a God who demands exclusive worship" (Exodus 20:5).[34]

3:17   The Christian beliefs that Jesus was God incarnate,[35] and mediator between God and man,[36] are clearly idolatrous.[37] A

28. Ramban, *Torath HaAdam*, *"Shaar HaSakanah"* (7b), *Milchamoth HaShem* on Rif, *Sanhedrin* 18a; Ran, *Pesachim* (Rif 6a) *s.v. Chutz; Nimukey Yosef, Sanhedrin* (Rif 18a) *s.v. Haikhi; Sifethey Cohen* 157:11; *Turey Zahav* 157:5.

29. *Tosafoth, Sanhedrin* 74b *s.v. VeHa, Yevamoth* 53b *s.v. Ein, Yoma* 82a *s.v. Mah;* Ran, *Pesachim* (Rif 6a) *s.v. Kasha;* Rosh, *Kethuvoth* 1:4; *Yoreh Deah* 157:1 in *Hagah*. See *Lechem Mishneh, Yesodey HaTorah* 5:4, that Rambam disputes this; *Cf. Birkey Yosef, Yoreh Deah* 157:1.

30. *Sifethey Cohen* 157:9.

31. By imprisonment, for example; *Nimukey Yosef, Sanhedrin* (Rif 17b) *s.v. Karka Olam;* Ran, *Shabbath* (Rif 22b) *s.v. U'Makshu; Teshuvoth Rivash* 387; *Turey Zahav* 157:4.

32. *Minchath Chinukh* 296 (p. 223d), from *Shabbath* 49a, 130a; *Berakhoth* 61b; *Avodah Zarah* 18a. See *Tifereth Yisrael, Berahkoth* 1:3, quoted in *Pith'chey Teshuvah* 157:3. Others maintain that martyrdom is not required in these cases; Ran *loc. cit.;* Maharsha, *Berakhoth* 61b *s.v. Yesh; Lechem Mishneh, Yesodey HaTorah* 5:4; *Kesef Mishneh ad. loc.* 5:1 (end).

33. *Minchath Chinukh* 296 (p. 224a).

34. *Sanhedrin* 7:6 (60b); *Yad, Avodath Kokhavim* 3:6; *Sefer HaMitzvoth*, Negative Commandment 6.

35. John 5:22, 10:9; 1 Corinthians 8:6, 15:26; 1 Timothy 2:5; Col. 1:13.

36. John 1:14; 2 Corinthians 5:19; *cf.* Nicene Creed.

37. *Yad, Avodath Kokhavim* 2:1; *Moreh Nevukhim* 1:36.

Jew must therefore be martyred rather than embrace Christianity.[38] However, since Islam is not idolatrous, and merely requires a verbal confession of belief in a false prophet, one need not be martyed rather than accept Mohammed as prophet, although martyrdom is commendable in such a case.[39]

3:18 In the case of murder, one must be martyred rather than kill any Jew, whether he be a newly born child or a very old man.[40] However, if the victim is wounded so badly that he will certainly die of his injuries, one need not be martyred to avoid ending his life.[41] Similarly, one need not be martyred rather than take the life of an unborn child.[42]

3:19 One must be martyred rather than hand a fellow Jew over to be killed, since this is akin to murder.[43] In such a case, one is more than a mere accomplice, since this is expressly forbidden by the commandment, "Do not stand still when your neighbor's life is in danger" (Leviticus 19:16).[44]

3:20 Destroying a person psychologically is comparable to killing him physically, since the mind controls even the most basic bodily functions.[45] Therefore, rather than publicly shame a person, thereby causing him permanent psychological damage, one must give his life.[46]

3:21 Sexual crimes include all forms of adultery, incest,[47] and forbidden intercourse with a Jewish woman.[48] Also included is

38. *Cf. Teshuvoth Rivash* 4, 11; *Teshuvoth Rabbi Yosef ibn Lev (Rival)* 1:15.
39. Rambam, *Iggereth HaShmad,* p. 17.
40. *Cf. Niddah* 5:3 (44a); *Yad, Rotzeach* 2:6.
41. *Minchath Chinukh* 296 (p. 224d). *Cf. Yad, Rotzeach* 2:8, from *Makkoth* 7a; *Sanhedrin* 78a.
42. *Minchath Chinukh loc. cit.* See below, 4:9.
43. See below, 3:24.
44. Expressed idiomatically as, "Do not stand still over your neighbor's blood"; *Sifra,* Rashi, *loc. cit.; Sefer HaMitzvoth,* Negative Commandment 296; *Minchath Chinukh* 296 (p. 225a); *Sefer Mitzvoth Gadol,* Negative Commandment 165 (p. 59d). *Cf. Yad, Rotzeach* 2:2, *Chovel* 8:9; *Choshen Mishpat* 388:9, from *Gittin* 7a.
45. *Bava Metzia* 58b; *Zohar* 3:85a. *Cf.* Bertenoro, *Avoth* 3:11; *Sefer Chasidim* 40, 54; *Menorath HaMaor* 2:5:1 (57).
46. Rabbenu Yonah, *Avoth* 3:11 and *Shaarey Teshuvah* 3:139, from *Bava Metzia* 59a; *Berakhoth* 43b; *Kethuvoth* 67b; *Sotah* 10b; *cf. Tosafoth ad. loc. s.v. Noach Lo; Chinukh* 240; *Menorath HaMaor* 2:5:2 (58). *Cf.* Genesis 38:25, Rashi *ad. loc.*
47. For listing, see below, Chapter 13 (end), Tables 13:4, 13:6.
48. Since even an unmarried woman is usually menstrually unclean; *cf. Niddah* 10b.

sexual contact with a menstrually unclean woman, even one's wife.[49] In all these cases, one must be martyred not only for intercourse, but for all forms of indecent bodily contact[50] which are included in the negative commandment, "No person shall [even] approach a close relative to commit a sexual offense" (Leviticus 18:6).[51]

3:22 A woman need not be martyred rather than submit to rape, even where a sexual crime is involved, as long as she is not forced to actively participate.[52]

3:23 Intercourse between a non-Jew and an unmarried Jewish girl is only forbidden by rabbinical decree[53] and, therefore, the girl need not be martyred, even if she is compelled to actively participate.[54] However, if the woman is married, it is considered a sexual crime for which she must be martyred rather than actively participate.[55] Intercourse between a Jewish man and non-Jewish woman is considered a sexual crime and is therefore forbidden.[56]

3:24 The value of life does not depend upon number, since one life may be worth more to God than many others.[57] Therefore, even an entire community[58] must be martyred before they kill

---

49. *Cf. Chayay Adam* 21:13; *Chokhmath Adam* 88:1; see below, Table 13:4, no. 7.

50. *Sifethey Cohen* 157:10, 195:20. *Cf. Beth Sh'muel (Bash), Evven HaEzer* 101; *Teshuvoth Chavath Yair* 182, quoted in *Pith'chey Teshuvah* 157:11.

51. *Yad, Issurey Biyah* 11:1; *Sefer HaMitzvoth,* Negative Commandment 353; *Sefer Mitzvoth Gadol,* Negative Commandment 126; *Chinukh* 188, from *Sifra ad. loc.* (85c); *cf. Shabbath* 13a. In Hebrew, this is *LeGaloth Erva,* literally "to uncover nakedness," since this is the first part of the sexual act; Ralbag *ad. loc.;* Ramban on Leviticus 20:17. The root *Galah* here may also mean "be exiled," and hence *LeGaloth Erva* may be translated, "to exile nakedness" or "to pervert sexuality"; *cf. Targum Yonathan ad. loc.*

52. *Cf. Chinukh* 296. See above, 3:14, note 29.

53. *Tosafoth, Sanhedrin* 74b *s.v. Hah; Kethuvoth* 3b *s.v. VeLidrosh;* Ran, *Yoma* (Rif 3b) *s.v. Chutz; cf. Yad, Issurey Biyah* 12:1; *Evven HaEzer* 15:1.

54. *Sifethey Cohen* 157:13.

55. *Sifethey Cohen* 157:14.

56. Ramban, *Torath HaAdam,* "Shaar HaSakanah" (7b); *Nimukey Yosef, Sanhedrin* (Rif 18a) *s.v. Haikhi,* maintain that one must be martyred even privately. However, *Sifethey Cohen, Yoreh Deah* 157:12, *Teshuvoth Noda BeYehudah, Evven HaEzer* 2:150, quoted in *Pith'chey Teshuvah* 157:12, consider this a sexual crime only when it is committed in public; see below, 14:10, note 28. *Cf. Evven HaEzer* 16:2 in *Hagah;* HaGra *ad. loc.* 16:9; *Turey Zahav, Yoreh Deah* 157:6. See below, 4:6, notes 19, 20; 13:66, note 220.

57. See *Kesef Mishneh, Yesodey HaTorah* 5:5 (end), that this was a tradition, and *Lechem Mishneh ad. loc. Cf. Sanhedrin* 4:5 (37a).

58. *Chinukh* 296; even thousands.

a single Jew, or even hand him over to others to be killed[59] or tortured.[60] Experience has shown us that when Jews are not ready to defend and die for their fellows, an even greater number are killed in the end.[61]

3:25 If the individual being sought is a criminal, however, he may be handed over,[62] since he placed both himself and the community in danger.[63]

3:26 Sin and shame are similarly not measured by number. If a group of women are given the choice of giving up one of their number for immoral purposes or all being raped, they must all submit rather than hand over the one.[64] In such a case it makes no difference whether the individual is single or married,[65] or even if she is otherwise immoral, since she may have repented her former deeds and should not be punished for them now.[66] However, the group need not give their lives rather than hand one over, since even she need not be martyred in such a case.[67]

3:27 In private, where there is no government decree, one need not be martyred for any law other than the three cardinal sins. Regarding other laws, the Torah states, "Keep My decrees and laws, since a person can [truly] live only by keeping them" (Leviticus 18:5) — live by keeping them and not die by keeping them.[68] Therefore, one need not be martyred if there is any question of its being

59. *Tosefta, Terumoth* 7:23; *Yerushalmi, Terumoth* 8:4 (47a); *Yad, Yesodey HaTorah* 5:5; *Sefer Mitzvoth Gadol,* Negative Commandment 165; *Yoreh Deah* 157:1 in *Hagah;* Rashi, *Sanhedrin* 72b *s.v. Yatza;* Ran, *Yoma* (Rif 4a) *s.v. U'Mihu;* Rash, *Terumoth* 8:12; Rosh *ad. loc.; Tosefoth Yom Tov, Ohaloth* 7:6; Rashi, Radak, on 2 Samuel 20:22; *Yalkut Shimoni* 2:152; *Sefer Chasidim* 699; *Chokhmath Adam* 88:15. *Cf. Bereshith Rabbah* 94:9.
60. *Turey Zahav, Yoreh Deah* 157:8, from *Kethuvoth* 33b. *Cf. Maggid Mishneh, Ishuth* 21:11.
61. As during the Nazi oppression.
62. See above, note 59.
63. *Turey Zahav* 157:7; *Sefer Chasidim* 700. *Cf.* Judges 15:12; *Metzudoth David ad. loc.; Choshen Mishpat* 388:12, 435:1 in *Hagah.* See also *Bereshith Rabbah* 94:9 (end).
64. *Terumoth* 8:12; *Yad, Yesodey HaTorah* 5:5; *Yoreh Deah* 157:1 in *Hagah.*
65. *Sefer Chasidim* 699; *Teshuvoth Chesed Avraham, Yoreh Deah* 1:45.
66. Rashba, quoted in *Kesef Mishneh, Yesodey HaTorah* 5:5 and *Beth Yosef, Yoreh Deah* 157. *Cf. Yerushalmi, Terumoth* 8:4 (46b); *Marah HaPanim ad. loc. Cf. Dagul Me'rvavah, Yoreh Deah* 157:1; *Teshuvoth Noda BeYehudah, Yoreh Deah* 2:74.
67. *Turey Zahav* 157:9. See above, 3:22-23.
68. *Sanhedrin* 74a; *Yad, Yesodey HaTorah* 5:1; *Sifra ad. loc.* (86b).

required.[69] In any case, the decision must be made by the individual alone, since no authority today can decide a question of life.[70]

3:28   In any case of religious persecution[71] or public display,[72] one may be martyred even when not required,[73] if an example is needed, and especially if one is a known religious leader.[74] However, if one gives his life when not required, in private and where no persecution is intended, he is considered culpable for his own death.[75]

3:29   Wherever one is required to be martyred, he must also suffer torture and mutilation to sanctify God.[76] However, a person may take his own life to avoid suffering and torture.[77]

3:30   If one breaks under pressure and is incapable of martyring himself when required, he is guilty of desecrating God's name,[78] and has lost the opportunity to sanctify God, which is the greatest merit a person can acquire.[79] However, he is not punishable for any sin he may have committed, since it was done under duress,[80] as

69.   *Terumath HaDeshen* 199, quoted in *Sifethey Cohen* 157:1. See above, 3:5.
70.   *Teshuvoth Besamim Rosh* 301, quoted in *Gilyon Maharsha, Yoreh Deah* 157:1.
71.   *Yoreh Deah* 157:1; *Tur*, quoting Rabbenu Yerocham.
72.   *Perishah* 157:3, quoted in *Sifethey Cohen* 157:2. But *Bayith Chadash* maintains that intent of persecution is required.
73.   *Tosafoth, Avodah Zarah* 27b *s.v. Yakhol, Eruvin* 21b *s.v. Mutav;* Ran, *Shabbath* (Rif 22b) *s.v. U'Makshey;* Rosh, *Avodah Zarah* 2:9, from *Yerushalmi, Sanhedrin* 3:6 (16b); see *Marah HaPanim ad. loc.* See *Yad, Yesodey HaTorah* 5:4; *Kesef Mishneh, Lechem Mishneh, ad. loc.,* where Rambam apparently maintains that one may never be unncessarily martyred. But see *Iggereth HaShmad* (p. 17) regarding Islam, where he seems to contradict this.
74.   *Sifethey Cohen* 157:2.
75.   *Ibid.; Beer HaGolah* 157:3. *Cf. Yad, Yesodey HaTorah* 5:4.
76.   *Tosafoth, Kethuvoth* 33b *s.v. Ilmaley, Pesachim* 57b *s.v. Mah. Cf. Pesikta* 10 (87a); *Yalkut Shimoni* 2:667; Ramban on Genesis 32:2.
77.   *Tosafoth, Gittin* 57b *s.v. Kaftzu, Avodah Zarah* 18a *s.v. VeAl. Cf. Yoreh Deah* 345:3, from *Bereshith Rabbah* 34:19. See Ramban, *Torath HaAdam "Inyan HaHesped"* (20b); Rosh, *Moed Katan* 3:94; Radak on 1 Samuel 31:5. See also *Yam Shel Shlomo, Bava Kama* 8:58.
78.   *Yad, Yesodey HaTorah* 5:4. However, *Nimukey Yosef, Sanhedrin* (Rif 17b), maintains that desecration is only in public; see *Minchath Chinukh* 296 (p. 224a). Furthermore, *Sefer Mitzvoth Gadol,* Negative Commandment 2, does not count such a case as a desecration at all.
79.   See *Lechem Mishneh, Yesodey HaTorah* 5:4; *Sefer HaMitzvoth,* Positive Commandment 9, who maintain that one does not violate the commandment to sanctify except in public; *cf. Teshuvoth Rivash* 4, 11, 171.
80.   *Yad, Yesodey HaTorah* 5:4; *Yoreh Deah* 157:1 in *Hagah; Tosafoth, Shabbath* 72b *s.v. Rava, Yoma* 82a *s.v. Mah, Yevamoth* 53b *s.v. Ein Ones L'Ervah, Avodah Zarah* 54a *s.v. Matkif;* Mordecai, *Yevamoth* 112. *Cf. Sifra* on Leviticus 20:3 (91c). See also Raavad,

the Torah states in the case of a girl who is victimized by a rapist: "You must not impose any penalty upon the girl, since she has not committed a sin worthy of death" (Deuteronomy 22:26).[81] The same is true of one who cannot hold up under the psychological strain of being forced to do something which is forbidden by the Torah and thereby desecrates God's name. Even if he now commits a sin, it is considered involuntary and he is not punished.[82]

3:31   However, a person who has an opportunity to escape or avoid a predicament where he may be forced to sin, and does not take advantange of this opportunity because of monetary or other considerations, bears full responsibility for his actions. Even if he is then forced to sin,[83] he is guilty of any sin committed in addition to that of desecrating God's name.[84] With regard to such an individual, it is written, "Like a dog that returns to its vomit, so is a fool who repeats his folly" (Proverbs 26:11).[85]

3:32   One who is martyred sanctifies God, and none is as dear in His eyes.[86] Even if he committed evil all his life, he attains the highest eminence before God as a martyr.[87] Regarding such a person, the Psalmist said, "Gather My pious ones to Me, those who have made a covenant with Me by [self] sacrifice" (Psalms 50:5).[88]

3:33   One who is publicly martyred fulfills the commandment, "I shall be sanctified among the children of Israel" (Leviticus 22:22), and should therefore say the blessing: בָּרוּךְ אַתָּה... אֲשֶׁר קִדְּשָׁנוּ בְּמִצְוֹתָיו וְצִוָּנוּ לְקַדֵּשׁ שְׁמוֹ בָּרַבִּים. "Blessed are You... Who has sanctified us with His commandments and instructed us to publicly sanctify

Avodath Kokhavim 3:6. Regarding the Marranos, see Rashi, *Pardes* (p. 23d); *Teshuvoth Rivash* 4, 11; *Chemdah Genuzah,* p. 14*ff.; Yoreh Deah* 124:9.

81.   *Avodah Zarah* 54a; *Bava Kama* 28b; *Nedarim* 27a. See *Yad, Sanhedrin* 20:2; *Sefer HaMitzvoth,* Negative Commandment 294; Ramban *ad. loc.; Sefer Mitzvoth Gadol,* Negative Commandment 201; *Chinukh* 556.
82.   See *Teshuvoth Noda BeYehudah* 2:72, quoted in *Minchath Chinukh* 296 (p. 225c); *Iggereth HaShmad,* pp. 15-16; *Chinukh* 296 (end).
83.   *Cf. Kethuvoth* 51b; *Yad, Ishuth* 24:20.
84.   *Iggereth HaShmad,* p. 19.
85.   *Yad, Yesodey HaTorah* 5:4; *Yoreh Deah* 157:1 in *Hagah,* 124:9 in *Hagah.*
86.   *Cf. Pesachim* 50b.
87.   *Iggereth HaShmad,* p. 15.
88.   *Cf. Sanhedrin* 110b; *Yad, Yesodey HaTorah* 5:4.

His Name."[89] With his last breath, he should have the *Sh'ma* on his lips.[90]

3:34   Although the merit of a martyr is very great, he should not expect any miraculous deliverance.[91] However, if he goes to his death with full love of God, he will feel no pain, as no delight in life is as great and as perfect as that of a martyr.[92]

3:35   One who is killed because he is Jewish, even though he is not given any choice, is considered a martyr. Even an evildoer who goes to his death as a Jew sanctifies God and is considered holy. Regarding such a person, it is written, "For He who avenges blood has remembered them; He has not forgotten the cry of the humble" (Psalms 9:13).[93]

3:36   One who resolves to give his life for God if called upon has the merit of an actual martyr,[94] since God considers a good intention as an accomplished deed.[95]

3:37   Since public humiliation is equivalent to death,[96] a Jew who suffers shame for the sake of his religion is considered a martyr.[97]

3:38   The greatest respect should be paid to the memory of our martyrs. Where possible, the place of their death should be preserved as a memorial, and even their bloodstains should not be removed. It is thus written, "O earth, do not cover my blood, and

89. *Sh'nei Luchoth HaB'rith, Shaar HaOthioth* 1:98a, quoting Recanti 70, quoted in *Pith'chey Teshuvah* 157:6. A similar blessing is found in the morning prayers after the preliminary *Sh'ma; cf. Tana DeBei Eliahu Rabbah* 21 (95a); *Yalkut Shimoni* 1:836; *Tosafoth, Berakhoth* 46a, *Pesachim* 105b *s.v. Kol; Tur, Orach Chaim* 46 (end); *Magen David* 46:9; HaGra 46:9.

90. Cf. *Berakhoth* 61b; *Yerushalmi, Berakhoth* 9:5 (67b); *Yerushalmi, Sotah* 5:5 (25a).

91. *Sifra* on Leviticus 22:32 (99d) and Rashi *ad. loc. Cf. Taanith* 18b; *Iggereth HaShmad,* p. 19.

92. *Taamey HaMinhagim* 351 (p. 161, note quoting *Arvey Nachal*). *Cf. Yerushalmi, Berakhoth* 9:5 (67b).

93. *Midrash Tehillim* 9:13 (44b). *Cf. Zohar* 1:39a; *Pesachim* 59b; Psalms 110:2. See *Mevakshey Emunah* (Rabbi Aaron Roth), pp. 27-28.

94. *Teshuvoth Rashba* 5:55, from Psalm 44:23; Ibn Ezra *ad. loc.; Sefer Chasidim* 222, 704; *Bayith Chadash, Orach Chaim* 61; *Chayay Adam* 21:13 (end); *Mishnah Berurah, Orach Chaim* 61:3; Rabbi Elimelekh of Lizensk, *Tzetel Katan* 1; *Cheredim,* Positive Commandments 1:16.

95. *Kiddushin* 40a.

96. See above, 3:20.

97. *Sefer Chasidim* 40.

give my cry no resting place!" (Job 16:18), and "I have placed her blood upon a bare rock, that it not be covered" (Ezekiel 24:8).[98]

3:39   The weapon used to kill a martyr should be buried with him or her and never again used.[99]

3:40   Concerning our martyrs, the Psalmist wrote: "If we had forgotten the name of our God, or spread forth our hands to a strange god, would God not search this out? He knows the secrets of the heart. But [You know O God,] for Your sake we are killed all the day and considered as sheep for the slaughter" (Psalms 44:21-23).

98.   *Sefer Chasidim* 449. *Cf. Yalkut Shimoni* 2:364; *Tosefta, Maaser Sheni* 5:9; *Yerushalmi, Maaser Sheni* 5:1 (28b).
99.   *Sefer Chasidim* 1113. *Cf.* Ezekiel 32:27; *Sanhedrin* 45b; *Avodah Zarah* 62b; *Yad, Sanhedrin* 15:9. See also *Teshuvoth Yaabetz* 2:158, quoted in *Pith'chey Teshuvah* 8:1.

FOUR

ULTIMATE SACRIFICE

4:1   God has commanded us in His Torah, "Keep My decrees and laws, since it is only by keeping them that a person can [truly] live" (Leviticus 18:5).[1] Thus, if one's life is in danger, he may violate any law to save or heal himself.[2] The only exception to this rule are the three cardinal sins — idolatry, murder and sexual crimes — for which one must die rather than transgress. We are called upon to give our lives rather than transgress any law which is even associated with these three sins.[3]

4:2   It is therefore forbidden to resort to any idolatrous faith healer or shrine, even when one is dangerously ill and a psychological cure may be effected.[4] One may receive treatment from a non-Jewish physician, even if he is an idolater,[5] but not from an atheistic or idolatrous psychiatrist.[6]

4:3   It is only forbidden to save a life through idolatrous means when some religious motivation is suspected.[7] Where no religious motivation is involved, it is permitted to make material use of objects associated with idolatry to save a life.[8] Therefore, it is

1.   See above, 3:27, note 68. See also Kaplan, *Torah Anthology*, Volume 11, p. 399.
2.   Regarding saving life; *Yoma* 82a. *Cf. Pith'chey Teshuvah, Yoreh Deah* 157:2; *Turey Zahav* 159:4. Regarding healing; *Pesachim* 25a; Rif, *Pesachim* 6a, *Avodah Zarah* 9a; *Yad, Yesodey HaTorah* 5:6; *Yoreh Deah* 155:3.
3.   See above, 3:12, notes 26, 27.
4.   *Avodah Zarah* 27b; *Yoreh Deah* 155:1.
5.   *Ibid.,* since he is publicly licensed and charges a fee; *cf. Sifethey Cohen* 155:3, 6.
6.   Rosh, *Avodah Zarah* 2:9, from *Yerushalmi, Avodah Zarah* 2:2 (10b); *Koheleth Rabbah* 10:7.
7.   *Turey Zahav* 157:11, quoting *Teshuvoth HaRosh* 19:17.
8.   *Tosafoth, Avodah Zarah* 27b *s.v. Shani;* Rosh, *Avodah Zarah* 2:9, from *Yerushalmi, Avodah Zarah* 2:2 (10b); *cf. Marah HaPanim ad. loc.* and *Yerushalmi, Shabbath* 14:4 (76b); *Yoreh Deah* 155:2; *Sifethey Cohen* 155:11; HaGra 155:14. Ran, *Avodah Zarah* (Rif 9a) *s.v. Bakhol,* disputes this. *Cf. Yoreh Deah* 150:3 in *Hagah.*

permitted to heal with drugs used in idolatrous rites, or seek asylum in a church when one is being pursued.[9]

4:4 One who is prepared to die for his Jewishness sanctifies God.[10] Conversely, denying that one is Jewish is akin to idolatry, since it implies a denial of our fundamental beliefs.[11] Therefore, in time of danger, it is forbidden to save one's life by denying that he is Jewish.[12] It is permitted to make an ambiguous statement,[13] to act like a non-Jew,[14] or to disguise oneself as such.[15] It is forbidden to disguise oneself as a priest, however, since this is the same as an outright denial of one's Jewishness.[16]

4:5 A woman may deny that she is Jewish or disguise herself as a nun to avoid being raped, since there is no sanctification of God in being raped.[17] In such a case, she may also disguise herself as a man.[18]

4:6 It is likewise forbidden to save life through any forbidden sexual pleasure. Therefore, if a man's psychological condition is deteriorating because of his desire for a particular woman even though she may be single or non-Jewish,[19] he must be allowed to die rather than even speak to her or see her.[20] However, he

9. *Shabbath* 116a, *Yoreh Deah* 157:3; *HaGra* 157:26; *Chokhmath Adam* 88:14. See above, 1:28. Still, during a time of religious persecution, this too is forbidden; *HaGra* 157:27.
10. See above, 3:35.
11. *Cf. Rosh, Avodah Zarah* 2:4.
12. *Ibid.; Or Zarua* 1:747; *Terumath HaDeshen* 196; *Yoreh Deah* 157:2; *Chokhmath Adam* 88:13. *Cf. Yerushalmi, Avodah Zarah* 2:1 (9b).
13. *Yoreh Deah* 157:2 in *Hagah,* from *Nedarim* 62b.
14. *Ibid.,* from *Avodah Zarah* 18b. *Cf.* Rambam, *Iggereth HaShmad,* p. 8.
15. *Nimukey Yosef, Bava Kama* (Rif 40a) *s.v. Omar,* from *Bereshith Rabbah* 82:9; *cf. Yalkut Shimoni* 1:136, 2:396; *Sefer Chasidim* 199. *Cf. Taanith* 22a; *HaGra, Yoreh Deah* 157:20. See also *Sefer HaEshkol* (Raavad) 3:118; *Teshuvoth Tashbatz* 417; *Teshuvoth Maharik* 88; *Teshuvoth Radbaz* 4:137; *Terumath HaDeshen* 197; *Teshuvoth Maharam Mintz* 102; *Teshuvoth Tzemach Tzedek* 90.
16. *Sefer Chasidim* 199. *Cf.* Rashi, *Nedarim* 62b *s.v. Avda D'Nura; Beer HaGolah, Yoreh Deah* 157:10; *Kenesseth HaGedolah ad. loc.*
17. *Sefer Chasidim* 702. *Cf. Yerushalmi, Avodah Zarah* 2:1 (9b).
18. *Sefer Chasidim* 200-201.
19. *Chokhmath Adam* 88:1. See above, 3:23, note 56.
20. *Sanhedrin* 75a; *Yerushalmi, Avodah Zarah* 2:2 (11a); *Yerushalmi, Shabbath* 14:4 (76b); *Yad, Yesodey HaTorah* 5:9; *Beth Yosef, Yoreh Deah* 157. See *Beth Sh'muel* (Bash), *Evven HaEzer* 20:1; *Mishneh LeMelekh, Yom Tov* 1:17; *Teshuvoth Zera Avraham, Yoreh Deah* 5; *Minchath Chinukh* 296 (p. 225c). *Cf. Kiddushin* 44a.

may marry her,[21] or his own wife may be substituted without his knowledge, if his condition can thereby be alleviated.[22]

4:7   A doctor may treat a woman patient in any manner dictated by good medical practice, since he does not derive any pleasure from it.[23]

4:8   It is forbidden to destroy one life to save another.[24] One may therefore not end a dying person's life by removing an organ needed for a transplant to save another. However, one may remove the organ as soon as he stops breathing, even though his heart is still beating, since the Torah considers life directly connected to breathing. This is brought out in the context of the Flood, regarding which it is written, "Everything on dry land whose life was sustained by breathing died" (Genesis 7:22).[25] This is true only when the donor has no possible chance of living.

4:9   An unborn child is considered part of its mother's body[26] and not a living person in its own right.[27] Therefore, if a woman's life is endangered by childbirth, it is permissible to destroy the unborn child to save the mother's life.[28] However, as soon as the child's head emerges[29] or, in the case of a breach, the majority of its body,[30] it is forbidden to destroy the child since it is considered a living person in its own right.[31]

21. *Ibid.*

22. *Nimukey Yosef. loc. cit.; Yoreh Deah* 157:2 in *Hagah.*

23. *Kitzur Shulchan Arukh* 192:8, from *Yoreh Deah* 195:15, 16 in *Hagah; Chokhmath Adam* 88:12; *Sifethey Cohen* 195:20; *Darkey Teshuvah* 157:8, 195:55; *Kereithi U'Pelethi* 195:17. *Cf. Teshuvoth Ramban* 127; *Terumath HaDeshen* 252; also *Teshuvoth Binyan Tzion* 1:75; *Teshuvoth Radbaz* 1:2; *Teshuvoth Besamim Rosh* 118; *Teshuvoth Chinukh Beth Yehudah* 66; *Beth Sh'muel (Bash), Evven HaEzer* 20:1.

24. *Sanhedrin* 72b; *Ohaloth* 7:6.

25. *Yoma* 85a; *Yerushalmi, Yoma* 8:5 (41b); *Yad, Shabbath* 2:19; *Orach Chaim* 329:4.

26. *Chullin* 58a; *Gittin* 23b; *Nazir* 51a; *Tosafoth, Sanhedrin* 80b *s.v. Ubar; Yad, Maakhaloth Assuroth* 5:15.

27. Rashi, *Sanhedrin* 72b *s.v. Yatza.*

28. *Yad, Rotzeach* 1:9, gives the reason because he is an assailant; see below, 4:10, 4:17. The reason for this is discussed in *Chidushey Rabbi Chaim HaLevi ad. loc.; Teshuvah Chavath Yair* 31, quoted in *Pith'chey Teshuvah, Choshen Mishpat* 425:1; *Minchath Chinukh* 296 (p. 223b). *Cf. Yerushalmi, Sanhedrin* 8:9 (42a); *Yerushalmi, Avodah Zarah* 2:2 (11a); *Yerushalmi, Shabbath* 14:4 (77a); *Chinukh* 600; *Sefer Mitzvoth Gadol,* Negative Commandment 164; *Teshuvoth Geoney Bathrey* 45 (2a); *Pri Megadim, Mishbetzoth Zahav, Orach Chaim* 328:1; *Nishmath Chaim* 2:18.

29. *Bekhoroth* 8:1 (46a); *Rash, Ohaloth* 7:6; *cf. Chullin* 4:1 (68a).

30. *Niddah* 3:5 (28a); *Chullin* 68b. See *Pith'chey Teshuvah, Choshen Mishpat* 425:2; *Chasdey David* on *Tosefta, Yevamoth* 9:9.

4:10   Nevertheless, it is forbidden to wantonly destroy even an unborn embryo,[32] since it will eventually be born and live.[33] Only when the physical[34] or mental[35] health of the mother is at stake, may she have an abortion.[36]

4:11   One is innocent of sin only when forced bodily or under threat of death to do a specific act,[37] and only when the sin itself is the source of danger.[38] However, it is forbidden to attempt to save oneself from sickness[39] or danger[40] by violating one of the three cardinal sins. In such cases, one is considered guilty, since he is not being coerced to transgress.

4:12   This distinction is also applicable in the case of money. It is forbidden to save one's life with another's money, unless one has the intention of repaying it.[41] If one is forced under pain of death or torture to hand over another's money, however, he need not repay it,[42] since it is considered involuntary.[43] Still, if there

31.   *Ohaloth* 7:6; *Tosefta, Yevamoth* 9:9; *Sanhedrin* 72b; *Yerushalmi, Sanhedrin* 8:9 (42a); *Yad, Rotzeach* 1:9; *Choshen Mishpat* 425:2. Cf. *Teshuvoth Noda BeYehudah* 2:59.
32.   *Tosafoth, Sanhedrin* 59a *s.v. Lekha, Chullin* 33a *s.v. Echad; Terumath HaDeshen* 58; *Teshuvoth Chavath Yair* 31 (p. 37a); *Teshuvoth Beth Yaakov* 51.
33.   Cf. *Nazir* 51a; *Yad, Tumath Meth* 3:5. See above, note 31. See also *Sanhedrin* 8:6 (72a).
34.   *Teshuvoth Rabbi Yosef Trani (Maharit)* 99.
35.   Rabbi Meir Mizrachi, *Teshuvoth Pri HaAretz, Yoreh Deah* 21.
36.   Cf. *Sanhedrin* 84b, from Exodus 21:12; Rashi, *Mekhilta* (80a), *ad. loc.*; *Sifra* (104d) on Leviticus 24:17; Meiri, *Sanhedrin* 72b; *Shabbath* 107b; *Sefer Meirath Eynayim (Sema), Choshen Mishpat* 425:5; Mizrachi on Exodus 21:12, that killing an unborn child is not considered murder. Some make the additional distinction that once the woman is in labor and the birth process has commenced, the child may not be destroyed except to save the mother's life, since it is considered a separate individual; *cf. Arakhin* 1:4 (7a); *Teshuvoth Rama* 40, quoted in *Machtzith HaShekel* 330:10; *Teshuvoth Chavath Yair loc. cit.* However, all feticide is equivalent to murder for a non-Jew; *cf. Yad, Melakhim* 9:4, from *Sanhedrin* 57b; *Tosafoth, Sanhedrin, Chullin, loc. cit; Bereshith Rabbah* 34:19.
37.   *Minchath Chinukh* 296 (p. 222d); *HaFla'ah* on *Tosafoth, Kethuvoth* 19a *s.v. DeAmar.*
38.   Cf. *Milchamoth HaShem* (Ramban), *Bava Kama* (Rif 43a); *Nimukey Yosef ad. loc.* 44a.
39.   *Yad, Yesodey HaTorah* 5:6.
40.   *Pith'chey Teshuvah* 157:17, quoting *Mishnath Chakhamim.*
41.   *Bava Kama* 60b; *Tosafoth ad. loc. s.v. Mahu;* Rosh, *Bava Kama* 6:12; *Choshen Mishpat* 359:4; *Sefer Meirath Eynayim (Sema) ad. loc.* 359:10. Cf. Rashi, *Yoma* 83b *s.v. Kipchey;* Maharatz Chajas *ad. loc.;* *Yerushalmi, Avodah Zarah* 2:2 (11a); *Parashath Derakhim, "Derekh Chaim."*
42.   *Bava Kama* 117a; *Yerushalmi, Bava Kama* 8:8 (37a); see *Marah HaPanim ad. loc.;* Rosh, *Bava Kama* 10:27; Raavad, *Chovel* 8:4; *Sifethey Cohen, Choshen Mishpat* 388:24, quoting Rav Hai Goan and Rabbenu Chananel, all maintain that this is true even if one hands over the money. Others exempt him only if he merely shows them

is no direct coercion, and one saves life or limb with another's money, he must make restitution.

4:13   If one is being pursued or attacked and causes damage while escaping, he must therefore make complete restitution to everybody involved with the exception of his assailant. Where one causes damage by saving another's life, however, the courts exempt him from payment so that people should not hesitate to come to the rescue of others.[44]

4:14   Although it is forbidden to save one life with another, it is permitted to kill in self-defense, since the assailant forfeits his life[45] and there is no guilt in killing him.[46] We are therefore taught, "If one comes to kill you, rise up and kill him first."[47]

4:15   Even where the assailant does not directly threaten one's life, as with a burglar[48] or armed robber,[49] he may be killed in self-defense, where it may be assumed that he will kill if provoked.[50] The Torah says, "If a burglar is caught in the act of breaking in, and is struck and killed, it is not considered an act of murder" (Exodus 22:1).[51] We derive all cases of self-defense from this case.[52]

4:16   Just as one may kill in self-defense, so is it required to kill one who is pursuing or attacking another with murderous intent.[53] Of course, if it is possible, one must save the person being pursued by injuring the attacker. Only when this cannot be done must we have no pity and kill the attacker.[54]

the money; *cf.* Rif, *Bava Kama* 43a; *Yad, Chovel* 8:3-4; *Choshen Mishpat* 388:2. For reason, see *Yam Shel Shlomo, Bava Kama* 10:47.

43.   *Cf. Tosafoth, Bava Kama* 4a *s.v. Kevan; Nimukey Yosef, Bava Kama* (Rif 11a) *s.v. U'Meshalem,* from *Yerushalmi, Bava Kama* 2:8 (11b). See also *Tosafoth, Bava Kama* 27b *s.v. Sh'muel, Bava Bathra* 93b *s.v. Chayav, Sanhedrin* 76b *s.v. Rotzeach.*

44.   *Bava Kama* 117b; *Sanhedrin* 74a; *Yad, Chovel* 8:13; *Choshen Mishpat* 380:3.

45.   Rashi on Exodus 22:1 and *Sanhedrin* 72a *s.v. Mai; Sefer Meirath Eynayim (Sema)* 425:6.

46.   Ibn Ezra on Exodus 22:1; *Targum Yonathan ad. loc.; Yad, Genevah* 9:7.

47.   *Sanhedrin* 62a; *Berakhoth* 58a, 62b; *Yoma* 85b; *BaMidbar Rabbah* 21:5, from Numbers 25:17. *Cf.* Radak on 1 Samuel 24:11.

48.   *Sanhedrin* 8:6 (72a). For details concerning burglary, see *Tur, Choshen Mishpat* 425.

49.   *Sefer Mitzvoth Gadol,* Negative Commandment 160 (p. 59a).

50.   *Sanhedrin* 62a; *Yoma* 85b.

51.   The expression *Ein Lo Damim,* literally "he has no blood," is interpreted according to note 46.

52.   Rashi, *Bava Kama* 117b *s.v. MiGufo.* This is compared to the general law of an assailant (*rodef*) in *Berakhoth* 58a, 62b; *Sanhedrin* 72b; *Yad, Genevah* 9:9.

53.   *Sanhedrin* 8:7 (73a); *Tosafoth ad. loc. s.v. Af.*

54.   *Sifri, Ki Tetze* 25:160, *Yalkut Shimoni* (1:938, p. 329a), *ad. loc.; Yad, Rotzeach* 1:7,

4:17   Similarly, any assailant who might kill when provoked, such as a burglar or armed robber, must be killed by any bypasser to save the victim.[55] Extending this to include all cases of endangering life, even a young child who does not know better,[56] or an unborn baby,[57] must be killed, since the life of the victim must be saved by any means.[58]

4:18   We are taught that rape is equivalent to murder.[59] Therefore, if one is attacking a woman with the intent of raping her, he may be killed to save her as long as he has not completed the act. Regarding a woman being sexually attacked, the Torah states, "Only the rapist shall be put to death... Since he attacked the betrothed girl in the field, even if she had cried out, there would have been no one to come to her aid" (Deuteronomy 22:25, 27), which implies that if a rescuer is present, he may use any means to save her, even if it means killing the attacker. One may similarly save a man from homosexual attack.[60]

4:19   An informer who denounces a fellow Jew to the government to be killed, imprisoned, or even fined is likened to an assailant, since being arrested can be a dangerous and traumatic experience. It is in recognition of this danger that the prophet lamented, "Your sons have fainted, they lie at the head of every street, as an antelope trapped in a net" (Isaiah 51:20).[61] Therefore, one who

8; *Hagahoth Maimonioth ad. loc.* 2. According to others, however, this is speaking of a case where the woman has no deadly intent, and "cutting off her hand" denotes that she must pay for the humiliation caused her victim; Rabbi Yehudah, *Sifri, Ki Tetze* 25:161; Rashi on Deuteronomy 25:12. See *Sefer Mitzvoth Gadol,* Negative Commandment 164, Positive Commandment 77, and *Hagahoth Maimonioth loc. cit.* See also *HaTorah VeHaMitzvah* (Malbim) on *Sifri ad. loc.*

55. *Sanhedrin* 72b; *Yad, Genevah* 9:7. *Cf. Minchath Chinukh* 296 (p. 225c).
56. *Ibid.; Yad, Rotzeach* 1:6.
57. See above, 4:9, and note 25.
58. Rabbi Yishmael, *Sanhedrin* 73a, from law of rape; *cf.* Rashi, *Sanhedrin* 72b *s.v. Nithan.*
59. See above, 3:11.
60. *Sanhedrin* 8:7 (73a); *Yad, Rotzeach* 1:10- 12; *Choshen Mishpat* 425:3.
61. The law regarding an informer is from *Yad, Chovel* 8:10; *Choshen Mishpat* 388:10. Based on this, *Sefer Meirath Eynayim (Sema) ad. loc.* (388:29), writes: "The belongings of the Jewish people are likened to an antelope. Just as no one has mercy on the antelope once it is already trapped, so also no one has mercy on our belongings once they have been dispossessed. We are often libeled to such an extent that our very lives are endangered. It is for this reason that an informer is considered as dangerous as an actual assailant"; *cf. Bava Kama* 117a.

is preparing to denounce another is considered an assailant, and may be killed as such as soon as his intention is known.[62]

4:20 In all the above cases, one should attempt to warn the assailant[63] when possible.[64] If he does not heed the warning, he should be stopped by being wounded or incapacitated, and only killed as a last possible resort.[65] One who kills an assailant where he could have just as easily stopped him without taking his life, is considered a murderer.[66]

4:21 One is only considered an assailant before he completes the act of murder, rape[67] or informing.[68] Once the deed is done, however, it becomes a case for the courts, and one may not take the law into his own hands.

4:22 A criminal whose activities endanger the community is considered an assailant, and after being duly warned, may be denounced to the authorities.[69] If he accepts the warning, however, he cannot be denounced for his previous actions. This is true of anybody who endangers others, even without intent.[70]

4:23 Any object that endangers life is judged as an assailant, and may be destroyed without monetary liability.[71]

4:24 "The commandment divides into two parts. "Cut off [the assailant's] hand" (Deuteronomy 25:12) is a positive

62. *Yad, Chovel* 8:10; *Choshen Mishpat* 388:10, from *Berakhoth* 58a; *Bava Kama* 117a; *Sefer Mitzvoth Gadol,* Negative Commandment 160 (p. 59a), Positive Commandment 70 (p. 148c); *Chinukh* 236; *Hagahoth Maimonioth, Genevah* 9:9; *Sefer Chasidim* 686; *Teshuvoth Rivash* 473; Mordecai, *Bava Kama* 195; *Teshuvoth HaRosh* 17:1, 8; *Teshuvoth Rashba* 181; *Tosafoth, Avodah Zarah* 10b *s.v. Chad.*

63. *Yad, Rotzeach* 1:7; *Choshen Mishpat* 425:1, from *Sanhedrin* 72b. For the law regarding an informer, see above, note 61.

64. *Maggid Mishneh, Chovel* 8:10; *Choshen Mishpat* 388:10 (in *Hagah*) from *Berakhoth* 58a. *Cf. Teshuvoth Rivash* 238, quoted in *Mishneh LeMelekh, Chovel* 8:10, that the victim need not give any warning.

65. Regarding an informer, see *Choshen Mishpat* 388:10 (in *Hagah*) from Mordecai, *Bava Kama* 195; *Teshuvoth Maimoni, Nezikin* 66.

66. *Sanhedrin* 74a; *Yad, Rotzeach* 1:13; *Tur, Choshen Mishpat* 425. Rashi, *Sanhedrin* 74a *s.v. VaYekhol,* maintains that this even applies to the victim, but this is disputed by *Mishneh LeMelekh loc. cit.; cf. Minchath Chinukh* 600 (p. 371b). *Cf. Teshuvoth Noda BeYehudah, Evven HaEzer* 1:95.

67. *Sanhedrin* 73a; *Yad, Rotzeach* 1:12; *Sefer Meirath Eynayim (Sema)* 425:10.

68. *Yad, Chovel* 8:11; *Choshen Mishpat* 388:11; Mordecai, *Bava Kama* 196.

69. *Choshen Mishpat* 388:12, 425:1 (in *Hagah*); *Chokhmath Adam* 88:15; *Kitzur Shulchan Arukh* 185:9.

70. HaGra, *Choshen Mishpat* 425:11, from *Bava Kama* 117b.

71. *Cf. Yad, Chovel* 8:15; *Choshen Mishpat* 380:4, from *Bava Kama* 117b.

commandment to save a victim from the hands of his assailant.[72] "Do not show any mercy" (*ibid.*) is a negative commandment not to hesitate to wound or even kill an assailant when necessary.[73]

4:25   In any case, one who neglects to save a life when the opportunity presents itself is guilty of violating the commandment, "Do not stand still when your neighbor's life is in danger" (Leviticus 19:16).[74] Therefore,[75] one is obliged to spend any amount of money necessary to save a Jewish life,[76] but the victim must repay it if and when he is able.[77] Nevertheless, one need not endanger life or limb to save another.[78]

4:26   If several persons are in danger where all cannot be saved, a religious scholar is given priority.[79] Similarly, one should give precedence to his own parents[80] or other relatives,[81] as well as his teachers.[82]

4:27   In case of imminent danger, the life of a man must be saved before that of a woman,[83] because it is assumed that he will

---

72. *Yad, Rotzeach* 1:15; *Sefer HaMitzvoth,* Positive Commandment 247; *Sefer Mitzvoth Gadol,* Positive Commandment 77 (p. 155d); *Chinukh* 600. See above, 4:16.

73. *Yad loc. cit.; Sefer HaMitzvoth,* Negative Commandment 293; *Sefer Mitzvoth Gadol,* Negative Commandment 164 (p. 59c); *Chinukh* 601.

74. *Yad, Rotzeach* 1:14-15; *Sefer HaMitzvoth,* Negative Commandment 283; *Sefer Mitzvoth Gadol,* Negative Commandment 165 (p. 59d); *Chinukh* 237; *Choshen Mishpat* 326:1. *Sefer Mitzvoth Gadol* questions whether this also applies in the case of an assailant; *cf. Sanhedrin* 73a.

75. Similar to any other negative commandment; see below, 6:3.

76. *Sanhedrin* 74a; *Yad, Rotzeach* 1:14; *Choshen Mishpat* 326:1.

77. Rosh, *Sanhedrin* 8:2; *Tur, Choshen Mishpat* 326; *Sefer Meirath Eynayim (Sema)* 326:1. *Cf. Yoreh Deah* 252:12 in *Hagah; Tosafoth, Bava Kama* 58a *s.v. Iy Nami.*

78. *Sefer Meirath Eynayim (Sema)* 326:2; *Teshuvoth Radbaz* 3:627; *Agudath Ezov* 3a; *Teshuvoth Yad Eliahu* 43, quoted in *Pith'chey Teshuvah, Yoreh Deah* 157:15; *Minchath Chinukh* 296 (p. 225b); *Kometz Minchah* 296; *Beer Hetiv, Orach Chaim* 329:6; *"Rav" Shulchan Arukh* 329:8; *Mishnah Berurah* 329:19; *Pith'chey Teshuvah, Choshen Mishpat* 426:2. *Kesef Mishneh, Rotzeach* 1:14 (end) disputes this.

79. *Horayoth* 3:8 (13a); *Yad, Matnoth Ani'im* 8:18; *Yoreh Deah* 251:9. *Cf. Teshuvoth Yad Elihau* 43.

80. *Yad, Yoreh Deah, loc. cit.,* from *Bava Metzia* 2:11 (3a); *Yerushalmi, Horayoth* 3:4 (18a).

81. *Yoreh Deah* 252:12 in *Hagah;* Mordecai, *Bava Metzia* 367. *Cf. Tana DeBei Eliahu Rabbah* 27 (105b). See HaGra, *Yoreh Deah* 151:4.

82. See sources quoted in note 80.

83. *Horayoth* 3:7 (13a); *Yoreh Deah* 252:8 in *Hagah. Cf. Sifethey Cohen* 251:11; *Beer HaGolah* 251:11. See also *Teshuvoth Yaabetz* 1:68.

perform more commandments in his lifetime.[84] In all other cases not involving a life or death situation, as for instance when a woman's honor is at stake, whether it be for food[85] or clothing,[86] she takes precedence, since the shame she could suffer is potentially greater.[87]

4:28 Just as we are required to save a fellow Jew from danger, so too we must rescue any non-Jew who worships God,[88] such as a Christian[89] or Moslem.[90] The Torah thus states, "Help him survive, whether he is a proselyte or a resident alien" (Leviticus 25:35).[91] This implies that we are required to sustain these non-Jews and provide them with charity and food,[92] as the Torah further states, "You may give it to a resident alien in your settlements so that he may eat it" (Deuteronomy 14:21).[93] However, there is no religious obligation to preserve the life of a Jewish atheist or an idolater.[94]

4:29 One need not give his life to save another, as the Torah states, "Let your brother live alongside you" (Leviticus 25:36), which

---

84. Rambam, Bertenoro, on *Horayoth* 3:7; *Turey Zahav* 252:6.

85. *Kethuvoth* 67a; *Tosefta, Kethuvoth* 6:8; *Yad, Matnoth Ani'im* 8:15; *Yoreh Deah* 251:8, 252:8.

86. *Horayoth* 3:7 (13a).

87. Bertenoro *ad. loc.; Sifethey Cohen* 251:12, quoting *Perishah. Cf. Kethuvoth* 67a end.

88. *Avodah Zarah* 20a; *Yad, Shabbath* 2:12; *Sifethey Cohen* 158:2; *Teshuvoth Rivash* 119; *Teshuvoth Noda BeYehudah*, introduction; *Tifereth Yisrael, Bava Kama* 4:4. Cf. *Bava Kama* 117b. See Ramban, additions to *Sefer HaMitzvoth*, Positive Commandment 16.

89. See Volume 1, 1:16.

90. See above, 3:17. Cf. *Magen Avraham* 330:4; *"Rav" Shulchan Arukh* 330:2; *Biur Halakhah* 330:2 s.v. *Kuthith.*

91. In Hebrew, this is *Ger VeToshav VaChai Imakh.* The expression *VaChai Imakh* means literally "he shall live with you." In the context of this verse, the word *Ger* seems to refer to "proselytes," or valid converts to Judaism, while *Toshav* refers to those who have forsworn their belief in idolatry, accepted upon themselves the seven Noahide commandments, and continue to eat non-kosher food. It is for this reason that a *Toshav* is considered a "resident alien"; Rashi, *Sifethey Chakhamim, ad. loc.* See, however, *Avodah Zarah* 20a s.v. *LaGer,* where Rashi equates *Ger* (in Deuteronomy 14:21) with *Ger Toshav.*

92. *Gittin* 61a; *Yad, Matnoth Ani'im* 7:7, *Avodath Kokhavim* 10:5; *Yoreh Deah* 151:12, 251:1 in *Hagah.*

93. Rashi *ad. loc.; Yad, Melakhim* 10:12, from *Avodah Zarah* 20a. "It" refers back to the first half of this verse, "Since you are a holy nation to God your Lord, you may not eat any [mammal or bird] which has not been properly slaughtered. You may give it [this non-kosher food] to the resident alien." See note 91.

94. *Avodah Zarah* 26a-b; *Sanhedrin* 57a; *Tosefta, Bava Metzia* 2:13; *Yad, Avodath Kokhavim* 10:1, *Rotzeach* 4:10; *Yoreh Deah* 158:1-2; *Choshen Mishpat* 425:5; *Chokhmath Adam* 88:16.

implies that one's own life comes first. Therefore, for example, if two persons are in a desert, and one has just enough water for himself, he need not share it with the other.[95] Similarly, one need not endure excessive pain or suffering to save another's life.[96] Although it is not required, it is an act of piety to give one's life to save a community[97] or a great religious leader.[98]

4:30   There is nothing more precious and irreplaceable than life in the eyes of God. Therefore, one who saves a single life is counted as if he had saved the entire world.[99]

95. *Bava Metzia* 62a; *Sifra* (109c), Ramban, on Leviticus 25:26; Ran, *Nedarim* 80b *s.v. Maayan; Sifethey Cohen* 252:10; *Yoreh Deah* 251:3 in *Hagah;* HaGra *ad. loc.* 251:6; *Chelkath Mechokek* 80:22. *Cf. Tosefta, Bava Kama* 10:13; *Minchath Chinukh* 296 (224d); *Tosafoth, Sanhedrin* 74b *s.v. VeHa, Yoma* 82a *s.v. Mah.*

96. *Cf. Nedarim* 80b; *Tosefta, Bava Metzia* 11:14; *Yerushalmi, Nedarim* 11:1 (36b); *Yerushalmi, Shevi'ith* 8:5 (23b); *Yad, Ishuth* 21:11; *Beth Sh'muel (Bash), Evven HaEzer* 80:15; *Beer Hetiv, Evven HaEzer* 80:14; *Pith'chey Teshuvah, Yoreh Deah* 157:15; *Minchath Chinukh* 296 (225b).

97. *Kuzari* 3:19 (28a).

98. *Sefer Chasidim* 698; *Teshuvoth Zekher Yehosef* 78:15; *Teshuvoth Yad Eliahu* 43; *Atereth Tzvi, Choshen Mishpat* 426.

99. *Sanhedrin* 4:5 (37a); *Yad, Rotzeach* 1:16.

FIVE

PRESERVATION OF LIFE

5:1   Along with the wisdom to cure illness, God has given the physician permission to heal,[1] as the Torah states in the case of bodily injury, "[The offender] must provide for his [victim's] complete cure" (Exodus 21:19) — that is, by a doctor.[2] Therefore, the physician need not fear that he is usurping a prerogative of God,[3] nor need he be apprehensive that he may injure or kill his patient, as long as he does his best.[4]

5:2   A doctor who heals a patient fulfills the commandment, "You must return [your brother's loss] to him" (Deuteronomy 22:2). If we are commanded to restore another's possessions, how much more so his life and health.[5]

5:3   Although it is forbidden to rely upon miracles,[6] one must realize that without God's help no physician can preserve life. It is thus written concerning Asa, king of Judah, "He became severely ill, but even in his sickness, instead of beseeching God, he sought his physicians... and he died" (2 Chronicles 16:12). One should always seek the best possible medical help, but still pray to God for divine aid.[7]

1.   *Bava Kama* 85a; *Berakhoth* 60a; *Yoreh Deah* 336:1; *Kitzur Shulchan Arukh* 192:3.
2.   *Targum*, Rashi, *ad. loc.*
3.   Rashi, *Bava Kama* 85a *s.v. Nithneal Reshuth; Tosafoth ad. loc. s.v. Sh'Nithnah;* Ramban on Leviticus 26:11 and *Torath HaAdam, "Shaar HaSakanah"* 9a.
4.   Ramban *loc. cit.; Sifethey Cohen* 336:1, 3. Cf. *Tosefta, Bava Kama* 6:6.
5.   *Sifri ad. loc. s.v. VeHaShevotho Lo; Sanhedrin* 73a; *Bava Kama* 81b; Rambam, Bertenoro, on *Nedarim* 4:4; Ran, *Nedarim* 41b *s.v. Eleh;* Rosh, *Nedarim* 4:8; *Sifethey Cohen* 336:4; *Turey Zahav* 336:2. Cf. *Yad, Nedarim* 6:8.
6.   See above, 1:33-34.
7.   Ramban *loc. cit.;* Rambam, Bertenoro, *Pesachim* 4:10; Rashi, *Berakhoth* 60a *s.v. SheEin; Chovoth HaLevavoth* 4:4 (132b); *Teshuvoth Rashba* 414, 416; *Tur, Yoreh Deah* 336; *Turey Zahav, Yoreh Deah* 336:1.

5:4   With the exception of the three cardinal sins, one must violate any religious law to save a life, as the Torah states, "Keep My decrees and laws, since a person can [truly] live only by keeping them" (Leviticus 18:5) — live by keeping them and not die by keeping them.[8]

5:5   Although keeping the Sabbath is considered a foundation of our religion, it may be violated in any manner necessary to save a life.[9] In such a case, it is a meritorious deed to violate the Sabbath, and one who hesitates is guilty of bloodshed.[10]

5:6   Where the Sabbath is violated in a case of danger, it must be done by responsible adults, and not by children or non-Jews,[11] even where possible.[12] However, if it is possible to avoid violating the Sabbath without causing any delay, it is permissible to do so.[13]

5:7   Similarly, a dangerously sick or starving person may eat any forbidden food necessary to preserve his life. In such a case, all is permitted, even pork products, and bread on Passover.[14]

5:8   Although *Yom Kippur* is our most sacred Day of Atonement, one whose life may be endangered by fasting is forbidden to do so.[15] In such a case, one obtains atonement even without fasting.[16]

8.   *Sifra ad. loc.* (86b); *Yoma* 85b; *Yad, Yesodey HaTorah* 5:1. See above, 3:27, 4:1.
9.   *Yoma* 8:6 (85a); *Yad, Shabbath* 2:1; *Orach Chaim* 328:2; *Chayay Adam* 68:1; *Kitzur Shulchan Arukh* 92:1. Cf. *Mekhilta* on Exodus 21:14 (80b), 31:13 (103b).
10.   *Yerushalmi, Yoma* 8:5 (41b); *Maggid Mishneh, Shabbath* 2:3.
11.   *Yoma* 84b; *Yerushalmi, Yoma* 8:5 (41b); *Yerushalmi, Shabbath* 16:7 (81a); *Yad, Shabbath* 2:3; *Orach Chaim* 328:12. Cf. Rambam on *Shabbath* 18:3; Ran, *Shabbath* (Rif 39b) s.v. *VeNimtzeth; Teshuvoth Tashbatz* 1:58; *Mishnah Berurah* 328:34.
12.   *Turey Zahav* 328:5; *Beer Hetiv* 328:5; "*Rav*" *Shulchan Arukh* 328:13; *Mishnah Berurah* 328:27; *Kitzur Shulchan Arukh* 92:1. Some maintain that gentiles should be engaged in any case if possible without delay; *Orach Chaim* 328:12 in *Hagah; Chayay Adam* 68:2; cf. *Tosafoth, Yoma* 84b s.v. *Eleh.* The same rule applies in the case of leaven on Passover; cf. *Magen Avraham* 450:9; *Shaarey Teshuvah* 450:11; *Mishnah Berurah* 450:18; "*Rav*" *Shulchan Arukh* 466:5, 450:26. However, others maintain that in this case also a gentile should be engaged whenever possible; cf. *Chokhmath Adam* 88:10. See also *Shaarey Teshuvah, Orach Chaim* 465:2; *Magen Avraham* 343:3; *Teshuvoth Nachalath Shivah* 14; *Teshuvoth Bayith Chadash* 43.
13.   *Orach Chaim* 328:12 in *Hagah; Mishnah Berurah* 328:25; cf. *Shabbath* 19:2 (133a); Bertenoro *ad. loc. s.v. Lo'es; Tosafoth ad. loc.* 133b *s.v. Lo'es;* Ramban, *Torath HaAdam* 6b.
14.   *Pesachim* 25a; *Yad, Yesodey HaTorah* 5:6; *Yoreh Deah* 155:3; *Chokhmath Adam* 88:2; *Kitzur Shulchan Arukh* 192:7. Cf. *Yad, Maakhaloth Assuroth* 14:13.
15.   *Yoma* 8:5 (82a); *Yad, Shevithath Assor* 2:8; *Orach Chaim* 618:2; *Chayay Adam* 145:29; *Kitzur Shulchan Arukh* 133:14.
16.   Cf. *Shevuoth* 13a; *Kerithoth* 7a; *Mishnah Berurah* 618:5, quoting *Teshuvoth Binyan Tzion.*

5:9 In all cases of sickness or injury, we rely upon the opinion of a physician.[17] As soon as he says that there is even a question of danger, any religious law may be violated to preserve life,[18] even if it is not certain that a given cure will help.[19]

5:10 In any case where there is disagreement between medical authorities, one should make the same decision that one would make if no religious prohibition were involved,[20] since where any question of danger is concerned, all religious laws must be completely ignored.[21]

5:11 If the patient himself feels that his life is in danger, his word must be taken against any number of physicians. Regarding such a case, it is written, "The heart knows its own bitterness" (Proverbs 14:10).[22]

5:12 If any lay person claims to recognize a sickness or injury as being dangerous, his word must be taken,[23] even if he is not certain,[24] as long as he is not contradicted by a competent physician.[25]

5:13 In any case, one should not violate religious law to provide a remedy unless it is prescribed by a physician or is otherwise known to be effective.[26] Still, if the patient insists that a certain remedy is necessary, it may be administered for its psychological effect,[27] as long as it is not known to be injurious to his health.[28]

---

17. *Orach Chaim* 328:10, 618:1, from *Yoma* 8:5 (84a); *cf.* Rambam, Bertenoro, *ad. loc.; Yad, Shabbath* 2:1.
18. Even if the patient does not feel he is in danger; *Yerushalmi, Yoma* 8:4 (41a); *Orach Chaim* 618:5.
19. Ran, *Shabbath* (Rif 40a) *s.v. VeEin; Turey Zahav* 328:5; *"Rav" Shulchan Arukh* 328:2.
20. Therefore, one may violate the law even if two doctors disagree; *Yoma* 83a; *Yad, Shabbath* 2:1; *Orach Chaim* 328:10, 618:2. If two physicians say that there is danger, no number can contradict them; *Yad, Shevithath Assor* 2:8; *Orach Chaim* 618:4.
21. See note 32.
22. *Yoma* 83a; *Orach Chaim* 618:1. *Cf.* Mordecai, *Shabbath* 417; *Teshuvoth Radbaz* 4:66. *Magen Avraham* 328:6; *Mishnah Berurah* 328:25.
23. *Orach Chaim* 328:10, from *Tur, Orach Chaim* 328; *Hagahoth Maimonioth, Shabbath* 2:1 no. 2; *Darkey Moshe, Orach Chaim* 618; *Mishnah Berurah* 618:1.
24. *"Rav" Shulchan Arukh* 328:10; *Kitzur Shulchan Arukh* 92:2.
25. *Magen Avraham* 328:7; *Mishnah Berurah* 328:27.
26. *Yoreh Deah* 155:3 in *Hagah,* from *Yoma* 49a. *Hagahoth Maimonioth, Maakhaloth Assuroth* 14:15 no. 2; *Magen Avraham* 466:2; *Turey Zahav* 328:5; *Chokhmath Adam* 88:7; *"Rav" Shulchan Arukh* 328:2, 466:5.
27. *Teshuvoth Radbaz* 4:66; *Magen Avraham* 328:6; *Chokhmath Adam* 88:8. *Biur Halakhah* 328:10 *s.v. VeRofe* discusses this at length. *Cf. Teshuvoth Rashba* 4:284; *Shiltey Gibborim, Shabbath* (Rif 51b) no. 2.
28. *Cf. Magen Avraham* 618:3; *Machtzith HaShekel* 328:6; *Chayay Adam* 155:29, that

5:14 If a physician maintains that a certain remedy is necessary, he must be heeded even though the patient may insist that he has no need of it.[29] In such a case, the patient may even be forced to take it.[30] One who goes aginst his physician's advice and refuses to violate any religious law when required is considered among the foolishly pious. He is held accountable for endangering his own life.[31] Regarding such a case, we are warned, "Do not be overly righteous" (Ecclesiastes 7:16).

5:15 When life is endangered, all religious laws may be totally disregarded. Therefore, even things that are not necessary to preserve the patient's life are permitted, as long as they enhance his well-being.[32] Nevertheless, one should not violate any religious law if treatment can be effected equally well without doing so.[33] Similarly, one should violate the least serious law whenever possible,[34] but when the danger is imminent and speed is essential, one need not concern oneself with these questions.[35]

5:16 Even when danger is not imminent, religious law may be violated to prevent the risk of future danger.[36] It is forbidden to hesitate in any case where such a delay may imperil life.[37]

5:17 An internal injury is generally considered dangerous, and one

regarding eating on *Yom Kippur* the patient is his own best judge, and may eat even if the physicians say that it will be harmful. However, this certainly does not apply when he has a known malady for which food is actually harmful.

29. *Yoma* 83a; *Orach Chaim* 618:1.
30. *Magen Avraham* 328:6; *Chayay Adam* 68:8.
31. *Beer Hetiv* 328:1; *Mishnah Berurah* 328:6; *Pith'chey Teshuvah, Yoreh Deah* 155:4, citing *Teshuvoth Radbaz* 1:67; *Kitzur Shulchan Arukh* 92:2.
32. *Orach Chaim* 328:4, from *Torath HaAdam* 7a; *Ran, Shabbath* (Rif 40a) *s.v. Makah; Maggid Mishneh, Shabbath* 2:14; *Magen Avraham* 328:4; *Pri Megadim ad. loc.; Teshuvoth Radbaz* 1:30; "*Rav*" *Shulchan Arukh* 328:4; *Teshuvoth Tzemach Tzedek, Orach Chaim* 35. This opinion is questioned, however, by *Mishnah Berurah* 328:14 and *Biur Halakhah* 328:4 *s.v. Kol; cf. Teshuvoth Tashbatz* 1:54; Recanti 104. Also see *Yad, Shabbath* 2:2.
33. *Yoreh Deah* 155:3 in *Hagah; HaGra ad. loc.* 155:24; *Chokhmath Adam* 88:9; *cf. Yad, Shabbath* 2:1; *Kesef Mishneh ad. loc.; Menachoth* 64a. See above, note 13.
34. *Yoma* 83a; *Tosefta, Yoma* 4:5; *Yad, Maakhaloth Assuroth* 14:16; *Orach Chaim* 618:9. *Cf. Orach Chaim* 328:16. See also *Teshuvoth Tashbatz* 3:38; *Teshuvoth Radbaz* 3:441; *Teshuvoth Noda BeYehudah, Orach Chaim* 1:36; *Teshuvoth Besamim Rosh* 39.
35. *Orach Chaim* 328:16 in *Hagah,* citing *Hagahoth Mordecai; Chayay Adam* 68:1.
36. *Rosh, Yoma* 8:13; *Magen Avraham* 618:2; *Mishnah Berurah* 3289:17; *Kitzur Shulchan Arukh* 92:2.
37. *Turey Zahav* 328:5. See above, notes 12, 35.

may violate the Sabbath or any other law without question to obtain medical aid.[38] However, even in the case of an extreme internal pain,[39] one may not violate the Sabbath unless it may be a warning of a serious illness[40] such as a heart attack or acute appendicitis.

5:18 Similarly, any injury to the teeth,[41] gums[42] or eyes[43] is always considered dangerous. One may likewise violate the Sabbath in the case of any injury that might damage exposed blood vessels, as on the back of the hand or the feet,[44] as well as any wound caused by a deadly weapon.[45] In any case where there is danger of excessive bleeding or shock, immediate medical attention is required.

5:19 One may similarly violate the Sabbath to bring medical aid to a person suffering from a very high fever,[46] as well as one bitten by a rabid dog[47] or other animal.[48]

5:20 A woman in childbirth is considered to be in danger unless the proper medical steps are taken.[49] Therefore, she may be taken to the hospital, and medical aid may be summoned, as soon as labor commences,[50] even on the Sabbath.

5:21 Similarly, a new born child is considered to be in danger unless it receives the proper medical attention.[51] Therefore, one may

38. *Avodah Zarah* 28a; *Yerushalmi, Avodah Zarah* 2:2 (10b); *Yerushalmi, Shabbath* 14:4 (76a); *Yad, Shabbath* 2:5; *Orach Chaim* 328:3.
39. *"Rav" Shulchan Arukh* 328:3. See below, 5:34.
40. *Biur Halakhah* 328:2 *s.v. VeDavka.*
41. See note 38.
42. *Mishnah Berurah* 328:7, from *Tosafoth, Avodah Zarah* 28a *s.v. Kekhi;* cf. Rambam, *Yoma* 8:6.
43. *Orach Chaim* 328:9.
44. *Shabbath* 109a; *Orach Chaim* 328:6.
45. *Avodah Zarah* 28a; Rashi *ad. loc. s.v. Padaatha; Tosafoth ad. loc. s.v. Makah;* Mordecai *ad. loc.* 815. *Cf. Tevuoth Shor, Yoreh Deah* 44:4.
46. *Pesachim* 25b; *Orach Chaim* 328:7.
47. *Avodah Zarah* 28b; *Orach Chaim* 328:6.
48. *Ibid.; Shabbath* 121b.
49. *Shabbath* 18:3 (128b); *Yad, Shabbath* 2:1; *Orach Chaim* 330:1.
50. *Turey Zahav* 330:2; *"Rav" Shulchan Arukh* 330:3; *Chayay Adam* 68:16; *Mishnah Berurah* 330:9; *Kitzur Shulchan Arukh* 93:1.
51. *Yad, Shabbath* 2:14. *Cf. Biur Halakhah* 330:7 *s.v. HaVlad,* who follows this opinion and therefore permits the violation of even Biblical prohibitions, thereby disputing *Magen Avraham* 330:13, from *Tosafoth, Shabbath* 129b *s.v. Kol.*

violate the Sabbath to do whatever is usually required for the infant.[52]

5:22   If a woman dies in labor, the Sabbath may be violated in any manner to save her unborn child, as long as there is the slightest chance that it is still alive.[53] As soon as the mother dies, the living child is considered to be born, lying in her body as in any other lifeless container.[54] If there is a chance that she is still alive, however, the mother may not be harmed in any way whatsoever, even on a weekday.[55]

5:23   Where there is any question of saving life, the Sabbath may be violated in any manner necessary. Therefore, if a fire breaks out, it may be extinguished wherever life may be endangered. Similarly, if a building collapses, one may dig into the rubble to save the victims. Likewise, if a person falls into a well, or is in danger of drowning, all that is necessary may be done to save them. Even where a child locks himself into a room or closet where he may hurt himself or be dangerously frightened, the door may be broken down, or any help summoned.[56]

5:24   Similarly, if a ship is in danger of sinking, or an individual is being pursued or attacked, the Sabbath may be violated in any way to save life.[57]

5:25   In case of war, one may violate the Sabbath in any way to fight back, since many lives may be at stake.[58]

5:26   One who violates the Sabbath in an attempt to save a life is worthy of merit[59] even if it turns out that his services were not

52. *Shabbath* 18:3 (128b); *Orach Chaim* 330:7.
53. *Arakhin* 7a; *Yad, Shabbath* 2:15; *Orach Chaim* 330:5.
54. *Tosafoth, Niddah* 44a *s.v. Ihu; Torath HaAdam* 6a; *Ran, Yoma* (Rif 3b) *s.v. VeKathuv.*
55. *Orach Chaim* 33:5 in *Hagah. Cf. Machtzith HaShekel* 330:11, quoting *Sefer Tosefeth Shabbath.* It appears that in such a case the test of breath alone is not enough; see above, 4:8; below, 5:28. Regarding a case where the mother is mortally wounded, see *Teshuvoth Rama* 5; *Teshuvoth Rabbi Yosef Trani (Maharit) 1:94; Eshel Avraham* 330:6.
56. *Yoma* 84b; *Yad, Shabbath* 2:17; *Orach Chaim* 329:1; *Magen Avraham* 328:8.
57. *Tosefta, Eruvin* 3:7; *Yad, Shabbath* 2:24; *Orach Chaim* 329:8. *Cf. Sanhedrin* 72b; *Yad, Genevah* 9:7.
58. *Cf. Eruvin* 45a; *Tosefta, Eruvin* 3:5; *Yad, Shabbath* 2:23; *Orach Chaim* 330:6.
59. *Orach Chaim* 328:15.

needed or in vain.[60] Similarly, one who unintentionally saves a life while purposely violating the Sabbath is free of all blame.[61]

5:27   One may violate the Sabbath where there is any chance, however miniscule, of saving a life. For example, one may search through the rubble of a collapsed building for survivors, even though the building may have been empty,[62] or all the occupants killed,[63] as long as there is any chance at all of a living person being trapped. Where life is at stake, we do not assume probabilities,[64] since the commandment to "live by keeping them"[65] does not permit any situation where observance should lead to death.[66]

5:28   Similarly, the commandment to "live by keeping them" requires us to prolong life wherever possible, even temporarily.[67] Therefore, if someone is dying[68] or mortally injured, the Sabbath may be violated to prolong his life even for minutes.[69]

5:29   One may violate the Sabbath to save the life of a very young child or an imbecile, since the commandments apply to them, but they are exempt due to their lack of understanding.[70] Similarly, one may violate the Sabbath to save an unborn fetus or embryo, since it will eventually live to keep many Sabbaths.[71]

5:30   Like all the other laws of the Torah, the commandment to "live

60.   *Menachoth* 64a; *Yad, Shabbath* 2:8.
61.   Rabbah, *Menachoth* 64a; *Yad, Shabbath* 2:16; *cf.* Raavad, *Maggid Mishneh, Migdal Oz, ad. loc.; Shegagoth* 2:15. See *Orach Chaim* 328:13; *Shaar HaTziun ad. loc.* 328:17. *Cf. Pri Megadim, Eshel Avraham* 328:8.
62.   *Mishnah Berurah* 329:9.
63.   *Yoma* 85a; *Yad, Shabbath* 2:18; *Orach Chaim* 329:3.
64.   *Yoma* 84b; *Yad, Shabbath* 2:20; *Orach Chaim* 329:2.
65.   See above, 5:4.
66.   Rashi, *Yoma* 85b *s.v. DeSh'muel; Tosafoth, Yoma* 85a *s.v. U'LeFakeach HaGal; "Rav" Shulchan Arukh* 329:3; *Mishnah Berurah* 329:5. *Cf. Pri Megadim, Mishbetzoth Zahav* 329:1; *Shaar HaTziun* 329:6. See also *Yad, Shabbath* 2:3.
67.   Ramban, *Torath HaAdam* 7a; *Pri Megadim, Mishbetzoth Zahav* 329:2. Meiri, *Yoma* 85a, gives the reason that he may repent in his last moments; *cf.* Maharatz Chajas, *Shabbath* 30a. But we may prolong life even where this reason does not apply, as in the case of a very young child or imbecile; *cf. Biur Halakhah* 329:4 *s.v. Eleh.*
68.   *Tosafoth, Niddah* 44a *s.v. Ihu; Pri Megadim, Biur Halakhah, loc. cit.*
69.   *Yoma* 85a; *Yad, Shabbath* 2:18; *Orach Chaim* 329:4.
70.   *Biur Halakhah loc. cit.* See below, 11:8*ff.*
71.   *Halakhoth Gedoloth,* quoted in *Torath HaAdam* 6a; Ran, *Yoma* (Rif 3b) *s.v. VeKathuv;* Rosh, *Yoma* 8:13; Ritva, *Niddah* 44a; *"Rav" Shulchan Arukh* 330:8; *Biur Halakhah* 330:7 *s.v. O Safek; cf. Magen Avraham* 330:15; *Pri Megadim, Mishbetzoth Zahav* 328:1; *Minchath Chinukh* 296 (p. 223c). Rosh gives a further reason that when

by keeping them" only applies to the Jewish people.[72] Therefore, one may not violate the Sabbath for the sake of a non-Jew, even though he may be in danger.[73] A physician should therefore prepare a non-Jewish substitute for the Sabbath, and not call on his non-Jewish patients, even in an emergency.[74] In a case of extreme danger, however, some authorities maintain that one may violate a rabbinical law for a non-Jew.[75]

5:31   In a city where Jews live, even where they are a minute minority, an unknown person in mortal danger, who cannot be asked, may be assumed to be Jewish in order to save his life on the Sabbath.[76] Similarly, if a disaster occurs in a city where Jews live, one may assume that Jews are involved and assist in rescue operations on the Sabbath.[77]

5:32   In the case of a plane, train or other transportation accident, if the point of origin is a city where Jews live, it may be assumed that there are Jews aboard in order to save lives.[78] However, if the point of origin is unknown, one may not violate the Sabbath to help,[79] unless there is some indication that a Jewish passenger is aboard.[80]

5:33   Where life is not endangered, one may not violate any Biblical prohibition, though one is ill or in pain.[81]

the fetus is endangered so is the mother, in which case *Pri Megadim* permits it without question.

72. Cf. *Tosafoth, Sanhedrin* 74b *s.v. Ben.* See Kaplan, *The Jew* (in *Kaplan Reader,* pp. 159-169).

73. *Yoma* 8:7 (83a); *Avodah Zarah* 27a; *Yad, Shabbath* 2:12; *Orach Chaim* 330:2; *Turey Zahav, Yoreh Deah* 154:5.

74. *Mishnah Berurah* 330:8.

75. Cf. *Pri Megadim, Eshel Avraham* 330:4; *Biur Halakhah* 330:2 *s.v. Kuthith.*

76. *Evven HaEzer* 4:34 in *Hagah,* from *Yoma* 85a; *Kethuvoth* 15b; *HaGra ad. loc.* 4:92; *Beth Sh'muel (Bash) ad. loc.* 4:58; *Turey Zahav ad. loc.* 4:19; *Mishnah Berurah* 329:6; *Pri Megadim, Eshel Avraham* 329:2; *Binath Adam, Shaar Kavuah* 41. Where the victim is unconscious or otherwise unable to answer, he is considered the same as an infant in the above sources.

77. *Yoma* 84b; *Yad, Shabbath* 2:20 and commentary *ad. loc.; Orach Chaim* 329:2. *Hagah, Evven HaEzer* 4:34 asserts that an entire city is considered like the courtyard discussed in this case; *cf. Mishnah Berurah, Orach Chaim* 329:6. If the disaster occurs indoors, this is a unanimous opinion; see *Tosafoth, Kethuvoth* 15a *s.v. Dilma; Beth Sh'muel (Bash) loc. cit.*

78. *Ibid.,* considering the city of origin to be like the courtyard under question.

79. *Pri Megadim, Mishnah Berurah, loc. cit.*

80. Rabbi Akiba Eiger, *Orach Chaim* 329:8.

81. *Orach Chaim* 329:1; *Yoreh Deah* 155:3; *Chokhmath Adam* 88:3.

5:34   If any part of the body is in danger of being permanently damaged without immediate attention, all rabbinical prohibitions may be violated to treat it, even though there is no mortal danger.[82] Therefore, for example, it is permitted to set a broken[83] or dislocated[84] limb on the Sabbath. However, where a Biblical law must be violated, it may only be done by a non-Jew.[85]

5:35   If one is sick enough to be bedridden,[86] or in such pain as to feel sick all over,[87] he may be treated by violating any rabbinical law on the Sabbath, as long as it is not done in the usual manner.[88] Similarly, he may take any necessary medication[89] or be treated by a non-Jew in any necessary manner.[90] Therefore, for example, one who has a severe toothache on the Sabbath may have it treated by a non-Jewish dentist.[91]

5:36   One who has a simple ache or pain, or other minor illness, is forbidden to take any remedy on the Sabbath, even where there is no violation at all.[92] All such cases are forbidden by rabbinical law, in order that one should not confuse them with cases of mortal danger and violate the Sabbath by preparing a remedy.[93] Similarly, one may not be treated by a non-Jew, since rabbinical law forbids

82. Ramban, *Torath HaAdam* 4b; Ran, *Shabbath* (Rif 39b) *s.v. U'MeHa;* Rosh, *Avodah Zarah* 2:10, from *Avodah Zarah* 28b; *Orach Chaim* 328; *Turey Zahav* 328:11; *Magen Avraham* 328:13; *Chayay Adam* 69:13; *Mishnah Berurah* 328:57; *"Rav" Shulchan Arukh* 328:19. But see *Yad, Shabbath* 2:10; *Maggid Mishneh, Kesef Mishneh, ad. loc.*
83. *Shabbath* 148a; *Orach Chaim* 328:47.
84. *Chayay Adam* 69:7; *Mishnah Berurah* 328:145, citing *Sefer Shulchan Atzey Shittim,* though in the case of a mere dislocation this is disputed by *Magen Avraham* 328:51 and *"Rav" Shulchan Arukh* 328:52.
85. *Nishmath Adam* 69:1; *Mishnah Berurah* 328:51.
86. Ran, *Shabbath* (Rif 39b) *s.v. U'Meha.*
87. *Avodah Zarah* 28a; *Maggid Mishneh, Shabbath* 2:10.
88. Ramban, *Torath HaAdam* 4a, cited in *Tur;* Rashba, *Shabbath* 129a; *Orach Chaim* 328:17, third opinion; *Turey Zahav* 328:7; *Mishnah Berurah* 328:57.
89. *Orach Chaim* 328:37 in *Hagah; Magen Avraham* 328:44; *Chayay Adam* 69:11; *"Rav" Shulchan Arukh* 328:19; *Kitzur Shulchan Arukh* 91:17. However, *Mishnah Berurah* 329:121 citing Radbaz maintains that one may only take a remedy which may otherwise be eaten as food; *cf. Biur Halakhah;* HaGra 328:37 *s.v. VeKhen; Turey Zahav* 328:25.
90. *Shabbath* 129a; *Betza* 28a; *Yad, Shabbath* 2:10.
91. *Orach Chaim* 328:3 in *Hagah.*
92. *Shabbath* 14:3 (109b), 14:4 (111a); Ran, *Shabbath* (Rif 39b) *s.v. U'Meha; Orach Chaim* 328:1.
93. *Shabbath* 53b; Rashi *ad. loc. s.v. Gezera; Yad, Shabbath* 21:20; Bertenoro, *Shabbath* 14:3 *s.v. SheEin.*

us from having a non-Jew do anything prohibited to a Jew, in order to preserve the sanctity of the Sabbath.[94] God thus enjoins us through His prophet, "Refrain from pursuing your own affairs on My holy day..." (Isaiah 58:13).[95] It is only in cases of extreme pain or illness that exceptions were made.[96]

5:37　However, in a case where medicine is never used[97] and there is no question of preparing a remedy,[98] one may relieve pain on the Sabbath. Therefore, for example, one may remove a splinter, even with a needle,[99] or press down a bruise with a knife or with ice.[100]

5:38　It is forbidden to eat, or even swallow[101] any forbidden food as a remedy when one is not dangerously sick. However, the Biblical prohibitions regarding forbidden foods only apply when they are eaten in an enjoyable manner,[102] since this is the normal connotation of eating.[103] When they are mixed with a very bitter substance, or eaten in any other manner which eliminates the possibility of deriving pleasure from them, they are forbidden only by rabbinical law,[104] and may be eaten as a remedy, even when there is no danger.[105]

5:39　It is permitted to swallow any forbidden food encased in an

---

94. *Shabbath* 150a; *Yad, Shabbath* 6:1.
95. *Ibid.;* Rashi, *Avodah Zarah* 6a *s.v. V'Lifney Iver; Kitzur Shulchan Arukh* 90:14.
96. *Mishnah Berurah* 328:50.
97. *Cf. Turey Zahav* 328:28; *Mishnah Berurah* 328:130, that in a case where any medicine may be used, all remedies are forbidden, even without medicine.
98. *Orach Chaim* 328:43; *Chayay Adam* 69:5.
99. *Shabbath* 17:2 (122b), 107a; *Yad, Shabbath* 25:8; *Orach Chaim* 308:11; *Magen Avraham* 328:32; *Kitzur Shulchan Arukh* 92:15. See *Biur Halakhah* 308:11 *s.v. HaKotz,* that it is permitted even where one may cause bleeding.
100. *Chayay Adam* 69:5.
101. *Teshuvoth Noda BeYehudah, Yoreh Deah* 1:35, cited in *Pith'chey Teshuvah* 155:6. *Cf. Teshuvoth Besamin Rosh* 141.
102. *Pesachim* 24b; *Yad, Maakhaloth Assuroth* 14:10.
103. *Chokhmath Adam* 88:3. However, where the prohibition does not specify eating, such as meat cooked in milk or mixed species, it is forbidden even without enjoyment, and may not be used as a remedy in any case where there is no danger; *Pesachim* 25a. *Cf. Lechem Mishneh, Maakhaloth Assuroth* 9:2.
104. *Tosafoth, Avodah Zarah* 12b *s.v. Eleh;* Ran, *Pesachim* (Rif 6b) *s.v. VeRa'ithi;* Rosh, *Pesachim* 2:2. However, Mordecai, *Pesachim* 545, maintains that without enjoyment it is absolutely permitted; see HaGra, *Yoreh Deah* 155:22.
105. *Pesachim* 25b; *Yad, Yesodey HaTorah* 5:8; *Yoreh Deah* 155:3; *Magen Avraham* 466:2; *Chokhmath Adam* 88:3; *Kitzur Shulchan Arukh* 192:5.

inedible capsule as a remedy,[106] since it does not touch[107] one's mouth or throat[108] while being swallowed. Similarly, one may take a medicine made of forbidden foods which have been burned[109] or chemically reduced,[110] since they are no longer considered to be food.[111]

5:40 We are commanded to preserve our health and well-being, as the Torah states, "Take heed and guard your life very carefully" (Deuteronomy 4:9),[112] and "Guard your lives very carefully" (*ibid.* 4:15).[113] It is therefore forbidden for a person to deliberately injure himself[114] or endanger his life or health in any way. Torah law itself requires that we be more strict concerning a danger to our physical well-being than concerning a violation of its own commandments.[115]

5:41 One who places either his own or another's life in danger is guilty of violating the commandment, "Do not allow a dangerous situation to remain in your house" (Deuteronomy 22:8).[116] For this reason, one should keep his property clear of anything that might cause a serious accident.[117]

106. *Chokhmath Adam* 88:6; *Binath Adam, Issur VeHeter* 91; *Mishneh LeMelekh, Maakhaloth Assuroth* 14:12, from *Pesachim* 115b; *Yad, Chametz U'Matzah* 6:2; *Orach Chaim* 475:3. See also *Yerushalmi, Shevuoth* 3:3 (13a); Ridbaz, *Korban HaEdah, ad. loc.* .

107. *Tosafoth, Sotah* 18a *s.v. Ba'ey.* However, if it is encased in a food substance, it is forbidden, since a similar substance is not considered an intervention; *Sukkah* 37b; *Zevachim* 110a. We find a similar distinction in *Tosefta, Zavim* 5:6; *cf. Yad, Avoth HaTumoth* 3:5; *Kesef Mishneh ad. loc.,* from Rash, *Zavim* 5:11. See *Pri Chadash, Orach Chaim* 475:3, cited in *Mishnah Berurah* 475:33.

108. Although it touches the stomach when the capsule dissolves; *Chullin* 103b; *Yad, Maakhaloth Assuroth* 14:3.

109. Mordecai, *Pesachim* 545; *Teshuvoth Rivash* 255; *Yoreh Deah* 155:3 in *Hagah,* from *Temurah* 34a; see *Tosafoth ad. loc.* 33b *s.v. HaNisrafim; Yad, Pesuley HaMukdashin* 19:13; HaGra, *Yoreh Deah* 155:21.

110. *Cf. Yoreh Deah* 87:10, 90:2 in *Hagah,* from Rash, *Kilayim* 7:1; HaGra, *Yoreh Deah* 87:29. See also *Teshuvoth Shevuth Yaakov* 2:70, cited in *Pith'chey Teshuvah* 155:6; *Teshuvoth Tifereth Tzvi, Yoreh Deah* 73, cited in *Pith'chey Teshuvah* 87:20.

111. *Cf. Pesachim* 15b; *Taharoth* 8:6.

112. *Berakhoth* 32b (end); *Shevuoth* 36a; *Yad, Rotzeach* 11:4; *Choshen Mishpat* 427:5; *Chokhmath Adam* 68:4; *Sefer Mitzvoth Gadol,* Positive Commandment 79 (156b); *Chinukh* 546; Ran, *Shevuoth* (Rif 10a) *s.v. Malkin.* See *Minchath Chinukh* 546 (350c) and *Kometz Minchah,* for discussion of how this can count as a commandment.

113. *Berakhoth* 32b; *Kitzur Shulchan Arukh* 32:1.

114. *Bava Kama* 8:6 (90b), 91b; *Yad, Chovel* 5:1; HaGra, *Yoreh Deah* 236:6, 239:17. *Cf. Tosafoth, Shevuoth* 36a *s.v. U'Shemor.*

115. *Chullin* 10a; *Yoreh Deah* 116:5 in *Hagah; Kitzur Shulchan Arukh* 33:7.

116. Literally, "Prevent any blood from being spilt in your house"; *Chokhmath Adam* 68:4.

117. *Sifri ad. loc.; Yalkut Shimoni* 1:939 (320b); *Bava Kama* 15b; *Sefer HaMitzvoth,* Positive

5:42   It is an extremely serious sin to cause one's own death, whether by intent or negligence. One who does so is considered a murderer, as the Torah states, "I will surely demand an account for [spilling] your own life's blood" (Genesis 9:5).[118]

Commandment 184, Negative Commandment 239; *Sefer Mitzvoth Gadol,* Negative Commandment 167 (58d); *Yad, Choshen Mishpat, loc. cit.*

118. Rashi, Ramban, *ad. loc.; Bava Kama* 91b; *Bereshith Rabbah* 34:19; *Yalkut Shimoni* 1:61 (16b); *Yad, Rotzeach* 2:2; Ran, *Shevuoth* (Rif 10a) *s.v. Malkin; cf. Yoreh Deah* 345:1.

SIX

FINANCIAL SACRIFICE

6:1   One's love for God must exceed his love for all material things. We are commanded, "Love God your Lord... with all your might" (Deuteronomy 6:5) — that is, even at the cost of all your wealth.[1] Therefore, there are times when a person must be ready to sacrifice all his possessions for the sake of God, even though he is not required to give his life.

6:2   If one lives in a place where it is impossible to keep our religion, he must move to a place where it is possible, whatever the expense or loss.[2]

6:3   One must sacrifice all one's possessions rather than actively[3] violate any negative commandment in the Torah.[4]

6:4   For example, if the cost of Kosher food is many times that of non-Kosher foods, one must spend any amount of additional money rather than eat something forbidden.[5] Similarly, in case of a fire, where no life is endangered, one may not violate the Sabbath to save one's possessions.[6]

6:5   One should not work or do business on the Sabbath, even if he is

---

1. *Targum,* Rashi, Ramban, *ad. loc.; Berakhoth* 9:5 (54a), 61a.
2. Rambam, *Iggereth HaShmad,* p. 19.
3. But not passively; *Pri Megadim, Eshel Avraham* 656:8; *Pith'chey Teshuvah* 157:3, quoting *Mishnath Chakhamim; Gilyon Maharsha, Yoreh Deah* 157:1 *s.v. Tzarikh.*
4. Ran, *Sukkah* (Rif 16a top) *s.v. U'LeHidur Mitzvah; Teshuvoth Rivash* 387; *Yoreh Deah* 157:1 in *Hagah; Orach Chaim* 656:1 in *Hagah. Cf. Shabbath* 16:6 (121a); *Betza* 22a; *Chullin* 49b, 56a; *Bekhoroth* 40a; *Chayay Adam* 21:13.
5. *Cf. Teshuvoth Radbaz* 1:145, cited in *Pith'chey Teshuvah* 157:4.
6. *Shabbath* 16:6 (121a); *Yerushalmi, Shabbath* 16:3 (80b); *Tosefta* 14:5; *Yad, Shabbath* 12:3; *Orach Chaim* 334:26 in *Hagah; Chayay Adam* 45:4ff.; *Kitzur Shulchan Arukh* 86:8. Some permit the violation of certain rabbinical laws; *Orach Chaim* 334:2, 301:33 in *Hagah; cf. Chayay Adam* 45:8. The majority forbid it; *Magen Avraham* 301:46; *Turey Zahav* 301:23; HaGra, *Orach Chaim* 334:2; *Yoreh Deah* 157:4; *Pri Megadim, Eshel Avraham* 334:31; *Mishnah Berurah* 334:76; *Biur Halakhah* 334:2 *s.v. D'BeMakom.*

thereby reduced to poverty. We are told that a person should beg for his bread and rely on charity rather than violate the Sabbath in any manner.[7] One should therefore never do business where the Sabbath is the main market day, since he may succumb to the temptation of gaining extra profit on the Sabbath.[8] Relying on charity, however, only relates to violating the Sabbath. Regarding the commandment to honor the Sabbath with special food and clothing,[9] it is preferable to treat the Sabbath as a weekday rather than rely on charity.[10]

6:6   Although one must impoverish himself rather than actively sin, one need not do so for the sake of doing good. From the two agricultural tithes, we learn that God does not intend for us to use more than a fifth of our means for religious purposes.[11] Therefore, one need not spend more than a fifth of his money in order to perform a positive commandment,[12] even if he will never have another chance to do it.[13] For example, one need not spend more than this amount for a *Tallith* or *Tefillin,* a *Sukkah* or *Ethrog* for *Sukkoth,* or *Matzah* for Passover.

6:7   Similarly, a fifth of one's income is considered a generous contribution to charity,[14] and should not be exceeded. It is forbidden to impoverish oneself by distributing all of one's wealth to charity,[15] and one who does so is counted among the foolishly pious who bring destruction to the world.[16] However, one may

---

7.   *Mishnah Berurah* 656:10.
8.   *Sefer Chasidim* 262; *Magen Avraham* 307:3; *Mishnah Berurah* 307:15; *"Rav" Shulchan Arukh* 307:9.
9.   *Shabbath* 25b; *Yad, Shabbath* 30:1ff.
10. *Shabbath* 118a; *Pesachim* 112a; *Tana DeBei Eliahu Rabbah* 26 (104b); *Yad, Shabbath* 30:6; *Orach Chaim* 242:1.
11. *Kethuvoth* 50a; *Yerushalmi, Kethuvoth* 4:8 (29a); *Yerushalmi, Peah* 1:1 (2b); *Rash, Peah* 1:1; *Sefer Mitzvoth Gadol,* Positive Commandment 162 (207b).
12. The same holds for a negative commandment that is only violated passively; *Chatham Sofer, Orach Chaim* 656:1; *Pri Megadim, Eshel Avraham* 656:7; *Teshuvoth Chavath Yair* 139; *Chomoth Yerushalayim* 196 (end), cited in *Pith'chey Teshuvah* 157:4.
13. *Tosafoth, Bava Kama* 9b *s.v. Ilemah;* Rosh, *Bava Kama* 1:7; Ran, *Sukkah* (Rif 15a) *s.v. U'LeHidur Mitzvah; Orach Chaim* 656:1 in *Hagah; Biur Halakhah ad. loc. s.v. Afilu.* See also *Sifethey Cohen* 157:3.
14. *Yad, Matnoth Ani'im* 7:5; *Yoreh Deah* 249:1; *cf. Beer HaGolah ad. loc.* 249:2.
15. *Arakhin* 8:4 (28a); *Yad, Arakhin* 8:13; *Iggereth Teiman,* p. 32.
16. *Sotah* 3:4 (20a).

leave as much as one third[17] of his estate to charity in his will.[18]

6:8   In any case, a minimum of one tenth of one's income belongs to God, and should be used for charity[19] or other religious purposes.[20] This is a measure handed down from the Patriarchs, as Jacob himself said to God, "Of all that You give me, I will set aside a tenth to You" (Genesis 28:22).[21] Similarly, the Talmud learns that we must give one tenth of our income to charity from the verse, "Honor God with your wealth, and with the firstfruits of all your produce" (Proverbs 3:9).[22]

6:9   If there is an urgent need for charity[23] or to perform any other commandment,[24] one must sacrifice a fifth, or at least a tenth, of all his possessions. After the first time, however, one need only tithe from his yearly income.[25] In any case, the very wealthy should give as much as is needed.[26]

6:10   It is a positive commandment to give charity, as the Torah states, "Open your hand generously, and extend to [your needy brother] any credit he needs to take care of his wants" (Deuteronomy 15:8).[27] The minimum that one can give to fulfill this commandment

17. *Chokhmath Adam* 144:12, quoting *She'ilthoth, Ki Tavo* (end); *Kitzur Shulchan Arukh* 34:4.
18. *Kethuvoth* 67b; Rif, *Kethovoth* 18a; *Yoreh Deah* 249:1 in *Hagah*.
19. Regarding monetary tithing, see *Sifri* on Deuteronomy 14:22, cited in *Tosafoth, Taanith* 9a *s.v. Asser Taasser; cf. Tanchuma, Ki Tavo* 4, quoted in *Sh'nei Luchoth HaB'rith* 2:223b; *Turey Zahav, Yoreh Deah* 331:32; *Teshuvoth Shaar Ephraim* 84; *Teshuvoth Chavath Yair* 224; *Teshuvoth Yaabetz* 1:6, quoted in *Pith'chey Teshuvah* 331:12; *HaGra, Yoreh Deah* 249:2. See, however, *Teshuvoth Rabbi Meir of Rothenberg* (Prague, 1608) 74, that tithing is merely a custom; *cf. Bayith Chadash, Yoreh Deah* 331; *Teshuvah MeAhavah* 1:87; *Mishnath Chakhamim, "Yesoday HaTorah"* (17a). Similarly, Ramban on Deuteronomy 14:22 writes that the scriptural support of this is artificial.
20. *Beth Yosef, Orach Chaim* 656, citing Rabbenu Yerocham; *Magen Avraham* 656:7; *Mishnah Berurah* 656:8; *Biur Halakhah ad. loc. s.v. Yother MiChomesh.*
21. *Pesikta* 11 (98a); *Yalkut Shimoni* 1:75 (20b), 1:892 (305c); *Menorath HaMaor* 3:7:2:4 (192).
22. *Yerushalmi, Peah* 1:1 (2b), cited in Mordecai, *Bava Kama* 192.
23. *Yoreh Deah* 249:1.
24. *Magen Avraham* 656:7.
25. *Yerushalmi, Peah loc. cit.; Tosafoth, Kethuvoth* 50a *s.v. Al;* Rosh, *Kethuvoth* 4:5.
26. *Chokhmath Adam* 144:10, from *Yoreh Deah* 249:1
27. *Yad, Matnoth Ani'im* 7:1; *Sefer HaMitzvoth,* Positive Commandment 195; *Sefer Mitzvoth Gadol,* Positive Commandment 162; *Chinukh* 479.

is one third of a shekel[28] per year. It is thus written, "We have accepted upon ourselves to donate a third of a shekel annually for the service of the house of our God" (Nehemiah 10:33).[29] This amount must be given by the poorest of the poor, since he would otherwise violate the commandment of charity.[30] However, a person of ordinary means who gives less than a tenth of his income to charity is considered a miser.[31]

6:11 If one is accustomed to use his tithe for charity alone, he may not use this money for any other religious purpose.[32] However, he may use it to buy religious articles or books, which he will also lend to the poor, as long as they are clearly designated as such.[33]

6:12 We are required to perform God's commandments in the choicest and most beautiful manner possible, as the Torah states, "This is my God and I will glorify Him" (Exodus 15:2).[34] Therefore, whenever possible, one should not use the cheapest religious articles available, but should spend as much as a third more to obtain better ones.[35] Whenever one has the choice between two such articles, he should spend a third more to buy the better one.[36] For example, rather than buy a cheap *Tallith,* one should spend a third more for a better one.

6:13 One who spends more than the required extra third to enhance his observance of the commandments is assured that God will amply repay him here on earth.[37] Therefore, any unanticipated income should be used for this purpose.[38]

28. That is, about 34 cents.
29. *Bava Bathra* 9a; *Tosafoth ad. loc. SheNeemar;* Ibn Ezra *ad. loc.; Yad, Matnoth Ani'im* 7:5; *Yoreh Deah* 249:2.
30. *Gittin* 7b; *Yad loc. cit.; Yoreh Deah* 248:1.
31. *Yad loc. cit.; Yoreh Deah* 249:1.
32. *Teshuvoth Chatham Sofer* 231; *Pith'chey Teshuvah* 249:2.
33. *Sifethey Cohen* 249:2; *Turey Zahav* 249:1; *Chokhmath Adam* 144:11.
34. *Mekhilta,* Rashi, *ad. loc.* (37a); *Shabbath* 133b; *Yad, Sefer Torah* 7:4, *Lulav* 7:6.
35. *Bava Kama* 9b; *Tosafoth ad. loc. s.v. Ad; Sefer Mitzvoth Gadol,* Positive Commandment 44 (121b); Rosh, *Bava Kama* 1:7; *Orach Chaim* 656:1, first opinion.
36. *Yerushalmi, Peah* 1:1 (2b); Rashi, *Bava Kama* 9b *s.v. BeHidur Mitzvah; cf. Yeffeh Eynayim ad. loc.; Nimukey Yosef, Bava Kama* (Rif 4a) *s.v. Garsinan;* Rosh, *Sukkah* 3:12; *Orach Chaim* 656:1, second opinion; *Turey Zahav* 656:1.
37. Rashi, *Bava Kama* 9b *s.v. MiKhan V'Elekh; Tosafoth ad. loc. s.v. Mishel; Mishnah Berurah* 656:6; *Shaar HaTziun* 656:71.
38. *Rabbenu Chananel ad. loc.; Nimukey Yosef loc. cit.*

6:14   One should always give his best for God, as we find, "The choicest belongs to God" (Leviticus 3:16).[39] Thus, when a congregation builds a synagogue, it should be constructed as beautifully as possible, as the scripture intimates, "Our God has granted us favor... in order to raise up high the House of our God" (Ezra 9:9).[40] There should be no show of poverty, false economy, or skimping in building a House dedicated to God's Torah.[41] Nevertheless, this should never be done at the expense of other charitable works, nor of denying affiliation to those of lesser means.

6:15   However, even where sacred things are concerned, lavishness and richness should be dictated by aesthetics and good taste, and not by mere ostentation and the desire to spend money. For example, one should not use gold where silver would do just as well.[42] We are taught that the Torah has regard for our money, and it should not be spent wastefully. We find this in the case of a plagued house, where it is stated, "The priest shall give orders that the house be emptied out before [any] priest comes to see the mark, so that everything in the house will not become unclean. Only then shall a priest come to see the house" (Leviticus 14:36).[43] Similarly, we find that God performed miracles, not only to save our lives, but also our possessions, as when He caused water to flow in the wilderness both for the Israelites and their livestock.[44]

6:16   It is forbidden to wastefully destroy any useful object,[45] as we learn from the commandment, "You must not destroy [the

---

39.   *Yad, Issurey Mizbeach* 7:11; *Yoreh Deah* 248:8; *Kitzur Shulchan Arukh* 34:5; *cf. Yalkut Shimoni* 1:895.
40.   *Shabbath* 11a; *Yad, Tefillah* 11:2; *Orach Chaim* 150:2.
41.   *Shabbath* 102b; *Tamid* 29a. See *Yad Malachi,* "Talmudic Rules" 229 (33a); *Tosafoth, Menachoth* 89a *s.v. Ein Aniuth.*
42.   *Rosh HaShanah* 27a; *Yoma* 39a.
43.   *Sifra* (73a), Rashi, *ad. loc.;* Rashi, *Yoma* 39a *s.v. HaTorah.*
44.   Numbers 20:11; *Menachoth* 76b.
45.   From *Sefer HaMitzvoth,* Negative Commandment 57, it appears that all cases are Biblically forbidden, but *Mishneh LeMelekh, Melakhim* 6:8, writes that except in the case of trees it is only a rabbinical prohibition; *cf. Minchath Chinukh* 529. See also *Tosefoth Yom Tov, Bava Kama* 8:6.

city's] trees" (Deuteronomy 20:19).[46] One who wantonly destroys furniture or utensils, tears clothing, or wastes good food, is guilty of violating this commandment.[47] Furthermore, if he does so in anger, it is considered as if he had committed idolatry.[48] One should not destroy anything over which a blessing can be said, as it is written, "Do not destroy [the grapevine] for the blessing [over its wine] is in it" (Isaiah 65:8).[49]

6:17 All such destruction is only forbidden when it is without purpose. If there is any logical reason or use for it, it is permitted.[50] Furthermore, where there is any question of health, it is certainly better to destroy one's possessions than one's well-being.[51]

6:18 It is similarly forbidden to damage or destroy another's property,[52] or to do anything which might even indirectly cause such damage.[53] If one causes damage, he is required to make restitution,[54] as it is written, "If one kills an [other's] animal, he must pay for it, [the value of] a life for a life" (Leviticus 24:18).[55]

6:19 It is forbidden to rob,[56] steal[57] or illegally hold on to any property or money,[58] as we are commanded, "Do not steal... Do not [unjustly] withhold that which is due your neighbor. Do

46. *Makkoth* 22a; *Yad, Melakhim* 6:8; *Sefer Mitzvoth Gadol*, Negative Commandment 229 (68b); *Chinukh* 529.
47. *Kiddushin* 32b; *Chullin* 7b; *Yad, Melakhim* 6:10; *Turey Zahav, Yoreh Deah* 116:6; *Teshuvoth Yaabetz* 76; *Kitzur Shulchan Arukh* 190:3. *Cf.* Rabbenu Yonah, *Shaarey Teshuvah* 3:82.
48. *Shabbath* 105b; *Tosefta, Bava Kama* 9:10; *Yad, Deyoth* 2:3; *Kitzur Shulchan Arukh* 29:4.
49. *Sefer Chasidim* 850.
50. *Tosafoth, Avodah Zarah* 11a *s.v. Okrin; Sefer Chasidim* 667; *Turey Zahav, Yoreh Deah* 117:4; *Teshuvoth Tzemach Tzedek* 41.
51. *Shabbath* 129a, 140b.
52. *Choshen Mishpat* 378:1; *Sefer Meirath Eynayim (Sema)* 378:1; *cf.* Radbaz, *Melakhim* 6:8.
53. *Bava Bathra* 23a; *Kitzur Shulchan Arukh* 183:1.
54. *Bava Kama* 2:6 (26a); *Choshen Mishpat* 378:1.
55. *Yad, Chovel* 6:1.
56. *Yad, Gezelah* 1:1; *Sefer HaMitzvoth*, Negative Commandment 245; *Sefer Mitzvah Gadol*, Negative Commandment 157; *Chinukh* 229; *Choshen Mishpat* 359:1; *Kitzur Shulchan Arukh* 182:1.
57. *Yad, Genevah* 1:1; *Sefer HaMitzvoth*, Negative Commandment 244; *Sefer Mitzvoth Gadol*, Negative Commandment 155; *Chinukh* 224; *Choshen Mishpat* 348:1.
58. *Yad, Gezelah* 1:4; *Sefer HaMitzvoth*, Negative Commandment 247; *Sefer Mitzvoth Gadol*, Negative Commandment 156; *Chinukh* 228; *Choshen Mishpat* 359:9; *Kitzur Shulchan Arukh* 182:4; *cf. Sifra* on Leviticus 19:13 (88d).

not rob" (Leviticus 19:11, 13) One must therefore be extremely careful not to take illegal possession of any money or property in any manner, no matter how trivial its worth,[59] whether it be from an adult or a child.[60]

6:20 It is forbidden to steal as a joke or to tease, even if one intends to return it immediately.[61] The prophet thus says, "If a wicked man... pays for what he stole" (Ezekiel 33:15), from which we learn that stealing is considered wicked even if the thief originally intended to pay for or replace the stolen article.[62]

6:21 We are commanded to return any property that is illegally in our possession, as the Torah states, "He must return the stolen article, the withheld funds, the article left for safekeeping, the found article" (Leviticus 5:23).[63] If the stolen article is available and intact, it must be returned, otherwise, restitution must be made for its value at the time of the theft.[64] If the owner has moved to a distant town, we are not required to bring the stolen article to him, but must inform him so that he can come and get it.[65] If the owner dies, restitution should be made to his heirs.[66]

6:22 One who robs or cheats the public has no one to repay[67] and can never actually rectify his crime.[68] However, he should do his best to work for the public welfare and supply public needs, in order that those from whom he stole can benefit indirectly.[69] If

59. *Yad, Genevah* 1:2, *Gezelah* 1:2; *Choshen Mishpat* 348:1, 359:1; *cf.* Rashi, *Sanhedrin* 57a *s.v. Tzaara B'Shaata.*
60. *Yad, Genevah* 1:1; *Choshen Mishpat* 248:2, from *Bava Kama* 109b.
61. *Bava Metzia* 61b; *Tosefta, Bava Kama* 10:15; *Sifra* on Leviticus 19:11 (88c); *Yad, Genevah* 1:2; *Choshen Mishpat* 248:2, 359:2; *Kitzur Shulchan Arukh* 182:3. See *Ketzoth HaChoshen* 348:2.
62. *Bava Kama* 60b.
63. *Yad, Gezelah* 1:5; *Sefer HaMitzvoth,* Positive Commandment 194; *Sefer Mitzvoth Gadol,* Positive Commandment 73; *Chinukh* 130; *Choshen Mishpat* 360:1; *Kitzur Shulchan Arukh* 182:6.
64. *Bava Kama* 9:1 (93b); *Yad, Gezelah* 2:1; *Choshen Mishpat* 353:1, 360:5, 363:1.
65. *Bava Kama* 103b; *Yad, Gezelah* 7:9; *Choshen Mishpat* 367:1; *Sifethey Cohen ad. loc.* 367:3.
66. *Bava Kama* 9:5 (103a); *Tosefta* 10:6; *Yad, Gezelah* 8:1; *Choshen Mishpat* 367:4.
67. *Cf. Choshen Mishpat* 231:19; *Sefer Meirath Eynayim (Sema)* 231:34; *Kitzur Shulchan Arukh* 182:7.
68. *Bava Bathra* 88b; *Tosafoth ad. loc. s.v. Hatham; Tosefta, Bava Kama* 10:8; *Yad, Teshuvah* 4:3; *Chovoth HaLevavoth* 7:9.
69. *Bava Kama* 94b; *Betza* 29a; *Yerushalmi, Betza* 3:8 (16a); *Choshen Mishpat* 34:29, 366:2.

he is able, he should also make a public confession and ask forgiveness.[70]

6:23 It is forbidden to buy a stolen article, as one thereby becomes an accomplice to the thief and encourages him to steal more.[71] Regarding this it is written, "One who shares with a thief hates his own soul" (Proverbs 29:24).[72] It is likewise forbidden to make use of a stolen article or derive any benefit from it.[73] One should therefore not buy anything that is likely to have been stolen or obtained dishonestly.[74] One who deals with stolen property in any way is considered like one who robs the public, and his repentance is extremely difficult.[75]

6:24 Borrowing without permission is considered the same as stealing.[76] It is therefore forbidden to make any use of another's property or possessions without permission. This is true even when he is certain that such permission would readily be granted.[77]

6:25 If one's coat or other possessions are accidently exchanged at a public gathering or party, he must restore the article to its rightful owner, even though his own might be irrevocably lost. Similarly, if another person's clothing is returned in the laundry, or any similar situation, one should not use it in the interim, but rather make every attempt to restore it to its owner.[78]

6:26 One should not accept anything that is given out of duress or shame.[79] Accepting a present that is not given wholeheartedly is akin to theft. Regarding this we are cautioned, "He who is greedy of gain destroys his own house, but he who hates gifts shall live" (Proverbs 15:27).[80] Therefore, one should not eat in a home where there is not enough food,[81] or where the invitation

70. *Cf. "Rav" Shulchan Arukh* 607:4; *Shaar HaTziun* 607:3. See below, 15:52, 16:14, 17:40.
71. *Yad, Gezelah* 5:1; *Choshen Mishpat* 369:1, from *Bava Kama* 10:9 (118b).
72. *Yad, Genevah* 5:1; *Choshen Mishpat* 356:1; *Kitzur Shulchan Arukh* 182:8.
73. *Yad, Gezelah* 5:2; *Choshen Mishpat* 369:2; *Kitzur Shulchan Arukh* 182:9.
74. *Yad, Genevah* 6:1; *Choshen Mishpat* 358:1.
75. *Yad, Teshuvah* 4:3.
76. *Bava Metzia* 43b; *Bava Bathra* 88a; *Yad, Gezelah* 3:15; *Choshen Mishpat* 359:5.
77. *Kitzur Shulchan Arukh* 182:13.
78. *Bava Bathra* 46a; *Yad, Gezelah* 6:6; *Choshen Mishpat* 136:1-2; *Kitzur Shulchan Arukh* 182:12.
79. *Bava Metzia* 22a; *Nedarim* 62a; *Rosh ad. loc. s.v. MiShum.*
80. Rashi *ad. loc.; Kiddushin* 59a; *Bava Bathra* 13b; *Sefer Chasidim* 316.
81. *Yad, Teshuvah* 4:4, *Zohar Chadash, Ruth* 76b.

is insincere, as we are taught, "Do not eat the bread of a stingy man" (Proverbs 23:6).[82]

6:27 It is forbidden to desire another's possessions, as we are commanded, "Do not desire your neighbor's house, his field, his servant... or anything else that is your neighbor's" (Deuteronomy 5:18).[83] If one forces the issue where an article is not for sale, and convinces the owner to sell it against his will,[84] he is also guilty of violating the parallel commandment, "Do not be envious of your neighbor's house... or anything else that is your neighbor's" (Exodus 20:14).[85] Both of these laws are in the Ten Commandments, and apply even where no dishonesty is involved.[86]

6:28 It is forbidden to be dishonest or cheat in any business transaction,[87] as we are commanded, "When you sell... or buy [property] from your neighbor, do not cheat one another" (Leviticus 25:14).[88] Maintaining strict honesty in business dealings is equivalent to upholding the entire Torah,[89] and is the first thing for which one is judged in the heavenly court.[90]

6:29 Just as it is forbidden to be dishonest to a fellow Jew, so is it forbidden to rob,[91] cheat[92] or steal[93] from a non-Jew in

82. *Sefer Chasidim loc. cit.*
83. *Yad, Gezelah* 1:10; *Sefer HaMitzvoth,* Negative Commandment 266; *Chinukh* 416; *Choshen Mishpat* 359:10; *Kitzur Shulchan Arukh* 182:5.
84. Even if one pays the full price. However, some dispute this; *cf.* Raavad, *Gezelah* 1:9; *Tosafoth, Sanhedrin* 25b *s.v. Melkara; cf. Minchath Chinukh* 38.
85. *Bava Metzia* 5b; *Mekhilta* on Exodus 20:14 (71a); *Yad, Gezelah* 1:9; *Sefer HaMitzvoth,* Negative Commandment 265; *Chinukh* 416. However, *Sefer Mitzvoth Gadol,* Negative Commandment 158 (58d), counts both of these as a single commandment.
86. *Cf. Yad, Gezelah* 1:12; *Choshen Mishpat* 359:12.
87. *Cf. Choshen Mishpat* 227:16, 35, 36; *Kitzur Shulchan Arukh* 62:2.
88. *Bava Metzia* 51a; *Yad, Mekhirah* 12:1; *Sefer HaMitzvoth,* Negative Commandment 250; *Sefer Mitzvoth Gadol,* Negative Commandment 170; *Chinukh* 337; *Orach Chaim* 156:1; *Choshen Mishpat* 227:1; *Kitzur Shulchan Arukh* 62:1.
89. *Mekhilta* on Exodus 15:26 (46a); Ramban *ad. loc.*
90. *Shabbath* 31a (end).
91. *Bava Metzia* 87b; *Tosafoth ad. loc. s.v. Ela, Bekhoroth* 13b *s.v. KeMan; Yad, Gezelah* 1:2; *Choshen Mishpat* 359:1; *Sifethey Cohen ad. loc.* 359:2; *Teshuvoth Noda BeYehudah, Yoreh Deah* 81.
92. *Yad, Genevah* 7:8; Mordecai, *Bava Kama* 158, from *Yerushalmi, Bava Metzia* 2:5 (8a); *Choshen Mishpat* 348:2 in *Hagah;* HaGra *ad. loc.* 348:13.
93. *Choshen Mishpat* 348:2; *Sefer Meirath Eynayim (Sema)* 348:2; *Sifethey Cohen* 348:2; *Beth Sh'muel (Bash)* 28:5; *Chelkath Mechokek* 28:3; *HaGra, Evven HaEzer* 28:5; *Kitzur Shulchan Arukh* 182:1, citing *Tana DeBei Eliahu Rabbah* 15. See *Nethivoth*

any manner. In many cases, this is worse than stealing from a fellow Jew, since it gives our people a bad reputation[94] and is a desecration of God's name.[95]

6:30   One's honesty should go far beyond the mere requirements of the Law, and all of one's dealings should be with absolute integrity and fairness to all. In all walks of life, one must be aware that he is constantly watched by God, and act accordingly. We are therefore commanded, "Do what is upright and good in God's eyes" (Deuteronomy 6:18).[96]

6:31   It is forbidden to use dishonest money for charity or any other religious purpose, as God told His prophet, "For I, God, love justice, I hate robbery" (Isaiah 61:8).[97] The Psalmist similarly teaches us, "The robber blesses, but [in so doing] scorns God" (Psalms 10:3).[98] Similarly, one who has excessive debts should repay them before intemporately contributing to charity.[99]

6:32   It is a blessing to be able to earn our own way in the world and thereby enjoy the fruits of our own labor, as the Psalmist writes, "You shall eat the fruit of your effort — you shall be happy and it shall be well with you" (Psalms 128:2).[100] Still, one's business or career should always be secondary to his duties towards God.[101] One who places material considerations before his service of God is guilty of violating the commandment to love God above all.[102]

HaMishpat 348:1. However, Rashi, *Sanhedrin* 57a *s.v. Yisrael,* maintains that this is only forbidden by rabbinical law; but see HaGra *ad. loc.,* and HaGra, *Choshen Mishpat* 348:8.

94. *Sefer Chasidim* 600; *Teshuvoth Chavath Yair* 213.
95. *Tosefta, Bava Kama* 10:8.
96. Rashi, Ramban, *ad. loc.; Bava Metzia* 16b, 35a, 108a.
97. *Sukkah* 30a; *Yad, Issurey Mizbeach* 5:7; *Sefer Chasidim* 317.
98. *Bava Kama* 94a; *Yerushalmi, Sanhedrin* 1:1 (2b); *Yerushalmi, Challah* 1:5 (9a); *Midrash Tehillim* 10:4 (47b); *Sefer Chasidim* 772; *Kesef Mishneh, Berakhoth* 1:19.
99. *Sefer Chasidim* 397, from *Arakhin* 23b.
100. Rashi *ad. loc.; Berakhoth* 8a; *cf. Avoth* 2:2; *Kiddushin* 4:14 (82a).
101. *Avoth* 4:10; *Berakhoth* 35b; *Yad, Talmud Torah* 3:7; *Orach Chaim* 156:1; *Yoreh Deah* 246:21 in *Hagah.* See *Teshuvoth Devar Sh'muel* 138, cited in *Beer Hetiv* 231:1 and *Biur Halakhah ad. loc. s.v. BeKhol; cf.* also *Nefesh HaChaim* 1:78.
102. *Chinukh* 418; *Chayay Adam* 1:5 (4).

SEVEN

FEAR OF GOD

7:1   We are commanded to fear God, as the Torah states, "Fear God
your Lord, serve Him, cling to Him" (Deuteronomy 10:20).[1] This
commandment depends upon thought and can be fulfilled at
any time.[2] However, the main observance for this commandment
occurs when one actually refrains from sinning because of his fear
of God.[3]

7:2   Although one serves God most perfectly out of love, fear is also
essential in one's spiritual life.[4] Love and fear are our two spiritiual
wings,[5] and just as a bird cannot fly with only one wing, so can
we not serve God with love alone.[6] It is fear more than anything
else which prevents a person from giving in to sinning.[7] The Torah
thus states, "God came to raise you up, so that His fear would
[always] be before you, and you would not sin" (Exodus 20:17).
It is also written, "Fear God and depart from evil" (Proverbs
3:7). Fear therefore precedes love,[8] in the sense that a person will
naturally do more out of fear of punishment than out of the
expectation of reward.[9]

1.   *Yad, Yesodey HaTorah* 2:1; *Sefer HaMitzvoth,* Positive Commandment 4; *Raya
Mehemna, Zohar* 3:157a; *cf. Sanhedrin* 56a. See also Deuteronomy 6:13.
2.   *Chinukh* 432; *Chayay Adam* 1:5 no. 5.
3.   *Chinukh loc. cit.* Both the *Chinukh* and *Sefer HaMitzvoth* write that the main
commandment is to fear God's punishment; *cf. Minchath Chinukh, Kinath Sofrim, ad
loc.* However, the *Zohar* (1:11b) seems to indicate that the chief observance is fulfilled
by the awe and reverence of God; see below, notes 16, 17; *Nefesh HaChaim* 3a:8.
4.   *Tikuney Zohar* (p. 151); *Reshith Chokhmah, Shaar HaYirah* 1 (6d).
5.   *Likutey Amarim (Tanya), Sefer Shel Benonim* 40 (55b).
6.   *Ibid.* 57b.
7.   *Yerushalmi, Berakhoth* 9:5 (67a); *Tosafoth, Sotah* 22b *s.v. Perush;* Rambam, *Avoth* 1:3;
Rokeach, Shoresh LeYirah; Sefer Chasidim 37.
8.   *Tikuney Zohar* (p. 62); *Reshith Chokhmah, Shaar HaYirah* 1 (6d).
9.   *Sefer Chasidim* 767.

7:3   One who believes in God's omnipotence[10] should fear to rebel against Him, lest he be punished.[11] Regarding this, the Psalmist said, "My flesh shudders for fear of You; I am fearful of Your judgments" (Psalms 119:120).[12] More than anything else, it is this fear of divine punishment which can prevent people from sinning.

7:4   It is the fear of divine punishment that first brings a person to serve God. Regarding this fear the Torah says, "And now, Israel, what does God want of you? Only that you you remain in awe of God your Lord, so that you will follow all His paths and love Him, serving God your Lord with all your heart and with all your soul" (Deuteronomy 10:12). Similarly, the Psalmist taught us, "The beginning of wisdom is the fear of God" (Psalms 111:10).[13]

7:5   It is only through the fear of God that our religious heritage can be transmitted from generation to generation, as we find, "Remain in awe of God your Lord, so that you will keep all His rules and laws... You, your children and your children's children [must keep them] as long as they live, so that you will long endure" (Deuteronomy 6:2). Judaism taught as an abstract philosophy or as a meaningless set of observances cannot survive. Only true fear and reverence for God and His teachings give inexhaustable vitality and meaning to our religion.[14] The Psalmist thus exclaimed, "Come children, listen to me, I will teach you the fear of God" (Psalms 34:12).

7:6   Fear of punishment is thus merely a first step in serving God.[15] As a person grows spiritually, he can attain a higher degree of fear, where he is filled with awe and reverence before God.[16] He can then realize that, "His dominion is an everlasting dominion, and

10. *Tikuney Zohar* 5b (end).
11. *Chovoth HaLevavoth* 8:3 26; *Reshith Chokhmah, Shaar HaYirah* 14 (41a); *Likutey Amarim (Tanya), Sefer Shel Benonim* 4 (8a).
12. Radak *ad. loc.; Midrash Tehillim* 119:52 (250b).
13. Commentary to *Yad, Yesodey HaTorah* 2:1; *Likutey Amarim, Sefer Shel Benonim* 43 (61b), from *Avoth* 3:17.
14. *Cf. Berakhoth* 6b; *Etz Yosef ad. loc.* (*Eyn Yaakov* 25); *Menorath HaMaor* 4:3:1:3 (264).
15. *Tikuney Zohar* 6, 62; *Reshith Chokhmah, Shaar HaYirah* 14 (41a); *Mesilath Yesharim* 24.
16. *Cheredim,* Positive Commandments 1:3; *Likutey Amarim, Sefer Shel Benonim* 3 (7b).

His kingdom is from generation to generation. All the inhabitants of the world are considered as naught [in His presence]" (Daniel 4:32).[17] It is of such fear that the Torah speaks when it says, "Only that you remain in awe of God your Lord... [For] the heaven, the heaven of heaven, the earth and everything in it, all belong to God" (Deuteronomy 10:12, 14).[18] Similarly, the Psalmist speaks of this awe and humility in the presence of the Creator when he exclaims, "I look at Your heavens, the work of Your fingers, the moon and the stars which You have established — What is man that You think of him? What is mortal man that You even consider him?" (Psalms 8:4-5).

7:7   True awe and reverence for God can only be achieved through the study and observance of His commandments. The Torah says as much when it states, "This is the mandate... that God your Lord commanded to teach you... Remain in awe of God your Lord, so that you will keep all His rules and laws" (Deuteronomy 6:1-2).[19]

7:8   When a person realizes God's greatness, how He fills and sustains all creation, seeing and knowing all,[20] he will be ashamed[21] to do anything wrong before Him, just as one is ashamed to make even the slightest error in the presence of a great person.[22] Therefore, all that one does should be with the realization that it is being done before God. This is what the Psalmist meant when he said, "I have set God before me at all times" (Psalms 16:8).[23]

7:9   One of the highest degrees in serving God is called the fear of sin.[24] This is only attained when one realizes the great spiritual

17. *Zohar* 1:11b.
18. *Reshith Chokhmah, Shaar HaYirah* 2 (10a).
19. *Zohar* 1:7b; *Tikuney Zohar* 5b; commentary to *Yad, Yesodey HaTorah* 2:1; *Likutey Amarim, Sefer Shel Benonim* 23 (29b), 43 (62a).
20. Cf. *Avoth* 2:1; Rabbenu Yonah *ad. loc.; Chovoth HaLevavoth* 8:3 10; *Reshith Chokhmah, Shaar HaYirah* 1 (8d); *Mesilath Yesharim* 25; *Likutey Amarim, Sefer Shel Benonim* 41 (56a).
21. *Nedarim* 20a; *Mekhilta* on Exodus 20:17 (72a); *Yerushalmi, Kiddushin* 4:1 (42b); *BaMidbar Rabbah* 8:4; *Tikuney Zohar* 6; *Reshith Chokhmah, Shaar HaYirah* 3 (13d); *Sh'nei Luchoth HaB'rith, BeAsarah Maamaroth* 1:75b.
22. *Berakhoth* 28b; *Zohar* 3:46a; *Moreh Nevukhim* 3:52, cited in *Orach Chaim* 1:1 in *Hagah; Menorath HaMaor* 4:3:1:2 (263).
23. See Volume 1, 1:20.
24. *Avodah Zarah* 20b; *Tosafoth ad. loc. s.v. Ahavah. Cf. Sotah* 21a.

harm wrought by sin,[25] and achieves a constant aversion for even the most minor infraction.[26] Regarding this fear it is written, "The fear of God is to detest evil" (Proverbs 8:13). Fearing sin furthermore implies a constant alertness not to do wrong. Regarding this it is written, "Happy is the man who always fears" (Proverbs 28:14) — not worldly things, but the possibility of going against God's will.[27] This apprehension of not being perfect with God,[28] though designated as fear, is really very close to the true love of God.[29]

7:10　　We are taught that covering the head is conducive to fearing God.[30] As a sign of respect and modesty,[31] it constantly reminds us that God is above us.[32] It is therefore a custom[33] for a male not to walk as much as four steps with his head uncovered.[34] Wearing a *Yarmulka* is a normative sign of an observant Jew,[35] which is meant to constantly remind him of his obligations toward God. Some say that the word *Yarmulka* comes from the Aramaic words *Yare Malka,* which means "fear of the King."

7:11　　One should fear God at least as much as he fears his fellow men,[36] and therefore not do anything in private that he would not do before other people. A hypocrite who sins secretly thrusts God aside as if to deny His omnipresence.[37] Regarding such a person it is written, "Cursed is he who is deceitful in the performance

25.　*Reshith Chokhmah, Shaar HaYirah* 3 (13b), from *Berakhoth* 4a; *Nefesh HaChaim* 1:3.
26.　*Raya Mehemna, Zohar* 3:278b; *Reshith Chokhmah, Shaar HaYirah* 3 (14a), *Shaar HaAhavah* 11 (96c); *Likutey Amarim, Sefer Shel Benonim* 10 (15a), 42 (60a).
27.　*Berakhoth* 60a; *Mesilath Yesharim* 24.
28.　*Sefer Chasidim* 12; *Rokeach, Shaar LeYirah* (end); *Reshith Chokhmah, Shaar HaYirah* 14 (43c).
29.　*Sotah* 31a; *cf. Tosefoth Yom Tov* 9:15 *s.v. VeAnavah.*
30.　*Shabbath* 156b; Maharsha *ad. loc. s.v. Giluy Resha; Orach Chaim* 2:6; *Hagah, Magen Avraham, Machtzith HaShekel, ad. loc.; Kitzur Shulchan Arukh* 3:6; *Mishnah Berurah* 2:1. See *Orach Chaim* 91:3; *Biur Halakhah ad. loc. s.v. VeYesh Omrim.*
31.　*Kiddushin* 33a; *Sofrim* 14:15; *Yad, Tefillah* 4:5; *"Rav" Shulchan Arukh* 2:6. See below, 8:25, notes 89, 90.
32.　*Kiddushin* 31a; *Sefer Chasidim* 53; *Makor Chesed ad. loc.* 53:13, 14.
33.　*Teshuvoth Maharshal* 72; *HaGra, Orach Chaim* 8:2. *Cf. Nedarim* 30b; *Bereshith Rabbah* 17:13.
34.　*Kiddushin* 31a; *Shabbath* 118b; *Raya Mehemna, Zohar* 3:122b, 245b; *Yad, Deyoth* 5:6; *Orach Chaim* 2:6; *Chayay Adam* 1:9.
35.　*Turey Zahav, Orach Chaim* 8:3.
36.　See above, note 22.
37.　*Chagigah* 16a; *Kiddushin* 31a; *Zohar* 1:68a; *Reshith Chokhmah, Shaar HaYirah* 7 (21c).

of God's work" (Jeremiah 48:10).[38] Nothing is as despicable as a hypocrite,[39] and we are taught that they bring destruction to the world, as it is written, "Hypocrites in heart increase anger" (Job 36:13).[40] A hypocrite is actually worse than an idolater, since an idolater only places one object above God, while the hypocrite does so with many people.[41] One should therefore be honest in his faith,[42] serving God with integrity, both inwardly and outwardly.[43]

7:12 We are taught that we should publicize hypocrites in order that they not be considered righteous and cause a desecration of God's name.[44] It is thus written, "Though his hatred be concealed with deception, his wickedness shall be revealed before the congregation" (Proverbs 26:26).[45]

7:13 A person is only considered a hypocrite when he deceitfully shows himself to be more righteous than he really is. Mere inconsistency, on the other hand, is not the same as hypocrisy. For example, one who eats non-Kosher food occasionally should not do so all the time to avoid being called a hypocrite, since the designation does not apply to him at all. The exact opposite is actually true. One should do as much as possible to serve God, and if he is sincere, he need not worry at all about being inconsistent or a hypocrite.[46]

7:14 Similarly, one is not considered a hypocrite if he hides his wrongdoings in order to avoid desecrating God's name. It is better to sin secretly than to desecrate God's name through false integrity.[47]

7:15 The fear of God implies that one should give Him the greatest

38. *Koheleth Rabbah* 4:2.
39. *Sotah* 22b; Rashi *ad. loc. s.v. Tzevuyim; Avoth DeRabbi Nathan* 25:5; *Binyan Yehoshua ad. loc.; Midrash Tehillim* 18:3. Cf. Isaiah 29:13; Psalms 5:20, 55:22; Radak on Psalms 50:16.
40. *Sotah* 41b.
41. *Chovoth HaLevavoth* 5:4.
42. *Bava Metzia* 49a.
43. *Berakhoth* 28a; *Yoma* 72b; *Tikuney Zohar,* p. 227; *Reshith Chokhmah, Shaar HaKedushah* 7 (148a), 12 (172c).
44. *Yoma* 86b; *Tosefta* 4:12; *Yalkut Shimoni* 2:341. Cf. *Yad, Deyoth* 6:8.
45. Rashi *ad. loc.; Midrash Tehillim* 52:3; *Yalkut Shimoni* 2:961. Cf. *Sotah* 9a.
46. *Shabbath* 31b, from Ecclesiastes 7:17; see Rashi *ad. loc.; Koheleth Rabbah* 7:34.
47. *Chagigah* 16a; *Tosafoth ad. loc. s.v. VeYaaseh, Kiddushin* 31a *s.v. Khol.* This is not to be taken as permission to sin; see *Tosafoth, Moed Katan* 17a *s.v. Im, Kiddushin* 49a *s.v. VeYaaseh; Reshith Chokhmah, Shaar HaTeshuvah* 7 (126c).

respect and honor. Our reverence for God should far exceed the respect that we have for even the most exalted mortal kings and rulers.[48] Therefore, one should not honor or respect any person more than he reveres God.[49] One should not even obey his parents if they tell him to sin, since the honor due to God comes before that due to one's parents.[50] Similarly, one should not be ashamed to serve God when scoffers laugh and make fun of him.[51] One's consideration for God should always come before that of mortal men, as the prophet says, "Refrain from [fearing] man whose soul is a mere breath in his nostrils" (Isaiah 2:22).[52]

7:16   Reverence for God also implies respect for those associated with Him.[53] We are therefore told to honor our religious leaders even as we honor God Himself.[54]

7:17   The fear of God is the outer door through which one enters into God's presence to serve Him.[55] It is the thread upon which all virtues are strung together like pearls. If the thread is broken, they are all scattered and lost.[56] We are taught that the fear of God is His most precious treasure,[57] for which all was created.[58] King Solomon thus said, "The sum of the matter, when all has been heard: Fear God and keep His commandments, for this is all of man" (Ecclesiastes 12:13).[59]

48. *Chovoth HaLevavoth* 8:3 (10); *Reshith Chokhmah, Shaar HaYirah* 15 (45d); *Tur, Orach Chaim* 1; *Chayay Adam* 1:2; *Kitzur Shulchan Arukh* 1:4; *Mishnah Berurah* 1:1.
49. *Cf. Kiddushin* 33b; *Yad, Talmud Torah* 6:8; *Turey Zahav, Yoreh Deah* 242:12.
50. *Bava Metzia* 2:10 (32a); *Yevamoth* 6a; *Tana DeBei Eliahu Rabbah* 27 (106a); *Yad, Mamrim* 6:12; *Yoreh Deah* 240:15; *Kitzur Shulchan Arukh* 143:11.
51. *Tur, Orach Chaim* 1, from *Avoth* 5:20; *Orach Chaim* 1:1 in *Hagah; cf. Biur Halakhah ad. loc. s.v. VeLo; Kitzur Shulchan Arukh* 1:3.
52. *Cf. Berakhoth* 14a; *Kitzur Shulchan Arukh* 5:5.
53. *Pesachim* 22b; *Kiddushin* 57a; *Bava Kama* 41b; *Tosafoth ad. loc. s.v. LeRaboth; Bekhoroth* 6b; *Yerushalmi, Berakhoth* 9:5 (67b); *Yerushalmi, Sotah* 5:5 (25b).
54. *Avoth* 4:12; *Yad, Talmud Torah* 5:1; *Mesilath Yesharim* 26.
55. *Shabbath* 31b; *Yoma* 72b.
56. *Orchoth Tzaddikim*, Introduction.
57. *Yerushalmi, Berakhoth* 2:8 (20b); *Koheleth Rabbah* 12:15.
58. *Berakhoth* 6b; *Shabbath* 30b, 31b.
59. When our sages say that the world was created for the fear of God, they are not contradicting the principle that it was created as a vehicle for His good. What they are doing is expressing what this good ultimately is. It is a closeness to God and an intimate knowledge of Him that is most perfectly expressed by the reverence and awe we call the "fear of God"; Rabbi Moshe Cordevero, *Shiur Komah, Erekh Torah* 13:3; *Etz Chaim, Shaar HaKelalim* 1; *Sh'nei Luchoth HaB'rith, Beth Acharon* 1:21b, all quoted in Kaplan, *Moreh Or* (Moznaim, 1992) 1:3 (pp. 9-10).

EIGHT

RESPECTING GOD IN SPEECH

8:1   Just as we revere God Himself, so must we show the greatest respect for His name, as the Torah states, "[You must] fear this glorious, awesome Name of God your Lord" (Deuteronomy 28:58).[1] The commandment to revere God[2] includes the injunction not to use His name unnecessarily.[3] It is the basis of the commandment, "Do not take the Name of God your Lord in vain" (Exodus 20:7).[4]

8:2   The commandment to respect God's name refers specifically to the ten[5] Hebrew names by which God is designated in the Bible.[6] [They are listed in Table 8:1, at the end of this chapter.] These names should never be pronounced except in prayer or in study.[7] In all other cases, the colloquial pronunciation is used.

1. *Yerushalmi, Shevuoth* 3:10 (18b); *Peney Moshe, Korban HaEdah, ad. loc. s.v. LeYirah; Yad, Shevuoth* 12:11; Maharsha, *Rosh HaShanah* 33a *s.v. DeAsrinan; cf.* Maharatz Chajas *ad. loc.;* HaGra, *Temurah* 4a (no. 1); but see *Shita Mekubetzeth ad. loc.* no. 14; *Chayay Adam* 5:1; *Kitzur Shulchan Arukh* 6:3.
2. "Fear God your Lord" (Deuteronomy 6:13, 10:20); see above, 7:1.
3. *Sanhedrin* 56a; *Temurah* 4a; *Tosafoth, Rosh HaShanah* 33a *s.v. Ha;* Ran, Rosh, *Nedarim* 7b *s.v. HaShamea;* Rabbenu Yonah, *Shaarey Teshuvah* 3:13; *Sefer Mitzvoth Gadol* (Positive 4) indicates that this commandment deals primarily with God's name; see also *Rokeach, Shaar LeYirah.*
4. Ramban *ad. loc.;* Ran, *Tosafoth, Nedarim* 7b *s.v. SheBeKhol Makom; Reshith Chokhmah, Shaar HaKedushah* 14 (182b). Although this commandment actually deals with a false or vain oath (see below, 8:29), since it uses the more inclusive phrase *Lo Tissa* ("do not take") rather than *Lo Tishba* ("do not swear"), it also includes this case; *cf. Menorath HaMaor* 2:9:1:1 (70).
5. *Avoth DeRabbi Nathan* 34:2. However, *Yad, Yesodey HaTorah* 6:2 lists only seven, since he does not differentiate all forms; *cf. Kesef Mishneh ad. loc.* For significance, see *Sh'nei Luchoth HaB'rith, Beth HaShem* 1:5a. See Volume 1, 7:78-80.
6. *Shevuoth* 35a; HaGra *ad. loc.; Yerushalmi, Megillah* 1:9 (12b); *Sofrim* 4:1; *Avoth DeRabbi Nathan* 34:2; HaGra *ad. loc.; Yad, Yesodey HaTorah* 6:2; *Yoreh Deah* 276:9. *Cf. Sefer Yetzirah* 5 (end).
7. *Chayay Adam* 5:1; *Mishnah Berurah* 215:19, citing *Teshuvoth Rivash. Cf. Avodah Zarah* 18a; *Tosafoth, Rosh HaShanah loc. cit.*

8:3   It is permissible to pronounce a word that is identical to a divine name, as long as its connotation implies a secular meaning.[8] For example, it is permissible to pronounce the word *Elohim* when it is an obvious reference to human judges[9] or false gods,[10] or *Tzevaoth* when it refers to armies.

8:4   *Halleluyah* is a composite word meaning "praise God,"[11] and should not be used except in prayer since the last syllable is a divine name.[12] At other times, it is customary to pronounce it *Hallelukah.*

8:5   When a divine name is part of another proper name, it is no longer sacred, since it is not translated separately. For example, one may always pronounce such names as Jeremiah, Hezekiah, Zechariah, etc., though the final syllable is the divine name *Yah.*[13] This is true even when the divine name appears as a separate word, such as in *Beth El,*[14] since it is still translated as part of the proper name.[15]

8:6   It is permitted to pronounce divine names when reading Biblical verses,[16] even if only part of the verse is quoted.[17] Therefore, when one comes across a Biblical quotation in his studies, it may be read as written, even if it contains God's proper name.[18] In

8.   *Cf. Shevuoth* 35b; *Yad, Yesodey HaTorah* 6:9.
9.   Exodus 21:6; *cf. Sanhedrin* 66a.
10.   We therefore say *Elokei HaElohim,* since it is translated "God of gods" or "God of judges," and the second word is not a divine name; *cf. Targum* on Deuteronomy 10:17; *Targum Yonathan ad. loc.* See also *Sofrim* 4:4; *Beth Yosef, Yoreh Deah* 276; Rabbi Akiba Eiger, *Yoreh Deah* 276:9; *HaGra* 276:20; *Kuzari* 4:3 (10b); Ibn Ezra, Radak, on Psalms 136:2.
11.   From *Hallelu* meaning "praise," and *Yah,* "God" or "Lord."
12.   Rabbah, *Pesachim* 117a; *Yerushalmi, Sukkah* 3:10 (16a); *Peney Moshe, Marah HaPanim, ad. loc.; Yerushalmi, Megillah* 1:9 (13a); *Sofrim* 5:10; *Midrash Tehillim* 1:6; *Tosefoth Yom Tov, Sukkah* 4:5; *Birkey Yosef, Yoreh Deah* 276; *Teshuvoth Zikney Peney Yehoshua, Orach Chaim* 6; *Teshuvoth Shevuth Yaakov* 56; *Teshuvoth Rabbi Moshe Mintz* 8; *Shaar HaMelekh, Gerushin* 4:12; Radak on Psalms 104:35; *Minchath Shai ad. loc.; Zohar* 1:178b; *Nitzotzey Oroth ad. loc.* 1:232b.
13.   Maharsha, *Pesachim* 117a *s.v. Hallelukah; Kiryath Sefer* (Meiri), p. 18a; *Beth Sh'muel* ("Rules of Names") 129 (end).
14.   *Teshuvoth Chatham Sofer* 270, cited in *Pith'chey Teshuvah* 276:14. *Cf. Sofrim* 5:10; *Yad, Sefer Torah* 5:12; *Yerushalmi, Megillah loc. cit.*
15.   *Cf. Targum* on Genesis 12:8.
16.   *Turey Zahav* 621:2 (end).
17.   *Chayay Adam* 5:2; *cf. Magen Avraham* 422:6, from *Sotah* 5:4 (27b).
18.   *Shaarey Teshuvah, Orach Chaim* 215:4; *Pri Megadim, Eshel Avraham* 215:5; *Mishnah Berurah* 215:14.

other cases, however, especially when reading a blessing,[19] the colloquial pronunciation should be used.

8:7 Similarly, when one is teaching young children to read or say their blessings, it is permissible to pronounce God's name wherever necessary.[20]

8:8 Just as we must have reverence for God's Hebrew names, so must we have the greatest respect for His name in any language.[21] It is therefore customary not to pronounce God's name in any language, except in prayer or study, or when proclaiming His deeds.[22] It is disrespectful to use God's name as part of a curse, an oath, or any other expletive such as in the common expressions "G-d damn" or "for G-d's sake."[23]

8:9 One who takes God's name in vain or otherwise uses it disrespectfully deserves to be placed under ban.[24] Regarding those who have reverence for God's name, the scripture states, "But for you who fear My Name, a sun of righteousness shall shine with healing in its wings" (Malachi 3:20).[25]

8:10 The Tetragrammaton is called God's "proper name" (*Shem HaMeforash*, שֵׁם הַמְפֹרָשׁ). Although God Himself is absolutely unknowable and unnamable, the Tetragrammaton is His highest emanation in creation.[26] It is therefore considered most sacred, and is never pronounced as it is written, even in prayer.[27] We are taught

---

19. *Magen Avraham* 215:5, from Rambam, *Mishnah Berakhoth* 9:1; *cf. Machtzith HaShekel ad. loc.;* but *Teshuvoth Yaabatz* 81, cited in *Shaarey Teshuvah loc. cit.,* permits even this case.
20. *Yad, Berakhoth* 1:15; *Orach Chaim* 215:3, from *Berakhoth* 53b.
21. Rabbenu Yerocham 14:8, cited in *Chayay Adam* 5:1; *Kitzur Shulchan Arukh* 6:3; *Mishnah Berurah* 215:19.
22. *Cf. Sefer Chasidim* 1094, cited in Rabbi Akiba Eiger, *Orach Chaim* 5; *Mishnah Berurah* 5:3, 215:19.
23. *Cf. Sefer Chasidim* 1093.
24. *Nedarim* 7b; *Yad, Shevuoth* 12:9; *Yoreh Deah* 334:37; *Chokhmath Adam* 172:31. However, the custom is not to use the ban; Rabbi Akiba Eiger, *Yoreh Deah* 334:37, from *Sefer Mitzvoth Gadol,* Negative Commandment 241 (70d); *Teshuvoth Rama* 132:4.
25. *Nedarim* 8b.
26. See Volume 1, 2:51, notes 65, 66. See also Rambam, *Mishnah Sotah* 7:6; *Yad, Yesodey HaTorah* 6:2, *Tefillah* 14:10; *Moreh Nevukhim* 1:62.
27. *Cf. Midrash Tehillim* 91:8 (200b); *Yalkut Shimoni* 2:843. See also Rash, *Mishnah Yadayim* 4:8, citing *Tosefta* 2:9; *cf.* HaGra *ad. loc.* no. 25. See Kaplan, *Torah Anthology*, Volume 4, p. 93.

that one who pronounces the Tetragrammaton[28] disrespectfully[29] is worthy of death[30] and has no portion in the World to Come.[31]

8:11 According to tradition, whenever the Tetragrammaton is written יְהוָה,[32] it is read *Adonai.*[33] However, when it occurs in conjunction with the name אֲדֹנָי *(Adonai),*[34] it is read *Elohim.*[35]

8:12 The only place where the Tetragrammaton was ever pronounced as it is written was in the Temple in Jerusalem, as the Torah states a number of times, "God your Lord will appoint a place to link His Name there" (Deuteronomy 12:5, 12:11, 12:21).[36] It was pronounced daily in the priestly blessing[37] in the Temple, as well as ten times[38] during the *Yom Kippur* service in the public confessions.[39]

8:13 In the daily priestly blessing, the Tetragrammaton was vocalized with the vowel points associated with the name *Adonai.* In the *Yom Kippur* service, on the other hand, the High Priest would pronounce the Tetragrammaton with its own unique vowel points.[40]

28. *Chayay Adam* 5:27, first opinion, from Rambam, Bertenoro, *Sanhedrin* 10:1; *Tosafoth, Avodah Zarah* 18a *s.v. Hogeh,* according to Rabbi Yaakov Emdin (Maharibatz) *ad. loc.;* Rosh, *Yoma* 8:19.

29. *Sanhedrin* 101b; Rashi *ad. loc. s.v U'VeLashon; Yerushalmi, Sanhedrin* 10:1 (50b); *Sefer Mitzvoth Gadol,* Positive Commandment 4.

30. *Pesikta* 22 (148a).

31. *Sanhedrin* 10:1 (90a); *Avodah Zarah* 18a; *Tosefta, Sanhedrin* 12:5; *Tanchuma, VaEra* 1. See Rabbi Yechezkel Landau, *Tzion LeNefesh Chayah, Rosh HaShanah* 17a, that although this is the individual opinion of Abba Shaul, we decide accordingly; *cf. Yoreh Deah* 179:8. See also *Tosefta, Sanhedrin* 12:1.

32. That is, with *Sheva-Kamatz-Cholam,* the vowel-points of the Name *Tzevakoth; cf. Sh'nei Luchoth HaB'rith, Beth HaShem* 1:5a.

33. *Pesachim* 59b; *Yerushalmi, Sanhedrin* 10:1 (50b); *Yalkut Shimoni* 1:171; *Shemoth Rabbah* 3:9; *Zohar* 3:230a, 3:281a; *Tikuney Zohar* 69 (101a); *cf.* also *Tosefta, Zohar* 2:27b, 3:309a; Rashi on Exodus 3:15; *Magen Avraham* 5:1.

34. With *Segol-Cholam-Chirik,* the vowel-points of *Elokim.*

35. HaGra, *Orach Chaim* 5:1 *s.v. VeYiKaven.*

36. *Sotah* 39a; *Sifri,* cited in *Tosafoth ad. loc. s.v. Harey; Yalkut Shimoni* 1:870. See also *Mekhilta,* Rashi, on Exodus 20:21 (73b); *Yalkut Shimoni* 1:305.

37. *Sotah* 7:6 (38a); *Tamid* 7:2 (33b); *Sifri Zuta* on Numbers 6:27, quoted in *Yalkut Shimoni* 1:711; Rashi *ad. loc.; Yad, Tefillah* 14:10; *Moreh Nevukhim* 1:61. *Cf. Chagigah* 16a; *BaMidbar Rabbah* 11:10.

38. *Yoma* 39b; *Tosefta* 2:2; *Yerushalmi, Yoma* 3:7 (18b); *Yad, Avodath Yom HaKippurim* 2:6; *"Rav" Shulchan Arukh* 621:8; *Teshuvoth Radbaz* 2:810.

39. *Yoma* 3:8 (35b), 37a; *Tosafoth Yeshenim* 39a *s.v. Esser;* Rosh 8:19; *Tur, Orach Chaim* 621; *Turey Zahav* 621:2; *Teshuvoth Bayith Chadash* 293.

40. *I.e. Cholam-Segol-Kamatz-Segol;* Rabbi Moshe Cordevero (Ramak), quoted in *Tosefoth Yom Tov, Yoma* 6:2 *s.v. KeSheHayu. Cf. Sh'nei Luchoth HaB'rith, Beth HaShem* 1:5a, quoting *Tikuney Zohar.*

8:14   Whenever the Tetragrammaton was pronounced in the Holy
        Temple, all present would respond, "Blessed be the Name of His
        glorious Kingdom for ever and ever,"[41] as we find, "[Israel] shall
        bless Your glorious Name, though You Yourself are exalted above
        all blessing and praise" (Nehemiah 9:5).[42] On *Yom Kippur,*[43] those
        standing closest to the High Priest[44] would prostrate themselves
        in awe and reverence as the transcendent name of God was
        pronounced.[45] In commemoration of this, we also prostrate
        ourselves when the High Priest's confessions are recalled during
        the *Mussaf* Service of *Yom Kippur.*[46] According to tradition, one
        of the ten miracles that occurred regularly in the First Temple
        was that all present had enough space to bow, even though they
        stood tightly packed together during the service.[47]

8:15   Originally, the Tetragrammaton was used by all the priests in
        their blessing. However, there is a tradition that after Shimon the
        Saint died in 3470 (291 b.c.e.), its use was discontinued,[48] since
        the Divine Presence *(Shekhinah)* was no longer manifest in the
        Temple[49] and the other priests felt themselves unworthy.[50] However,

41. *Yoma* 3:8 (35b), 4:1 (39a), 62 (66a); *Taanith* 16b; *Yerushalmi, Berakhoth* 9:5 (67b);
     Yerushalmi, Taanith 2:10 (11b); *Mekhilta* on Exodus 13:3 (19b); *Yad, Taanith* 4:15;
     Bertenoro, *Berakhoth* 9:5; *Tosefoth Yom Tov, Sotah* 7:6 *s.v.* *U'BeMikdash,* from
     Rashi, *Sotah* 49b *s.v.* *VeYiVarkhu* and *Tosafoth ad. loc. s.v. VeKhol.* This was also
     the response after the priestly blessing, but *Yad, Tefillah* 14:9 and *Sefer Mitzvoth
     Gadol,* Positive Commandment 20 (103d), write that they responded "Blessed be
     God, the God of Israel, from everlasting to everlasting"; *cf. Berakhoth* 9:5 (54a).
42. *Berakhoth* 63a; *Taanith* 16a; *Sotah* 40b; for the reason, see Maharsha *ad. loc.; Yalkut
     Shimoni* 2:1071. Ralbag *ad. loc.* maintains that this verse was the actual response; *cf.
     Bigdey Yesha,* Mordecai, *Yoma* 727:7.
43. See *Tosefoth Yom Tov, Yoma* 6:2 for reason why not during priestly blessing.
44. *Yerushalmi, Yoma* 3:7 (18b); *Tosafoth, Sotah loc. cit.; Koheleth Rabbah* 3:15.
45. *Yoma* 6:2 (66a); *Yad, Avodath Yom HaKippurim* 2:7; Mordecai, *Yoma* 727.
46. *Orach Chaim* 621:4 in *Hagah.*
47. *Avoth* 5:5; *Yoma* 21a; Rashi *ad. loc. s.v. Mishtachavim,* from *Bereshith Rabbah* 5:6,
     "In order that they not hear each other praying," and *VaYikra Rabbah* 10:9, "There
     was a space of four cubits between them"; *cf. Avoth DeRabbi Nathan* 35:8.
48. *Yoma* 39a; *Menachoth* 109b; *Tosefta, Sotah* 13:8; *Yad, Tefillah* 14:10. However, Rashi
     maintains that they only stopped using it temporarily, whereas its general use continued
     until the destruction of the Temple; *cf.* Rashi, *Eruvin* 18b *s.v. MiYom;* Maharatz
     Chajas *ad. loc.* In *Moreh Nevukhim* 1:62, Rambam maintains that the 12 Letter
     Name, which was inferior to the Tetragrammaton, was used in the priestly blessing;
     cf. Kiddushin 71a. However Rashi *ad. loc. s.v. Mavliyim,* writes that the 12 Letter
     Name was used by the High Priest, while the others used the Tetragrammaton.
     Radal *ad. loc.* writes that the High Priest used it in a special prayer, but not in the
     priestly blessing.
49. *Tosafoth, Sotah* 38a *s.v. Harey.*

as long as the Temple stood, it was used by the High Priest[51] in the *Yom Kippur* service.[52] Still, it was pronounced in such a low voice[53] that it was drowned out by the singing of the other priests[54] in order that it not be learned by the unworthy.

8:16   As a sign of reverence, the Tetragrammaton was mentioned as infrequently as possible. Therefore, during this period, its precise pronunciation[55] and significance[56] was taught only to the worthiest students just once every seven years.

8:17   Some authorities maintain that it is forbidden to pronounce the spelling of the Tetragrammaton just as it is forbidden to pronounce the name itself. When spelling the name out therefore, we change the letter *Heh* to *Keh,* and read *Yud-Keh-Vav-Keh.* Similarly, we read the spelling of the name *Yah,* as *Yud-Keh.*[57]

8:18   There is also a name of God consisting of 12 letters,[58] as well as combinations of 42 letters,[59] and 72 letters[60] or triads,[61] which

50. Rashi, *Yoma* 39b *s.v. MiLeVarekh.*
51. Maharsha, *Kiddushin* 71a *s.v. Shem.*
52. Rashash, *Sotah* 38a *s.v. Harey.*
53. *Yerushalmi, Yoma* 3:7 (18b); *Yad, Avodath Yom HaKippurim* 2:6; *Lechem Mishneh ad. loc.; Zohar* 3:146a; *Or Zarua* 2:281; *Avodath Yisrael* 108b; *Mayim Chaim (Pri Chadash),* p. 30a.
54. *Kiddushin* 71a; *Koheleth Rabbah* 3:15.
55. *Kiddushin* 71a; *Yad, Tefillah* 14:10. *Cf.* HaGra, *Orach Chaim* 5:1 *s.v. VeYiKaven.*
56. *Moreh Nevukhim* 1:62; Maharsha, *Kiddushin* 71a *s.v. Shem. Cf. Sefer Chasidim* 471. See below, Table 8:1, note 6.
57. *Chayay Adam* 5:27 (second opinion), from *Tosafoth, Avodah Zarah* 18a, according to Maharsha *ad. loc.,* and *Sukkah* 5a *s.v. Yod; cf.* Maharam *ad. loc.,* and *Shevuoth* 35a *s.v. BeAleph.*
58. *Kiddushin* 71a. See above, note 48.
59. *Ibid.; Zohar* 1:1a, 2:175b, 2:234b, 3:256b; *Tikuney Zohar* 66b, 82b, 104a, 131b; Rashi, *Avodah Zarah* 17b *s.v. Lama, Sanhedrin* 60a *s.v. Shem,* 101b *s.v. U'VeLashon; Tosafoth, Sukkah* 5a *s.v. Yod, Chagigah* 11b *s.v. Ein Dorshin, Avodah Zarah* 18a *s.v. Hage.* Rav Hai Gaon maintained that this was the Name used in the *Yom Kippur* service; see Rosh, *Yoma* 8:19; *Taam Zekenim,* p. 55; *Teshuvoth Bayith Chadash* 293. This Name is contained in the initial letters of the words of the prayer *Ana BeKoach,* attributed to the author of the *Sefer Bahir,* Rabbi Nehuniah ben HaKana; Radal, *Kiddushin* 71a. Also see *Moreh Nevukhim* 1:62.
60. *Avoth DeRabbi Nathan* 13:3; *Bereshith Rabbah* 44:22; *VaYikra Rabbah* 23:2; *Devarim Rabbah* 1:0; *Shir HaShirim Rabbah* 2:6, from Deuteronomy 4:34; *Tanchuma, VaYera* 4; *Pesikta* 5 (52b); *Yalkut Shimoni* 1:77; *Zohar* 2:234b; *Tikuney Zohar* 8b.
61. *Bahir* 94, 107, 110; *Zohar* 2:51b, 2:270a; Rashi, *Tosafoth, Sukkah* 45a *s.v. Ani; Tosefoth Yom Tov, Sukkah* 4:5 *s.v. Ani; Pesikta Zutrata* on Exodus 33:21; Ibn Ezra on Exodus 14:19, 33:21. This Name is derived from the three 72-letter verses, Exodus 14:19, 20 and 21. It is vocalized in *Pardes Rimonim* 21:5. For an explanation of this Name, see *Raziel HaMalakh* (Margolioth edition), pp. 54*ff.;* see also Kaplan, *Meditation and the Bible* (Weiser, 1978), pp. 41-2.

are considered divine names. There is a tradition that these names have miraculous powers if used properly.[62] However, our sages were extremely careful to avoid using them altogether,[63] since one who uses them improperly[64] is worthy of death[65] and forfeits his portion in the World to Come.[66]

8:19   One must be extremely circumspect with respect to all mystical matters. Therefore, one may never pronounce the names of any angels not mentioned in the Bible. Since they have a hidden mystical significance, they may only be contemplated silently.[67] Some maintain that they should not be pronounced even when they are found in certain prayers.[68] Those found in the Bible, on the other hand, such as Michael, Gabriel, Raphael, Uriel, etc., and used as personal names, may be pronounced at any time.[69] Even these names were not revealed until after the Babylonian exile,[70] when there was no longer any danger of them being used for idolatrous purposes.[71]

8:20   Although it is permissible to pronounce the name *Adonai* in prayer, it must be done with the utmost awe and respect.[72] One

62. *Sifethey Cohen, Yoreh Deah* 179:18; Maharal, *Beer HaGolah*, p. 11a; *Derekh HaShem* 3:2:5, from Exodus 20:21. For examples, *cf. Yevamoth* 49a; *Gittin* 68b; *Sanhedrin* 95a; *Bekhoroth* 8b; *Shemoth Rabbah* 1:35; Rashi, Ramban, on Exodus 2:14; *Koheleth Rabbah* 3:15; *Midrash Tehillim* 36:8; Rashi on Isaiah 29:12, Jeremiah 21:4; *Midrash Tehillim* 91:8; *Pesikta* 19 (140a); *Yalkut Shimoni* 2:336. See *Moreh Nevukhim* 1:62.

63. *Cf. Taanith* 3:8 (19a); Bertenoro, *Tosefoth Yom Tov, ad. loc. s.v. Niduy;* Rav Hai Gaon, quoted in *Taam Zekenim*, pp. 55-58; *Tosafoth, Berakhoth* 7a *s.v. HaHu; Sefer Chasidim* 205, 484; *Ikkarim* 1:18; Rabbi Chaim Vital, *Shaar Ruach HaKodesh*, p. 13b; Rabbi Yaakov Emdin (Maharibatz), *Eruvin* 43a; *Chokhmath Adam* 89:8; *Teshuvoth Rashba* 1:220; *Teshuvoth Chatham Sofer, Orach Chaim* 197-98; *Teshuvoth Yakhin U'Boaz* 135 (54c). *Cf. Sanhedrin* 106a, from Exodus 24:23.

64. *Derekh HaShem* 3:2:7.

65. *Avoth DeRabbi Nathan*12:13; *Yoreh Deah* 246:21 in *Hagah*, from *Avoth* 1:13. *Cf. Yoreh Deah* 179:16 in *Hagah*.

66. Rashi, *Tosafoth*, cited in note 59.

67. *Chayay Adam* 5:27. *Cf. Tosefta, Zohar* 3:310a; *Tikuney Zohar* 97a, 131b.

68. *Ibid.*, citing *Likutey Torah* (HaAri); *Kitzur Shulchan Arukh* 129:15, citing *Matteh Ephraim* 590:37.

69. *Taamey HaMinhagim*, p. 497, citing *Kitzur Sh'nei Luchoth HaB'rith; ibid.* p. 538, citing *Livushey Mikhlul* 18, *Shulchan Arukh HaAri.*

70. *Yerushalmi, Rosh HaShanah* 1:2 (6a); *Bereshith Rabbah* 48:9.

71. *Sefer Chasidim* 192; *cf. Yoma* 69b. See Kaplan, *Meditation and the Bible*, pp. 151-152; *Jewish Meditation*, pp. 42-44.

72. *Sefer Chasidim* 46; *Menorath HaMaor* 2:9:1:1 (70); *Orach Chaim* 5:1; *Chayay Adam* 5:1; *Kitzur Shulchan Arukh* 6:1.

who reads the services as if they were meaningless words is guilty of showing gross disrespect to God.

8:21 Similarly, we are warned to adhere to the traditional prayers and not overdo our praises of God,[73] since there are no words which can describe His greatness.[74] Accordingly, the Psalmist exclaims, "Who can express God's mighty acts, or tell all His praise?" (Psalms 106:2).[75]

8:22 It was therefore decreed[76] that one should not say any unnecessary blessing, since it is considered taking God's name in vain.[77] For this reason, in any case where there is a question or doubt about whether a particular blessing is required, the rule is that it should not be said.[78] The only exception is the Blessing after Meals (*Birkath HaMazon*, בִּרְכַּת הַמָּזוֹן), which, because it is a Biblical commandment,[79] must be said even where there is a question of its being required.[80]

8:23 If one accidentally says an unnecessary blessing, or otherwise pronounces God's name in vain, he should show his reverence and make it into a praise by adding, "Blessed be the Name of His glorious Kingdom for ever and ever."[81]

8:24 It is logically inconsistent to bless God for a sin, as it is written, "The robber blesses, but [in so doing] mocks God" (Psalms

73. *Berakhoth* 33b; *Megillah* 18b; *Yerushalmi, Berakhoth* 9:1 (61b); *Midrash Tehillim* 19:2; *Yalkut Shimoni* 1:855; *Yad, Tefillah* 9:7; *Orach Chaim* 113:9.
74. See Volume 1, 2:51, note 67.
75. Cf. *Pirkey Rabbi Eliezer* 3.
76. *Tosafoth, Rosh HaShanah* 33a *s.v. Ha;* Ran, *Rosh HaShanah* (Rif 10b) *s.v. U'LeInyan;* Rabbenu Yonah, *Berakhoth* (Rif 39b) *s.v. Khol;* Rosh, *Kiddushin* 1:49; *Chinukh* 430 (end); *Magen Avraham* 215:6; *Nishmath Adam* 5:1.
77. *Berakhoth* 33a; *Yad, Berakhoth* 1:15; *Orach Chaim* 215:4; *Sh'nei Luchoth HaB'rith, Mesekheth Shevuoth* 2:102a. See above, 8:1.
78. *Yad, Berakhoth* 11:16, *Milah* 3:6; Raavad, *Kesef Mishneh, ad. loc.; She'ilthoth, Yithro* 52, quoted in Rosh, *Berakhoth* 3:15. Cf. *Magen Avraham* 581:3, 652:1; *Pri Chadash, Orach Chaim* 67:1; HaGra, *Orach Chaim* 67:1 *s.v. U'Mevarekh,* 688:4 *s.v. VeLe; Yoreh Deah* 28:3; *Chayay Adam* 5:24.
79. From Deuteronomy 8:10; *Berakhoth* 20b; *Yad, Berakhoth* 1:1; *Sefer HaMitzvoth,* Positive Commandment 19; *Sefer Mitzvoth Gadol,* Positive Commandment 27; *Chinukh* 430.
80. *Orach Chaim* 209:3; *Kitzur Shulchan Arukh* 6:6.
81. *Yerushalmi, Berakhoth* 9:1 (43b); *Yad, Shevuoth* 12:11; Rosh, *Berakhoth* 6:20; *Orach Chaim* 206:6; *Chayay Adam* 5:1; *Kitzur Shulchan Arukh* 6:4; *Tosafoth, Berakhoth* 39a *s.v. BeTzar.* See above, 8:14.

10:3).[82] Therefore, one should not say a blessing over any forbidden or stolen food,[83] since this is not a blessing but a blasphemy. However, in a situation where non-Kosher food is permitted because of mortal danger,[84] one should recite a blessing,[85] since he fulfills God's will by eating it.[86] Similarly, one who must eat on *Yom Kippur*[87] should recite the proper blessing over his food if he is able.[88]

8:25 Covering one's head has customarily been a sign of respect and reverence before God.[89] For this reason, it is forbidden to pray or to pronounce God's name in any manner with one's head uncovered.[90] Since the custom only applies to a man, a woman need not cover her head to pray.[91] Even when a woman does cover her hair, it is forbidden for her to wear a *Yarmulka,* since she may not wear any garment usually worn by a male.[92]

8:26 It is forbidden to pray in a lavatory or bathroom, or any place where people are not properly dressed, as the Torah states, "You must designate a place outside the camp to use as a lavatory... for God your Lord makes His presence known in your camp... Your camp must therefore be holy. Let no nakedness be seen in your midst, lest He turn away from you" (Deuteronomy 23:13-15).[93] It is likewise forbidden to discuss or even contemplate religious matters in an unclean place.[94] Similarly, if one hears a blessing

82. *Bava Kama* 94a; *Sanhedrin* 6b; *Tosefta* 1:3; *Yerushalmi, Sanhedrin* 1:1 (2b); *Yerushalmi, Challah* 1:5 (9a); *Midrash Tehillim* 10:4.
83. *Berakhoth* 7:1 (45a); *Rosh* 7:2; *Tosefta, Demai* 2:14; *Yad, Berakhoth* 1:19, Raavad, *Kesef Mishneh, ad. loc.; Orach Chaim* 196:1; *Turey Zahav* 196:1.
84. See above, 5:7, 5:38.
85. *Orach Chaim* 196:2, 204:9.
86. *Magen Avraham* 204:21; HaGra 204:9; *Mishnah Berurah* 196:5.
87. See above, 5:8.
88. *Orach Chaim* 618:10; *Hagahoth Maimonioth, Shevithath Assor* 2:9 (no. 9).
89. See above, 7:10.
90. *Sofrim* 14:15; *Yad, Tefillah* 4:5; *Orach Chaim* 91:3.
91. Cf. *Orach Chaim* 75:2.
92. From Deuteronomy 22:5; *Yad, Avodath Kokhavim* 12:10; *Sefer HaMitzvoth,* Negative Commandment 39; *Sefer Mitzvoth Gadol,* Negative Commandment 59; *Chinukh* 542; *Yoreh Deah* 182:5.
93. *Berakhoth* 25a; *Shabbath* 150a; *Yad, Keriath Sh'ma* 3:2ff.; *Orach Chaim* 76:1ff.; *Chayay Adam* 3:6; *Kitzur Shulchan Arukh* 5:1; cf. *Cheredim,* Positive Commandments 1:40; Rabbenu Yonah, *Shaarey Teshuvah* 3:44.
94. *Berakhoth* 24b; *Shabbath* 40a; *Avodah Zarah* 44b; *Yad, Keriath Sh'ma* 3:4; *Orach Chaim* 85:2.

while in an unclean place, he may not respond by saying *Amen.*[95]

8:27　There is a tradition that the word *Shalom,* meaning "Peace," is also one of God's names, as we find, "And he called [the altar] Adonai-Shalom" (Judges 6:24).[96] It was ordained that we use Shalom[97] as a greeting,[98] in order to constantly recall God's name, and because it is an expression of peace. Still, since the word Shalom refers to God, it is never used in an unclean place.[99]

8:28　Since the Bible is God's Word, it must be respected as such. Therefore, Biblical verses should only be recited in reverence, and not used for jokes,[100] games,[101] or common songs.[102] This does not apply to songs sung at religious gatherings, since they are sung to honor God. Similarly, sacred prayers, such as the *Kaddish* should not be used as common songs.[103]

8:29　It is a very serious sin[104] to swear falsely, as the Torah states, "Do not swear falsely by My Name; [if you do so,] you will be desecrating God's Name" (Leviticus 19:12).[105] Similarly, one who swears in vain violates one of the Ten Commandments, "Do not take the Name of God your Lord in vain" (Exodus 20:7).[106] We

95. *Yerushalmi, Shabbath* 3:3 (24a); Ran, *Shabbath* (Rif 19a) *s.v. VeAshme'inan; Orach Chaim* 84:1 in *Hagah.*
96. *Shabbath* 10b; *Zohar* 3:10b; *Derekh Eretz Zuta* 11; *VaYikra Rabbah* 9:9; *BaMidbar Rabbah* 11:7; *Yalkut Shimoni* 2:62; *Minchath Shai ad. loc.; Shulchan Arukh, Orach Chaim* 89:2.
97. Rambam, *Berakhoth* 9:5; Rashi, *Makkoth* 23b *s.v. She'elath.*
98. *Berakhoth* 9:5 (54a); *Yerushalmi, Berakhoth* 9:5 (67b); *Ruth Rabbah* 4:7; *Midrash Tehillim* 57:2; *Yalkut Shimoni* 2:18, from Ruth 2:4. *Cf. Teshuvoth Radbaz* (new) 202, cited in *Pith'chey Teshuvah* 276:28.
99. *Tosefta, Berakhoth* 2:21; *Shabbath* 10a; *Derekh Eretz Rabbah* 10; *Kesef Mishneh, Kriath Sh'ma* 3:5; *Orach Chaim* 84:1. When it is not used as a greeting, see *Bayith Chadash, Orach Chaim* 84; *Turey Zahav* 84:3; *Magen Avraham* 84:2; *Chayay Adam* 3:36; *Kitzur Shulchan Arukh* 5:14; "*Rav*" *Shulchan Arukh* 84:1; *Mishnah Berurah* 84:6.
100. *Turey Zahav, Orach Chaim* 560:5.
101. *Sefer Chasidim* 644; *B'rith Olam* (Chida) *ad. loc.*
102. *Sanhedrin* 101a; Rashi *ad. loc. s.v. HaKerei; Mesekhta Khallah* 1; *Magen Avraham* 560:10; *Mishnah Berurah* 560:16; *Tosefta, Sanhedrin* 12:5; *Yerushalmi, Sotah* 35a; Maharsha, *Eruvin* 18b *s.v. Nothen.*
103. *Turey Zahav, Orach Chaim* 560:5; *Mishnah Berurah* 560:15. Regarding tapes, diskettes and records, *cf. Makor Chesed* (on *Sefer Chasidim*) 4:1, from *BaMidbar Rabbah* 12:21.
104. *Shevuoth* 39a; *Yoma* 86b; *Yad, Teshuvah* 1:2; *Reshith Chokhmah, Shaar HaKedushah* 14 (182a); *Teshuvoth Besamim Rosh* 204, quoted in Maharatz Chajas, *Bava Metzia* 5b.
105. *Shevuoth* 20b; *Yad, Shevuoth* 1:3; *Sefer HaMitzvoth,* Negative Commandment 61; *Sefer Mitzvoth Gadol,* Negative Commandment 239; *Chinukh* 227. *Cf. Sifra* (88c), Rashi, *ad. loc.*
106. *Shevuoth* 3:7 (27b); *Yad, Shevuoth* 1:7; *Sefer HaMitzvoth,* Negative Commandment 62;

are taught that the earth trembled when God pronounced this commandment.[107]

8:30 There are four types of vain oaths which are forbidden by this commandment. The first two involve a present situation and refer to swearing about that which is either manifestly false or trivially true. The other two involve the future and refer to an oath to do the impossible or to violate a Biblical commandment.[108]

8:31 Because of their extreme seriousness, one should avoid all oaths entirely.[109] One should therefore not use such common expressions as, "I swear to G-d." Similarly, one should not swear on the life of his children,[110] or on his portion in the World to Come.[111] Whenever possible, one should even avoid speaking to a person who habitually swears.[112]

8:32 It is an extremely serious sin to curse God in any manner, as the Torah states, "Anyone who curses God shall bear his sin" (Leviticus 24:15).[113] If one curses God using the Tetragrammaton,[114] he is worthy of death, as it is written, "But if one blasphemes the Name *YHVH,* he shall be put to death" *(ibid.).*[115]

8:33 One who hears a fellow Jew cursing God in any manner[116] must rend his clothing as in mourning.[117] This is not required, however, if the curse is pronounced by a nonreligious Jew[118] or a gentile.[119]

Sefer Mitzvoth Gadol, Negative Commandment 238; *Chinukh* 30. *Cf. Mekhilta* (35b), Rashi, *ad. loc.*
107. *Shevuoth* 39a.
108. *Shevuoth* 3:8 (29a); *Yad, Shevuoth* 1:4-7; *Yoreh Deah* 236:4.
109. *Gittin* 35a; *Shevuoth* 39b; *Yerushalmi, Shevuoth* 6:5 (31a); *BaMidbar Rabbah* 22:1; *Zohar* 1:165a; *Yad, Shevuoth* 12:12; *Sefer Chasidim* 10, 418, 788, 1110; Ramban, *Sefer HaMitzvoth,* Positive Commandment 7, commentary to Deuteronomy 6:13; Rabbenu Yonah, *Shaarey Teshuvah* 3:45; *Cheredim,* Negative Commandments 4:5; *Kitzur Shulchan Arukh* 67:2.
110. *Gittin* 35a; *Bava Metzia* 85a; *Sefer Chasidim* 416.
111. *Sefer Chasidim* 1091. *Cf.* Mordecai, *Bava Metzia* 354; *Yoreh Deah* 228:45.
112. *Sefer Chasidim* 417.
113. *Shevuoth* 36a; *Sefer HaMitzvoth,* Negative Commandment 60; *Sefer Mitzvoth Gadol,* Negative Commandment 16; *Chinukh* 70.
114. *Yad, Avodath Kokhavim* 2:7; *Kesef Mishneh ad. loc.; Tosefoth Yom Tov, Sanhedrin* 7:5 *s.v. Hakeh, Shevuoth* 4:12 *s.v. HaMekallel. Cf. Sifra* on Leviticus 24:15 (104c).
115. *Sanhedrin* 7:5 (56a).
116. *Nimukey Yosef, Sanhedrin* (Rif 16a) *s.v. VeTu; Pith'chey Teshuvah* 340:16.
117. *Sanhedrin* 60a; *Yad, Avodath Kokhavim* 2:10; *Yoreh Deah* 340:37.
118. *Nimukey Yosef, Sanhedrin* (Rif 16a) *s.v. VeTu; Sifethey Cohen* 340:54.
119. *Cf. Sifethey Cohen* 340:53.

8:34   It is forbidden to curse one's fellow,[120] especially if one uses God's name in any language,[121] as the Torah states, "Do not curse the deaf" (Leviticus 19:14) — even a deaf man who cannot hear the curse and is not bothered by it.[122] One should avoid cursing another even indirectly, for example by saying, "May you not be blessed."[123] Therefore, one should be extremely careful not to use such expressions as "G-d damn you" or "G-d should only punish you," even if they are not meant seriously.

8:35   Just as one may not curse another, so is it forbidden to curse oneself,[124] as the Torah states, "Take heed and guard your life very carefully" (Deuteronomy 4:9).[125] One should therefore be careful not to use such common expressions as "I'll be damned."

8:36   One must be even more careful not to curse one's parents. One who curses his parents using any one of God's names is worthy of death, as we find, "Any person who curses his father or mother shall be put to death. Since he has cursed his father or mother, he shall be stoned to death" (Leviticus 20:9).[126]

8:37   There are other ways in which we are forbidden to injure another with words. Thus, we are commanded not to slander, gossip, or talebear, as the Torah states, "Do not go around as a gossiper among your people" (Leviticus 19:16).[127] Concerning a slanderer, the Psalmist entreated, "May God cut off all slandering

120. Even without God's name; *Choshen Mishpat* 27:2; *Kitzur Shulchan Arukh* 6:3.
121. *Shevuoth* 4:13 (35a); *Yad, Sanhedrin* 26:2; *Choshen Mishpat* 27:1.
122. *Shevuoth* 36a; *Temurah* 4a; *Yad, Sanhedrin* 26:1; *Sefer HaMitzvoth,* Negative Commandment 318; *Sefer Mitzvoth Gadol,* Negative Commandment 211; *Chinukh* 321. *Cf. Zohar* 3:85a; *Sefer Chasidim* 76; *Reshith Chokhmah, Shaar HaKedushah* 13 (181b).
123. *Shevuoth* 4:13; *Choshen Mishpat* 27:2; *Ketzoth HaChoshen* 27:2.
124. *Shevuoth* 36a; *Yad, Sanhedrin* 26:3; *Choshen Mishpat, Kitzur Shulchan Arukh* 6:3; *Zohar* 1:14b, 2:266a, 3:155b; *Reshith Chokhmah, Shaar HaKedushah* 12 (181c). *Cf. VaYikra Rabbah* 15:7.
125. *Shevuoth* 36a; *Sefer Mitzvoth Gadol* (Negative 212) counts this as a separate commandment; *cf. Cheredim,* Negative Commandments 4:15. See above, 5:40.
126. "He shall be stoned" is expressed idiomatically by the Torah as, "his blood is in him." This indicates that he was to be killed by a method that induced internal bleeding, namely, stoning; see below, 13:62. See Leviticus 20:27; Exodus 21:17; *Sanhedrin* 7:4 (53a), 7:8 (66a); *Yad, Mamrim* 5:1; *Sefer Mitzvoth Gadol,* Negative Commandment 219; *Yoreh Deah* 241:1.
127. *Kethuvoth* 46a; *Yad, Deyoth* 7:1; *Sefer HaMitzvoth,* Negative Commandment 301; *Sefer Mitzvoth Gadol,* Negative Commandment 9; *Chinukh* 236; *Menorath HaMaor* 2:4:1:2 (49); *Kitzur Shulchan Arukh* 31:1.

lips, every tongue that speaks distortions" (Psalms 12:4),[128] thereby warning us that this is among the most serious of sins.[129]

8:38   It is likewise forbidden to cause pain, anguish or suffering, or tease another, or embarrass him in any way, as the Torah states, "Do not vex your fellow man, but rather fear your God" (Leviticus 25:17).[130]

8:39   It is forbidden to cause dissent and argument, as the Torah states, "Do not be like Korach and his party" (Numbers 17:5) — who wrought dissent in Israel.[131]

8:40   One should avoid lying and deception, as the Torah states, "Keep far away from anything false" (Exodus 23:7).[132] Similarly, we are enjoined by the prophet, "Let each man speak the truth with his fellow" (Zechariah 8:16). We are likewise taught that God's seal and emblem is Truth (*Emeth*, אֱמֶת). It is thus written, "The Lord God is Truth" (Jeremiah 10:10).[133] Although it is permissible to hide or slightly alter the truth for the sake of fostering peace and harmony, this should still be avoided as there is a danger that a person might make a habit of lying.[134]

8:41   Since all forms of idolatry are an abomination to God, one should avoid pronouncing the name of any idolatrous deity, as the Torah states, "Make no mention of the name of other gods" (Exodus 23:13).[135] However, this only refers to gods whose names are reverenced by their followers, and not those whose names are

128. *Arakhin* 15b; *Yerushalmi, Peah* 1:1 (4a); *Yad, Deyoth* 7:2.
129. *Tosefta, Peah* 1:2; *Yerushalmi, Peah loc. cit.;* see below, 14:16.
130. *Bava Metzia* 4:10 (58b); *Yad, Mekhirah* 14:12; *Sefer HaMitzvoth,* Negative 251; *Sefer Mitzvoth Gadol,* Negative 171; *Chinukh* 338; *Choshen Mishpat* 428:1; *Menorath HaMaor* 2:3:2:2 (47); *Kitzur Shulchan Arukh* 63:1; *PeleYo'etz, s.v. Onaath Devarim.*
131. *Sanhedrin* 110a; *Rif* 20a; *Rosh* 11:8; *Rabbenu Yonah, Shaarey Teshuvah* 3:48; *Sefer HaMitzvoth,* Negative 45; *Cheredim,* Negative Commandments 4:42.
132. *Cheredim,* Positive Commandments 4:26; *Menorath HaMaor* 2:2:1:1 (34).
133. *Shabbath* 55a; *Yoma* 69b; *Sanhedrin* 64a; *Bereshith Rabbah* 81:2. Truth is also one of three pillars upon which the world stands; *Avoth* 1:18. See *Sanhedrin* 89b: "One of the punishments of a liar is that even when he speaks the truth, no one pays attention to him"; quoted in *Mesilath Yesharim* 11. Cf. Proverbs 12:22.
134. *Yevamoth* 63a, 65b; *Bava Metzia* 87a; *Derekh Eretz Zuta* 11; *VaYikra Rabbah* 9:9; *BaMidbar Rabbah* 11:7; *Chazon Ish, Emunah U'Bitachon,* p. 13.
135. *Mekhilta* (101a), Rashi, *ad. loc.; Sanhedrin* 63b; *Rosh* 7:3; *Yad, Avodath Kokhavim* 5:10-11; *Sefer HaMitzvoth,* Negative 14; *Sefer Mitzvoth Gadol,* Negative 32; *Chinukh* 86; *Yoreh Deah* 147:1; *Turey Zahav* 147:1; *Chokhmath Adam* 87:1; *Kitzur Shulchan Arukh* 167:9. Cf. *Sefer Chasidim* 194.

used in common speech or in personal names.[136] Similarly, it is permitted to pronounce the name of any deity mentioned in the Bible.[137]

8:42　It is forbidden to use any foul or improper language,[138] as the Torah is interpreted to say, "Let Him not find a vulgar word [spoken] among you" (Deuteronomy 23:15).[139]

8:43　The power of speech is a gift from God. Only man is distinguished with the ability to speak; this ability should not be taken lightly or used for anything degrading.[140] With this in mind, a God-fearing person will carefully guard his speech, as the Psalmist taught us, "Who is the person who truly desires life, who loves the days [of this world] in order to see [eternal] good: Guard your tongue from evil and your lips from speaking deceit!" (Psalms 34:13-14).[141]

TABLE 8:1 — THE BIBLICAL NAMES OF GOD

	Name	Transliteration	Colloquial Pronunciation	Translation
1.	יהוה	Yod-Keh-Vav-Keh[1]	HaShem[2]	Tetragrammaton God/Eternal
2.	אדני	Adonai	HaShem[2]	God/Lord
3.	יה	Yah[3]	Kah	God/Lord

136. Mordecai, *Avodah Zarah* 809; *Hagahoth Maimonioth, Avodath Kokhavim* 5:10 no. 3; *Yoreh Deah* 147:2; *Teshuvoth Shaar Ephraim* 24.
137. *Sanhedrin* 63b; *Yoreh Deah* 147:4.
138. *Pesachim* 3a; *Shabbath* 33a; *Kethuvoth* 8b; *Chagigah* 5b; *Bereshith Rabbah* 32:5; *VaYikra Rabbah* 26:1; *BaMidbar Rabbah* 19:2; *Midrash Tehillim* 1:3, 12:4; *Zohar* 2:249b, 2:263b; *Yad, Deyoth* 5:4; *Turey Zahav, Yoreh Deah* 124:1; *Mishnah Berurah* 156:4; *Menorath HaMaor* 2:4:2:2 (56); *Reshith Chokhmah, Shaar HaKedushah* 12 (180b); *Sh'nei Luchoth HaB'rith, Shaar HaOthioth* 1:175a.
139. *Zohar* 1:76a; *Cheredim*, Negative Commandments 4:49. *Cf. Yerushalmi, Terumoth* 1:4 (6b); *HaGra ad. loc.* no. 1; *Ridbaz ad. loc.;* Mordecai, *Eruvin* 512. The word *Davar* means both "thing" and "word" in Hebrew. The expression *Davar Erva* can therefore be translated "erotic thing" or "vulgar word."
140. *Moreh Nevukhim* 3:8.
141. Rabbi Nachman of Breslev, *Sefer HaMidoth s.v. Merivah.*

1.　In order to prevent vocalization, the letters *Y-H-V-H* are not punctuated; see above, 8:10.
2.　Literally "The Name"; *cf. Yoma* 3:8, 4:2, 6:2, and not the meaningless *Adoshem; Turey Zahav, Orach Chaim* 621:2 (end); *Kitzur Shulchan Arukh* 6:3.
3.　Included only in lists of *Avoth DeRabbi Nathan* 34:2, and Rif, *Shevuoth* 16a. See

4.	אלהים	*Elohim*	*Elokim*	*God/Lord*
5.	אלוה	*Elo'ah*[4]	*Elokah*	*God/Lord*
6.	אלהי	*Elohei*[5]	*Elokei*	*God of*
7.	אל	*El*	*Kel*	*God*
8.	אהיה	*Eheyeh*[6]	*Ekeyeh*	*I Am/I Will Be*
9.	שדי	*Shadai*	*Shakai*	*God/Almighty*
10.	צבאות	*Tzevaoth*[7]	*Tzevakoth*	*Hosts*

also *Nachalath Yaakov, Sofrim* 4:1; HaGra, *Yoreh Deah* 276:19. Rabbi Shimon ben Gamliel may dispute this in *Bereshith Rabbah* 12:9, *Midrash Tehillim* 114:3, *Yalkut Shimoni* 2:794; *cf.* Ramban on Genesis 43:20. From *Yerushalmi, Chagigah* 2:1 (10b), however, this does not appear to be the case, and in any case, *Menachoth* 29b agrees with Rabbi Eliezer who considers it a divine name; *cf.* Rashi on Genesis 2:4, Psalms 68:5. For a complete discussion, see *Tosefoth Yom Tov, Sukkah* 4:5; *cf. Midrash Tehillim* 113:3; *Eruvin* 18b; Ibn Ezra on Exodus 15:2; Rashi on Exodus 17:16; Radak on Isaiah 26:4; *Minchath Shai* on Psalms 94:7, 118:5; *Kuzari* 4:3 (9a); *Moreh Nevukhim* 1:63.

4. Often mispronounced *Eloha.*
5. *Tur, Yoreh Deah* 276; *Turey Zahav* 276:7. This includes all possessive forms, such *Elokai, Elokenu, Elokecha, Elokechem*, etc.
6. Not included in *Yad;* see *Kesef Mishneh ad. loc.; Tur loc. cit.; Yoreh Deah* 276:9; *cf.* HaGra *ad. loc.* 276:19. The phrase *Ekeyeh Asher Ekeyeh,* "I am that I am," or "I will be who I will be," occurs only in Exodus 3:14 and the entire phrase constitutes a divine name; *cf. Targum ad. loc.; Bava Bathra* 73a; *Moreh Nevukhim loc. cit.* However, *Ekeyeh* alone is also a divine name; *cf.* HaGra 276:20; *Pilpula Charifta* on Rosh, *Shevuoth* 4:22 (no. 1); Rif *loc. cit.* who includes *Ekeyeh* alone. See *Kuzari loc. cit.;* Ibn Ezra on Exodus 3:14, 15:2. Also see Rashbam on Exodus 3:15, where the *Atbash* (את‬ב״ש) code is deciphered to read, "He calls Himself *EHYH,* 'I will be,' and we call Him *YHYH,* 'He will be' with a *Vav* in place of the [second] *Yod* [to make] *YHVH,* 'He was, is and will be,' as we find, *Ki meh hoveh la-adam* (Ecclesiastes 2:22)." See Volume 1, 7:80, note 194.
7. *Cf. Tosafoth, Shevuoth* 35a *s.v. Hakhi Garsinan;* Ran, *Shevuoth* (Rif 16a) *s.v. Amar.*

NINE

REVERENCE OF THE SACRED

9:1   Just as we are commanded to revere God Himself, so must we respect places and objects which are associated with His worship. The Torah teaches this through juxtaposition, as God says, "Revere My sanctuary — I am God" (Leviticus 19:30, 26:2).[1] One should therefore[2] show the utmost respect for a synagogue,[3] which is also considered a sanctuary, as God told His prophet, "Although I have removed them far off among the nations, and although I have scattered them among the peoples, still, I have provided them with a *miniature sanctuary* in the countries where they have been exiled" (Ezekiel 11:16).[4]

9:2   It is forbidden to destroy anything associated with God's worship. This is learned from another juxtaposition in the Torah: "You must *tear down* their altars, *break* their stone pillars, *burn* their sacred groves, and *cut down* the statues of their gods... But you must never do anything like this to [the sacred objects of] God your Lord" (Deuteronomy 12:3-4).[5] Accordingly, it is

1.   *Sifra* (90d), Rashi, *ad. loc.; Yevamoth* 6b; *Yad, Beth HaBechirah* 7:1; *Sefer HaMitzvoth,* Positive Commandment 21; *Sefer Mitzvoth Gadol,* Positive Commandment 164; *Chinukh* 252.
2.   *Sefer Mitzvoth Gadol loc. cit.* (210c); *Sefer Yereyim* 394; *Cheredim,* Positive Commandments 1:19; *Chayay Adam* 17:6; *Kitzur Shulchan Arukh* 13:1.
3.   *Megillah* 3:3 (28a); *Yad, Tefillah* 11:5; *Orach Chaim* 151:1.
4.   *Targum,* Rashi, *Metzudoth David, ad. loc.; Megillah* 29a, all understand the phrase *VaEhi Lahem LeMikdash Me'at* (literally, "I have been for them a miniature sanctuary"), as an allusion to the synagogues and houses of study which were established in Babylon after the destruction of the First Temple. *Metzudoth David* paraphrases thus: "I will cause My Presence to rest in their synagogues, and though they will be far removed from the Great Sanctuary in Jerusalem, the synagogue will serve as a Miniature Sanctuary in its stead."
5.   *Sifri, Yalkut Shimoni* (878), Rashi, Ramban, *ad. loc.; Makkoth* 22a; *Yad, Yesodey HaTorah* 6:7; *Sefer HaMitzvoth,* Negative Commandment 65; *Sefer Mitzvoth Gadol,* Negative Commandment 3; *Chinukh* 437.

forbidden to wantonly destroy a synagogue,[6] or anything else which is used in worship.[7]

9:3   Similarly, it is forbidden to destroy even a single letter of any of the ten divine names of God.[8] This is learned from the continuation of the same verse: "You must obliterate their names from that place. But you must never do anything like this to God your Lord" (ibid.).[9] It is therefore forbidden to erase a divine name written on parchment or paper, unravel one embroidered in cloth,[10] or melt down a piece of metal[11] or a seal[12] upon which a divine name is engraved or impressed.

9:4   If any word resembling a divine name is written with the specific intent that it have a secular meaning,[13] or if its context unambiguously implies that it is not a divine name,[14] it may be erased. However, if it is written with no specific intent, it may not be destroyed.[15]

9:5   As soon as one writes a divine name, any suffix[16] added on to it is also considered sacred and may not be erased. On the other hand, it is permitted to erase a prefix attached to a divine name.[17]

9:6   It is forbidden to destroy a divine name, even if it has already

6.   Yad, Minyan HaMitzvoth, Negative Commandment 65; Mordecai, Megillah 826; Orach Chaim 152:1 in Hagah; Magen Avraham 152:6; Turey Zahav 151:3; Chayay Adam 17:10; Chokhmath Adam 86:15; Mishnah Berurah 152:11. See Pri Megadim, Eshel Avraham 152:6, for whether this is considered a Biblical or rabbinical law; cf. Nimukey Mahari, Yesodey HaTorah 6:1.

7.   See Chatham Sofer, Orach Chaim 152:1; Pri Megadim, Mishbetzoth Zahav 151:3; Biur Halakhah 152:1 s.v. Davar, that "all things used in worship are considered extensions of the synagogue"; cf. Yerushalmi, Megillah 3:1 (23b); Yad, Tefillah 11:15; Orach Chaim 154:3; Makkoth 22a; Avodah Zarah 51b. However, Machtzith HaShekel 152:6, and Chayay Adam 17:10, apply this exclusively to things attached to a synagogue; cf. Biur Halakhah 152:1 s.v. VeAssur. Cf. Magen Avraham 154:9; Pri Megadim ad. loc.

8.   See above, Table 8:1.

9.   Makkoth 22a; Sofrim 5:6; Yad, Yesodey HaTorah 6:1; Yoreh Deah 176:9; Chokhmath Adam 86:14.

10. Pith'chey Teshuvah 276:17.

11. Yad, Yesodey HaTorah 6:6; Hagahoth Maimonioth ad. loc. 6:1 no. 1.

12. Teshuvoth Chavath Yair 15, cited in Pith'chey Teshuvah loc. cit.

13. Yad, Yesodey HaTorah 6:8.

14. Cf. Pith'chey Teshuvah 276:24.

15. Sifethey Cohen 176:12.

16. As long as it is meaningful; Turey Zahav 276:7.

17. Shevuoth 35b; Yad, Yesodey HaTorah 6:3; Yoreh Deah 276:9.

been partially erased.[18] If a divine name is written on a wall, some authorities maintain that it is forbidden to paint over it.[19] One should likewise be careful not to perforate a divine name in any way.[20]

9:7 It is only forbidden to destroy a divine name when it is written on a single object or sheet. However, if it is merely put together with alphabet blocks or movable type, it may be separated. Similarly, those who spell out the divine name *Shadai* with their *Tefillin* straps may undo the straps without being concerned about destroying the name, although the custom itself is not proper.[21]

9:8 Similarly, it is only forbidden to erase a divine name that is written in a normal fashion. However, where it is written in mirror image, as on a rubber stamp or immovable type, it may be destroyed.[22] For this reason, it is permissible to destroy a phonograph record,[23] or to erase or copy over a sound or video tape, even though a divine name may be recorded on it.

9:9 The commandment not to destroy God's name applies only to the ten specific divine names. [See above, Table 8:1.] Therefore, any other appellation or adjective used to designate God may be erased.[24] Similarly, it is permitted to erase God's name written in any language other than Hebrew.[25]

9:10 It is likewise permitted to erase any abbreviation of a divine name, such as the double *Yod*[26] or *Heh*[27] used to abbreviate the

18. *Pith'chey Teshuvah* 276:15.
19. *Meil Tzedakah* 23-24, cited in *Pith'chey Teshuvah* 276:9. However, *Panim Meiroth* 1:45, writes that it is permitted, as we find that the Torah was written on stones and covered with lime in Joshua 8:35; *cf. Sotah* 35b according to Rabbi Yehudah. However, see Radak *ad. loc.*, quoting Rav Saadiah Gaon, that this is no proof.
20. *Sefer Chasidim* 932, 933, from *Sanhedrin* 56a.
21. *Pith'chey Teshuvah* 276:17, citing *Beney Yonah. Cf. Teshuvoth Chavath Yair* 15.
22. *Ibid.*
23. *Makor Chesed* on *Sefer Chasidim* 4:1.
24. *Shevuoth* 35a; *Yad, Yesodey HaTorah* 6:5.
25. *Teshuvoth Tashbatz* 1:2; *Sifethey Cohen* 179:11; *Pith'chey Teshuvah* 276:11. *Cf. Sanhedrin* 60a; *Nedarim* 10a; *Yad, Sanhedrin* 26:3; *Choshen Mishpat* 27:1; *Sefer Meirath Eynayim (Sema)* 27:3. See *Teshuvoth Chavath Yair* 106, that no name of God written in Hebrew letters should be destroyed, irrespective of the original language of this name.
26. *Sefer Chasidim* 935; *Yoreh Deah* 276:10 in *Hagah; HaGra ad. loc.* 276:24. See *Teshuvoth Pri HaSadeh* 4:3; *Teshuvoth Maharasham* 1:87.
27. *Pith'chey Teshuvah* 276:16.

Tetragrammaton, as long as the abbreviation itself is not a divine name.[28] However, some maintain that even the first two letters of *Adonai* or *Eheyeh* should not be erased when used as an abbreviation.[29]

9:11   Although it is permissible to erase God's name in a langauge other than Hebrew, it is forbidden to desecrate such a name in any manner.[30] Therefore, it is forbidden to throw a paper upon which such a name is written in the garbage or any other place where it may be desecrated.[31] If one has letters or notes with God's name written in a language other than Hebrew, one may burn them to save them from desecration.[32]

9:12   One should therefore be careful not to write God's name in any language on a letter or note which may be thrown away.[33] In such a case, it is customary to abbreviate God's name as G-d or L-rd.

9:13   It is customary to write ב"ה (abbreviation of *Barukh HaShem*, "Blessed be the Name") or בע"ה (*BeEzrath HaShem*, "With the Help of the Name") in the upper right hand corner of letters.[34] However, some people prefer the abbreviation בס"ד (*BeSiyatta DeShamaya*, Aramaic for "With the Help of Heaven") in order to avoid writing any allusion to God's name in a letter that might be thrown out.[35]

9:14   It is permitted to erase names like Jeremiah, Isaiah, or Zechariah, even though the last two letters of such names spell out the divine name *Yah*, since the entire name is considered a single word.[36] Nevertheless, it is customary to abbreviate such names,

---

28. *Shevuoth* 35b; Raavad, *Yesodey HaTorah* 6:4; *Yoreh Deah* 276:10.
29. *Tosafoth, Shevuoth* 35a *s.v. U'BeFerush; Yad, Yesodey HaTorah* 6:4; *Yoreh Deah* 276:10 in *Hagah*. However, see *Yerushalmi, Megillah* 1:9 (12b) and HaGra 276:23, where this case is completely permitted.
30. *Cf. "Rav" Shulchan Arukh* 85:3; *Mishnah Berurah* 85:10.
31. *Urim VeThumim* 27:2; *Nethivoth HaMishpat* 27:2; *Kitzur Shulchan Arukh* 6:3.
32. However, it is preferable to place them in *Genizah* (storage); see below, 9:23. If the names are written in Hebrew, they may not be burned. *Cf. Teshuvoth Kenesseth Yechezkel* 37, quoting Rabbi Akiba Eiger; *Magen Avraham* 154:9.
33. *Cf. Rosh HaShanah* 18b (end); *Yoreh Deah* 276:13 in *Hagah*.
34. *Cf. Berakhoth* 9:5 (54a).
35. *Beth Lechem Yehudah, Yoreh Deah* 176:10; *Pith'chey Teshuvah* 176:16.
36. See above, 8:5.

leaving out the final *Heh,* so as not to desecrate a divine name in any manner whatsoever. Similarly, it is customary to write Yehudah with an *Aleph* (יהודא) rather than a final *Heh* (יהודה), lest one accidentally leave out the letter *Daleth* and write the Tetragrammaton.[37]

9:15 It is likewise customary to write the Hebrew number 15 as ט״ו rather than יה״, which is a divine name. Similarly, 16 is written as ט״ז rather than as יו״, which resembles a divine name. These changes are made even when they are part of a larger number such as 115, 416, etc. It is likewise customary to transpose the letters of numbers which might otherwise spell out a word with a negative connotation, such as in the case of 270 (רע, which means "evil") or 304 (שֵׁד, which spells the word for "demon").

9:16 Some authorities maintain that one should avoid writing the greeting Shalom[38] in a letter which may be thrown away,[39] but the custom is to ignore this opinion.[40]

9:17 It is forbidden to make personal use of anything upon which a divine name is written.[41] For example, it is forbidden to drink from a vessel[42] or wear a ring[43] upon which such a name is written or engraved. However, if such a ring or locket is worn as a sign of divine protection, it is permissible as long as the divine name is covered.[44]

9:18 A divine name only sanctifies the surface upon which it is written.[45] Therefore, if it is written on any object, the name may be carefully cut or shaved off and set aside, after which the article

---

37. *Cf. Sofrim* 5:2-3; *Shabbath* 104b; *Hagahoth Maimonioth, Tefillin* 1:16 no. 40; *Yoreh Deah* 276:12.
38. See above, 8:27.
39. *Tosafoth, Sotah* 10a *s.v. Eleh; Yoreh Deah* 276:13 in *Hagah; Nekudoth HaKesef ad. loc. Cf. Minchath Shai* on Judges 6:24.
40. *Teshuvoth HaRosh* 3:15; *Sifethey Cohen* 276:13; *Pith'chey Teshuvah* 276:28; *Shaarey Teshuvah* 84:2. *Cf. Teshuvoth Tashbatz* 1:177; *Teshuvoth Rashbash* 267; *Rashbash* 2:220; *Teshuvoth Zaken Aaron* 72, 188; *Teshuvoth Beth Ephraim, Evven HaEzer* 86 (p. 162b).
41. See below, note 46.
42. *Teshuvoth Panim Meiroth* 2:132, quoted in *Pith'chey Teshuvah* 176:25.
43. *Teshuvoth Chavath Yair* 16, quoted in *Pith'chey Teshuvah* 276:27; *Beth Lechem Yehudah* 276:10.
44. *Teshuvoth Yaabetz,* quoted in *Pith'chey Teshuvah loc. cit.*
45. *Arakhin* 6a.

may be used.[46] However, some maintain that the reason for this limitation is because a vessel is an improper place on which to write, whereas if a divine name is written on a proper place such as parchment or paper, then the entire sheet is sanctified and may no longer be used.[47]

9:19   It is forbidden to bring anything containing a divine name into a place where it may not be read,[48] as the Torah states, "[This scroll] must always be with [the king], and he shall read from it all the days of his life" (Deuteronomy 17:19). That is, it shall be with him only when he may read from it.[49] It is therefore forbidden to stand naked before a divine name,[50] or carry anything upon which it is written into a lavatory or bath, unless the name is completely covered.[51]

9:20   Just as we are commanded to show respect for God's name, so also must we revere His teachings. We are commanded, "Stand up before the wise elder and give respect to the aged. You shall thus fear your God" (Leviticus 19:32).[52] Just as we respect our elders who study sacred books, we must honor the books themselves.[53]

9:21   One should therefore keep his sacred books and other religious articles on nice shelves or cabinets[54] apart from his secular books.[55] One should also be careful not to store sacred books

---

46. *Ibid.; Shabbath* 61b; *Sofrim* 5:13; *Tosefta, Megillah* 2:10; *Minchath Bikkurim ad. loc.; Yad, Yesodey HaTorah* 6:6; *Yoreh Deah* 276:13.

47. Rashi, *Arakhin* 6a *s.v. Shem; Sefer Mitzvoth Gadol,* Negative Commandment 3, quoting *Halakhoth Gedoloth,* from *Moed Katan* 26a; *cf.* Rabbi Akiba Eiger on *Sifethey Cohen* 276:13. See also *Tosafoth, Arakhin* 6a *s.v. Yegud; Magen Abraham* 32:26 (end).

48. See above, 8:26.

49. *Sanhedrin* 21b; *Tosefta* 4:5; Rashi, *Shabbath* 120b *s.v. MiKlal,* derives this law from Deuteronomy 23:15, but this link is still needed since that passage only speaks of reading. See also *Teshuvoth Besamim Rosh* 21; Maharatz Chajas, *Shabbath* 61b.

50. *Shabbath* 120b; *Yad, Yesodey HaTorah* 6:6. *Cf. Teshuvoth Noda BeYehudah, Orach Chaim* 2:17, quoted in *Pith'chey Teshuvah* 276:9 (end).

51. *Shabbath* 62a; *Yoma* 7b; *Yad, Sefer Torah* 10:5; *Yoreh Deah* 282:6.

52. *Kiddushin* 32b; *Yad, Talmud Torah* 6:1; *Sefer HaMitzvoth,* Positive Commandment 209; *Sefer Mitzvoth Gadol,* Positive Commandment 13; *Chinukh* 257; *Yoreh Deah* 244:1. See above, 7:16, below, 12:5, note 18.

53. *Kiddushin* 33b; *Yerushalmi, Megillah* 4:1 (27b); *Sefer Mitzvoth Gadol,* Positive Commandment 13; *cf. Teshuvoth Yad Eliahu* 64; *Reshith Chokhmah, Shaar HaYirah* 15 (45a).

54. Rabbi Yehudah ibn Tibon, *Tzavaah; Sefer Chasidim* 129, 275; *Reshith Chokhmah ibid.* 45a.

55. *Sefer Chasidim* 429.

near food where they may be stained or attacked by mice and vermin.[56]

9:22   When picking up a sacred book which has fallen to the ground, it is customary to kiss it as a sign of love and respect for God's teachings.[57] For the same reason, it is customary to kiss a sacred book when closing it and putting it away. It is likewise customary to kiss one's *Tefillin* when putting them on and taking them off.[58]

9:23   It is forbidden to destroy or desecrate any sacred or religious book, whether it is written in Hebrew or any other language.[59] One must similarly be careful with worn or torn books,[60] and even with loose and torn pages from sacred books.[61] All these should be set aside in a special *Genizah* (storage)[62] and eventually buried.[63]

9:24   Sacred books and religious articles should always be handled with respect.[64] One should avoid shaking a sacred book or *Tefillin* out of its container,[65] and it is forbidden to throw them.[66] Similarly, one should always be careful to place a sacred book right side up.[67] If one leaves the room in the midst of his study, it is customary not to leave the book open, but to either close or cover it.[68]

---

56. *Sefer Chasidim* 910; *cf. Shabbath* 14a; *Yad, Avoth HaTumah* 9:5; *Teshuvoth Beth Ephraim, Yoreh Deah* 62; Rambam, Bertenoro, *Mishnah Zavim* 5:12.
57. *Sefer Chasidim* 932, 274.
58. *Orach Chaim* 28:3.
59. *Yad, Yesodey HaTorah* 6:8; *Sefer HaMitzvoth,* Negative Commandment 64. See Rashi, *Shabbath* 115a *s.v. Teunah.*
60. *Hagahoth Asheri, Shabbath* 9:2. This is true even if the writing is faded; *cf. Teshuvoth Beer Sheva* 43; *Yeshuoth Yaakov, Orach Chaim* 154:3, quoted in *Pith'chey Teshuvah* 182:6.
61. *Sefer Chasidim* 97, *B'rith Olam* (Chida) *ad. loc.,* 911; *Reshith Chokhmah, Shaar HaYirah* 15 (44d).
62. *Shabbath* 16:1 (115a).
63. See below, 9:35.
64. *Sofrim* 3:12.
65. *Sefer Chasidim* 273; *Magen Avraham* 28:4 (end); *"Rav" Shulchan Arukh* 28:9; *Mishnah Berurah* 28:9.
66. *Eruvin* 98a; *Sofrim* 3:12; *Yad, Sefer Torah* 10:5; *Yoreh Deah* 282:5; *Chayay Adam* 31:45; *Kitzur Shulchan Arukh* 28:6.
67. *Sefer Chasidim* 943; *Yoreh Deah* 282:5 in *Hagah. Cf. Eruvin* 98a; *Sofrim* 3:14 (end); *Yad, Tefillin* 1:17; *Yoreh Deah* 277:1.
68. In order that it not get soiled; Rashi, *Eruvin* 98a *s.v. LaHafokh; Reshith Chokhmah, Shaar HaYirah* 15 (44d). *Cf. Yerushalmi, Eruvin* 10:3 (60b); *Yerushalmi, Megillah* 1:9 (12a end); *Sofrim* 3:16; *Turey Zahav* 277:1; *Sifethey Cohen* 277:1.

9:25 Sacred books should always be placed in a respectful place. Therefore, one should not lay them on the floor,[69] nor sit upon a bench where they are lying.[70] However, if the book is placed on some object and somewhat raised,[71] one may sit on the bench, especially if there is no other place for the books.[72] Likewise, one should avoid sitting on a trunk or case containing sacred books,[73] unless there is no other place.[74]

9:26 Just as it is forbidden to be waited upon by a religious scholar,[75] it is prohibited[76] to make use of a sacred book for anything other than for what it is intended.[77] Therefore, one should not use a book as a sunshade,[78] prop,[79] or line marker.[80] Similarly, it should not be used as a bookmark,[81] or to hide anything in it.[82] Likewise, one should not hit anybody with a sacred book,[83] nor hide behind one.[84]

9:27 Just as we respect sages according to their rank, so do we honor books according to their importance. Therefore, we place books of the Torah on top of those of the Prophets and Writings, and not vice versa.[85] However, the Prophets and Writings are considered

69. *Yoreh Deah* 282:7 in *Hagah; cf.* HaGra *ad. loc.* 282:18.
70. *Menachoth* 32b; *Moed Katan* 25a; *Sofrim* 3:13; *Yad, Sefer Torah* 10:6; *Yoreh Deah* 282:7; *Chayay Adam* 31:43; *Kitzur Shulchan Arukh* 28:4. *Cf. Sefer Chasidim* 157; *Beer Sheva* 38.
71. *Yerushalmi, Berakhoth* 3:5 (28a); *Tosafoth, Menachoth* 32a *s.v. Assur;* Raavad, *Sefer Torah* 10:6; *Sifethey Cohen* 282:8. But see *Tosafoth, Moed Katan* 25a *s.v. VeKhaf.*
72. *Sifethey Cohen* 282:9.
73. *Teshuvoth Rama* 34; *Turey Zahav* 282:4. *Cf. Yerushalmi, Berakhoth* 3:5 (27b); *Piskey Tosafoth, Menachoth* 81.
74. *Kitzur Shulchan Arukh* 28:4; *cf. Nekudoth HaKesef* on *Turey Zahav loc. cit; Beer Hetiv, Yoreh Deah* 282:7.
75. *Avoth* 1:13; *Megillah* 28b; *Sefer Mitzvoth Gadol,* Positive Commandment 12; *Yoreh Deah* 143:6 in *Hagah; Sifethey Cohen* 146:23.
76. See above, 9:20.
77. *Sefer Chasidim* 904; *Chayay Adam* 31:45; *Kitzur Shulchan Arukh* 28:9; *Mishnah Berurah* 154:31. *Cf. Yerushalmi, Megillah* 3:1 (23a).
78. *Ibid.*
79. *Turey Zahav, Yoreh Deah* 182:13; *Orach Chaim* 315:6; *Magen Avraham* 154:14 (end).
80. *Sefer Chasidim* 101, 902, 903.
81. *Pith'chey Teshuvah* 282:17.
82. *Sefer Chasidim* 899, 907.
83. *Sefer Chasidim* 276; *Beth Lechem Yehudah, Yoreh Deah* 282:7.
84. *Sefer Chasidim* 906.
85. *Megillah* 27a; *Tosefta* 3:12; *Yerushalmi, Megillah* 3:1 (23b); *Yad, Sefer Torah* 10:5; *Yoreh Deah* 282:19. *Cf. Magen Avraham* 28:4.

equal[86] and may be placed in any order.[87] Similarly, Biblical books are considered more sacred than Talmudic books,[88] and the former should always be placed on top.[89] This rule only applies when the books are bound separately. If they are bound together,[90] a lesser one may be placed on top.[91] Some maintain that *Tefillin* should not be placed on top of a prayer book.[92]

9:28   The Torah is the testimony of the covenent between God and Israel, as it is written, "Take this Torah scroll... that it may serve as a testimony for you" (Deuteronomy 31:26).[93] A Torah scroll must be treated with the utmost respect.[94] We are taught that whoever honors the Torah will himself be honored.[95]

9:29   The Torah should be placed in a special ark, as we find, "Take this Torah scroll, and place it in the Ark by the [Tablets of the] Covenant" (*ibid.*).[96] The ark should be made as richly and beautifully as the congregation can afford.[97] Nothing else should be placed in the ark, even other sacred books.[98] Invalidated Torah scrolls are an exception to this rule; these may be placed in the ark[99] in the same way that the broken tablets were placed next to the unbroken ones in the original Ark of Testimony.[100]

---

86. *Cf. Yerushalmi, Megillah loc. cit.; Magen Avraham* 153:2.
87. *Tosafoth, Bava Bathra* 13b *s.v. Rabbi; Ran, Megillah* (Rif 8b) *s.v. Menichin; Yoreh Deah* 282:19 in *Hagah.*
88. *Cf. Mishnah Berurah* 334:30; *Magen Avraham* 334:15, from *Sefer Chasidim* 858.
89. *Zohar* 1:72a (top); *Nitzotzey Oroth ad. loc.* no. 1; *Sefer Chasidim* 141, 909.
90. *Bava Bathra* 13b; *Yerushalmi, Megillah, loc. cit.; Yad, Sefer Torah* 7:16; *Yoreh Deah* 183:1.
91. *Tosafoth, Bava Bathra* 13b *s.v. Madbik;* Mordecai 511; *Yoreh Deah* 182:19 in *Hagah; Sifethey Cohen* 183:1.
92. *Shaarey Teshuvah, Orach Chaim* 28:3, from *Sefer Meirath Eynayim (Sema)* 87:40. But see *Sifethey Cohen, Choshen Mishpat* 87:42; *Turey Zahav ad. loc.; Beer Hetiv* 87:39; HaGra 87:50.
93. *Yad, Sefer Torah* 10:11.
94. *Ibid.* 10:2; *Yoreh Deah* 182:1; *Chayay Adam* 31:42; *Kitzur Shulchan Arukh* 28:3; *Reshith Chokhmah, Shaar HaYirah* 15 (44d).
95. *Avoth* 4:6.
96. Rashi, *Avoth* 4:6; *Bava Bathra* 14a; *Yerushalmi, Sotah* 8:3 (35a).
97. *Yad, Sefer Torah* 10:10.
98. *Bayith Chadash, Orach Chaim* 154; *Magen Avraham* 154:14; *Turey Zahav* 154:7; *Mishnah Berurah* 154:31; *Teshuvoth Noda BeYehudah, Orach Chaim* 1:9.
99. *Sefer Chasidim* 934.
100. *Berakhoth* 8b; *Bava Bathra* 14b; *Menachoth* 99a; *Yerushalmi, Shekalim* 6:1 (25a); *Yerushalmi, Sotah* 8:3 (35a); *BaMidbar Rabbah* 4:21.

9:30   One must show the same respect before a Torah that one would show before an important person.[101] Therefore, it is forbidden to do anything disrespectful in the presence of a Torah.[102]

9:31   Just as we are commanded to stand before a sage,[103] so also, when seeing a Torah scroll being carried, we must rise and remain standing until it is brought to its destination or is no longer in our line of vision.[104]

9:32   When the Torah is taken out in the synagogue, the entire congregation must stand as long as it is being carried. It should also be accompanied by worshippers. This is implied in the Torah's command to, "Walk after God your Lord" (Deuteronomy 13:5).[105] It is customary to kiss the Torah as it passes by.[106]

9:33   When a Torah must be transported, it is preferable that it be accompanied by a person who will hold it in his arms the entire journey.[107] However, where this is impossible, it may be wrapped up and transported or shipped in any respectful manner.[108] When a Torah is carried locally from one synagogue to another, it should be accompanied by ten men.[109]

9:34   Out of respect and reverence, one should never touch the parchment[110] of a Torah scroll with one's bare hands.[111] This is permissible when one is repairing a Torah.[112]

9:35   When a Torah is no longer usable, it should be placed in a waterproof container[113] and buried, preferably[114] together with a

---

101. *Kiddushin* 33b.
102. *Yad, Sefer Torah* 10:10; *Yoreh Deah* 182:1.
103. *Kiddushin* 33b.
104. *Yad, Sefer Torah* 10:9; *Yoreh Deah* 182:2.
105. *Sotah* 39b; *Orach Chaim* 149:1 in *Hagah; Magen Avraham* 149:3.
106. *Orach Chaim* 149 in *Hagah,* citing *Or Zarua.*
107. *Berakhoth* 18a; *Yerushalmi, Berakhoth* 3:5 (28a); *Yad, Sefer Torah* 10;11; *Yoreh Deah* 182:3. *Cf. Bayith Chadash, Yoreh Deah* 182.
108. *Cf. Sifethey Cohen* 182:5.
109. *Beth Lechem Yehudah ad. loc.,* quoting *Piskey Recanti.*
110. But it is permissible to hold the handles; *Magen Avraham* 147:0; *Turey Zahav* 147:1; *Mishnah Berurah* 147:4.
111. *Shabbath* 14a; *Megillah* 32a; *Sofrim* 3:16; *Yad, Sefer Torah* 10:6; *Rash, Yedayim* 3:2; *Orach Chaim* 147:1; *Yoreh Deah* 282:4. *Cf.* Bertenoro, *Yedayim* 4:6 *s.v. Af.* See Rosh, Rash, *ad. loc.,* for reasons.
112. *Pri Megadim, Mishbetzoth Zahav* 147:1; *Mishnah Berurah* 147:1.
113. *Turey Zahav, Orach Chaim* 154:4; *Yoreh Deah* 282:6; *Mishnah Berurah* 154:23. *Cf.* Jeremiah 32:14. See *Teshuvoth Kenesseth Yechezkel* 37.

religious scholar.[115] Similarly, articles used with a Torah, such as mantles and ties, should be buried when no longer usable.[116]

9:36   If a Torah is dropped, it is customary for all those present[117] to fast at least one day, especially the one who dropped it.[118] If one drops *Tefillin* when not in their container, it is also customary to fast.[119] In all these cases, one may redeem the fast with charity.[120]

9:37   One who sees a Torah forcibly burned or desecrated[121] must rend his clothing as in mourning.[122] Two tears should be made, one for the writing, and another for the parchment.[123] This rule also applies to other sacred books[124] and to *Tefillin.*[125]

9:38   Some maintain that a printed Hebrew Bible or Torah is as sacred as a written Torah.[126] Still, one may never make use of a printed Torah, *Tefillin,* or *Mezuzah* for sacred purposes.[127]

9:39   All the above laws regarding a Torah scroll apply only when it is written in holiness by a religious man who is also a qualified scribe. However, a Torah written by an atheist or apostate who does not believe in our faith is not considered sacred and may be burned.[128] It is even permitted to destroy the divine names

114. But not necessarily; *Pri Megadim, Mishbetzoth Zahav* 154:5; *Biur Halakhah* 154:5 *s.v. VeGonzin.*
115. *Megillah* 26b; *Yad, Sefer Torah* 10:3; *Orach Chaim* 154:5; *Yoreh Deah* 282:10.
116. *Ibid.; Orach Chaim* 154:4; *Yoreh Deah* 282:11.
117. *Sheyarey Berakhah, Yoreh Deah* 282:1.
118. *Teshuvoth Misphetey Sh'muel* 12; *Magen Avraham* 44:5; *Kitzur Shulchan Arukh* 28:12; *Mishnah Berurah* 40:3.
119. *Ibid.; Kitzur Shulchan Arukh* 10:14.
120. *Ibid.; cf. Orach Chaim* 334:26 in *Hagah; Mishnah Berurah* 334:81.
121. *Sifethey Cohen* 340:56; *Turey Zahav* 340:24; *Teshuvoth Radbaz* 2:646; *Teshuvoth Chakham Tzvi* 17.
122. *Moed Katan* 26a; *Yerushalmi, Moed Katan* 3:7 (17b); *Yad, Avel* 9:2; *Yoreh Deah* 340:37; Ramban, *Torath HaAdam, "Shaar HaKeriah"* (16b). *Cf.* Radak on Jeremiah 36:24.
123. *Ibid.; Sefer Mitzvoth Gadol,* Negative Commandment 3; *Sifethey Cohen* 340:57; *Turey Zahav* 340:23.
124. Rosh, *Moed Katan* 3:64; *Pith'chey Teshuvah* 340:21. See sources cited in note 92.
125. *Yoreh Deah loc. cit.; Beer HaGolah* 340:82.
126. *Turey Zahav, Yoreh Deah* 271:8; *Teshuvoth Shevuth Yaakov* 3:15; *Shaarey Teshuvah, Orach Chaim* 334:1. *Cf. Yoma* 3:11 (38a); *Tosefoth Yom Tov,* Maharatz Chajas, *ad. loc.; Teshuvoth Mas'ath Binyamin* 99, that printing is considered the same as writing, even though an entire sheet is printed at once.
127. *Teshuvoth Chavath Yair* 184; *Teshuvoth Panim Meiroth* 1:45; *Beney Chayay* 281, quoted in *Pith'chey Teshuvah* 271:20.
128. *Shabbath* 115a; *Gittin* 45b; *Yad, Yesodey HaTorah* 6:8; *Orach Chaim* 334:21; *Yoreh Deah* 281:1.

in it, since they were written without sacred intent.[129] A Torah
written by an irreligious Jew[130] or non-Jew, on the other hand,
should be put aside, and neither used nor destroyed.[131] This same
rule applies to *Tefillin* and *Mezuzoth*.[132] It is preferable that all
religious articles and books[133] be made by religious Jews.

9:40   The respect we show for sacred writings includes all Biblical
verses written in any language.[134] Because these verses are the word
of God, they should not be desecrated or taken into any unclean
place.[135] For this reason, it is forbidden to embroider a scriptural
verse or passage on any article of clothing,[136] even a *Tallith*.[137] In
addition, because of this, it was customary to underline Biblical
verses written in correspondence,[138] so that they be recognized and
not discarded.[139]

9:41   The special Ashurith script used for writing the Torah
is considered holy[140] and should therefore not be used for
secular purposes.[141] It should not be used in advertisements or
signs.[142] Similarly, one should not use books or newspapers written
in Hebrew script for any unclean or degrading purpose, even
though they contain nothing of a sacred nature.[143] It was for this

129. *Yad, Yesodey HaTorah* 6:8. See above, 9:4.
130. *Teshuvoth Radbaz* 2:774; *Teshuvah MeAhavah* 1:110; *Biur Halakhah* 39:4 *s.v.*
     SheKathvam.
131. See sources cited in note 128; *Sofrim* 1:13.
132. *Yad, Tefillin* 1:13; *Orach Chaim* 39:4.
133. *Teshuvoth Zaken Aaron* 171, quoted in *Birkey Yosef, Yoreh Deah* 281:1; *Pith'chey
     Teshuvah* 281:1.
134. *Teshuvoth Radbaz* 1:45, cited in *Gilyon Maharsha* 283:4.
135. *Sifethey Cohen* 283:6.
136. *Turey Zahav* 283:3; *Teshuvoth Ginath Veradim, Orach Chaim* 1:2:25; *Teshuvoth Maharit,
     Orach Chaim* 2:3.
137. *Yoreh Deah* 283:4. For this reason, one should not buy a *Tallith* with blessings
     embroidered on it. *Cf. Magen Avraham* 45:2.
138. *Gittin* 6b; *Yerushalmi, Megillah* 3:2 (24b); *Yad, Sefer Torah* 7:16, *Yibum* 4:35;
     Yoreh Deah 184:1-2. See also *Tosafoth, Gittin* 6b *s.v. Amar; Sotah* 17b *s.v. Kathva;
     Menachoth 32b *s.v. Ha; Teshuvoth Rashba* 779, 1191; *Teshuvoth Tashbatz* 1:2; *Teshuvoth
     Radbaz* 3:647.
139. Rabbi Yaakov Emdin (Maharibatz), *Gittin* 6b.
140. *Cf.* Rosh, *Megillah* 2:2 (end), citing Ramban. See Volume 1, 7:58.
141. *Yoreh Deah* 284:2 in *Hagah; Teshuvoth Radbaz* 1:45; *Teshuvoth Divrey Yosef* 41;
     Orchoth Chaim 21, quoted in *Taamey HaMinhagim*, p. 73.
142. *Gilyon Maharsha ad. loc.*
143. *Pith'chey Teshuvah* 271:20.

reason that a different form of Hebrew script was used for secular purposes.[144]

9:42 All accessories used with sacred articles may not be thrown away or burned,[145] but must be carefully put aside and stored or buried.[146] This rule applies to such accessories as Torah mantles, ties and decorations, the ark and its hanging, as well as *Tefillin* straps and bags.[147]

9:43 Accessories used for religious observances such as a *Sukkah, Lulav, Shofar,* or *Tallith,* may be discarded or burned after they are used[148] since they are not sacred in themselves.[149] However, they should not be thrown in the garbage or any other degrading place,[150] but should be used for a good purpose where possible.[151] We are taught that something used for one observance should preferably be used for another.[152]

9:44 As long as an accessory is being used for a religious observance, it may not be used for any other purpose, out of respect for God's commandments.[153] After the observance is finished, however, it is permissible to make use of it,[154] although it should not be put to any unclean or degrading use.[155]

9:45 Although we are commanded to respect sacred articles, it is not the objects that we revere, but God who makes them sacred.[156] Accordingly, the Torah states, "Revere My sanctuary — I am God" (Leviticus 19:30, 26:2). That is, I, God, require this reverence.

144. *Tur, Yoreh Deah* 274; *Beer HaGolah, Yoreh Deah* 284:2.
145. *Magen Avraham* 154:9.
146. *Megillah* 26b; *Yad, Sefer Torah* 10:4; *Orach Chaim* 154:3; *Yoreh Deah* 282:12.
147. *Ibid.*
148. *Megillah* 26b; *Yad, Tzitzith* 3:9; *Orach Chaim* 21:1. For detailed discussion of this entire subject, see *Pri Megadim, Mishbetzoth Zahav* 153:15 (end).
149. *Bayith Chadash, Orach Chaim* 21; *Mishnah Berurah* 21:1.
150. *Hagahoth Asheri, Megillah* 4:1; *Orach Chaim* 21:1, in *Hagah* 664:8.
151. *Magen Avraham* 21:1; *Turey Zahav* 21:2; *Kitzur Shulchan Arukh* 9:19, 138:3; *Mishnah Berurah* 21:6. *Cf. Mesekhta Tzitzith* (end).
152. *Turey Zahav, Orach Chaim* 394:1, 525:14; *cf. Orach Chaim* 394:2, 664:9 in *Hagah; Sukkah* 5:3 (51a); *Berakhoth* 39b (end); *Shabbath* 117b.
153. *Shabbath* 22a; *Tosafoth ad. loc. s.v. Sukkah; Turey Zahav, Orach Chaim* 21:1.
154. *Shabbath* 35b (end); *Pri Megadim loc. cit.*
155. *Ran, Shabbath* (Rif 48b) *s.v. Shiyurey; Orach Chaim* 21:2.
156. *Yevamoth* 6b; *Tosafoth ad. loc. s.v. Yakhol; Yad, Beth HaBechirah* 7:1.

TEN

KEEPING THE COMMANDMENTS

10:1 Since the commandments were given by God in order to bestow His highest good upon us, they should be observed in a thankful spirit befitting such a gift. One should therefore keep the commandments out of love and reverence for God,[1] not because of one's preferences or logic,[2] or for any other ulterior worldly motive.[3] In all observance, one's only motive should be to serve God, as the Psalmist exclaimed, "To do Your will, my God, is my desire, and Your Torah is in my insides" (Psalms 40:9).[4]

10:2 A person should always consider the significance of the commandments and not let their observance degenerate into mere habit and rote. Regarding such insincere lipservice, God said, "These people draw near with their mouths and honor Me with their lips, but their hearts are far from Me, and their reverence for Me is that of men who perform a commandment by rote" (Isaiah 29:13).[5]

10:3 Nevertheless, one should not abandon the commandments merely because he suspects his own intentions. Even insincere observance is better than none at all, since all the commandments

---

1. *Tikuney Zohar* 21 (51a); *Reshith Chokhmah, Shaar HaYirah* 1 (6d); *Cheredim,* introduction no. 2-3 (p. 16), quoted in *Sh'nei Luchoth HaB'rith, Teshuvah* 2:185b.
2. See Volume 1, 5:31-33; *Chayay Adam* 68:18.
3. *Chayay Adam* 68:17. Cf. *Horayoth* 10b, Rashi *ad. loc. s.v. Leshem; Reshith Chokhmah, Hakdamah LePerek HaMitzvoth* 241d. However, *Tosafoth Rosh ibid. s.v. VeEchad,* disputes this interpretation.
4. *Reshith Chokhmah, Perek HaMitzvoth* 7 (245b).
5. *Chovoth HaLevavoth, Cheshbon HaNefesh* 3:9; *Sefer Chasidim* 46, 785, quoted in *Sh'nei Luchoth HaB'rith, Tefillah* 2:219b; *Kitzur Shulchan Arukh* 6:1; *Kaf HaChaim, Orach Chaim* 5:1.

are sacred and will ultimately lead a person back to the right path.[6]

10:4 Realizing the deep significance of the commandments, one should observe them with joy and happiness, as the Psalmist exclaims, "Serve God with joy, come before Him with song" (Psalms 100:2).[7] When such joy is missing, it implies a lack of appreciation for the blessings that God bestows upon us. Accordingly, God cautioned Israel to serve Him, "With joyfulness and gladness of heart for the great abundance [He would grant them]" (Deuteronomy 28:47).[8] We are similarly taught that the *Shekhinah* (Divine Presence) only resides in Israel through the merit of observing God's commandments with joy.[9]

10:5 One should therefore eagerly anticipate each observance[10] and carefully prepare for it,[11] as the prophet states, "Prepare to meet your God, O Israel" (Amos 4:12).[12] In order to put oneself in the proper frame of mind, it is customary to introduce each observance with the words, "Behold, I am prepared and ready to do this in order to perform the will of my Creator."[13]

10:6 The blessings that were legislated before[14] each observance are part of the observance and therefore compulsory.[15] However,

---

6. *Pesachim* 50b; *Nazir* 23b; *Sotah* 22b, 47a; *Sanhedrin* 105b; *Horayoth* 10b; *Arakhin* 16b; *Yerushalmi, Chagigah* 1:7 (6b); *Eikhah Rabbah,* introduction:2; *Pesikta* 15 (121a); *Yad, Talmud Torah* 3:5, *Teshuvah* 10:5; *Yoreh Deah* 246:20.
7. *Rokeach, Shoresh Ahavah,* quoted in *Reshith Chokhmah, Shaar HaAhavah* 1 (52a); *Cheredim loc. cit.* no. 4 (p. 16); *Chayay Adam* 68:13; see above, 2:8. *Cf. VaYikra Rabbah* 34:8; *Reshith Chokhmah, Hakdamah LePerek HaMitzvoth* 241bf.; Bachya on Deuteronomy 28:47 ("One should always perform a commandment with a *joyous* heart"), although the reading in *Ruth Rabbah* 5:6 and *Yalkut Shimoni* 2:604 is *complete* rather than *joyous* heart.
8. *Yad, Lulav* 8:15; *Ikkarim* 3:33; *Cheredim loc. cit.; Reshith Chokhmah, Shaar HaAhavah* 9 (85c).
9. *Shabbath* 30b; *Zohar* 1:216b; *Reshith Chokhmah loc. cit.*
10. *Cheredim loc. cit.* no. 13 (p. 18, bottom); *Chayay Adam* 68:15.
11. *Asarah Maamaroth, Chag HaPesach* 3:11; *Chayay Adam* 68:25.
12. *Cf. Berakhoth* 23a, 51b; *Tosefta, Berakhoth* 2:19; *Shabbath* 10a.
13. *Chayay Adam loc. cit. Cf. Taamey HaMinhagim* 9 (p. 4). See below, note 41.
14. *Pesachim* 7b, 119b; *Megillah* 21b; *Sukkah* 39a; *Menachoth* 35b; *Niddah* 63a; *Yerushalmi, Berakhoth* 9:3 (66a); *Yad, Berakhoth* 1:3, 11:3, *Tefillin* 4:7; *Orach Chaim* 25:8, 158:11; *Rif, Tefillin* 8a; *Tosafoth, Sukkah* 39a *s.v. Over;* *Rosh, Kethuvoth* 1:12; *Teshuvoth HaRosh* 36:1; *Rokeach* 219, 350.
15. *Tosefta, Berakhoth* 6:14; *Yad, Berakhoth* 1:3, 11:2; Rambam makes no distinction between whether the commandment is an individual obligation or not. See, however, *Sh'nei Luchoth HaB'rith, Shaar HaOthioth* 1:98b *s.v. U'BeReshith Iyuni,* where this possibility is considered.

this only includes positive[16] commandments[17] involving the completion[18] of a religious ritual[19] directed primarily towards God.[20] All such blessings begin with the words, "Blessed are You, O God our Lord, King of the Universe, Who has made us holy with His commandments and instructed us..." This legislation also included rabbinical commandments.[21]

10:7 There are two basic wordings that we find in all blessings over commandments. In some cases, the blessing is expressed in a verb form, as in, "to put on *Tefillin,*" and "to dwell in the *Sukkah.*" In others, it is expressed in a noun form, as in, "on the commandment of *Eruv,*" and "on the washing of the hands." The rule is[22] that whenever the obligation devolves upon the individual,[23] but the

16. As opposed to negative commandments; *cf.* Ran, *Kethuvoth* 2a *s.v. VeHethir;* Rosh, *Kethuvoth* 1:12; Maharatz Chajas, *Niddah* 51b. Thus, no blessing is said over removing the sciatic nerve *(gid ha-nasheh,* גיד הנשה); *Pri Megadim, Eshel Avraham* 415:4. See Volume 1, 4:30 (note 81), 5:8.

17. Except such commandments that are already contained in a service, such as the *Sh'ma; Pri Megadim, Mishbetzoth Zahav* 239:2; *Taamey HaMinhagim* 66 (p. 38).

18. *Menachoth* 42b; *Yad, Berakhoth* 11:8. For this reason, we do not say a blessing before making *Tzitzith, Tefillin, Sukkah,* or *Lulav,* although this is disputed in *Yerushalmi, Berakhoth* 9:3 (66a). *Cf. Tosafoth, Sukkah* 46a *s.v. HaOseh.* This is also the reason why we do not say a blessing before the *Chupah* in marriage; Ran, *Kethuvoth* (Rif 2b, top); *Beth Yosef, Evven HaEzer* 34; *Pri Megadim,* introduction to *Hilkhoth Berakhoth* 22; *Taamey HaMinhagim* 997 (p. 420).

19. And not over logical commandments, such as the command to "be fruitful and multiply" (Genesis 1:28); *Taamey HaMinhagim* 997 (p. 420).

20. *Yad, Berakhoth* 11:2, *Kesef Mishneh ad. loc.* This is the reason why no blessing is said before giving charity, passing judgment, returning stolen articles, etc., even though these are Biblical commandments; *Sh'nei Luchoth HaB'rith, Shaar HaOthioth* 1:98a, quoting Abudarham. This also explains why no blessing is said before sending *Mishloach Manoth* on Purim, although a different reason is given in *Taamey HaMinhagim* 897 (p. 383), quoting *Teshuvoth Mor VeOhaloth.* For general discussion, see HaGra, *Orach Chaim* 8:1 *s.v. VaYibarekh; Teshuvoth Ramban* 189.

21. *Shabbath* 23a; *Yad, Berakhoth* 11:3, *Kesef Mishneh ad. loc.;* Ran, *Kethuvoth* (Rif 2a) *s.v. VeAssar.* The seven rabbinical commandments requiring a blessing are: washing the hands, the Sabbath and Festival candles, the *Eruv,* the *Hallel,* the *Chanukah* light, and the *Megillah.*

22. For general discussion, see *Pesachim* 7b; *Tosafoth, Sukkah* 39a *s.v. Over;* Rosh, *Pesachim* 1:10; Ran, *Pesachim* (Rif 3b) *s.v. VeKashia;* Mordecai, *Pesachim* 538; *Yad, Berakhoth* 11; *Rokeach* 363 (p. 253); *Sh'nei Luchoth HaB'rith, Shaar HaOthioth* 1:98af.; *Teshuvoth Tamim Dey'im* 179, 186; *Teshuvoth Ravan* 35; *Chok Yaakov, Orach Chaim* 432:2.

23. In *Pesachim* 7b, it is indicated that the verbal form implies an individual obligation. For this reason, Riva holds that any commandment which must be done by the individual requires the verbal form, while those which can be done by others require the noun form. Similarly, in *Yad, Berakhoth* 11:11, the distinction is made that when one does a commandment for oneself, the verb form is used, while when it

primary focus is on the result,[24] the verb form of the blessing is used.[25] [See Table 10:1 at end of this chapter.] However, where the primary focus is on the deed itself, whether the obligation devolves upon the individual or not,[26] the noun form is used. Similarly, in any case where the blessing is said after the observance is initiated, only the noun form is used.[27] [See Table 10:2 at end of this chapter.]

10:8 In order to further express joyfulness in observing God's commandments, it was instituted that one treat an annually[28] occurring observance[29] as a special joyous occasion, reciting the blessing, "Blessed are You... Who has kept us alive,

is done for others, the noun form is used. This is also indicated by *Yerushalmi, Berakhoth* 9:3 (66a), according to the reading of HaGra, *Sukkah* 46a. [However, neither of these explain the use of the noun form for the commandments of *Matzah* and *Maror* where, according to our distinction, the focus is primarily on the act of eating; see below, Table 10:2, note 12.] The verb form certainly indicates that the obligation falls on the particular individual, but the reason for this is because the focus is primarily on the result. This explains why, if there were no individual obligation, no blessing at all would be recited; *cf. Menachoth* 42a; *Tosafoth, Shabbath* 25b *s.v. Chovah;* Rosh, *Shabbath* 2:18; *Teshuvoth Rashba* 18; Maharatz Chajas, *Makkoth* 8a.

24. In *Pesachim* 7b, it is likewise indicated that the noun form is used for the commandment of the Four Species because the main observance is the taking, rather than the holding, of the *Lulav; cf. Tosafoth, Sukkah* 39a *s.v. Over.* Because of this, Rabbenu Tam distinguishes between the commandment being done all at once or in installments in order to determine whether the noun or verbal form is used; *cf.* Rosh, Mordecai, *Rokeach, loc. cit.* Since this rule is contradicted by numerous cases, however, we follow a similar interpretation, but, again, make the distinction depend on whether the focus is on the action or the result.

25. *Yad, Berakhoth* 11:14 makes another distinction, namely, that if the commandment is done both for oneself and others, it depends on whether one also wishes to fulfill his personal obligation or not to determine if the verb or noun form is used. [If one does want to fulfill his personal obligation, the verb form is used.]

26. But also when it is thus an individual obligation, how answering such contradictions to Riva's and Rambam's distinctions as *Matzah* and *Maror.*

27. In *Pesachim* 7b, it is indicated that the noun form implies either the future or the past while the verb form refers only to a future observance. *Cf. Yad, Berakhoth* 11:15; *Kesef Mishneh ad. loc.* 11:11.

28. *Cf. Eruvin* 40b; *Tosafoth, Sukkah* 46a *s.v. HaOseh;* Rosh, *Sukkah* 4:2; Ran, *Sukkah* (Rif 22b) *s.v. VeKathvu;* Mordecai, *Sukkah* 769; *Tosafoth, Menachoth* 42a *s.v. VeIhu; Yad, Berakhoth* 11:9; *Rokeach* 371; *Teshuvoth Rashba* 126.

29. The same applies to an observance that is part of the cycle of life, notably, *Pidyon HaBen,* "redemption of the first-born"; *cf. Tosafoth, Rokeach,* Ran, *loc. cit.; Yoreh Deah* 305:10; *Sifethey Cohen loc. cit.* 265:17. Although *Yad loc. cit.* maintains that the blessing is also said by circumcision, the majority dispute this; the reasons are quoted in the above references as well as in HaGra, *Yoreh Deah* 265:36; *Taamey HaMinhagim* 910 (p. 388). For the reason why it is not said by marriage, see *Tevuoth Shor* 28:4, quoting Abudarham; *Taamey HaMinhagim* 2:106 (p. 532); see above, note 18.

sustained us, and allowed us to reach this occasion."[30] Similarly, the observance of a commandment for the first time in a person's life should be treated as a joyous occasion, with the recitation of the same blessing.[31]

10:9   When an observance does not result in any physical enjoyment it is particularly easy to become lax and perform it without the proper intent. It was therefore instituted that such observances be performed while standing if they require a blessing.[32] One must therefore stand while performing such commandments as *Tzitzith,*[33] *Tefillin,*[34] *Shofar,*[35] *Lulav,*[36] Counting the *Omer,*[37] and Circumcision.[38] In all these cases we likewise find that the Torah lays particular stress on their being "for you" — that is, for your own spiritual benefit.[39]

10:10   All religious observances must be performed deliberately for the sake of obeying God's commandment.[40] It is preferable to express this intent verbally if possible.[41] Mere action without intent is as dead as a body without a soul.[42]

30. *Cf. Tosefta, Berakhoth* 6:15; *Sukkah* 46a; *Menachoth* 42a; *Yerushalmi, Berakhoth* 9:3 (66a); *Yerushalmi, Sukkah* 1:2 (4b), 3:4 (14a).

31. *Cf. Berakhoth* 37b; *Tosafoth, Menachoth* 75b s.v. *Hayah; Rokeach* 371; *Maharik Shoresh* 128; *Yoreh Deah* 28:2 in *Hagah; Sifethey Cohen, Pri Megadim, loc. cit.* 28:5; *Tevuoth Shor* 28:4; *Biur Halakhah* 22:1 s.v. *Kana.* Regarding *Tallith* and *Tefillin,* see *Orach Chaim* 22:1; *Magen Avraham, Turey Zahav, Beer Hetiv,* HaGra, *ad. loc.; Taamey HaMinhagim* 11 (p. 6, note). See also *Taamey HaMinhagim* 260 (p. 125), citing *Yaabetz,* that a bride says this blessing the first time she kindles the Sabbath lights and the first time she separates *Challah; cf. Challath Lechem* 7:1.

32. Abudarham, quoted in *Taamey HaMinhagim* 11 (p. 6, note); *Pri Megadim, Eshel Avraham* 8:2, 690:1. See Rosh, *Pesachim* 10:41; *Hagahoth HaGriv ad. loc.* no. 3; *Hagahoth HaRaf* on *Sefer Mitzvoth Katan* 92, 145; *Kesef Mishneh, Temidim U'Musafim* 7:23; *Zohar* 2:183b, *Nitzotzey Oroth ad. loc.; Raya Mehemna, Zohar* 3:97b; *Teshuvoth Nefesh Chayah* 489; HaGra, *Orach Chaim* 8:1 s.v. *Yit'atef, s.v. MeUmad; Pri Megadim,* introduction to *Hilkhoth Berakhoth* 18.

33. *Sefer Mitzvoth Katan* 92; *Orach Chaim* 8:1; *Magen Avraham, Turey Zahav,* HaGra, *ad. loc.*

34. *Orach Chaim* 25:11 in *Hagah.* This is disputed by some.

35. *Orach Chaim* 585:1.

36. *Orach Chaim* 551:5 in *Hagah.*

37. Rosh, *Sefer Mitzvoth Katan, Zohar, loc. cit.; Orach Chaim* 489:2; *Turey Zahav loc. cit.* With regard to reading the *Megillah,* see *Magen Avraham* 690:1.

38. *Sefer Mitzvoth Katan loc. cit.*

39. Abudarham, quoted in *Taamey HaMinhagim* 11 (p. 6, note); *Hagahoth HaRaf* on *Sefer Mitzvoth Katan* 145; *Pri Megadim, Mishbetzoth Zahav* 8:1.

40. *Berakhoth* 13a; *Eruvin* 95b; *Pesachim* 114b; *Yad, Shofar* 2:4; *Orach Chaim* 60:4. Others dispute this; see *Beer HaGolah,* HaGra, *Orach Chaim loc. cit.*

41. *Reshith Chokhmah, Shaar HaAhavah* 9 (85a), quoting *Zohar* 2:88a, 3:50a.

42. *Zohar* 2:93b, top; *Agra DeParka* 178. *Cf. Reshith Chokhmah, Perek HaMitzvoth* 7 (245b).

10:11 Therefore, any religious observance,[43] whether of Biblical or rabbinical origin,[44] that is performed without the specific intent of observing a divine commandment, is considered invalid and does not release one from his obligation.[45] In such a case, the observance must be repeated, although the blessing is omitted.[46]

10:12 If one performs a religious observance without being aware of his obligation, his observance is totally invalid and must be repeated with the proper blessing.[47] The same is true of an observance performed with the specific intent of not fulfilling one's religious obligation.[48]

10:13 If one performs a religious observance to practice or teach others, he does not fulfill his religious obligation unless he has the specific intent to do so.[49] Therefore, one who has not already fulfilled an observance and wishes to practice or teach it, should either do so with a definite positive intent and say its blessing, or with a specific negative intent in order that he may recite the blessing upon a later observance.[50]

10:14 If an observance is performed in its usual manner, such as after reciting its blessing, or together with the congregation, then it is assumed that it was done with the proper intent, though one may not have thought of it at the time.[51]

10:15 Some authorities maintain that a commandment which depends entirely on eating does not require specific intent since the result

43. But not a prerequisite of an observance; cf. *Teshuvoth Radbaz* 1:34; *Teshuvoth Chakham Tzvi* 1; Maharatz Chajas, *Chagigah* 19a.
44. *Mishnah Berurah* 60:10. Others do not require specific intent for rabbinical commandments; cf. *Teshuvoth Radbaz* 1:2; *Meil Tzedakah* 2:62; *Kenesseth HaGedolah* 589; *Magen Avraham* 60:3; *Chokhmath Shlomo* 60:4; *Chayay Adam* 68:9.
45. *Mishnah Berurah* 60:8.
46. *Ibid.,* because some maintain that the obligation is fulfilled even without intent. Others are of the opinion that if the entire observance consists of words, even the blessing must be repeated; cf. *Beth Yosef* 60, 589; *Pri Chadash, ibid.; Chayay Adam* 68:9; *Magen Avraham* 60:3; *Biur Halakhah loc. cit.; Makor Chesed* (on *Sefer Chasidim*) 46:3; *Tikuney Zohar,* introduction (6a).
47. *Biur Halakhah* 60:4 *s.v. Yesh Omrim.*
48. *Tosafoth, Sukkah* 39a *s.v. Over;* Ran, *Rosh HaShanah* (Rif 7b) *s.v. Aval; Magen Avraham* 651:12; *Chayay Adam* 68:9; *Biur Halakhah loc. cit.; Mishnah Berurah* 489:22.
49. *Rosh HaShanah* 4:8 (32b); *Yad, Shofar* 2:4; *Orach Chaim* 589:8; *Mishnah Berurah* 60:9. See also Ran, *Rosh HaShanah* (Rif 9b) *s.v. VeEin;* Maharatz Chajas, *Berakhoth* 13a, *Yoma* 46b.
50. *Biur Halakhah* 60:4 *s.v. LaTzeth.*
51. *Chayay Adam* 68:9; *Mishnah Berurah* 60:10. Cf. *Teshuvoth Radbaz* 1:160; *Magen Avraham* 589:4; *"Rav" Shulchan Arukh* 589:9; *Mishnah Berurah* 589:16.

is accomplished when the food remains in the body.[52] Therefore, if one is forced to eat *Matzah,* for example, his obligation for the first night of Passover is fulfilled, even if it was eaten without the proper intent.[53] Nevertheless, if one is unaware that it is Passover,[54] or if he has a specific intent not to fulfill his religious obligation,[55] then the observance is not considered valid.

10:16 Although there are many other special intentions associated with various commandments, based on Talmudical or Kabbalistic sources, the main prerequisite for all observance is that it be done for the sake of God.[56]

10:17 When a person truly loves God, he does not attempt to get by with a minimal observance, but tries to maximize his observance as an expression of this love.[57]

10:18 One should therefore constantly try to do more than is required of an observance, and accordingly, we are taught that the dispensable parts of a commandment shield one from troubles.[58] Nevertheless, one should be sure that there is some reason for the non-required observance,[59] since we are taught that one who does that which is not required is considered a fool,[60] especially if it may lead to a violation of the law[61] or to pious vanity.[62]

10:19 One should[63] observe a commandment in the most aesthetic and

---

52. Rashi, *Sanhedrin* 62b *s.v. SheKhen; Tosafoth, Pesachim* 115a *s.v. Matkif;* Ran, *Rosh HaShanah* (Rif 7b) *s.v. Garsinan; Orach Chaim* 475:4; *Magen Avraham* 475:14. Others dispute this; *cf. Pri Chadash* 475:4; *Mishnah Berurah* 475:34; *Biur Halakhah* 60:4 *s.v. Yesh Omrim.*
53. *Rosh HaShanah* 28a; *Yad, Chametz U'Matzah* 6:3; *Orach Chaim* 475:4.
54. *Orach Chaim* 475:4. See above, note 47.
55. *Mishnah Berurah* 475:36. See above, note 48.
56. *Nefesh HaChaim* 1:22 (end), 3b (beginning).
57. *Mesilath Yesharim* 18 (24b).
58. *Sukkah* 38a, top; *Pirkey Rabbi Eliezer* 20 (47a); *Radal ad. loc.* 20:25; Mordecai, *Yoma* 723; *Tur, Orach Chaim,* 299; *Mesilath Yesharim* 19 (25a).
59. *Shita Mekubetzeth,* Meiri, Maharatz Chajas, *Bava Kama* 87a.
60. *Yerushalmi, Shabbath* 1:2 (7a); *Tosafoth, Gittin* 6b *s.v. Amar Rabbi Yitzchak; Orach Chaim* 639:7 in *Hagah.*
61. *Olath Sh'muel* 98, quoted in *Biur Halakhah* 639:7 *s.v. VeKhol.*
62. Maharatz Chajas, *Sukkah* 26b.
63. Some maintain that this is a Biblical law; *cf.* Rashi, *Sukkah* 29b *s.v. Yavesh; Teshuvoth Shaagath Aryeh* 50; Maharatz Chajas, *Sukkah* 11b. Others maintain that it is merely a preference; *cf. Tosafoth, Sukkah* 29b *s.v. Lulav;* Mizrachi on *Sefer Mitzvoth Gadol,* Positive Commandment 44; *Chayay Adam* 68:4.

beautiful way possible, as the Torah states, "This is my God and I will glorify Him" (Exodus 15:2).[64] One should therefore even be prepared to spend extra money to perform an observance in the choicest manner possible.[65]

10:20 One should eagerly anticipate each religious observance, as the prophet teaches us, "Let us run to know God" (Hosea 6:3).[66] One should therefore hasten to observe a commandment, following the advice of the Psalmist, "I run the way of Your commandments, for You have expanded my heart" (Psalms 119:32).[67]

10:21 Similarly, one should attempt to perform each observance as soon as it is possible to do so, setting aside personal needs until later,[68] as we find with the Patriarchs, "Abraham arose early in the morning and saddled his donkey..." (Genesis 22:3).[69] It is a great merit to be the first among many to perform a commandment.[70]

10:22 It is forbidden to degrade a religious observance which is at hand by setting it aside or delaying it.[71] This is alluded to in the verse, "You shall observe the *Mitzvoth*" (Exodus 12:17).[72] Similar to the dough of *Matzoth* (unleavened bread), the *Mitzvoth* (commandments) of the Torah should not be left to grow sour.[73]

64. *Mekhilta (BeShalach) ad. loc.; Shabbath* 133b; *Sukkah* 11b; *Nazir* 2b; *Yerushalmi, Peah* 1:1 (2b); *Sofrim* 3:13; *Yad, Sefer Torah* 7:4, *Lulav* 7:6; *Orach Chaim* 656:1; *Chayay Adam* 68:4; *Reshith Chokhmah, Perek HaMitzvoth* 5 (244d); *Cheredim,* introduction no. 14 (p. 19, top); *Sh'nei Luchoth HaB'rith, Teshuvah* 2:185b.

65. *Orach Chaim, ibid.* See above, 6:12.

66. *Berakhoth* 6b; *Yerushalmi, Berakhoth* 5:1 (37b); *Rif, Shabbath* 42b; *Yad, Tefillah* 8:2, *Shabbath* 24:5; *Orach Chaim* 90:12, 301:1; *Sh'nei Luchoth HaB'rith loc. cit.; Mesilath Yesharim* 7 (10b).

67. *Cheredim loc. cit.* no. 7 (p. 18); *Chayay Adam* 68:14.

68. *Reshith Chokhmah, Perek HaMitzvoth* 4 (244c).

69. Rashi, *Yad, loc. cit.; Pesachim* 4a; *Rosh HaShanah* 32b; *Yoma* 28b; *Sifra* on Leviticus 12:3; *Tanchuma, VaYera* 22; *Yalkut Shimoni* 1:86; *Tosafoth, Pesachim* 4a *s.v. SheNe'emar, Yoma* 28a *s.v. Omer, Bava Kama* 60b *s.v. LeOlam; Yad, Milah* 1:8; *Cheredim loc. cit.* no. 15 (p. 19); *Sh'nei Luchoth HaB'rith loc. cit.; Chayay Adam* 68:6.

70. *Nazir* 23b (end); *Horayoth* 11a; *Bava Kama* 38b; *Makkoth* 10a; *Menorath HaMaor* 3:10:1:3 (232); *Reshith Chokhmah, Perek HaMitzvoth* 3 (244a); *Mesilath Yesharim* 7 (10b).

71. Cf. *Mekhilta, Targum Yonathan,* Rashi, on Exodus 1:12.

72. The actual reading is "You shall watch the *Matzoth.*" Without the vowel points, however, the word *Mitzvoth* (commandments) is spelled exactly the same as *Matzoth* (unleavened bread).

73. *Mekhilta,* Rashi, *ad. loc.;* Rashi, *Yoma* 33a *s.v. Ein Ma'Avirin; Orach Chaim* 625:1 in *Hagah;* HaGra *ad. loc.; Reshith Chokhmah, Shaar HaAhavah* 11 (90b), *Perek*

10:23   As a sign of eagerness to obey God, religious observance should be performed as deftly and swiftly as possible.[74] It is thus written, "If you see a man quick in his work, [know that] he shall stand before kings" (Proverbs 22:29).[75] It is likewise taught, "Be bold as a leopard, light as an eagle, swift as a deer, and strong as a lion, to do the will of your Father in heaven."[76]

10:24   Similarly, religious observance should be done with vigor, as we find, "All my bones shall say, 'O God, who is like You?'" (Psalms 35:10). It is for this reason that some people sway or shake during prayer and religious study.[77]

10:25   One should strive to maximize the effort expended in a religious observance, as we are taught, "According to the effort is the reward."[78] Thus, for example, one should travel as far as practical to synagogue in order to maximize one's effort.[79] Similarly, whenever possible, one should spend one's money in order to fulfill a religious observance rather than get by for nothing.[80] It is for this reason that it is customary to make a charitable donation in honor of a religious observance as, for instance, when one is called up to the reading of the Torah.[81]

10:26   Out of the joy of serving God one should let oneself go and not be overly scrupulous about one's dignity.[82] This is what King David meant when he said, "Before God I will make merry, and I will be even more vile than this, and will be base in my own sight"

HaMitzvot 3 (244a); Cheredim loc. cit. no. 12 (p. 18); Sh'nei Luchoth HaB'rith loc. cit.; Chayay Adam 68:1.

74. BaMidbar Rabbah 10:17; Mesilath Yesharim 7 (11a).
75. Ralbag, Metzudoth David, ad. loc.; Mesilath Yesharim loc. cit.
76. Avoth 5:20; Reshith Chokhmah, Shaar HaAhavah 11 (90b); Tur, Orach Chaim 1; Kitzur Shulchan Arukh 1:3.
77. Yerushalmi, Berakhoth 4:3 (33b); Orach Chaim 48:0 in Hagah. Cf. Berakhoth 31a; Tosefta, Berakhoth 3:7; Tur, Orach Chaim 104; Zohar 3:119a; Kuzari 2:79-80 (86b); Asarah Maamaroth, Em Kol Chai 33; Baal HaTurim on Exodus 20:18; Magen Avraham 48:4; Mishnah Berurah 48:5.
78. Avoth 5:23; Rambam ad. loc.; Chayay Adam 68:14.
79. Sotah 22a; Bava Metzia 107a; Tana DeBei Eliahu Zuta 17 (35a).
80. Zohar 2:128a; Cheredim loc. cit. no. 17 (p. 19); Sh'nei Luchoth HaB'rith, Teshuvah 2:185b.
81. Taamey HaMinhagim 927 (p. 395).
82. Reshith Chokhmah, Perek HaMitzvoth 4 (244c); Yad, Lulav 8:15. Cf. Sukkah 53a; Kethuvoth 17a; Bikkurim 3:4.

(2 Samuel 6:21-22). Certainly, one should not let pride or dignity prevent him from observing a commandment correctly.[83]

10:27 With regard to any question of law, one should always strive to take the stricter course whenever practical.[84] This is especially true if one is a known religious scholar or leader, and others would be likely to learn from his example.[85]

10:28 Nevertheless, one should not be overly strict in order to make a show of piety.[86] If one wishes to be stringent beyond the requirements of either the law or local custom, he should only do so privately, unless he is a recognized religious leader.[87] This is the intent of the verse, "The glory of God is to hide a thing" (Proverbs 25:2).[88] Similarly, the prophet teaches us, "He has told you, O man, what is good, and what God requires of you: Only to do justly, and to love mercy, and to walk humbly with your God" (Micah 6:8).[89] We are likewise taught that one who does good secretly will be rewarded openly.[90]

10:29 One should perform every religious observance with great care, fulfilling all its prerequisites.[91] This includes even those prerequisites whose observance are not absolutely required.[92]

10:30 One must be careful to observe every commandment exactly as it was given, without adding to or diminishing anything from it. We are thus commanded, "Do not add to the word that I am commanding you, and do not subtract from it" (Deuteronomy 4:2).[93] For example, the *Tefillin* contain four parchments; this commandment prohibits us from making a pair containing either

---

83. *Chayay Adam* 68:2. *Cf. Orach Chaim* 651:7; *Pesachim* 57b; *Kerithoth* 28b.
84. *Mesilath Yesharim* 14 (22a). *Cf. Chullin* 37b, 44b.
85. *Cf. Shabbath* 142b; *Moed Katan* 11b, 12b; *Bava Metzia* 73a; *Avodah Zarah* 8b; *Beer Sheva* 110d; *Teshuvoth Divrey Yosef* 48; *Yad Malachi* 6 (2b).
86. *Bava Kama* 59b; *Maharatz Chajas ad. loc.; Taanith* 10b; *Magen Avraham* 575:3, 581:9; *Mishnah Berurah* 575:3.
87. *Yerushalmi, Chagigah* 2:2 (11a); *Teshuvoth Tashbatz* 102; *Reshith Chokhmah, Shaar HaTeshuvah* 6 (123a); *Yalkut Shimoni* 2:244.
88. *Sefer Chasidim* 8.
89. *Ibid.; Orach Chaim* 1:1 in *Hagah; Yad Ephraim ad. loc.; Mishnah Berurah* 1:7. *Cf. Sukkah* 49b.
90. *Sefer Chasidim* 46. *Cf. Targum Yonathan* on Ecclesiastes 12:13.
91. *Cheredim loc. cit.* no. 16 (p. 19); *Sh'nei Luchoth HaB'rith, Teshuvah* 2:185b.
92. *Tosafoth, Gittin* 28b *s.v. VeHa; Chayay Adam* 68:24.
93. *Rosh HaShanah* 28b. See *Yad, Mamrim* 2:9.

five or three parchments. Similarly, it forbids us to add or subtract from the number of *Tzitzith*,[94] the number of species taken on *Sukkoth*,[95] or the number of priestly blessings.[96]

10:31 If one uses more ritual objects than required by the law, he is guilty of violating this commandment. It is forbidden, for example, to wear two pair of valid *Tefillin* simultaneously.[97]

10:32 Nevertheless, it is permitted to perform a valid ritual as many times as desired, since this is not considered an addition to the law. One may therefore put on *Tefillin*, read the *Sh'ma*, eat *Matzah* on Passover, or blow the *Shofar* on *Rosh HaShanah*, as many times during the day as one wishes.[98]

10:33 Just as it is forbidden to add to a ritual itself, it is forbidden to add to the time span alloted to the ritual. For example, if done for the sake of religious observance, it is forbidden to eat *Matzah* or dwell in a *Sukkah* after the festival is over.[99] Similarly, one who puts on *Tefillin* on the Sabbath or Festivals, when we are exempt from them, is guilty of adding to the law.[100]

10:34 One does not violate the commandment not to add unless he has the specific intention of acting in fulfillment of a divine commandment.[101] This is true whether or not the commandment is performed during its alloted time.[102] For example, it is permitted to eat *Matzah* all year around, as long as one does not do so with the intention of fulfilling the commandment to eat *Matzah* on Passover.

10:35 A person does not violate the commandment not to add if

---

94. Where the required number is four, see Rashi on Deuteronomy 4:2, 13:1, from *Sifri; Yoma* 88b; *Chayay Adam* 68:23.
95. Where four species are required; Leviticus 23:40; *Orach Chaim* 651:14.
96. That is, the three blessings in Numbers 6:24-26. *Cf. Rosh HaShanah* 28b; *Yad, Nesiuth Kapayim* 14:12; *Orach Chaim* 128:27.
97. *Eruvin* 95b; *Tosafoth ad. loc. s.v. Iy KaSavar; Chinukh* 454; *Magen Avraham* 34:3; *Turey Zahav*, HaGra, 34:2; *Mishnah Berurah* 34:8.
98. *Tosafoth, Rosh HaShanah* 16b *s.v. VeTok'im,* 28b *s.v. U'Mina; Pri Megadim,* introduction 1:35; *Minchath Chinukh* 454; *Chayay Adam* 68:23. *Cf.* Maharatz Chajas, *Chagigah* 7a.
99. *Rosh HaShanah* 28b; *Chinukh* 454.
100. *Eruvin* 96a; *Menachoth* 36b; *Yad, Tefillin* 4:10; *Orach Chaim* 31:1.
101. *Rosh HaShanah* 28b; *Tosafoth, Menachoth* 40b *s.v. MeHai; Magen Avraham* 666:2; *Turey Zahav* 666:1; *Mishnah Berurah* 666:5.
102. *Cf. Magen Avraham* 651:23; *Chayay Adam* 68:23; *Biur Halakhah* 651:14 *s.v. MiShum.*

he observes a commandment from which he is exempt because of personal reasons. For example, women are permitted to observe those commandments[103] from which they are normally exempt.[104] They may also recite the blessings over such commandments.[105] Similarly, a non-Cohen does not violate the commandment not to add if he recites the priestly blessing. Still, he may not assume the priestly prerogative,[106] and therefore must not recite the introductory blessing.[107]

10:36 Any observance involving a ritual article that is fastened together to form a single unit may not be altered in any way. In such a case, it is forbidden to increase the number of its regular components, even if no additional component is added. For example, it is forbidden to double any of the parchments of the *Tefillin* or to take a greater number of any of the Four Species of *Sukkoth* than is actually required.[108]

10:37 However, in a case where a commandment does not involve a single ritual article, the number of its regular components may be increased. For example, a Cohen may repeat any of his three blessings, as long as he does not add a fourth.[109]

10:38 The Sanhedrin had the power to add to an observance in order to safeguard the Torah.[110] For example, the custom of adding a second day to all Biblical Festivals was instituted as a safeguard

103. See below 11:3, 11:5.
104. *Cf. Eruvin* 96b; *Rosh HaShanah* 33a; *Chagigah* 16b; *Chullin* 15a; *Sifra* on Leviticus 1:2; Raavad *ad. loc.; Tosafoth, Eruvin* 96a *s.v. Mikhol; Orach Chaim* 17:2 in *Hagah; Pri Megadim,* introduction 1:40; *Yad, Tzitzith* 3:9; *Minchath Chinukh* 454.
105. *Tosafoth, Rosh HaShanah* 33a *s.v. Ha;* Ran, *Kiddushin* (Rif 12b) *s.v. Tze'u;* Rosh, *Kiddushin* 1:49; Mordecai, *Shabbath* 286; *Magen Avraham* 17:1; *Mishnah Berurah* 17:4. See below, 11:5, note 12.
106. *Kethuvoth* 24b; Rashi *ad. loc. s.v. DeIssur; Orach Chaim* 128:1 in *Hagah; Biur Halakhah ad. loc. s.v. DeZar.*
107. *Tosafoth, Shabbath* 118b *s.v. Ilu; Magen Avraham* 128:1; *Turey Zahav* 128:2; *Mishnah Berurah* 128:4. See also *Teshuvoth Noda BeYehudah, Orach Chaim* 1:6; *Shaar HaMelekh, Shabbath* 19:23; *Atzey Arazim* 3:2.
108. *Orach Chaim* 651:15; *Cf. Sanhedrin* 88b; *Tosafoth ad. loc. s.v. Iy; Sukkah* 31a, 36b; *Yad, Lulav* 7:7; Raavad, *Maggid Mishneh, Lechem Mishneh, ad. loc.; Pri Megadim,* introduction 1:35; *Machtzith HaShekel* 651:27; *Mishnah Berurah* 34:8, 651:59. As distinct from note 95 above, this prohibition does not involve adding a fifth species, for example, on *Sukkoth,* but to increasing the number of individual components in each species, i.e. two citrons or two palm branches instead of one.
109. *Pri Megadim loc. cit.* See above, note 96.
110. *Pri Megadim,* introduction 1:38; *Minchath Chinukh* 454.

for their observance.[111] Nevertheless, where a single ritual article is involved, even the Sanhedrin may not add to or subtract from any of its components.[112]

10:39 Just as it is forbidden to add to any observance, it is forbidden to subtract from it. This includes the actual failure to observe a positive commandment. Besides violating the commandment itself, one also violates the commandment not to subtract from the commandments of the Torah.[113]

10:40 When one begins a religious duty, he should diligently strive to complete it. We are taught that one is punished for neglecting to finish a religious act,[114] and furthermore, if a second person completes it, the latter receives the entire credit.[115]

10:41 Since the commandments are our only means of fulfilling God's purpose, they must be respected accordingly.[116] It is therefore forbidden to perform any religious act in any manner which may even seem to be derogatory.[117] For example, it is forbidden to cover the blood of a ritually slaughtered animal with one's foot, since this indicates a lack of reverence for the commandment.[118] Similarly, it is forbidden to make personal use of any ritual object that is still needed for religious observance.[119]

10:42 In order to show proper respect for each commandment, it is forbidden to perform two or more rituals simultaneously. The commandments are not meant to be taken up in bundles.[120]

---

111. *Cf. Orach Chaim* 668:1; *Magen Avraham* 668:2; *Chayay Adam* 153:5; *Mishnah Berurah* 668:6; *Shaar HaTziun ad. loc.* 668:4.
112. *Pri Megadim,* introduction 1:36.
113. Rabbenu Yonah, *Shaarey Teshuvah* 3:11; *Minchath Chinukh* 455, citing Rashba, *Sifri.*
114. *Sotah* 13b; *Bereshith Rabbah* 85:4; *Devarim Rabbah* 8:5; *Tanchuma, Ekev* 10; *Yalkut Shimoni* 1:144, 2:35; *Sefer Chasidim* 726; *Menorath HaMaor* 3:10:1:3 (232); *Mesilath Yesharim* 7 (11a).
115. *Sotah* 13b; Rashi on Deuteronomy 8:1; *Cheredim,* introduction no. 5 (p. 14); *Sh'nei Luchoth HaB'rith, Teshuvah* 2:185b.
116. *Tanchuma, VaYigash* 6.
117. *Cheredim loc. cit.* no. 11 (p. 18); *Sh'nei Luchoth HaB'rith, Teshuvah* 2:185b; *Reshith Chokhmah, Perek HaMitzvoth* 4 (244c); *Chayay Adam* 68:2. *Cf. Sukkah* 42a; *Yad, Lulav* 7:11; *Orach Chaim* 651:7.
118. *Shabbath* 22a; *Chullin* 87a; *Sifra* on Leviticus 17:13; *Yad, Shechitah* 14:16; *Yoreh Deah* 28:6; *Reshith Chokhmah, Perek HaMitzvoth* 4 (244b); *Sh'nei Luchoth HaB'rith, Teshuvah* 2:186a.
119. *Kitzur Shulchan Arukh* 28:9.
120. *Sotah* 8a; *Berakhoth* 49a; *Pesachim* 102b; *Cheredim loc. cit.* no. 10 (p. 18); *Sh'nei*

10:43   The merit associated with the commandments was not revealed in order that people would observe all of them equally, and not pick and choose those offering the greatest reward.[121] It is therefore forbidden to forego a commandment at hand in order to observe another commandment[122] that can be done at a later time.[123]

10:44   It is also for this reason[124] that one who is engaged in performing a religious duty is exempt from all other observance.[125] This is only true, however, when the effort involved in the observance may tend to delay the religious duty at hand. If both can be done equally well, there is no exemption.[126]

10:45   Each commandment is best done at the time it comes to hand.[127] It should therefore not be delayed,[128] even if it seems that postponing it will enhance its observance.[129] This is what the Psalmist meant when he said, "I made haste [in order] not to delay the observance of Your commandments" (Psalms 119:60).[130]

Luchoth HaB'rith, Teshuvah 2:185b; *Magen Avraham* 147:11; *Chayay Adam* 68:3; *Nismath Adam ad. loc.* no. 2; *Mishnah Berurah* 147:24.

121.   *Avoth* 2:1; *Menachoth* 44a; *Yerushalmi, Kiddushin* 1:7 (20b); *Yerushalmi, Peah* 1:1 (3b); *Yalkut Shimoni* 2:937, from Proverbs 4:23; *Midrash Tehillim* 4:3; *Pesikta Rabathai* 23 (121b); *Menorath HaMaor* 3:10:1:2 (231); *Reshith Chokhmah, Perek HaMitzvoth* 2 (242c).

122.   *Pesachim* 64b; *Yoma* 33a, 58b, 70a; *Megillah* 6b; *Menachoth* 64a; *Tosafoth, Yoma* 33b *s.v. Avurey;* Maharatz Chajas, *ibid.; Tosafoth, Zevachim* 51a *s.v. Asher; Teshuvoth Radbaz* 522; *Magen Avraham* 147:11; *Chayay Adam* 68:1; *Mishnah Berurah* 25:3; *Menorath HaMaor, Reshith Chokhmah, loc cit.; Cheredim, loc. cit.* no. 9 (p. 18); *Sh'nei Luchoth HaB'rith, Teshuvah* 2:185b.

123.   See below, note 129.

124.   *Reshith Chokhmah, Perek HaMitzvoth* 1 (242c).

125.   *Berakhoth* 11a, 16a; *Sukkah* 25a; *Sotah* 44b; *Orach Chaim* 640:7; *Biur Halakhah ad. loc.; Teshuvoth Chatham Sofer* 119; *Chayay Adam* 68:4.

126.   *Orach Chaim* 38:8 in *Hagah; Magen Avraham* 38:9, 648:14; *Mishnah Berurah* 640:38.

127.   *Pesachim* 68b, 105b; *Kiddushin* 53a; *Menachoth* 72a; *Chullin* 54b; *Yad, Maaseh HaKorbanoth* 4:3.

128.   *Yevamoth* 39a, 47b; *Mekhilta* on Exodus 17:12; *Magen Avraham* 25:2; *Mishnah Berurah* 25:7.

129.   *Sefer Chasidim* 878; *Magen Avraham, Pri Megadim* 25:2; *Mishnah Berurah* 25:7. *Cf. Yevamoth* 39a; *Arakhin* 24a; *Tosefta, Arakhin* 2:7; Rashi, *Sukkah* 25b *s.v. SheChal; Tosafoth, Arakhin* 17b *s.v. Aval; Teshuvoth Radbaz* 4:1087, 7:2286; *Teshuvoth Chakham Tzvi* 106; *Teshuvoth Yaabetz* 1:48; *Shevuth Yaakov* 1:34; *Mishneh LeMelekh, Megillah* 1:1; *Ketzoth HaChoshen* 104:2 (end); *Teshuvoth Beth Shlomo, Yoreh Deah* 145; *Teshuvoth Zekher Yehosef* 223; *Beth Yitzchak, Yoreh Deah* 2:108, *Evven HaEzer* 1:121 (end); *Teshuvoth Nefesh Chayah* 595; Maharatz Chajas, *Moed Katan* 9a. *Chayay Adam* 68:1 disputes this; *cf. Nishmath Adam ad. loc.* no. 1; *Orach Chaim* 426:2; HaGra *ad. loc.; Terumath HaDeshen* 35; Rashi, *Moed Katan* 9b *s.v. U'BeMitzvah;* Maharsha *ad. loc.*

130.   *Sefer Chasidim* 878.

10:46 It is only forbidden to abandon an individual observance for another. If one is merely participating in a communal service, however, he may forego it for an individual duty.[131]

10:47 It is only forbidden to forego one commandment for another when it is ultimately possible to do both. In a case where only one commandment may be observed, a commandment of lesser importance may be abandoned in favor of one of greater importance.[132] As long as the delay is not more than a day or two,[133] one may even forego a commandment at hand in order to be able to observe a more important one at a later time.[134] Regarding such a case, King Solomon said, "While it is good to grab hold of one, do not withdraw your hand from the other, for he who fears God fulfills all his obligations" (Ecclesiastes 7:18).[135]

10:48 An observance which occurs regularly (*tadir*, תָּדִיר) takes precedence over an occasional observance,[136] and should be observed first,[137] even when the latter pertains to the entire congregation.[138] Whenever it is necessary to forego one commandment in favor of another, the regularly occurring one should be observed.[139]

10:49 Similarly, a personal obligation (*gavra*, גַּבְרָא) takes precedence over one which pertains to a situation or object (*cheftza*, חֶפְצָא).[140] For example, *Tefillin*, which is a personal

---

131. *Chayay Adam* 68:1 from *Yoma* 70a; Rashi *ad. loc. s.v. KaMashma Lan.*

132. *Moed Katan* 9b; Rashi, Maharsha, *ad. loc. s.v. U'BeMitzvah; Tosafoth ad. loc. s.v. Kan;* Maharatz Chajas, *ibid.; Yalkut Shimoni* 2:31; *Tosafoth, Yoma* 33a *s.v. Ein; Magen Avraham* 656:8; *Chayay Adam* 68:1. *Cf. Kiddushin* 29b; *Yad, Bikkurim* 11:4.

133. *Chayay Adam loc. cit.; Nishmath Adam ad. loc. no.* 1. The reason for this is because one may die while waiting if the delay is too long; *cf. Tosafoth, Yevamoth* 26a *s.v. Iy.*

134. *Chayay Adam,* Maharatz Chajas, *loc. cit.; Teshuvoth Chakham Tzvi* 106. *Cf. Teshuvoth Radbaz* 1:10, 4:13; *Teshuvoth Rival* 2:53; *Magen Avraham* 248:14; *Zevachim* 91a.

135. *Sefer Chasidim* 529.

136. *Yerushalmi, Nazir* 7:1 (24b); *Teshuvoth Rama* 38:2.

137. *Horayoth* 3:6 (12b); *Berakhoth* 27a, 51b; *Pesachim* 104a; *Zevachim* 91a; *Tosefta, Berakhoth* 5:25; *Yerushalmi, Berakhoth* 8:1 (56b); *Yerushalmi, Pesachim* 10:2 (69b); *Beth Yosef, Orach Chaim* 25; *Turey Zahav* 25:1; *Yad Ephraim* 25:1; *"Rav" Shulchan Arukh* 25:2; *Kitzur Shulchan Arukh* 10:2; *Teshuvoth Shaagath Aryeh* 28.

138. *Yerushalmi, Yoma* 2:2 (12b).

139. *Chayay Adam* 68:1.

140. *Chayay Adam* 68:1. *Cf. Beer Hetiv, Orach Chaim* 25:1; *Chayay Adam* 14:28; *Mishnah Berurah* 25:2; *Teshuvoth Yad Eliahu* 41; *Teshuvoth Rabbi Akiba Eiger* 9.

obligation, takes precedence over *Mezuzah,* which is an obligation pertaining to a dwelling.[141]

10:50 A commandment which must be done at a given time takes precedence over one which can be done at any time.[142] For example, buying an *Ethrog* for *Sukkoth* takes precedence over redeeming one's first born son, since the former must be done before the *Sukkoth* Festival, while the latter can be done at any time.[143]

10:51 The reward for obeying a positive commandment is infinite, while the punishment for violating a negative commandment is of finite duration. When it is impossible to keep both,[144] it is therefore preferable to violate a negative commandment than to forego a positive one.[145] By the same token, if a negative commandment stands in the way of a positive observance, one must violate the negative rather than forego the positive.[146]

10:52 One may violate a negative commandment in order to observe a positive only when both acts occur simultaneously,[147] unless the negative will be violated anyway as a matter of course.[148] Nevertheless, if the positive commandment is known to be of great importance,[149] or if it involves an entire congregation,[150] it takes precedence even when both acts do not occur simultaneously.

141. *Yerushalmi, Megillah* 4:12 (34a); Rosh, *Tefillin* 30; *Orach Chaim* 38:12; HaGra *ad. loc.; Magen Avraham* 38:15; *Mishnah Berurah* 38:37; *Yoreh Deah* 285:1 in *Hagah;* HaGra *ad. loc.* 285:4; *Teshuvoth Rabbi Akiba Eiger ibid.*
142. *Kiddushin* 29b; *Berakhoth* 27a; *Tosefta, Bekhoroth* 6:3; *Tosafoth, Shabbath* 9b *s.v. LeMan D'Amar; Yad, Bikkurim* 11:4; *Chayay Adam* 68:1; *Teshuvoth Shaagath Aryeh* 19.
143. *Magen Avraham* 656:8; *Beer Hetiv* 656:6.
144. *Shabbath* 132b; *Betza* 8a; *Kethuvoth* 40b; *Teshuvoth Beth Ephraim, Orach Chaim* 4; *Maharatz Chajas, Nedarim* 31b.
145. *Reshith Chokhmah, Perek HaMitzvoth* 2 (243c); *Likutey Amarim (Tanya), Iggereth HaTeshuvah* 1 (90b). Some maintain that a positive commandment is more important than a negative; *cf.* Ramban on Exodus 20:8; *Megillath Esther* (on *Sefer HaMitzvoth*), *Shoresh* 4 (42a); *Rosh Yosef, Choshen Mishpat* 34:4. Others dispute this; *cf. Yad Malachi* 515 (85b). From the general discussion, it appears that while the sin of violating a negative commandment is more serious than that of foregoing a positive, the loss of reward for the positive outweighs the punishment for the negative.
146. *Yevamoth* 3b*ff.; Chayay Adam* 68:22.
147. *Tosafoth, Pesachim* 59a *s.v. Ati; Chayay Adam loc. cit.; Turey Aven, Chagigah* 2a; *Teshuvoth Noda BeYehudah, Yoreh Deah* 2:10; *Teshuvoth Sho'el U'Meshiv* 3:2:4; Maharatz Chajas, *Shabbath* 137b; *Makor Chesed* (on *Sefer Chasidim*) 31:4.
148. *Chayay Adam loc. cit.,* from Rashba, *Shabbath* 130b. *Cf. Tosafoth ibid. s.v. SheLo.*
149. *Tosafoth, Pesachim* 59a *s.v. Ati; Chayay Adam loc. cit. Cf. Menachoth* 40a.
150. *Magen Avraham* 426:2; *Chayay Adam loc. cit;* Maharatz Chajas, *Rosh HaShanah* 38b. *Cf.*

10:53   A positive commandment only takes precedence over a simple negative, but not over one which is associated with another positive,[151] or one which incurs a penalty of death or excision.[152]

10:54   Except in cases where negative commandments are formally nullified by positive precepts, all religious observances must be without taint of sin.[153] Any observance which is tainted by sin is absolutely invalid. Regarding this it is written, "The robber blesses, but [in so doing] scorns God" (Psalms 10:3).[154]

10:55   Torah law allows any person to appoint an agent to take his place.[155] Still, an agent's power is limited by his appointment and therefore one cannot appoint an agent to do something which he himself may not do.[156] Furthermore, since every agent has a prior responsibility to God,[157] no agent can be appointed to carry out a sinful act.[158] Similarly, no agent can take the place of one's own body, and therefore, any religious duty which involves one's person cannot be done by proxy.[159] In any case, even where a religious duty can be fulfilled by proxy, it is preferable to do it oneself.[160]

Berakhoth 47b; Maharatz Chajas *ad. loc.;* Rosh, *Berakhoth* 7:20; *Magen Avraham* 90:30; *Teshuvoth Besamim Rosh* 155; *Teshuvoth Shaagath Aryeh* 96, 97.

151. *Rosh HaShanah* 38b; *Bava Metzia* 30a.
152. *Yevamoth* 3b; *Teshuvoth Rashdam, Yoreh Deah* 231.
153. *Cf. Teshuvoth Shaagath Aryeh ibid.;* Maharatz Chajas, *Berakhoth* 47b.
154. *Berakhoth* 47b; *Sukkah* 30a; *Bava Kama* 94a; *Yerushalmi, Challah* 1:5 (9a); *Yerushalmi, Shabbath* 13:3 (72b); *Chayay Adam* 68:10; *Nishmath Adam* 3:7. *Cf. Orach Chaim* 11:6, 649:1.
155. *Berakhoth* 34b; *Chagigah* 10b; *Nedarim* 72b; *Nazir* 12b; *Kiddushin* 41b, 43a; *Bava Metzia* 96a; *Menachoth* 93b; *Mekhilta* on Exodus 12:3, 12:6; Rashi on Leviticus 24:14; *Yad, Sheluchin* 1:1; *Choshen Mishpat* 182:1; *Sefer Meirath Eynayim (Sema)* 182:1.
156. *Nazir* 12b; *Bava Kama* 110a; Maharatz Chajas *ad. loc.; Ketzoth HaChoshen* 123:5, 126:16.
157. *Kiddushin* 42b; *Bava Kama* 56a; *Sanhedrin* 29a; *Temurah* 25a; *Niddah* 14b; *Sefer Meirath Eynayim (Sema)* 182:2.
158. *Kiddushin* 42b; *Bava Kama* 51a, 79a; *Bava Metzia* 10b; *Yad, Me'ilah* 7:2; *Choshen Mishpat* 182:1 in *Hagah,* 410:8; Maharatz Chajas, *Bava Metzia* 10b; *Mishneh LeMelekh, Rotzeach* 2:2; *Pri Megadim,* introduction 3:28; *Teshuvoth Noda BeYehudah* 1:78-79.
159. *Ketzoth HaChoshen* 182:1, from Rosh, *Nedarim* 72b *s.v. VeHa;* Maharatz Chajas *ad. loc. Cf. Teshuvoth Rambam (P'er HaDor)* 52, quoted in *Lechem Mishneh, Shofar* 1:1; *Teshuvoth Rabbi Moshe Alshaker* 8-10; *Tosafoth, Nazir* 11a; Maharatz Chajas *ad. loc.; Ketzoth HaChoshen* 123:5.
160. *Kiddushin* 41a; *Shabbath* 119a; *Yad, Shabbath* 30:6; *Cheredim,* introduction no. 8 (p. 18); *Sh'nei Luchoth HaB'rith, Teshuvah* 2:185b; *Chayay Adam* 68:7; *Teshuvoth Mabit* 49. *Cf. Sifethey Cohen, Choshen Mishpat* 382:4; *Kereithi U'Pelethi* 108:3; *Ketzoth*

10:56 Whenever applicable, it is preferable to perform any religious observance as part of a group. It is thus written, "In a multitude of people is the King's glory" (Proverbs 14:28).[161] Although this requirement is fulfilled by a group of three,[162] a full congregation, containing ten adult men, is preferable.[163] We are taught that the Divine Presence rests upon a congregation of ten, in accord with the verse, "God stands in the Godly congregation" (Psalms 82:1).[164] It is therefore particularly important to pray with a congregation,[165] and for this reason, many prayers were inaugurated specifically as congregational prayers.[166]

10:57 If one is aware of a religious observance which is generally neglected, he should strive to fulfill it, as such an observance is particularly dear to God.[167] Furthermore, when any commandment is generally neglected, it disrupts the entire relationship between Israel, God and His Torah.[168]

10:58 Every person should choose at least one commandment and attempt to fulfill it faithfully[169] and perfectly all his life.[170] We are

HaChoshen 382:1; *Gilyon Maharsha, Yoreh Deah* 260:1; *Mishnath Chakhamim, Kuntres Maaloth HaMidoth* p. 136, quoted in *Pith'chey Teshuvah, Yoreh Deah* 270:7. See also *Yoreh Deah* 305:10 in *Hagah*, from *Teshuvoth Rivash* 131; *Sifethey Cohen, Turey Zahav,* 305:11; HaGra 305:17.

161. *Pesachim* 64b; *Yoma* 27a, 70a; *Zevachim* 14b; *Yad, Korban Pesach* 1:14; *Cheredim*, introduction no. 16 (p. 19); *Sh'nei Luchoth HaB'rith, Teshuvah* 2:185b; *Chayay Adam* 68:11. See also *Berakhoth* 53a; *Tosefta, Berakhoth* 5:33; *Orach Chaim* 298:14; *Magen Avraham* 298:18; *Turey Zahav* 298:10; *Mishnah Berurah* 298:36; *Tosefta, Berakhoth* 6:20; *Orach Chaim* 8:5; *Mishnah Berurah* 8:13; *Chayay Adam* 5:17; *Orach Chaim* 432:2; *Biur Halakhah* 167:11 *s.v. Echad; Kesef Mishneh, Berakhoth* 1:12 (end).

162. *Menachoth* 62a; *Chayay Adam loc. cit. Cf. Avoth* 3:6; *Berakhoth* 6a, 45a (7:1); *Yad, Berakhoth* 5:2; *Orach Chaim* 192:1.

163. *Megillah* 23b; *Berakhoth* 21b; *Sanhedrin* 74b, from Leviticus 22:32, Numbers 14:27; *Yerushalmi, Berakhoth* 7:3 (55a) from Genesis 42:3; *Yerushalmi, Sanhedrin* 1:4 (8b), 3:5 (16a); *Yerushalmi, Shevi'ith* 4:2 (10b); *Sofrim* 10:7; *Bereshith Rabbah* 91:3. *Cf.* Genesis 18:32, Exodus 18:21, Judges 6:27, Ruth 4:2.

164. *Avoth* 3:7; *Berakhoth* 6a; *Mekhilta* on Exodus 21:21; *Yalkut Shimoni* 2:548.

165. *Berakhoth* 6a; *Yad, Tefillah* 8:1; *Orach Chaim* 90:9.

166. *Berakhoth* 7:3 (49b); *Megillah* 4:3 (23b); *Yad, Tefillah* 8:4; *Orach Chaim* 69:1.

167. *Sefer Chasidim* 105, 261; *Sh'nei Luchoth HaB'rith, Teshuvah* 2:188b; *Chayay Adam* 68:20. *Cf. VaYikra Rabbah* 32:1; *Midrash Tehillim* 12:5; *Sefer Chasidim* 529.

168. *Sefer Chasidim loc. cit.; Yerushalmi, Sanhedrin* 2:6 (13a); *Shemoth Rabbah* 6:1; *VaYikra Rabbah* 19:2. See Volume 1, 4:54.

169. *Mekhilta* on Exodus 14:31; *Yalkut Shimoni* 1:240.

170. *Emunoth VeDeyoth* 5:4 (71a); *Sefer Chasidim* 529; *Taamey HaMinhagim*, p. 516. *Cf. Shabbath* 118b; *Kiddushin* 39b; *Yerushalmi, Kiddushin* 1:9 (22b); *Menorath HaMaor* 3:8:3:5 (213); *Maggid Mesharim, Tazria* (end). Also see *Koheleth Rabbah* 5:8;

taught that a person who fulfills even one commandment without ulterior motive all his life is assured of his portion in the World to Come.[171]

TABLE 10:1 — BLESSINGS FOR COMMANDMENTS — VERBAL FORM

1. *Tallith Gadol*[1] To wrap oneself in *Tzitzith*[2]
2. Hand *Tefillin*[3] To put on *Tefillin*[4]
3. Priestly Blessing[5] To bless His people Israel with love[6]
4. *Hallel*[7] To read the *Hallel*[8]

Rashi on Ecclesiastes 5:9; *Magen Avraham* 154:23 *s.v. BeRabbah; Machtzith HaShekel ad. loc.*

171. *Yerushalmi, Kiddushin* 1:9 (22b); Rambam, *Makkoth* 3:16; *Reshith Chokhmah, Perek HaMitzvoth* 2 (242b). *Cf. Sotah* 3b.

1. Numbers 15:38; *Sefer HaMitzvoth,* Positive 14; *Sefer Mitzvoth Gadol,* Positive 26.
2. *Berakhoth* 60b; *Yerushalmi, Berakhoth* 9:3 (66a); *Tosefta* 6:15; *Yad, Tzitzith* 3:8; *Orach Chaim* 8:5. Both according to Rabbenu Tam and Riva, this is a classical example of the verbal form; see notes 23, 24. Similarly, according to *Yad, Berakhoth* 11:12, this is a good example of a commandment done for and by oneself. According to our distinction, the verbal form is used because the primary focus is on wearing the *Tallith,* not on putting it on.
3. Deuteronomy 6:8; *Sefer HaMitzvoth,* Positive 13; *Sefer Mitzvoth Gadol,* Positive 21.
4. *Menachoth* 36a, 42a; *Berakhoth* 60b; *Tosefta* 6:15; *Yad, Tefillin* 4:4; *Orach Chaim* 25:5. This is also a classical example of the verbal form according to all distinctions.
5. Numbers 6:22; *Sefer HaMitzvoth,* Positive 26; *Sefer Mitzvoth Gadol,* Positive 21.
6. *Sotah* 39a; *Yad, Tefillah* 14:12; *Orach Chaim* 128:11. According to both Riva and Rambam, this is a classical case, since the commandment is and must be done by the individual, in this case the Cohen. However, the verbal form is difficult to understand according to Rabbenu Tam's distinction, although one may justify it because of frequent interruptions, as in the case of *Hallel.* Similarly, according to our distinction, the verbal form is used, since the emphasis is on the blessing having been given rather than on how it is given or read, exactly as in the case of *Hallel.*
7. This is a rabbinical law; *cf. Pesachim* 117a; Ramban on *Sefer HaMitzvoth, Shoresh* 1 (p. 9b); *Yad, Berakhoth* 11:16; *Tosafoth, Berakhoth* 14a *s.v. Yamim, Arakhin* 10a *s.v. Shemonah Esreh Yamim; Pri Megadim,* introduction 1:41.
8. *Sukkah* 39a; *Tosafoth ad. loc. s.v. Aval; Pesachim* 119b; *Yad, Chanukah* 3:10; *Mordecai, Shabbath* 285; *Orach Chaim* 422:2. According to Riva, the verbal form is used because it must be said by the individual. Even though the obligation can be fulfilled by hearing the *Hallel,* each individual must repeat the responses. Likewise, according to *Yad, Berakhoth* 11:12, this is a good example of an observance where the obligation and the fulfillment devolve upon the same person. Since the *Hallel* is interrupted by the responses, it is not considered a single prayer, and therefore, the verbal form is used according to Rabbenu Tam. Furthermore, the emphasis is on the content rather than the form, and for this reason, the *Hallel* can be said whenever events warrant it; *cf. Rosh, Pesachim* 1:10. This also justifies the verbal form according to

5.	Sabbath Lamp[9]	To kindle the Sabbath Lamp[10]
6.	Festival Lamp[11]	To kindle the Festival Lamp[12]
7.	*Yom Kippur* Lamp[13]	To kindle the *Yom Kippur* Lamp[14]
8.	*Shofar*[15]	To hear the sound of the *Shofar*[16]

our distinction. In this respect, it is unlike the *Megillah*, where the emphasis is also on the form of the reading.

9.   This is also a rabbinical law; *cf. Shabbath* 25b.

10.   *Tosafoth, Shabbath* 25b *s.v. Chovah*, quoted in *Siddur Rav Amram Gaon* 1:24; *Sefer HaYashar* 619, 622; Rosh, *Shabbath* 2:18; Ran, *Shabbath* (Rif 11b) *s.v. Gemara;* Mordecai 294; *Yad, Shabbath* 5:1; *Orach Chaim* 263:5. In Mordecai, *Shabbath* 273, *Or Zarua, Hilkhoth Erev Shabbath* 41, and *Hagahoth Maimonioth* on *Yad, Shabbath* 5:1, we find that *Yerushalmi, Betza* 4 and *Yerushalmi, Berakhoth* 9, are given as sources for this blessing (*cf. HaKobetz, Shabbath* 5:1; HaGra, *Orach Chaim* 263:5), although neither source is in our editions (*cf. Beney Binyamin, Shabbath* 5:1; *HaShmatoth MiYerushalmi, Berakhoth* 9:3 [66a], *Betza* 4:4 [18a]). Furthermore, from *Sefer HaYashar, loc. cit.*, it is evident that this blessing was not in the editions of the *Yerushalmi* used by Rabbenu Tam. According to both Rabbenu Tam and Riva, this is a classical case; see below, note 20. *Yad, Berakhoth* 11:12 also gives this as an example of a commandment where both obligation and fulfillment are incumbent upon the same individual. According to our distinction, this is also a classical case, since the emphasis is on the light (the result) rather than on the act of lighting.

11.   Rabbinical law; see note 12.

12.   *Orach Chaim* 263:5; Mordecai, *Hagahoth Maimonioth loc. cit.; Or Zarua* 2:361; *Hagahoth Asheri, Betza* 4:8. Here again, however, the references from the *Yerushalmi* are not in our editions.

13.   Rabbinical custom; *cf. Pesachim* 4:4 (53b); Rashi, *ibid. s.v. Bein; Yerushalmi, Pesachim* 4:4 (28a); *Tosefta* 3:11; Rosh, *Yoma* 8:27; *Yad, Shevithath Assor* 3:10; *Orach Chaim* 610:1.

14.   Rosh, *Yoma* 8:27; *Orach Chaim* 610:2. In *Orach Chaim* 263:5, however, this is debated, and Mordecai, *Yoma* 728, *Shabbath* 273, writes that no blessing should be said since it is a mere custom; *cf.* HaGra, *Orach Chaim* 610:2.

15.   Numbers 29:1; *Sefer HaMitzvoth*, Positive 170; *Sefer Mitzvoth Gadol*, Positive 42.

16.   *Yad, Shofar* 3:10, *Berakhoth* 11:14; *Orach Chaim* 585:2. The blessing is also mentioned in *Pesachim* 7b, *Yerushalmi, Berakhoth* 9:3 (66a), although its wording is not given. See *HaMaor HaKatan* and *Milchamoth HaShem* (Ramban), *Rosh HaShanah* (Rif 10b), for a discussion as to whether this blessing existed in the time of the Talmud, or whether the blessing mentioned in the above sources refers to the blessings in the *Mussaf* service. Rosh, *Rosh HaShanah* 4:10, quotes Rabbenu Tam that the blessing is in the noun form, e.g. "on sounding the *Shofar*"; *cf. Korban Nethanel ad. loc.* no. 3. However, according to Rosh, *Pesachim* 1:10, even Rabbenu Tam uses the verbal form, since the sounding is interrupted by the *Mussaf* service; *cf. Rokeach* 363 (p. 253, bottom). According to Riva, this is a classical example, since each person must hear the *Shofar*. Similarly, *Yad, Berakhoth* 11:14 uses this as an example of an individual obligation that one does both for himself and others. The reason why (unlike the *Megillah*) the blessing refers to hearing rather than sounding is given by Ran, *Pesachim* (Rif 4a) *s.v. VeTu:* the main commandment is to hear the *Shofar* blown, not how it is blown. Another reason is because the *Shofar* must actually be heard, while the *Megillah* can be read silently; *cf. Taamey HaMinhagim* 872 (p. 374), quoting Abudarham. According to our distinction, the verbal form is used because the emphasis is on the *Shofar* being heard (the result), rather than on the act of hearing it.

9. *Sukkah*[17]   To dwell in the *Sukkah*[18]
10. *Chanukah* Lamp[19]   To kindle the *Chanukah* Lamp[20]
11. Sanctification of Name[21]   To sanctify His Name publicly[22]
12. *Mezuzah*[23]   To affix a *Mezuzah*[24]
13. Battlement[25]   To make a battlement[26]

17. Leviticus 23:42; *Sefer HaMitzvoth,* Positive 168; *Sefer Mitzvoth Gadol,* Positive 43.
18. *Pesachim* 7b; *Menachoth* 42a; *Yerushalmi, Berakhoth* 9:3 (66a); *Tosefta, Berakhoth* 6:14; *Yad, Sukkah* 6:12, *Berakhoth* 11:12; *Orach Chaim* 641:1. This is a classical example of the verbal form according to all opinions.
19. Rabbinical law; *cf. Shabbath* 21b. Also see 1 Maccabees 4:59, 2 Maccabees 10:8; *Megillath Chashmonayim* 1:71.
20. *Shabbath* 23a; *Sukkah* 46a; *Sofrim* 20:6; *Yad, Chanukah* 3:4; *Orach Chaim* 676:1. According to Rabbenu Tam, the verbal form is used because the light must burn for a designated time; *cf.* Rosh, *Pesachim* 1:10; *Mordecai* 538; *Rokeach* 363. Likewise, according to Riva, it is an individual obligation, and although it can be done through another, the preference is on the individual (*cf.* Rosh *loc. cit.*), and furthermore, one must go into partnership with another who lights it; *cf.* Ran, *Pesachim* (Rif 4a) *s.v. U'Mihu.* Likewise, according to our distinction, the verbal form is used, since the emphasis is on the light rather than on the lighting. However, in *Yerushalmi, Sukkah* 3:5 (14a), we find the blessing in the noun form, e.g. "on the commandment of the *Chanukah* lamp"; *cf. Likutey Amarim (Tanya), Sefer Shel Benonim* 35; *Pardes Rimonim* 42; *Anshey Shem* on Ran *loc. cit.*
21. Leviticus 22:32; *Sefer HaMitzvoth,* Positive 9; *Sefer Mitzvoth Gadol,* Positive 5.
22. *Sh'nei Luchoth HaB'rith, Shaar HaOthioth* 1:98a-99a; *Korban Nethanel, Pesachim* (Rosh 1:10) no. 20. According to Riva and Rambam, the verbal form should be used, since both the obligation and its fulfillment are incumbent on the individual. Similarly, according to our distinction, the emphasis is on the result, also requiring the verbal form. According to Rabbenu Tam, however, the commandment is done all at once and therefore requires the noun form, e.g. "on the sanctification of the Name," and this is indeed the form found in *Piskey Recanti* 70 as quoted by *Sh'nei Luchoth HaB'rith* and *Korban Nethanel loc. cit.*
23. Deuteronomy 6:9; *Sefer HaMitzvoth,* Positive 15; *Sefer Mitzvoth Gadol,* Positive 23.
24. Rif, *Hilkhoth Mezuzah* 5a; *Yad, Muzuzah* 5:7; *Yoreh Deah* 289:1. However, in *Yerushalmi, Berakhoth* 9:3 (66a), the blessing is given in noun form, "on the commandment of *Mezuzah*"; *cf. Rokeach* 363; HaGra, *Yoreh Deah* 289:2. It is necessary to clarify this wording, since, according to both Rabbenu Tam and Riva, this should be a classical case of the noun form, both because it is done all at once and because it can be done by another. The justification for the verbal form, however, is the fact that the actual commandment is to live in a house bearing a *Mezuzah, cf. Magen Avraham, Orach Chaim* 19:1; *Beer Hetiv* 19:2; *Mishnah Berurah* 19:4, and this observance is both individual and long lasting, *cf. Korban Nethanel loc. cit.* no. 300. In *Yad, Berakhoth* 11:12-13, the usual distinction is made that, when one affixes a *Mezuzah* on his own doorpost, the verbal form is used, while for another, the noun form, "on affixing a *Mezuzah*" is used. According to our distinction, this is a classical case where the focus is on the result, namely, having a *Mezuzah* on the house.
25. Deuteronomy 22:8; *Sefer HaMitzvoth* 184; *Sefer Mitzvoth Gadol* 79.
26. *Yad, Berakhoth* 11:8, 11:12; *Chayay Adam* 15:25, quoting Abudarham; *Pith'chey Teshuvah, Choshen Mishpat* 427:1; Rabbi Akiba Eiger *ad. loc. Or Zarua* 1:225 quotes this blessing from *Yerushalmi, Berakhoth* 9:3 (66a), but see *HaShmatoth MiYerushalmi ad. loc.* that this is absent from our editions. In *Korban Nethanel, Pesachim* (Rosh

14. Proselyte Circumcision[27]	To circumcise proselytes[28]
15. Slave Circumcision[29]	To circumcise slaves[30]
16. *Challah*[31]	To separate *Challah*[32]
17. *Terumah*[33]	To separate *Terumah*[34]
18. *Ma'aser*[35]	To separate *Ma'aser*[36]

1:10) no. 300, we find that this is likened to the blessing for the *Mezuzah*, however, in no. 20, he writes that the custom according to Rabbenu Tam is to use the noun form, "on making a battlement," although *Nishmath Adam* 15:3 disputes this. In *Yad, Berakhoth* 11:12, we find the customary distinction whether one makes it for oneself, in which case the verb form is used, or for others, in which case the noun form is used. According to our distinction, the verbal form is justified since the focus is primarily on the result.

27. See Volume 1, 5:14, note 35.

28. *Shabbath* 137b; *Rosh, Shabbath* 19:11; *Yad, Milah* 3:4; *Yoreh Deah* 268:8. However, in *Shabbath* 137b, the noun form, "on the circumcision," is used, while in *Sefer Mitzvoth Gadol*, Positive 28, the wording is "on the circumcision of converts," and this would also be the correct reading according to Rabbenu Tam. According to Riva, the verbal form is used because the obligation is incumbent upon every Jew equally, and therefore, no proxy is possible; *cf. Tosafoth, Pesachim* 7b *s.v. Lo; Kesef Mishneh, Milah* 3:5; *Gilyon Maharsha, Yoreh Deah* 268:8. It is for this same reason that, according to our distinction, the blessing is in the verbal form.

29. Genesis 17:12; *cf. Tosafoth, Shabbath* 137b *s.v. BeMitzvothav.*

30. *Shabbath* 137b; *Yad, Milah* 3:5; *Yoreh Deah* 267:12. This is exactly the same as the above case. However, in *Yad* and *Yoreh Deah loc. cit.*, we find the distinction that if one circumcises his own slaves, he uses the verbal form, whereas if he circumcises another's slaves, the noun form, "on the circumcision of slaves," is used; *cf. Pith'chey Teshuvah, Yoreh Deah* 267:2, quoting *Teshuvoth Rashbash* 89.

31. Numbers 15:20; *Sefer HaMitzvoth*, Positive 133; *Sefer Mitzvoth Gadol*, Positive 141.

32. *Yad, Bikkurim* 5:11; *Rokeach* 359 (p. 243); *Or Zarua* 1:225; *Yoreh Deah* 328:1 in *Hagah; Kitzur Shulchan Arukh* 35:1. *Cf. Rash, Challah* 2:3. Others, however, use the wording, "to separate *Terumah*," in this case also; *cf. She'ilthoth, Tzav;* Raavad, *Bikkurim* 5:11; *Sefer Mitzvoth Gadol*, Positive 141; Abudarham (p. 156b); *Yoreh Deah* 228:1; HaGra *ad. loc.* 228:2; *Sifethey Cohen, Turey Zahav, ad. loc.* 228:1. According to *Sefer Mitzvoth Katan,* cited in *Sifethey Cohen, Turey Zahav, ad. loc.*, the wording is "to separate the *Terumah* of *Challah*." For the reason the verb form is used, see note 34.

33. Deuteronomy 18:4; *Sefer HaMitzvoth*, Positive 126; *Sefer Mitzvoth Gadol*, Positive 133. For the *Terumah* taken from the Levites' Tithe, see Numbers 18:26; *Sefer HaMitzvoth*, Positive 129; *Sefer Mitzvoth Gadol*, Positive 134.

34. *Yerushalmi, Berakhoth* 9:3 (66a); *Tosefta* 6:19; *Yad, Terumah* 2:16, *Berakhoth* 11:12; *Yoreh Deah* 331:78; Rash, Bertenoro, *Maaser Sheni* 5:11; Rashi, *Berakhoth* 40b *s.v. MiLeVerakhakhah.* However, in *Rosh, Pesachim* 1:10, we find that Rabbenu Tam used the noun form, "on the separation of *Terumah*," since it is done in a single act; *cf. Korban Nethanel ad. loc.* no. 100. Although *Terumah* can be separated by proxy, it is not a true proxy since it requires both the knowledge and consent of the owner. The blessing is therefore in the verbal form according to Riva; *cf. Ran, Pesachim* (Rif 4a) *s.v. VeIkha; Korban Nethanel loc. cit.* no. 20. In *Yad, Berakhoth* 11:12, we find the customary distinction, where the verb form is used if one does it for himself, and the noun form is used if it is done for another. According to our distinction, this is a classical case where the focus is on the result.

35. Numbers 18:24, Leviticus 27:30; *Sefer HaMitzvoth*, Positive 127; *Sefer Mitzvoth Gadol*, Positive 135.

36. *Yerushalmi, Berakhoth* 9:3 (66a); *Tosefta* 6:18; *Yad, Maaseroth* 1:16; *Yoreh Deah* 331:78.

19. *Ma'aser Sheni*[37]   To separate *Ma'aser Sheni*[38]
20. *Ma'aser Tzedakah*[39]   To separate *Ma'aser Tzedakah*[40]
21. Passover Sacrifice[41]   To slaughter the Passover Sacrifice[42]
22. Festival Sacrifice[43]   To slaughter the Festival Sacrifice[44]
23. Eating *Terumah*[45]   To eat *Terumah*[46]

TABLE 10:2 — BLESSINGS FOR COMMANDMENTS — NOUN FORM

1. *Tallith Katan*[1]   On the commandment of *Tzitzith*[2]
2. Head *Tefillin*[3]   On the commandment of *Tefillin*[4]

37. Deuteronomy 14:22; *Sefer HaMitzvoth*, Positive 128; *Sefer Mitzvoth Gadol*, Positive 136.
38. Rash, *Maaser Sheni* 5:11. A special blessing is also indicated by *Yerushalmi, Demai* 5:2 (20b). See *Yad, Maaser* 1:16; HaGra, *Orach Chaim* 25:5; *Teshuvoth Rivash* 384.
39. Deuteronomy 14:28; *Sefer HaMitzvoth*, Positive 130; *Sefer Mitzvoth Gadol*, Positive 137.
40. See note 38.
41. Exodus 12:6; *Sefer HaMitzvoth*, Positive 55; *Sefer Mitzvoth Gadolm*, Positive 223.
42. *Yad, Berakhoth* 11:12 (end). *Cf. Pesachim* 7b, Rashi *ad. loc. s.v. Pesach; Lechem Mishneh, Chametz U'Matzah* 3:6. According to Rashi and Ran, the blessing would be in the noun form, similar to circumcision. According to our distinction, however, the verb form may be used here, since the focus is on the result, namely, the sacrifice of the Passover offering, while when one slaughters for food in general, the focus is on the act.
43. Deuteronomy 16:16; *Sefer HaMitzvoth*, Negative 156; *Sefer Mitzvoth Gadol*, Negative 360.
44. See above, note 42.
45. *Cf.* Radbaz, *Terumoth* 15:22.
46. *Yad, Terumoth* 15:25, *Bikkurim* 1:2; *Sefer Mitzvoth Gadol*, Negative 158 (76b).

1. See Table 10:1, note 1. Regarding the *Tallith Katan*, see *Orach Chaim* 8:3; Mordecai, *Hilkhoth Ketanoth* 943; Maharik, *Shoresh* 149.
2. *Nimukey Yosef, Hilkhoth Tzitzith* 12a *s.v. Amar; Kol Bo* 22; *Orach Chaim* 8:6 in *Hagah; cf. Nedarim* 49b (end). The usual reason given for this wording is that the *Tallith Katan* is not the primary observance and therefore the blessing is only recited for the commandment in general; *cf. Darkey Moshe, Orach Chaim* 8, quoted in *Turey Zahav* 8:7; *Pri Megadim ad. loc.; Levush* 8; *Beer Hetiv, Shaarey Teshuvah* 8:7; *Chayay Adam* 12:4. Another reason may be because the *Tallith Katan* is usually put on the first thing in the morning, while the blessing is not said until later. Thus, the noun form is used as in every other case where the blessing is said after the observance has begun.
3. Deuteronomy 6:8; *Sefer HaMitzvoth*, Positive 12; *Sefer Mitzvoth Gadol*, Positive 22.
4. *Menachoth* 36a; *Yad, Tefillin* 4:4; *Orach Chaim* 25:5. For whether the blessing is said only when there is an interruption between the two *Tefillin*, see *Yad, Orach Chaim, loc. cit; Tosafoth, Menachoth* 36a *s.v. Lo; Rif, Hilkhoth Tefillin* 8a; Rosh, *Hilkhoth Tefillin* 14; Mordecai, *Hilkhoth Ketanoth* (p. 12a, middle of second column). According to *Tosafoth, Berakhoth* 60b *s.v. Asher*, the reason for the noun form is that

3. Washing Hands[5] On the washing of hands[6]
4. *Eruv*[7] On the commandment of *Eruv*[8]
5. Destroying *Chametz*[9] On destroying *Chametz*[10]

the commandment has already begun when the hand *Tefillin* are put on. This answer relates, however, to the problem of whether this blessing applies to both *Tefillin; cf. Turey Zahav* 25:6; *Magen Avraham* 25:9; *Beer Hetiv* 25:4; *Mishnah Berurah* 25:20. Rosh, *Pesachim* 1:10, states that the reason for this wording is because the sages did not wish to make both blessings the same, and furthermore, because this is the ending of the observance; *cf. Levush, Orach Chaim* 432. In *Yerushalmi, Berakhoth* 9:3 (66a), we find only this form; *cf. Rokeach* 363 (p. 254, end); Ramban, *Niddah* 51a.

5. Rabbinical commandment; *cf. Eruvin* 21b. For washing before prayer, see Psalms 26:6; *Berakhoth* 15a; *Yad, Tefillah* 4:2; *Teshuvoth Rashba* 191; *Beth Yosef, Orach Chaim* 4; *Orach Chaim* 4:1; *Kitzur Shulchan Arukh* 2:1; see also *Zohar* 1:184b. For washing before a meal, see *Chullin* 105a; *Yad, Berakhoth* 6:1; *Orach Chaim* 158:1. Similarly, for washing before eating wet fruit, see *Pesachim* 115a, *Tosafoth ad. loc. s.v. Kol; Yad, loc. cit.; Rif, Berakhoth* 41a; Rosh, *Chullin* 8:10; *Orach Chaim* 158:4. Some maintain that no blessing should be said when washing the hands for wet fruit; *cf. Tosafoth, Orach Chaim loc. cit.; Turey Zahav* 158:6; *Mishnah Berurah* 158:20. Others do require a blessing; *cf. Yad loc. cit.; Tur, Orach Chaim* 473; *HaGra, Orach Chaim* 158:4.

6. For washing the hands before prayer, see *Berakhoth* 60b; *Yad, Tefillah* 7:4; *Orach Chaim* 4:1, 46:1. For washing before eating, see *Yad, Berakhoth* 6:2; *Orach Chaim* 158:2. According to Rabbenu Tam, the noun form is used because the observance is done all at once. According to Riva, however, even though it is an individual obligation, the noun form is used, since the blessing is said after the washing; *cf. Tosafoth, Pesachim* 7b *s.v. Al, Sukkah* 39a *s.v. Over;* Rosh, *Pesachim* 1:10; Ran, *Pesachim* (Rif 4a) *s.v. Aval.* Nevertheless, since according to *Yad, Berakhoth* 6:2, the blessing is said before washing the hands, in *Yad, Berakhoth* 11:15, the reason given for the noun form is because there is no obligation to wash if one does not wish to eat.

7. Rabbinical commandment; *cf. Eruvin* 21b.

8. For *Eruv Chatzeroth*, see *Yad, Eruvin* 1:16; *Orach Chaim* 366:14, 395:1. See also *HaGra, Orach Chaim* 366:14, who interprets the expression in *Shabbath* 23a, "to bless over it," to refer to the blessing for the *Eruv* rather than that over the food. For *Eruv Techumin*, see *Yad, Eruvin* 6:24; *Orach Chaim* 415:4. However, Raavad *ad. loc.,* disputes this and writes that no blessing should be said in this case; *cf. Maggid Mishneh, Migdal Oz, ad. loc.; Magen Avraham, Pri Megadim* 415:4; *Mishnah Berurah* 415:13. For *Eruv Tavshilin,* see *Yad, Yom Tov* 6:8; *Orach Chaim* 527:12. In Mordecai, *Betza* 672; *Hagahoth Maimonioth, Yom Tov* 6:3 no. 2; *Or Zarua* 347; *HaGra, Orach Chaim* 527:2, this blessing is quoted from *Yerushalmi, Betza* 2. It is not found in our editions; *cf. Yeffeh Eynayim, Betza* 16b; *HaShmatoth MiYerushalmi, Betza* 2:1. According to both Rabbenu Tam and Riva, this is a classical case of the noun form, since the observance is a single act and can be done by proxy. In *Yad, Berakhoth* 11:14, this is used as an example of an observance which is not an individual obligation and is performed both for oneself and others. According to to our distinction, this blessing was put in the noun form in order to place the focus on the deed rather than the result. See also *Taamey HaMinhagim* 25 (p. 14).

9. Exodus 12:15; *Sefer HaMitzvoth,* Positive 156; *Sefer Mitzvoth Gadol,* Positive 39.

10. See *Pesachim* 7b, where this is the classical case, initiating the entire discussion of the form of blessings; *Tosafoth ad. loc. s.v. VeHilkhatha; Yad, Chametz U'Matzah* 3:6; *Orach Chaim* 432:1. This is also a classical case according to both Rabbenu Tam and Riva. However, Rosh, *Pesachim* 1:10, writes that the noun form is used to indicate that the actual commandment is not to be observed until much later

6. *Matzah*[11]   On the eating of *Matzah*[12]
7. *Bitters*[13]   On the eating of *Maror*[14]
8. Counting the *Omer*[15]   On the counting of the *Omer*[16]
9. Four Species of *Sukkoth*[17] On taking the *Lulav*[18]

(which is the case here where the leaven is not burned until the next morning); *cf. Korban Nethanel ad. loc.* no. 90. In *Yad, Berakhoth* 11:15, Rambam explains that the noun form is used when a blessing is recited after its observance has already been initiated. In the present case, the commandment is essentially fulfilled with one's resolve to destroy the leaven; *cf. Kesef Mishneh ad. loc.* 11:11. According to our distinction, the noun form is used because the focus is on the action. The result is already required by the commandment not to possess *Chametz* on Passover, and therefore, the commandment to destroy it focuses on the act itself.

11. Exodus 12:18; *Sefer HaMitzvoth,* Positive 157; *Sefer Mitzvoth Gadol,* Positive 40.
12. *Pesachim* 115a; *Yad, Chametz U'Matzah* 8:8; *Orach Chaim* 475:1. According to Rabbenu Tam, this is a classical example of a commandment which is fulfilled in a single act. According to Riva, however, this is an individual obligation, and therefore, the verbal form, "to eat *Matzah,*" must be used; *cf. Rosh, Pesachim* 1:10; *Ran, Pesachim* (Rif 4a) *s.v. VeKashia;* Raavad, *Berakhoth* 11:15. Several attempts to justify the noun form according to Riva are given in *Migdal Oz, Berakhoth* 11:15; *cf. Kesef Mishneh ad. loc.; Levush, Orach Chaim* 432; *Taamey HaMinhagim* 909 (p. 387, note 8); *Chok Yaakov, Orach Chaim* 475:1, citing *Teshuvoth Mahari Mintz* 77. According to our distinction, however, the noun form is used since the focus is on the act of eating.
13. Exodus 12:8. However, the commandment of *Maror* is part of the Passover sacrifice rather than a separate commandment; it is therefore only a rabbinical law nowadays; *cf. Pesachim* 120a; *Yad, Chametz U'Matzah* 7:12, *Korban Pesach* 8:2.
14. *Pesachim* 114b; *Yad, Chametz U'Matzah* 8:8; *Orach Chaim* 475:1. See note 12 for the form of the blessing. For the reason why no blessing is said over *Charoseth,* see *Lechem Mishneh, Chametz U'Matzah* 7:11; Rambam, *Tosefoth Yom Tov, Pesachim* 10:3; *Tur, Orach Chaim* 475.
15. Leviticus 23:15; *Sefer HaMitzvoth,* Positive 161; *Sefer Mitzvoth Gadol,* Positive 200.
16. *Yad, Tamidim U'Mussafim* 7:25; *Orach Chaim* 489:2. According to Rabbenu Tam, this is a classical example of an observance done in a single action. According to Riva, on the other hand, it is a personal obligation and should require the verbal form. Nevertheless, the noun form is used because the main observance is fulfilled with the bringing of the *Omer, cf. Ran, Pesachim* (Rif 4a) *s.v. VeIkha,* or because the reader usually says this blessing on behalf of the congregation; *Rosh, Pesachim* 1:10. According to our distinction, the noun form is used because the focus is on the act itself. For a discussion why a woman need not bless over the counting of the days before her immersion, see *Tosofoth, Kethuvoth* 72a *s.v. VeSafrah; Menachoth* 65b *s.v. U'Sefartem; Ran, Pesachim* (Rif 27b) *s.v. U'MeChayavin; Teshuvoth Radbaz* 1:27; *Beer Hetiv, Orach Chaim* 489:5; *Chok Yaakov* 489:6; *Pri Chadash, Pri Megadim, Mishbetzoth Zahav* 489:1. For a discussion whether it is a commandment at all, see *Sh'nei Luchoth HaB'rith, Shaar HaOthioth* 1:161b; *Teshuvoth Noda BeYehudah, Yoreh Deah* 2:123; *Teshuvoth Maharam Ben Barukh* 152; *Pith'chey Teshuvah, Yoreh Deah* 196:4.
17. Leviticus 23:40; *Sefer HaMitzvoth,* Positive 169; *Sefer Mitzvoth Gadol,* Positive 44.
18. *Pesachim* 7b; *Sukkah* 46a; *Yerushalmi, Berakhoth* 9:3 (66a); *Tosefta* 6:15; *Yad, Lulav* 7:6, *Berakhoth* 11:9; *Orach Chaim* 651:5. According to Rabbenu Tam, this is a classical case of a commandment done all at once, from which this rule is derived; *cf. Tosafoth, Sukkah* 39a *s.v. Over.* According to Riva, however, the noun form is used because

10. *Megillath Esther*[19]	On reading the *Megillah*[20]
11. Ritual Slaughter[21]	On the *Shechitah*[22]
12. Covering the Blood[23]	On covering the blood with dust[24]
13. Circumcision[25]	On the circumcision[26]

the blessing is usually said after one has lifted the *Lulav; cf. Tosafoth, Pesachim* 7b *s.v. BeIdna;* Rosh, *Pesachim* 1:10. *Yad, Berakhoth* 11:15, gives the same reason, but writes that if one says the blessing before lifting the *Lulav,* he should use the verbal form, "to take the *Lulav*"; *cf.* Raavad *ad.loc.; Kesef Mishneh, Lulav* 7:6. According to our distinction, this is the classical case; see 10:7, note 24.

19. Rabbinical law; *cf.* Esther 9:20, 9:32; *Eruvin* 2b (end); *Tosefta, Megillah* 2:4; Ramban on *Sefer HaMitzvoth, Shoresh* 1 (9a).
20. *Megillah* 4:1 (21a); Rambam, Bertenoro, *ad. loc.,* 21b; *Yad, Megillah* 1:3; *Orach Chaim* 692:1. According to Rabbenu Tam, the noun form is used because the entire reading of the *Megillah* is considered a single uninterrupted act, in contrast to the *Hallel* which is interrupted by the responses. Likewise, according to Riva, it is not completely an individual obligation, since one can fulfill his obligation by hearing it from another; *cf.* Rosh, *Pesachim* 1:10. The reason why the blessing is on the reading, rather than on the hearing as in the case of the *Shofar,* is either because it must be read from a proper scroll, Ran, *Pesachim* (Rif 4a) *s.v. VeTu,* or because it can also be read silently; *cf.* Abudarham, quoted in *Taamey HaMinhagim* 872 (p. 374). According to our distinction, the primary focus is on the act of reading. Some authorities maintain that a blessing must also be said when reading the other scrolls on the holidays; *cf. Sofrim* 14:3; *Nachalath Yaakov, ad. loc.;* Mordecai, *Megillah* 783; HaGra, *Orach Chaim* 490:9. The majority of later authorities do not require a blessing; *cf. Teshuvoth Rama* 35; *Orach Chaim* 490:19 in *Hagah; Turey Zahav* 490:6; *Magen Avraham, Beer Hetiv* 490:9; *"Rav" Shulchan Arukh* 490:19; *Mishnah Berurah* 490:17. Although *Sofrim ad. loc.* omits Ecclesiastes from the list of scrolls requiring a blessing, it is added in *Nus'chaoth HaGra ad. loc.; cf. Machtzith HaShekel* 490:9; HaGra *ad. loc.*
21. Deuteronomy 12:13; *Sefer HaMitzvoth,* Positive 146; *Sefer Mitzvoth Gadol,* Positive 103.
22. *Yerushalmi, Berakhoth* 9:3 (66a); *Tosefta, Berakhoth* 6:16; *Yad, Shechitah* 1:2; *Yoreh Deah* 19:1. According to both Rabbenu Tam and Riva, this is a classical example of the noun form, since the observance is a single act and not an individual obligation. In *Yad, Berakhoth* 11:15, it is given as an example of an observance which is only required as a means to an end; *cf. Kesef Mishneh ad. loc.* 11:11. According to our distinction, there is a separate negative commandment requiring the result, and therefore, the positive commandment focuses on the action.
23. Leviticus 17:13; *Sefer HaMitzvoth* 147; *Sefer Mitzvoth Gadol* 104.
24. *Yerushalmi, Berakhoth* 9:3 (66a); *Tosefta* 6:15; *Yad, Shechitah* 14:1; *Yoreh Deah* 28:2. This is also a classical example both according to Rabbenu Tam and Riva. Similarly, according to our distinction, the focus is on the act; *cf. Chullin* 87a; *Yad, Shechitah* 14:7; *Yoreh Deah* 28:11; *Magen Avraham* 586:6.
25. Genesis 17:10, Leviticus 12:3; *Sefer HaMitzvoth,* Positive 215; *Sefer Mitzvoth Gadol,* Positive 28.
26. *Pesachim* 7b; *Shabbath* 137b; *Menachoth* 42a; *Yerushalmi, Berakhoth* 9:3 (66a); *Tosefta* 6:17; *Yad, Milah* 3:1; *Yoreh Deah* 265:1. According to both Rabbenu Tam and Riva, this is a classical case of the noun form; *cf. Levush, Yoreh Deah* 265:1; *Taamey HaMinhagim* 909 (p. 387). According to *Yad, Berakhoth* 11:12-13, *Milah* 3:1; *Yoreh Deah* 265:2, on the other hand, the noun form is only used when one circumcises another man's child. When circumcising one's own son, the verb form, "to circumcise the son," must be used. Although this is evidenced from *Pesachim* 7b, still, Rashi *ad.*

14. First-Born Redemption[27]   On redeeming the first-born[28]
15. Firstling Ass Redemption[29] On redeeming the firstling ass[30]
16. Immersion[31]   On the immersion[32]
17. Vessel Immersion[33]   On the immersion of vessels[34]
18. Redeeming *Ma'aser*[35]   On redeeming *Ma'aser Sheni*[36]

loc. s.v. VeHilkhetha; Ran (Rif 3b) *s.v. VeKashia; Hagahoth Maimonioth, Milah* 3:1 no. 2, indicate that this is only according to Rav Pappi who uses the verb form for *Chametz*, but not according to Rav Pappa who uses the noun form. For this reason, *Hagah, Yoreh Deah* 265:2, decides to use the noun form in all cases. Nevertheless, see *Beth Yosef, Yoreh Deah* 265, who defends the position of the *Yad*. According to our criterion, the noun form is used since the focus is on the deed rather than on the result.

27. Numbers 18:15, Leviticus 15:16; *Sefer HaMitzvoth,* Positive 80; *Sefer Mitzvoth Gadol,* Positive 144.

28. *Pesachim* 121b; *Yad, Bikkurim* 11:5; *Yoreh Deah* 305:10. According to both Rabbenu Tam and Riva, this is a classical case of the noun form, since it is done all at once and can be done by proxy; *cf. Turey Zahav, Yoreh Deah* 305:8. The accepted opinion is that the noun form is used without distinction whether one redeems oneself or another person; *cf. Yoreh Deah* 305:10 in *Hagah; Teshuvoth Rivash* 131; *Beer HaGolah* 305:17. However, according to *Yad loc. cit.,* one who redeems himself must use the verb form, "to redeem the first-born"; *cf. HaGra, Yoreh Deah* 305:15. According to our distinction, the noun form indicates that the primary obligation is on the act of redemption, to be performed by the father.

29. Exodus 13:13; *Sefer HaMitzvoth,* Positive 81; *Sefer Mitzvoth Gadol,* Positive 145.

30. *Yoreh Deah* 321:6; *Tosafoth, Bekhoroth* 11a *s.v. VeHilkhatha;* Rosh, *Bekhoroth* 1:14. Nevertheless, we do not say a blessing when giving other firstlings to the Cohen, since they are never actually in the possession of the giver; *cf. Perishah, Yoreh Deah* 321; *Turey Zahav* 321:7.

31. Leviticus 15:16; *Sefer HaMitzvoth,* Positive 109; *Sefer Mitzvoth Gadol,* Positive 248.

32. *Berakhoth* 51a; *Pesachim* 7b; *Yad, Berakhoth* 11:7; *Yoreh Deah* 200:1, 268:2. According to Rabbenu Tam, this is a classical case because it is all done in a single action. According to Riva, however, the noun form is used even though personal immersion cannot be done by proxy. He explains that since the immersion of vessels can be done by anyone, the noun form was used for all cases; *cf.* Rosh, *Pesachim* 1:10. Furthermore, in the case of a proselyte, the noun form must be used because the blessing cannot be recited until after the immersion. It is for this reason that the noun form is always used; *cf.* Rosh *loc. cit.;* Ran, *Pesachim* (Rif 4a) *s.v. Aval; Yad, Berakhoth* 11:15. According to our criterion, the result of immersion is already required by the various laws of purity; the specific positive commandment therefore focuses on the act itself.

33. Numbers 31:23; *Avodah Zarah* 5:11 (75b); *Yad, Maakhaloth Assuroth* 17:3; *Yoreh Deah* 120:1.

34. Rosh, *Pesachim* 1:10; Mordecai, *Pesachim* 538, *Avodah Zarah* 849 (note); *Yoreh Deah* 120:3.

35. Deuteronomy 14:26.

36. *Yerushalmi, Demai* 1:4 (3b); *Yad, Maaser Sheni* 4:3; *Rokeach* 363 (p. 353); Rash, *Maaser Sheni* 5:11. Also mentioned is the blessing "on profaning the second tithe." According to Rabbenu Tam, this is a classical example of a precept accomplished in a single action; *cf. Rokeach loc. cit.*

19. Eating Passover Sacrifice[37] On eating the Passover sacrifice[38]
20. Eating Festival Sacrifice[39] On eating the sacrifice[40]
21. Counting Jubilee[41] On counting the *Yovel*[42]

---

37. Exodus 12:8; *Sefer HaMitzvoth,* Positive 56; *Sefer Mitzvoth Gadol,* Positive 225.
38. *Yad, Chametz U'Matzah* 8:7. However, many others use the verb form, "to eat the *Pesach*"; *cf. Tosefta Pesachim* 10:8; Ran, *Pesachim* (Rif 4a) *s.v. VeKashia;* Rambam, Bertenoro, on *Pesachim* 10:9 (120a); Rashbam *ibid. s.v. Birkath;* Rashi, *Zevachim* 37a *s.v. Berakh.* Furthermore, Rashi, *Pesachim* 121a *s.v. Birkath,* has the reading "on the eating of *Pesachim.*"
39. Leviticus 7:15-16.
40. See note 38. According to Rashi *loc. cit.,* the blessing is "on the eating of *Shelamim.*" See *Tosefta, Berakhoth* 7:23.
41. Leviticus 25:8; *Sefer HaMitzvoth,* Positive 140; *Sefer Mitzvoth Gadol,* Positive 150.
42. *Tosafoth, Menachoth* 65b *s.v. U'Sefartem.* However, the wording of the blessing is not mentioned.

ELEVEN
INDIVIDUAL RESPONSIBILITY

11:1   The negative commandments of the Torah apply to men and women alike. The Torah thus equates the two in terms of personal responsibility: "If a man or woman sins against his fellow man... they must confess the sin they have committed and make restitution" (Numbers 5:6-7).[1] A woman is accordingly required to refrain from sin and heed all negative commandments just like a man.[2]

11:2   There are three exceptional negative commandments which do not apply to women.[3] Women are not enjoined to refrain from rounding the corners of the hair,[4] from shaving the corners of the beard,[5] nor, in the case of a female Cohen, from defiling themselves by contact with the dead.[6]

11:3   Women and men are equally responsible to observe any positive commandment, on the condition that its performance is not restricted to a specific time. This is because a woman's schedule does not always permit interruption,[7] and she is therefore exempt

1.   *Kiddushin* 35a; *Pesachim* 43a; *Sukkah* 28a; *Yevamoth* 84b; *Bava Kama* 15a; *Temurah* 2b; *Niddah* 48b; *Yerushalmi, Bava Kama* 1:3 (6b); *BaMidbar Rabbah* 8:5.
2.   *Kiddushin* 1:7 (29a); *Yad, Avodath Kokhavim* 12:3.
3.   *Ibid.; Tosefta, Sotah* 2:8.
4.   Leviticus 19:27.
5.   *Ibid.*
6.   This is based on Leviticus 21:1-2 which states, "God told Moses to declare the following to the sons of Aaron the priest: Let no priest defile himself [by contact with] the dead among his people, except for such close blood relatives as his mother, father, son, daughter or brother..." The Talmud (*Kiddushin* 35a) learns that the phrase "the sons of Aaron" comes to exclude "the daughters of Aaron." The concept of defilement by contact with a corpse is based on Numbers 19:11: "If one has contact with any dead human being, he shall become ritually defiled for seven days."
7.   *Taamey HaMinhagim* 788 (p. 346), quoting Abudarham.

from positive commandments which must be performed at fixed times.[8]

11:4 Nevertheless, there are six exceptional positive commandments having fixed times which women must keep. All of these have special reasons. [They are listed in Table 11:1, at the end of this chapter.][9]

11:5 Although women are exempt from having to perform many commandments, they are permitted to observe them on a voluntary basis.[10] They may even recite the blessings which are associated with such commandments,[11] although some authorities maintain that it is preferable not to do so.[12]

11:6 A proselyte or convert is considered exactly the same as another Jew[13] and has exactly the same responsibilities.[14] As soon as a proselyte is accepted into the Jewish fold,[15] he is considered a child of Abraham, as God promised, "No longer shall you be called Abram. Your name shall become Abraham, for I have established you as the father of a horde of nations" (Genesis 17:5).[16]

11:7 A proselyte is considered like a newly born babe,[17] and is therefore not morally accountable for any sin or crime committed

---

8. *Kiddushin* 1:7 (29a); *Berakhoth* 20b; *Shabbath* 62a; *Eruvin* 27a; *Chagigah* 4a; *Rosh HaShanah* 30a; *Menachoth* 43a; *Tosefta, Sotah* 2:8; *Tosefta, Kiddushin* 1:8; *Yerushalmi, Berakhoth* 3:3 (25a); *Yerushalmi, Pesachim* 8:1 (58a); *Yad loc. cit.* Regarding rabbinical laws having set times, see *Tosafoth, Berakhoth* 20b s.v. *BeTefillah.*
9. *Yad loc. cit.; Kesef Mishneh ad. loc.* .
10. See above, 10:35, note 104. Others, however, forbid this; *cf.* Rashi, *Rosh HaShanah* 33a s.v. *Ha;* Maharsha, *Peney Yehoshua, ad. loc.;* Rashi, *Eruvin* 96a s.v. *VeLo; Tosafoth ibid. s.v. Mikhol; Teshuvoth Shaagath Aryeh* 104; Maharatz Chajas, *Chagigah* 4a, 16a, *Sukkah* 2b.
11. See above, 10:35, note 105.
12. *Yeshuoth Yaakov* 17:1; *Birkey Yosef* 654:2, cited in *Taamey HaMinhagim* 456 (note, p. 201); Raavad, *Tzitzith* 3:9; *Hagahoth Maimonioth ad. loc.*
13. *Tosefta, Nedarim* 2:5; *Yad, Nedarim* 9:23; *Yoreh Deah* 217:42; *Teshuvoth Shaagath Aryeh* 49.
14. *Yerushalmi, Shekalim* 1:4 (5a); *Sifra* on Leviticus 1:2 (4c), 17:3 (84c), 17:8 (84d); *Or HaChaim* on Leviticus 17:3; *Yevamoth* 47a; *Yad, Issurey Biyah* 13:14, 14:1; *Yoreh Deah* 268:2.
15. That is, with immersion and circumcision; see Volume 1, 5:14.
16. *Yerushalmi, Bikkurim* 1:4 (3b); *Tosafoth, Bava Bathra* 81a s.v. *LeMiut; Yad, Bikkurim* 4:3; Rosh, *Nedarim* 30b s.v. *Assur;* Maharatz Chajas *ad. loc.; Yoreh Deah* 217:40; *Turey Zahav* 217:35; Maharatz Chajas, *Chagigah* 3a.
17. *Yevamoth* 22b, 48b, 62a, 97b; *Bekhoroth* 47a.

before his conversion,[18] although in some cases legal and criminal responsibility may remain.[19] However, a proselyte can fulfill the commandment to have children[20] with those born before his conversion.[21]

11:8 In order for a person to have any religious responsibility, he must understand what he is doing, and for whom he is doing it, as the Torah states, "You must realize that I, God, am setting you aside and making you holy" (Exodus 31:13).[22] Therefore, one who is so feeble minded[23] or psychotic[24] that he exhibits a usual[25] erratic,[26] violent,[27] or confused[28] behavior, or an otherwise total lack of responsibility,[29] is exempt from all religious, moral, and legal responsibilities.[30]

11:9 An individual who suffers periods of temporary insanity, but is otherwise not affected,[31] has the status[32] and responsibilities[33] of a normal person when not suffering from a spell. However, during periods of temporary insanity, he is considered irresponsible, and any observance performed at such time is considered invalid.[34] Furthermore, although such a person has no legal

18. *Yevamoth* 48b; Rashi *ad. loc. s.v. KeKatan;* Maharatz Chajas *ad. loc.; Tosafoth, Sanhedrin* 71b *s.v. Ben Noah; Teshuvoth Yad Eliahu* 40; *Teshuvoth Beth Yaakov* 3; *Sefer Chasidim* 691; *Teshuvoth Chelkath Yoav* 2:14.
19. *Sanhedrin* 71b; *Yad, Melakhim* 10:4; *Sefer Chasidim* 691; *Teshuvoth Chaim Sha'al* 49; *Teshuvoth Chavath Yair* 79; *Teshuvoth Shevuth Yaakov, Choshen Mishpat* 1:177.
20. Genesis 1:22; *Sefer HaMitzvoth,* Positive Commandment 212; *Sefer Mitzvoth Gadol,* Positive Commandment 49; *Chinukh* 1; *Evven HaEzer* 1:1.
21. *Yevamoth* 62a; Maharatz Chajas *ad. loc.; Yad, Ishuth* 15:6; *Evven HaEzer* 1:7; *Turey Aven, Rosh HaShanah* 28a; *Teshuvoth Noda BeYehudah, Evven HaEzer* 1:6.
22. *Mekhilta ad. loc.* (103b).
23. *Yad, Eduth* 9:19; *Choshen Mishpat* 35:10; *Sefer Meirath Eynayim (Sema)* 35:21; *Sefer Halttur* 100, from *Teshuvoth HaRif.*
24. *Yad, Eduth* 9:9; *Choshen Mishpat* 35:8; *Yad Avraham, Yoreh Deah* 1:5.
25. HaGra, *Choshen Mishpat* 35:14, from *Kethuvoth* 21a; *Sifethey Cohen, Yoreh Deah* 1:23.
26. Such as sleeping in a cemetery; *Chagigah* 3b; *Tosefta, Terumoth* 1:4; *Yerushalmi, Terumoth* 1:1 (2a); *Yerushalmi, Gittin* 7:1 (38b); *Yoreh Deah* 1:5.
27. Such as tearing his clothing; *ibid.*
28. HaGra, *Choshen Mishpat* 35:13, from *Niddah* 13b.
29. Such as losing what is given to him; see note 26.
30. Rashi, *Chagigah* 3b *s.v. Aizehu;* Maharatz Chajas *ad. loc.; Tosafoth ibid. s.v. Derekh; Pri Megadim,* introduction 2:6; Maharatz Chajas, *Niddah* 45b.
31. HaGra, *Choshen Mishpat* 35:18, from *Gittin* 7:1 (67b); Rashi *ad. loc. s.v. Bodkim.*
32. *Yevamoth* 31a (end); *Tosefta, Terumoth* 1:3; *Yerushalmi, Gittin* 7:1 (38b); *Yad, Eduth* 9:9; *Choshen Mishpat* 35:9; *Evven HaEzer* 121:3.
33. *Rosh HaShanah* 28a; *Turey Aven,* Maharatz Chajas, *ad. loc.*
34. *Yad, Chametz U'Matzah* 6:3; *Orach Chaim* 475:5; *Mishnah Berurah, Shaar HaTziun* 475:39.

responsibility for actions performed while temporarily insane, he does have a moral responsibility to make restitution for any damage done. The same is true of damage done while drunk.[35]

11:10 Understanding religious responsibility involves the ability to grasp verbal concepts, as the Torah states, "You must listen to His commandments" (Exodus 15:26).[36] Therefore, because a deaf mute has no understanding of verbal concepts,[37] he is exempt from all religious[38] and legal responsibility.[39] This is true even if he is of normal or superior intelligence[40] and can communicate in writing.[41]

11:11 A person who is only deaf or only mute can comprehend verbal concepts and is therefore considered perfectly normal and fully responsible.[42] Similarly, one who can hear even slightly is not considered deaf.[43]

11:12 A person who is born normal but becomes a deaf mute later in life is assumed to lose his verbal understanding[44] and is therefore exempt from all religious responsibility.[45] Some maintain that this is questionable,[46] and therefore, the stricter course should be taken whenever possible.[47]

11:13 Although the mentally deficient and deaf mutes are not religiously responsible, it is forbidden to actively cause them to

35. *Sefer Chasidim* 692.
36. *Yerushalmi, Terumoth* 1:2 (4a); Rabbenu Chananel, *Megillah* 20a. *Cf.* Sforno on Deuteronomy 6:4.
37. *Chagigah* 2b; *Yevamoth* 99b; *Gittin* 23a; *Menachoth* 93a; *Arakhin* 5b.
38. *Chagigah* 1:1 (2a); Rashi *ad. loc. s.v. Cheresh; Chullin* 1:1 (2a); *Yerushalmi, Terumoth* 1:1 (1a); *Parah* 5:4; *Makhshirim* 7:1, 8:3; *Tosafoth, Chullin* 12b-13a *s.v. VeTiva'ey; Yoreh Deah* 1:5; *Orach Chaim* 55:8.
39. *Bava Kama* 39a; *Yad, Nizkey Mamon* 6:3, *Chovel* 4:20; *Choshen Mishpat* 406:5, 424:8.
40. *Teshuvoth Tzemach Tzedek* 77, cited in *Pri Megadim,* introduction 2:3 (end).
41. *Evven HaEzer* 120:5, 121:6; *Choshen Mishpat* 235:17.
42. *Terumoth* 1:2; *Tosefta* 1:2; *Chagigah* 2b; *Gittin* 71a; *Niddah* 13b; *Yerushalmi, Terumoth* 1:1 (1b); *Yerushalmi, Yevamoth* 12:4 (68b); *Yad, Ishuth* 2:26, *Gerushin* 2:16; *Mekhirah* 29:2; *Orach Chaim* 55:8; *Evven HaEzer* 121:6; *Choshen Mishpat* 235:18.
43. *Choshen Mishpat* 235:19, from *Teshuvoth HaRosh* 85 (end).
44. *Beth Yosef, Evven HaEzer* 121, cited in *Pri Megadim,* introduction 2:4.
45. *Sifethey Cohen, Yoreh Deah* 1:22; *Pri Megadim ad. loc.,* introduction 2:4; *Biur Halakhah* 55:8 *s.v. Hu; cf. Tosefta, Terumoth* 1:1 (end); *Gittin* 71b; *Yevamoth* 110b, 112b; *Yerushalmi, Terumoth* 1:1 (1b); *Yerushalmi, Gittin* 7:1 (39a end); *Evven HaEzer* 121:6; *Pith'chey Teshuvah* 121:5.
46. *Cf.* Rambam, Bertenoro, on *Terumoth* 1:2.
47. *Pri Megadim,* introduction 2:5.

violate any commandment. However, if they violate any law on their own accord, an onlooker is not required to stop them.[48]

11:14 A minor is exempt from all religious and legal responsibility.[49] However, a child who is intelligent enough to understand the issues at stake does have some moral responsibility.[50]

11:15 A boy remains a minor until he attains adolescence at the age of 13,[51] when he becomes a *Bar Mitzvah,* literally "son of the commandment."[52] This age is given by tradition[53] as the time when the first signs of physical maturity appear,[54] and when the child's mental development is complete enough to understand his religious responsibility.[55]

11:16 Since a girl matures earlier than a boy, both physically and mentally,[56] she attains adolescence a year younger at the age of 12.[57]

11:17 When a child's age is not known, he attains puberty as soon

48. *Maggid Mishneh, Shabbath* 20:7; *Magen Avraham* 266:8; *"Rav" Shulchan Arukh* 266:14; *Mishnah Berurah* 266:10; *Teshuvoth Maharil* 196, cited in *Tevuoth Shor* 1:49; *Pri Megadim,* introduction 2:1; *Mishbetzoth Zahav* 343:1; *Sifethey Da'ath* 1:27. *Cf. Tosafoth, Shabbath* 153a *s.v. Mi.*
49. See note 38. *Cf. Sifra* on Leviticus 17:14 (84c).
50. *Sefer Chasidim* 543; *Makor Chesed ad. loc. Cf.* Rosh, *Gittin* 9:11 (end), quoting Rabbenu Chananel; Maharsha, *Berakhoth* 31b *s.v. HaMorah; Peneach Raze,* Riva, on Genesis 38:7. See below, 11:27*ff.*
51. *Avoth* 5:21; *Niddah* 5:6 (45b), 46a; *Yoma* 82a; *Yad, Ishuth* 2:10; *Orach Chaim* 55:9, 616:2.
52. *Cf. Orach Chaim* 225:2 in *Hagah.*
53. See *Teshuvoth HaRosh* 16:1; Rashi, *Avoth* 5:21; *Chayay Adam* 66:1; *Mishnah Berurah* 55:40; Maharatz Chajas, *Yoma* 82a, *Sukkah* 5b, *Niddah* 45a; *cf. Niddah* 32a; *Teshuvoth Chavath Yair* 192, all of whom state that it is of Sinaic origin. Some find a hint for the age of 13 from the fact that Levi was called a man at this age; *cf.* Rashi, *Machzor Vitri,* on *Avoth* 5:21; *Bereshith Rabbah* 80:9; *Yalkut Shimoni* (1:135) on Genesis 34:25. Others obtain it from the numerical value of the word *Zu* (זו) in Isaiah 43:21; *cf. Magen Avoth,* on *Avoth loc. cit.* See also Rashi, *Baaley Tosafoth,* on Genesis 25:27; *Taamey HaMinhagim* 2:76 (p. 525).
54. *Niddah* 6:11; Rashi on *Avoth* 5:21.
55. Rosh, *Gittin* 9:11 (end). It is therefore said that a person first receives his Good Urge *(Yetzer Tov)* at this age; *cf. Avoth DeRabbi Nathan* 16:2; *Koheleth Rabbah* 4:15; *Midrash Tehillim* 9:5; *Yalkut Shimoni* 2:971; Rashi on Ecclesiastes 4:13. *Cf. Pirkey Rabbi Eliezer* 26 (60b).
56. *Niddah* 45b; *Bereshith Rabbah* 18:1; Rambam on *Yoma* 8:4.
57. *Yad, Ishuth* 2:1; see note 51.

as the first signs of physical maturity appear,[58] that is, the first adolescent growth of hair on the body.[59]

11:18 However, when a child's age is known, the ordinary signs of physical maturity can be ignored. If the physical signs appear before puberty is reached, they are assumed to be spurious,[60] while as soon as this age is reached, the physical signs are assumed to be present.[61]

11:19 It is customary to solemnize a boy's coming of age with a *Bar Mitzvah* celebration and feast.[62] The boy is usually called up to the Torah reading and asked to lead the service as a sign of having reached adulthood.[63] Because he is being welcomed as an adult member of the Jewish people, a *Bar Mitzvah* boy's Torah reading takes precedence over all others except that of a bridegroom.[64] After the *Bar Mitzvah* boy is called up to the Torah, it is customary for the father to say, "Blessed is He who has absolved me from responsibility for this child's punishment."[65]

11:20 Although it is not traditional to celebrate a girl's coming of age,[66] some celebration of her becoming a *Bath Mitzvah*, "daughter of the commandment," has become customary.

11:21 All calculations regarding a child's birthday are made according

58. *Mishnah Berurah* 55:4. *Cf. Kiddushin* 63b; *Tosafoth ad. loc. s.v. Beni; Evven HaEzer* 155:14 in *Hagah; Beth Sh'muel* 155:22; *Pith'chey Teshuvah* 155:7; *Mishneh LeMelekh, Ishuth* 2:19; *Teshuvoth Rashba* 1216.
59. Usually given as the first two hairs; *cf. Niddah* 6:1 (52a). With regard to the size of these hairs, *cf. Niddah* 6:12 (52b); *Yad, Ishuth* 2:16, *Parah Adumah* 1:4, *Tumath Tzaraath* 2:1; *Evven HaEzer* 155:18. Whether childbirth is a sign of maturity, *cf. Yevamoth* 12b; *Yad, Ishuth* 2:9; *Evven HaEzer* 155:12; *Beth Sh'muel* 155:18.
60. *Kiddushin* 16b; *Niddah* 46a; *Yad, Ishuth* 2:18; *Evven HaEzer* 155:14.
61. *Yevamoth* 13a; *Niddah* 46a; *Yad, Ishuth* 2:20; *Evven HaEzer* 155:20; *Chayay Adam* 66:1; *Mishnah Berurah* 55:50, 616:12. *Cf. Orach Chaim* 55:5 in *Hagah*, from *Maharik Shoresh* 49; *HaGra ad. loc.; Yerushalmi, Berakhoth* 7:2 (53a); *Bereshith Rabbah* 91:3; *Matnath Kehunah ad. loc. s.v. Ein*, quoting Rashi.
62. *Yam Shel Shlomo, Bava Kama* 7:37, from *Bava Kama* 87a; *Magen Avraham* 225:4; *Machtzith HaShekel ad. loc.; Kitzur Shulchan Arukh* 61:8; *Mishnah Berurah* 225:6; *Taamey HaMinhagim* 503 (p. 385). *Cf. Sofrim* 18:5.
63. *Magen Avraham, Kitzur Shulchan Arukh, Mishnah Berurah, loc. cit.*
64. *Magen Avraham* 282:18 (end); *Kitzur Shulchan Arukh* 78:11.
65. *Orach Chaim* 225:2, from *Bereshith Rabbah* 63:14; *Yalkut Shimoni* (1:110) on Genesis 25:27; *Magen Avraham* 225:5; *Chokhmath Shlomo, Eliahu Rabbah, Levush, ibid.; Chayay Adam* 65:3; *Kitzur Shulchan Arukh* 78:11; *Taamey HaMinhagim* 206 (p. 94).
66. *Pri Megadim, Eshel Avraham* 225:5; *Taamey HaMinhagim* 107 (p. 95).

to the Hebrew calendar, which is based on the intercalation of the solar and lunar cycles.[67] Even in a leap year, when an extra month is added, the child must wait until the month in which he was born.[68]

11:22 A child who was born during the month of Adar in an ordinary year, but becomes a *Bar Mitzvah* in a leap year when Adar is doubled, celebrates his birthday in the second Adar.[69] However, if he was born in the first Adar of a leap year, his birthday is always celebrated in the first Adar.[70]

11:23 It is therefore possible for a younger boy to become *Bar Mitzvah* before an older one. If both children are born in a leap year — one at the end of the first Adar, and the other at the beginning of the second — then if the 13th year is not a leap year, both *Bar Mitzvah* rites will fall in the same month, with that of the second child occurring first.[71]

11:24 Although a minor has no religious responsibility, his father is required to provide him with a religious education, as we are commanded, "Teach your children to speak of these [words of Torah], when you are at home, when traveling on the road, when you lie down and when you get up" (Deuteronomy 11:19).[72]

---

67. *Yad, Ishuth* 2:21. *Cf. Rosh HaShanah* 6b; *Yoma* 65b; *Arakhin* 31b; *Sifra* on Leviticus 25:30 (108d); *Yad, Shemittah* 12:1, *Bekhoroth* 1:12; *Yoreh Deah* 306:10.

68. *Orach Chaim* 55:9; *HaGra ad. loc.,* from *Hagahoth Mordecai, Yevamoth* 115-116, from *Bava Metzia* 8:8 (102a); *Yerushalmi, Kethuvoth* 1:2 (4a); *Yerushalmi, Nedarim* 6:8 (23b); *Yerushalmi, Sanhedrin* 1:2 (6a); *Yalkut Shimoni* (2:775) on Psalms 57:3; *Maggid Mishneh, Ishuth* 2:21; *Kol Yehudah* (on *Kuzari*) 3:41 (50a); Ridbaz, *Yerushalmi, Megillah* 7a. *Cf. Nedarim* 8:8 (63a); Ran *ad. loc.*

69. *Yerushalmi, Megillah* 1:5 (7a); *Sefer Chasidim* 55:10 in *Hagah; Pri Chadash ibid.; Teshuvoth Mahari Mintz* 9; *Teshuvoth Chatham Sofer, Orach Chaim* 163. Some dispute this and maintain that it should be celebrated in the first Adar; *cf. Teshuvoth Rash HaLevi, Orach Chaim* 16, cited in *Pri Chadash loc. cit.* See also *Nedarim* 8:8 (63a); *Tosefoth Yom Tov ad. loc.; Yad, Nedarim* 10:6; *Yoreh Deah* 220:8; *Evven HaEzer* 126:6 in *Hagah; Megillah* 1:4 (6b); *Yad, Megillah* 1:12; *Tur, Orach Chaim* 688; *Tosafoth, Rosh HaShanah* 19b *s.v. Adar.*

70. *Levush, Eliahu Rabbah, Orach Chaim* 685; *Beer Hetiv* 55:11; *Shaarey Teshuvah ibid.; Chayay Adam* 66:1; *Kitzur Shulchan Arukh* 15:2; *Mishnah Berurah* 55:43; *Teshuvoth Shevuth Yaakov* 1:9; *Teshuvoth Meil Tzedakah* 21; *Teshuvoth Beth Ephraim, Evven HaEzer* 59. However *Magen Avraham* 55:10 disputes this, and maintains that it is always in the second Adar.

71. *Orach Chaim* 55:10, from *Arakhin* 31b; *cf. Yad, Shemittah* 12:6, *Bekhoroth* 1:12; *Yoreh Deah* 306:11; *Sifethey Cohen* 306:16; *Turey Zahav* 306:8.

72. *Kiddushin* 29b; *Bava Bathra* 21a; *Yad, Talmud Torah* 1:1; *Sefer Mitzvoth Gadol,* Positive

11:25 The parents[73] of a minor child[74] are likewise required to instruct him in religious observance,[75] as we are taught, "Educate a child in the way he should go, and when he is old, he will not depart from it" (Proverbs 22:6).[76]

11:26 A child should be introduced to a religious observance as soon as he is physically and mentally capable of doing it properly.[77] Nevertheless, a child's parents are required to keep him from violating any religious prohibitions as soon as he can understand what they are telling him.[78]

11:27 Just as parents are required to instruct their children religiously, so are they required to instruct and discipline them morally.[79]

11:28 As soon as a child begins to talk, he or she should be taught simple prayers and Biblical verses.[80] Children should also be taught

Commandment 12; *Yoreh Deah* 245:1. *Cf.* Deuteronomy 6:7; *Sefer HaMitzvoth,* Positive Commandment 11; *Chinukh* 419.

73. Including the mother; *cf. Sukkah* 2b; Rashi, *Chagigah* 2a *s.v. Aizehu;* Rashba, Meiri, *Yoma* 82a; *Eliahu Rabbah, Bikkurey Yaakov, Orach Chaim* 640; *Orach Mishor, Nazir* 28a; *Machtzith HaShekel* 343:1, 616:2, 640:3; *Chikrey Lev* 70; *Mishnah Berurah* 343:3, 616:5, 640:5; *Chayay Adam* 66:2. Others maintain that training does not include the mother; *cf. Nazir* 29a; *Tosafoth Yeshenim, Yoma* 82a *s.v. Ben; Terumath HaDeshen* 94; *Teshuvoth Maharam DeKrakow* 200; *Magen Avraham* 343:1, 616:2, 640:3; *"Rav" Shulchan Arukh* 343:4, 616:4; *cf. Pri Megadim,* introduction 2:10. Compare *Kiddushin* 29b; *Yad, Talmud Torah* 1:1; *Yoreh Deah* 246:6 in *Hagah.* See also *Yad, Maakhaloth Assuroth* 17:28, *Avel* 3:12; *Orach Chaim* 343:1.

74. Including both boys and girls; *Yoma* 8:4 (82a); *Nazir* 29a; *Tosafoth ad. loc.* 28b *s.v. Ben; Tosafoth Yeshenim loc. cit.; Chayay Adam* 66:2; *Kitzur Shulchan Arukh* 165:1; HaGra, *Orach Chaim* 616:2; *Pri Megadim,* introduction 2:9. See Rambam on *Nazir* 4:6; Maharatz Chajas, *Nazir* 29a, that although an exception is made for girls, this is not a question of religious training.

75. *Yoma* 8:4 (82a); *Sukkah* 2:8 (28a), 3:15 (42a); *Yerushalmi* 3:12 (17b); *Arakhin* 2b; *Tosefta, Chagigah* 1:3; *Yad, Tzitzith* 3:9, *Tefillin* 4:13, *Shevithath Assor* 2:10, *Chametz U'Matzah* 6:10, *Sukkah* 6:1, *Lulav* 7:19, *Megillah* 1:1, *Shavuoth* 12:7; *Orach Chaim* 17:3, 37:3, 616:2, 657:1, 677:12, 689:1; *Yoreh Deah* 233:1 in *Hagah.*

76. Rambam on *Yoma* 8:4; *Yad, Maakhaloth Assuroth* 17:28; *Chayay Adam* 66:1; *Kitzur Shulchan Arukh* 165:1; *Mishnah Berurah* 343:2. This is a rabbinical law; *cf. Sukkah* 18b; Rashi, *Sukkah* 42a *s.v. Chayav. Cf. Makkoth* 8b, from Proverbs 29:17.

77. *Tosafoth, Sukkah* 28b *s.v. Kan BeKatan, Arakhin* 2b *s.v. SheHigiyah;* Ran, *Sukkah* (Rif 13a) *s.v. Haikhi; Magen Avraham* 343:3 (end); *Chayay Adam* 66:2; *"Rav" Shulchan Arukh* 343:3; *Kitzur Shulchan Arukh* 165:1; *Mishnah Berurah* 343:3.

78. *Issur VeHether* 348; *Magen Avraham* 343:2; *Chayay Adam* 66:3; *"Rav" Shulchan Arukh* 343:3; *Kitzur Shulchan Arukh* 165:1; *Mishnah Berurah* 343:3; *Shaar HaTziun ad. loc.* no. 6. *Cf. Yevamoth* 114a; *Sifethey Cohen, Yoreh Deah* 81:26.

79. *Chayay Adam* 66:5; *Kitzur Shulchan Arukh* 165:1; *Mishnah Berurah* 343:3. *Cf. Yad, Genevah* 1:10; *Choshen Mishpat* 349:5; *Sefer Chasidim* 864.

80. *Sukkah* 42a; *Sifri* on Deuteronomy 11:19; *Yad, Talmud Torah* 1:6; *Yoreh Deah* 245:5; *Chayay Adam* 66:2; *Kitzur Shulchan Arukh* 165:10.

to answer *Amen* after blessings at a very early age, since we are taught that a child has a portion in the World to Come from the time it answers *Amen*.[81]

11:29 If a child is not willing to obey his parents, they should apply as much psychological or physical pressure as necessary, as we are taught, "Correct your son, and he will give you peace" (Proverbs 29:17).[82] However, parents should never beat their children brutally, sadistically or with a vengeance, but with wisdom according to necessity.[83] Similarly, they should not threaten their children with undue or exaggerated punishments.[84] In every case, at the same time that a child is being pushed toward obedience, care should be taken never to alienate him.[85]

11:30 The community has a responsibility for the religious education[86] and training[87] of its children. Therefore, as soon as a child's religious training begins,[88] every Jew is required to prevent him from violating religious law.[89] However, before the child's

81. *Sanhedrin* 110b; *Yerushalmi, Shevi'ith* 4:8 (13a); *Amudey Yerushalayim ad. loc.,* citing *Beer Sheva* 77a; *Or Zarua, Milah* 104; *Orach Chaim* 124:7 in *Hagah; Chayay Adam* 66:1; *Kitzur Shulchan Arukh* 185:2. *Cf. Tanchuma, Tzav* 7; *Sefer Chasidim* 883. For the meaning of *Amen,* see *Sefer Chasidim* 18; *Makor Chesed ad. loc.* 18:89.
82. *Cf. Makkoth* 8b; *Iggeroth Moshe, Yoreh Deah* 2:103.
83. "Teachers must not administer beatings like cruel enemies, with a whip, or with a rod; instead, a little strap should be used"; *Yoreh Deah* 245:10. *Cf. Bava Bathra* 21a; *Yad, Talmud Torah* 2:2; *"Rav" Shulchan Arukh* 343:13; *Chayay Adam* 66:1; *Kitzur Shulchan Arukh* 165:13. See also Ritva, *Moed Katan* 17a; *Sh'nei Luchoth HaB'rith, Shaar HaOthioth, Derekh Eretz* 1:103a; *Teshuvoth Kiryath Chanah* 22, cited in *Pith'chey Teshuvah* 245:4.
84. *Semachoth* 2:4-5; Rosh, *Moed Katan* 3:94; *Kitzur Shulchan Arukh* 165:7.
85. *Sanhedrin* 107b; *Sotah* 47a; *Semachoth* 2:6; *Sefer Chasidim* 565, 919; *Kitzur Shulchan Arukh loc. cit.*
86. *Sifri, Yalkut Shimoni* (1:841), Rashi, on Deuteronomy 6:7; *Yad, Talmud Torah* 1:2; *Yoreh Deah* 245:3; *HaGra* 245:5; *Bava Bathra* 21a; *Yalkut Shimoni* 1:870; *Yad, Talmud Torah* 2:1; *Yoreh Deah* 245:7.
87. Since the community has exactly the same responsibility as the child's parents; *cf. Tosafoth, Nazir* 28b *s.v. Beno; Tosafoth Yeshenim, Yoma* 82a *s.v. Ben,* citing Rabbi Eliezer MiMitz; *Nimukey Yosef, Yevamoth* (Rif 42a) *s.v. Gezera; Magen Avraham* 640:3; *Chayay Adam* 66:3. Others maintain that the parents alone are responsible; *cf. Tosafoth, Tosafoth Yeshenim, loc. cit.,* according to Rabbi Yitzchak; *Yad, Shabbath* 12:7, *Maakholoth Assuroth* 17:27, *Avel* 3:13; *Orach Chaim* 343:1; *Yoreh Deah* 373:1 in *Hagah.* See also *Kesef Mishneh, Shevithath Assor* 1:5.
88. At the age of 6 or 7 years; *cf. Bava Bathra* 21a; *Yad, Talmud Torah* 2:2; *Yoreh Deah* 245:5, 8; *Mishnah Berurah* 269:1. However, *cf. Tosafoth, Arakhin* 2b *s.v. Ein.*
89. *Tosafoth, Shabbath* 121a *s.v. Sh'ma; Orach Chaim* 343:1 in *Hagah; Magen Avraham* 640:3; *Mishnah Berurah* 343:6; *Chayay Adam* 66:3.

religious training begins, this obligation does not extend[90] beyond his parents.[91]

11:31 Even when a community is not responsible for a child's religious training, they are responsible for his moral training.[92] Therefore, they must take steps to prevent children from stealing or doing damage.[93] Similarly, children must be prevented from doing things which may cause others to sin.[94]

11:32 If a child's parents are lax about his religious training, it is the community's responsibility to correct them, especially in cases where Biblical prohibitions are involved.[95]

11:33 It is forbidden to cause[96] or tell[97] a child to violate any[98] religious law,[99] regardless of how young the child is.[100] For example, it is

---

90. *Shabbath* 121a; *Yevamoth* 114a; *Gittin* 55a; *Niddah* 46b; *Yad, Orach Chaim, Yoreh Deah,* cited in note 87; *Yad, Shabbath* 24:11; *"Rav" Shulchan Arukh* 343:1; *Chayay Adam* 66:3.
91. See above, 11:25.
92. *Maggid Mishneh, Genevah* 1:10; *Beer HaGolah* on *Choshen Mishpat* 349:5 no. 10.
93. *Yad, Genevah* 1:10; *Choshen Mishpat* 349:5.
94. Ran, *Rosh HaShanah* (Rif 9b) *s.v. VeHani Mili; Magen Avraham* 343:0; *Beer Hetiv* 343:1; *"Rav" Shulchan Arukh* 343:1.
95. *Yad, Shabbath* 24:11; *Kesef Mishneh ad. loc.;* Radbaz, *Kesef Mishneh, Maakhaloth Assuroth* 17:28; *Magen Avraham* 343:2; *Turey Zahav* 343:1; *Chayay Adam* 66:3; *Mishnah Berurah* 343:3.
96. *Nimukey Yosef, Yevamoth* (Rif 42a) *s.v. Gezera,* citing Ritva; *Orach Chaim* 343:1; *Chayay Adam* 66:6.
97. *Machtzith HaShekel* 640:3; *"Rav" Shulchan Arukh* 343:5; *Mishnah Berurah* 343:5, 640:5.
98. According to some, this only applies to those cases mentioned in *Yevamoth* 114a; *cf. Tur, Yoreh Deah* 373; *Lechem Mishneh, Avel* 3:12. However, the majority apply it to all cases; *cf. Turey Zahav* 343:1; *Pri Megadim ad. loc.; Chayay Adam* 66:6; *Mishnah Berurah* 343:3; *Teshuvoth Beth Ephraim, Orach Chaim* 23; *Yoreh Deah* 61-62; *Tosafoth, Pesachim* 88a *s.v. Seh.* See *Sifra* (93c); *Yalkut Shimoni* (1:636); Rashi, Ramban, on Leviticus 21:1; *Yad, Avel* 3:12; Rosh, *Tumah* 1; *Yoreh Deah* 373:1. For whether this applies to positive commandments, see *Hagahoth Maimonioth, Shabbath* 39:8 no. 40; *Magen Avraham* 269:1.
99. Even rabbinical laws; *cf. Tosafoth, Rosh HaShanah* 33a *s.v. Tanya; Nimukey Yosef loc. cit.; Orach Chaim* 343:1; *Chayay Adam* 66:6. Others maintain that one may cause them to violate rabbinical laws; *cf. Teshuvoth Rashba* 92, cited in *Nimukey Yosef loc. cit.;* Ran, *Shabbath* (Rif 45b) *s.v. Aval;* HaGra, *Orach Chaim* 343:1 *s.v. VeAfilu.* See also *Yad, Shofar* 2:7; Raavad *ad. loc.; Mishneh LeMelekh, Maakhaloth Assuroth* 17:27; *Biur Halakhah* 345:1 *s.v. MiDivrey Sofrim.*
100. *Magen Avraham* 343:2; *"Rav" Shulchan Arukh* 343:6; *Chayay Adam* 66:6; *Mishnah Berurah* 343:4. *Cf. Yerushalmi, Kethuvoth* 5:6 (36b); Rosh, *Kethuvoth* 5:18; *Yoreh Deah* 81:7; *Sifethey Cohen* 81:21. See *Teshuvoth Beth Yehudah* 45, cited in *Eshel Avraham, Orach Chaim* 343:1.

forbidden to cause a child to eat forbidden food[101] or to violate the Sabbath.[102]

11:34 If a child violates a law for the sake of an adult,[103] it is the same as if he did so at the adult's request.[104] Therefore, even if a very young[105] child does so of his own accord, he must be stopped.[106] However, where only a rabbinical law is involved and it is apparent that the child is also doing it for his own sake, it is permitted.[107]

11:35 It is forbidden even indirectly to cause a child to violate a negative Biblical commandment. Thus, for example, one may not give a child forbidden food to play with, lest he eat it.[108] However, in cases where only rabbinical law[109] or a positive commandment[110] is concerned, this is permitted.

11:36 Some authorities maintain that it is permitted to cause a child to violate a rabbinical law if the child himself requires this for health[111] or other reasons.[112] It is therefore permitted to cause a child to violate a law for the sake of his own religious training[112] or

101. *Yevamoth* 114a; *Sifra* (50b); *Yalkut Shimoni* (1:537); Rashi on Leviticus 11:13; *Sifra* (57b) on Leviticus 11:42; *Sifra* (84c); *Yalkut Shimoni* (1:583); Rashi on Leviticus 17:12; Rashi, *Shabbath* 90b *s.v. Dilma; Yad, Maakhaloth Assuroth* 17:27; *Tosefoth Yom Tov, Shabbath* 9:7.

102. *Mekhilta* (69b); *Yalkut Shimoni* (1:296); Rashi on Exodus 20:10. *Cf. Shabbath* 16:6 (121a); *Yad, Shabbath* 12:7; *Teshuvoth Mutzal MeEsh* 4.

103. Even his father; *Mishnah Berurah* 334:66, citing *Beth Yosef; "Rav" Shulchan Arukh* 334:26.

104. Rashi, *Yevamoth* 114a *s.v. BeOseh;* Ran, *Shabbath* (Rif 45b) *s.v. Aval; Turey Zahav* 334:19; *Magen Avraham* 334:29; *Mishnah Berurah* 34:65.

105. *Tosafoth, Shabbath* 121a *s.v. Sh'ma; "Rav" Shulchan Arukh* 334:26; *Mishnah Berurah* 334:64.

106. *Shabbath* 16:6 (121a); *Yerushalmi* 16:7 (81b); *Yevamoth* 114a; *Yad, Shabbath* 12:7; *Orach Chaim* 334:25; *Chayay Adam* 66:4. *Cf. Teshuvoth Rabbi Akiba Eiger* 15, cited in *Kitzur Shulchan Arukh* 165:5; *Biur Halakhah* 343:1 *s.v. MiDivrey Sofrim.*

107. *Shabbath* 153a; *Tosafoth ad. loc. s.v. Mi; Yad, Shabbath* 20:6; *Orach Chaim* 266:5-6, 362:7 in *Hagah; Magen Avraham* 266:8, 362:15.

108. *Shabbath* 90b; *Hagahoth Asheri, Shabbath* 9:2; *Magen Avraham* 343:3; *"Rav" Shulchan Arukh* 343:9; *Chayay Adam* 66:7; *Mishnah Berurah* 343:4.

109. *"Rav" Shulchan Arukh* 343:10. *Cf.* Mordecai, *Shabbath* 369; *Magen Avraham* 340:5; *Turey Zahav* 340:2; *"Rav" Shulchan Arukh* 340:4; *Mishnah Berurah* 340:14.

110. *Machtzith HaShekel* 640:3; *Shaar HaTziun* on *Mishnah Berurah* 640:8.

111. *Teshuvoth Rabach* 1:112; *Magen Avraham* 343:3; *Beer Hetiv* 343:4.

112. *Tosafoth, Pesachim* 68a *s.v. Seh; "Rav" Shulchan Arukh* 343:7. *Cf. Rosh HaShanah* 33a; *Yad, Shofar* 2:7; Raavad, *Maggid Mishneh, Kesef Mishneh, Lechem Mishneh, ad. loc.*

for the sake of the community,[113] as long as this is not done habitually.[114]

11:37 In any case, we are not required to prevent a child from violating something that is only temporarily[115] forbidden by rabbinical law.[116] Thus, for example, a child may be given food to eat before *Kiddush* on a Sabbath or Festival,[117] or on minor fast days.[118]

11:38 Since anything that is forbidden to a Jew may not be done through a non-Jew,[119] it is forbidden to tell a non-Jew to cause a child to violate any law.[120]

11:39 If a child is sick, however, even if there is no danger,[121] it is permissible to tell a non-Jew to give him forbidden food.[122] If there is no non-Jew present, it may be given through another child.[123]

11:40 If a non-Jew wishes to give a child forbidden food, any member of the community should stop him if a Biblical prohibition is involved and the child's religious training has begun. However, if the child has not yet begun his religious training, or only a

113. *"Rav" Shulchan Arukh* 343:6. *Cf. Magen Avraham* 269:1; *Tosafoth, Eruvin* 40b *s.v. Dilma;* Mordecai, *Eruvin* 493; *Orach Chaim* 621:3 in *Hagah; Magen Avraham* 621:3.
114. *Eruvin* 40b; *Tosafoth,* Mordecai, *loc. cit.; Magen Avraham* 269:1, citing *Teshuvoth Rashba* 72, 303; *Turey Zahav* 621:1.
115. *Beth Yosef, Orach Chaim* 343; *Magen Avraham* 269:1, from *Tosafoth, Pesachim* 106b *s.v. Ishtelai; "Rav" Shulchan Arukh* 269:3; *Chayay Adam* 66:10; *Kitzur Shulchan Arukh* 165:4.
116. But not Biblical law, even if only involving a positive commandment; *cf. Magen Avraham* 616:2, 640:3; *Mishnah Berurah* 616:5, 640:5. Others make the distinction only because a positive commandment is involved; *Chayay Adam* 66:10; *Kitzur Shulchan Arukh* 165:4.
117. *"Rav" Shulchan Arukh* 343:6; *Chayay Adam* 66:10, from *Orach Chaim* 296:1; *Eruvin* 40b.
118. *Chayay Adam* 66:10-11. *Cf. Magen Avraham* 550:2; *Mishnah Berurah* 550:5.
119. *Bava Metzia* 90a; *Rosh ad. loc.* 7:6; *Tosafoth, Rosh HaShanah* 24b *s.v. Shani; Avodah Zarah* 43b *s.v. Shani;* Raavad, *Kilayim* 1:3; *Maggid Mishneh, Sekhiruth* 13:3; *Choshen Mishpat* 338:6 in *Hagah; Sifethey Cohen ad. loc.* 338:1; *Beer HaGolah* on *Evven HaEzer* 5:15 no. 3; *Beth Sh'muel* 5:16; HaGra 5:32; *Turey Zahav, Yoreh Deah* 197:1. *Cf. Shabbath* 150a; *Eruvin* 67b; *Gittin* 8b; *Bava Kama* 80b; *Yad, Shabbath* 6:1; *Orach Chaim* 367:2; *Yad, Issurey Biyah* 16:13; *Moed Katan* 12a; *Yad, Yom Tov* 7:24; *Orach Chaim* 543:1; *Kesef Mishneh, Kilayim* 1:3.
120. *"Rav" Shulchan Arukh* 343:5; *Chayay Adam* 66:8; *Mishnah Berurah* 343:5.
121. See above, 5:15.
122. *Magen Avraham* 343:3, 450:8; *"Rav" Shulchan Arukh* 343:5; *Chayay Adam* 66:9; *Mishnah Berurah* 343:5, 450:18.
123. *Chayay Adam* 66:9. *Cf. Mishnah Berurah* 450:18.

rabbinical prohibition is involved, no action need be taken except by the child's own parents.[124]

11:41 Even in cases where it is permissible to allow a child to eat forbidden food, every effort should be made to avoid this, since what he eats is incorporated into his body and can adversely affect his later spiritual life.[125] Similarly, since a nursing mother's diet is reflected in her milk,[126] a child should not be allowed to nurse from a non-Jewess,[127] or from a Jewish woman who has eaten non-Kosher food,[128] even if she was forced to do so for health reasons.[129]

11:42 A person should repent for his childhood sins,[130] since even a child has some moral responsibility.[131] Therefore, though one is legally obligated to return a childhood theft only when the stolen object is still in his possession,[132] one has a moral obligation to make restitution for any damage[133] or theft[134] committed as a child. Although childhood sins may have been done without knowledge, they still can cause spiritual damage. It is thus written, "Even

---

124. *"Rav" Shulchan Arukh* 343:5; *Chayay Adam* 66:8; *Mishnah Berurah* 343:6.
125. *Or Zarua* 2:48; *Hagahoth Asheri, Avodah Zarah* 2:6, from *Yerushalmi, Chagigah* 2:1 (9b); *Tosafoth, Chagigah* 15a *s.v. Shuvu; Yoreh Deah* 81:7 in *Hagah; Kitzur Shulchan Arukh* 165:8. *Cf. Yoma* 29a.
126. *Yoma* 75a; Rashi, *Sotah* 12b *s.v. Davar.*
127. Ran, *Avodah Zarah* (Rif 7b) *s.v. MiDeAmrinan,* citing Rashba, from *Sotah* 12b; Maharatz Chajas *ad. loc.; Shemoth Rabbah* 1:30; *Yoreh Deah, Kitzur Shulchan Arukh, loc. cit;* HaGra 81:31; *cf. Tosafoth, Avodah Zarah* 10b *s.v. Omer Leh.*
128. *Hagahoth Asheri, Yoreh Deah, Kitzur Shulchan Arukh, loc. cit.*
129. *Sifethey Cohen, Yoreh Deah* 81:25; *Turey Zahav* 81:12.
130. *Piskey Maharia* 62; *Orach Chaim* 343:1 in *Hagah; "Rav" Shulchan Arukh* 343:11; *Chayay Adam* 66:5; *Kitzur Shulchan Arukh* 165:6; *Pith'chey Teshuvah, Choshen Mishpat* 349:2; *Teshuvoth Beth Yaakov* 3; *Teshuvoth Rabbi Akiba Eiger* 147.
131. See above, 11:14. *Cf. Magen Avraham* 343:4, from *Sanhedrin* 55b; *Chokhmath Shlomo ibid.,* from *Kerithoth* 16b; HaGra *ibid. s.v. MiKhol Makom. Cf. Bava Metzia* 10b; *Nedarim* 35b; *Tosefta, Sanhedrin* 14:1; *Tosafoth, Pesachim* 91b *s.v. Ish; Tosefoth Yom Tov, Chagigah* 1:1; *Tevuoth Shor* 11:50; *Teshuvoth Rabbi Akiba Eiger* 134; *Teshuvoth Chatham Sofer, Yoreh Deah* 184, *Evven HaEzer* 2:172; *Teshuvoth Radbaz* 2:2094 on *Yad, Shegagoth* 9:3; *Issurey Biyah* 3:17; Raavad *ad. loc.*
132. *Yad, Genevah* 1:8, *Chovel* 4:20; *Choshen Mishpat* 349:3, 424:8; HaGra *ad. loc.* 349:2, from *Bava Kama* 112a; *Bava Metzia* 102a. *Cf. Bava Kama* 8:4 (87a); *Rosh* 8:9.
133. *Hagahoth Asheri, Bava Kama* 8:9, from Rashi, *Bava Kama* 98b *s.v. Rafram; Turey Zahav, Orach Chaim* 343:2; *Choshen Mishpat* 439:1; *Mishnah Berurah* 343:9; *cf. Shabbath* 56b.
134. *Sefer Chasidim* 692; *Teshuvoth Shevuth Yaakov* 1:176; *Chayay Adam, Kitzur Shulchan Arukh, loc. cit.*

without knowledge, a soul [can become] no good" (Proverbs 19:2).[135]

TABLE 11:1 — POSITIVE COMMANDMENTS HAVING FIXED TIMES AND APPLICABLE TO WOMEN

1. *Kiddush* ("Sanctification") of the Sabbaths and Festivals.[1]
2. Eating *Matzah* on the first night of Passover.[2]
3. Eating the Passover Sacrifice (when the Temple is standing).[3]
4. Slaughtering the Passover Sacrifice.[4]
5. Gathering to hear the Torah at the Temple.[5]
6. Rejoicing on the Festivals.[6]

135. *Cf. Yalkut Shimoni* (2:958); *Metzudoth David ad. loc.; Chayay Adam, Kitzur Shulchan Arukh, loc. cit.*

1. *Berakhoth* 20b. See above, note 9.
2. *Pesachim* 43a; *Kiddushin* 34a.
3. *Yerushalmi, Pesachim* 8:1 (58b).
4. *Pesachim* 8:1 (87a).
5. *Kiddushin* 34a.
6. *Ibid.*

TWELVE
MUTUAL RESPONSIBILITY

12:1 The Jewish people accepted their religion together as one unit,[1] and continue to function as a community rather than as mere individuals.[2] All Jews[3] are therefore responsible for one another.[4] Even the responsibility for individual obligations does not rest upon the individual alone, but upon the entire community. It is for this reason that one Jew may recite a blessing for another even if he has already fulfilled his own obligation.[5]

12:2 When a single Jew sins, it is not he alone who suffers, but the entire Jewish people. In the Midrash, this is likened to passengers on a single huge ship. Though all the passengers may be very careful not to damage the hull, if one of them takes a drill and begins drilling holes under his own seat, the ship will sink,

---

1. *Sefer Chasidim* 233. *Cf. Sotah* 37b; *Mekhilta,* Rashi, on Exodus 20:2 (66b).
2. Thus, the entire Jewish people can be looked upon as a single organic whole, like a great body encompassing all of its individuals; *Cf. Kuzari* 3:19; *Zohar* 3:218a; Rabbenu Yonah, *Shaarey Teshuvah* 3:168; *Derekh Mitzvotekha, Mitzvath Ahavath Yisrael* (p. 28a). If any part of the body is infected, or if poison is injected into even a single extremity, then the individual as a whole suffers, and every other part of the body is affected. The same is true of the Jewish people; if even a single Jew does not keep the Torah, all of us suffer. See Kaplan, *Reaching Out* (NCSY, 1974), pp. 17-18.
3. For discussion whether converts are included, see Rashi, *Niddah* 13b *s.v. KeSapachat; Tosafoth, Yevamoth* 47b, *Kiddushin* 70b *s.v. Kashim,* from *Sotah* 37b.
4. *Shevuoth* 39a; *Sanhedrin* 27b; *Sifra* (112a), Rashi, on Leviticus 26:37; Rashi, *Sotah* 37b *s.v. Amar; Sefer Chasidim* 233, 601; *Reshith Chokhmah, Shaar HaYirah* 14 (41d).
5. "The reason for this is because every Jew is responsible as a "co-signer"for every other Jew with regard to the observance of the commandments"; Rashi, *Rosh HaShanah* 29a *s.v. Af Al Pi.* "Therefore, as long as another person has not fulfilled his obligation, it is the same as if he himself had not fulfilled it"; Ran, *Rosh HaShanah* (Rif 8a) *s.v. Tani; Pesachim* (Rif 27b top) *s.v. SheYekhol; Tosefoth Yom Tov, Rosh HaShanah* 3:8 *s.v. Zeh,* 4:9 *s.v. Kakh; Magen Avraham* 167:40; *Mishnah Berurah* 167:92, 213:14; *Chayay Adam* 5:18.

and all will drown.[6] In the same manner, whenever any Jew does not keep the Torah, all others are affected spiritually.[7] Such actions may even precipitate physical suffering for the Jewish people.[8]

12:3 Each Jew's moral responsibility extends beyond the Jewish people to the entire human race, as moral corruption in any place affects the entire world.[9] It is for this reason that Jonah was sent to correct the people of Nineveh, even though theirs was a pagan city.[10]

12:4 Nevertheless, we are not required to proselytize and attempt to convert others to Judaism,[11] since a good non-Jew is spiritually better off than a bad Jew.[12] Furthermore, proselytes have always been a source of trouble to our people.[13] The prophet therefore warned, "But the proselyte shall join [Israel], and become a plague[14] for the house of Jacob" (Isaiah 14:1).[15]

12:5 It is forbidden to cause another to sin in any manner, as we are commanded, "Do not place a stumbling block before the blind" (Leviticus 19:14).[16] The Torah does not refer here to one who is actually blind, but to one who is blind to the truth and can stumble

---

6. *VaYikra Rabbah* 4:6; *Tana D'Bei Eliahu Rabbah* 11 (66b); *Yalkut Shimoni* 2:334, 2:920; *Reshith Chokhmah, Shaar HaYirah* 7 (22b).
7. *Mekhilta* (63a), *Yalkut Shimoni* (1:276), on Exodus 19:6.
8. *Cf.* Rashi, *Sanhedrin* 44a *s.v. Akhan;* Joshua 22:20; *Sefer Chasidim* 601; *Akedath Yitzchak* 83; *Metzudoth David* on Joshua 7:11.
9. *Sefer Chasidim* 1124. *Cf. Yad, Melakhim* 8:10; Rashi, *Sanhedrin* 75a *s.v. VeIm.*
10. *Sefer Chasidim loc. cit. Cf.* Ibn Ezra, Radak, on Jonah 1:2; Radak on Amos 3:2.
11. *Yad, Melakhim* 8:10. *Cf. Yevamoth* 109b; *Yad, Gerim* 1:1.
12. *Cf. Yevamoth* 47a; *Yad, Issurey Biyah* 14:2; *Yoreh Deah* 268:2.
13. *Yevamoth* 47b, 109b; *Kiddushin* 70b; *Niddah* 13b; *Yad, Issurey Biyah* 13:18; *Sifethey Cohen, Turey Zahav, Yoreh Deah* 268:3.
14. Based on the double meaning of the Hebrew root *Sapach* (ספח), the word *VeNispechu,* usually translated "they shall become joined or attached," also means "they shall become a plague or scab"; see Leviticus 13:2, 14:56.
15. *Yalkut Shimoni* (2:417) *ad. loc.; Yevamoth* 47b; *Kiddushin* 70b.
16. *Sifra* (88d), *Yalkut Shimoni* (1:609), *Zohar* (3:85a), Rashi, *ad. loc.; Sefer HaMitzvoth,* Negative Commandment 299; *Sefer Mitzvoth Gadol,* Negative Commandment 168; *Chinukh* 232; *Pesachim* 22b; *Moed Katan* 17a; *Nedarim* 62b; *Kiddushin* 32a; *Bava Metzia* 5b, 5:11 (75b); *Avodah Zarah* 6b, 22a; *Tosafoth, Bava Metzia* 10b *s.v. DeOmer; Yad, Rotzeach* 12:14, *Malveh* 2:7, *Mamrim* 6:9, *Kilayim* 10:31, *Neziruth* 5:20, *Avel* 3:5; *Sefer Chasidim* 673; *HaGra, Orach Chaim* 196:1; *Mishneh LeMelekh, Beth HaMikdash* 3:21; *Sifethey Cohen, Yoreh Deah* 303:3; *HaGra* 303:3. *Cf. Tosefta, Makkoth* 3:7.

into sin.[17] This is indicated by the conclusion of the verse, "You must fear your God; I am God," which is only said concerning something which is hidden from the eyes of other human beings.[18]

12:6   God Himself regards with contempt anyone who purposely causes another to sin, as it is written, "Cursed is he who misdirects the blind on the way" (Deuteronomy 27:18). Here again the intention is not literal, but refers to a person who is morally or conceptually blinded by another.[19] Furthermore, we are taught that one who causes his fellow to sin is worse than one who murders him.[20]

12:7   Since any sin is considered a stumbling block, one is guilty of violating this commandment whether he is an accomplice to a Biblical or to a rabbinical prohibition.[21]

12:8   The Biblical prohibition only applies to a true accomplice to the sin, i.e. where the sin could not be done without the help[22] of another Jew,[23] or where one actually brings the sin to a person[24] or tells him to do it.[25] It also includes a case in which one person causes another to sin unknowingly[26] or through an incorrect decision.[27] However, merely giving aid in the performance of a

17. Rambam, *Tosefoth Yom Tov,* on *Mishnah Shevi'ith* 5:6. *Cf. Zohar* 3:85a; *Minchath Chinukh* 232:4; *Minchath Pittim, Orach Chaim* 156; *Makor Chesed* (on *Sefer Chasidim*) 673:1.

18. Maharal, *Gur Aryeh,* quoted in *Mesoreth HaTalmud* on *Sifra loc. cit.*

19. *Mesilath Yesharim* 11 (16a). *Cf.* Rashi, *Targum Yonathan, ad. loc.*

20. *BaMidbar Rabbah* 21:5; *Tanchuma, Pinchas* 3.

21. *Tosafoth, Avodah Zarah* 22a *s.v. Tepuk;* Rosh, *Bava Metzia* 5:42; *Yoreh Deah* 179:1 in *Hagah;* HaGra 170:2; *Nachalath Tzvi ibid.; Orach Chaim* 163:2 in *Hagah; Pri Megadim, Eshel Avraham* 163:2; *Chokhmath Shlomo, Orach Chaim* 347:1; *Kenesseth HaGedolah, Yoreh Deah* 55; *Teshuvoth Mishpetey Sh'muel* 134; *Teshuvoth Chavath Yair* 185; *Yad Malachi* 364 (57b); *Kometz Minchah* (on *Chinukh*) 232, 238. However, see *Teshuvoth Radbaz* 2:3:215, who apparently disputes this.

22. *Avodah Zarah* 6b; *Bava Kama* 117a. *Cf. Marah HaPanim* on *Yerushalmi, Demai* 3:1 (12a).

23. Even if it could be done with the help of a non-Jew; *Mishneh LeMelekh, Malveh* 4:2; *Minchath Chinukh* 232:3.

24. *Pri Chadash, Orach Chaim* 496, "Rules of Customs" no. 23; *Teshuvoth Mishpetey Sh'muel* 134; *Derekh HaKodesh* (on *Esser Kedushoth*), p. 10a; *Teshuvoth Chavath Yair* 185; *Yad Malachi* 362 (57b).

25. *Teshuvoth Mishpetey Sh'muel* 134; *Yad Malachi* 365 (58a).

26. *Teshuvoth Mishpetey Sh'muel loc. cit.; Teshuvoth Rabbi Betzalel Ashkenazi* 3; *Yad Malachi* 366 (58a); *Kometz Minchah* (on *Chinukh*) 232.

27. *Zohar* 3:85a. *Cf. Avodah Zarah* 19b; *Zohar* 1:5a, 3:42a; *Yad, Talmud Torah* 5:4; *Yoreh Deah* 242:13.

sin which would otherwise have been done does not make one a true accomplice, although it is nevertheless forbidden.[28]

12:9 One is guilty of acting as an accomplice even when no wrong is actually committed.[29] It is therefore forbidden to provoke a person, thereby causing him to sin in anger, even though it is not certain that he will do so. It is for this reason that a father may not strike his grown son, since the boy is liable to strike him back.[30]

12:10 It is forbidden to cause another to sin, even if this does not result immediately.[31] Similarly, it is forbidden to place another in a predicament in which he may be tempted to sin. For example, it is forbidden to grant a loan without witnesses, since the borrower may be tempted to deny it at a later date.[32]

12:11 Non-Jews are required to live a moral life in obedience to the seven commandments given to all mankind.[33] Just as it is forbidden to cause another Jew to sin, so is it forbidden to cause a non-Jew to violate any of these commandments.[34]

28. By rabbinical legislation; *Tosafoth, Shabbath* 3a *s.v. Baba;* Rosh 1:1; Ran, *Shabbath* (Rif 1b) *s.v. U'Makshei, Avodah Zarah* (Rif 1b) *s.v. Dayka Nami; Magen Avraham* 347:4; *"Rav" Shulchan Arukh* 347:3; *Mishnah Berurah* 347:7; *Sifethey Cohen, Yoreh Deah* 151:6; HaGra 151:8; *Teshuvoth Mishpetey Sh'muel loc. cit.; Teshuvoth Zaken Aaron* 88; *Turey Aven, Avney Milu'im, Chagigah* 13a *s.v. Ein; Teshuvoth Noda BeYehudah, Evven HaEzer* 1:75; *Yad Malachi* 361 (57b); Maharatz Chajas, *Shabbath* 3a, *Bava Metzia* 10b. However, in *Sefer HaMitzvoth*, Positive Commandment 205, we find it forbidden by a positive commandment. See also *Shevi'ith* 5:9; *Gittin* 5:9 (61a); *Yad, Shemittah* 8:1; *Shaar HaTziun* on *Mishnah Berurah* 347:5 no. 8; *Pri Megadim, Eshel Avraham* 163:2.
29. *Yad Malachi* 367 (58a); *Makor Chesed* (on *Sefer Chasidim*) 566:2. Cf. *Teshuvoth HaRan* (Rome) 73, (Constantinople) 89; Ritva, *Avodah Zarah* 15a *s.v. Mi Dami; Shita Mekubetzeth, Bava Metzia* 5a *s.v. DeIm;* Maharam, *Sanhedrin* 63b *s.v. Assur; Teshuvoth Beth Yitzchak, Orach Chaim* 29:3; *Teshuvoth Nefesh Chayah* 169:2; *Teshuvoth Zaken Aaron* 88; *Teshuvoth Mahara Sasson* 162.
30. *Moed Katan* 17a; *Kiddushin* 32a; *Zohar* 2:85a; *Yad, Mamrim* 6:9; Raavad, *Talmud Torah* 6:14; *Sefer Chasidim* 566.
31. *Pilpula Charifta, Bava Metzia* (Rosh 5:80) no. 100.
32. *Bava Metzia* 75b; *Yad, Malveh* 2:7; *Choshen Mishpat* 70:1; *Sefer Meirath Eynayim (Sema)* 70:1.
33. See Volume 1, 4:8.
34. *Pesachim* 22b; *Avodah Zarah* 6b; *Tosafoth, Sanhedrin* 63b *s.v. Assur, Bekhoroth* 2b *s.v. Sh'ma; Sifethey Cohen, Yoreh Deah* 27:1, 62:2, 151:6; *Turey Zahav* 62:1; *Pith'chey Teshuvah* 62:1, 151:1; *Teshuvoth Zikhron Yitzchak* 108; *Teshuvoth Peney Aryeh* 74; *Teshuvoth Beth Ephraim, Yoreh Deah,* introduction; *Teshuvoth Chatham Sofer* 19; *Tevath Gomer, Shemoth* 1; *Teshuvoth Chavath Yair* 136. Whether a non-Jew is forbidden to be an accomplice; cf. *Tosafoth, Avodah Zarah* 15b *s.v. LeOved; Piskey Tosafoth, Sanhedrin* 125; Maharsha, *Sanhedrin* 63b *s.v. Assur.*

12:12 Even if a person has left the Jewish fold,[35] or is completely irreligious, it is still forbidden to help[36] or cause him to sin. For example, it is forbidden to even pass[37] non-Kosher food to a Jew who is likely to eat it.[38]

12:13 Similarly, it is forbidden to sell or lend anything to a person who is likely to use it in committing a sin.[39] For example, one may not sell or lend tools to a person who is likely[40] to use them in violation of the Sabbath.[41]

12:14 Similarly, it is forbidden to ask a fellow Jew to do any work if it is likely that he will do it on the Sabbath. It is likewise forbidden to invite him to one's home or synagogue if he is liable to violate the Sabbath in traveling there. This is particularly true if the person habitually violates the Sabbath.

12:15 Where it is reasonable to assume that no sin will be committed, it is permissible to make such an assumption. For example, it is permitted to lend or sell something which can be used in committing a sin, as long as it is reasonable to assume that no sin will be committed.[42] However, if the object cannot be obtained from any other source, such an assumption may not be made.[43]

35. Tosafoth, Avodah Zarah 6b s.v. Minayin; Sefer Mitzvoth Gadol, Negative Commandment 168; Magen Avraham 347:4; Machtzith HaShekel ad. loc.; Pri Megadim, Sifethey Da'ath, Yoreh Deah 65:11 (end); Teshuvoth Chavath Yair 185; Teshuvoth Mishpetey Sh'muel 134. Others do not consider an apostate a Jew in such a case; cf. Sifethey Cohen, Yoreh Deah 151:6; Beer Hetiv 151:5; Dagul Me'rvavah, Gilyon Maharsha, ibid. See Sanhedrin 44a.

36. Even if he can do it without help; cf. Yoreh Deah 151:1 in Hagah; HaGra 151:8; Birkey Yosef ibid.; Pith'chey Teshuvah 151:2, 160:1; Pri Megadim, Eshel Avraham 347:4; Mishnah Berurah 347:7; Emunoth Sh'muel 14. Others maintain that it is permitted if he can do it without help; cf. Avodah Zarah 6a, Tosafoth loc. cit., Avodah Zarah 14b s.v. Makom; Mordecai, Avodah Zarah 795; Rosh 5:18. Cf. Rashi, Avodah Zarah 55a s.v. Dorkhin; Tosafoth, Chagigah 13a s.v. Ein. See Machtzith HaShekel loc. cit. who equates an apostate and a non-Jew in such a case.

37. Even if it belongs to him; Tosafoth loc. cit., Pesachim 22a s.v. VeEver; cf. Yerushalmi, Demai 3:1 (12a); Yad, Maaser 10:13; Rabbenu Yonah, Shaarey Teshuvah 3:81; Magen Avraham 163:2; "Rav" Shulchan Arukh 163:2; Mishnah Berurah 163:12.

38. "Rav" Shulchan Arukh 347:3.

39. Shevi'ith 5:6; Rambam, Rash, ad. loc.; Yad, Shemittah 8:2.

40. But if it is not known that he will violate the Sabbath, then it is permitted; cf. Yerushalmi, Shevi'ith 5:3 (14b); Yad, Shemittah 8:4.

41. Magen Avraham 347:4, from Yerushalmi, Demai 3:1 (12a); cf. Gilyon HaShas ad. loc.; "Rav" Shulchan Arukh 347:4; Mishnah Berurah 347:7.

42. Avodah Zarah 15b; Shevi'ith 5:8; Rash, Bertenoro, ad. loc.; Yerushalmi, Shevi'ith 5:4 (15a); Tosafoth, Gittin 61a s.v. Mishalath Ishah; Yad, Shemittah 8:2, 6; Ran, Nedarim 62b s.v. Rov; Rash, Tosefoth Yom Tov, Shevi'ith 5:9; Magen Avraham, "Rav" Shulchan Arukh, Mishnah Berurah, loc. cit.

43. "Rav" Shulchan Arukh 347:4.

12:16 Even where a sin is likely to be committed, it is permitted to ignore this possibility in order to preserve peace. It is therefore permissible to lend something with which a sin is likely to be committed, if such a loan is required to keep the peace.[44] Nevertheless where a sin is certain to be committed, it is forbidden even in such a case.[45] Furthermore, some maintain that preserving the peace only applies to a loan, but not to a sale.[46]

12:17 Where it is known that a person will not gain any benefit from sinning, it is logical to assume that he will not do so.[47]

12:18 Even where it is certain that a person will sin without our help, it is forbidden to render him any aid or assistance in committing the sin.[48] It is also forbidden to give any kind of verbal encouragement to a person engaged in violating a religious law.[49]

12:19 Although it is forbidden to be an accomplice to a sin, the Biblical prohibition does not forbid one from being an accomplice to an accomplice.[50] For example, it is permitted to sell something to a non-Jewish merchant, even though he will later sell it to another non-Jew who will use it in committing a sin.[51]

12:20 Nevertheless, it is forbidden to be an accomplice to a Jewish accomplice, since a Jewish accomplice is himself committing a sin. In such a case, one is not merely an accomplice to an accomplice, but an accomplice to an actual sin.[52]

12:21 Since it is forbidden to cause a Jew to sin in any manner, one may not even be an accomplice to a non-Jew who may cause another Jew to sin.[53] For example, it is forbidden to give or sell

44. *Shevi'ith* 5:9; *Gittin* 5:9 (61a); *Tosafoth*, Rash, *Magen Avraham*, *"Rav" Shulchan Arukh*, *Mishnah Berurah*, loc. cit.
45. *Yerushalmi, Shevi'ith* 5:4 (15a); Bertenoro on *Shevi'ith* 5:9; *Tosafoth*, Rash, *Tosefoth Yom Tov*, *"Rav" Shulchan Arukh*, loc. cit.
46. *Tosafoth* loc. cit.
47. *Bava Metzia* 5b; *Yad Malachi* 362 (57b). *Cf. Kiddushin* 63b; *Shevuoth* 42b; *Arakhin* 23a.
48. *Shevi'ith* 5:9; *Gittin* 5:9 (61a); *Yad, Shemittah* 8:1. *Cf. Tosafoth, Avodah Zarah* 14a s.v. *Makom.*
49. *Gittin* 62a; *Yerushalmi, Shevi'ith* 4:4 (15b); *Yad, Shemittah* 8:1, 8:8; Rambam, Bertenoro, on *Gittin* 5:9; *Magen Avraham* 347:4; *"Rav" Shulchan Arukh* 347:4; *Mishnah Berurah* 347:7.
50. *Avodah Zarah* 14a, 21a; *Sifethey Cohen, Yoreh Deah* 151:3.
51. *Tosefta, Avodah Zarah* 1:4; *Yerushalmi, Avodah Zarah* 1:5 (5b); *Yoreh Deah* 151:1.
52. *Tosafoth, Avodah Zarah* 15b s.v. *LeNokhri; Minchath Chinukh* 232:2.
53. Rosh, *Avodah Zarah* 1:14; *Turey Zahav, Yoreh Deah* 151:3; *Beer Hetiv* 151:2; *Kometz Minchah* (on *Chinukh*) 232.

forbidden articles to a non-Jew if he might in turn sell them to an unsuspecting Jew and thereby cause him to sin.[54]

12:22   Nevertheless, it is permitted to sell a forbidden article to a non-Jew if it is not likely to be resold. For example, it is permitted to sell him small amounts of forbidden food (like non-Kosher meat) since it is assumed that he will eat it himself.[55]

12:23   It is assumed that the average Jew will not sin deliberately. Therefore, it is also permitted to sell or give a forbidden article to a non-Jew in the presence of a Jew, as long as it is readily apparent that the object is forbidden.[56]

12:24   Even if a person considers something to be permitted, it is forbidden for him to cause another who considers it forbidden to inadvertently violate his convictions. For example, if there is a question whether certain food is Kosher, one who considers it permissible may not serve it to another who considers it forbidden.[57] Nevertheless, since according to his opinion no sin is committed, he is not considered an accomplice to a sin if he does serve it.[58]

54.   *Pesachim* 40b; *Avodah Zarah* 65b; *Niddah* 61b; *Chullin* 64a, 94a; *Tosefta, Chullin* 3:8; *Yerushalmi, Orlah* 3:1 (18a); *Yerushalmi, Avodah Zarah* 3:13 (25a); *Tosafoth, Chullin* 95a *s.v. U'VeNimtza, Avodah Zarah* 49b *s.v. Arag, Yevamoth* 81b *s.v. Kulan; Zevachim* 72a-b *s.v. Ve'NithArvu; Yad, Chametz U'Matzah* 5:9, *Kilayim* 1:27; *Orach Chaim* 467:1; *Yoreh Deah* 57:21, 84:5 in *Hagah*, 86:10, 112:11, 134:5, 301:8; *Sifethey Cohen* 84:15; *Turey Zahav* 84:7, 134:6; *Pith'chey Teshuvah* 112:3, 301:8; HaGra 84:15; *"Rav" Shulchan Arukh* 367:2; *Teshuvoth Noda BeYehudah, Orach Chaim* 2:70, *Yoreh Deah* 2:186; *Teshuvoth Panim Meiroth* 3:35; Bertenoro on *Orlah* 3:6; *Tosefoth Yom Tov ibid.* and on *Avodah Zarah* 3:9.

55.   *Pesachim* 40b; *Magen Avraham* 467:2; *"Rav" Shulchan Arukh* 467:2; *Mishnah Berurah* 467:4; *Sifethey Cohen, Yoreh Deah* 84:17; *Turey Zahav* 134:6.

56.   The example given involves a Jewish butcher who gives the hind-quarters of a kosher animal containing the forbidden sciatic nerve to a non-Jew in the presence of another Jew. If the hind-quarters are whole, in which case it is readily apparent that the nerve has not been removed, we do not suspect that the Jew who witnessed the transaction will attempt to buy it from the non-Jew. If, on the other hand, the hind-quarters have been cut up (and the prohibition is not readily apparent), one may not give it to the non-Jew in the presence of a Jew until he has removed the nerve, lest the Jew mistakenly assume that the nerve has been removed; *Chullin* 7:2 (93b); Rambam, Bertenoro, *ad. loc.; Pesachim* 22a; *Yad, Maakhaloth Assuroth* 8:14; *Maggid Mishneh ad. loc.; Yoreh Deah* 65:11; *Tosafoth, Niddah* 61b *s.v. Lo; Magen Avraham* 467:0; *Turey Zahav* 467:1; *"Rav" Shulchan Arukh* 467:4; *Mishnah Berurah* 467:1; *Chayay Adam* 124:28.

57.   *Hagahoth Mordecai, Yevamoth* 96; *Sifethey Cohen, Yoreh Deah* 119:20; HaGra 119:21; *cf. Yevamoth* 14a; *Chullin* 111b.

58.   *Pri Chadash, Orach Chaim* 496, "Rules of Customs" no. 23; *Yad Ephraim, Yoreh*

12:25   Where a question of law is concerned, it is permitted to cause a person who is known to accept a stricter viewpont to violate this opinion, if it is apparent that he does so accepting the more lenient opinion. For example, it is permitted to serve questionable food to one who forbids it, as long as the question is obvious.[59] In such a case, if the one taking the stricter view eats it, it is obvious that in doing so he has changed his opinion.[60]

12:26   However, one may not abandon a stricter viewpoint which is upheld because of community or ancestral custom. In such a case, it is forbidden to serve him what he considers prohibited, even where the question is obvious.[61] Still, if there is a definite custom not to take the stricter opinion when served by others, then he may partake in any case.[62]

12:27   We do not normally suspect a person of causing others to violate their convictions. It is therefore permitted for one who takes the stricter viewpoint to partake of the food of another who does not,[63] as long as the latter knows of his custom and is not suspect of violating it.[64]

12:28   If a person sees another Jew[65] sinning[66] or following the wrong path, he is required to correct him and attempt to set him right. We are thus commanded, "You must correct your neighbor" (Leviticus 19:17).[67] Even though this commandment specifically

Deah 62:1; *cf. Teshuvoth Levi ibn Chaviv* 121; *Beer Sheva* 84c-d. However, *Hagahoth Mordecai, Sifethey Cohen, loc. cit.,* appear to dispute this.

59.   *Sifethey Cohen, loc. cit.; Beer Hetiv* 119:12; *Pith'chey Teshuvah* 119:1.
60.   *Pri Chadash loc. cit.*
61.   *Sifethey Cohen loc. cit.*
62.   *Ibid. Cf. Issur VeHether* 4 (end).
63.   *Hagahoth Mordecai loc. cit.; Yoreh Deah* 119:7 in *Hagah,* from Rashi, *Yevamoth* 14a *s.v. DeModey; Pri Chadash loc. cit.* no. 24; *Chokhmath Adam* 71:9.
64.   *Sifethey Cohen, Yoreh Deah* 119:20.
65.   But not a non-Jew; *cf.* Rashi, *Sanhedrin* 75a *s.v. VeIm.*
66.   Even in violation of a positive commandment; *cf. Sefer Chasidim* 5; *Makor Chesed ad. loc.* 5:1; *Ginath Veradim, Orach Chaim* 3:15.
67.   *Sifra, Yalkut Shimoni* (1:613), *Zohar* (3:85b), Ramban, *ad. loc.; Arakhin* 16b; Rif, *Bava Metzia* 17a; *Yad, Deyoth* 6:7; *Sefer HaMitzvoth,* Positive Commandment 205; *Sefer Mitzvoth Gadol,* Positive Commandment 11; *Chinukh* 239; *Sefer Chasidim* 5; *Reshith Chokhmah, Shaar HaAnavah* 5 (227d). Also see *Teshuvoth Mishpetey Sh'muel,* "*Shemate'ta DeTokhacha*" (Vilna, 1916), pp. 40a-44a; *Mitzvath Tokhacha* (Jerusalem, 1951). The exact Hebrew wording in the Torah is *Hokheach Tokhiach,* literally, "Correct, you shall correct." The double wording strengthens the phrase and indicates that this is something that we *must* do, and not merely moral advice. It is for this

only refers to a person violating a Biblical commandment, we are required to correct any person who is doing wrong.[68]

12:29 Just as a person makes every attempt to save a friend from physical harm, so should he attempt to save him from spiritual harm.[69] We can learn this from God Himself, as it is written, "God corrects those whom He loves, just like a father [corrects] a child whom he cherishes" (Proverbs 3:12).[70] A person should desire for his friends the same spiritual benefits that he wishes for himself, and it is thus written, "Let your springs be dispersed abroad" (Proverbs 5:16).[71]

12:30 A person should correct himself before he attempts to correct others.[72] Otherwise, they will not accept his correction.[73]

12:31 Just as we are required to correct others, so are we required to accept correction. The Torah thus states, "Therefore, cut away the thickening of your hearts, and stiffen your necks no more" (Deuteronomy 10:16).[74]

12:32 It is therefore very important to accept correction, as the scripture teaches us, "Correction brings delight, and a good blessing shall come upon them" (Proverbs 24:25).[75] A person who accepts correction is considered wise, as we find, "Correct a wise man and he will love you" (Proverbs 9:8).[76] On the other hand,

reason that we loosely translate the phrase as "you must correct." Most English translations render the word *Hokheach* as "admonish" or "rebuke." This, however, is not a precise translation. The words "admonish" or "rebuke" have the connotation that one should "tell off" the person doing wrong, speaking to him in a harsh, stern manner. It is for this reason that we translate the word as "correct." As most authorities explain, the best way to fulfill this commandment and "correct" another person is not with harsh words, but by drawing him to God with love and affection; see Kaplan, *Reaching Out,* pp. 26-27.

68. *Berakhoth* 31b; *Tosafoth ad. loc. s.v. Davar.*
69. *Mesilath Yesharim* 19 (28b). *Cf. Sifra loc. cit.; Arakhin* 16b; *Bereshith Rabbah* 54:3; *Yalkut Shimoni* 1:95.
70. *Zohar* 3:85b; *Reshith Chokhmah ibid.* 228a.
71. Rambam, *Pirkey HaHatz'lachah* 1.
72. *Bava Metzia* 107b; *Bava Bathra* 60b; *Sanhedrin* 18a, 19a; *Yerushalmi, Taanith* 2:1 (8b); Rashi, Radak, Mahari Kara, on Zephaniah 2:1.
73. *Sefer Chasidim* 5. *Cf. Bava Bathra* 15b; *Arakhin* 16b; Rif, *Bava Metzia* 17a; Rashbam, *Bava Bathra* 60b *s.v. HithKosheshu.*
74. *Sefer Mitzvoth Katan* 9, cited in *Cheredim,* Positive Commandments 1:32 (p. 62). *Cf.* Ramban *ad. loc.*
75. *Tamid* 28a; Rashi *ad. loc. s.v. SheNe'emar; Yalkut Shimoni* 2:961; *Reshith Chokhmah, Shaar HaAnavah* 5 (228b); *Sh'nei Luchoth HaB'rith, Toldoth Adam* 1:3a.
76. *Arakhin* 16b; Rif, *Bava Metzia* 17a; *Sefer Mitzvoth Katan loc. cit.*

one who refuses to accept correction is not likely to repent,[77] and he will die with his sin, as it is written, "He who hates correction shall die" (Proverbs 15:10).[78]

12:33 It is therefore the responsibility of every community to encourage its spiritual leaders to speak out and correct them.[79] A congregation that discourages its spiritual leaders from correcting them is considered a congregation of sinners. Regarding them it is written, "They mocked the messengers of God and despised His words... until God's wrath rose against His people and there was no remedy" (2 Chronicles 36:16).[80]

12:34 Just as one is required to correct others with regard to sins against God, so should he do so with respect to sins against his own person. Therefore, if a person has been wronged, he should not keep the hurt to himself, but should speak out to the person who wronged him.[81] We can learn this lesson from Abraham, as we find, "And Abraham admonished Abimelekh" (Genesis 21:25).[82] It is forbidden to bear hatred because of such a wrong, as the Torah states, "Do not hate your brother in your heart,[83] [rather] you must correct your neighbor" (Leviticus 19:17).[84]

12:35 It is therefore forbidden to carry a grudge and refuse to speak to the person who has committed this wrong.[85] We are thus taught that the one who refuses to speak to his neighbor for three days is considered his enemy,[86] and is guilty of violating this commandment not to hate.[87]

77. *Yad, Teshuvah* 4:2.
78. Rabbenu Yonah, *Shaarey Teshuvah* 2:11. *Cf.* Ralbag *ad. loc.*
79. *Yad, Teshuvah* 4:2; *Sefer Chasidim* 19. *Cf. Yalkut Shimoni* 2:533.
80. *Cf. Yalkut Shimoni* 2:1085; Proverbs 1:25.
81. *Arakhin* 16b; *Yad, Deyoth* 6:6; *Sefer Mitzvoth Gadol,* Negative Commandment 5; *Kitzur Shulchan Arukh* 29:15. *Cf. Tana DeBei Eliahu Rabbah* 18 (91a).
82. Ramban on Leviticus 19:17; *Reshith Chokhmah, Shaar HaAnavah* 5 (227d). *Cf. Bereshith Rabbah* 54:3; *Yalkut Shimoni* 1:95.
83. *Pesachim* 113b; *Nedarim* 9:4 (62b); *Sotah* 3a; *Arakhin* 16b; *Yad, Deyoth* 6:5; *Sefer HaMitzvoth,* Negative Commandment 302; *Sefer Mitzvoth Gadol,* Negative Commandment 5; *Chinukh* 238; *Kitzur Shulchan Arukh* 29:15.
84. *Yad, Deyoth* 6:6.
85. *Yad loc. cit.; Bereshith Rabbah* 84:8; *Midrash Tehillim* 28:8; *Yalkut Shimoni* 2:149; Rashi on Genesis 37:4; Ralbag on 2 Samuel 13:22.
86. *Sanhedrin* 3:5 (27b); *Yad, Rotzeach* 6:10; *Choshen Mishpat* 7:7 in *Hagah;* Bertenoro on *Makkoth* 2:3. *Cf.* Rashash, *Sanhedrin loc. cit.,* from Deuteronomy 19:4.
87. *Cheredim,* Negative Commandments 1:19 (p. 117).

12:36 It is similarly forbidden to attempt to cover up one's hurt while keeping it in his heart. It is thus written, "Draw me not away with the wicked... who speak peace with their neighbors, but have evil in their hearts" (Psalms 28:3).[88] Nevertheless, if one wishes to forgive the wrongdoer in his heart and not say anything, it is commendable to do so.[89]

12:37 When first correcting a person, one should begin as politely and gently as possible,[90] speaking to him privately,[91] so as not to shame him in any way.[92] If one knows that the person will be ashamed at the mention of the sin, he should not even correct him privately, but should merely hint at the sin and try to draw the person away from it.[93]

12:38 If the wrongdoer accepts correction immediately, no more is required, and he should be blessed.[94] If it is not accepted, however, one must correct him as many times as necessary in order to bring him to the right path.[95]

12:39 One is required to correct a wrongdoer as long a there is any chance that it might have a positive effect. However, if he shows signs of anger,[96] becomes insulting,[97] scornful,[98] or simply refuses

88. *Midrash Tehillim* 28:8. *Cf.* Jeremiah 9:7.
89. *Arakhin* 16b; *Tosafoth ad. loc. s.v. VeAnavah; Yad, Deyoth* 6:9; *Kitzur Shulchan Arukh* 29:18.
90. *Zohar* 3:85b; *Yad, Deyoth* 67; *Sefer Mitzvoth Gadol*, Positive Commandment 11; *Sefer Chasidim* 5; *Reshith Chokhmah, Shaar HaAnavah* 5 (228a); *Kitzur Shulchan Arukh* 29:15. *Cf. Shabbath* 24a; *Gittin* 7a; *Orach Chaim* 260:4; *Magen Avraham* 260:2; *"Rav" Shulchan Arukh* 260:5; *Mishnah Berurah* 260:10.
91. *Zohar, Yad, loc. cit.*
92. *Arakhin* 16b; *Tanchuma, Mishpatim* 7.
93. *Zohar* 3:86a; *Reshith Chokhmah, Shaar HaAnavah* 5 (228a).
94. *Devarim Rabbah* 1:6, from Proverbs 24:25; *Tana DeBei Eliahu Rabbah* 3 (30b); *Reshith Chokhmah, Shaar HaAnavah* 5 (228b).
95. *Bava Metzia* 31a; *Arakhin* 16b; Rif, *Bava Metzia* 17a; *Yad, Deyoth* 6:7; *Sefer Mitzvoth Gadol*, Positive Commandment 11; *Sefer Chasidim* 5.
96. *Chinukh* 239; *Minchath Chinukh ad. loc.* 239:2; *Biur Halakhah* 608:2 *s.v. Ad.*
97. *Arakhin* 16b; *Yad, Deyoth* 6:7; *Kesef Mishneh, Lechem Mishneh, ad. loc.; Orach Chaim* 608:2 in *Hagah; Mishnah Berurah* 608:11; *Shaar HaTziun ad. loc.* no. 13. Others require that correction should be continued until the other person actually strikes back physically; *cf. Hagahoth Maimonioth, Deyoth* 6:7 no. 5, from *Eikhah Rabbah* 2:4; *Tanchuma, Tazria* 9; *Zohar* 1:68a; *Birkey Yosef, Machzik Berakhah, Orach Chaim* 608; *Teshuvoth Chaim Sha'al* 2:43.
98. *Sh'nei Luchoth HaB'rith, Toldoth Adam* 1:2b, from Proverbs 9:8.

to listen,[99] one must stop.[100] It is thus written, "Do not correct a scorner, lest he hate you" (Proverbs 9:8).[101]

12:40 If a person does not accept correction privately, one should correct him in the presence of his friends.[102] If this still does not have any effect, one should correct him publicly,[103] shame him,[104] or do anything else in his power to bring him back to the right path.[105]

12:41 One is only required to begin correcting a person privately if he sins privately. If one is committing a sin in public, however, where others may learn from him, then he should be publicly corrected.[106]

12:42 Where only personal injury is involved,[107] one may only speak up privately, and under no condition shame the person who has committed this wrong. The Torah thus says, "You must correct your neighbor, [but] do not bear a sin because of him" (Leviticus 19:17). That is, you should not bear a sin by publicly shaming him.[108]

12:43 Although one is required to prevent another from sinning in any way possible, one is not required to expose himself to any harm in the process. Therefore, one is not required to correct another if he fears that the latter will take revenge and harm him.[109]

---

99. *Yad, Deyoth* 6:7.
100. *Yevamoth* 65b; *Yerushalmi, Terumoth* 5:3 (30b); *Yerushalmi, Sotah* 8:2 (34b). *Cf. Maaseh Choshev, Arakhin* 16b, quoted in *Makor Chesed* (in *Sefer Chasidim*) 413:4.
101. *Magen Avraham* 608:3; *"Rav" Shulchan Arukh* 608:6; *Mishnah Berurah* 608:11; *Kitzur Shulchan Arukh* 29:16.
102. *Zohar* 3:85b; *Reshith Chokhmah, Shaar HaAnavah* 5 (228a).
103. *Ibid.;* Maharsha, *Arakhin* 16b *s.v.* Yakhol.
104. *Yad, Deyoth* 6:8; *Lechem Mishneh ad. loc.; Sefer Mitzvoth Gadol,* Negative Commandment 6; *Chinukh* 240; *Kitzur Shulchan Arukh* 29:17. *Cf. Berakhoth* 19b; *Yad, Kilayim* 10:24; *Yoreh Deah* 303:1.
105. *Yad loc. cit.* Others maintain that a person should only be publicly corrected one time; *cf. Zohar loc. cit.; "Rav" Shulchan Arukh* 608:5; *Bava Kama* 92b.
106. *Sefer Mitzvoth Katan* 112; *Magen Avraham* 608:3; *"Rav" Shulchan Arukh* 608:5; *Mishnah Berurah* 608:10.
107. *Cf. Minchath Chinukh* 240:1.
108. *Arakhin* 16b; *Tanchuma, Mishpatim* 7; Rif, *Bava Metzia* 17a; *Yad, Deyoth* 6:8; *Sefer HaMitzvoth,* Negative Commandment 303; *Sefer Mitzvoth Gadol,* Negative Commandment 6; *Chinukh* 240; *Sefer Chasidim* 1125.
109. *Sefer Chasidim* 413; *Chinukh* 239; *Minchath Chinukh ad. loc.* 239:1; *Magen Avraham* 608:3; *Pri Chadash* 608:3; *Mishnah Berurah* 608:7; *Biur Halakhah ibid. s.v.*

12:44 When a person must correct an entire congregation, he may speak out and not be concerned lest he shame them.[110] However, one is only required to correct a congregation where there is a chance that they might accept it.[111] If one is certain that his words will go unheeded, he is only required to correct them once, in order that they not be able to plead ignorance.[112] Beyond that, we are taught that just as one has an obligation to speak up when his words will be accepted, so must he refrain from speaking up when they will not.[113]

12:45 If one sees his father, rabbi, or teacher[114] violating any law,[115] he is required to correct him, just as he must correct any other person. Even though this might appear disrespectful, God's honor comes before that of any human being,[116] as we are taught, "There is no wisdom, understanding or counsel against God" (Proverbs 21:30).[117] Nevertheless, out of respect, one should do this as indirectly as possible, preferably posing it as a question, "Have you not taught us that this is wrong?"[118]

12:46 If a person sees his rabbi or teacher engaged in a questionable action, if Torah law is involved, he should question the action

Chayav; *Teshuvoth Zekher Yehosef* 214; *Teshuvoth Chavath Yair* 164 (end); *K'tav Sofer, Evven HaEzer* 47. *Cf. Tana DeBei Eliahu Rabbah* 18 (91a); *Yalkut Shimoni* 1:613; *Reshith Chokhmah, Shaar HaAnavah* 5 (228a); *Yoreh Deah* 334:48 in *Hagah,* citing *Teshuvoth Mahariv* 157; *Pith'chey Teshuvah ad. loc.* 334:19, citing *Bekhor Shor, Sotah* 47b; *Choshen Mishpat* 12:1 in *Hagah;* HaGra *ad. loc.* 12:4, from *Kiddushin* 71a.

110. *Sefer Chasidim* 1125. *Cf. Akedath Yitzchak* 20.

111. *Turey Zahav, Orach Chaim* 608:2.

112. Ritva, *Yevamoth* 65b; *Nimukey Yosef, Yevamoth* (Rif 21b) *s.v. Davar; Orach Chaim* 608:2 in *Hagah,* from *Shabbath* 55a; *Eikhah Rabbah* 2:4. *Cf. Sh'nei Luchoth HaB'rith, Toldoth Adam* 1:2b (note); *Mishnah Berurah* 608:9; *Birkey Yosef* 608:2; *Biur Halakhah ibid. s.v. Mochin.*

113. *Yevamoth* 65b; *Yerushalmi, Terumoth* 5:3 (30b); *Yerushalmi, Chagigah* 1:8 (8a); *Yerushalmi, Sotah* 8:2 (34b).

114. *Bava Metzia* 31a; *Rif* 17a; *Lechem Mishneh, Mishneh LeMelekh, Deyoth* 6:7; *Minchath Chinukh* 239:4.

115. Even a rabbinical law; *Terumath HaDeshen* 43; *Yoreh Deah* 242:22 in *Hagah; Sifethey Cohen* 242:42; *HaGra* 242:58; *Maharatz Chajas, Berakhoth* 16b.

116. *Sefer Chasidim* 5.

117. *Berakhoth* 19b; *Eruvin* 68a; *Shevuoth* 30b; *Sanhedrin* 82a; *Yad, Eduth* 1:2.

118. Regarding a parent, see *Kiddushin* 32a; *Sanhedrin* 81a; *Yad, Mamrim* 6:11; *Chayay Adam* 68:10; *Kitzur Shulchan Arukh* 143:10. Regarding a teacher or rabbi, see *Yad, Talmud Torah* 5:9; *Yoreh Deah* 242:22. *Cf. Berakhoth* 2:5-7 (16a-b); *Tosafoth, Chullin* 30b *s.v. Lamdenu;* HaGra, *Yoreh Deah* 242:58; *Maharatz Chajas, Berakhoth* 16b, *Chullin* 30b.

immediately. Where only rabbinical law is involved, however, he should not question it until after the fact.[119]

12:47   Even though it is normally forbidden to render any decision in the presence of one's teacher or rabbi, one may do so to prevent another from sinning. Where God's name may be desecrated, we do not render honor, even to a rabbi.[120]

12:48   If a person is knowingly violating any law, one is required to correct him, even though he is certain that he will be ignored.[121] If he is certain that his words will be useless, however, then he is not punished for the other's sin if he neglects to correct him.[122]

12:49   Even if a person is doing something wrong unknowingly, and it is certain that he will ignore any correction, one is still required to correct him where any law written expressly in the Torah is concerned.[123] When a law is written in the Torah, ignorance of the law is no excuse.[124]

12:50   If a law is not written in the Torah, however, then the oath regarding mutual responsibility does not apply to it.[125] Therefore, in such a case, if one is doing wrong unknowingly, and it is certain that the correction will be ignored, then nothing need be said.[126] In such a case, we say that it is better for people to do wrong unknowingly, than to do so knowingly.[127]

119. *Eruvin* 67b; *Yoreh Deah* 242:22 in *Hagah. Cf. Pith'chey Teshuvah* 242:12, quoting *Yom Teruah* (p. 10), *s.v. Amar.*

120. *Eruvin* 63a; *Yad, Talmud Torah* 5:3; *Yoreh Deah* 242:11.

121. *Sefer Yereyim* 223; *Sefer Mitzvoth Katan* 112; *Sefer Mitzvoth Gadol*, Positive Commandment 11; *Hagahoth Maimonioth, Deyoth* 6:7; *Magen Avraham* 608:3; *Mishnah Berurah* 608:5. Others do not require correction in such a case; *cf. Sefer Mitzvoth Gadol, Hagahoth Maimonioth, loc. cit.; Tosefta, Bava Bathra* 2:6; *Pri Megadim, Eshel Avraham* 608:1; *Eliahu Rabbah, Orach Chaim* 608.

122. *Ibid.*, from *Shabbath* 65a.

123. Rashba, Meiri, *Betza* 30a; Ran, *Betza* (Rif 16b) *s.v. VeHakh;* Rosh, *Betza* 4.2, citing *Sefer Halttur; Orach Chaim* 608:2 in *Hagah;* "*Rav*" *Shulchan Arukh* 608:5; *Pri Megadim*, introduction 4:9; *Minchath Chinukh* 239:3.

124. Rashba *loc. cit.; Mishnah Berurah* 608:6. *Cf. Horayoth* 4a; *Sanhedrin* 33b; Rambam on *Horayoth* 1:3; *Yad, Sanhedrin* 10:9; *Sh'nei Luchoth HaB'rith, Toldoth Adam* 1:2b; *Kiddushin* 24b; HaGra, *Orach Chaim* 608:2. *Cf. Chokhmath Shlomo, Orach Chaim* 608:2, from *Yevamoth* 49b; *Tosafoth ad. loc. s.v. Ashivehu.*

125. *Cf.* Volume 1, 5:12-13; Ran, *Nedarim* 8a *s.v. Ha, Shevuoth* (Rif 10a) *s.v. Malkin; Yoreh Deah* 239:6; *Sifethey Cohen* 236:3; HaGra 608:2.

126. *Sefer Mitzvoth Gadol*, Positive Commandment 11; *Sefer Chasidim* 39; *Orach Chaim* 608:2 in *Hagah; Biur Halakhah* 608:2 *s.v. VeDavka.* See Ritva, *Makkoth* 20b, that this only applies to a positive commandment; *cf. Mitzvath Tokhachah* 9; *Makor Chesed* (on *Sefer Chasidim*) 39:3.

127. *Shabbath* 148b; *Betza* 30a; *Bava Bathra* 60b; *Yad, Shevithath Assor* 1:7; *Orach*

12:51   Where people become accustomed to doing something publicly, it is assumed that they will not accept correction regarding it.[128] However, if there is even a chance that they are doing wrong knowingly,[129] or that the correction will have a positive effect,[130] then one is required to speak up, even where only a rabbinical law is concerned.[131]

12:52   We only say that it is better for people to sin unknowingly where very few minor trangressions are involved. However, where people are violating many laws unknowingly, we must correct them in every case,[132] lest our entire religion gradually be forgotten.[133]

12:53   Similarly, we only say that it is better for people to sin unknowingly where an old established custom[134] involving all the people is concerned. Where only a few people are involved, they must be corrected, in order that others not learn from them.[135]

12:54   Although one is required to correct another even where it will be ignored, one is not required to correct a person who is completely nonreligious or nonbelieving. Similarly, one need not correct a person who habitually sins out of spite.[136] The Torah tells us, "You must correct your *neighbor*" (Leviticus 17:19) — and such individuals are not considered "your neighbor."[137] Nevertheless,

Chaim 339:3 in *Hagah,* 356:6, 608:2; *Yoreh Deah* 239:3; *Sifethey Cohen, Yoreh Deah* 39:37, 293:7; *Sefer Chasidim* 262; Rabbenu Yonah, *Shaarey Teshuvah* 3:146. Cf. *Teshuvoth Shevuth Yaakov* 3:1.

128. *Teshuvoth Meil Tzedakah* 19, cited in *Machtzith HaShekel* 608:2; *Hagahoth Barukh Frankel* 608:2; *Biur Halakhah* 608:2 *s.v. VeDavka.*

129. *Shita Mekubetzeth, Betza* 30a, quoting Ritva, cited in *Machtzith HaShekel* 608:3.

130. *Tosafoth, Shabbath* 55a *s.v. Af, Bava Bathra* 60b *s.v. Mutav, Avodah Zarah* 4a *s.v. SheHayah;* Rosh, *Betza* 4:2; *Teshuvoth HaRosh* 3:6; *Magen Avraham* 608:1.

131. *Levushey Serad* 608:2; *Mishnah Berurah* 608:3. Cf. *Orach Chaim* 365:6; *Magen Avraham* 365:12; *Machtzith HaShekel, Pri Megadim, ad. loc.; Mishnah Berurah* 365:30.

132. *Shita Mekubetzeth loc. cit.,* cited in *Machtzith HaShekel* 608:3; *Yad Malachi* 2:434 (153b).

133. *Teshuvoth Tashbatz* 2:47, cited in *Shaar HaTziun* (on *Mishnah Berurah*) 608:3.

134. Mordecai, *Betza* 689. Cf. Rashi, *Betza* 30a *s.v. Henakh.*

135. *Teshuvoth Tashbatz loc. cit.,* cited in *Yad Malachi* 2:437 (153b); *Shaar HaTziun loc. cit.; Chokhmath Shlomo, Orach Chaim* 608:2. Cf. *Sefer Chasidim* 262; *Magen Avraham* 263:30.

136. Regarding one who sins habitually out of desire, cf. *Biur Halakhah* 608:2 *s.v. Aval* (end). See *Dagul Me'rvavah, Yoreh Deah* 151.

137. *Kli Yekar ad. loc.; Tana DeBei Eliahu Rabbah* 18 (91a); *Yalkut Shimoni* 1:613; *Reshith Chokhmah, Shaar HaAnavah* 5 (228a); *Minchath Chinukh* 239:4; *Biur Halakhah loc. cit.* Cf. *Bava Metzia* 58b; *Shevuoth* 30a.

if there is any chance whatsoever that one may have a good influence on them, one is required to make every effort.[138]

12:55 However, a person who has been brought up in a nonreligious environment[139] where he never had the opportunity to learn about Judaism,[140] is like a child who was abducted by gentiles,[141] and is not considered to be doing wrong purposely.[142] Even if he is later exposed to authentic Judaism, he is not to be blamed for rejecting it, since it is almost impossible to overcome one's childhood upbringing.[143] Therefore, such a person is not to be counted among the nonbelievers,[144] and he should be approached with love and with every attempt to bring him back to the teachings of our faith.[145]

12:56 Just as one is required to correct a wrongdoer verbally, so is one required[146] to physically stop or prevent a person from

---

138. *Minchath Chinukh loc. cit.*
139. *Cf. Tosefta, Sanhedrin* 14:1; *Yad, Avodath Kokhavim* 4:6; *Migdal Oz, Kesef Mishneh, Pri Chadash, ad. loc.;* Mordecai, *Sanhedrin* 716; *Yoreh Deah* 340:5 in *Hagah,* 345:6; *Dagul Me'rvavah ad. loc.;* *Pith'chey Teshuvah* 340:5, 345:4; *HaGra* 340:13, 345:9; *Chokhmath Adam* 156:7; *Kitzur Shulchan Arukh* 201:7; *Teshuvoth Avodath HaGershoni* 48. See also *Semachoth* 3:5; *Yoreh Deah* 344:6.
140. For example, the children of the Karaites; *cf. Yad, Mamrim* 3:3; *Hagahoth Mordecai, Yevamoth* 107; *Yoreh Deah* 159:3. Others count later generations of Karaites as apostates; *cf.* Radbaz, *Mamrim* 3:3; *Sifethey Cohen, Yoreh Deah* 159:6, 266:17, 267:59; *Choshen Mishpat* 175:33; *Yad Avraham, Yoreh Deah* 159:3; *Mishnah Berurah* 55:47; *Teshuvoth Rabbi Aaron ibn Chaim* 113, 125; *Teshuvoth Mabit* 2:38; *Teshuvoth Rabbi Betzalel Ashkenazi* 3 (end). Other sources seem to indicate that the later generations of Karaites were worse than the earlier ones; *cf. Tosafoth, Avodah Zarah* 26b *s.v. Ani;* Rosh, *Avodah Zarah* 2:7, from *Yerushalmi, Avodah Zarah* 5:4 (34a). See also Rambam on *Chullin* 1:1.
141. *Shabbath* 68a-b; *Shevuoth* 5a; *Yerushalmi, Shabbath* 7:1 (40a); *Yad, Shegagoth* 2:6, 7:2; *Yoreh Deah* 159:6 in *Hagah.*
142. *Yad, Mamrim* 3:3; *Sefer Mitzvoth Gadol,* Negative Commandment 217 (end). *Cf. Bava Metzia* 33b.
143. *Cf. Kethuvoth* 41b; *Yerushalmi, Sotah* 4:4 (20a); *BaMidbar Rabbah* 9:10; *Yad, Issurey Biyah* 1:9. See *Magen Avraham* 204:20; *Biur HaGra ibid. s.v. Im Ansuhu.* Also see *Terumath HaDeshen* 223.
144. Regarding their portion in the World to Come, see *Sanhedrin* 110b; *Tosefta, Sanhedrin* 13:1; *Yalkut Shimoni* 2:874; *Sotah* 48a (end). From Rashi, *Sotah* 48b, *Sanhedrin* 110b, *s.v. Ketaney,* this would appear to refer only to those who die as children. *Cf. Koheleth Rabbah* 4:1; *Zohar* 2:113a. Also see *Zohar* 2:96a, 3:234a.
145. Rambam, *Iggereth HaShmad,* p. 20, from Proverbs 6:30; *Yad, Mamrim* 3:3; *Sefer Mitzvoth Gadol,* Negative Commandment 217 (end); *Teshuvoth Rashbash* 68, cited in *Pith'chey Teshuvah* 268:10; *Chazon Ish, Yoreh Deah* 13:28, *Evven HaEzer, Yibum* 71, commentary on *Yad, Deyoth* 6:3.
146. *Sefer HaMitzvoth,* Positive Commandment 205; *Maharatz Chajas, Shabbath* 3a. *Cf. Shaar HaTziun* (on *Mishnah Berurah*) 347:5.

sinning wherever possible.[147] However, if a person is sinning unknowingly[148] or only violating a rabbinical law,[149] he need not be stopped where it would involve a public spectacle.[150] In such cases, we say that preserving human dignity comes even before preventing sin.[151] Nevertheless, if the sin is likely to be continued long afterwards, and this is the only opportunity, one is required to act even in such cases.[152] In any event, where such action is likely to violate the law of the land, no action need be taken.[153]

12:57 One who has the ability to influence others and prevent them from doing wrong is considered responsible for their sins if he fails to do whatever he can. This is true whether he can only influence the members of his own family, or whether he can influence the entire community.[154] Concerning this, God told His prophet, "If you do not speak up to warn the wicked man of his evil ways so that he may live, then that wicked man shall die with his sin, but I will seek his blood from your hand" (Ezekiel 3:18).[155] One who neglects to prevent others from sinning is also included in the

147. *Yad, Kilayim* 10:29; *Yoreh Deah* 303:1, from *Berakhoth* 19b, 20a; *Yerushalmi, Kilayim* 9:1 (40a); *Yalkut Shimoni* 1:911, 1:932; Rash on *Kilayim* 9:4. Cf. *Bava Kama* 28a; *Yad, Avadim* 3:5. Also see *Teshuvoth Shaagath Aryeh* 58.

148. Rosh, *Niddah* ("Laws of Mixed Species") 9:6; *Yoreh Deah* 301:1 in *Hagah, 372:1 in Hagah; Sifethey Cohen* 303:2; *Terumath HaDeshen* 285. Others dispute this and require action even in such a case; see *Teshuvoth Shaagath Aryeh* 58; *Pith'chey Teshuvah* 303:1; *Yad Avraham, Yoreh Deah* 159:3.

149. *Berakhoth* 19b; Rashi *ad. loc. s.v. Kol; Menachoth* 38a; Rabbenu Yonah, *Berakhoth* (Rif 11b) *s.v. Poshto; Yoreh Deah* 303:1; *Orach Chaim* 13:3.

150. But otherwise, one must take action even in such cases; *Nachalath Tzvi, Yoreh Deah* 303:1; *Pith'chey Teshuvah* 303:2.

151. *Berakhoth* 19b; *Shabbath* 81b, 94a; *Eruvin* 41b; *Megillah* 3b; *Menachoth* 37b; *Yad, Kilayim* 10:29.

152. *Teshuvoth Noda BeYehudah, Orach Chaim* 1:35, cited in *Yad Avraham loc. cit.* Cf. *Teshuvoth Panim Meiroth* 2:56; *Teshuvoth Chavath Yair* 95.

153. *Sefer Chasidim* 405; *Yoreh Deah* 334:48 in *Hagah; Choshen Mishpat* 12:1 in *Hagah.* See above, note 109.

154. *Shabbath* 54b; *Avodah Zarah* 18a; *Shevuoth* 39b; *Yerushalmi, Kethuvoth* 13:1 (68a); *Shemoth Rabbah* 27:8; *Tanchuma, Mishpatim* 7, *Tazria* 9; *Midrash Tehillim* 12:2; *Yalkut Shimoni* 2:264; Rif, *Bava Metzia* 17a; *Yad, Deyoth* 6:7; *Yoreh Deah* 157:1 in *Hagah,* 334:48 in *Hagah; Sefer Chasidim* 5; Rabbenu Yonah, *Shaarey Teshuvah* 3:195. Cf. *Avodah Zarah* 4a; *Sanhedrin* 20a; *Yerushalmi, Sotah* 1:8 (7b); *Eikhah Rabbah* 2:4; *Pesikta* 4 (33a); *Yalkut Shimoni* 2:656. Also see *Eikhah Rabbah* 1:34; *Yalkut Shimoni* 1:1012; *Zohar* 3:46b, 3:218a; *Zohar Chadash Ruth* 77a; *Mesilath Yesharim* 19 (28b).

155. Radak *ad. loc.; Sefer Yereyim* 223; *Sefer Mitzvoth Gadol,* Positive Commandment 11. Cf. *Ezekiel* 33:8.

Biblical malediction, "Cursed is the man who does not uphold all the words of this Torah" (Deuteronomy 27:26).[156]

12:58 Nevertheless, as soon as a person corrects another according to the law, he is released from his responsibility.[157] God thus continues, "But if you warn the wicked man, and he does not turn back from his wickedness, then he shall die with his sins, but you will have saved your own soul" (Ezekiel 3:19).[158] Even when the correction has no effect, one is still rewarded for the attempt.[159] It is thus written, "He who corrects a man shall in the end find more favor than he who flatters with the tongue" (Proverbs 28:23).[160]

12:59 One who in any way causes another to do some good, or assists him in doing it, shares the other's reward.[161] Therefore, for example, one can support another who is engaged in Torah study in return for a share of his merit.[162] This is only true, however, before the good deed is completed. After the deed is done, all the money in the world cannot buy a share of its merit.[163]

12:60 Conversely, one who causes another to sin shares the responsibility for the sin.[164] If one causes another to sin

---

156. Ramban *ad. loc.* When all Israel answered Amen to this statement, in effect they made an oath to keep the Torah for all generations. But this oath was not just that each individual should keep the Torah. It was that the entire Jewish nation as a whole should live by it. It is for this reason that the oath speaks of "the man who does not *uphold* the words of this Torah." The Jerusalem Talmud asks, "Can the Torah then fall down," that it needs to be upheld? It answers that this means that the oath was for every individual to make sure that the Torah is upheld by every other Jew; *Yerushalmi, Sotah* 7:4 (31a); *VaYikra Rabbah* 25:1; *Magen Gibborim* 149. See Kaplan, *Reaching Out,* p. 14.

157. *"Rav" Shulchan Arukh* 608:5.

158. *Sefer Chasidim* 5. *Cf. Ezekiel* 33:9; Isaiah 49:4-5; *Zohar* 1:58a.

159. *Yerushalmi, Sotah* 7:4 (31a); *VaYikra Rabbah* 25:1; *Sefer Chasidim* 5.

160. *Tamid* 28a; *Tanchuma, Mishpatim* 7.

161. *BaMidbar Rabbah* 9:46; *Yoreh Deah* 246:1 in *Hagah; Sh'nei Luchoth HaB'rith, Mesekhta Shavuoth* 2:96a; *Birkey Yosef, Yoreh Deah* 246:1; *Pith'chey Teshuvah* 246:3; Rabbenu Yerocham 52; *Teshuvoth Maharam Alshaker* 101; *Teshuvoth Maaseh Chiyah* 16. *Cf. Bava Bathra* 9a; *Shemoth Rabbah* 35:3; *Yad, Matnoth Ani'im* 10:6; *Yoreh Deah* 249:5.

162. *Bereshith Rabbah* 99:1; *VaYikra Rabbah* 25:1; *Zohar* 3:150a; *Yoreh Deah* 246:1 in *Hagah; HaGra ad. loc.* 246:7. *Cf. Bereshith Rabbah* 75:5; *Pesachim* 53b; Rashi on Genesis 49:13; *Targum Yonathan,* Rashi, on Deuteronomy 33:18; *Yalkut Shimoni* 2:934; Rashi, *Sotah* 21a, *Zevachim* 2a, *s.v. Shimon;* Bertenoro, *Zevachim* 1:2, *Taharoth* 8:7, *s.v. Shimon; Seder HaDoroth,* p. 121a.

163. *Sotah* 21a (end), from Song of Songs 8:7; *Yoreh Deah, Sh'nei Luchoth HaB'rith, loc. cit.*

164. *Cf. Zohar Chadash* 33a, cited in *Reshith Chokhmah, Shaar HaYirah* 13 (37b).

unknowingly, he can often bear legal as well as moral responsibility for it.[165] It is written, "He who causes the upright to go astray on an evil way, shall himself fall into his own pit" (Proverbs 28:10).[166]

12:61 Although one is required to make every effort to prevent another from sinning, one is not required to put out any money to do so.[167] Nevertheless, where one is bringing another back to Judaism completely, then he must make any expenditure necessary, since this comes under the heading of loving God with all one's possessions.[168] One is not required to jeopardize life or limb to prevent another from sinning.[169] However, where there is no actual probability of danger, one may not refrain from acting merely because of an unfounded fear or timidity.[170] The Torah thus commands us, "You shall not be afraid of any man" (Deuteronomy 1:17).[171]

12:62 One is not allowed to sin in order to benefit another.[172] Therefore, one should not violate even a minor law in order to prevent another person from purposely committing a greater sin.[173]

12:63 However, where one may be responsible for the other person's sin,[174] or where one has a special responsibility toward the

---

165. *Tosefta, Makkoth* 3:7-9; *Yad, Kilayim* 10:31, *Nazir* 5:20, *Avel* 3:5; Radbaz, *Kesef Misheh, Lechem Mishneh, ad. loc.;* HaGra, *Yoreh Deah* 303:3; *Minchath Chinukh* 263:14, 551:2; *Or HaChaim* on Leviticus 21:1. *Cf. Nazir* 44a; *Yad, Avodath Kokhavim* 12:16. Regarding *Kareth*, see *Sifra* on Leviticus 17:14.
166. *Cf.* Proverbs 26:27.
167. *Yoreh Deah* 157:1 in *Hagah*, 334:48 in *Hagah*, from *Teshuvoth Mahariv* 156; HaGra 157:5, from *Sanhedrin* 73a. See *Pith'chey Teshuvah* 157:5.
168. See *Chomath HaDa'ath*, introduction, no. 1.
169. *Choshen Mishpat* 12:1 in *Hagah*; HaGra *loc. cit.*, from *Kiddushin* 71a.
170. *Bekhor Shor, Sotah* 47b, cited in *Pith'chey Teshuvah* 334:19.
171. *Cf. Sanhedrin* 6b; *Yad, Sanhedrin* 22:1; *Sefer HaMitzvoth*, Negative Commandment 276; *Sefer Mitzvoth Gadol*, Negative Commandment 207; *Chinukh* 415; *Choshen Mishpat* 12:1; Rabbenu Yonah, *Shaarey Teshuvah* 3:33.
172. *Shabbath* 4a; *Kiddushin* 55b; *Menachoth* 48a; *Tosefta, Challah* 1:8; *Magen Avraham* 454:21, 596:3, 655:0; *Chayay Adam* 148:18; *Mishnah Berurah* 655:3; *Shaar HaTziun ad. loc.* 655:5.
173. *Magen Avraham* 254:21; *"Rav" Shulchan Arukh* 254:12; *Mishnah Berurah* 254:40; *Teshuvoth Tashbatz* 3:37-38; *Teshuvoth Besamim Rosh* 38; *Teshuvoth Beth Yaakov* 88; Maharatz Chajas, *Shabbath* 4a.
174. *Tosafoth, Shabbath* 4a *s.v. VeKhi, Eruvin* 32b *s.v. VeLo;* Maharatz Chajas *ad. loc. Cf. Yoreh Deah* 334:3 in *Hagah;* HaGra *ad. loc.* 334:5, from *Kiddushin* 72b; *Turey Zahav* 334:1; *Pith'chey Teshuvah* 334:1; *Teshuvoth Tashbatz* 2:47; *Teshuvoth Shemesh Tzedakah, Yoreh Deah* 48; *Teshuvoth Chavath Yair* 141; *Teshuvoth Yaabetz* 1:79; *Teshuvoth Radbaz* (new) 187; *Teshuvoth Chatham Sofer* 322. See also *Sefer Chasidim* 263;

wrongdoer,[175] then one may violate a minor law[176] in order to prevent a serious sin.[177]

12:64 Similarly, if another person is being forced to sin, it is permitted to violate a lesser law to save him.[178] If the situation arose through that person's purposeful negligence, however, then he is considered a purposeful wrongdoer.[179]

12:65 Before violating any law for the sake of another, one must be very careful to gauge which is the more important. Thus, for example, violating the Sabbath is considered among the very worst sins,[180] and therefore, one may not violate the Sabbath[181] in order to save another person[182] who is being forced to commit even a most serious[183] sin.[184] If something is only prohibited by rabbinical law on the Sabbath, however, the law may be violated in order to prevent another from transgressing a negative commandment,[185] as long as he is not doing it purposefully.[186]

12:66 Although one may not violate the Sabbath in order to prevent an individual from sinning, one may do so in order to save an entire community that is being forced to sin.[187]

Makor Chesed ad. loc. 263:1; *Magen Avraham* 638:4; *Beer Hetiv* 638:4; *Mishnah Berurah* 638:11; *Bikkurey Yaakov* 638:9.

175. *Magen Avraham* 596:3; *Pri Megadim ad. loc.*

176. Some say only a rabbinical law; cf. *Teshuvoth Beth Yaakov* 88 (end); *Mishneh LeMelekh, Terumoth* 3:17; *Maharatz Chajas, Eruvin* 32b.

177. *Eruvin* 32b.

178. *Tosafoth, Shabbath, Eruvin, loc. cit., Gittin* 41b, *Chagigah* 2b, *s.v. Kofin;* Maharatz Chajas *ad. loc.; Hagahoth Asheri, Shabbath* 1:3; *Magen Avraham* 306:29; *Machtzith HaShekel* 254:21.

179. *Magen Avraham* 252:21; *"Rav" Shulchan Arukh* 306:29.

180. *Eruvin* 69b; *Chullin* 5a; *Yerushalmi, Nedarim* 3:9 (12b); *Tanchuma, Ki Tissa* 33; *Zohar* 2:47a; *Yad, Shabbath* 30:15; Rabbenu Yonah, *Shaarey Teshuvah* 3:142; *Magen Avraham* 306:29; *Kitzur Shulchan Arukh* 72:1.

181. For a discussion whether this includes things which are not actually work, see *Machtzith HaShekel* 306:29; *Pri Megadim, Eshel Avraham* 306:29; *Shaar HaTziun* (on *Mishnah Berurah*) 306:50.

182. Regarding saving oneself, see *Pri Megadim, Mishbetzoth Zahav, Orach Chaim* 328:5.

183. This even included idolatry; cf. *Magen Avraham* 306:29; *Mishnah Berurah* 306:58, 328:31. Others apparently dispute this; see *Levush* 306, cited in *Pri Megadim, Mishbetzoth Zahav* 306:5.

184. *Orach Chaim* 328:10 in *Hagah; Magen Avraham* 306:29; *Turey Zahav* 306:5, 328:4; HaGra, *Orach Chaim* 306:14.

185. But not for a positive commandment; see *"Rav" Shulchan Arukh* 306:29. Cf. *Rosh HaShanah* 4:8 (32b); *Yad, Shofar* 1:4; *Orach Chaim* 586:21; *Magen Avraham* 586:23; *Turey Zahav* 655:2; *"Rav" Shulchan Arukh* 586:22; *Mishnah Berurah* 586:83.

186. *"Rav" Shulchan Arukh* 306:29.

187. *Tosafoth, Shabbath, Eruvin, Gittin, loc. cit., Pesachim* 88b *s.v. Kofin,* from

12:67 If a person is being forced to leave the fold of Judaism completely, it is permitted to violate the Sabbath in any manner[188] in order to save him,[189] since it is better to violate one Sabbath, in order that he may keep many.[190] This is true even where it is not certain that he can be saved.[191]

12:68 Even where a community is not responsible for a very young child's religious training,[192] they must violate the Sabbath to save him from leaving the fold of Judaism,[193] since if he is estranged from Judaism as a child, he is likely to remain estranged as an adult.[194] If a child's parents do not wish to violate the Sabbath to save their child, they can be forced to do so by the community.[195]

12:69 If a person wishes to leave the Jewish fold voluntarily, without coercion, then he is considered to be a purposeful sinner, and we may not violate the Sabbath to save him.[196] In such a case, however, it is permitted to violate any rabbinical law in order

Berakhoth 47b. See above, 10:52, note 150; *Magen Avraham* 306:29, citing *Teshuvoth Beth Yosef* 2; "*Rav*" *Shulchan Arukh* 306:29; *Chayay Adam* 68:14. Also see *Magen Avraham* 426:2; Maharatz Chajas, *Rosh HaShanah* 38b. *Cf.* Rosh, *Berakhoth* 7:20; *Magen Avraham* 90:30; *Teshuvoth Besamim Rosh* 155; *Teshuvoth Shaagath Aryeh* 96, 97; Maharatz Chajas, *Berakhoth* 47b.

188. Even where actual work is involved; "*Rav*" *Shulchan Arukh* 306:29; *Chayay Adam* 68:12; *Mishnah Berurah* 306:57.

189. *Orach Chaim* 306:14, 329:8 in *Hagah*, from *Tosafoth loc. cit.; Magen Avraham* 306:28; *Turey Zahav* 306:5; *Kitzur Shulchan Arukh* 92:10.

190. *Shabbath* 151b; *Yoma* 85b; *Yerushalmi, Yoma* 8:5 (41b); *Magen Avraham* 396:29; "*Rav*" *Shulchan Arukh* 306:29; *Chayay Adam* 68:12; *Mishnah Berurah* 306:57.

191. *Pri Megadim, Mishbetzoth Zahav* 306:5; "*Rav*" *Shulchan Arukh* 306:29; *Kuntres Acharon ad. loc.* no. 1; *Chayay Adam, Kitzur Shulchan Arukh, loc. cit.*

192. See above, 11:30, note 90.

193. Even when the minor wishes to voluntarily leave the Jewish fold, his actions are not considered purposeful; *Shaar HaTziun* (on *Mishnah Berurah*) 306:49. *Cf.* *Machtzith HaShekel* 596:3. See *Yevamoth* 33b, 61b; *Yerushalmi, Pesachim* 8:1 (57b); *Yerushalmi, Sotah* 1:2 (3a), 2:1 (9a); *Tosafoth, Kethuvoth* 9a *s.v. VeIy,* 40b *s.v. Hah;* Raavad, *Sotah* 2:4, *Issurey Biyah* 3:2.

194. *Magen Avraham* 306:29; *Mishnah Berurah* 306:57; "*Rav*" *Shulchan Arukh* 306:29; *Kitzur Shulchan Arukh* 92:10. Others only allow the violation of a Biblical law in the case of a minor when it is certain that he will be saved; *Chayay Adam* 66:3; *Nishmath Adam ad. loc.* no. 1. *Cf. Eliahu Rabbah* 306, from *Eruvin* 103b.

195. *Orach Chaim* 306:14; *Pri Megadim, Mishbetzoth Zahav* 306:5; "*Rav*" *Shulchan Arukh* 306:29.

196. Some authorities, however, maintain exactly the reverse opinion, namely, that one may only violate the Sabbath for a person who wishes to leave the fold willingly; *cf. Bayith Chadash, Orach Chaim* 306; *Magen Avraham* 306:29; *Machtzith HaShekel ad. loc.; Pri Megadim loc. cit.* See also *Kethuvoth* 3b.

to save him.[197] Nevertheless, if he is likely to remain irreligious and cause others to sin, no attempt should be made to stop him even if this does not require the violation of any law on our part. It is thus written, "Ephraim has joined himself to idols, let him alone" (Hosea 4:17).[198]

---

197. *Eliahu Rabbah, Orach Chaim* 306:33; *Beer Hetiv* 305:5, citing *Teshuvoth Nachalath Shiva* 83; *Shaarey Teshuvah* 306:19; *Mishnah Berurah* 306:56; *Shaar HaTziun ad. loc.* 306:47, from *Tosafoth loc. cit.; Pri Megadim, Chayay Adam, Kitzur Shulchan Arukh, loc. cit.* Others dispute this; *cf. Teshuvoth Shevuth Yaakov* 1:16, cited in *Shaarey Teshuvah loc. cit.*
198. *Sefer Chasidim* 188. *Cf.* Radak *ad. loc.*

THIRTEEN

MORALITY AND SIN

13:1   For thousands of years, the world's greatest philosophers and thinkers have wrestled with the problem of good and evil. Man instinctively knows that some things are right and others wrong, some moral and others immoral. Yet, when it comes to giving an objective definition of what is right and wrong, philosophy has found itself at a loss. There have been many attempts at such a definition, but each succeeding generation of philosophers has amply pointed out the shortcomings of its predecessors. Thus, without any true objective philosophical standard, morality has often become nothing more than a matter of custom and convention.[1] In order for any objective morality to exist, there must exist some universal standard. There must be an authority whose very word can define good and evil. Thus, the only successful objective system of morality has been one that begins with the concept of a God who has revealed a definition of right and wrong.

13:2   Judaism accepts the Torah as the standard of morality revealed by God. In this system, good is synonymous with God's will as revealed to man. Sin, on the other hand, is defined as anything that goes against God's revealed will. This is what the Torah means when it says, "If a person sins by violating any one of God's prohibitory commandments... he bears full responsibility for his act" (Leviticus 5:17).[2]

---

1.   *Cf. Ikkarim* 1:6*ff.* Also see *Kuzari* 1:79, 2:49; *Chovoth HaLevavoth* 3:3, no. 5; *Emunoth VeDeyoth* 3:3.
2.   Although we deduce human responsibility in general from this verse, it applies

[158]

13:3   The morality of the Torah might often not conform to that of a particular time and place. In many instances, the Law might seem unduly harsh, or out of tune with the times. Many things that the Torah reckons as serious sins may not appear wrong at all from a contemporary viewpoint. Still, it is important to remember that this contemporary viewpoint is largely a matter of custom and convenience. It has neither a strong philosophical base, or is it even well thought out. In general, people tend to blindly follow the values of their contemporary society, especially with regard to questions of morality. The values set forth by the Torah, on the other hand, are God-given and eternal. Emanating from God as they do, they stand above contemporary judgment. Far from being "out of date" or "old fashioned," these values are timeless.

13:4   Many things that contemporary man may consider of little value therefore have great meaning and depth in the realm of truth. This is particularly true of the rituals of the Torah, such as the Sabbath and Kashruth, which play a most important role in God's plan, but are not even taken into account by contemporary morality.³ Our sages thus speak of, "Things that stand in the heights of the universe, but are taken lightly by ordinary people."⁴

13:5   Even if an individual knows something to be wrong, the more he violates his conscience, the more his sense of morality becomes numbed. Even things known to be sinful begin to appear inconsequential when people become habituated to them. The Talmud thus teaches us that once a person repeats a sin, it begins to appear permissible to him.⁵

13:6   Sin itself furthermore tends to harden a person's heart and make him insensitive to moral feelings.⁶ In this manner, sin draws one

---

specifically to sins carrying a penalty of *Kareth,* "cutting off" (see below, 13:48*f.*), where there is a question as to whether or not there was a violation; Rashi *ad. loc.;* *Kerithoth* 2a; *Yad, Shegagoth* 1:1. *Cf.* Leviticus 4:2, 26:14; Deuteronomy 38:15.

3.   *Reshith Chokhmah, Shaar HaYirah* 4 (17b); Maharal, *Tifereth Yisrael* 6; *Nefesh HaChaim* 1:3.

4.   *Berakhoth* 6b; *Midrash Tehillim* 12:5; *Keter Shem Tov* 138; *Nefesh HaChaim* 2:13.

5.   *Yoma* 86b; *Moed Katan* 27b; *Sotah* 22a; *Kiddushin* 20a, 40a; *Arakhin* 30b; Rabbenu Yonah, *Shaarey Teshuvah* 1:5.

6.   *Yoma* 39a; *Yoreh Deah* 81:7 in *Hagah.*

away from godliness, as the prophet said, "Only your sins have separated you from your God" (Isaiah 59:2).[7] Sin thus reinforces itself.[8] It makes a permanent mark on one's personality,[9] and can render him totally insensitive to spiritual values.[10] Our sages thus teach us that small sins beget larger ones.[11] They also teach that sin may enter as a guest, but it can end up staying as one's master.[12]

13:7   It is for this reason that our moralists have stressed that an individual should avoid all sin, no matter how small or inconsequential it may appear.[13] Even though some sins may be less serious than others, all are reckoned in the end,[14] and none are overlooked.[15] This is the meaning of the Talmudic teaching that, "The sins a person may tread underfoot during his lifetime are the ones which surround him at the time of his final judgment."[16]

13:8   One should therefore not consider the relative smallness of any sin, but the greatness of the One against whom it is committed.[17] Every sin is a rebellion against God, and only a fool would knowingly rebel against a God who is all-powerful,

7.   *Sanhedrin* 65b; *Bahir* 196; Rambam, *Shemonah Perakim* 8; *Sefer Chasidim* 35 (end); *Reshith Chokhmah, Shaar HaYirah* 7 (22d); *Nefesh HaChaim* 1:18. See Volume 1, 5:50.
8.   *Chovoth HaLevavoth* 7:7.
9.   Ben Sirah 19:29, cited in *Bereshith Rabbah* 73:12; *Sefer Chasidim* 35 (end); *Makor Chesed ad. loc.* 35:5. *Cf. Zohar* 1:73b, 3:75b, 3:76a. Also see Isaiah 3:9; *Shabbath* 55a.
10. *Sefer Chasidim ad. loc.*
11. *Sukkah* 52a; *Bereshith Rabbah* 22:11. *Cf. Avoth* 4:2; Rabbenu Yonah, *Tosefoth Yom Tov, ad. loc.; Midrash Tehillim* 10:1; *Yalkut Shimoni* 2:1066; *Mekhilta* on Exodus 15:26 (46a); Rashi on Deuteronomy 11:13; *Nefesh HaChaim* 1:6 note (8a). Also see *Yoma* 39a; *Derekh Eretz Zuta* 3; Rashi on Deuteronomy 29:18.
12. *Sukkah* 52a; *Bereshith Rabbah* 22:11; *Zohar* 3:268a.
13. *Avoth* 4:2.
14. *Chagigah* 5a; *Reshith Chokhmah, Shaar HaYirah* 7 (21b); *Mesilath Yesharim* 4 (7b). *Cf. Sotah* 44b; *Menachoth* 36a.
15. *Bava Kama* 50a; *Yerushalmi, Shekalim* 5:1 (21b); *Yerushalmi, Betza* 3:8 (16a); *Yerushalmi, Taanith* 2:1 (9a); *Bereshith Rabbah* 67:4; *BaMidbar Rabbah* 14:17; *Esther Rabbah* 7:25, 8:1; *Midrash Tehillim* 10:3; *Tanchuma, Ki Tissa* 26; *Pesikta* 25 (161b); *Yalkut Shimoni* 1:115, 2:535, 2:648; *Magen Avoth* (on *Avoth*), p. 76b; *Nefesh HaChaim* 1:12.
16. *Avodah Zarah* 18a; *Zohar* 1:199a (top); *Sefer Chasidim* 31; *Reshith Chokhmah, Shaar HaYirah* 6 (20c); *Pirkey Rabbi Eliezer* 34 (81a), on Psalms 49:6.
17. *Chovoth HaLevavoth* 7:7.

all-knowing, and all-good. Our sages thus teach us that no man
sins unless he is overcome by a spirit of folly.[18]

13:9   God judges a person for all his deeds, whether they be good
or evil. A person may do much good, but this does not diminish
the liability for his sins. The Torah says, "God does not give
special consideration or take bribes" (Deuteronomy 10:17). But
how can one bribe God? What is there that one can give Him?
Our sages answer this by teaching that God does not even accept
the bribery of good deeds to overlook the evil that an individual
might have done.[19] In many ways, sin can even undermine the
merit of one's good deeds. In the Talmud, sin is likened to water
which can extinguish the flame of good deeds.[20]

13:10   There are some places where the Torah specifically allows one
to ignore a prohibition in order to observe a commandment. Thus,
for example, we have the rule that a mandatory commandment
takes precedence over a prohibition of the Torah. Only in such
cases is it permissible to violate a commandment in the pursuit of
good.[21] In all other instances, the ends do not justify the means,
and this in itself is considered a sin. It is therefore a cardinal
principle of the Torah that a good deed which comes through sin
does not incur any merit. One cannot steal something and then
legitimately use it in the service of God. The Psalmist speaks
of this when he says, "The robber blesses, but [in so doing]
scorns God" (Psalms 10:3).[22] In general then, sin can even reduce
the merit of one's good deeds. The more one is immersed in
wrongdoing, the more he divorces himself from his Creator and

18.   *Sotah* 3a; *BaMidbar Rabbah* 9:3. *Cf.* Proverbs 3:32, 9:16.
19.   Ramban, Sforno, *ad. loc.;* Rambam, Rabbenu Yonah, Bertenoro, *Midrash Sh'muel,*
      Tosefoth Yom Tov, on *Avoth* 4:22; *Reshith Chokhmah, Shaar HaYirah* 14 (42b); *Makor*
      Chesed (on *Sefer Chasidim*) 605:8. *Cf.* 2 Chronicles 19:7; *Midrash Tehillim* 17:5; *Yalkut*
      Shimoni 2:670, 2:947; *Midrash Mishley* on Proverbs 11:21. The only way that sin can
      be eradicated is by sincere repentance before God; see Chapter 15.
20.   *Sotah* 21a; Rashi *ad. loc. s.v. BeIdna; Tosafoth ibid. s.v. VeHa; Raya Mehemna,*
      Zohar 3:28b; *Tikuney Zohar* 21 (52b); *Tikuney Zohar Chadash* 97a; *Sefer HaChaim,*
      "*Geulah VeYeshua*" 5:5; *Midrash Sh'muel* on *Avoth* 4:22; Rabbenu Yonah, *Shaarey*
      Teshuvah 1:41.
21.   See above, 10:52.
22.   See above 8:24, 10:54.

ceases to be a recipient of His goodness.[23] Even his good deeds are no longer acceptable to God, as the Psalmist again says, "To the wicked, God says, 'Why do you declare My statutes?'" (Psalms 50:16).[24]

13:11   Although any individual sin is bad, it is much worse when an entire community sins. In such a case, the general tone of immorality tends to reinforce itself, generating a general climate of godlessness. Like a virus that becomes more virulent during an epidemic, sin incurs greater guilt when an entire community transgresses.[25]

13:12   The moral fortitude required to overcome temptation is counted as virtue in God's eyes. Our sages thus teach us that a person who has the opportunity to sin, but refrains from doing so, has the same merit as one who does a good deed.[26]

13:13   Since the entire concept of morality and sin emanates from God, the main consequences of immorality are in the spiritual realm. Therefore, even though most sins involve action, it is also possible to sin in thought. In some ways, lascivious thoughts can be more harmful than immoral acts,[27] since the former affect man's highest faculty, namely his mind,[28] and thus can harm the highest reaches of his spiritual being.[29] Besides being sinful in their own right, lustful thoughts are also likely to bring a person to the actual commission of sin.[30] The Torah therefore warns us, "Do not stray after your hearts and after your eyes, which lead you to immorality" (Numbers 15:39).[31] Reiterating the injunction against

---

23.   *Yerushalmi, Rosh HaShanah* 1:3 (7b); *Avoth DeRabbi Nathan* (B) 32; *Shaarey Teshuvah* 1:41. Cf. *Nefesh HaChaim* 4:5.

24.   *Reshith Chokhmah, Shaar HaTeshuvah* 2 (108b); *Derekh HaShem* 4:2:6.

25.   *Avodah Zarah* 5a; *Tosafoth ad. loc. s.v. U'Tzerikha;* Maharam *ad. loc.; Teshuvoth Shaar Ephraim* 50.

26.   *Makkoth* 3:15 (23b); Rambam *ad. loc.; Kiddushin* 39b; *Yerushalmi, Kiddushin* 1:9 (22b); *Tana DeBei Eliahu Rabbah* 9 (64b).

27.   The Talmud thus states that, "Thoughts of sin are more severe than sin itself"; *Yoma* 26a. Cf. *Yoma* 74b; *Berakhoth* 12b; *Ikkarim* 4:28; *Cheredim, Teshuvah* 4 (p. 231).

28.   *Moreh Nevukhim* 3:8 (12a); *Ikkarim* 4:28; *Cheredim, Teshuvah* 4 (p. 231); Maharatz Chajas, *Yoma* 29a.

29.   *Nefesh HaChaim* 1:14. Cf. *Tikuney Zohar* 70 (124a).

30.   *Avodah Zarah* 20b.

31.   *Sifri ad. loc.; Berakhoth* 13a.

lascivious thoughts, the Torah states, "You must avoid every immoral thing" (Deuteronomy 23:10).[32]

13:14   When the Torah says that one can sin through thought, it is only referring to cases where the individual actually dwells on such thoughts and derives sensual pleasure from them. In general, however, mere intent is not considered sinful. The Psalmist thus said, "If I had [merely] regarded sin in my heart, God would not have paid attention (Psalms 66:18).[33] If the intent actually results in sin, however, then the individual can be held accountable for the thought as well as the deed. This is what God meant when He told His prophet, "Behold, I will bring evil upon this people for the *fruit* of their thoughts" (Jeremiah 6:19).[34] This has an important consequence. If a person is doing something permissible, but thinks that it is a sin, then he is considered to have sinned.[35] The very fact that the deed was accompanied by a sinful thought places it in the category of a sinful act. Still, of course, it is not as serious as an actual sin.[36] There is one exception to the rule that one is not held accountable for mere intent. This involves all things that affect one's belief in God, such as atheism and idolatry. In such cases, one can be held liable for intent as well as deed, as we find, "These people have set up idols in their hearts" (Ezekiel 14:3).[37]

13:15   In all cases, liability for sin depends upon one's mental

---

32. *Kethuvoth* 46a; *Avodah Zarah* 20b; Rabbenu Yonah, *Shaarey Teshuvah* 3:40; *Cheredim*, Negative Commandments 1:30 (p. 101). Also see *Bava Bathra* 165a; *Sefer Chasidim* 123.

33. *Kiddushin* 39b, 40a; *Chullin* 142a; *Yerushalmi, Peah* 1:1 (5a); *Tosefta, Peah* 1:4; *Zohar* 2:150b; *Emunoth VeDeyoth* 5:8 (74a); *Teshuvoth Divrey Yosef* 60. Regarding idolatry, however, mere intent is considered sinful; *Yerushalmi, Peah loc. cit.; Tosafoth, Kiddushin* 39b *s.v. Machshavah.*

34. *Ibid. Cf.* Rosh, *Rosh HaShanah* 1:5 (p. 36a); *Korban Nethanel ad. loc.* no. 1.

35. *Nazir* 4:3 (17a); *Kiddushin* 81b; *Tosefta, Nazir* 3:6; *Yerushalmi, Nazir* 4:3 (17a); *Tosafoth, Kiddushin* 32a *s.v. DeMachil Leh; Reshith Chokhmah, Shaar HaYirah* 4 (15a); *Turey Zahav, Yoreh Deah* 157:10; *Beer Hetiv* 157:13.

36. *Nimukey Yosef, Bava Kama* (Rif 40a) *s.v. Omer; Yoreh Deah* 157:2 in *Hagah.*

37. *Kiddushin* 40a; *Yerushalmi, Tosefta, loc. cit.,* from Ezekiel 14:5; *cf.* Radak *ad. loc.; Zohar* 2:150b. See note 33 (end). When God commanded us, "You shall have no other gods before Me" (Exodus 20:3), He was giving us a commandment that depends essentially upon thought; *Yad, Yesodey HaTorah* 1:6; *Sefer HaMitzvoth,* Negative Commandment 1; *Sefer Mitzvoth Gadol,* Negative Commandment 1; *Chinukh* 26.

involvement.[38] Therefore, for example, a premeditated sin is worse than one done without prior intent in the heat of momentary passion.[39]

13:16 Similarly, the seriousness of a sin depends on one's motive. A person who sins because he is overcome by desire is not as bad as one who does wrong without any overriding compulsion.[40] Likewise, one who does wrong for material gain, convenience, or comfort, is not as reprehensible as one who sins merely because he does not care.[41] Although neither passion nor material gain is a true mitigating factor, the fact that a person has some benefit from an immoral act makes it less an act of rebellion, and more a response to his baser human nature.

13:17 The worse possible kind of sin is one done out of spite, as a demonstration that one does not believe in God or the Torah.[42] A person who rebels in this manner is counted as a renegade and an apostate,[43] even for a single[44] violation of a relatively minor law.[45] Such a person is considered worthy of death,[46] as the Torah states, "The person who acts defiantly... denounces God, and that person shall be cut off [spiritually] from among his people" (Numbers 15:30).[47]

13:18 At the other extreme is one who is forced to sin. Such an individual is not considered liable for his actions at all, as the

38. *Nefesh HaChaim* 1:14.
39. *Sefer Chasidim* 174.
40. Ran, *Chullin* (Rif 1a) *s.v. U'LeInyan; Anshey Shem ad. loc.* no. 1; *Yoreh Deah* 2:5 in *Hagah;* HaGra *ad. loc.* 2:16; *Magen Avraham* 39:3.
41. *Gittin* 46a; Rashi, *Avodah Zarah* 26b *s.v. LeTeavon; Sefer Meirath Eynayim (Sema), Choshen Mishpat* 425:20.
42. *Moreh Nevukhim* 3:41 (53b).
43. *Avodah Zarah* 26b; *Horayoth* 11a; *Yad, Gezelah VeAvedah* 11:2; *Yoreh Deah* 2:5; HaGra *ad. loc.* 2:13; *Choshen Mishpat* 266:2; *Magen Avraham, Orach Chaim* 39:3; *Mishnah Berurah* 39:6; *Biur Halakhah* 39:2; *Pith'chey Teshuvah, Yoreh Deah* 158:3; *Teshuvoth Avodath HaGershoni* 18 (end).
44. *Yam Shel Shlomo, Chullin* 1:16; *Sifethey Cohen, Yoreh Deah* 2:16.
45. For whether this applies solely to a violation of a negative commandment, or also includes a positive, *cf. Tevuoth Shor, Yoreh Deah* 2:18; *Pri Megadim*, introduction 4:2; *Eshel Avraham* 37:1. *Cf.* Rashi, *Chullin* 4b *s.v. Mumar; Rosh Yosef ad. loc.; Kesef Mishneh, Shechitah* 4:14.
46. *Avodah Zarah* 26b; *Yad, Rotzeach* 4:10; *Yoreh Deah* 158:2; *Choshen Mishpat* 425:5; *Moreh Nevukhim* 3:41 (53b).
47. *Moreh Nevukhim* 3:41 (53b); *Chovoth HaLevavoth* 7:7; Rabbenu Yonah, *Shaarey Teshuvah* 3:143.

Torah states concerning a victim of rape, "You must not impose any penalty whatsoever upon the girl, since she has not committed a sin worthy of death" (Deuteronomy 22:26).[48] A very similar situation exists where there is no way that a person can ascertain that an act is sinful or forbidden, and therefore sins inadvertantly or through ignorance.[49] The same is also true in every other case where a sinful act cannot possibly be avoided.[50]

13:19 Thus, when a person sins accidently and without intent,[51] he is not considered liable for his action.[52] The only exception to this rule is where the individual derives bodily pleasure from his act,[53] as in the case of sexual activity or the eating of forbidden food.[54] In such cases, the enjoyment itself is counted as intent.[55]

13:20 In general, man has the responsibility of controlling his desires, and therefore the fact that one is overcome by desire is no excuse to sin, and he bears full responsibility for it.[56] There is, however, one exception to this rule. If one is forced to sin, and is then overcome by desire and sins willingly, he is not considered responsible for his willingness. In such a case, since the desire itself was coerced, it is a mitigating factor.[57]

---

48. See above, 3:30; *Moreh Nevukhim* 3:41 (53b). If one is in danger and saves himself by sinning, *cf. Mishnath Chakhamim, Avodath Kokhavim,* introduction; *Pith'chey Teshuvah* 147:2, 147:14; *Turey Zahav* 179:4; *Tosafoth, Kethuvoth* 19a *s.v. DeOser; HaFla'ah ad. loc.*
49. *Cf. Pith'chey Teshuvah, Yoreh Deah* 185:9, citing *Teshuvoth Chatham Sofer* 155.
50. *Shevuoth* 18a; Rashi *ad. loc. s.v. MiShum; Tosafoth, Yevamoth* 35b *s.v. VeNimtzeth;* Mordecai, *Hilkhoth Niddah* 731, in *Shevuoth; Yad, Shegagoth* 5:6; *Yoreh Deah* 185:4 in *Hagah;* HaGra *ad. loc. Deah* 185:12-13; *Pith'chey Teshuvah* 185:15; *Teshuvoth Meir Nethivim* 73; *Teshuvoth Chatham Sofer* 155, 156, 163, 188.
51. *Cf. Tosafoth, Kiddushin* 24a *s.v. MiBa'eh.*
52. *Kerithoth* 4:3 (19a); *Shabbath* 72b; *Sanhedrin* 62b; *Horayoth* 5a; Rashi, *Kerithoth* 19b *s.v. Mith'asek; Tosafoth ibid. s.v. DeHah; Ikkarim* 4:27.
53. Therefore, Rashi, *Shabbath* 73b *s.v. DeSabur,* writes that in violating the Sabbath there is no bodily pleasure. However, *Tosafoth, Sanhedrin* 62b *s.v. LeHagbia,* maintains that because "thoughtful work" or "work which involves thought" is required, one is exempt on Sabbath even if one does have pleasure.
54. *Shabbath* 72b; *Sanhedrin* 72b; *Yerushalmi, Shabbath* 11:6 (68a); *Yad, Shegagoth* 2:7.
55. Rashi, *Sanhedrin* 62b *s.v. SheKen.*
56. *Yam Shel Shlomo, Yevamoth* 6:5; *Pith'chey Teshuvah, Evven HaEzer* 6:11; *Maharatz Chajas, Shevuoth* 17b. Also see *Teshuvoth Noda BeYehudah, Evven HaEzer* 2:150; *HaFla'ah, Peney Yehoshua, Kethuvoth* 51b.
57. *Kethuvoth* 51b; *Yerushalmi, Sotah* 4:4 (20a); *Tosafoth, Bava Kama* 41a *s.v. KeMaan, Shevuoth* 17b *s.v Iy; Yad, Issurey Biyah* 1:9; *Beth Sh'muel, Evven HaEzer* 6:23; *Beer Hetiv ibid.* 6:20; *Teshuvoth Chatham Sofer* 155; *Pith'chey Teshuvah, Yoreh Deah* 185:9.

13:21 Where there is the slightest question of a sin or prohibition, one is required to investigate as thoroughly as possible before acting.[58] In any such case where a person neglects to investigate, he is considered liable even for an inadvertant sin.[59] This is considered a spiritual blemish on a person's soul,[60] for which atonement is required.[61] It is of inadvertant sins such as these that the Torah is speaking when it says, "If an individual commits an inadvertant sin by violating one of God's prohibitory commandments... the sacrifice for his violation shall be brought... as a sin offering to God" (Leviticus 4:2-3).[62] Scripture likewise states, "Even without knowledge, a soul [can become] no good" (Proverbs 19:2).[63] It is also written, "Do not plead before the [punishing] angel, 'It was only an error!'" (Ecclesiastes 5:5).[64] The sin itself may have been inadvertant, but such "errors" are most usually brought about by general moral and religious laxity.[65]

13:22 Ignorance of the Law is no excuse for sin.[66] Every individual has the duty to study and make himself aware of his basic obligations, and therefore one who sins out of ignorance of the Law is as blameful as any other inadvertant sinner.[67] In the case of a scholar, however, the Torah is even more stringent, since the greater the

---

58. *Yad, Shegagoth* 5:6. *Cf. Niddah* 2:2 (14a), 57b; *Shevuoth* 18a; *Kerithoth* 17b; *Sifethey Cohen, Yoreh Deah* 184:7; *Pith'chey Teshuvah* 184:2, 185:14. See also *Tosafoth, Betza* 25b *s.v. Orach Ara; Ran, Pesachim* (Rif 1a) *s.v. Ela; Yoreh Deah* 1:1 in *Hagah; Teshuvoth Noda BeYehudah* 2:85, 2:96.

59. *Moreh Nevukhim* 3:41 (53b); *Tanchuma, VaYikra* 7; *Yalkut Shimoni* 1:464; *Reshith Chokhmah, Shaar HaYirah* 4 (14b); *Pri Megadim,* introduction 3:13.

60. *Reshith Chokhmah, Shaar HaYirah* 4 (14b). *Cf. Tosafoth, Yevamoth* 58a *s.v. VeNakeh; Mishneh LeMelekh, Sotah* 2:8. *Cf. Sanhedrin* 55b; *Yad, Issurey Biyah* 1:18.

61. *Cf. Yoreh Deah* 185:4 in *Hagah.*

62. Alshekh, *Taamey HaKorbanoth ad. loc.;* Abarbanel, introduction to Leviticus; Radak on Jeremiah 7:22. *Cf. Berakhoth* 23a; *Sefer Chasidim* 228. See *Chagigah* 5a; *Yerushalmi, Chagigah* 2:1 (8b), from Ecclesiastes 12:14; see below, 13:57.

63. *Midrash Mishley ad. loc.,* cited in *Yalkut Shimoni* 2:959; *Metzudoth David ibid.; VaYikra Rabbah* 4:3; *Koheleth Rabbah* 12:15; *Tanchuma, VaYikra* 6; see above, 11:42, note 135.

64. *Sefer Chasidim* 228.

65. *Yalkut Shimoni* 2:959; Rashi on Deuteronomy 39:18; *Sefer Chasidim* 177; *Makor Chesed* (on *Sefer Chasidim*) 7:7.

66. *Makkoth* 7b, 9a; Rashi, *Shabbath* 68b *s.v. Patur, Sanhedrin* 62b *s.v. Ela; Tosafoth, Makkoth* 7b *s.v. Ela, Shabbath* 68b *s.v. Aval Tinok,* 72b *s.v. BeOmer; Yad, Rotzeach* 5:4, 6:10; *Teshuvoth Shoel U'Meshiv* 1:1:16. See above, 12:49, notes 123, 124.

67. *Cf. Shabbath* 7:1 (67b); *Yad, Shegagoth* 7:2.

individual, the greater his responsibility.[68] Therefore, for example, a scholar who sins because of his own misinterpretation of the Law is considered as blameful as if he had purposely sinned.[69]

13:23 At the opposite extreme is the individual who is raised in a totally nonreligious environment. Such a person can grow up in complete ignorance of the Torah's teachings. He is thus not considered a purposeful sinner, but rather, like a child kidnapped as an infant who never had access to the truth.[70] Although such an individual might bear some responsibility for his general ignorance, he is in no way to blame for each individual act.[71] Even if he is later exposed to the Torah's teachings, it is still counted as if he is acting out of ignorance,[72] since it is all but impossible to overcome one's upbringing.[73] However, even such an individual is responsible for moral sins, such as murder and robbery, since these can be readily deduced from common sense.[74]

13:24 Occasionally, an individual may commit a sin thinking that he is actually doing a good deed.[75] In such a case, if it was impossible for him to ask or otherwise ascertain the truth, then he has the merit of the good deed.[76] With regard to such cases, our sages teach us that, "A sin committed for [God's] sake can be better than a good deed not done for [God's] sake."[77] On the other hand, if the individual was able in any way to have ascertained the true nature of his deed but neglected to do so,[78] he has both the

---

68. *Bava Bathra* 15a; *Zohar* 3:176a; *Tikuney Zohar* 70 (124a). *Cf. Devarim Rabbah* 7:4.
69. *Avoth* 4:13; *Bava Metzia* 33b; *Sanhedrin* 103b.
70. *Shabbath* 68b; *Yerushalmi, Shabbath* 7:1 (40a); *Yad, Shegagoth* 2:6, 7:2. However, see Bertenoro, *Tosefoth Yom Tov*, on *Kerithoth* 1:2.
71. *Ibid.*
72. *Cf. Bava Metzia* 33b; Maharsha *ad. loc.*
73. See above, 12:55, notes 142, 143.
74. *Moreh Nevukhim* 3:13; Ramban, Meiri, *Makkoth* 7b; *Sefer Chasidim* 153.
75. *Cf. Shabbath* 19:4 (137a); *Pesachim* 72b; *Menachoth* 64a; *Yad, Shegagoth* 2:8, *Shabbath* 2:16.
76. *Sefer Chasidim* 153, 645; Maharatz Chajas, *Berakhoth* 63b. *Cf. Tosafoth, Berakhoth* 24b *s.v. MiBa'eh.* Also see *Kiddushin* 39a; *Yerushalmi, Peah* 1:1 (5a); *Tosefta, Peah* 1:4.
77. *Nazir* 23b; *Tosafoth ad. loc. s.v SheMiTokh; Horayoth* 10b; *Beney Chayay* 188b, cited in *Orach Mishor, Nazir loc. cit. Cf. Beth HaMeir, Evven HaEzer* 178:3; *Teshuvoth Shevuth Yaakov* 2:116; *Beer Hetiv, Evven HaEzer* 6:20; *Pith'chey Teshuvah* 6:11.
78. *Sefer Chasidim* 153, 489, 645. *Cf. Taanith* 22b.

merit of his good intention and the blame for his sinful act.[79] If he was forewarned, however, then he has no merit at all, even for his good intentions.[80]

13:25 The Torah prescribes many penalties and punishments for various sins, and these once played a very important role in Judaism. Although these are no longer practiced, they can give us a deeper insight into the Jewish concept of morality in general. While the Temple or *Beth HaMikdash* stood in Jerusalem, animal sacrifices were required for a number of minor sins.[81] In one sense, they served almost like a monetary fine.[82] Animal sacrifice was furthermore a common mode of worship from the most ancient times,[83] and the Torah incorporated this practice in providing for such offerings.[84] On a deeper level, the death and burning of the animal presented a strong visual symbol of the punishment that unmitigated justice might exact from a sinner.[85] In this way, sacrifice gave the sinner a vicarious taste of death, and vividly portrayed the tenuousness of mortal life.[86] It thus strengthened man spiritually and helped reconcile his animal and spiritual natures.[87]

13:26 Sacrifice did not serve as an end in itself, but merely as a means by which man could expiate his sins.[88] No sacrifice could atone for sin unless it was accompanied by repentance.[89] In any event,

---

79. *Sefer Chasidim* 489. Regarding being rewarded and punished for the same deed, see *Sanhedrin* 101b; *Makor Chesed* (on *Sefer Chasidim*) 489:3.
80. *Ibid. Cf. Teshuvoth Chatham Sofer, Orach Chaim* 177; *Machaneh Ephraim, Sekhiruth* 17; *Teshuvoth Ramatz, Yoreh Deah (HaShmatoth)* 2:11.
81. *Cf.* Leviticus 4:1*ff.* See *Tal Torah, Chullin* 130b; *HaShmatoth* on *Yerushalmi, Yevamoth* 1:1 (47d); *Menachoth* 73b; *Taanith* 32a; *Shevuoth* 12b; *Zohar* 2:12a, 3:20a.
82. Radak on Jeremiah 7:23.
83. *VaYikra Rabbah* 22:5; *Moreh Nevukhim* 3:32 (45a); *Shem Tov ad. loc.;* Radak *loc. cit.*
84. *Cf. Bereshith Rabbah* 16:5; *VaYikra Rabbah* 2:9; *Zohar* 1:141b, 1:199b, 2:5a, 2:165b, 3:263a; *Zohar Chadash* 18c; *Nitzotzey Zohar* 1:27a no. 7.
85. *Tanchuma, VaYikra* 8; Ramban on Leviticus 1:9; *Chinukh* 95.
86. *Zohar* 1:89b, 1:244a, 2:5b, 3:18a; *Sh'nei Luchoth HaB'rith, Or Torah MeInyan HaAvodah* 2:140a-b, citing Recanti.
87. *Etz Chaim, Shaar Kitzur ABYA* 2; *Likutey Amarim (Tanya), Iggereth HaTeshuvah* 7 (97a).
88. Radak on Jeremiah 7:23.
89. *Shevuoth* 13a; *Kerithoth* 7a; *Tosefta, Yoma* 4:8; *Yad, Teshuvah* 1:1. *Cf.* Rashi, *Yoma* 85b *s.v. Chatath;* Bertenoro, *Tosefoth Yom Tov,* on *Yoma* 8:8.

God did not require the sacrifice *per se,*[90] but preferred that man not sin, and not bring any sacrifice.[91]

13:27 The idea of animal sacrifice might seem repugnant to us, and perhaps rightly so. The sacrificial system would be brutal and barbaric unless administered in an atmosphere permeated by dedication to God, where its full spiritual and mystical nature is thoroughly appreciated. Therefore, only a nation of the highest moral and spiritual caliber could be worthy of offering sacrifices to God.[92] When the Jewish people no longer maintained this standard,[93] the sacrificial system was abolished by God through the destruction of the Temple in the year 77 c.e.[94]

13:28 Now that the Temple no longer stands, study and prayer take the place of sacrifice. The prophet thus foretold, "We will offer the words of our lips instead of calves" (Hosea 14:3).[95] Therefore, one who commits a sin requiring sacrifice should read the Biblical portion dealing with that particular sacrifice, or study its Talmudic laws.[96] Furthermore, since an obligation for the sacrifice still remains, he should keep a record of the sin,[97] as well as its

---

90. *Sifri* (54a), *BaMidbar Rabbah* 21:16, *Pesikta* 6 (57a), *Yalkut Shimoni* (2:761, 2:955), on Numbers 28:2; *Kuzari* 2:26 (41a).

91. *Berakhoth* 22a; *Chagigah* 7a; *Targum* on Ecclesiastes 4:17; *Zohar* 2:55b; *Raya Mehemna, Zohar* 3:240a.

92. *Cf.* Isaiah 1:11; Jeremiah 7:11; Psalms 50:12.

93. Forty years before the destruction of the Temple, the sacrifices began to lose their efficacy; *Yoma* 39b.

94. *Cf. Yoma* 9b; *Tosefta, Menachoth* 13:4; *Yerushalmi, Yoma* 1:1 (4b); *BaMidbar Rabbah* 7:10.

95. *Siddur, "Yehi Ratzon"* before *"Aizehu Mekoman,"* in the first section of the *Shacharith* morning service; *cf.* Rabbi Yaakov Emdin, *Siddur Beth Yaakov ad. loc.* (p. 38a); *Pesikta* 6 (60b); *Yalkut Shimoni* 2:479; Rabbenu Yonah, *Shaarey Teshuvah* 1:41. *Cf. Yoma* 86b; *Shemoth Rabbah* 38:4. Study and prayer are much more spiritual modes of worship than sacrifice, and therefore, much less likely to be corrupted. Even these cannot affect atonement, however, without sincere repentance, which is required to expiate all sin; see Chapter 15.

96. *Menachoth* 110a; *Taanith* 27b; *Megillah* 31a; *Zohar* 1:100a, 1:101b, 3:32a, 3:35a; Rosh, *Rosh HaShanah* 4:14; *Orach Chaim* 1:5; *Magen Avraham* 1:8, 1:11; *Sh'nei Luchoth HaB'rith, Mesekheth Taanith* 2:124b, citing *Hagahoth Yesh Nochlin; Pri Megadim,* introduction 3:20. Regarding reading the sacrificial portions as part of the daily service, see *VaYikra Rabbah* 7:2; *Tosafoth, Avodah Zarah* 19b s.v. *YeShalesh, Kiddushin* 30a *s.v. Lo; Orach Chaim* 50:1; HaGra *ad. loc.*

97. *Shabbath* 12b; *Tosafoth, Shevuoth* 26a *s.v. Eth; Sh'nei Luchoth HaB'rith, Teshuvah* 2:184b; *Magen Avraham* 334:33; *Beer Hetiv* 334:24; *Shaarey Teshuvah, Orach Chaim* 603:1, citing *Yad Eliahu* 29. *Cf. Sefer Chasidim* 21.

circumstances.[98] If the Temple is then rebuilt during his lifetime, he will be obliged to bring the appropriate sacrifice.

13:29   Just as some transgressions required sacrifice, others required the atonement of physical punishment administered by the courts.[99] In practice, however, these punishments were almost never invoked, and existed mainly as a deterrent and to indicate the seriousness of the sins for which they were prescribed.[100] The rules of evidence and other safeguards that the Torah provides to protect the accused made it all but impossible to actually invoke these penalties.[101]

13:30   The courts could only inflict a punishment where it was specifically outlined in the Torah, and never on the basis of inference alone.[102] The reason for this was because an analogous sin may be serious enough to lie outside the domain of the courts and incur a more severe punishment by the hand of God.[103] Likewise, the punishment served as an atonement, and a more serious sin might not have been atoned for by such punishment.[104] Furthermore, besides being a gauge of the seriousness of a sin, the severity of punishment also depended upon how frequently it was likely to be committed, the amount of temptation involved, and the facility for doing it secretly.[105]

13:31   As in the case of sacrifice, the system of judicial punishments could become brutal and barbaric unless administered in an atmosphere of the highest morality and piety. When these standards declined among the Jewish people,[106] the Sanhedrin, which was the

---

98. Yoma 80a; Yerushalmi, Peah 1:1 (2a); Gilyon HaShas ad. loc.; Yerushalmi, Chagigah 1:2 (4b).
99. Moreh Nevukhim 3:41 (53a).
100. Sanhedrin 71a; Tosefta, Sanhedrin 14:1; Zohar 3:197b.
101. Makkoth 1:10 (7a); Yad, Sanhedrin 14:10.
102. Sanhedrin 54a, 73a, 74a; Makkoth 5b, 14a, 17a; Zevachim 196b; Sifra on Leviticus 20:17 (92d).
103. Maharsha, Sanhedrin 64b (Halakhoth) s.v. Gemara; Maharatz Chajas, Nedarim 4b, Makkoth 5b. Cf. Rambam, Mishnah Terumoth 7:1, Mishnah Meilah 6:2; Sefer Mitzvoth Gadol, Negative Commandment 40; Maharshal ad. loc.; Kesef Mishneh, Eduth 2:2; Yad Malachi 378 (60a); Mishneh LeMelekh, Yesodey HaTorah 6:8 s.v. VeDa, Naziruth 2:17; Beer Yaakov ("Rules," end of volume) no. 15. See also Temurah 3b; Kethuvoth 37b; Sefer Chasidim 406, 591.
104. Cf. Makkoth 2b; Tosafoth, Pesachim 32b s.v. Meilah.
105. Moreh Nevukhim 3:41 (53a).
106. Avodah Zarah 8b; Rashi, Sanhedrin 41a (end) s.v. Ela Dinei Nefashoth.

Jewish supreme court and legislative body, voluntarily abolished this system of penalties.[107] As the nation's religious and moral standards diminished, it was no longer worthy of having such a ready means of atonement as afforded by the courts.[108]

13:32 The system of penalties still provides us with a gauge as to the relative severity of various sins. Thus, as we shall explain, there were many sins that were punishable by flogging. Other more serious sins incurred the penalty of excision or *Kareth,* where the Torah states that a person should be "cut off from his people." Still more serious were sins punishable by the death penalty. Again, although these penalties were rarely if ever invoked, they teach us the relative severity of the sins for which they were prescribed. There are a number of instances where it is important to know this. One important case involves the rule that one may commit a lesser sin in order to avoid a greater one.[109] Thus, for example, if one has an uncontrollable desire to sin, he may commit a lesser sin in order to assuage this desire, although even the lesser sin requires atonement.[110] This, however, is only true where the greater sin is certain, or the desire absolutely uncontrollable. When it is not certain, the lesser sin may not be violated.[111]

13:33 Now that we have gone into the concept of sin in general, we can look at specifics. Any violation of Jewish law is considered improper behavior. If it only involves religious custom[112] or religious etiquette,[113] however, such behavior is not considered

---

107. This took place in the year 30 c.e.; *Shabbath* 15a; *Sanhedrin* 41a; *Avodah Zarah* 8b; *Yerushalmi, Sanhedrin* 1:1 (1b); *Yad, Sanhedrin* 14:13.
108. See note 104; *Likutey Amarim, Iggereth HaTeshuvah* 7 (96b).
109. *Shabbath* 4a; *Yad, Shabbath* 9:5; *Orach Chaim* 254:6; *Magen Avraham* 254:21-22; *Mishnah Berurah* 254:39. Cf. *Pri Megadim, Mishbetzoth Zahav* 328:4.
110. *Sefer Chasidim* 176; *Chelkath Mechokek* 23:1; *Beth Sh'muel* 23:1, from *Targum Yonathan* on Genesis 49:24; *Sotah* 36b; *Yerushalmi, Horayoth* 2:5 (10b). Cf. Rambam on *Horayoth* 2:4. See also *Avodah Zarah* 64a; *Tosafoth, Chagigah* 16a s.v. *VeYaaseh.*
111. *Teshuvoth Rivash* 755; *Teshuvoth Radbaz* 1:187; *Turey Zahav, Yoreh Deah* 334:1; *Sefer Chasidim* 620; *Makor Chesed ad. loc.* 620:3; *Birkey Yosef, Evven HaEzer* 5:13. Cf. *Menachoth* 48a; *Sotah* 48a; Bertenoro, *Demai* 3:5 s.v. *Ein.*
112. Cf. *Pri Megadim,* introduction 1:41.
113. *Ibid.* 1:42.

sinful. Accordingly, we never find any punishment for such a transgression.[114]

13:34 As the supreme court of the Jewish people, the Sanhedrin was empowered by the Torah to legislate laws. These laws are called "Rabbinical Commandments" (*Mitzvoth DeRabbanan*, מִצְוֹת דְּרַבָּנָן). The least severe transgression that is considered sinful[115] is the violation of any of these rabbinical laws.[116] However, even in such a case, if one transgresses out of blatant disregard for the law, he is considered a most serious sinner.[117]

13:35 The courts were empowered to judge and administer punishment to any individual who violated a rabbinical law.[118] If one violated legislation instituted to safeguard Torah law,[119] it was customary to flog him,[120] as the court would see fit.[121] However, if one consistently refused to obey the law, he could be physically coerced into obedience, even at the expense of his life.[122]

13:36 More serious is the violation of a law which had been legislated for its own sake.[123] Such a violation was[124] punishable by

114. *Ibid.* 1:41.
115. See Volume 1, 11:29, note 67. Also see Volume 1, 5:22, 11:24.
116. Rabbenu Yonah, *Shaarey Teshuvah* 3:4. See Kaplan, *Torah Anthology*, Volume 11, p. 418.
117. *Ibid.* 3:5. See Volume 1, 11:29, note 68.
118. *Pri Chadash, Orach Chaim* 496:1.
119. Ran, *Pesachim* (Rif 17b) *s.v. VeIkhah; Kesef Mishneh, Talmud Torah* 6:14; *Magen Avraham* 496:1; *"Rav" Shulchan Arukh* 496:2; *Sifethey Cohen, Yoreh Deah* 334:70; *Pith'chey Teshuvah* 334:14, 16; *Teshuvoth Kenesseth Yechezkel, Orach Chaim* 19 (end); *Teshuvoth Panim Meiroth* 1:90.
120. *Makkoth Marduth; Shabbath* 40b; *Yevamoth* 52a; *Kethuvoth* 45b; *Nazir* 4:3 (23a), 58b; *Chullin* 141b; *Yad, Shabbath* 1:2, *Issurey Biyah* 17:7, *Sanhedrin* 18:5; *Pri Megadim,* introduction 1:23.
121. Rashi, *Chullin* 141b *s.v. Makkoth;* Rambam, Bertenoro, *Nazir* 4:3; Ran, *Kethuvoth* (Rif 16b) *s.v. VeHaMotzi; Nimukey Yosef, Makkoth* (Rif 4b) *s.v. LeGaon;* Rabbenu Yonah, *Shaarey Teshuvah* 3:8; *Pri Chadash* 471:1; *Beer Hetiv, Orach Chaim* 496:1; HaGra, *Choshen Mishpat* 271:12; Ramban, *Megillath Esther, Sefer HaMitzvoth, Shoresh* 1:6 (6a). Others maintain that this consists of 39 lashes, as with Biblical sins; *Teshuvoth Rivash* 90, cited in *Pri Chadash loc. cit.; Bayith Chadash* on Ran *loc. cit.* no. 5. Still others maintain that it consists of 13 lashes; *Magen Avraham* 496:2; *Bayith Chadash loc. cit.*
122. *Arukh s.v. Marad,* cited in Ran *loc. cit.; Yad, Chametz U'Matzah* 6:12; Bertenoro on *Nazir* 4:3.
123. See note 119. Excommunication was a more severe form of punishment than lashes; cf. *Moed Katan* 17a; *Kiddushin* 70b; Rashi, *ad. loc. s.v. DeAdifa; Yad, Talmud Torah* 7:1, *Yom Tov* 1:22; *Orach Chaim* 496:1; *Kesef Mishneh, Talmud Torah* 6:14; *Sifethey Cohen, Yoreh Deah* 334:70; *Sefer Meirath Eynayim (Sema), Choshen Mishpat* 8:23; *Beer Hetiv,*

excommunication,[125] where the sinner was barred from all social intercourse[126] and obliged to observe the customs of mourning[127] for a period of seven days.[128] This punishment was also meted out in other cases involving God's honor or the community's general welfare. [See Table 13:1, at end of this chapter.]

13:37 More severe than this is the sin of failing to observe a mandatory Biblical commandment.[129] One must be particularly careful regarding positive commandments, since even repentance cannot make up the loss of merit incurred.[130] Regarding such a loss, it is written, "That which is crooked cannot be made straight, and that which is missing cannot be counted" (Ecclesiastes 1:15).[131] One who habitually ignores any positive commandment can therefore be counted among the worst of sinners.[132]

13:38 The courts had the power to compel a person to obey a positive commandment, even at the cost of his life.[133] Still, regarding cases in which the Torah mentions the reward for a mandatory commandment, the court was not obliged[134] to force compliance.[135]

Choshen Mishpat 8:7; *Mishnah Berurah* 496:3; *Shaar HaTziun ad. loc.* 496:5; *Pri Megadim,* introduction 3:27.

124. It is not applied today; *cf. Yoreh Deah* 334:48 in *Hagah.*

125. *Cherem* or *Niduy,* also known in English as the "Ban" or "Anethema"; see *Eduyyoth* 5:6; *Berakhoth* 19a; *Yerushalmi, Moed Katan* 3:1 (10b).

126. *Bava Metzia* 59b; *Yerushalmi loc. cit.; Yad, Talmud Torah* 7:4; *Yoreh Deah* 334:1.

127. *Moed Katan* 15a; *Yad, Talmud Torah* 7:4; *Yoreh Deah* 334:2.

128. *Moed Katan* 16a; *Yad, Talmud Torah* 7:6; *Yoreh Deah* 334:1.

129. Rabbenu Yonah, *Shaarey Teshuvah* 3:9. For discussion whether violation of a positive or negative commandment constitutes a more serious sin, see above, 10:51; Maharatz Chajas, *Yevamoth* 7a, *Bava Kama* 9b.

130. *Sh'nei Luchoth HaB'rith, Meseketh Rosh HaShanah, Amud HaDin* 2:160b, quoting *Sefer HaMussar.*

131. *Berakhoth* 26a; *Sukkah* 2:6 (27a); *Chagigah* 1:6 (9a); *Reshith Chokhmah, Shaar HaYirah* 14 (41b).

132. *Rosh HaShanah* 17a; *Ritva ad. loc.; Ran, Rosh HaShanah* (Rif 4a) *s.v. Benonim;* Ramban, *Torath Adam, Shaar HaGamul* 70a. *Cf.* Rabbenu Yonah, *Shaarey Teshuvah* 3:11; *Pri Chadash, Orach Chaim* 612:6; *Teshuvoth Chut HaShani* 18; *Choshen Mishpat* 34:2; Maharatz Chajas, *Yevamoth* 20a. Also see *Sanhedrin* 99a; *Menachoth* 41a.

133. *Kethuvoth* 85b; *Chullin* 132b; Rashi, *Chullin* 110b *s.v. SheMathan; Tosafoth, Menachoth* 41a *s.v. Anishto;* Ramban on Exodus 20:8; *Choshen Mishpat* 97:15 in *Hagah; Teshuvoth Rivash* 484; Mizrachi on Exodus 18:20; *Teshuvoth Rashba* 472; HaGra, *Yoreh Deah* 261:7. *Cf. Yad, Malveh* 11:8; *Choshen Mishpat* 107:1.

134. But they may coerce if they see fit; *cf. Yerushalmi, Bava Bathra* 5:5 (18a); *Tosafoth, Bava Bathra* 8b *s.v. Ikh'pey, Kiddushin* 32a *s.v. Oru;* Mordecai, *Bava Bathra* 490, *Kethuvoth* 159; *Teshuvoth Maimoni (Kinyan)* 27; *Teshuvoth Ramban* 88; *Teshuvoth Rashba* 745; *Choshen Mishpat* 97:16 in *Hagah; Turey Zahav, Yoreh Deah* 240:1;

13:39 More serious than a simple mandatory commandment[136] is a negative commandment whose transgression is rectifiable by observing a corresponding positive commandment.[137] There is no physical punishment penalizing the transgression of such a negative commandment,[138] unless it becomes impossible to fulfill the accompanying positive.[139]

13:40 In a similar category is a negative commandment which is rectifiable by monetary compensation.[140] In any case where a single act incurs both physical punishment and monetary compensation, only a single penalty may be applied.[141] Except where a monetary penalty is specified, such as in the case of stealing, robbery,[142] or bodily injury,[143] only the physical punishment is meted out.[144]

13:41 More severe than this is the violation of a negative commandment which does not involve action.[145] The violation of such a commandment does not incur any physical punishment,[146] except in the case of swearing falsely, violating a vow, or cursing one's fellow.[147]

Sefer Meirath Eynayim, Choshen Mishpat 97:36, 107:2; *Sifethey Cohen ibid.* 97:10, 107:1; *Ketzoth HaChoshen* 97:9, 107:1; *Chokhmath Shlomo, Choshen Mishpat* 107:1; HaGra, *Choshen Mishpat* 97:54; *Teshuvoth Maharam Mintz* 32; *Teshuvoth Rabbi Moshe Alshekh* 15; *Teshuvoth Maharit* 72; *Teshuvoth Chatham Sofer, Choshen Mishpat* 177; *Hagahoth Maimonioth, Ishuth* 12:15 no. 20; *Mishneh LeMelekh, Avadim* 3:14; *Shaar HaMelekh, Ishuth* 12:14; Maharatz Chajas, *Chullin* 110b.

135. *Chullin* 110b; *Yerushalmi, Bava Bathra* 5:5 (18a); *Mekhilta* on Exodus 20:12 (70a); *Raya Mehemna, Zohar* 3:82b; *Yoreh Deah* 240:1 in *Hagah; Choshen Mishpat* 97:16 in *Hagah; Sefer Meirath Eynayim* 97:35. See also *Tosafoth, Chullin* 110b *s.v. Kol, Kethuvoth* 49b *s.v. Ikh'pey; Sifethey Cohen, Yoreh Deah* 248:3.

136. *Cf. Pri Megadim,* introduction 1:7.

137. Such as the return of a stolen article; *cf. Leviticus 5:23; Rabbenu Yonah, Shaarey Teshuvah* 3:24.

138. *Chullin* 12:4 (141a); *Makkoth* 3:4 (17a), 16a; *Tosefta, Makkoth* 4:6; *Yad, Sanhedrin* 18:2; *Lechem Mishneh ad. loc.*

139. *Chullin* 141b; *Yad, Sanhedrin* 16:4.

140. *Makkoth* 16a; *Tosafoth ad. loc. s.v. Hatham; Yad, Sanhedrin* 18:2; *Kesef Mishneh ad. loc. s.v. Kol.*

141. *Kethuvoth* 32b.

142. *Ibid.; Yad, Genevah* 3:1.

143. *Kethuvoth* 32b; *Sanhedrin* 85a; *Makkoth* 9a; *Yad, Sanhedrin* 16:12, 19:4 no. 131; *Choshen Mishpat* 420:2; *Sefer Meirath Eynayim* 420:5; *Yad, Chovel* 4:11; *Choshen Mishpat* 350:1; *Sifethey Cohen, Sefer Meirath Eynayim,* 350:1.

144. *Kethuvoth* 32b; *Yad, Genevah* 3:1, *Naarah Bethulah* 1:11, *Terumoth* 6:6.

145. Rabbenu Yonah, *Shaarey Teshuvah* 3:26, from *Yoma* 85b.

146. *Sanhedrin* 63a; *Bava Metzia* 91a; *Makkoth* 4b, 16a, 20b; *Temurah* 3a; *Zevachim* 29b; *Yad, Sanhedrin* 18:1.

147. *Shevuoth* 21a; *Tosefta, Makkoth* 4:5; *Yerushalmi, Shevuoth* 3:10 (18b), 4:10 (22b); *Yad loc. cit.*

13:42   In a similar category is a negative commandment which is given in general terms, for which there is no physical punishment.[148]

13:43   More severe than these are those negative commandments which are punishable by flogging.[149] This category includes all negative commandments except those which do not involve action, which are stated in general terms, which serve as a warning for a death penalty, or which are rectifiable by fulfilling an accompanying positive commandment, or by monetary compensation.[150] In all, of the 365 prohibitive commandments in the Torah, 207 are penalized by such corporal punishment. Of these, 21 are also punishable by *Kareth,* 18 by divine execution, and 168 have no other punishment.[151]

13:44   Flogging was executed with a doubled calfskin scourge, a handbreath in width.[152] Lashes were given in groups of three, according to how many the accused could withstand without endangering his life, with a maximum of 39.[153] A person guilty of an offense incurring lashes is considered worthy of death, but the flogging takes the place of the death penalty.[154]

13:45   No physical punishment[155] could be imposed except by a duly ordained court,[156] upon the testimony of at least two competent witnesses.[157] Similarly, no such penalty could be imposed unless the accused was forewarned of his liability,[158] since otherwise there

148. *Pesachim* 24a, 41b; *Nazir* 38b; *Bava Metzia* 115b; *Sanhedrin* 63a; *Menachoth* 58b; *Temurah* 7b; *Kerithoth* 4a, 5a; *Yad, Sanhedrin* 18:2-3; *Yad Malachi* 391 (61a).
149. *Shaarey Teshuvah* 3:75; *Yad Malachi* 378 (59b), from *Temurah* 4b; *Makkoth* 17a; *Yerushalmi, Kilayim* 3:1 (14b). For a conflicting opinion, see *Gufey Halakhoth (Maharash Algazi)* 313, from *Tosafoth, Makkoth* 13b *s.v. Rabbi Yitzchak; Mishneh LeMelekh, Yesodey HaTorah* 5:8 *s.v. VeDa; Rosh Yosef, Choshen Mishpat* 34:2 (end); *Pri Megadim,* introduction 1:7.
150. Rambam on *Makkoth* 3:1; *Yad, Sanhedrin* 18:2.
151. *Yad, Sanhedrin* 19:1, 2, 4.
152. *Makkoth* 3:12-13 (22b); *Yad, Sanhedrin* 16:8.
153. *Makkoth* 3:10-11 (22a); *Yad, Sanhedrin* 17:1-2.
154. *Sanhedrin* 10a; Rashi *ad. loc. s.v. Malkoth; Yad, Sanhedrin* 16:1; *Kesef Mishneh ad. loc.*
155. Regarding *Makkoth Marduth* given for a rabbinical transgression, see *Pri Megadim,* introduction 1:24; *Yad, Sanhedrin* 16:3.
156. See Volume 1, 10:25, 11:2.
157. Numbers 35:30; Deuteronomy 17:6, 19:15; *Sanhedrin* 4:1 (32a); *Yad, Sanhedrin* 12:1, 16:4.
158. *Sanhedrin* 40b; *Tosafoth ad. loc. s.v. Minayin; Yad, Sanhedrin* 16:4, *Issurey Biyah* 1:3.

was a possibility that the sin was committed without knowledge of its penalty.[159]

13:46 Still more severe is the violation of a negative commandment which also serves as a warning for a death penalty. The violation of such a commandment could not incur the penalty of flogging,[160] since it is too severe a sin to be atoned by lashes.[161]

13:47 Next in order of severity are sins punishable by premature death by the hand of God.[162] There are 18 sins which incur this punishment, and they are punishable by lashes when committed with warning in the presence of witnesses.[163] [See Table 13:2.] There are also 14 sins which are punishable by premature death alone. [See Table 13:3.]

13:48 More severe than these are sins punishable by *Kareth,* literally, "excision" or "cutting off."[164] This punishment is entirely in the hand of God. It means that a person's soul is "cut off" from its Source, and suffers a kind of spiritual atrophy.[165]

13:49 The effect of this atrophy varies with each individual. If a person is on such a high spiritual level that he cannot exist without a close relationship to God,[166] then *Kareth* can cause his lifespan to be shortened.[167] Although this is very much like death by the hand of God, our traditions teach us that *Kareth* entails an earlier[168] and

159. *Yad, Sanhedrin* 12:2; *Kesef Mishneh, Lechem Mishneh, ad. loc. Cf. Sanhedrin* 8b, 41a, 72b; *Makkoth* 6b, 9b; Maharatz Chajas, *Sanhedrin* 41a.
160. *Shabbath* 154a; *Eruvin* 17b; *Bava Kama* 74b; *Sanhedrin* 86b; *Shevuoth* 4a; *Makkoth* 13b; *Yad, Sanhedrin* 18:2; Ramban, *Megillath Esther, Sefer HaMitzvoth, Shoresh* 1 no. 3 (5a); *Yad Malachi* 583 (60b).
161. *Minchath Chinukh* 364 (272a); *Urim VeThumim* 34. See notes 103, 104.
162. Rabbenu Yonah, *Shaarey Teshuvah* 3:107. *Cf. Pesachim* 32b.
163. *Yad, Sanhedrin* 19:2.
164. Genesis 17:14; Exodus 12:15, 19, 30:33, 38, 31:14; Leviticus 7:20, 21, 25, 17:4, 9, 10, 14, 19:8, 20:17, 22:3, 9; Numbers 9:13, 15:30, 31, 19:13, 20.
165. *Zohar* 1:236b, 2:142b; *Shaarey Kedushah* 3:5; *Sh'nei Luchoth HaB'rith, Shaar HaOthioth, Taharah* 1:108a; *Nefesh HaChaim* 1:18; *Likutey Amarim, Iggereth HaTeshuvah* 5 (95b); *Or HaChaim* on Leviticus 17:10. See Kaplan, *Innerspace,* p. 175f.
166. *Likutey Amarim, Iggereth HaTeshuvah* 6 (96a).
167. *Cf. Mekhilta* on Exodus 12:15 (9b), 12:19 (10b), 31:14 (104a); *Sifra* on Leviticus 20:5 (91c), 23:30 (102a); *Emunoth VeDeyoth* 9:9 (98a); Ramban on Leviticus 18:29; Abarbanel on Numbers 15:22; *Kesef Mishneh, Milah* 1:2.
168. *Moed Katan* 28a; *Tosafoth ad. loc. s.v. U'Mithah B'Yedey Shamayim; Yerushalmi, Bikkurim* 2:1 (6b); *Marah HaPanim,* HaGra, *ad. loc.; Semachoth* 3:8; *Tosafoth, Shabbath* 25a *s.v. Kareth, Yevamoth* 2a *s.v. Esheth Achiv;* Ibn Ezra on Genesis

more sudden death.[169] In some cases, the punishment of *Kareth* can also result in the death of one's very young children.[170]

13:50 Another major difference between these two divine punishments is that death by the hand of God atones for the sin even without repentance, the premature death itself being the atonement.[171] In the case of *Kareth,* on the other hand, death without repentance does not expiate the sin, and the sin is also punishable after death.[172] In such a case, full spiritual achievement in the future life would entail unbearable guilt pangs, and therefore, in His mercy, God keeps the sinner on a lower spiritual level, where the feelings of guilt are not as severe.[173]

13:51 If a person is not on a sufficiently high spiritual level so as to be punished in this life,[174] then the main penalty of *Kareth* is exacted after death, and is all the more severe.[175] In any case, a

17:14; *Kesef Mishneh, Biyath HaMikdash* 4:4; *Pri Megadim,* introduction 3:18; *Yad Malachi* 2:350 (151a); Ramban, *Torath HaAdam, Inyan HaPetirah* 11b.

169. *Semachoth ibid.* 3:9; *Tosafoth Yeshenim, Yevamoth* 2a no. 3.

170. This is specified in Leviticus 20:20-21; *cf.* Targum, *Sifra* (93a-b), Rashi, *Sifethey Chakhamim, ad. loc.* According to Rashi *loc. cit.,* this applies to all cases of *Kareth; cf.* Rashi on Genesis 17:14, Leviticus 17:19; Ibn Ezra on Genesis 17:14; Rashi, *Shabbath* 25a *s.v. VeKareth, Chullin* 31a (end) *s.v. Tumah, Kerithoth* 2a *s.v. VeKareth;* Rabbenu Tam, *Tosafoth loc. cit.; Shaarey Teshuvah* 3:107, 3:119; Bertenoro, *Sanhedrin* 9:6; *Asarah Maamaroth* 1:1:19; *Pri Megadim,* introduction 3:18. However, Riva, *Tosafoth loc. cit.,* maintains that this is only true in the two cases mentioned in the Torah. *Cf. Yevamoth* 55a; *Tosafoth Yeshenim, Shabbath* 25a. In general, we find that young children may die for their parents' sins; see *Yad, Teshuvah* 6:1; *Sotah* 49a; *Tanchuma, Ki Tetze* 2; *Tana DeBei Eliahu Rabbah* 10; *Yalkut Shimoni* 2:600; *Zohar* 1:118b, 2:113b; *Or HaChaim* on Exodus 22:5, 22:14.

171. Rambam, Bertenoro, on *Sanhedrin* 9:6; *Asarah Maamaroth* 1:1:19; *Pri Megadim,* introduction 3:18; *Maharatz Chajas, Yevamoth* 2a.

172. *Sanhedrin* 64b, 90b; *Sifri, Yalkut Shimoni* (1:749), on Leviticus 15:31; *Yad, Teshuvah* 8:1; *Hagahoth Maimonioth, Kesef Mishneh, ad. loc.;* Ramban, *Torath HaAdam, Shaar HaGamul* 79a; *Raya Mehemna, Zohar* 3:218a. Others, however, write that this is only true of the sin of idolatry; *cf.* Ramban on Leviticus 18:29; *Shaarey Teshuvah* 3:121. See *Zohar* 2:170b; *Nishmath Chaim* 1:4.

173. *Emunoth VeDeyoth* 9:9 (98a); Ramban on Leviticus 15:31, 18:29, *Shaar HaGamul* 78a, from *Rosh HaShanah* 17a; Abarbanel on Leviticus 15:23; Bachya on Leviticus 18:25. The concept that the higher a person is raised spiritually the more acute his awareness of the gravity of his former sins and the more he suffers inwardly, is brought out in the parable of the Baal Shem Tov about a peasant who rebelled against a wise and beneficent king. Instead of punishing him, the king elevated the peasant step by step until he became the king's chief assistant. This caused the peasant to suffer, for he realized that he had reblled against such a great, merciful king; *Toldoth Yaakov Yosef, Bo* (50d); see Kaplan, *The Light Beyond* (Moznaim, 1981), pp. 351-352.

174. *Shaarey Teshuvah* 3:122.

175. *Emunoth VeDeyoth, Ramban, loc. cit..*

person is not judged by God in this life[176] until he reaches the age of 20.[177] When a person dies before the age of 20, it is therefore never the result of divine punishment. At times, the reason may be to prevent him from sinning further, so that he may die with some degree of righteousness.[178]

13:52 Of course, as in the case of all sins, if one repents, he is completely forgiven by God. Although repentance does not help to exempt one from the punishments inflicted by the courts, it does help to prevent the punishment of *Kareth* and death by the hand of God.[179] Repentance alone does not atone for a sin punishable by *Kareth* without some additional suffering.[180] If a person is punished by the courts and repents, however, he is immediately forgiven, even if he is worthy of *Kareth*.[181]

13:53 In all, there are 45 sins punishable by *Kareth*.[182] All such sins may also be punishable by death or flogging under the proper legal conditions, and by *Kareth* alone only when the court cannot

---

176. But in the afterlife, individuals are punished for sins committed even before age 20; *cf. Teshuvoth Chakham Tzvi* 49; *Teshuvoth Noda BeYehudah, Orach Chaim* 8, *Yoreh Deah* 2:164; *Teshuvoth Chatham Sofer, Yoreh Deah* 155; *Teshuvoth Chavath Yair (HaShmatoth)* 156; *Teshuvoth Tifereth Tzvi, Orach Chaim* 5:6; *Pith'chey Teshuvah, Yoreh Deah* 185:9, 376:3. However, from *Shabbath* 89b, it appears that such punishment will take place in the Ultimate Future after the resurrection; *cf. Teshuvoth Halakhoth Ketanoth* 2:273. See below, 17:26, that this is true only when one has not repented before death. Sincere repentance before death, on the other hand, can absolve even a very wicked person from all suffering beyond death.

177. Rashi on Numbers 14:29; *Avoth* 5:21; Rashi, Bertenoro, *ad. loc.; Shabbath* 89b; Rashi *ad. ioc. s.v. Dal;* Maharatz Chajas *ad. loc.; Yerushalmi, Bikkurim* 2:1 (6b); *Yerushalmi, Sanhedrin* 11:5 (56b); *Bereshith Rabbah* 58:1; Rashi on Genesis 23:1; Mizrachi, *Sifethey Chakhamim, Gur Aryeh* (Maharal), *ad. loc.; BaMidbar Rabbah* 18:3; Rashi on Numbers 16:28; *Zohar* 1:118b, 2:98a (top), 2:101a, 2:113a, 2:148b, 3:293b; *Tikuney Zohar* 40 (81a); *Bahir* 195; *Tosafoth, Taanith* 28a *s.v. Meth;* Rambam on *Sanhedrin* 7:4 (end); *Yad Shaul* 265; *Asarah Maamaroth* 1:2:23; *Yaaroth Devash* 2, "Lecture for 7th of Adar"; *Pri Megadim, Eshel Avraham* 219:1; *Pith'chey Teshuvah, Yoreh Deah* 5:3; *Yad Avraham, Yoreh Deah* 261:1.

178. *Zohar* 1:118b; *Asarah Maamaroth* 1:2:23; *cf. Shaar HaGamul* 76a. See below, 20:51.

179. *Sanhedrin* 90b; *Makkoth* 13b; *Emunoth VeDeyoth* 9:9 (98a); *Yad, Teshuvah* 6:2; Rashi on Numbers 15:31; *Yalkut Shimoni* 1:749; *Pri Megadim,* introduction 3:19.

180. See below, 17:16-18.

181. *Makkoth* 3:15 (23a); Rambam, Bertenoro, *ad. loc.; Megillah* 7b; *Yad, Sanhedrin* 17:7; *Mishneh LeMelekh ad. loc.; Pri Megadim,* introduction 3:21, "Introduction to Laws of Sabbath" *s.v. VeYesh Lishol.*

182. *Kerithoth* 1:1 (2a); Rambam *ad. loc.; Yad, Shegagoth* 1:4; *Lechem Mishneh ad. loc.*

act.[183] Of the 45 sins punishable by *Kareth,* 24 are otherwise punishable by death, and 21 by flogging.[184] [See Table 13:4.]

13:54 When the courts are unable to inflict punishment, all sexual crimes are punishable by *Kareth.* Thus, after enumerating these crimes, the Torah clearly states, "Whenever anyone does any of these perversions, their souls shall be cut off [spiritually] from the midst of their people" (Leviticus 18:29).[185] Of the 25 sexual crimes so designated, 18 are otherwise punishable by death, and 7 by flogging.

13:55 There are only two positive commandments whose neglect is so serious that they are punishable by *Kareth.* They are circumcision[186] and the bringing of the Passover lamb while the Temple stood.[187]

13:56 One who violates a negative commandment punishable by *Kareth* three times is considered among the inveterately wicked,[188] and there is a tradition[189] that he should be put to death indirectly by the courts.[190] Regarding such a person, it is written, "The wicked will end up being killed by their own evil" (Psalms 34:22).[191]

13:57 A person who inadvertently violated a negative commandment punishable by *Kareth* was required to bring a sin offering while the Temple stood,[192] and today should give the value of such a sacrifice to charity.[193]

---

183. *Cf. Yad, Avodath Kokhavim* 3:1, 6:1, 6:3, *Shabbath* 1:1, *Issurey Biyah* 1:1; Rashi, *Kerithoth* 2a *s.v. VeKareth.*
184. *Yad, Sanhedrin* 19:1.
185. *Kerithoth* 2b; *Yad, Issurey Biyah* 1:1; *Sefer HaMitzvoth,* Negative Commandment 352.
186. Genesis 17:14; *Kerithoth* 1:1 (2a); *Eruvin* 96b; *Zevachim* 106b; *Yad, Milah* 1:1, *Shegagoth* 1:2; *Yoreh Deah* 261:1; *cf. Shabbath* 133b.
187. Numbers 9:13; *Yad, Korban Pesach* 1:1, 5:2.
188. *Sanhedrin* 81b, Rashi *ad. loc. s.v. Averoth; Tosafoth ibid. s.v. U'Mar.*
189. Rashi, *Sanhedrin* 81b *s.v. VeHeikhi.*
190. *Sanhedrin* 9:5 (81b), 82b; *Yevamoth* 64b; *Tosefta, Sanhedrin* 12:4; *Yad, Sanhedrin* 18:4-5; *Pri Megadim,* introduction 3:24.
191. Rashi *ad. loc.; Sanhedrin* 81b.
192. *Kerithoth* 1:2 (2a); *Yad, Shegagoth* 1:1.
193. *Orach Chaim* 334:26 in *Hagah; Piskey Mahari* 60; *Tur, Yoreh Deah* 185; *Magen Avraham* 334:34; *Mishnah Berurah* 334:80; *"Rav" Shulchan Arukh* 334:28; *Chayay Adam* 9:12; *cf. Zevachim* 48a. Regarding fasting for such a sin, see *Orach Chaim*

13:58   There were a number of sins for which the Torah prescribed a death penalty to be administered by the courts, and these are considered more severe than those incurring the penalty of *Kareth*.[194] The four death penalties provided by the Torah were stoning, burning, decapitation, and strangulation.[195] These punishments were rarely carried out in practice, having been written into the Law mainly as deterrents against sin.[196] They were formally abolished by the courts in the year 30 c.e.[197]

13:59   Least severe of the death penalties was strangulation,[198] specified for the 6 sins listed in Table 13:5. It was also the penalty inflicted whenever the Torah does not specify the mode of death.[199] It was executed by immersing the accused in dung up to his armpits to reduce struggling. The two witnesses who had warned the accused, and according to whose testimony the court had convicted him, would then place a hard cloth wrapped in a soft one around his neck, and draw upon it until he died of strangulation.[200]

13:60   More severe than this was decapitation,[201] which was specified for murder[202] and communal apostasy.[203] It was administered with a sword while the accused stood erect.[204]

13:61   Still more severe was burning,[205] which was specified for the 10 sins listed in Table 13:6. It was administered in the same manner as strangulation, except that the witnesses would only draw the cloth until the accused was forced to open his mouth, after which

loc. cit.; *Yoreh Deah* 185:4; *Orach Chaim* 568:4; *Magen Avraham* 568:12; *Rokeach, Teshuvah* 7 (26b), 14 (27a), 28 (35a).

194. Rabbenu Yonah, *Shaarey Teshuvah* 3:126.
195. *Sanhedrin* 7:1 (49b); *Yad, Sanhedrin* 14:1; *Tanchuma, VaYera* 9.
196. See above, 13:29.
197. See Volume 1, 10:38; above 13:31, note 107.
198. *Sanhedrin* 50a; *Yad, Sanhedrin* 14:4; *Shaarey Teshuvah loc. cit.*
199. *Sanhedrin* 52b, 84b, 89a; *Yerushalmi* 7:1 (30b), 7:4 (31b); *Mekhilta* on Exodus 21:15, 21:16 (81b); *Yad, Sanhedrin* 14:1.
200. *Sanhedrin* 7:3 (52b); *Mekhilta loc. cit.; Yad, Sanhedrin* 15:5.
201. See note 198.
202. *Sanhedrin* 9:1 (76b), 52b; *Tosefoth Yom Tov, Sanhedrin* 9:1; *Yad, Sanhedrin* 15:12; Rabbenu Yonah, *Shaarey Teshuvah* 3:128.
203. *Ibid.,* from Deuteronomy 13:16.
204. *Sanhedrin* 7:3 (52b); Ramban, Bertenoro, *Tosefoth Yom Tov, ad. loc.;* Rashi *ibid. s.v. Nivul Hu Zeh; Yad, Sanhedrin* 15:4. *Cf. Tosefta, Sanhedrin* 9:3 (end).
205. See note 198.

molten lead or tin was poured down his throat, scalding his insides.[206]

13:62 Most severe was the penalty of stoning,[207] specified for the 18 sins listed in Table 13:7. This was administered by binding the accused and casting him from a platform twice his height. If he was still alive, a large stone would be thrown on his chest, and if this did not kill him, all present would pelt him to death.[208]

13:63 All sins incurring capital punishment are also punishable by *Kareth,* with the exception of the 11 listed in Table 13:8. Nevertheless, if a person is to be judged for his sins in this world,[209] he may die a death analogous to that of which he is guilty. Thus, for example, one who is guilty of a sin punishable by stoning may die by falling or some analogous accident. Similarly, death by fire or poisoning may be related to burning, death in war or by murder to decapitation, and drowning and sickness to strangulation.[210]

13:64 The community presently has no formal means of punishing a person who violates a commandment punishable by death. Still, such a person should be totally excommunicated and barred from all social intercourse within the community until he repents.[211]

13:65 More severe than these are sins for which a person may be killed without benefit of trial.[212] This category includes[213] stealing from the Temple,[214] cursing God in the name of a pagan diety,[215] and public fornication with a non-Jewess.[216] In such a case, one who

206. *Sanhedrin* 7:2 (52a); *Yad, Sanhedrin* 15:3.
207. *Sanhedrin* 49b; see note 198.
208. *Sanhedrin* 6:4 (45a); *Yad, Sanhedrin* 15:1.
209. *Tosafoth, Kethuvoth* 30b *s.v. Din, Sanhedrin* 37b *s.v. MiYom;* Ritva on *Eyn Yaakov, Kethuvoth* 10. *Cf. Eruvin* 54a; *Tosefoth Yom Tov, Avoth* 5:8.
210. *Kethuvoth* 30a; *Sotah* 8b; *Sanhedrin* 37b; *BaMidbar Rabbah* 14:7; *Tosafoth, Zevachim* 88b *s.v. HaMikhaperim; Shaarey Teshuvah* 3:130. See also *Perishah, Yoreh Deah* 345; *Yoreh Deah* 345:6; *Teshuvoth Maharil* 65; *Teshuvoth Chatham Sofer, Evven HaEzer* 2:132, *Yoreh Deah* 333; *Teshuvoth Beth Yaakov* 148; *Kol Bo, "Al Aveluth"* 3:2:35 (p. 195).
211. *Choshen Mishpat* 425:0 in *Hagah; Tur, Choshen Mishpat* 8, citing Rav Natrunai Gaon; *HaGra ad. loc.* 425:5.
212. Rabbenu Yonah, *Shaarey Teshuvah* 3:131. See below, note 220.
213. *Sanhedrin* 9:6 (81b); *Yad, Sanhedrin* 18:6.
214. *Sanhedrin* 81b, 82b, from Numbers 4:20; *cf.* Ramban *ad. loc.*
215. Since this resembles cursing God; *Sanhedrin* 82b; *Tosefoth Yom Tov, Sanhedrin* 9:6.
216. Numbers 25:8; *Avodah Zarah* 36b; *Yad, Issurey Biyah* 12:4; *Evven HaEzer* 16:2 in

is zealous for God[217] may kill the sinner without benefit of trial, as long as he is in the act[218] and has been warned.[219]

13:66 Intercourse with a non-Jewess incurs a harsher form of *Kareth* than any other sexual crime.[220] Regarding such a sin, it is written, "He has had sexual intercourse with the daughter of a strange god... God will cut off the man who does this" (Malachi 2:11-12).[221] Our sages also taught, "Whoever has intercourse with a non-Jewish maidservant will end up being hung by the hair of his scalp, as it is written (Psalms 68:22), 'Surely God will cleave the head of his enemies, the hairy scalp of he who walks about [untroubled] in his sins.'"[222]

13:67 More serious still[223] are the cardinal sins,[224] which may not be committed even under pain of death. These include murder, sexual crimes, and idolatry,[225] as well as sins associated with them.[226] The laws of Judaism teach us that one must give his life rather than commit one of these cardinal sins. These are the sins that result in a most serious spiritual defilement,[227] and they are the classical sins of antiquity.[228] For an individual, they are punishable both

Hagah; Choshen Mishpat 425:4 in *Hagah; Sefer Meirath Eynayim* 425:13. Bertenoro on *Sanhedrin* 9:6 writes that she must also be the daughter of a non-Jew.

217. But if he asks, he should not be advised to kill; *Sanhedrin* 82a; *Yad loc. cit.* 12:5; *Choshen Mishpat loc. cit.; Sefer Meirath Eynayim* 435:14.

218. *Sanhedrin* 81a; *Yad, Choshen Mishpat, loc. cit. Cf. Chokhmath Shlomo* on *Evven HaEzer loc. cit.*

219. Raavad, *Issurey Biyah* 12:4; *Maggid Mishneh ibid.;* HaGra, *Choshen Mishpat* 425:17.

220. *Sefer Mitzvoth Gadol,* Negative Commandment 112; *Turey Zahav, Evven HaEzer* 16:2. *Cf. Eruvin* 19a; *Tosafoth ad. loc. s.v. Bar MiBa, Bava Metzia* 58b *s.v. Chutz; Zohar* 1:131b, 2:3b, 2:87b. See above, 3:23, note 56.

221. Rashi, Radak, *ad. loc.; Sanhedrin* 82a; Rambam, Bertenoro, *Tosefoth Yom Tov,* on *Sanhedrin* 9:6; *Yad, Issurey Biyah* 12:6; *Evven HaEzer* 16:2; *Beth Sh'muel* 16:4; *Beer Hetiv* 16:5.

222. *VaYikra Rabbah* 9:5, 25:8; *BaMidbar Rabbah* 10:4; *Shir HaShirim Rabbah* 5:15; *Yalkut Shimoni* 2:798; Rabbenu Yonah, *Shaarey Teshuvah* 3:133. For a possible connection between this sin and its punishment, see *Chidushey Radal* on *Vayikra Rabbah* 9:5 no. 14.

223. Rabbenu Yonah, *Shaarey Teshuvah* 3:136.

224. *Arakhin* 15b; *Yerushalmi, Peah* 1:1 (4a); *Midrash Tehillim* 12:2.

225. See above, 3:8.

226. See above, 3:12.

227. *Shevuoth* 7b; *Sifra* on Leviticus 16:16 (81c).

228. They were the sins responsible for the Flood; *Sanhedrin* 57a; *Tana DeBei Eliahu Zuta* 10 (15b); Rashi on Genesis 6:11. For the destruction of Sodom; *Tosefta, Sanhedrin* 13:1; *Yerushalmi* 10:3 (53a); *Targum Yonathan* on Genesis 13:13; *Bereshith Rabbah* 41:10;

in this world and the next.[229] For the Jewish people as a whole, it was the violation of these cardinal sins that resulted in the forfeiture of national existence,[230] as well as the termination of the special relationship with God which existed as long as the First Temple stood in Jerusalem.[231]

13:68   Though a Jew may commit an extremely serious sin, he is still considered a Jew.[232] However, there are some sins, outlined in the next chapter, which divorce a person from the Jewish people, both in this world and the next.

TABLE 13:1 — TWENTY FOUR OFFENSES PUNISHABLE BY EXCOMMUNICATION[1a]

1. Insulting a learned man, even after his death.[1]
2. Insulting a messenger of the court.[2]
3. Calling a fellow Jew a "slave."[3]
4. Refusing to appear before the court at the appointed time.[4]
5. Dealing lightly with Torah or rabbinical law.[5]

Tanchuma, VaYera 7. By Yishmael; *Tosefta, Sotah* 6:3; *Bereshith Rabbah* 53a; *Shemoth Rabbah* 1:1; Rashi, Ramban, on Genesis 21:9. By Esau; *Bava Bathra* 16b; *Bereshith Rabbah* 63:16; *Shemoth Rabbah* 1:1; *Midrash Tehillim* 9:7. By the Golden Calf; *Tosefta, Sanhedrin* 6:3; Rashi on Exodus 32:6.

229. *Tosefta, Peah* 1:2; *Yerushalmi* 1:1 (4a); *Yad, Deyoth* 7:3.

230. *Avoth* 5:9; *Tosefoth Yom Tov ad. loc.; Shabbath* 33a; *BaMidbar Rabbah* 7:10. *Cf.* Isaiah 1:21.

231. *Yoma* 9b; *Tosefta, Menachoth* 13:4; *BaMidbar Rabbah* 7:10.

232. *Sanhedrin* 44a, from Joshua 7:11; *Maharsha ad. loc.; Yalkut Shimoni* 2:17.

1a. These 24 offenses are mentioned in *Berakhoth* 19a; *Yerushalmi, Moed Katan* 3:1 (10b). For a listing, see *Yad, Talmud Torah* 6:14; *Yoreh Deah* 334:43; *Nimukey Yosef, Moed Katan* (Rif 9b); *Sefer Chasidim* 47. For other cases not given here, see Raavad, *Migdal Oz, Kesef Mishneh, Talmud Torah* 6:14 (end); *Nimukey Yosef loc. cit.*

1. *Berakhoth* 19a; *Yerushalmi, Moed Katan* 3:1 (10b); *Sifethey Cohen* 334:68; *Beer HaGolah* 334:80.

2. *Kiddushin* 70b; *Yad, Sanhedrin* 25:6; *Choshen Mishpat* 8:5; *Sifethey Cohen, Yoreh Deah* 334:69; *Beer HaGolah* 334:81. See also *Moed Katan* 16a; *Yevamoth* 54a; *Bava Kama* 112b; *Teshuvoth Binyamin Zeev* 226; *Atzmoth Yosef*, p. 37; *Kenesseth HaGedolah, Yoreh Deah* 334:43.

3. *Kiddushin* 28a, 70a.

4. *Bava Kama* 112b; *Yad, Sanhedrin* 25:8; *Choshen Mishpat* 11:1.

5. *Eduyyoth* 5:6; *Berakhoth* 19a; *Yerushalmi loc. cit.*

6. Refusing to abide by the court's decision.[6]
7. Keeping an injurious animal or object in one's possession.[7]
8. Selling Jewish land or property to a non-Jew without accepting full responsibility.[8]
9. Testifying against a fellow Jew in a non-Jewish court.[9]
10. Sale of priestly portions by a Cohen *Shochet.*[10]
11. Violating the second day of a Festival.[11]
12. Performing work on the afternoon before Passover.[12]
13. Taking God's name in vain.[13]
14. Causing others to profane God's name.[14]
15. Causing others to eat holy meat outside of Jerusalem.[15]
16. Calculating the calendar outside of the Land of Israel.[16]
17. Causing another to sin.[17]
18. Preventing the community from doing good.[18]
19. Selling forbidden meat as Kosher.[19]
20. Failure of a *Shochet* to let a rabbi examine his knife.[20]
21. Causing oneself to have an erection.[21]
22. Having business intercourse with one's divorced wife.[22]
23. Being the subject of scandal for a rabbi.[23]
24. Excommunicating a person unjustly.[24]

6. *Bava Kama* 113a; *Yad, Sanhedrin* 25:11; *Choshen Mishpat* 100:3.
7. *Bava Kama* 15b; *Kethuvoth* 41b.
8. *Bava Kama* 114a; *Yad, Shekhenim* 12:7; *Choshen Mishpat* 175:40.
9. *Bava Kama* 113b; *Choshen Mishpat* 28:3.
10. *Chullin* 132b; *Yoreh Deah* 61:24.
11. *Pesachim* 52a; *Yad, Yom Tov* 1:22; *Orach Chaim* 496:1.
12. *Pesachim* 50b; *Yad, Yom Tov* 8:17; *Orach Chaim* 468:1.
13. *Nedarim* 7b; *Yad, Shevuoth* 12:9; *Yoreh Deah* 334:37.
14. *Yerushalmi, Moed Katan* 3:1 (10a).
15. *Berakhoth* 19a; *Betza* 23a.
16. *Berakhoth* 63a; *Sifethey Cohen* 334:79.
17. *Moed Katan* 17a.
18. *Yerushalmi, Moed Katan* 3:1 (10a).
19. *Sanhedrin* 25a; *Yoreh Deah* 119:15.
20. *Chullin* 18a; *Yoreh Deah* 18:17.
21. *Niddah* 13a; *Evven HaEzer* 23:3.
22. *Kethuvoth* 28a; *Evven HaEzer* 119:5.
23. *Moed Katan* 17a; *Yoreh Deah* 334:42.
24. *Moed Katan* 17a; *Sifethey Cohen* 334:86; *Turey Zahav* 334:21.

TABLE 13:2 — SINS PUNISHABLE BY PREMATURE DEATH AND LASHES[1a]

1. A non-Cohen eating *Terumah*.[1]
2. A non-Cohen eating *Terumah* of the Tithe.[2]
3. A non-Cohen eating the First Fruits.[3]
4. A non-Cohen eating *Challah*.[4]
5. Eating untithed food.[5]
6. Eating bread from which *Challah* was not separated off.[6]
7. A unclean Cohen eating ritually pure *Terumah*.[7]
8. A Cohen entering the Holy of Holies in vain.[8]
9. A Cohen leaving the Temple during the service.[9]
10. A Levite performing a Cohen's service.[10]
11. A non-Cohen participating in the Temple service.[11]
12. An improperly vested Cohen participating in the Temple service.[12]
13. A ritually unclean Cohen serving in the Temple.[13]

1a. *Yad, Sanhedrin* 19:2; Rambam, Bertenoro, *Tosefoth Yom Tov*, on *Sanhedrin* 9:6; *cf. Sanhedrin* 83a; *Tosefta, Kerithoth* 1:2; *Tosefta, Zevachim* 12:8; Rabbenu Yonah, *Shaarey Teshuvah* 3:108.
1. *Bikkurim* 2:1; *Sanhedrin* 83b; Rashi *ad. loc. s.v. Lamah*, from Leviticus 22:9-10; *Yad, Terumoth* 10:1, 4; *Sefer HaMitzvoth*, Negative Commandment 133; *Lechem Mishneh, Sanhedrin* 19:2.
2. *Ibid.*
3. Once brought to Jerusalem; *Bikkurim* 2:1; *Yad, Bikkurim* 3:1. *Cf. Makkoth* 19a; Rashi *ad. loc. s.v. MeEimatai.*
4. *Ibid. Cf. Lechem Mishneh loc. cit.*, that all the above come under the category of *Terumah.*
5. *Sanhedrin* 83a; *Makkoth* 16b; *Yad, Maakhaloth Assuroth* 10:18; *Sefer HaMitzvoth*, Negative Commandment 153; *Lechem Mishneh loc. cit. s.v. HaOkhel.*
6. *Ibid.*
7. Leviticus 23:9; Rashi *ad. loc.; Yad, Terumoth* 7:1.
8. Leviticus 16:2; Rashi *ad. loc.; Menachoth* 27b; *Yad, Biyath HaMikdash* 2:3; *Sefer HaMitzvoth*, Negative Commandment 165.
9. Leviticus 10:7; Ramban *ad. loc.; Yad, Biyath HaMikdash* 2:5; *Sefer HaMitzvoth*, Negative Commandment 165.
10. Numbers 18:3; *Yad, K'ley HaMikdash* 3:11; *Sefer HaMitzvoth*, Negative Commandment 72. Regarding a Cohen who performs the service of a Levite, see Raavad, *Kesef Mishneh ad. loc.*
11. Numbers 1:51; *Sanhedrin* 9:6 (81b); *Yad, Biyath HaMikdash* 9:1; *Sefer HaMitzvoth*, Negative Commandment 74.
12. *Sanhedrin* 83b; *Yad, K'ley HaMikdash* 10:4. *Cf.* Exodus 28:35; Rashi *ad. loc.*
13. *Sanhedrin* 83b; *Shevuoth* 17b; *Yad, Biyath HaMikdash* 4:1; *Sefer HaMitzvoth* 74.

14. Serving in the Temple while intoxicated.[14]
15. An unclean person who has immersed by day serving in the Temple.[15]
16. An unclean person who has not brought the proper purification sacrifice serving in the Temple.[16]
17. Serving in the Temple with unshort hair.[17]
18. Serving in the Temple with torn vestments.[18]

TABLE 13:3 — SINS PUNISHABLE BY PREMATURE DEATH ALONE

1. Serving in the Temple without proper ablution.[1]
2. A prophet withholding his prophecy.[2]
3. A prophet disregarding his own prophecy.[3]
4. Disregarding a prophet.[4]
5. Mistreating an orphan or widow.[5]
6. Stealing from the poor.[6]
7. Giving another a bad name.[7]
8. Emitting semen in vain.[8]

14. Leviticus 10:9; *Sanhedrin* 22b, 83a; *Shevuoth* 36b; *Taanith* 17b; *Tosefta, Kerithoth* 1:12; *Yad, Biyath HaMikdash* 1:1; *Sefer HaMitzvoth* 73.
15. Leviticus 22:7, 9; *Sanhedrin* 83b; *Yad, Biyath HaMikdash* 4:4; Raavad, *Kesef Mishneh, Mishneh LeMelekh, ad. loc.; Sefer HaMitzvoth* 76.
16. *Yad loc. cit.;* Raavad, *Kesef Mishneh, ad. loc.; cf. Sefer Mitzvoth Gadol,* Negative 305; *Sanhedrin* 83b.
17. Leviticus 10:6; *Yad, Biyath HaMikdash* 1:8; *Sefer HaMitzvoth,* Negative Commandment 163.
18. *Yad ibid.* 1:14; *Sefer HaMitzvoth,* Negative Commandment 164.

1. Exodus 30:21; *Yad, Sanhedrin* 19:3, *Biyath HaMikdash* 5:1; *Sefer HaMitzvoth,* Positive Commandment 24.
2. *Yad, Sanhedrin* 19:3; see Volume 1, 8:25, note 43.
3. *Yad loc. cit.;* see Volume 1, 8:25.
4. *Yad loc. cit.;* see Volume 1, 8:3, note 5.
5. Exodus 22:20-23; Rabbenu Yonah, *Shaarey Teshuvah* 3:109; *Yad, Deyoth* 6:10; *Sefer HaMitzvoth,* Negative Commandment 256; *Chinukh* 65.
6. *Shaarey Teshuvah* 3:110, from Proverbs 22:22-23; *Bava Kama* 119a; *Bava Metzia* 112a; *Zohar* 286b.
7. Numbers 14:37; *Arakhin* 15a; *Shaarey Teshuvah* 3:111.
8. Genesis 38:10; *Niddah* 13b; *Shaarey Teshuvah* 3:112; *Yad, Issurey Biyah* 21:18; *Evven HaEzer* 23:1; *Kitzur Shulchan Arukh* 151:1; *Zohar* 1:19a, 1:59a, 1:69a, 1:188a, 1:119b.

9. Not attending the local synagogue.[9]
10. A rabbi not acting modestly.[10]
11. Going against one's rabbi's teachings.[11]
12. Rendering a decision in the presence of one's rabbi.[12]
13. Not paying a pledge to charity.[13]
14. Not giving charity when required.[14]

TABLE 13:4 — SINS PUNISHABLE BY KARETH AND FLOGGING[1a]

1. Incest with one's sister.[1]
2. Incest with one's father's sister.[2]
3. Incest with one's mother's sister.[3]
4. Incest with one's wife's sister.[4]
5. Incest with one's brother's wife.[5]
6. Incest with one's father's brother's wife.[6]
7. Intercourse with a menstrually unclean woman.[7]
8. Eating forbidden fats.[8]
9. Eating blood.[9]

---

9. *Derekh Eretz Rabbah* 11; *HaGriv* 300; *Nachalath Yaakov ad. loc.*, from Jeremiah 2:5; *cf.* HaGra *ibid.* 80; *Shaarey Teshuvah* 3:114. *Cf. Avoth DeRabbi Nathan* 36:5.
10. *Shabbath* 114a, from Proverbs 8:36; *Shaarey Teshuvah* 3:113.
11. *Sanhedrin* 110a; *Berakhoth* 27b; *Shaarey Teshuvah* 3:115; *cf. Yad, Talmud Torah* 5:1; *Yoreh Deah* 242:2.
12. *Eruvin* 62b; *Shaarey Teshuvah* 3:116; *Yad, Talmud Torah* 5:2; *Yoreh Deah* 242:4.
13. *Shaarey Teshuvah* 3:117, from *Avoth* 5:8-9; *cf.* Rabbenu Yonah *ad. loc.; Shabbath* 32b.
14. *Shaarey Teshuvah* 3:118; Rabbenu Yonah on *Avoth loc. cit.*, from Proverbs 22:22. Whether touching the Ark in the Holy Temple is punishable by death, see Numbers 4:15; Rashi *ad. loc.;* 2 Samuel 6:7.

1a. *Yad, Sanhedrin* 19:1; see above, 13:43.
1. Leviticus 20:17; *Sefer HaMitzvoth*, Negative 331.
2. Leviticus 20:19; *Sefer HaMitzvoth*, Negative 341.
3. Leviticus 20:19; *Sefer HaMitzvoth*, Negative 340.
4. Leviticus 18:18; *Sefer HaMitzvoth*, Negative 345.
5. Leviticus 20:21; *Sefer HaMitzvoth*, Negative 344.
6. Leviticus 20:20; *Sefer HaMitzvoth*, Negative 342.
7. Leviticus 20:18; *Sefer HaMitzvoth*, Negative 346.
8. Leviticus 7:23-25; *Sefer HaMitzvoth*, Negative 185.
9. Leviticus 7:27, 17:10; *Sefer HaMitzvoth*, Negative 184.

10. Eating leaven on Passover.[10]
11. Eating on *Yom Kippur.*[11]
12. Working on *Yom Kippur.*[12]
13. Eating leftover sacrifices.[13]
14. Eating defiled sacrifices.[14]
15. An unclean person eating sacrifices.[15]
16. An unclean person entering the Temple.[16]
17. Slaughtering sacrifices outside the Temple.[17]
18. Burning offerings outside the Temple.[18]
19. Preparing the anointing oil for private use.[19]
20. Using the anointing oil in vain.[20]
21. Compounding the incense for private use.[21]

TABLE 13:5 — SINS PUNISHABLE BY STRANGULATION[1a]

1. Adultery with a married woman.[1]
2. Wounding one's parent.[2]

10. Exodus 12:15, 12:19; *Sefer HaMitzvoth,* Negative 197.
11. Leviticus 23:30; *Sefer HaMitzvoth,* Negative 196.
12. Leviticus 23:29; *Sefer HaMitzvoth,* Negative 329.
13. Leviticus 7:18, 19:8; *Sefer HaMitzvoth,* Negative 131.
14. *Ibid.; Sefer HaMitzvoth,* Negative 132.
15. Leviticus 7:20; *Sefer HaMitzvoth,* Negative 129.
16. Numbers 19:13; *Sefer HaMitzvoth,* Negative 77, 78. *Cf.* Leviticus 15:31; Rashi *ad. loc.* Whether this applies to the Temple grounds now that the Temple is not standing is disputed. Rambam, *Yad, Beth HaBechirah* 6:14, maintains that it is; Raavad *ad. loc.* disputes this. *Cf. Shevuoth* 16a; *Chinukh* 184, 363; *Minchath Chinukh* 184:5.
17. Leviticus 17:4; *Sefer HaMitzvoth,* Negative 89. Whether this applies today, *cf. Tosafoth, Zevachim* 59b *s.v. Ad, Yoma* 63a *s.v. Shelamim; Minchath Chinukh* 186:2. *Cf. Yoreh Deah* 5:1.
18. Leviticus 17:9; *Sefer HaMitzvoth,* Negative 90. Whether this applies today is disputed in *Zevachim* 197b, and the opinion that it is is upheld in *Yad, Maaseh HaKorbanoth* 19:15; *cf. Mishneh LeMelekh ad. loc. Cf. Orach Chaim* 469:1.
19. Exodus 30:33; *Sefer HaMitzvoth,* Negative 83; *Yad, K'ley HaMikdash* 1:4. This applies even today; *cf. Chinukh* 109.
20. Exodus 30:33; *Sefer HaMitzvoth,* Negative 84; *Yad, K'ley HaMikdash* 1:5. This applies even today; *cf. Chinukh* 108.
21. Exodus 30:38; *Sefer HaMitzvoth,* Negative 85; *Yad, K'ley HaMikdash* 2:9. This also applies today; *cf. Chinukh* 110.

1a. *Sanhedrin* 11:1 (84b); *Yad, Sanhedrin* 15:13.
1.   Leviticus 20:10; Deuteronomy 22:22.
2.   Exodus 21:15.

3. Kidnapping.[3]
4. Insubordination to the Sanhedrin.[4]
5. False prophecy.[5]
6. Prophesying in the name of heathen dieties.[6]

TABLE 13:6 — SINS PUNISHABLE BY BURNING[1a]

1. Adultery for a Cohen's daughter.[1]
2. Incest with one's daughter.[2]
3. Incest with one's daughter's daughter.[3]
4. Incest with one's son's daughter.[4]
5. Incest with one's stepdaughter.[5]
6. Incest with one's stepdaughter's daughter.[6]
7. Incest with one's stepson's daughter.[7]
8. Incest with one's mother-in-law.[8]
9. Incest with one's mother-in-law's mother.[9]
10. Incest with one's father-in-law's mother.[10]

TABLE 13:7 — SINS PUNISHABLE BY STONING[1a]

1. Incest with one's mother.[1]
2. Incest with one's stepmother.[2]

3. Exodus 21:16.
4. *Zaken Mamreh;* Deuteronomy 17:12; see Volume 1, 11:56.
5. Deuteronomy 18:20; see Volume 1, 8:27.
6. Deuteronomy *loc. cit.;* see Volume 1, 8:50.

1a. *Sanhedrin* 9:1 (75a); *Yad, Sanhedrin* 15:11.
1. Leviticus 21:9.
2. *Sanhedrin* 71a.
3. Leviticus 18:10.
4. Leviticus 18:10.
5. Leviticus 18:17.
6. *Ibid.*
7. *Ibid.*
8. Leviticus 20:14.
9. *Sanhedrin* 75a.
10. *Ibid.* The last three are only culpable during the lifetime of one's wife.

1a. *Sanhedrin* 7:4 (53a); *Yad, Sanhedrin* 15:10.
1. Leviticus 18:7, 20:11.
2. Leviticus 18:8, 20:12.

3. Incest with one's daugher-in-law.[3]
4. Adultery with a betrothed virgin.[4]
5. Homosexual intercourse by men.[5]
6. Bestial intercourse by men.[6]
7. Bestial intercourse by women.[7]
8. Cursing God.[8]
9. Idolatry.[9]
10. Offering one's children to Molekh.[10]
11. Necromancy.[11]
12. Pythonism.[12]
13. Inticing individuals to idolatry.[13]
14. Instigating communities to idolatry.[14]
15. Witchcraft.[15]
16. Breaking the Sabbath.[16]
17. Cursing one's parents.[17]
18. Rebelling against parents.[18]

TABLE 13:8 — SINS PUNISHABLE BY DEATH, BUT NOT KARETH[1]

1. Inticing individuals to idolatry.
2. Instigating communities to idolatry.

3. Leviticus 10:12.
4. Deuteronomy 22:23-24.
5. Leviticus 20:13.
6. Leviticus 20:15.
7. Leviticus 20:16.
8. Leviticus 24:16.
9. Deuteronomy 17:2-7.
10. Leviticus 20:2.
11. *Ov;* Leviticus 20:27.
12. *Yid'oni; ibid.*
13. Deuteronomy 13:7-12.
14. Deuteronomy 13:2-6.
15. Exodus 22:17.
16. Numbers 15:32-36.
17. Leviticus 20:9.
18. Deuteronomy 21:18-21.

1. *Sifra* on Leviticus 4:3 (16a); *Sefer HaMitzvoth,* Negative 352.

3. False prophecy.
4. Prophesying in the name of heathen dieties.
5. Insubordination to the Sanhedrin.
6. Rebelling aginst parents.
7. Kidnapping.
8. Murder.
9. Wounding one's parent.
10. Cursing one's parent.
11. Witchcraft.[2]

TABLE 13:9 — CATEGORIES OF OBSERVANCE AND SIN

1. Custom.[1]
2. Rabbinical safeguards of Torah laws.[2]
3. Rabbinical laws.[3]
4. Mandatory positive commandments.[4]
5. Torah prohibition expiable by payment.[5]
6. Prohibition expiable by observing positive commandments.[6]
7. Prohibition not involving action.[7]
8. Prohibition stated in general terms.[8]
9. Prohibition punishable by flogging.[9]
10. Prohibition serving as warning for death penalty.[10]

2. This is not included in *Sefer HaMitzvoth loc. cit.* but is included in *Sifra loc. cit.* Similarly, it is not included among those sins punishable by *Kareth* in *Kerithoth* 1:1 (2a), although *Kareth* is indicated in *Sefer HaMitzvoth, Negative* 34; *Chinukh* 511. See *Mishneh LeMelekh, Shegagoth* 1:2; *Minchath Chinukh* 511:1. *Sifra loc. cit.* also counts false witnesses in this category.

1. See above, 13:33; Volume 1, 13:26-27.
2. See above, 13:35.
3. See above, 13:36.
4. See above, 13:37.
5. See above, 13:40.
6. See above, 13:39.
7. See above, 13:41.
8. See above, 13:42.
9. See above, 13:43.
10. See above, 13:46.

11. Sin punishable by premature death.[11]
12. Sin punishable by *Kareth*.[12]
13. Sin punishable by strangulation.[13]
14. Sin punishable by decapitation.[14]
15. Sin punishable by burning.[15]
16. Sin punishable by stoning.[16]
17. Sin punishable without benefit of trial.[17]
18. Cardinal sins for which one must be martyred.[18]
19. Sins for which one forfeits eternal life.[19]
20. Sins for which one loses his portion in the World to Come.[20]

11. See above, 13:47.
12. See above, 13:48.
13. See above, 13:59.
14. See above, 13:60.
15. See above, 13:61.
16. See above, 13:62.
17. See above, 13:65.
18. See above, 13:67.
19. See below, 14:2*ff.*
20. See below, 14:12*ff.*

FOURTEEN

FORFEITING ETERNITY

14:1   It is a foundation of our faith that every Jew has a share in God's eternal reward, even though he may have committed many serious sins.[1]

14:2   There are some sins, however, which are so ineradicable that they cannot be erased without altering a person's entire identity. The loss of one's eternal reward is therefore preferable to the shame and humiliation of standing before God permanently marked by such a sin.[2] In such cases, God in His mercy has decreed that such a person should die spiritually as well as physically, thereby being spared this eternal shame.[3] Regarding such an individual, the Torah states, "Because he has despised God's word and negated His commandment, that soul shall be utterly cut off [spiritually and] his sin shall remain upon him" (Numbers 15:31).[4]

14:3   Man's eternal reward is a closeness to God,[5] and therefore one who denies God cannot possibly partake of it. Similarly, one whose belief in God is so mistaken as to be idolatrous[6] is also denied all future reward.[7] This category[8] includes those who

1.   *Sanhedrin* 10:1 (90a), Bertenoro, Maharsha, *ad. loc.; Yad, Teshuvah* 3:5; *Zohar* 1:33a, 1:59b, 1:93a, 1:116a, 2:23a.
2.   See above, 13:50, note 173; below, 14:24, 23:17.
3.   *Cf. Yad, Teshuvah* 8:1; *Hagahoth Maimonioth, Kesef Mishneh, ad. loc.;* Ramban, *Shaar HaGamul* 79a.
4.   *Targum Yonathan,* Ramban, *ad. loc.; Sanhedrin* 64b, 90b, 99a; *Shevuoth* 13a; *Yerushalmi, Peah* 1:1 (4a); *Yad loc. cit.;* Rabbenu Yonah, *Shaarey Teshuvah* 3:143, 3:121.
5.   See Volume 1, 3:12, 3:15, 3:18.
6.   *Moreh Nevukhim* 1:36; *Lechem Mishneh, Teshuvah* 3:7.
7.   *Sanhedrin* 10:1 (90a); *Rosh HaShanah* 17a; *Yerushalmi, Peah* 1:1 (5a); *Yad, Teshuvah* 3:5.
8.   All these are given the name *Min* ("heretic") by Maimonides; *Yad, Teshuvah* 3:7.

deny the unity, the incorporeality,[9] or the eternity of God.[10] It also includes one who requires an intermediary between God and man.[11]

14:4   Furthermore, man's final reward stems largely from his satisfaction of accomplishment in having fulfilled God's revealed will.[12] Therefore, one whose philosophy of life excludes this concept is likewise excluded from this reward.[13] This category includes all those who deny revelation, who deny the Torah, or who deny God's omniscience.[14]

14:5   Since God's revelation can only be correctly understood as an integrated whole, one who denies any fundamental part of it is the same as one who denies it entirely. Therefore, one who denies the authenticity of even a single word of the Torah or Oral Law, or who believes that God has abrogated or changed any of His commandments, is considered the same as one who denies revelation completely.[15]

14:6   Similarly, one who does not believe in personal immortality is denied this eternal reward, since for him it does not exist.[16] Since

---

Cf. Avodah Zarah 26b, that this term is applied to an idolater; *cf.* Rashi *ad. loc. s.v. Minim; Tosafoth ibid. s.v. Aizehu;* Raavad, *Teshuvah* 3:9; Rashi, *Shabbath* 116a *s.v. Sifrey HaMinin, Chullin* 13b *s.v. Min, Gittin* 45b *s.v. Min, Berakhoth* 12b *s.v. Minuth, Rosh HaShanah* 17a *s.v. HaMinim;* Ran, *Shabbath* (Rif 43a) *s.v. VeSifrey, Rosh HaShanah* (Rif 4a) *s.v. VeHaMinim;* Maharatz Chajas, *Gittin* 45b; *Kesef Mishneh, Tefillin* 1:13; *Orach Chaim* 334:21; *Sifethey Cohen, Yoreh Deah* 281:1; *Gilyon Maharsha ad. loc.; Biur Halakhah* 39:4 *s.v. SheKathvam.*

9.   This is disputed by Raavad, *Teshuvah* 3:7; *cf. Kesef Mishneh, Lechem Mishneh, ibid.; Ikkarim* 1:2. See Volume 1, 2:21, note 24.

10.   Raavad *ibid.* also includes belief in creation ex nihilo in this category; *cf. Kesef Mishneh, Lechem Mishneh, ibid.* See also *Ikkarim* 1:2, 1:12. See *Milchamoth Hashem* 6:1 (p. 293), who disputes this, and *Shamayim Chadashim* (Abarbanel), which is entirely devoted to this question.

11.   See Volume 1, 1:14-15.

12.   See Volume 1, 3:13, 17.

13.   *Rosh HaShanah* 17a; *Yad, Teshuvah* 3:6; *Reshith Chokhmah, Shaar HaYirah* 13 (37c no. 5).

14.   These are given the name *Apikores* in *Yad, Teshuvah* 3:8; *cf. Hagahoth Maimonioth, Kesef Mishneh, ad. loc.; Yoreh Deah* 158:2; *HaGra ad. loc.* 158:11; Maharatz Chajas, *Eruvin* 69a. Since acceptance of the Torah predicates respect of the interpreters of God's revelation, one who shows them disrespect is also included in this category; *cf. Sanhedrin* 99b; Rabbenu Yonah, *Shaarey Teshuvah* 3:155; *Ikkarim* 3:10.

15.   *Sanhedrin* 10:1 (90a); *Rosh HaShanah* 17a; *Yad, Teshuvah* 3:8; *Reshith Chokhmah, Shaar HaYirah* 13 (37c).

16.   *Sanhedrin* 90a; *Shaarey Teshuvah* 3:154; *Reshith Chokhmah, Shaar HaYirah* 13 (37c).

belief in reward and punishment,[17] as well as in the Messiah,[18] is closely intertwined with this, the denial of these principles also precludes one's everlasting reward.

14:7   There are therefore 13 basic principles which are essential to Judaism. [These are listed in Table 14:1, at the end of this chapter.] They are the basic axiomatic beliefs supporting the entire system of Jewish theology and making it unique. Since each of these beliefs is absolutely essential to the entire structure of Judaism, a person who denies even a single one is completely divorced from Jewish tradition.[19]

14:8   One who abandons the Jewish religion abandons his eternal reward,[20] though he neither adopts nor accepts any idolatrous faith.[21] The same applies to one who abandons the practice of Judaism completely, though he maintains his identity as a Jew.[22]

14:9   Similarly, since both the initial acceptance of Judaism and its final reward include the entire Jewish people as a whole,[23] one who separates himself from the Jewish community is denied its final reward,[24] even though he maintains the practice of Judaism.[25]

14:10   Similarly, one who is a known spiteful sinner is denied his eternal reward, even if only a relatively minor sin is involved,[26] since such action attests to his denial of Judaism.[27] The same is true of

17. Thirteen Principles of Faith 11.
18. Thirteen Principles of Faith 12; *Yad, Teshuvah* 3:6; *Tziuney Maharan ad. loc.; cf. Ikkarim* 4:42; *Rosh Emunah* (Abarbanel) 14 (p. 18a). *Cf. Sanhedrin* 99a; *Ikkarim* 1:1. See below, Chapter 24.
19. Rambam on *Sanhedrin* 10:1 (end).
20. *Yad, Teshuvah* 3:9, from *Rosh HaShanah* 17a; *Chullin* 5a; *Avodah Zarah* 26b; *Horayoth* 11a. *Cf. Yad, Avodath Kokhavim* 10:1, *Maaseh HaKorbanoth* 3:4, *Gezelah VeAvedah* 11:2, *Rotzeach* 4:10; *Yoreh Deah* 158:2; *Choshen Mishpat* 266:2, 425:5.
21. *Migdal Oz, Kesef Mishneh, Teshuvah* 3:9. *Cf.* Rashi, *Chullin* 13b s.v. *Min; Tosafoth, Avodah Zarah* 26b s.v. *VeChad.*
22. *Tosefta, Sanhedrin* 12:5; *Yerushalmi, Peah* 1:1 (5a); *Yerushalmi, Sanhedrin* 10:1 (49a); Rabbenu Yonah, *Shaarey Teshuvah* 3:13. *Cf. Yad, Avel* 1:10; *Yoreh Deah* 345:5.
23. See above, 12:1.
24. *Rosh HaShanah* 17a; *Yad, Teshuvah* 3:11; *Shaarey Teshuvah* 3:168; Rashi, *Rosh HaShanah* s.v. *SheParshu;* Rosh 1:5, do not list it as a separate category, although it is listed separately by Rif, *Rosh HaShanah* 4a; *cf.* Ran *ad. loc. s.v. SheParshu,* who quotes *Yad loc. cit. Cf. Semachoth* 2:10; Rif, *Moed Katan* 18a; *Yad, Avel* 1:10; *Yoreh Deah* 345:5, 340:4 in *Hagah; Kitzur Shulchan Arukh* 201:4.
25. *Yad, Teshuvah* 3:11. However in *Yad, Avel, Yoreh Deah, loc. cit.,* it appears that this is only true of one who abandons the practice of Judaism.
26. *Yad, Teshuvah* 3:9. See above, 13:17.
27. *Cf. Yad, Avodath Kokhavim* 10:1, *Gezelah* 11:2.

one who makes a show of sinning,[28] or who demonstrates gross disrespect for the teachings of our faith.[29] All these are considered desecrations of God's name,[30] which is among the most serious of sins.[31]

14:11 One who causes the community to sin is denied his eternal reward, since the sin of the entire community is too great for a single individual to bear throughout eternity.[32] This is true whether he forces them to sin or seduces them, whether the sin be great or small.[33] Furthermore, it is all but impossible to repent this, since the damage is irreparable.[34] Regarding this it is written, "He who causes the upright to go astray on an evil way, shall himself fall into his own pit" (Proverbs 28:10).[35]

14:12 Similarly, one who terrorizes the community is condemned and has no portion in the Future World,[36] since he is guilty of usurping God's respect[37] and causing people to sin.[38] The prophet thus states, "They caused terror in the land of the living, they shall bear their shame with those who go down to the pit... their sins shall be upon their bones" (Ezekiel 32:25, 27).[39]

14:13 A murderer is condemned and has no portion in the Future World,[40] since he commits an immeasurable wrong against his

28. That is, one who sins highhandedly; *Yad, Teshuvah* 3:6, 3:11; *Lechem Mishneh ad. loc., Kesef Mishneh ibid.* 3:14. *Cf. Sanhedrin* 99a; Maharatz Chajas *ad. loc.; Yerushalmi, Peah* 1:1 (5a); *Yerushalmi, Sanhedrin* 10:1 (49a); *Avoth* 3:11; Rambam, Bertenoro, Rabbenu Yonah, *ad. loc.; Shaarey Teshuvah* 3:143. *Cf. Targum Onkelos* on Numbers 15:30, who interprets *Yad Ramah,* "highhandedly," to mean "publicly," while *Targum Yonathan* and Rashi interpret it to mean "spitefully," and Ibn Ezra, "brazenly." The same expression is found in Exodus 14:8, where it means "publicly"; *cf. Mekhilta* (17b); *Targum Onkelos,* Rashi, *ad. loc.* See also Numbers 33:3; *Zohar* 2:150b.
29. *Sanhedrin* 99b; Rashi, Bertenoro, on *Avoth* 3:11. *Cf. Emunoth VeDeyoth* 5:8 (74a).
30. See above, 2:20-21.
31. See above, 2:19.
32. *Rosh HaShanah* 17a; *Yad, Teshuvah* 3:10; *Shaarey Teshuvah* 3:161; *Zohar* 2:150b; *Reshith Chokhmah, Shaar HaYirah* 12 (36b); *Sefer Chasidim* 202, 688.
33. *Yad loc. cit.*
34. *Yoma* 87a; *Tosefta* 4:11; *Sanhedrin* 107b, from Proverbs 28:17; *cf.* Rashi *ad. loc.,* although others apply this passage to murder; see below, notes 43, 75.
35. Ralbag *ad. loc.;* see above, 12:60.
36. *Rosh HaShanah* 17a; *Yad, Teshuvah* 3:13; *Sanhedrin* 35:1, Radbaz *ad. loc.; Choshen Mishpat* 8:4; *Shaarey Teshuvah* 3:162. *Cf. Nedarim* 81a; *Zohar Chadash Ruth* 79c; *Reshith Chokhmah, Shaar HaYirah* 13 (37a).
37. Rabbenu Yonah, *Shaarey Teshuvah* 3:167.
38. *Ibid.* 3:166. *Cf. Gittin* 7a.
39. Rashi, Mahari Kara, Radak, *ad. loc.; Shaarey Teshuvah* 3:162.
40. *Yad, Teshuvah* 3:6; *Kesef Mishneh, Lechem Mishneh, Yad Ethan, Beney Binyamin,*

victim both spiritually and materially. We are thus taught that taking a single life is like destroying the entire world.[41] Murder is considered an even worse sin than idolatry or incest, since it is a crime against one's fellow,[42] for which there can be no forgiveness.[43] Concerning murder we are taught, "A man who is laden with the blood of any person shall hasten his steps into the pit, and none shall support him" (Proverbs 28:17).[44]

14:14 Since life and death belong to God alone, one who takes his own life is also considered a murderer.[45] The Torah thus warns, "I will surely demand an account for [spilling] your own life's blood" (Genesis 9:5).[46] Therefore, one who wantonly commits suicide has no portion in the Future World,[47] and for this reason is not to be mourned in any manner.[48] However, if one takes his own life out of fear of great pain[49] or torture,[50] as repentance for

Tziuney Maharan, ad. loc. Cf. Tosefta, Peah 1:2; *Yerushalmi* 1:1 (4a); *Avoth DeRabbi Nathan* 40:1, according to reading of Rambam on *Avoth* 1:17; *Yad, Deyoth* 7:3; *Sefer Mitzvoth Gadol,* Negative Commandment 9; *Menorath HaMaor* 2:4:2:2 (52). *Cf. Yerushalmi, Peah* 1:1 (5a); *Yerushalmi, Sanhedrin* 10:1 (49a). However, Rabbenu Yonah, *Shaarey Teshuvah* 3:141, writes that a murderer can have a portion in the World to Come. See below, note 75.

41. *Sanhedrin* 37a.
42. *Yad, Rotzeach* 4:9.
43. *Devarim Rabbah* 2:25. See *Yad Yosef* on *Devarim Rabbah* 2:17, note 44, citing *Torah Chaim* 99a, that murder is the most unforgivable of the three cardinal sins because one can never ask forgiveness from the person wronged.
44. Ibn Ezra, Ralbag, *Metzudoth David, ad. loc.; Yad, Rotzeach loc. cit.*
45. *Yad, Rotzeach* 2:3; *Chovoth HaLevavoth* 4:4; see above, 5:42.
46. Rashi, Ramban, *Baaley Tosafoth, ad. loc.; Bava Kama* 91b; *Tosefta, Bava Kama* 9:10; *Bereshith Rabbah* 34:19; *Yalkut Shimoni* 1:61; *Yad, Rotzeach loc. cit; Ramban, Torath HaAdam* 20b; Rosh, *Moed Katan* 3:94; Ran, *Shevuoth* (Rif 10a) *s.v. Malkin;* Radak on 1 Samuel 31:5; *Sifethey Cohen, Yoreh Deah* 345:1. *Cf.* Judges 9:53, 16:30; 1 Samuel 31:4; 2 Samuel 17:23; 1 Kings 16:18.
47. *Zohar* 3:127a; *Lechem Shamayim, Sanhedrin* 87; *Chidushey Maharit, Kethuvoth* 152; *Shevet Mussar* 20; *Teshuvoth Yabiah Omer, Yoreh Deah* 2:24; *Taamey HaMinhagim, Kuntres Acharon* 1058 (p. 464), from *Kuntres Keren Tzvi,* from *Midrash Tehillim* 120:4; *Kol Bo, "Al Aveluth"* 4:3:49 (p. 318), from *Kethuvoth* 103b; *Gittin* 57b; *Avodah Zarah* 18a; *Taanith* 29a; *Shaarey Zohar* 115d. *Cf.* Josephus, *The Jewish Wars* 3:8:5.
48. *Semachoth* 2:1; *Yad, Avel* 1:11; *Yoreh Deah* 345:1; *Chokhmath Adam* 156:1; *Kitzur Shulchan Arukh* 201:1; Ramban, *Torath HaAdam* 20b; Rosh, *Moed Katan* 3:94.
49. *Teshuvoth Besamim Rosh* 345; *Pith'chey Teshuvah, Yoreh Deah* 345:2; *Teshuvoth Yad Ephraim, Yoreh Deah* 76; *Har Avel,* p. 18; *Tuv Taam VeDa'ath* 202; *Kol Bo, "Al Aveluth"* 4:3:50 (p. 319). *Cf. Teshuvoth Chatham Sofer, Yoreh Deah* 326, from *Avodah Zarah* 19a, who disputes this.
50. *Bereshith Rabbah* 34:19; *Yoreh Deah* 345:3; *Sifethey Cohen ad. loc.* 345:6; *Beer Hetiv* 345:4; *Chokhmath Adam* 156:4; *Kitzur Shulchan Arukh* 202:3; Ramban, *Torath HaAdam* 20b; Rosh, *Moed Katan* 3:94; *Tosafoth, Gittin* 57b *s.v. Kaftzu;* Radak on

an unbearable sin,[51] or to prevent himself from sinning,[52] he is not considered a suicide.

14:15 Since the trauma of being arrested and handed over to the authorities can be as great as that of death itself, an informer is considered as serious a sinner as a murderer.[53] Furthermore, an informer separates himself from his people and sides with their enemies,[54] and is therefore considered among those who have no portion in the World to Come.[55]

14:16 A talebearer is condemned and has no portion in the World to Come,[56] since destroying another person's reputation can cause more pain than taking his life.[57] Regarding this sin, the Psalmist prayed, "May God cut off all slandering lips, every tongue that speaks distortions" (Psalms 12:4).[58]

14:17 Similarly, the pain of being publicly shamed can be as bad as that of death.[59] Therefore, one who habitually[60] shames his fellow has no portion in the World to Come.[61] The same is true of one

1 Samuel 31:5; cf. Yevamoth 78b; HaGra, Yoreh Deah 345:5. There are some who dispute this; cf. Da'ath Zikney Baaley Tosafoth on Genesis 9:5; Tosafoth, Avodah Zarah 18a s.v. VeAl; Teshuvoth Chaim Sha'al 46.

51. Bereshith Rabbah 65:18; Midrash Tehillim 11:7; Yuchasin HaShalem 14b; Shita Mekubetzeth, Kethuvoth 103b; Teshuvoth Shevuth Yaakov 2:111; Zakhur LeAvraham, Avel 40; Teshuvoth Evven Shoham 44; Beth Lechem Yehudah, Yad Avraham, Rabbi Akiba Eiger, Yoreh Deah 345:1; Pith'chey Teshuvah, Yoreh Deah 345:2.

52. Yad Avraham, Rabbi Akiba Eiger, loc. cit.; Tosafoth, Avodah Zarah 18a s.v. VeAl; Zakhur LeAvraham, Yoreh Deah, Avel 3:43.

53. Bava Kama 117a; Sefer Meirath Eynayim (Sema), Choshen Mishpat 388:29. See above, 4:19.

54. Cf. Gittin 45b; Rashi ad. loc. s.v. Mumar; Yad, Tefillin 1:13, Avel 1:10; Orach Chaim 39:1; Yoreh Deah 2:9 in Hagah, 119:10 in Hagah, 281:3, 345:5; Magen Avraham 39:4; Machtzith HaShekel ad. loc.; Beer Hetiv 39:3; Mishnah Berurah 39:7; Pith'chey Teshuvah, Yoreh Deah 281:5; Chomoth Yerushalayim 269.

55. Rosh HaShanah 17a; Yad, Teshuvah 3:6, Chovel 8:9; Choshen Mishpat 388:9; Sifethey Cohen ad. loc. 388:53.

56. Yad, Teshuvah 3:6; Deyoth 7:3; Derekh Eretz Rabbah 11; Pirkey Rabbi Eliezer 53 (126a); Radal ad. loc. 53:2. See above, note 40.

57. Arakhin 15b; Rashi, Tosafoth, ad. loc. s.v. Lishna; Yerushalmi, Peah 1:1 (4b); Rif, Shabbath 14a; VaYikra Rabbah 26:2; Midrash Tehillim 12:2, 120:4; Pesikta 4 (32a); Yad, Deyoth 7:3; Sefer Mitzvoth Gadol, Negative Commandment 9; Chinukh 236; Menorath HaMaor 24:2:1 (51). See above, 8:37.

58. Arakhin 15b; Yerushalmi, Peah 1:1 (4a); Devarim Rabbah 6:6 (end); Tanchuma, Metzorah 2; Tana DeBei Eliahu Rabbah 18 (90b); Yalkut Shimoni 1:558-559, 2:656, 2:953; Rashi on Leviticus 19:16; Sefer Chasidim 605.

59. See above, 3:20, 3:37; Zohar 3:85a; Tikuney Zohar 58 (92b).

60. Yad, Teshuvah 3:14; Kesef Mishneh ad. loc.

61. Avoth 3:11; Rambam, Bertenoro, ad. loc.; Bava Metzia 59a; Sanhedrin 99a, 107a;

who habitually makes up[62] or uses[63] embarrassing nicknames for others. Likewise, one who gains honor at the expense of another's reputation has no portion in the World to Come.[64]

14:18 Circumcision is the permanent sign that distinguishes the Jewish people, and as such is the most important of all commandments.[65] Therefore, one who disdains the covenant of circumcision divorces himself from Judaism and is counted among those who have no portion in the World to Come.[66] This applies both to a person who refuses to be circumcised,[67] as well as to one who has the mark of circumcision removed surgically or by other means.[68] This does not apply to one who cannot be circumcised for health reasons.[69]

14:19 Sexual crimes are akin to murder,[70] and can cause permanent

Pirkey Rabbi Eliezer 44 (105a); Radal *ad. loc.* 44:34; *Yad, Teshuvah* 3:14, *Deyoth* 6:8; *Sefer HaMitzvoth,* Negative Commandment 303; *Shaarey Teshuvah* 3:141; *Kitzur Shulchan Arukh* 29:17.

62. *Bava Metzia* 58b; *Yad loc. cit.; Choshen Mishpat* 228:5. However, *Tosafoth, Bava Metzia* 58b *s.v. Chutz,* maintains that such a person is only punished for 12 months.
63. *Yad loc. cit.; Kesef Mishneh ad. loc.; Zohar* 2:122a; *cf. Megillah* 28a.
64. *Yerushalmi, Chagigah* 2:1 (10a); *Bereshith Rabbah* 1:7; *Yad, Teshuvah* 3:14; *Kesef Mishneh ad. loc., ibid.* 4:4; *Makor Chesed* (on *Sefer Chasidim*) 19:17. *Cf. Megillah* 28a; *Yalkut Shimoni* 2:715.
65. See Volume 1, 4:24; *Nedarim* 32a; *Ran, Nedarim* 31b *s.v. SheHi; Tosafoth ibid. s.v. Hiney;* Maharatz Chajas *ad. loc.; Eyn Yaakov, Nedarim* 10; *Yoreh Deah* 260:1; *Sifethey Cohen* 260:1; *Yad Avraham ibid. Cf. Zohar* 1:196a, 2:61a, 3:13b; *Tikuney Zohar* 47 (87a); HaGra *ad. loc. s.v. LeMeevad* (94a), who writes that the numerical value of the word *B'rith* (בְּרִית) is 612, indicating that circumcision is a single commandment which equals the other 612 commandments in importance.
66. *Avoth* 3:11; *Sanhedrin* 99a; *Shevuoth* 13a; *Yad, Teshuvah* 3:14; *Milah* 3:8. *Cf. Eruvin* 19a; *Tosafoth ad. loc. s.v. Bar; Zohar* 1:8a, 1:93a, 1:95b; *Yam Shel Shlomo, Yevamoth* 8:4; *Chidushey HaRan, Moed Katan* 24b. Others maintain that this is simply punishable by *Kareth; cf. Tosafoth, Yoma* 86a *s.v. Chutz, Yevamoth* 9a *s.v. Mah.* See also *Yoreh Deah* 264:1 in *Hagah; Sifethey Cohen ad. loc.* 264:4; Rabbi Akiba Eiger *ibid. s.v. Mumar. Cf. Zohar* 1:94a.
67. Bertenoro, *Avoth* 3:11; *Yad, Milah loc. cit.,* include both cases. However, Rashi, *Avoth* 3:11 *s.v. HaMefir; Tosafoth, Yevamoth* 72a *s.v. U'MiDeRabanan,* only apply it to this case. See also *Yad, Milah* 1:2; Raavad, *Kesef Mishneh, ad. loc.; Yoreh Deah* 261:1 in *Hagah;* HaGra *ad. loc.* 261:2; *Yad Avraham ibid.,* from *Rosh HaShanah* 6b, for discussion as to whether *Kareth* applies only when one dies uncircumcised, or also when one delays it.
68. Rabbenu Yonah, *Avoth* 3:11. *Cf.* Rashi, *Sanhedrin* 44a *s.v. Moshekh.* See also *Yad, Terumoth* 7:10; *Tur, Yoreh Deah* 331.
69. *Chullin* 5a; *Yoreh Deah* 2:4, 164:1; *Sifethey Cohen* 2:21, 264:1; *Turey Zahav* 264:1; Rabbi Akiba Eiger *ibid.; Pith'chey Teshuvah* 2:11; *Teshuvoth Beth Ephraim, Yoreh Deah* 57. *Cf. Yevamoth* 64b; *Yad, Milah* 1:18; *Yoreh Deah* 263:2.
70. See above, 3:11.

damage[71] when they result in the birth of a bastard,[72] or cause a married woman to be forbidden to her husband.[73] In such cases, some say that an unrepentant sinner[74] has no portion in the World to Come.[75]

14:20 There are some sins, though not intrinsically very serious, which nevertheless indicate a gross disrespect for the teachings of Judaism. Therefore, one who regularly commits these sins psychologically divorces himself from Judaism and forfeits his portion in the World to Come.[76]

14:21 One who shows disrespect for rabbis and religious leaders indirectly shows disrespect for Judaism as a whole, and therefore has no portion in the World to Come.[77] The same is true for one who regularly reads atheistic or immoral books, since in giving them undue regard, he disregards our faith.[78]

14:22 Similarly, one who rejects the basic institutions of Judaism divorces himself from Judaism in general. Therefore, for example, one who neglects to keep our Festivals and Holy Days,[79] even the minor intermediate days,[80] has no portion in Israel's eternal reward. The same is true of one who despises our ancient sacrificial system, referring to it as an outdated primitive cult.[81]

71. *Chagigah* 9b; Rashi *ad. loc. s.v. Nitrad; BaMidbar Rabbah* 9:3. *Cf.* Maharshal, *Sotah* 4b.
72. *Yevamoth* 4:11 (49a); *Kiddushin* 64b; *Yad, Issurey Biyah* 15:1; *Evven HaEzer* 4:13.
73. *Yevamoth* 56b; *Kethuvoth* 51b; *Yad, Ishuth* 24:17.
74. *Tosafoth, Sotah* 4b *s.v. Hee,* from *Chagigah* 9b; Maharsha, *Bava Metzia* 59a *s.v. U'VeTzalei; cf. Tosafoth, Sanhedrin* 47a *s.v. VeAmai; Teshuvoth Maharam Shif, Bava Metzia* 58b, citing *Asarah Maamaroth* 1:3:2. All maintain that the statement in *Bava Metzia* 59a, *Sanhedrin* 197a, that they do have a portion in the World to Come, is only when they repent.
75. See above, note 40; *Nimukey Mahari* on *Yad, Teshuvah* 3:6; *Reshith Chokhmah, Shaar HaYirah* 37c (no. 6), 39b. Others maintain that he has a portion in the World to Come; *cf. Tosafoth, Bava Metzia* 58b *s.v. Chutz;* Maharshal, *Eruvin* 19a. See also *Berakhoth* 61a; *Tosafoth ad. loc. s.v. VeKol.*
76. *Yad, Teshuvah* 3:14; *Kesef Mishneh ad. loc.*
77. *Sanhedrin* 10:1 (90a), 99b; *Yad, Talmud Torah* 6:11; *Yoreh Deah* 343:6; Rabbenu Yonah, *Shaarey Teshuvah* 3:147, 3:155; *Ikkarim* 3:10; *cf. Shabbath* 119b.
78. See above, 1:23; *Zohar* 2:124a.
79. *Cf. Raya Mehemna, Zohar* 3:29b; *Yad, Yom Tov* 6:16; *Tosafoth, Chagigah* 18a *s.v. Choli; Machtzith HaShekel* 530:1, that some only apply it to actual holidays.
80. *Avoth* 3:11; Rashi, Bertenoro, Rabbenu Yonah, *ad. loc.; Sanhedrin* 99a; Rashi *ad. loc. s.v. HaMevazeh; Shaarey Teshuvah* 3:146, 3:11. *Cf. Makkoth* 23a; Rashi *ad. loc. s.v. Eth; Pesachim* 118a; Rashbam *ad. loc. s.v. Kol; Magen Avraham* 530:1; *Mishnah Berurah* 530:1; *Shaar HaTziun ad. loc.* 530:3.
81. *Avoth loc. cit.; cf.* Bertenoro, Rabbenu Yonah, *ad. loc.,* that this refers to making sacrifices unfit.

14:23 Showing disrespect for God's name indicates a definite lack of belief in Him, and one who does this has no portion in the World to Come. This is true of one who makes disrespectful use of the Tetragrammaton,[82] as well as one who makes unseemly use of any of God's names.[83]

14:24 Of those who have no portion in the World to Come, some are allowed to experience the shame of their sins, and are then relegated to a state of limbo with neither punishment nor reward,[84] or are totally destroyed.[85] It is thus written, "They that go down to the pit shall come up no more" (Job 7:9).[86] However, those who have some merit may retain enough of an identification with their people to vicariously partake of their reward.[87]

14:25 The worst of these are people who intentionally rebel against God and are not even deemed worthy of His mercy. These are condemned to eternal shame and disgrace, as the prophet tells us, "They will go forth and look at the dead bodies of the men who have rebelled against Me; for their worms will not die, nor will their fire be quenched; and they will be a disgusting sight to all mankind" (Isaiah 66:24).[88]

14:26 All this is only true if such people die without repenting. If they repent, however, we are taught that, "Nothing can stand up before repentance."[89] No matter what a person does, if he repents, then he is forgiven and accepted by God.[90]

---

82. See above, 8:10.
83. *Sanhedrin* 10:1 (90a), 101a; *Shevuoth* 15b; *Tosefta, Zohar* 3:306b; *Yad, Avodath Kokhavim* 11:12; *Kesef Mishneh ad. loc.; Yoreh Deah* 179:8; *Sifethey Cohen* 179:10; *Turey Zahav* 179:5-6; Rabbi Yechezkel Landau (in Vilna Shas), *Rosh HaShanah* 17a.
84. *Tosafoth, Bava Metzia* 58b *s.v. Chutz.* See below, 23:14, note 19.
85. *Yad, Teshuvah* 8:1. See above 13:50, note 172.
86. *Tanchuma, Bereshith* 5; *Zohar* 1:177b, 2:150b, 3:286a; *Reshith Chokhmah, Shaar HaYirah* 13 (37c no. 5).
87. *Ramathayim Tzofim* (on *Tana DeBei Eliahu Rabbah*) 15 (64a); *Taamey HaMinhagim, Kuntres Acharon* 536 (p. 232), 149 note (p. 63).
88. *Rosh HaShanah* 17a; Rabbi Yechezkel Landau (in Vilna Shas) *ad. loc.; Tosafoth loc. cit.; Reshith Chokhmah, Shaar HaYirah* 13 (37c no. 7); *cf. Yad, Teshuvah* 3:6; Ramban, *Shaar HaGamul* 79a.
89. See below, 15:5.
90. Rif, *Rosh HaShanah* 4a; *Tosafoth ibid.* 17a *s.v. Karkafta; Yad, Teshuvah* 3:14. *Cf.* Sforno on Numbers 15:31.

TABLE 14:1 — THE THIRTEEN BASIC UNIQUE BELIEFS OF JUDAISM[1a]

1. God exists. He is the Creator and Ruler of the universe. He alone has made, does make, and will make all things.[1]
2. God is One. There is no unity that is in any way like His. He alone is our God — He was, He is, and He will be.[2]
3. God does not have a body. Physical concepts do not apply to Him. There is nothing whatsoever that resembles Him.[3]
4. God is eternal, first and last.[4]
5. No intermediary is required between God and man. It is therefore only proper to pray to God. One may not pray to anyone or anything else.[5]
6. All the words of the prophets are true. The Torah, Prophets and Writings are the word of God.[6]
7. The prophecy of Moses is absolutely true. He was the greatest of all prophets, both before and after him.[7]
8. The entire Torah that we now have, both written and oral, is that which was given to Moses by God.[8]
9. God will not change nor exchange the Torah.[9]
10. God knows all of man's deeds and thoughts.[10]
11. God ultimately rewards good and punishes evil.[11]

1a. Rambam on *Sanhedrin* 10:1; Prayer Book; Thirteen Principles of Faith; *Yigdal; Ikkarim* 1:3-4; Abarbanel, *Rosh Emunah* 1 (4a); *Sh'nei Luchoth HaB'rith, Shaar HaOthioth* 1:94a. *Minchath Kinaoth* 4 (p. 7) lists three principles: belief in God, in His Torah, and in creation and providence. *Or HaShem* (Crescas) 3, introduction (61a), lists numbers 1, 11, 13, 9, 7 and 12, as well as belief in immortality and prophecy through the *Urim VeThumim,* among his eight basic beliefs. *Ikkarim* lists 1, 8, and 11, as basic beliefs, and 2, 3, 4, 5, 6, 7, 9, 10, 12, and 13, as well as the belief in the reward of the soul, as secondary beliefs. For discussion of the lists of *Or Hashem* and *Ikkarim,* see *Rosh Emunah* 2 (5b).
1. See Volume 1, 2:1, 2:13, 1:10.
2. See Volume 1, 2:7, 2:11.
3. See Volume 1, 2:11; above 14:3, note 9.
4. See Volume 1, 2:28.
5. See Volume 1, 1:14-15.
6. See Volume 1, 6:4-5.
7. See Volume 1, 7:3.
8. See Volume 1, 7:14, 7:20, 9:1.
9. See Volume 1, 7:16-17, 8:41 (note 82).
10. See Volume 1, 2:44-46.
11. See below, Chapter 18.

12. The Messiah will come. No matter how long it takes, we await his coming every day.[12]
13. The dead will be brought back to life when God wills it to happen.[13]

---

12. See below, Chapter 24. This rejects the Christian belief that the Messiah has already come.
13. *Sanhedrin* 10:1 (90a).

FIFTEEN

REPENTANCE

15:1   There are many people who feel that they can set their own standards of morality. They try to live by their own definitions of good and evil, without any recourse to divine revelation. What these individuals are doing is following an unsuccessful course paved by many generations of philosophers. For after 2500 years of probing, philosophy finally has come to the conclusion that unless revealed by some higher power, no objective standard of good and evil exists.

15:2   But when a person tries to live by his own moral standards, he is also likely to encounter another serious problem. As long as he is successful, everything is fine. But then, there may come a time when a person fails to live up to his own ethical standards. There are times when he can fail in a very extreme sense, and in all such cases, he has no recourse. No authority can forgive his guilt. This is one reason why unassuaged guilt has become such an important part of the contemporary human condition.

15:3   Judaism, however, recognizes God as the supreme authority of all morality. Good and evil are defined as revealed by God. Thus, God also has the power to forgive sin and eradicate any evil that a person may commit.[1] The same Authority that declares something evil and sinful, can also declare it forgiven — "the voice that binds is also the voice that loosens."[2] If sin is spiritual sickness,

---

1. Cf. *Pesikta* 25 (157a); *Yalkut Shimoni* 2:506; *Menorath HaMaor* 5:1:1:1 (276); *Reshith Chokhmah, Shaar HaTeshuvah* 1 (104c). Also see *Midrash Tehillim* 32:4, 57:1; *Reshith Chokhmah ibid.* 2 (107b). Cf. *Targum*, Rashi, *Baaley Tosafoth*, on Exodus 34:7; *Rosh HaShanah* 17a; *Yoma* 86a.
2. *Kethuvoth* 2:2 (17a).

then God has provided repentance as its cure.[3] Just as God may have decreed something impure, so has He decreed the means of its purification.[4]

15:4 Therefore, one of the fundamental teachings of Judaism is that when any person repents, his sins are forgiven. The Torah thus states, "If you return to God your Lord and listen to His voice... God will then accept your repentance and have compassion on you" (Deuteronomy 30:2-3).[5] The doors of repentance are open to every human being, Jew and non-Jew alike.[6]

15:5 Repentance is effective for any sin, no matter how serious, and our sages teach us, "Nothing can stand before repentance."[7] It helps no matter how often a sin may have been repeated.[8] It is equally effective for an entire lifestyle as it is for individual sins.

---

3. *Ikkarim* 4:25; *Midrash Tehillim* 51:2. *Cf.* Isaiah 57:18; Jeremiah 3:22; Hosea 14:4; Psalms 41:4; 2 Chronicles 7:14; *Yoma* 86b; *Tana DeBei Eliahu Zuta* 22 (45b).

4. *Yoma* 8:9 (85b); *Tosefoth Yom Tov ad. loc.; Pesikta loc. cit.; Midrash Tehillim* 4:9, 51:2.

5. *Targum Yonathan ad. loc.* Some count this as a commandment; *cf. Zohar* 3:122a; Ramban on Deuteronomy 30:11; *Ikkarim* 4:25; *Sefer Mitzvoth Katan* 2:53; *Beth Elokim* (Mabit) 2:17; *Minchath Chinukh* 364. Others, however, merely consider as it a promise; see *Yad, Teshuvah* 7:5; Rabbenu Yonah, *Shaarey Teshuvah* 1:1. The only commandment associated with repentance is then confession; see below, 15:20, 16:1.

6. As we find in the case of Nineveh; Jonah 3:10; *Pesikta* 25 (161a); *Menorath HaMaor* 5:1:2:5 (284); *Yerushalmi, Sanhedrin* 11:5 (56b); *Mekhilta* on Exodus 12:1 (1b); *Pirkey Rabbi Eliezer* 10 (24a); Radal *ad. loc.* 10:7; *Tanchuma, VaYikra* 8, *Tzav* 14; *Yalkut Shimoni* 2:550; Rashi on Jonah 1:3; Ibn Ezra on 1:2; Radak on 1:1. Also see *Pirkey Rabbi Eliezer* 43 (103a) with regard to Pharaoh. In other places, however, it appears that repentance does not help for non-Jews; *cf. Yerushalmi, Nazir* 9:1 (42a); *Pesikta* 24 (156a); *Tanchuma, VaYikra* 5, *HaAzinu* 4; *Tikuney Zohar* 21 (54b). See *Minchath Chinukh* 364 (p. 273d); Abarbanel on Jonah 4:10. In any case, there is a special mercy that God extends to Israel alone; *cf. Ikkarim* 4:38; *Kuzari* 2:44 (53b); *Rosh HaShanah* 17a (end); *Avodah Zarah* 4a; *Tosafoth, Shabbath* 44a *s.v. Ketzef; Bereshith Rabbah* 82:9; *Yalkut Shimoni* 1:126, 2:396; *Tanchuma, VaYetze* 2, *Nitzavim* 1, *Kedoshim* 1; Rashi on Isaiah 3:13.

7. *Yerushalmi, Peah* 1:1 (5a); *Yerushalmi, Sanhedrin* 10:1 (49a); *Zohar* 2:106a; *Emunoth VeDeyoth* 5:6; *Yad, Teshuvah* 3:14; *Teshuvoth Maharit* 2:8; *Teshuvoth Radbaz* 5:6; *Reshith Chokhmah, Shaar HaTeshuvah* 1 (105a). *Cf. Avodah Zarah* 4b, 5a, 17a; *Shabbath* 65a; *Moed Katan* 16b, Rashi *ad. loc. s.v. SheChakim; Midrash Tehillim* 40:2, 51:3; *VaYikra Rabbah* 5:8; *Midrash Tehillim* 19:17; *Yalkut Shimoni* 2:677, from Psalms 19:14; *cf. Sanhedrin* 107a. Regarding Onanism, see *Zohar* 1:291b, *Nitzotzey Oroth ad. loc.* no. 3; *cf. Zohar* 1:62a, 2:214b, 3:3b; *Tikuney Zohar* 22 (66a); *Reshith Chokhmah, Shaar HaKedushah* 17 (204c); *Sh'nei Luchoth HaB'rith, Shaar HaOthioth* 1:158a; *Likutey Amarim (Tanya), Iggereth HaTeshuvah* 4 (93b); Rabbi Yaakov of Tzozmer, *Teshuvoth Beth Yaakov* (Dyherenfurth, 1696) 222.

8. *Tana DeBei Eliahu Rabbah* 22 (96b); *Sh'nei Luchoth HaB'rith, Shaar HaOthioth* 2:156b.

Even if a person has lived an absolutely evil life,[9] denying[10] and blaspheming God,[11] he can still be forgiven.[12] God thus told His prophet, "The evil of the wicked man shall not trip him up on the day he turns away from his wicked way" (Ezekiel 33:12).[13]

15:6   In order to understand how repentance is so powerful, we must realize that God created the universe for the ultimate good of mankind. Evil and sin exist only in order to allow man to have free will, and therefore are neither part of God's primary purpose nor do they have permanence.[14] All things that tend to detract from man's ultimate good are thus eradicable.[15] God may have allowed for the existence of evil, but it is like a blot in the fabric of creation, and as such, it is readily eradicated by repentance.[16] Our sages therefore teach us that repentance was part of God's original plan for creation.[17]

15:7   Since God created man as a fallible creature with free choice

---

9. Maharal, *Nethivoth Olam, Teshuvah* 4 (157b), 5 (161b). It could even help for one as evil as King Menasseh; *cf.* 2 Chronicles 33:13; *Sanhedrin* 103a; *Yerushalmi, Sanhedrin* 10:2 (51b); *Avoth DeRabbi Nathan* 36:5; *Targum* on 2 Chronicles 33:7; *BaMidbar Rabbah* 14:1; *Devarim Rabbah* 2:13; *Ruth Rabbah* 5:6; *Pesikta* 25 (162a); *Pirkey Rabbi Eliezer* 43 (102a); *Reshith Chokhmah, Shaar HaTeshuvah* 1 (105c). Another similar example is Ahab; see *Pirkey Rabbi Eliezer* 43 (101a); *Pesikta* 25 (160b); *Menorath HaMaor* 5:1:2:5 (284); *Reshith Chokhmah, Shaar HaTeshuvah* 7 (124a).

10. *Pesikta* 25 (163b); *Yalkut Shimoni* 2:532; *Yad, Teshuvah* 3:14; *Menorath HaMaor* 5:1:1:1 (276); *Sh'nei Luchoth HaB'rith, Shaar HaOthioth* 2:156b. However, see *Avodah Zarah* 17a; *Kesef Mishneh, Lechem Mishneh, Avodath Kokhavim* 2:5; Maharal, *Nethivoth Olam, Teshuvah* 8 (168a).

11. *Tana DeBei Eliahu Rabbah* 22 (96b).

12. See Rif, *Rosh HaShanah* 4a; *Tosafoth, Rosh HaShanah* 17a *s.v. Karkafta, Bava Metzia* 58b *s.v. Chutz; Sefer Chasidim* 606; *Sh'nei Luchoth HaB'rith, Shaar HaOthioth* 1:157a; *Yad, Teshuvah* 3:14; *Chovoth HaLevavoth* 7:10 (62b); Maharal, *Nethivoth Olam, Teshuvah* 4 (157b).

13. *Kiddushin* 40a; *Tosefta* 1:11; *BaMidbar Rabbah* 10:1; *Yalkut Shimoni* 2:979; *Yad, Teshuvah* 1:3, 2:1.

14. See Volume 1, 3:5, 3:26; *Innerspace*, pp. 71 (note 51), 171.

15. See Volume 1, 3:24. *Cf.* Isaiah 1:18, 43:25, 44:22.

16. *Shemoth Rabbah* 23:11; *Shir HaShirim Rabbah* 1:38; *Zohar* 1:73b; *Reshith Chokhmah, Shaar HaTeshuvah* 5 (116d). *Cf.* Psalms 51:4.

17. *Ikkarim* 4:28. *Cf. Pesachim* 54a; *Nedarim* 39a; *Bereshith Rabbah* 1:5; *Tanchuma, Naso* 11; *Pirkey Rabbi Eliezer* 3 (6a-b); Radal *ad. loc.* 3:14, 3:19; *Tana DeBei Eliahu Rabbah* 31; *Midrash Tehillim* 90:3, 93:3; *Zohar* 1:90a, 1:134b, 3:34b; *Zohar Chadash* 8a, 85a; *Menorath HaMaor* 4:0 (238), 5:0 (275); *Orchoth Tzadikim* 26 (p. 146); *Reshith Chokhmah, Shaar HaTeshuvah* 1 (101b).

and free will,[18] it is all but inevitable that man should sin. It is thus written, "There is no man who does not sin" (1 Kings 8:46). If there were no means of erasing sin, man's guilt would accumulate until he would cry out with the anguish of Cain, "My sin is too great to bear!" (Genesis 4:13).[19] For this reason, God gave man repentance as a means of eradicating his sins.[20]

15:8   Man's primary purpose in existence is to obey God's will. Therefore, when a man sins, justice might decree that he be destroyed, like anything else that goes against the very purpose of its being.[21] God's love and mercy, however, override His justice, and He is always ready to forgive man, as the Psalmist sang, "God is good and upright, He shows sinners the way [to return]" (Psalms 25:8).[22] This is all in accordance with God's ultimate purpose, as He told His prophet, "'As I live,' says God, 'I have no pleasure in the death of the wicked, but [I desire] that he turn from his way and live'" (Ezekiel 33:11).[23]

15:9   Therefore, although God is all-powerful and has the power to retaliate immediately when a person sins against Him, He bides His time,[24] and gives man a chance to repent before punishing him.[25] He thus told us through His prophet, "For My name's sake, I will be patient; and for My praise, I will restrain [My anger] from you, that I not cut you off" (Isaiah 48:9).[26]

18. See Volume 1, 3:16.
19. *Cf. Bereshith Rabbah* 22:25; *Pirkey Rabbi Eliezer* 21 (49b).
20. *Pirkey Rabbi Eliezer* 11 (27b); *Zohar* 1:134b, 1:205a, 3:35b. *Cf. Pirkey Rabbi Eliezer* 20 (47b); Radal *ad. loc.* 20:35; *Reshith Chokhmah, Shaar HaTeshuvah* 1 (101b).
21. *Yerushalmi, Makkoth* 2:6 (7a); *Pesikta* 25 (158b); *Yalkut Shimoni* 2:358, 2:702; *Teshuvoth Meah Shearim* 46; *Orchoth Chaim, "Rosh HaShanah."*
22. *Ibid.;* Rashi, Radak, *ad. loc.; Midrash Tehillim* 25:10; Rabbenu Yonah, *Shaarey Teshuvah* 1:1; *Menorath HaMaor* 5:0 (275).
23. *Cf.* 2 Samuel 14:14; Ezekiel 18:28, 18:33; *Shemoth Rabbah* 9:1; *BaMidbar Rabbah* 10:1; *Midrash Tehillim* 5:7; *Yad, Rotzeach* 13:14; *Menorath HaMaor* 5:0 (275). Also see *Berakhoth* 10a; *Taanith* 23b; *Sotah* 14a; *Niddah* 70b.
24. See Exodus 34:6; Numbers 14:18, Rashi *ad. loc.;* Psalms 86:15; *Sanhedrin* 111a; *Tosafoth, Eruvin* 22a, *Bava Kama* 50b, *s.v. Erekh Apayim; Avoth* 5:2; *Bereshith Rabbah* 32:10; Rashi on Genesis 6:3.
25. *Yerushalmi, Taanith* 2:1 (9a); *Pesikta* 25 (161b); *Midrash Tehillim* 26:7; *Menorath HaMaor* 5:1:2:3 (282). *Cf. Shabbath* 32a.
26. *Cf. BaMidbar Rabbah* 5:6; *Tanchuma, BaMidbar* 24; Radal (on *Pirkey Rabbi Eliezer*) 11:26.

15:10 Since repentance forms an integral part of God's plan, its doors are always open.[27] Even when strict justice would shut the gates of repentance in a sinner's face, God is ready to admit him.[28] However, just as a person must seek out waters in which to cleanse himself, so must one who wants to repent make the first move to seek out God. Our sages thus teach us, "When one comes to cleanse himself, then [God] helps him."[29]

15:11 It is often asked how repentance can help, since it does not undo the damage caused by a sin. If a person murders another, or destroys his life, how can repentance undo the damage? The answer is that to a great extent, the guilt associated with sin depends upon its motives and the conditions under which it was committed. Thus, for example, murder in self defense or in defense of another is not considered a sin, even though a human being is killed. There are even cases where motivation alone may neutralize an otherwise sinful act[30] or transform it into a good deed.[31] Therefore, when a person repents, even though his act remains the same, his intent is retroactively changed.[32] Although repentance cannot undo the deed itself, it can retroactively undo the intent, and thus rectify the spiritual damage caused by the sin.[33] However, since earthly courts judge only deeds, repentance does not help to defer their penalties.[34]

15:12 Even if a person is wicked all his life, God still gives him the opportunity to repent. Every moment of life is like a precious coin with which to pay our fare across the river of this world. Even if many coins have been wasted, as long as one remains,

27. *Devarim Rabbah* 2:7; *Eikhah Rabbah* 3:35; *Midrash Tehillim* 65:4; *Pesikta* 25 (157a); *Menorath HaMaor* 3:3:1:12 (102); *Sefer Chasidim* 7.
28. *Pesachim* 119a; Rashi, Rashbam, *ad. loc. s.v. Mipeney; Tana DeBei Eliahu Zuta* 22 (4b); *Yalkut Shimoni* 2:337; *Zohar* 2:75b, 2:260b; *Zohar Chadash* 39a, from Ezekiel 1:8.
29. *Shabbath* 104a; *Yoma* 38b; *Zohar* 1:54a, 1:62a, 1:77b, 1:88b, 1:142a, 2:79b, 3:53b, 3:126a, 3:155b. See *Midrash Tehillim* 4:9.
30. See above, 13:19.
31. See above, 13:24.
32. *Ikkarim* 4:27; *Nethivoth Olam, Teshuvah* 5 (160a); *Mesilath Yesharim* 4 (8a); *Etz Yosef* (on *Eyn Yaakov* 76) on *Yoma* 86b; see below, note 101.
33. *Zohar* 1:79b, 3:122a; *Reshith Chokhmah, Shaar HaTeshuvah* 2 (107d); *Cheredim, Teshuvah* 6 (p. 249); *Mesilath Yesharim* 4 (8a); *Nefesh HaChaim* 1:20.
34. Maharal, *Nethivoth Olam, Teshuvah* 2 (150b). See above, 13:52.

there is always hope of crossing over to our destination.[35] The prophet thus taught us, "When the wicked man turns away from his wicked way, and does what is just and right, then through this he shall live" (Ezekiel 33:19).[36]

15:13 In its most perfect sense, repentance consists of four elements:[37] changing one's ways,[38] sincere regret, confession to God,[39] and resolve not to repeat the sin. All of these are included in the prophet's warning, "Return, Israel, to God your Lord (1), for you have regretted your sin (2). Take along words (3), and return to God. Say to Him, '... we will no longer make gods out of the work of our hands (4)'" (Hosea 14:2, 4).[40]

15:14 Of these four, the last three are necessary to rectify the spiritual damage done to man's main faculties, thought, speech and action. Regret rectifies one's thoughts, confession is for speech, and resolve is for the action itself.[41]

15:15 The first prerequisite for repentance, however, is changing one's ways and abandoning the practice of sin. Repenting while still immersed in sin is like trying to cleanse oneself while still holding on to filth.[42] The initial and most important step of repentance is therefore changing one's way of life, as the prophet counsels, "Let the wicked man forsake his way" (Isaiah 55:7).[43] We are furthermore advised, "Cast away all your transgressions" (Ezekiel 18:31).[44] When one repents, his sin should therefore be irrevocably

35. *Chovoth HaLevavoth* 7:10 (end).
36. *Yerushalmi, Peah* 1:1 (5a); *Shemoth Rabbah* 31:1; *BaMidbar Rabbah* 10:1; *Shir HaShirim Rabbah* 6:1.
37. *Emunoth VeDeyoth* 5:5 (72a); *Chovoth HaLevavoth* 7:4; *Yad, Teshuvah* 2:2; *Sefer Chasidim* 42; Rabbenu Yonah, *Shaarey Teshuvah* 1:19; *Ikkarim* 4:26; *Cheredim, Teshuvah* 2 (p. 204); *Sh'nei Luchoth HaB'rith, Teshuvah* 2:168b. Cf. *VaYikra Rabbah* 3:3.
38. *Yad loc. cit.* appears to count the first and fourth element in a single category. The *Ikkarim* omits the first element, while *Shaarey Teshuvah* omits the fourth.
39. *Emunoth VeDeyoth* substitutes "petition for forgiveness" for "confession to God."
40. *Emunoth VeDeyoth loc. cit.*
41. *Ikkarim* 4:26. Cf. *Zohar* 1:79b; *Nefesh HaChaim* 1:20.
42. *Taanith* 16a; *Tosefta, Taanith* 1:8; *Yerushalmi, Taanith* 2:1 (8b); *Eikhah Rabbah* 3:33; *Pesikta Rabathai* 182b; *Yad, Teshuvah* 2:3; Rosh, *Yoma* 8:17; Rabbenu Yonah, *Shaarey Teshuvah* 1:11; *Menorath HaMaor* 5:1:2:1 (280). *Yad loc. cit.* applies this primarily to resolve.
43. *Yad, Teshuvah* 2:2; *Chovoth HaLevavoth* 7:4; *Shaarey Teshuvah* 1:11. Cf. *VaYikra Rabbah* 3:3.
44. Cf. Ezekiel 33:11; Isaiah 1:16.

cast away and discarded.[45] One's intention in doing this should be the fear of God,[46] and the shame for having sinned before Him.[47]

15:16   When a person has repented, he should be careful to keep himself even from permissible things that may cause him to sin.[48] He should carefully examine his entire lifestyle in order to abandon anything associated with his sinful ways, as we are taught, "Let us search and examine our ways, and return to God" (Lamentations 3:40).[49] When a person changes his ways, he is forgiven, as God told His prophet, "Let every man turn from his evil way, and I will forgive their sins and errors" (Jeremiah 36:3).[50] God likewise told Cain, "If you do good, you will be forgiven" (Genesis 4:7).[51]

15:17   The second element of repentance is the feeling of remorse and regret for one's sins.[52] It is thus written, "After I repented, I felt remorse" (Jeremiah 31:18).[53] Out of fear of God,[54] a person should be filled with humility[55] and contrition[56] for having transgressed His command.[57] He should constantly admonish himself for having

45. *Chovoth HaLevavoth* 7:5. Five conditions are given for abandoning sin: abandoning all forbidden things, abandoning permissible things that may lead to sin, being motivated by fear of God, being ashamed before God, and making one's abandonment final and absolute. These five are included in notes 45, 46, and 47. See *Sanhedrin* 25b; *Choshen Mishpat* 34:29-35; *Likutey Amarim, Iggereth HaTeshuvah* 1 (91a).
46. *Chovoth HaLevavoth* 7:5; *Shaarey Teshuvah* 1:16.
47. *Chovoth HaLevavoth* 7:5; *Shaarey Teshuvah* 1:21.
48. *Chovoth HaLevavoth* 7:5. *Cf.* Rambam, *Shemonah Perakim* 4; *Menorath HaMaor* 5:1:2:1 (280).
49. *Shaarey Teshuvah* 1:36. *Cf. Berakhoth* 4a; *Zohar* 1:228b.
50. *Cf.* Jeremiah 18:8; Jonah 3:8.
51. *Targum Yonathan*, Ibn Ezra, Ramban, *ad. loc.; Bereshith Rabbah* 22:11.
52. *Cf. Chagigah* 5a; *Tosafoth ad. loc. s.v. Hah, Shevuoth* 12b *s.v. Lo; Mayim Chayim* 44b *s.v. Nithkashti; Teshuvoth Panim Meiroth* 1:26; *Asarah Maamaroth* 1:1:17. *Cf. Shaarey Teshuvah* 1:10, 12; *Menorath HaMaor* 5:1:1:1 (276).
53. Radak *ad. loc.; Yad, Teshuvah* 2:2; *Menorath HaMaor* 5:1:2:2 (281).
54. *Chovoth HaLevavoth* 7:5. Five conditions of remorse are listed: fear of God's anger and punishment, humility and contrition, physical signs of remorse such as sackcloth and ashes, tears of regret, and self admonishment for having sinned. These are given in notes 54, 57, and 58.
55. *Sifra* on Leviticus 26:41 (112b); *Yad, Teshuvah* 7:8; *Shaarey Teshuvah* 1:23; *Sefer Chasidim* 54; *Sh'nei Luchoth HaB'rith, Mesekheth Rosh HaShanah* 2:156b; *Menorath HaMaor* 5:1:2:3 (282). *Cf.* Rashi on Leviticus 14:4.
56. *Sanhedrin* 43b; *Pesikta* 25 (158a); *Menorath HaMaor loc. cit.;* Maharal, *Nethivoth Olam, Teshuvah* 1 (148b).
57. *Chovoth HaLevavoth* 7:5.

sinned,[58] as the Psalmist lamented, "For I know my wrongdoings, and my sin is ever before me" (Psalms 51:5).[59]

15:18 When a person repents, he should experience deep shame because of his sins. We thus find, "And I said, 'O my God, I am mortified and ashamed to lift my face to You, my God, for our sins have mounted up above our heads'" (Ezra 9:6).[60] Shame is an important ingredient of the punishment for sin in the Future World,[61] and therefore, the person who stands in shame before God in this world, is spared the shame of the next world.[62] One who is truly ashamed of his sins is therefore forgiven all, as God told His prophet, "When you remember your ways and are ashamed... I will establish My covenant with you... and forgive all that you have done" (Ezekiel 18:61-63).[63]

15:19 Still, it is important that one not sink into depression because of his sin. Rather, he should rejoice, knowing how ready God is to forgive him. This is the meaning of King David's prayer when he repented and entreated, "A pure heart create for me, O God, a proper spirit renew in me. Cast me not away from Your presence, and take not Your *Holy Spirit* from me. Restore to me the joy of Your salvation, and let a willing spirit uphold me" (Psalms 51:12-14).[64]

15:20 The third element of repentance is confession before God, as the Torah states, "If a man or woman sins... they must confess the sin they have committed" (Numbers 5:6-7).[65] Confession such as this is before God alone, and is one of the commandments of the Torah.[66] King David thus said, "[At last] I admitted my sin to You, no [longer] concealing my guilt. I said, 'I will confess

58. *Ibid.*
59. *Menorath HaMaor* 5:1:2:2 (281); *Shaarey Teshuvah* 1:48. *Cf. Yoma* 86b; *Tosefta* 4:14; *Yerushalmi* 8:7 (42b); *Midrash Tehillim* 32:2; *Zohar* 1:73b.
60. *Shaarey Teshuvah* 1:21; *Menorath HaMaor* 5:1:2:2 (281). *Cf.* Daniel 9:7-8.
61. See below, 23:17, note 29.
62. *Yevamoth* 105b; *Kiddushin* 81a; *Bava Bathra* 75a; *Shemoth Rabbah* 30:15; *Midrash Tehillim* 6:6; *Zohar* 1:4a.
63. *Berakhoth* 12b; *Yalkut Shimoni* 2:140, 2:357; *Zohar Chadash* 19b; *Sefer Chasidim* 54.
64. *Likutey Amarim, Iggereth HaTeshuvah* 11 (100b end). *Cf.* Ibn Ezra, *Metzudoth David*, *ad. loc.*
65. See below, 16:2.
66. See below, 16:1.

my sin to God.' And You, You have forgiven the wrong of my sin" (Psalms 32:5).[67] When a person confesses his sin to God, then he is judged by God's mercy alone,[68] as we find, "He who covers up his sins shall not do so successfully, but he who confesses and forsakes them will find mercy" (Proverbs 28:13).[69] On the other hand, a person can be punished for denying his sin before God, as He told us through His prophet, "Behold, I will enter into judgment with you because you say, 'I have not sinned'" (Jeremiah 2:35).[70]

15:21 In addition to confessing, one must pray to God for forgiveness, as the prophet taught us, "Say to Him: 'Forgive all sin and grant us favor!'" (Hosea 14:3).[71] Thus, when Moses was seeking to atone for the sin of the Golden Calf, he said, "I pray... pardon our sins and errors" (Exodus 34:9).[72] When a person prays to God for forgiveness, he is sure to be answered,[73] as King Solomon declared in his dedication prayer, "If they turn to You, acknowledge Your name, and pray and supplicate to You... then You will hear in heaven, and forgive the sin of Your people" (1 Kings 8:33-34).[74]

15:22 One should also pray to God to help him repent. We thus find the prayer, "Bring me back and I will repent, for You are God my Lord" (Jeremiah 31:17).[75] It is particularly important to pray

---

67. *Chovoth HaLevavoth* 7:5; *Shaarey Teshuvah* 1:18; *Ikkarim* 4:26. *Cf. Pirkey Rabbi Eliezer* 20 (47b); *Zohar* 3:20a, 3:195a, 3:231a; *Akedath Yitzchak* 63 (62a).
68. *Tanchuma, Balak* 10; *BaMidbar Rabbah* 20:13; *Zohar* 2:41a, 3:231a; *Reshith Chokhmah, Shaar HaTeshuvah* 5 (118d). *Cf. Bava Kama* 14b.
69. Rashi, Ralbag, *ad. loc.; Shaarey Teshuvah* 1:18; *Chovoth HaLevavoth* 7:4; *Akedath Yitzchak* 63; *Ikkarim* 4:26. *Cf. Taanith* 16a; *Tosefta* 1:8; *Yoma* 86b; *Shir HaShirim Rabbah* 6:17; *Pesikta* 25 (159a); *Midrash Tehillim* 100:2; *Zohar* 3:231b, 3:275a; *Yalkut Shimoni* 2:961, 2:854; *Yad, Teshuvah* 2:5.
70. Mahari Kara, Radak, *Metzudoth David, ad. loc.; Yerushalmi, Taanith* 2:7 (11a); *Tzion Yerushalayim ad. loc.; Midrash Tehillim* 80:1; *Yalkut Shimoni* 2:482, 2:268, 2:533; *Chovoth HaLevavoth* 7:4; Rabbenu Yonah, *Shaarey Teshuvah* 1:18; *Binah LeItim* 50. *Cf. Midrash Tehillim* 51:2.
71. Rabbenu Yonah, *Shaarey Teshuvah* 1:41.
72. *Menorath HaMaor* 5:1:2:3 (282). *Cf.* Daniel 9:3; Psalms 106:6; *Shaarey Teshuvah* 1:42.
73. *Midrash Tehillim* 51:2; *Yalkut Shimoni* 2:764; *Sefer Chasidim* 605; *Reshith Chokhmah, Shaar HaTeshuvah* 5 (118d).
74. *Cf.* Amos 7:2-3; *Tana DeBei Eliahu Rabbah* 6.
75. *Shaarey Teshuvah* 1:53. *Cf.* Lamentations 5:21. See also *Sefer Mitzvoth Gadol,* Positive Commandment 16.

that one should not die without fully repenting, as the Psalmist requested, "Do not gather my soul together with sinners, nor take my life together with men of blood" (Psalms 26:9).[76]

15:23 The fourth and final element of repentance is the resolve not to repeat the sin, as we find, "If I do not see, show me — if I have done wrong, I will do it no more" (Job 34:32).[77] A person's resolve should be so sincere that God, probing his innermost conscience, should be able to bear witness to it.[78] It is thus written, "Let God be a true and faithful witness against us if we do not do everything that God our Lord sends you to tell us" (Jeremiah 42:5).[79]

15:24 In his resolve to abandon sin, one should go as far as practical in the opposite direction, doing good in the same way he sinned.[80] We are thus taught, "If you have done bundles of sins, now do bundles of good deeds."[81] If possible, one should attempt to do good deeds with the same parts of the body with which he sinned.[82]

15:25 Although the initial steps of repentance consist of abandoning sin, remorse and confession, a higher form of repentance involves doing good deeds.[83] The Psalmist thus counsels, "Depart from evil, do good, seek peace and pursue it" (Psalms 34:15).[84] An essential part of this higher repentance is prayer,[85] deeds of kindness to others,[86] and the study of Torah.[87] Regarding this, it is written,

76. *Midrash Tehillim* 26:7; *Menorath HaMaor* 5:1:2:3 (282); *Akedath Yitzchak* 22.
77. *Chovoth HaLevavoth* 7:4.
78. *Yad, Teshuvah* 2:2; *Kesef Mishneh, Lechem Mishneh, ad. loc. Cf. Pesikta* 25 (164b); *Yalkut Shimoni* 2:532; *Zohar* 3:240a; *Midrash David* on *Avoth* 4:13.
79. See Genesis 31:50.
80. *Shemoth Rabbah* 23:3; Rabbenu Yonah, *Shaarey Teshuvah* 1:35, 4:5; *Menorath HaMaor* 5:1:2:1 (280); *Sh'nei Luchoth HaB'rith, Teshuvah* 2:169b, from *Bava Bathra* 4a; *Emek Berakhah* 106a. Cf. *Sanhedrin* 70b; *Tosafoth ad. loc. s.v. Bah.*
81. *VaYikra Rabbah* 21:4; *Shaarey Teshuvah* 1:35; *Sh'nei Luchoth HaB'rith, Mesekheth Rosh HaShanah, Amud HaDin* 2:157b; *Sichoth HaRan* 89. Cf. *Midrash Tehillim* 32:3.
82. *Yalkut Shimoni* 2:42; *Chovoth HaLevavoth* 7:9; *Shaarey Teshuvah* 1:35; *Menorath HaMaor* 5:1:2:3 (282); *Reshith Chokhmah, Shaar HaTeshuvah* 7 (124c); *Sh'nei Luchoth HaB'rith, Mesekheth Rosh HaShanah, Amud HaDin* 2:157b.
83. *Zohar* 3:123a; *Reshith Chokhmah, Shaar HaTeshuvah* 2 (108b); *Likutey Amarim (Tanya), Iggereth HaTeshuvah* 9 (98b).
84. Cf. Rashi *ad. loc.; Shaarey Teshuvah* 1:49; Genesis 4:7.
85. *Emunoth VeDeyoth* 5:5 (72b). Cf. *Yerushalmi, Rosh HaShanah* 2:5 (13a); *Yerushalmi, Sanhedrin* 1:2 (4a).
86. *Berakhoth* 5b; *Yalkut Shimoni* 2:954; *Cheredim, Teshuvah* 3 (p. 212); *Likutey Amarim, Iggereth HaTeshuvah* 9 (99a).

"By [deeds of] kindness and truth, sin is forgiven" (Proverbs 16:6).[88] Measures such as these constitute a higher degree of repentance that can help even when all others fail.[89] Good deeds do not help to atone for sin, however, until all the other basic prerequisites have been fulfilled.[90]

15:26 An important aspect of such repentance is bringing other people back to God, as the Psalmist said, "Then I will teach wrongdoers Your ways, and sinners will return to You" (Psalms 51:15).[91] The merit of bringing others to do good can outweigh the guilt that results from one's sins.[92]

15:27 It is a custom for one repenting a very serious sin to undergo ritual immersion in a *Mikvah* as a sign of purification and repentance.[93] In a sense, immersing in the *Mikvah* is like returning to the womb, and emerging is a symbolic rebirth.[94] Thus, for example, a convert must immerse when entering the Jewish faith as a sign that he is experiencing a spiritual birth,[95] and the same is true of one repenting a particularly serious sin.[96] For this

87. *Ibid.; Tana DeBei Eliahu Rabbah* 18 (90a); *Sefer Chasidim* 589; *Sh'nei Luchoth HaB'rith, Mesekheth Rosh HaShanah, Amud HaDin* 2:157b. *Cf. Sotah* 21a; *Tikuney Zohar* 21 (52b); *Tikuney Zohar Chadash* 97a; *Nefesh HaChaim* 1:20 (end).
88. *Berakhoth* 5b; *Emunoth VeDeyoth* 5:5 (72b); Rabbenu Yonah, *Shaarey Teshuvah* 4:11; Maharal, *Nethivoth Olam, Yissurin* 2 (177a).
89. *Reshith Chokhmah, Shaar HaKedushah* 17 (204c); *Likutey Amarim, Iggereth HaTeshuvah* 4 (93b). *Cf. Shaarey Teshuvah* 4:16; *Rosh HaShanah* 18a; *Yevamoth* 105a; *Yerushalmi, loc. cit.,* from 1 Samuel 3:14; Mahari Kara, Radak, *ad. loc.*
90. *Akedath Yitzchak* 97, cited in *Sh'nei Luchoth HaB'rith, Mesekheth Rosh HaShanah, Amud HaDin* 2:157b; *Reshith Chokhmah, Shaar HaTeshuvah* 2 (108b). *Cf. Sefer Chasidim* 589.
91. *Emunoth VeDeyoth* 5:5 (72b); *Chovoth HaLevavoth* 7:5; *Shaarey Teshuvah* 1:50; *Reshith Chokhmah, Shaar HaTeshuvah* 7 (124d); *Sh'nei Luchoth HaB'rith, Mesekheth Rosh HaShanah* 2:161a. *Cf.* Rashi, Radak, on Ezekiel 18:30. See also *Bava Metzia* 107b; *Bava Bathra* 60b; *Sanhedrin* 18a, 19a; *Yerushalmi, Taanith* 2:1 (8b), from Zephaniah 2:1; Radak *ad. loc.*
92. See *Yoma* 87a; *Tosefta, Yoma* 4:11.
93. *Reshith Chokhmah, Shaar HaTeshuvah* 11 (92a); *Sh'nei Luchoth HaB'rith, Shaar HaOthioth* 1:167b, 2:166a. *Cf. Pirkey Rabbi Eliezer* 20 (47b); *Magen Avraham* 606:8; *Mishnah Berurah* 606:21.
94. Kaplan, *Waters of Eden,* p. 13 (note 20). See *Yad, Mikvaoth* 1:1; *Sefer HaMitzvoth,* Positive Commandment 109; *Sefer Mitzvoth Gadol,* Positive Commandment 248; *Chinukh* 175.
95. See Volume 1, 5:14-15, notes 36, 39; *Waters of Eden,* p. 20f.
96. Maharil, *Hilkhoth Erev Yom Kippur* (44a); *Darkey Moshe, Orach Chaim* 606:3; *Machtzith HaShekel* 606:8; *"Rav" Shulchan Arukh* 606:12; *Kitzur Shulchan Arukh* 131:6. See *Tosefoth Yom Tov, Pesachim* 8:8.

reason, one who has left the fold of Judaism, should immerse when he returns and repents.[97] Similarly, it is a custom to immerse before *Yom Kippur* as a sign of repentance.[98]

15:28 In order to be effective, all repentance should involve the following seven concepts: one must accept total responsibility for having done wrong, recognize the seriousness of having sinned, realize that he cannot escape God's punishment, acknowledge God's omniscience and knowledge of his sin, know that repentance is his only chance to be healed, recognize God's goodness, and desire to achieve closeness to God.[99]

15:29 There are, however, two basic thoughts that can motivate a person to repent. He can be stricken with the realization that God can and will punish him for his evil ways and repent out of dread of this punishment. This is called "repentance out of fear." On the other hand, a person can grow to love God and His teachings to such an extent that he sincerely regrets ever having violated them. This is called "repentance out of love."[100] As discussed earlier, repentance may not help undo the deed itself, but it helps to retroactively rectify the intent accompanying the sin. When a person repents out of fear, he essentially wishes he had never committed any of his wrong or sinful acts. In such a case, God retroactively applies this intent to the sin,[101] and counts it as if it were done unintentionally.[102] Still, further atonement is required,[103] just as in the case of any other unintentional sin.[104]

97. *Nimukey Yosef, Yevamoth* (Rif 16b) *s.v. Kedoshav; Yoreh Deah* 268:12 in *Hagah,* 267:8 in *Hagah; Turey Zahav, Yoreh Deah* 267:5; *Magen Avraham* 326:8; *Machtzith HaShekel ad. loc. Cf. Avoth DeRabbi Nathan* 8:8. Also see *Teshuvoth HaGeonim, Shaarey Tzedek* 3:6:8 (24b); *Teshuvoth Rashba* 5:6; *Makor Chesed* (on *Sefer Chasidim*) 203:1.

98. Mordecai, *Yoma* 723; Rosh 8:24; *Rokeach* 214; *Sefer Chasidim* 394; *Menorath HaMaor* 5:2:2:1 (295), from *Pirkey Rabbi Eliezer* 46; *Orach Chaim* 606:4; *Turey Zahav* 606:5; *Beer Hetiv* 606:8; *Teshuvoth Chavath Yair* 181. Cf. *Orach Chaim* 581:4 in *Hagah.*

99. *Chovoth HaLevavoth* 7:3. Cf. *Reshith Chokhmah, Shaar HaTeshuvah* 1 (104c).

100. Cf. *Yoma* 86a; *Zohar* 3:123a; *Reshith Chokhmah, Shaar HaYirah* 1 (6d). See also *Zohar* 3:287b, 1:119a, 2:114b, 3:15b, 3:16a, 3:100b, 3:122a, 3:185b.

101. See above, note 32.

102. *Yoma* 36b, 86b; *Ikkarim* 4:25; *Menorath HaMaor* 4:1:1:1 (276).

103. Sforno on Exodus 34:7. See below, 17:1, 17:3 (note 11).

104. See above, 13:28.

15:30   When a person repents out of love, however, all that he ever wants to do is obey God's will. He not only wishes that he had not done bad, but sincerely regrets not having used this same time and effort in serving his beloved God. Therefore, all sins repented because of such love are counted as if they were done with the intent to do good.[105] They are thus reckoned as good deeds,[106] and in this manner, all of one's evil can be transformed into good.[107] Regarding this, the Psalmist said, "You [now] love right and hate wrong, so God your Lord has anointed you above your fellows with the oil of joy" (Psalms 45:8).[108]

15:31   Just as repentance varies according to one's intent, so does it vary according to the circumstances. Just as special modes of cleansing can eradicate certain stains better than others, so can specific modes of repentance erase sin more effectively.[109] We are taught that there are seven levels of repentance, and they are given in Table 15:1 at the end of this chapter.

15:32   It is best to repent as soon as possible. The longer any sin abides with an individual, the more indelibly it becomes imprinted on his personality,[110] and the more difficult it becomes to repent.[111] One also gradually forgets the sin, and no longer feels its full gravity.[112] The more one delays repenting a particular sin, the less the chances of its ever being fully repented, for the individual may forget the sin completely,[113] or sudden death may prevent his ever repenting it.[114]

105. See above, note 32.
106. *Yoma* 86b; *Yerushalmi, Peah* 1:1 (5a); *Shemoth Rabbah* 31:1; *BaMidbar Rabbah* 10:1; *Shir HaShirim Rabbah* 6:1; *Ikkarim* 4:25; Sforno on Exodus 34:7; Maharal, *Nethivoth Olam, Teshuvah* 2 (153a); *Cheredim, Teshuvah* 3 (p. 211), 6 (p. 249); *Minchath Chinukh* 364 (273d).
107. *Cheredim, Teshuvah* 6 (p. 250).
108. Rashi, Radak, *ad. loc.;* see note 106.
109. Rabbenu Yonah, *Shaarey Teshuvah* 1:9; *Sh'nei Luchoth HaB'rith, Mesekheth Rosh HaShanah* 2:156b.
110. It is like the shell of a nut that hardens as it matures; *cf. Zohar* 3:227a; *Reshith Chokhmah, Shaar HaTeshuvah* 1 (103c).
111. *Shaarey Teshuvah* 1:2. *Cf. Pesikta* 25 (164a); *Yalkut Shimoni* 2:532; Rashi on Hosea 14:2.
112. *Shaarey Teshuvah* 1:4; *Sefer Chasidim* 82.
113. *Sefer Chasidim* 82.
114. *Ibid.; Yad, Teshuvah* 7:2. *Cf. Zohar* 1:220a, 3:33a; *Reshith Chokhmah, Shaar HaTeshuvah* 1 (102c).

15:33 If a person does something wrong, it is therefore best to repent immediately.[115] When one does so, it is like bathing a fresh stain before it has dried and set, which comes out immediately,[116] and this is therefore called the way of the wise.[117]

15:34 If one repents a sin immediately, he is also much less apt to repeat it. If he does not, on the other hand, it is likely to be repeated until he becomes inured to it, and it no longer seems wrong. Our sages thus teach us, "When a person sins and repeats it, then it begins to seem permissible to him."[118] King Solomon described this in the most derogatory terms, "Like a dog that returns to its vomit, so is a fool who repeats his folly" (Proverbs 26:11).[119]

15:35 Every sin is counted separately, and therefore each one must be repented.[120] This is true even if one repeats the same act numerous times.[121] One must be careful to repent even seemingly minor sins[122] as well as accidental transgressions.[123]

15:36 Just as one must repent sinful deeds, so must one repent sinful character traits, such as anger, hatred, jealousy, and greed.[124] One must be especially careful to repent in cases where the sin itself is questionable,[125] or where the average person is not aware of its being wrong.[126]

115. *Menorath HaMaor* 5:1:1:2 (277), 5:1:1:3 (278); *Sh'nei Luchoth HaB'rith, Mesekheth Rosh HaShanah* 2:156a, *Hilkhoth Teshuvah* 2:183a.

116. *Cf. Zohar Chadash* 7a.

117. *Shaarey Teshuvah* 1:3; *Menorath HaMaor* 5:1:1:1 (276), from *Berakhoth* 19a; *Midrash Tehillim* 125:5; *Yalkut Shimoni* 2:880; *Tana DeBei Eliahu Rabbah* 6; *Tikuney Zohar* 50 (141b).

118. *Yoma* 86b; *Moed Katan* 27b; *Sotah* 22a; *Kiddushin* 10a, 40a; *Arakhin* 30b; *Shaarey Teshuvah* 1:5.

119. *Yoma* 86b; *Yerushalmi, Yoma* 8:7 (42b).

120. *Sh'nei Luchoth HaB'rith, Mesekheth Rosh HaShanah, Amud HaDin* 2:158a, from *Shabbath* 7:1 (67b); *Yad, Shegagoth* 4-7. *Cf. Shemoth Rabbah* 23:3.

121. *Shaarey Teshuvah* 1:7, from *Makkoth* 3:7 (21a); *Kiddushin* 77b; *Chullin* 82b; *Nazir* 38b, 42a; *Yad, Nazir* 5:13, *Avel* 3:4, *Kilayim* 10:30; Rambam, *Tosefoth Yom Tov,* on *Mishnah Nazir* 6:2 (42a).

122. *Sh'nei Luchoth HaB'rith, Mesekheth Rosh HaShanah, Amud HaDin* 2:159b. *Cf. Shaarey Teshuvah* 1:38; *Chinukh* 364.

123. *Reshith Chokhmah, Shaar HaTeshuvah* 7 (126d). See above, 13:21.

124. *Yad, Teshuvah* 7:3; *Sefer Chasidim* 27, from Isaiah 55:7.

125. *Orach Chaim* 603:1 in *Hagah; Eshel Avraham ad. loc.;* Rabbenu Yonah, *Berakhoth* (Rif 3b) *s.v. VeHah* (end); *Kol Bo* 69; *Sh'nei Luchoth HaB'rith, Mesekheth Rosh HaShanah* 2:159b, *Hilkhoth Teshuvah* 2:178b. *Cf. Avoth DeRabbi Nathan* 30:2; *Nazir* 23a; *Kerithoth* 22b; Rashi, *Sanhedrin* 103a *s.v. SheLo; Yerushalmi, Kiddushin* 1:9 (22b).

126. *Sh'nei Luchoth HaB'rith, Mesekheth Rosh HaShanah* 2:159b.

15:37 It is therefore an act of piety to keep a written record of all one's wrongdoings, in order that all might be repented and none forgotten.[127] However, the sins should only be alluded to in the written record, lest it fall into the wrong hands.[128]

15:38 Rabbi Eliezer, one of the greatest sages of the Talmud, always used to say, "Repent a day before you die."[129] When his disciples asked him how it was possible to know the day of one's death in advance, he answered that one should therefore repent every day.[130] This is also alluded to in King Solomon's advice, "Let your garments always be white" (Ecclesiastes 9:8).[131] It is therefore a good custom to set aside a short time to review one's deeds every night before going to bed.[132]

15:39 Although one can always repent, God has set aside the ten days between *Rosh HaShanah* and *Yom Kippur* inclusively as the special Ten Days of Repentance.[133] It is therefore customary to say prayers of repentance during this period,[134] and to be somewhat more stringent in one's ethical and religious observance.[135] The prophet says, "Seek God when He can be found" (Isaiah 55:6), and our tradition teaches us that this refers to these Ten Days of Repentance.[136]

15:40 The Ten Days of Repentance are initiated by *Rosh HaShanah,* whose main symbolic commandment is the sounding

127. *Shaarey Teshuvah* 1:8; *Sefer Chasidim* 21; *Sh'nei Luchoth HaB'rith* 2:167b. See above, 13:28, notes 97, 98.
128. *Sefer Chasidim* 27.
129. *Avoth* 2:10; *Shabbath* 153a; *Midrash Tehillim* 90:16; *Zohar* 3:33a; *Chovoth HaLevavoth* 7:10; Maharal, *Nethivoth Olam, Teshuvah* 2 (151a).
130. *Ibid.; Zohar* 1:120a; *Sefer Chasidim* 30.
131. Rashi, Sforno, *ad. loc.; Shabbath* 153a; *Avoth DeRabbi Nathan* 15:4; *Koheleth Rabbah* 9:6; *Zohar* 2:155a, 3:187a; *Chovoth HaLevavoth* 7:10; *Yad, Teshuvah* 7:2; *Sefer Chasidim* 26.
132. *Zohar* 3:178a. *Cf. Sefer Chasidim* 8; see below, 16:17.
133. *Rosh HaShanah* 17b; *Tanchuma, HaAzinu* 4; *Pesikta* 25 (156b); *Zohar* 1:114b, 3:58a; *Tikuney Zohar* 21 (45b); *Yad, Teshuvah* 2:6; *Orach Chaim* 603:1 in *Hagah. Cf.* Rashi, Radak, on 1 Samuel 25:38; *Rosh HaShanah* 18a; *Yerushalmi, Bikkurim* 2:1 (6b); *Zohar* 3:104a; *Nitzotzey Oroth, Zohar* 2:23b no. 2; *Midrash Tehillim* 17:5; *Yalkut Shimoni* 2:670; *Rokeach* 206.
134. *Orach Chaim* 602:1; *Yad, Teshuvah* 3:4. *Cf. Rosh HaShanah* 18a.
135. *Yerushalmi, Shabbath* 1:3 (8b); *Korban HaEdah ad. loc. s.v. VeIm; Yad, Teshuvah* 3:4; Rosh, *Rosh HaShanah* 4:13 (end); *Orach Chaim* 603:1; *Magen Avraham* 242:4.
136. *Rosh HaShanah* 18a; *Yevamoth* 105a; *Pesikta* 24 (156b); *Chovoth HaLevavoth* 7:10; *Yad, Teshuvah* 2:6.

of the *Shofar*. One of the symbolisms of the *Shofar* is to awaken people's hearts to God.[137] The prophet thus said, "Shall a *Shofar* be sounded in a city, and the people not tremble?" (Amos 3:6).[138] Similarly, *Yom Kippur*, which concludes these Ten Days, is a particular day of repentance and prayer.[139]

15:41 It is best to repent while one is still young and full of vigor,[140] as it is written, "Remember your Creator in the days of your youth, before the evil days come" (Ecclesiastes 12:1).[141] Our sages thus teach us that a sign of true repentance is when a person has both the desire and opportunity to repeat his sins but refrains from doing so,[142] not out of fear of discovery or lack of ability, but because his repentance was complete.[143] However, one should certainly not purposely place himself in a situation where he might be tempted to sin,[144] since even without this, God knows if his repentance is perfect.[145]

15:42 Spontaneous repentance is better than repentance that is prompted by fear of suffering,[146] and certainly better than repentance that comes in the wake of God's punishment.[147] However, even the latter helps, as the Torah states, "When you are in distress and all these things have happened to

137. *Yad, Teshuvah* 3:4, *Lechem Mishneh ad. loc.; Pesikta* 25 (157b); *Tanchuma, VaYishlach* 2; *Menorath HaMaor* 5:2:1:4 (293).
138. *Pesikta* 25 (157a); *Yalkut Shimoni* 2:540.
139. *Yad, Teshuvah* 2:7.
140. *Avodah Zarah* 19a; *Zohar* 3:13b; *Zohar Chadash* 7a, 24b; *Reshith Chokhmah, Shaar HaTeshuvah* 1 (103b); *Sefer Chasidim* 7, 62.
141. *Shabbath* 151b; *Yerushalmi, Sotah* 2:2 (10b); *VaYikra Rabbah* 18:1; *Koheleth Rabbah* 12:1; *Eikhah Rabbah,* introduction:23; *Yad, Teshuvah* 2:1; Rashi on *Avoth* 3:1; *Zohar* 1:204a, 3:13b; *Menorath HaMaor* 5:1:1:2 (277); *Reshith Chokhmah, Shaar HaTeshuvah* 1 (103a).
142. *Yoma* 86b; *Kiddushin* 39b; *Yad, Teshuvah* 1:1; *Menorath HaMaor loc. cit.* Some require two such tests; *cf.* Rabbenu Chananel *ad. loc.; Shiltey Gibborim, Yoma* (Rif 5b) no. 1. Others do not require it; Rif, *Yoma* 5b; Rosh 8:17; *Lechem Mishneh, Teshuvah* 2:1.
143. *Yad, Teshuvah* 2:1.
144. *Sefer Chasidim* 167. *Cf. Sanhedrin* 107a.
145. Rabbenu Yonah, *Shaarey Teshuvah* 1:49; Maharal, *Nethivoth Olam, Teshuvah* 3 (155b).
146. *Koheleth Rabbah* 12:1; *Reshith Chokhmah, Shaar HaTeshuvah* 1 (103a); *Emunoth VeDeyoth* 5:6 (73a); *Menorath HaMaor* 5:1:1:2 (277). *Cf.* Sforno on Numbers 15:31.
147. *Emunoth VeDeyoth* 5:6 (73a); *Menorath HaMaor* 5:1:1:2 (277); *cf. Avoth* 4:11; *Pirkey Rabbi Eliezer* 43 (101a).

you, you will finally return to God your Lord and listen to His call" (Deuteronomy 4:30).[148]

15:43 Repentance when one has the ability to sin is better than that done because of the lack of power to do so.[149] One who repents because he lacks the ability to sin is like a thief who refrains from robbing because he cannot find a victim.[150] It is therefore better to repent when one is young and full of strength, than when one is old and has neither the desire nor ability to sin.[151]

15:44 Still, one can sincerely repent and be forgiven by God even in old age.[152] Even if one has been wicked and sinful all his life, he can repent on his deathbed and be forgiven.[153] Regarding this it is written, "You return man to the dust, and say, 'Return [to Me] you mortal beings'" (Psalms 90:3).[154] Even if a person has the intention to repent and is prevented from doing so by death, his intention helps,[155] since God counts a good intention as an accomplished deed.[156]

15:45 Therefore, if one knows that he is about to die, he should repent his sins with all his heart and being.[157] One who has the opportunity, and does not repent before death, is counted as one who denies God's judgment and mercy.[158]

15:46 The doors of repentance only remain open as long as a person is alive. After death, the doors are closed, as it is written, "Do whatever you can while you still have the strength, for in the

148. *Or HaChaim ad. loc. Cf.* 2 Chronicles 30:6.
149. *Avodah Zarah* 19a; *Shaarey Teshuvah* 1:9; *Eikhah Rabbah,* introduction:23.
150. *Cf. Sanhedrin* 22a; Rashi *ad. loc. s.v. Chasrei; Sefer Chasidim* 7.
151. *Shabbath* 151b; *Koheleth Rabbah* 12:1; *Yad, Teshuvah* 2:1; *Menorath HaMaor* 5:1:1:2 (277).
152. *Ibid.; Hagahoth Maimonioth, Teshuvah* 2:1 no. 1; *Zohar* 3:13b, 3:85a, 3:87b; *Tikuney Zohar* 69 (112a); *Sefer Mitzvoth Gadol,* Positive Commandment 16, quoted in *Sh'nei Luchoth HaB'rith, Mesekheth Rosh HaShanah* 2:156a; *Menorath HaMaor loc. cit.*
153. *Tana DeBei Eliahu Rabbah* 3 (30a), 21 (94b); *Emunoth VeDeyoth* 5:6 (73a); *Shaarey Teshuvah* 1:9; *Menorath HaMaor* 5:1:1:3 (278). *Cf. Avoth* 2:10; *Kiddushin* 40b.
154. *Targum ad. loc.; Yerushalmi, Chagigah* 2:1 (9b); *Ruth Rabbah* 4:6; *Koheleth Rabbah* 7:18; *Tosafoth, Chagigah* 15a *s.v. Shuvu; Shiltey Gibborim, Yoma* (Rif 5b) no. 1; *Shaarey Teshuvah* 1:9; *Menorath HaMaor* 5:1:1:2 (277).
155. *Zohar* 1:41a, 2:150b. See below, 16:5, 16:19.
156. *Berakhoth* 6a; *Shabbath* 63a; *Kiddushin* 40a; *Tosefta, Peah* 1:4; *Tana DeBei Eliahu Rabbah* 9; *Zohar* 1:167b, 2:150b, 2:158b, 2:277a.
157. See below, 16:19.
158. *Menorath HaMaor* 5:1:1:2 (277), quoted in *Sh'nei Luchoth HaB'rith, Mesekheth Rosh HaShanah* 2:156a.

grave where you are going, there is nothing that you can do, reckon [or accomplish] with knowledge and wisdom" (Ecclesiastes 9:10).[159] Neither repentance[160] nor atonement[161] exist after death, as we are taught, "When a wicked man dies, his hope perishes" (Proverbs 11:7).[162] After death, there is no way that a man can avoid his due judgment, as we find, "He will not consider any ransom" (Proverbs 6:35).[163] Our sages teach us that just as additional oil cannot rekindle an extinguished lamp, so repentance cannot redeem an extinguished life.[164] When one departs the shores of life, there is no turning back to repent.[165]

15:47 Even though a person is not completely responsible for his actions as a child, he should nevertheless repent his childhood sins to the best of his ability.[166] Similarly, a convert should repent any major sins committed before entering the Jewish faith.[167]

15:48 Although repentance helps for all sins, there are some for which it is extremely difficult. There is a tradition of 24[168] sins for which repentance is unlikely, and they are given in Table 15:2. Nevertheless, in no case is repentance impossible.[169]

15:49 There are some sins for which repentance is unlikely because they are not normally considered sinful.[170] Others, such as gossip, temper, evil thoughts, or wicked friends, involve habits that are

159. *Targum,* Rashi, *Yalkut Shimoni* (2:989), *ad. loc.;* Rambam on *Avoth* 4:17; *Menorath HaMaor* 5:1:1:2 (277); *Reshith Chokhmah, Shaar HaTeshuvah* 1 (103a); Radal (on *Pirkey Rabbi Eliezer*) 43:48.
160. *Targum* on Ecclesiastes 1:15, 3:19; *Yalkut Shimoni* (2:938) on Proverbs 6:6, quoted in *Reshith Chokhmah, Shaar HaTeshuvah* 1 (103a). *Cf. Avoth* 4:17; Bertenoro *ad. loc.; Shabbath* 32a; *Eruvin* 19a.
161. Rashi, *Nazir* 21b *s.v. VeHayinu; Sefer Chasidim* 1171. *Cf. Yoma* 50a; *Horayoth* 6b; *Temurah* 15a, 16a, 21b; *Yad, Pesuley HaMukdashim* 4:1.
162. *Koheleth Rabbah* 7:32; *Yalkut Shimoni* 2:979.
163. *Pirkey Rabbi Eliezer* 43 (103a); Radal *ad. loc.* 43:50; *Midrash Tehillim* 17:5; *Yalkut Shimoni* 2:670; *Reshith Chokhmah, Shaar HaTeshuvah* 3 (110a).
164. *Yalkut Shimoni* (2:989) on Ecclesiastes 9:10; *Reshith Chokhmah, Shaar HaTeshuvah* 1 (105a).
165. *Menorath HaMaor* 5:1:1:3 (278); *Sh'nei Luchoth HaB'rith, Teshuvah* 2:183a. *Cf. Ruth Rabbah* 3:3; *Koheleth Rabbah* 1:36, from Ecclesiastes 1:15.
166. See above, 11:42.
167. See above, 11:7, note 19.
168. For the possible significance of this number, *cf. Rokeach* 28, 216.
169. *Cf. Chovoth HaLevavoth* 7:10. See below, 15:56.
170. *Yad, Teshuvah* 4:4; Table 15:2, no. 15-19.

broken only with great difficulty.[171] Similarly, there are personality traits that preclude repentance, such as a general disregard for religion, disrespect for its teachers, disassociation from its adherents, or the inability to accept criticism.[172]

15:50   One who causes many to sin is prevented from repenting[173] by the fact that he cannot undo the sins of others,[174] and all are his responsibility.[175] However, it is still possible for him to repent by bringing about their repentance,[176] or, if this is not possible, by bringing many others to do good.[177]

15:51   Similarly, one who causes another to stray from the path of righteousness is prevented from repenting[178] unless he can bring him back.[179] The same is true of one who has the opportunity to prevent another from going astray and does not take advantage of it.[180]

15:52   One who robs or hurts many others or unknown persons,[181] can repent only with great difficulty,[182] since full restitution can never be made.[183] However, if he wishes to repent, he should do public works[184] from which his victims can benefit, thereby indirectly repaying them.[185] Nevertheless, even this is not perfect

171. *Ibid.* 4:5; Table 15:2, no. 19-24.

172. *Ibid.* 4:2; Table 15:2, no. 5-9.

173. *Avoth* 5:18; *Yoma* 87a; *Tosefta, Yoma* 4:11; *Sanhedrin* 107b; *Sotah* 47a; *Emunoth VeDeyoth* 5:8 (74b); *Chovoth HaLevavoth* 7:9; *Yad, Teshuvah* 4:1; Table 15:2, no. 1. Rambam on *Avoth loc. cit.* writes that he is prevented from repenting; see Volume 1, 3:49. *Tosefoth Yom Tov,* however, writes that God merely does not help him to repent; see above, 14:11.

174. *Sefer Chasidim* 613.

175. See above, 12:60.

176. *Sefer Chasidim* 202.

177. *Yalkut Shimoni* 1:391, quoted in *Reshith Chokhmah, Shaar HaTeshuvah* 7 (124d).

178. *Yad, Teshuvah* 4:1; Table 15:2, no. 2. See above, 12:6.

179. *Sefer Chasidim* 202.

180. *Yad, Teshuvah* 4:1; Table 15:2, no. 3. See above, 12:57.

181. *Yad, Teshuvah* 4:3; Table 15:2, no. 10-14.

182. *Yevamoth* 21a; *Bava Bathra* 88b; *Bava Kama* 94b, Rashi *ad. loc. s.v. Teshuvatham; Tosefta, Bava Kama* 10:5; *Chovoth HaLevavoth* 7:9; *Sefer Chasidim* 599; *Choshen Mishpat* 231:18.

183. *Yad, Genevah* 7:12; Maharsha, *Chagigah* 9a.

184. *Betza* 29a; *Bava Kama* 94b; *Choshen Mishpat* 34:29, 266:2; *Chovoth HaLevavoth* 7:10. *Cf.* Rosh, *Bava Kama* 9:2; *Yam Shel Shlomo* 9:3; *Pith'chey Teshuvah, Choshen Mishpat* 366:2; *Teshuvoth Shivath Tzion* 112.

185. Rashi, *Bava Kama* 94b *s.v. Boroth; Sefer Meirath Eynayim (Sema)* 366:5.

repentance[185] until he makes full restitution to every one whom he has possibly harmed.[187]

15:53 Similarly, one who indulges in sexual crimes and causes a bastard to be born will find it very difficult to repent,[188] since he has caused the birth of a person who will bear this stigma for his entire life.[189] However, even in such a case one can repent,[190] and God will help erase his guilt.[191]

15:54 God gave repentance and atonement to man in order to cleanse him from evil, and not to make it easier to sin, or to assuage his conscience.[192] Therefore, if one sins with the specific intention of later repenting, he perverts the entire concept of repentance, and is therefore not given the opportunity to do so.[193] The same is true of the other atonements that God has given man, whether they be prayers,[194] *Yom Kippur,*[195] suffering,[196] or even death itself.[197] If one sins with the presumption that these will atone for him, his

186. Rashi, *Yevamoth* 21a *s.v. Arayoth;* Rashbam, *Bava Bathra* 88b *s.v. Efshar; Tosafoth ibid. s.v. Hatham; Sefer Meirath Eynayim (Sema)* 231:34; *Pith'chey Teshuvah, Choshen Mishpat* 366:1; *Teshuvoth Mayim Chaim* 26.

187. *Yevamoth* 15:7 (118b); *Bava Metzia* 3:3 (37a); *Bava Kama* 103b; *Yad, Gezelah* 4:10; *Choshen Mishpat* 365:2.

188. *Chagigah* 1:7 (9a); *Yevamoth* 22b; *Tosafoth, Sotah* 4b *s.v. Hee; Chovoth HaLevavoth* 7:9; *Rokeach* 28. However, this is not included among the 24 things precluding repentance listed in Table 15:2.

189. Rashi, *Chagigah* 1:7 (9a) *s.v. VeHolid; Tosafoth ibid. s.v. Zeh;* Bertenoro, *Tosefoth Yom Tov, Chagigah* 1:7.

190. *Tosafoth, Bava Bathra* 88b *s.v Hatham.* However, Rashbam *ibid. s.v. Efshar,* and Rashi, *Yevamoth* 21a *s.v. Arayoth,* maintain that repentance is only possible when no bastard *(mamzer)* is born. *Cf. Yevamoth* 22b.

191. *Chovoth HaLevavoth* 7:10.

192. Maharal, *Nethivoth Olam, Teshuvah* 8 (169a). *Cf.* Rashi, *Yoma* 87a *s.v. Agav Shani.*

193. *Yoma* 8:9 (85b), 87a; *Avoth DeRabbi Nathan* 39:1; *Yad, Teshuvah* 4:1; Table 15:2, no. 4. On the basis of the Mishnah, some maintain that one is only prevented from repenting if he repeats this twice; *cf.* Bertenoro, *Tosefoth Yom Tov, ad. loc.,* from *Yoma* 87a; Rashash *ad. loc.; Pesikta Rabathai* 44, cited in *Yeffeh Eynayim ibid.* However, others maintain that even one time is enough, since if one repeats it twice, he himself loses the desire to repent since the sin begins to seem permissible to him; *cf. Lechem Mishneh, Teshuvah* 4:1; *Marah HaPanim, Yerushalmi, Yoma* 8:7 (42a); *Peney HaMenorah* 5:4. *Cf. Avoth DeRabbi Nathan* 40:4, where only one time is required, and 40:5, where Rabbi Eliezer disputes this and requires three times. See below, 17:28.

194. *Sefer Chasidim* 605.

195. *Yoma* 8:9 (85b), 87a; Rambam, *Yoma* 8:9; *Avoth DeRabbi Nathan* 40:4; *Yad, Teshuvah* 4:1. *Tosefoth Yom Tov, Yoma* 8:9 maintains that *Yom Kippur* also requires two times, while Rashash *loc. cit.* disputes this. *Cf. Emunoth VeDeyoth* 5:8 (74b).

196. *Asarah Maamaroth* 1:1:19.

197. *Ibid.; Avoth DeRabbi Nathan* 40:4.

intent destroys their effectiveness.[198] Even in such cases, however, the door to repentance is not completely closed,[199] since one can even regret his misguided intention to misuse repentance.[200]

15:55 There are times when a person can commit such a terrible sin that the opportunity to repent is taken away from him.[201] Regarding this it is written, "[God] opens their ears to discipline and commands that they return from sin. If they listen and serve Him, they shall spend their days in tranquility... But if they listen not, they shall perish and die without knowledge" (Job 36:10-12).[202] This is the meaning of such expressions in the Torah as, "God hardened Pharaoh's heart" (Exodus 7:13). Our sages therefore teach us that God may send an individual two or three warnings, but if they are ignored, the path to repentance is closed.[203] This, however, does not mean that the free will to repent is taken away. Rather, the individual is made oblivious to all warnings.[204]

15:56 Therefore, no matter how much a person may have sinned, it is always possible for him to repent.[205] Even if it has been decreed on high that he shall never return, the decree is reversible,[206] and, if necessary, God Himself will break through all barriers standing before the person who sincerely wants to change his ways.[207] It is an inviolable rule that nothing in the world can prevent a person from repenting.[208] God Himself promised that the gates of repentance will always remain open,[209] and that His hands

198. "If one says, 'I will sin and repent, I will sin and repent,' then he is not given the opportunity to repent"; *Yoma* 8:9 (85b), 87a; Rashi *ad. loc. s.v. Agav.*
199. *Likutey Amarim, Iggereth HaTeshuvah* 11 (100b).
200. *Asarah Maamaroth* 1:1:20, quoted in *Marah HaPanim* on *Yerushalmi, Yoma* 8:7 (42a); Rashash, *Yoma* 87a.
201. See Volume 1, 3:49.
202. *Shemoth Rabbah* 11:2. Cf. *Tanchuma, Re'eh* 2.
203. *Shemoth Rabbah* 13:4. Cf. *Ikkarim* 4:26. See also Exodus 7:22, 8:15, 9:12, 35, 10:20, 27, 11:10, 14:7, 8.
204. *Ikkarim* 4:25.
205. *Yad, Teshuvah* 4:6; *Asarah Maamarath* 1:1:20; *Shaarey Zohar, Sanhedrin* 103a.
206. Rabbenu Chananel, *Chagigah* 15a; *Reshith Chokhmah, Shaar HaKedushah* 17 (205a); *Sh'nei Luchoth HaB'rith, Shaar HaOthioth* 1:157b, *Rosh HaShanah* 2:156b; *cf. Avodah Zarah* 17a. Some base this on the saying "Do all that the host (God) tells you to do, except leave"; *Pesachim* 86b; *Derekh Eretz Rabbah* 6; *Zohar* 3:244a; *Magen Avraham* 170:10.
207. *Devarim Rabbah* 2:13; *Ruth Rabbah* 5:6.
208. See above, note 7.
209. See above, note 27.

will remain stretched out, rejecting no human being.[210] A person should therefore never give up because of his sins, but should trust in God, and in His promise that full repentance will always bring forgiveness.[211]

15:57 It is especially important that a person who has committed a serious sin not give up and sin further. The wise King Solomon warned, "Do not be *very* wicked" (Ecclesiastes 7:17).[212] Our sages asked why he added the word "very," and replied that even if one has done something wicked, he should not give up and use it as an excuse to do more evil. To do so, they say, is like a person who has burned himself once, going back and burning himself still more.[213]

15:58 Similarly, even though one may have committed many terrible sins, he should not give up doing good. His sins do not undo the good,[214] and his merit therefore remains complete when he repents.[215] Regarding this it is written, "If the spirit of the [evil] ruler rises up against you, do not abanon your place" (Ecclesiastes 10:4) — that is, do not give up whatever good you have been accustomed to doing.[216] On the other hand, if one regrets the good that he has done, then all the good is lost.[217] The prophet thus tells us, "But when the righteous man turns away from his righteousness... none of his good deeds shall be remembered" (Ezekiel 18:24).[218]

15:59 Even if one has lived a completely ungodly life, he should not give up hope and feel that it is impossible to change his way of life.[219] Our sages teach us that, "All beginnings are difficult."[220] God

210. *Midrash Tehillim* 120:7.
211. *Midrash Tehillim* 40:3. *Cf. Chovoth HaLevavoth* 7:10; *Reshith Chokhmah, Shaar HaKedushah* 17 (205a); *Teshuvoth Maharit* 2:8; Mahari Kara on Ezekiel 18:31.
212. *Shabbath* 31b; Maharatz Chajas *ad. loc.; Koheleth Rabbah* 7:34; *Midrash Tehillim* 1:7; *Sh'nei Luchoth HaB'rith, Teshuvah* 2:178b.
213. *Koheleth Rabbah* 7:34. *Cf. Ikkarim* 4:26 (end).
214. Rambam, *Iggereth HaShmad*, pp. 4, 18.
215. *Sefer Chasidim* 37; *Nefesh Chayah* 271.
216. *Targum ad. loc.*
217. *Kiddushin* 40b; *Tosefta, Kiddushin* 1:11; *Yerushalmi, Peah* 1:1 (5a); *Yad, Teshuvah* 3:3; *Teshuvoth Chavath Yair* 15.
218. *Sefer Chasidim* 37. *Cf.* Ezekiel 3:20, 33:12, 33:18.
219. *Cf.* Ramban on Deuteronomy 30:11; *Menorath HaMaor* 5:2:1:4 (293); *Reshith Chokhmah, Shaar HaTeshuvah* 1 (101c).

thus gives a person every opportunity,[221] and once he makes the initial effort to repent, he is given divine help.[222] God told His prophet, "Return to Me, and I will return to you" (Malachi 3:7).[223] Our sages teach us that God says, "Open for Me as the eye of a needle, and I will open wide for you the gates of heaven."[224]

15:60 Therefore, if a person repents and confesses all his known wrongs, he is also forgiven all his forgotten sins.[225] There is a rule that we do not open the windows of a dark house to search for any unclean blemish. In the same manner, God does not throw light on the forgotten sins of one who truly repents.[226]

15:61 One who does not know how to repent should seek the advice of a very learned and pious rabbi[227] in order to learn the ways of repentance.[228] It is thus written, "The way of the fool is correct in his own eyes, but he who is wise listens to advice" (Proverbs

---

220. *Mekhilta* on Exodus 19:5 (62d); Rashi *ibid.; Tosafoth, Taanith* 10b *s.v. Pesiah; Zohar* 2:174a, 2:187a.

221. *Bereshith Rabbah* 21:6; *BaMidbar Rabbah* 13:5; *Midrash Tehillim* 100:2; *Menorath HaMaor* 5:1:2:5 (283).

222. *Shabbath* 104a; *Yoma* 38b; *Avodah Zarah* 45a; *Menachoth* 29b; *Yerushalmi, Peah* 1:1 (5b); *Yerushalmi, Kiddushin* 1:9 (23a); *Yerushalmi, Shevuoth* 1:6 (7b); *Yerushalmi, Sanhedrin* 10:1 (49a); *Mekhilta* on Exodus 15:26 (46b), from Proverbs 3:34. *Cf. Zohar* 1:62a, 1:77b, 1:88b, 1:125b, 1:142b, 1:198b, 1:200a, 1:260a, 2:19b, 2:263a, 3:24b, 3:54a, 3:77a, 3:81, 3:86b, 3:126a, 3:240a; *Zohar Chadash* 10c, 20d, 24a; *Yad, Teshuvah* 6:5; *Sefer Chasidim* 7, 28; *Reshith Chokhmah, Shaar HaYirah* 13 (38d), *Shaar HaKedushah* 4 (134c); *Cheredim, Teshuvah* 7 (p. 253); *Sh'nei Luchoth HaB'rith, Teshuvah* 2:184d. Since God created the universe so that good must come from man's own actions, He deals with man reciprocally, whereby when man awakens his own awareness of Him, God awakens him further from above; see Volume 1, Chapter 5, note 119.

223. *Eikhah Rabbah* 5:22; *Midrash Tehillim* 85:3; *Zohar* 3:103b; *Reshith Chokhmah, Shaar HaTeshuvah* 1 (102c).

224. *Zohar* 3:95a. *Cf. Shir HaShirim Rabbah* 5:3; *Pesikta* 5 (46b), 25 (163b); *Zohar Chadash* 23d; *Reshith Chokhmah, Shaar HaTeshuvah* 1 (102c).

225. *Shemoth Rabbah* 31:1; *Zohar* 3:195b; *Nitzotzey Oroth ad. loc.* no. 1; *Asarah Maamaroth* 1:1:10. See below 16:12, 17:61.

226. *Ibid. Cf. Negaim* 2:3; *Sanhedrin* 92a; *Chullin* 10b; *Sifra* on Leviticus 14:35 (73a); *Yad, Tumath Tzaraath* 14:5. *Cf. Pesachim* 8a.

227. *Zohar* 3:20a; *Demesek Eliezer ad. loc.; Sefer Chasidim* 21, *Makor Chesed ad. loc.* 21:4; *Sh'nei Luchoth HaB'rith* 2:167b; *Shaarey Teshuvah, Orach Chaim* 607:2; Rabbi Nachman of Breslev, *Likutey Moharan* 4:8 (4a).

228. *Cf. Yad, Teshuvah* 4:2; *Emunoth VeDeyoth* 2:1. *Cf. Berakhoth* 35a; *Zohar* 2:106a.

12:15).[229] If a sage is not available, one can seek the advice of a person who himself has undergone repentance.[230]

15:62 A person who has been raised in a nonreligious atmosphere should not abandon hope of being acceptable before God. Our sages teach us that, "In the place where the one who has repented stands, even the perfectly righteous cannot stand."[231] Since they have tasted sin and abandoned it,[232] such individuals can achieve extreme spiritual heights. Furthermore, they are able to serve God in deep humility,[233] and with an enthusiasm and spirit that is often lacking among those who have been religious all their lives.[234]

15:63 Repentance only helps to remove evil, but it does not make up for any good that might have been lost.[235] Still, when one repents out of love for God, all his former wickedness is counted as good,[236] and therefore, he can acheive in an instant what others may need many years to attain.[237]

15:64 Although repentance can raise one to the loftiest spiritual heights,[238] there are some sins that are ineradicable in the eyes of man.[239] Therefore, one who has committed serious offenses may be barred from leading certain public services, even though

229. *Sh'nei Luchoth HaB'rith, Mesekheth Rosh HaShanah, Amud HaDin* 2:160a. *Cf.* Rambam, *Shemonah Perakim* 3 (end).
230. *Sefer Chasidim* 21.
231. *Berakhoth* 34b; *Sanhedrin* 99a, where this is the opinion of Rabbi Avahu, disputed by Rabbi Yochanan; *cf. Koheleth Rabbah* 1:27. *Cf. Tana DeBei Rabbi Eliahu* 3 (30a); *Yalkut Shimoni* 1:20; *Zohar* 1:39a, 2:106a, 2:113b, 3:16b, 3:202b; *Yad, Teshuvah* 7:4; *Chovoth HaLevavoth* 7:8; Rabbenu Tam, *Sefer HaYashar* 10, cited in HaGra, *Orach Chaim* 53:8 *s.v. Mi*; *Sefer Chasidim* 60; *Menorath HaMaor* 5:1:1:2 (277), 5:end (312); Maharal, *Nethivoth Olam, Teshuvah* 4 (156a). Also see *Pri Megadim, Eshel Avraham* 118:i; Rashi, *Sukkah* 53a *s.v. Elu.*
232. *Yad, Teshuvah* 7:4; *Sefer Chasidim* 60; *Menorath HaMaor* 5:1:1:2 (277); Maharsha, *Berakhoth* 34b.
233. *Chovoth HaLevavoth* 7:8.
234. *Tikuney Zohar* 69 (115b); *Reshith Chokhmah, Shaar HaTeshuvah* 6 (120a), that they have the additional Sabbath soul constantly; *cf. Menachoth* 29b; *Nethivoth Olam, Teshuvah* 4 (157b).
235. See above, 13:37; *Likutey Amarim, Iggereth HaTeshuvah* 1 (90b).
236. See above, 15:30.
237. *Zohar* 1:129b. *Cf. Avodah Zarah* 10b, 17a, 18a.
238. *Midrash Tehillim* 183, 32:1, 45:1; *Yalkut Shimoni* 2:671, 2:747; *Menorath HaMaor* 5:1:4:1 (288), 5:end (312).
239. *Cf.* Maharal, *Nethivoth Olam, Teshuvah* 4 (158a top), that penitents are only better than the righteous in the World to Come which is purely spiritual. See *Orach Chaim* 53:4; *Mishnah Berurah* 53:16; *Berakhoth* 27b.

he may have repented.[240] Nevertheless, a minor sin[241] which is repented immediately[242] does not leave any stigma.

15:65 An apostate who wishes to repent is immediately considered acceptable.[243] However, it is preferable that he formally confirm his repentance before a rabbinical court of three and undergo ritual immersion.[244]

15:66 It is an extremely serious sin to remind one who has repented of his former deeds, even in jest.[245] One who does so is guilty of violating the commandment, "You shall not vex one another" (Leviticus 25:17).[246]

15:67 Every person must repent, for no man is free of sin. It is thus written, "There is no man on earth who is so righteous that he [only] does good and does not sin" (Ecclesiastes 7:20).[247]

15:68 The call to repentance was one of the major missions of all the prophets.[248] Along with prayer and charity, repentance can banish any evil decree that may have been decreed against either an individual or a community.[249] God thus promised, "If My people...

240. Regarding leading a synagogue service; see *Orach Chaim* 53:5 in *Hagah; Magen Avraham* 53:8; *Turey Zahav* 53:3; *Beer Hetiv* 53:7. Regarding a Cohen who committed murder saying the priestly blessing; *cf. Berakhoth* 32b; *Yad, Tefillah* 15:3; *Hagahoth Maimonioth ad. loc.* no. 3; *Orach Chaim* 128:35; *Tosafoth, Menachoth* 109a *s.v. Lo, Sotah* 39a *s.v. Vekhi, Taanith* 27a *s.v. Khi;* Rosh, *Megillah* 3:1; *cf. Yerushalmi, Gittin* 5:9 (32b); *Zohar* 3:214a. Regarding an apostate Cohen; see *Menachoth* 13:10 (109a); *Yad, Biyath HaMikdash* 9:13; *Orach Chaim* 128:37; *Mishnah Berurah* 128:134; *Biur Halakhah ibid. s.v. VeIm.*

241. *Cf. Chovoth HaLevavoth* 7:8, that a penitent is only better where minor sins are involved. *Cf. Sefer HaYashar* 10, quoted in HaGra, *Orach Chaim* 53:8 *s.v. Mi; Sh'nei Luchoth HaB'rith, Teshuvah* 2:178a.

242. *Menorath HaMaor* 5:1:1:2 (277).

243. *Choshen Mishpat* 34:22 in *Hagah,* citing *Maharik Shoresh* 85; HaGra, *Orach Chaim* 34:50, from *Bekhoroth* 7:7 (48b); *Sefer Meirath Eynayim (Sema)* 34:54; *Sifethey Cohen* 34:21; *Beer Hetiv* 34:26; *Pith'chey Teshuvah* 34:32; *Terumath HaDeshen* 198; *Teshuvoth Chemdath Shlomo, Evven HaEzer* 6. *Cf. Tosafoth, Avodah Zarah* 7a, *Bekhoroth* 31a, *s.v. Vekhulan.*

244. See above, note 97.

245. *Orchoth Tzadikim* 15c.

246. See above 8:38, note 130; *Bava Metzia* 4:10 (58b); *Sifra* ad. loc. (108a); *Pesikta Rabathai* 42; *Yad, Teshuvah* 7:8, *Mekhirah* 14:13; *Choshen Mishpat* 228:4; *Sefer Chasidim* 7.

247. *Cf. Sanhedrin* 46a, 101a; *Tosafoth, Shabbath* 55b *s.v. Arba; Midrash Tehillim* 16:2; *Yalkut Shimoni* 1:930, 2:976; *Zohar* 2:54a; *Chovoth HaLevavoth* 7:introduction.

248. *Yad, Teshuvah* 7:5; Rabbenu Yonah, *Shaarey Teshuvah* 1:1; *Reshith Chokhmah, Shaar HaTeshuvah* 1 (104b).

249. *Rosh HaShanah* 17b; *Shir HaShirim Rabbah* 8:5; *Tanchuma, Noah* 8; *Menorath HaMaor* 5:1:4:1 (288); Maharal, *Nethivoth Olam, Teshuvah* 6 (163a).

shall humble themselves, pray, seek My face, and turn from their evil ways, then I will hear from heaven, I will forgive their sin and heal their land" (2 Chronicles 7:14).[250] Repentance thus intercedes for a person,[251] protecting him from evil,[252] and even lengthening his life.[253]

15:69 Repentance is one of the primary things that can break the barriers preventing the redemption.[254] The prophet thus said, "A redeemer shall come to Zion, to those who turn from transgression among Jacob's [children]" (Isaiah 59:20).[255] There is a tradition that if every Jew would repent and turn to God even for a single day, the redemption would immediately come.[256] The Torah thus states, "If you return to God your Lord, and listen to His voice, doing everything that I am commanding you *today*... God will then bring back your remnants and have mercy on you. God your Lord will once again gather you from among all the nations where He has scattered you" (Deuteronomy 30:2-3).[257]

TABLE 15:1 — SEVEN LEVELS OF REPENTANCE[1]

1. Repentance is most effective immediately after a sin.
2. When still in the same circumstances.

250. *Yerushalmi, Taanith* 2:1 (8b); *Yerushalmi, Sanhedrin* 10:2 (51b); *Bereshith Rabbah* 44:15; *Koheleth Rabbah* 5:4, 7:29; *Pesikta* 30 (191a); *Yalkut Shimoni* 2:971; *Menorath HaMaor* 3:3:1:11 (101). Cf. *Rosh HaShanah* 16b.
251. *Shabbath* 32a.
252. *Avoth* 4:11; *BaMidbar Rabbah* 14:17. See below, 17:2.
253. *Yoma* 86b.
254. *Yerushalmi, Taanith* 1:1 (3a); *Devarim Rabbah* 2:14; *Midrash Tehillim* 106:9; *Yalkut Shimoni* 1:827, 2:865; Rashi on Psalms 106:45.
255. *Yoma* 86b; Maharal, *Nethivoth Olam, Teshuvah* 2 (153a).
256. *Yad, Teshuvah* 7:5; *Sanhedrin* 97b; *Shir HaShirim Rabbah* 5:3; *Pesikta* 25 (163b); *Tana DeBei Eliahu Rabbah* 16 (78b); *Zohar* 2:188b, 3:122a, 3:270a, 3:278a; *Tikuney Zohar* 6 (22a); *Zohar Chadash* 8a, 23b.
257. *Yad, Teshuvah* 7:5. Cf. *Megillah* 29a.

1. *Menorath HaMaor* 5:1:1:2 (277), quoted in *Sh'nei Luchoth HaB'rith, Mesekheth Rosh HaShanah* 2:156a. With the exception of 1 and 6, all these levels are given in the same order in *Emunoth VeDeyoth* 5:6 (73a). The source of this order may be from *Koheleth Rabbah* 12:1; cf. Radal, quoted in *Yad Yosef ad. loc.* no. 3, where levels 3, 5, and 6 are given. See also anonymous Midrash quoted in *Menorath HaMaor* 5:1:1:3 (278) and *Sh'nei Luchoth HaB'rith, Teshuvah* 2:183a, where levels 1, 6, and 7 are given in order.

3.   While still young, but not in the same circumstances.
4.   Out of fear of suffering.
5.   Because of suffering that has already come.
6.   When old.
7.   Just before death.

TABLE 15:2 — OBSTACLES TO REPENTANCE[1a]

1.   Causing many to sin or preventing them from doing good.[1]
2.   Leading others away from Godliness.[2]
3.   Neglecting to prevent others from sinning.[3]
4.   Sinning with the intent of repenting.[4]
5.   Separating oneself from the community.[5]
6.   Disrespecting our religious teachings.[6]
7.   Deriding the commandments.[7]
8.   Disrespecting one's parents and teachers.[8]

1a. *Yad, Teshuvah* 4:1-5; Rif, *Yoma* 6a; Rosh 8:18; *Rokeach* 28, 216; *Sefer Chasidim* 19; Rabbenu Yonah, *Shaarey Teshuvah* 1:52; Meiri, *Chibur HaTeshuvah* (New York, 1950) 1:4; *Reshith Chokhmah, Shaar HaTeshuvah* 6 (119d); Maharal, *Nethivoth Olam, Teshuvah* 8 (169a). The order here is that of *Yad.* For the source of the list; *cf.* Ran on Rif *loc. cit.; Kesef Mishneh, Lechem Mishneh, Teshuvah* 4:1; *P'er HaDor* (Rambam) 12; *Teshuvoth HaRambam* (Jerusalem, 1934) 367; *B'rith Olam* (on *Sefer Chasidim*) 19, that there is no more ancient source to be found, although *Chinukh* 364 writes that it is from a *Tosefta. Cf. Avoth DeRabbi Nathan* 39:1; *Chovoth HaLevavoth* 7:9.
1. Rif no. 14; *Reshith Chokhmah ibid.* no. 11. Numbers 1-4 are in *Yad, Teshuvah* 4:1. Rif only has "preventing others from doing good." See 15:50.
2. Rif no. 15; *Reshith Chokhmah* no. 12. *Rokeach* no. 28 omits this and substitutes "despising the observant."
3. Rif no. 19; *Reshith Chokhmah* no. 16; *Chovoth HaLevavoth* 7:9.
4. Rif no. 8; *Reshith Chokhmah* no. 9. See 15:54.
5. Rif no. 10; *Reshith Chokhmah* no. 18. Numbers 5-9 are in *Yad, Teshuvah* 4:2. Because when the community repents, he is not with them; *Yad.* See above, 14:9.
6. Rif no. 21; *Reshith Chokhmah* no. 19. Rif has "disputing the sages," while *Reshith Chokhmah* substitutes "violating their teachings," and *Rokeach* has "disputing the Torah."
7. Rif no. 24; *Reshith Chokhmah* no. 23. Because he does not consider the commandments significant enough to repent their breach; *Yad. Cf. Eruvin* 21b; *Gittin* 57a; *Menorath HaMaor* 2:1:2:1 (33).
8. Rif no. 12; *Reshith Chokhmah* no. 10. In Rif's enumeration, "despising parents" and "despising teachers" are listed separately, but *Bayith Chadash ad. loc.* no. 2 indicates that they should be listed together. This is also indicated by the fact that some only list teachers; *Yad, Lechem Mishneh ad. loc.; Rokeach* 216; *Sefer Chasidim* no. 19; *Reshith Chokhmah* no. 10. Others only count parents; Rosh *loc. cit.; Rokeach* 28.

9. Inability to accept correction.[9]
10. Cursing the community.[10]
11. Dividing spoils with a thief.[11]
12. Not returning a lost article.[12]
13. Robbing or oppressing the poor.[13]
14. Accepting a bribe for judgment.[14]
15. Eating from a set table which does not suffice for the host.[15]
16. Using a poor man's pledge.[16]
17. Staring lewdly at women.[17]
18. Gaining honor at the expense of another.[18]
19. Suspecting the innocent.[19]
20. Gossip.[20]
21. Slander.[21]

9. Rif no. 23; *Reshith Chokhmah* no. 22. See above, 12:32.
10. Rif no. 13; *Reshith Chokhmah* no. 24. Numbers 10-14 are in *Yad, Teshuvah* 4:3. Because he cannot ask a specific person for forgiveness; *Yad.* See above, 15:52.
11. Rif no. 7; *Reshith Chokhmah* no. 8. Since it is like stealing from many; *Yad.*
12. Rif no. 18; *Reshith Chokhmah* no. 15. Because the owner will not be available later; *Yad. Cf. Tana DeBei Eliahu* 2.
13. Rif no. 20; *Reshith Chokhmah* no. 17. *Yad* reads *Shor,* the "ox" of the poor, referring to one who steals from them. However, the majority read *Shod,* the "spoil" or "sustenance" of the poor, referring to one who oppresses the poor or takes away their property; *cf.* Raavad, *Migdal Oz, Kesef Mishneh, Lechem Mishneh, ad. loc. Cf.* Job 24:3, 24:9.
14. Rif no. 17; *Reshith Chokhmah* no. 14. Since one does not know how far reaching the judgment will be; *Yad.*
15. Rif no. 5; *Reshith Chokhmah* no. 6. Numbers 15-19 are in *Yad, Teshuvah* 4:4, and the reason for all is because one does not normally consider them sins. Rambam writes that this is like stealing, even though one has eaten at the invitation of the host; *cf. Bava Metzia* 22a; *Nedarim* 62a; *Zohar Chadash* 79b; *Sefer Chasidim* 316, from Proverbs 23:16. *Rokeach* omits this and substitutes "despising the observant."
16. Rif no. 16; *Reshith Chokhmah* no. 13. Because one considers it inconsequential to use it while it is in his possession; *Yad. Cf.* Deuteronomy 24:12.
17. Rif no. 9; *Reshith Chokhmah* no. 7. Since one does not consider it sinful when no deed is done; *Yad.* But see Numbers 15:39; *Berakhoth* 12b; above, 13:13.
18. Rif no. 9; *Reshith Chokhmah* no. 20. Because one assumes that it is not sinful to shame one's fellow when he is not present; *Yad.* See above, 14:17.
19. Rif no. 22; *Reshith Chokhmah* no. 21. Because one does not deem this particularly harmful to one's fellow; *Yad. Cf. Berakhoth* 31b; *Shabbath* 97a; *Yoma* 19b.
20. Rif no. 1; *Reshith Chokhmah* no. 1. Numbers 20-24 are in *Yad, Teshuvah* 4:5, and the reason for all is because they are difficult habits to break; see above, 15:49. *Cf. Sanhedrin* 106b; *Menorath HaMaor* 2:4:1:3 (50); *Reshith Chokhmah, Shaar HaKedushah* 12 (178c); Rabbenu Yonah, *Shaarey Teshuvah* 3:204.
21. Rif no. 1; *Reshith Chokhmah* no. 2. *Cf. Yoma* 22b; *Zohar* 2:161a, 3:53a. Rif counts gossip and slander together, although the majority appear to count them separately. It would therefore appear preferable to count these separately and to combine 11 and 12; see note 8.

22. Evil temper.[22]
23. Evil thoughts.[23]
24. Associating with wicked friends.[24]

22. Rif no. 2; *Reshith Chokhmah* no. 3. *Cf. Pesachim* 66a.
23. Rif no. 3; *Reshith Chokhmah* no. 4. *Cf.* Jeremiah 11:19.
24. Rif no. 4; *Reshith Chokhmah* no. 5. *Cf. Negaim* 12:6; *Sukkah* 56b; *Kallah Rabbah* 3.

SIXTEEN

CONFESSION

16:1   It is a positive commandment to confess a sin to God as part of one's repentance. The Torah thus states, "If a man or woman sins against his fellow man, thus being untrue to God, and becoming guilty of a crime, they must confess the sin they have committed" (Numbers 5:6-7).[1]

16:2   Confession is an integral part of repentance,[2] as God said through His prophet, "Return, backsliding Israel... Just admit your sin, for you have rebelled against God" (Jeremiah 3:12-13).[3] Since God is all knowing, one's confession does not implicate him before God.[4] On the contrary, he thereby acknowledges his belief in God's omniscience and his own regret for the sin,[5] thus placing himself in the hands of God's mercy alone.[6] All that God requires is sincere words[7] acknowledging that one has sinned.[8]

16:3   Confession is required for all sins, whether they are violations of mandatory or prohibitive commandments, and whether they are committed by individuals or communities, no matter where they

---

1.   *Yad, Teshuvah* 1:1; *Sefer HaMitzvoth,* Positive Commandment 73; *Sefer Mitzvoth Gadol,* Positive Commandment 16; *Chinukh* 364; *Menorath HaMaor* 5:1:1:4 (279). See above, 15:13, 15:20; *cf.* Leviticus 5:5, 26:40.
2.   *Cf. Sifra* on Leviticus 26:40 (112b); *Pirkey Rabbi Eliezer* 19 (44a); *Zohar* 1:56a; *Reshith Chokhmah, Shaar HaTeshuvah* 1 (104d). However, others maintain that desire is enough for repentance; Rashi, *Yoma* 85b *s.v. Chatath, Kerithoth* 7a *s.v. Elah,* and that confession is a separate commandment; *cf. Minchath Chinukh* 364 for discussion.
3.   *Cf.* Mahari Kara, Radak, *ad. loc.*
4.   *Pesikta* 25 (159a); *Yalkut Shimoni* 2:854.
5.   *Chinukh* 364.
6.   See above, 15:20, note 68.
7.   *Yoma* 86b; *Pirkey Rabbi Eliezer* 43 (103b); Radal *ad. loc.* 43:80; *Akedath Yitzchak* 96; *Menorath HaMaor* 5:1:1:4 (279); Radak on Hosea 14:3.
8.   *Yerushalmi, Taanith* 2:7 (11a); *Yalkut Shimoni* 2:103, from 1 Samuel 7:6.

may be.[9] Even if one sins against his fellow, makes restitution, and gains forgivenenss from him, his sin is not atoned until he confesses before God.[10]

16:4   Confession is a prerequisite for all atonement. Therefore, in ancient times, one was required to confess over every sacrifice that was offered.[11] Similarly, one was required to confess when receiving punishment at the hand of the courts such as death or stripes.[12] Even when one is punished by the hand of God, his atonement is not complete without confession.[13]

16:5   Although repentance is primarily in the heart,[14] confession must be made verbally.[15] Confession in thought alone is not enough[16] unless one is unable to do otherwise.[17]

16:6   If a person is unable to confess, another can say his confession for him.[18] Similarly, one can confess on behalf of an entire community, as Moses said, "The people have committed a terrible sin by making themselves a golden idol" (Exodus 32:31).[19]

16:7   When one confesses, all that he need say is "I have sinned,"[20] and it is not necessary to specify every sin.[21] Nevertheless, it is preferable

9.   *Sifri Zuta,* quoted in *Yalkut Shimoni* 1:701 on Numbers 4:7, quoted in *Chinukh* 364. Cf. *Kesef Mishneh, Lechem Mishneh, Teshuvah* 1:1.
10. *Ibid.; BaMidbar Rabbah* 8:5; *Yad, Teshuvah* 1:1. Cf. *Shaar HaTziun* (on *Mishnah Berurah*) 607:13.
11. *Ibid.,* from Leviticus 5:5; *Sifra* (24a), *Yalkut Shimoni* (1:473), Ramban, *ad. loc.; Yad, Maaseh HaKorbanoth* 3:14-15. Cf. *Yoma* 3:8 (35b); *Kerithoth* 12a; *Taanith* 23a, Rashi *ad. loc. s.v. Par; Zohar* 3:12b, 3:63a; Rashi on Psalms 50:23, 2 Chronicles 30:22.
12. See notes 9, 10; *Sanhedrin* 6:2 (43b); *Yad, Sanhedrin* 13:1.
13. See below, 17:2, note 4.
14. See note 9, since it is required for *Kareth;* above, 13:50.
15. *Yad, Teshuvah* 2:2; *Chinukh* 364; *Minchath Chinukh ad. loc.* (270b).
16. *Pri Megadim,* Introduction 3:10.
17. *Midrash Tehillim* 45:4; *Yalkut Shimoni* 2:749; Ramban, *Torath HaAdam* 10a; *Chinukh* 364 (end); *Yoreh Deah* 338:3; HaGra *ad. loc.* 338:3; *Chokhmath Adam* 151:11; *Kitzur Shulchan Arukh* 193:13.
18. *Minchath Chinukh* 364 (271a). Cf. *Sefer Chasidim* 22, *Makor Chesed ad. loc.* 22:1.
19. Cf. Daniel 9:15; Ezra 9:6; *Yoma* 6:2 (66a); *Yad, Teshuvah* 1:2, *Avodath Yom HaKippurim* 4:2. See *Yerushalmi, Yoma* 6:2 (33a), where it is indicated that the name of the sinner should be mentioned.
20. *Yoma* 87b; *Yad, Teshuvah* 2:8; *Orach Chaim* 607:3 in *Hagah; Magen Avraham* 607:5; *"Rav" Shulchan Arukh* 607:4; *Mishnah Berurah* 607:5. Cf. *Yerushalmi, Taanith* 2:7 (11a); *Yalkut Shimoni* 2:103, from 1 Samuel 7:6; *Midrash Tehillim* 51:1; *Yalkut Shimoni* 2:764, from 2 Samuel 12:13. However, others interpret *Yoma loc. cit.* to refer to the entire traditional order of confession; cf. *Sh'nei Luchoth HaB'rith, Teshuvah* 2:171b; *Magen Avraham* 607:5; *Shaar HaTziun* (on *Mishnah Berurah*) 607:11. See note 24.
21. This is the opinion of Rabbi Akiba, disputed by Rabbi Yehudah ben Baba; *Yoma* 86b;

to specify one's sins,[22] especially if one is repenting for a particular transgression.[23]

16:8 It is customary to recall all three types of sins in one's confession.[24] In ascending order, these are: the accidental (*Chet*, חֵטְא), the purposeful (*Avon*, עָוֹן), and the spiteful (*Pesha*, פֶּשַׁע).[25] A traditional confession is, "O God,[26] I have erred, I have sinned, I have rebelled against You; I regret and am ashamed of my deeds, and will never again repeat my sin."[27] One may also include a specific sin in this confession.[28]

16:9 In confessing many sins, a person should confess the lighte. ones first.[29] However, the standard confessions are in alphabetical order,[30] and one need not be particular about this when they are used.[31]

Tosefta 4:14; *Yerushalmi* 8:7 (42b); Rif 5b; Rosh 8:17. The majority follow Rabbi Akiba; *Orach Chaim* 607:2; *Beth Yosef ibid.; Shiltey Gibborim* (Rif 5b) no. 3; *Sh'nei Luchoth HaB'rith* 2:167a; *Pri Chadash* 607:3; *Chayay Adam* 143:1; *Minchath Chinukh* 364 (271b). However, others follow Rabbi Yehudah that it is necessary to specify every sin; *cf. Yad, Teshuvah* 2:3; *Hagahoth Maimonioth ad. loc.* no. 2; *Kesef Mishneh, Lechem Mishneh, ad. loc.; Sefer Mitzvoth Gadol*, Positive Commandment 16; Rabbenu Yonah, *Shaarey Teshuvah* 4:21; *Menorath HaMaor* 5:1:1:4 (278).

22. *Orach Chaim* 607:2; *HaGra, Yoreh Deah* 338:6; *"Rav" Shulchan Arukh* 607:4; *Kitzur Shulchan Arukh* 131:9, since even Rabbi Akiba does not forbid it; *cf. Beth Yosef, Orach Chaim* 607; *Sh'nei Luchoth HaB'rith, Teshuvah* 2:171b; *Machtzith HaShekel* 607:2. See also *Zohar* 2:41b, 3:195b, 3:231; *Reshith Chokhmah, Shaar HaTeshuvah* 7 (127a); *Maavar Yavok* 1:4, 1:11; *Sh'nei Luchoth HaB'rith, Teshuvah* 2:171b; *Rokeach* 215. See Joshua 7:20.

23. *Turey Zahav, Orach Chaim* 607:1.

24. Some maintain that all of these categories must be included whenever one confesses; *cf. Lechem Mishneh, Teshuvah* 2:8; *Pri Chadash* 607:5; *Pri Megadim, Eshel Avraham* 607:5; *Mishnah Berurah* 607:2. On the other hand, some question this usage entirely for private confessions; *cf. Minchath Chinukh* 364 (270c); but see *Makor Chesed* (on *Sefer Chasidim*) 7:7, who answers his objections.

25. *Yoma* 36b; *Tosafoth Yeshenim ad. loc. s.v. Halakhah; Tosefta, Yoma* 2:1; *Yerushalmi, Yoma* 3:7 (18b); *Sifra* on Leviticus 16:5 (80c); *Yad, Avodath Yom HaKippurim* 2:6; Ramban, *Torath HaAdam* 10a; *Orach Chaim* 621:5; *Yoreh Deah* 338:2. Cf. Psalms 106:6; *Yoma* 3:8 (35b), 4:2 (41b), 6:2 (66a), and references in following note.

26. *Yoma* 37a; *Yad, Teshuvah* 1:1. Cf. *Minchath Chinukh* 364 (270c), who questions why this should be said in private. See *Yad, Maaseh HaKorbanoth* 3:15; Rabbenu Yonah, *Shaarey Teshuvah* 4:22; *Orach Chaim* 621:5; 1 Kings 8:47, where this is indeed omitted. However, see Daniel 9:5, where it is included.

27. *Yad, Teshuvah* 1:1. Cf. *Yoma* 8:7 (42b); *VaYikra Rabbah* 3:3; *Emunoth VeDeyoth* 5:6 (73a). See below, 15:23.

28. *Yad, Maaseh HaKorbanoth* 3:15.

29. *Yoma* 36b; Rashi *ad. loc. s.v. Chozer; Pesikta Rabbathai* 35 (160b); *Tur, Orach Chaim* 582; *Magen Avraham* 607:3; *"Rav" Shulchan Arukh* 607:6. Cf. *Magen Avraham* 621:5; *"Rav" Shulchan Arukh* 621:13; *Mishnah Berurah* 621:17.

30. Cf. *Orach Chaim* 607:2 in *Hagah; "Rav" Shulchan Arukh* 607:5. This includes both *Ashamnu* and *Al Chet; cf. Tosefoth Yeshenim, Yoma* 86b *s.v. VeTzarikh*. Regarding

16:10   It is customary to confess in the plural,[32] "we have sinned,"[33] since all Jews are responsible for one another.[34] For the same reason, one should confess all the sins in the standard order, even though he may be certain that he has not committed some of them.[35] It is likewise customary to confess ancestral sins, as it is written, "They will then confess their sins and the sins of their fathers" (Leviticus 26:40).[36]

16:11   Though one has confessed a sin once, he may[37] confess it again, as the Psalmist said, "For I know my wrongdoings, and my sin is ever before me" (Psalms 51:5).[38] This is especially true before a sin has been atoned,[39] after which one should confess in general terms.[40] However, in repeating a confession, one must be careful not to deny God's forgiveness, or neglect mentioning one's later sins.[41]

16:12   Even when a person is not required to repeat a confession, he should constantly pray for forgiveness lest his repentance not

the reason for the alphabetical order, see *Reshith Chokhmah, Shaar HaTeshuvah* 5 (118d); *Chayay Adam* 143:1.

31.   *Magen Avraham* 607:3.
32.   *Sefer Chasidim* 22, 601; *Taamey HaMinhagim* 683 (p. 304).
33.   See note 20.
34.   See above, 12:1, note 4.
35.   *Sefer Chasidim* 601; *B'rith Olam ad. loc; Ben Ish Chai, Ki Tissa* introduction, 1; *Kaf HaChaim, Orach Chaim* 131:16-17, quoting the Ari.
36.   Rabbenu Yonah, *Shaarey Teshuvah* 1:40; *Sh'nei Luchoth HaB'rith, Teshuvah* 2:171a; *Taamey HaMinhagim* 685 (p. 304). *Cf. Yad, Taanith* 5:1; Psalms 106:6; Maharsha, *Yoma* 36b *s.v. Chatanu.*
37.   Some maintain that this is praiseworthy; *Magen Avraham* 607:6; *"Rav" Shulchan Arukh* 607:9; *Mishnah Berurah* 607:14. Others dispute this; *Pri Chadash* 607:4; *Pri Megadim, Eshel Avraham* 607:6.
38.   Opinion of Rabbi Eliezer ben Yaakov, disputed by the Sages; *Yoma* 86b; *Tosefta* 4:15; *Yerushalmi* 8:7 (42b); Rif 5b; Rosh 8:17; and reversed in *Midrash Tehillim* 32:2; *Shaarey Teshuvah* 4:21. The majority concur with the first opinion; *cf. Yad, Teshuvah* 2:8; *Hagahoth Maimonioth ad. loc.* no. 6; *Orach Chaim* 607:4; *Rokeach* 215; *Sefer Chasidim* 621; *Sh'nei Luchoth HaB'rith* 2:167b; *Likutey Amarim, Iggereth HaTeshuvah* 11 (100b). Others, however, dispute it; *Shaarey Teshuvah loc. cit.,* as well as authorities quoted in notes 40 and 41.
39.   *Minchath Chinukh* 364 (271d); *cf.* Rashi, *Yoma* 86b *s.v. VeChatathi;* Maharsha *ibid. s.v. Kol Sheken.* Regarding sins between man and his fellow, see *Pri Megadim, Mishbetzoth Zahav* 607:1; *Mishnah Berurah* 607:12; *Chayay Adam* 144:10.
40.   Rabbi Yitzchak Geyuth, quoted in *Shiltey Gibborim, Yoma* (Rif 5b) no. 2; *Tur, Orach Chaim* 607; *Turey Zahav* 607:1; *Pri Chadash* 607:4; *Sh'nei Luchoth HaB'rith* 2:167b.
41.   *Midrash Tehillim* 32:2; *Shemoth Rabbah* 53:2, from Psalms 31:19; *Shaarey Teshuvah* 4:21; *Likutey Amarim, Iggereth HaTeshuvah* 11 (100a-b).

be complete and further punishment be required.[42] Similarly, one should ask God forgiveness for unknown and forgotten sins, as the Psalmist prayed, "Clear me from hidden faults" (Psalms 19:13).[43]

16:13 One should not publicize his sins, since this indicates lack of shame[44] and disrespect for God.[45] Regarding this, King David said, "Happy is the man whose transgression is forgiven, whose sin is *covered*" (Psalms 32:1).[46] However, one may publicize the fact that he has sinned and repented, as long as he does not specify the sin,[47] and for this reason there are standard confessions said publicly as part of the synagogue service.[48] One may also confess his sin to a person from whom he wishes to learn how to repent.[49]

16:14 If one's sin is publicly known, however, he should not deny it. Rather, he should make a public confession[50] feel ashamed,[51] and announce his repentance.[52] Similarly, if one sins against his fellow, he should make it known,[53] in order that he may gain

42. *Zohar* 1:73b; *Shaarey Teshuvah* 4:21.
43. Rashi, Radak, Ibn Ezra, *ad. loc.; Shaarey Teshuvah* 4:21. However, see Rashi, *Sanhedrin* 107a *s.v. Nistharoth;* Maharsha *ibid. s.v. Shegioth.* See above, 15:60.
44. *Berakhoth* 34b; *Tosafoth ad. loc. s.v. Kisuy; Sotah* 7b, *Tosafoth Shantz ad. loc.; Yad, Teshuvah* 2:5; *Hagahoth Maimonioth ad. loc.* no. 4; *Menorath HaMaor* 5:1:1:4 (279).
45. *Zohar* 2:168a; Rashi, *Yoma* 86b *s.v. BeChet.* See above, 3:4, 7:14.
46. "Covered" or "concealed" from the eyes of other human beings but not from God's eyes, as the Psalm continues: "Happy is the man whom God regards as sinless, whose [repenting] spirit is without deception. For as long as I was silent [and did not confess], my bones were wasting away... At last I admitted to You I had sinned, no longer concealing my guilt. I said, 'I will confess my transgression to God.' And You, You have forgiven the wrong of my sin" (Psalms 32:2-5). See *Yoma* 86b; *Zohar* 3:101a; Rav Nissim Gaon, *Berakhoth* 34b; *Yad, Teshuvah* 2:5; *Orach Chaim* 607:2 in *Hagah; Shaarey Teshuvah ad. loc.* 607:2; *Sh'nei Luchoth HaB'rith, Mesekheth Rosh HaShanah, Amud HaDin* 2:160b; *Teshuvoth Panim Meiroth* 2:178.
47. *Yad, Teshuvah* 2:5; *Minchath Chinukh* 364 (271b). *Cf.* Rashi, *Chullin* 41b *s.v. MeChuyav; Magen Avraham* 607:2; *Pri Megadim, Chatham Sofer, ad. loc.* 607:3.
48. *Menorath HaMaor* 5:1:1:4 (279); *cf.* Mordecai, *Yoma* 725; *Orach Chaim* 607:2 in *Hagah; "Rav" Shulchan Arukh* 607:5.
49. See above, 15:61; *Teshuvoth Panim Meiroth* 2:178; *Sotah* 32b.
50. Even a sin between man and God; Rav, *Yoma* 86b. This is disputed by Rav Zutra bar Tuvia, who allows a public confession only for sins against man; see note 53. See Raavad, *Kesef Mishneh, Teshuvah* 2:5; *Magen Avraham* 607:2; *Beer Hetiv* 607:2; *"Rav" Shulchan Arukh* 607:4; *Mishnah Berurah* 607:6; *Menorath HaMaor* 5:1:1:4 (279). However, others forbid formal public confession even if the sin is already known; *cf. Lechem Mishneh ibid.; Shaar HaTziun* (on *Mishnah Berurah*) 607:1.
51. Rashi, *Yoma* 86b *s.v. BeChet Mefursam; Tosafoth Shantz, Sotah* 7b.
52. *Menorath HaMaor* 5:1:1:4 (279); *Sefer Chasidim* 167.
53. Rav Zutra bar Tuvia, *Yoma* 86b; *Rabbenu Chananel ad. loc.; Rif* 5b; *Rosh* 3:17;

forgiveness.[54] Regarding this it is stated, "He who covers over his sin will not succeed, but he who admits and abandons his sin will gain mercy" (Proverbs 28:13).[55] Nevertheless, even in these cases, one need not confess publicly if he will suffer undue disgrace,[56] since even a person who has blasphemed God publicly may repent privately and be accepted by God.[57]

16:15 If one has committed a sin and another person is suspected, he should confess publicly in order to allay the suspicion against his fellow.[58] One should also make his repentance known to his accomplices, but not publicize their names.[59]

16:16 It is customary to confess while standing,[60] bowed and humble before God.[61] It is likewise customary to beat one's heart lightly, as if to say, "You have caused me to sin."[62]

16:17 One should examine his deeds and confess every night before

---

Yad, Teshuvah 2:5; *Menorath HaMaor* 5:1:1:4 (279). Others dispute this; *cf. Mishnah Berurah* 607:9; *Shaar HaTziun ad. loc.* 607:5.

54. Rashi, *Yoma* 86b *s.v. Averoth; Kesef Mishneh loc. cit.*
55. *Yoma loc. cit.*
56. *Cf. Sotah* 32b; *Magen Avraham* 607:2; Rashi, *Yoma* 21a *s.v. Mishtachavim;* Bertenoro on *Avoth* 5:6; *Minchath Chinukh* 364 (271c); *Zohar Chadash* 39a.
57. *Pesikta* 25 (163b); *Yalkut Shimoni* 2:532; *Menorath HaMaor* 5:1:1:1 (276). Although *Yad, Teshuvah* 2:5 writes that repentance is not complete without public confession, he does hold that it is acceptable; *cf. Kesef Mishneh ad. loc.; Yad, Teshuvah* 3:14; *Lechem Mishneh ad. loc.,* from *Avodah Zarah* 7b; *Rabbenu Chananel ad. loc.; Rif* 2a; *Rosh* 1:4.
58. *Sefer Chasidim* 22, 630, 631; *Yad Ephraim, Orach Chaim* 607:1; *Shaarey Teshuvah* 607:2; *Tevuoth Shor* 5:7, from *Sotah* 7b; *cf. Sanhedrin* 11a; *Marith HaAyin* (Chida) *ad. loc. s.v. Amad Sh'muel.* However, *Chokhmath Shlomo, Orach Chaim* 607:2, writes that this only applies to sin against man.
59. *Sefer Chasidim* 167.
60. *Zohar* 2:262a; *Ran, Yoma* (Rif 6a) *s.v. Sh'ma; Shiltey Gibborim ibid.* 5b no. 3; *Mordecai* 725; *Rosh* 8:18; Maharshal on *Sefer Mitzvoth Gadol,* Positive Commandment 16, from *Yoma* 87b; *Orach Chaim* 607:3; *Magen Avraham* 607:3; *Pri Chadash* 607:3; *"Rav" Shulchan Arukh* 607:7; *Mishnah Berurah* 607:10; *Kitzur Shulchan Arukh* 131:9. *Cf. Pri Megadim ad. loc.* whether this is an absolute requirement. Also see *Yoma* 3:8 (35b), 4:2 (41b), 6:2 (66a), 36a; *Tosefta, Menachoth* 10:3; *Yad, Maaseh HaKorbanoth* 3:14, where it is specified that the confession over a sacrifice is said standing. Also see above, 10:9.
61. *Sh'nei Luchoth HaB'rith* 2:167a, quoting Maharil, *Minhagey Yom Kippur,* quoting *Mahari Segel; Magen Avraham* 607:4; *Machtzith HaShekel ad. loc.; "Rav" Shulchan Arukh* 607:7; *Mishnah Berurah* 607:10; *Kitzur Shulchan Arukh* 131:9. *Cf. Shaar HaTziun* 607:6, that this is not an absolute requirement.
62. *Magen Avraham* 607:3; *Chatham Sofer ibid.; Mishnah Berurah* 607:11; *"Rav" Shulchan Arukh* 607:7; *Kitzur Shulchan Arukh* 131:9; *Taamey HaMinhagim* 694 (p. 304), 740 (p. 330). *Cf. Jeremiah* 17:9; *Bereshith Rabbah* 34:11, 67:7; *Koheleth Rabbah* 5:1; *Esther Rabbah* 10:3; *Midrash Tehillim* 14:2.

going to sleep.[63] At the same time, one should also forgive anyone who might have sinned against him or hurt him.[64] It is permissible to say such a confession even on the Sabbath, although it should not be said in great bitterness.[65]

16:18 *Yom Kippur* is a particular day of repentance, and therefore confession is mandatory on this day.[66] It is for this reason that orders of confession were made part of the regular service.[67]

16:19 If a person knows that he is about to die, he should repent and make his confession before God in order that he enter his future life free of sin.[68] If one cannot confess in words, he should at least repent in thought.[69]

16:20 Therefore, if a person is about to die, those with him should tactfully remind him to confess.[70] They can remind him that many have confessed and not died immediately, while others have died before they were able to confess. However, this should not be said in the presence of the unlearned lest they become overly frightened,[71] and if it is not customary, it should be omitted entirely.[72]

16:21 If possible, one should confess any major sins known to him,[73] since, if one repents and confesses, his death atones for all

63. *Zohar* 1:191a, 3:178a; *Sefer Chasidim* 603; *Magen Avraham* 230:7; *Beer Hetiv* 239:6; *Chayay Adam* 35:5; *Kitzur Shulchan Arukh* 71:3; *Mishnah Berurah* 239:9. See above, 15:38.
64. *Magen Avraham* 607:3; *Kitzur Shulchan Arukh* 131:9; *Mishnah Berurah* 607:11. *Cf. Megillah* 28a; see below, 17:52.
65. *Sh'nei Luchoth HaB'rith, Mesekheth Rosh HaShanah, Amud HaAvodah* 2:143a.
66. See *Chinukh* 364, that one who does not confess on *Yom Kippur* violates this commandment. *Cf.* Rabbenu Yonah, *Shaarey Teshuvah* 4:17.
67. *Yoma* 87b; *Tosefta* 4:13; *Yerushalmi* 8:7 (42b); *Pesachim* 3a; *Niddah* 8b; *Yad, Teshuvah* 2:7; *Orach Chaim* 607:1.
68. See above, note 12; Ramban, *Torath HaAdam, "Shaar HaSof"* 10a; *Kitzur Shulchan Arukh* 191:13; *Zohar* 3:33a.
69. See above, 16:5.
70. *Shabbath* 32a; *Hagahoth Maimonioth, Teshuvah* 1:1 no. 1; *Yoreh Deah* 338:1; *Sifethey Cohen, Beer Hetiv, ad. loc.* 338:1; *Chokhmath Adam* 151:11; *Maavar Yavok* 1:9.
71. *Ibid.;* Ramban, *Torath HaAdam "Shaar HaSof"* 10a, citing *Semachoth.* However, this is not in our editions of *Semachoth; cf.* HaGra, *Yoreh Deah* 338:1.
72. *Chokhmath Adam* 151:11.
73. *Ibid.* 151:12; Rashash, *Sanhedrin* 43b; *Maavar Yavok* 1:12.

his sins.[74] If one has committed any sin worthy of death,[75] he should also pray that his death be considered a complete atonement.[76]

16:22   A traditional confession before death is: "I acknowledge before You, O my God and God of my fathers, that both my healing and death are in Your hands. May it be Your will to heal me. But if You have decreed that I should die, let my death atone for all my errors, sins, and crimes. Shelter me under the shadow of Your wings, grant my portion in Paradise, and may I merit the resurrection and the World to Come which are prepared for the righteous."[77]

16:23   If one is able, he should also say the entire *Yom Kippur* confession,[78] as well as the other traditional prayers before death.[79] One should also attempt to say the *Sh'ma* with one's last breath.[80]

16:24   If a dying person cannot confess more fully, all he need say or think is, "I have erred, sinned, and transgressed;[81] may my death be an atonement for all my sins."[82]

16:25   Every person should make his confession to God before dying, since there is no man on earth who is completely free of sin.[83] No matter how greatly one may have sinned, if he repents and confesses before dying, he has a portion in the World to Come.[84]

74. Rambam, *Tosefoth Yom Tov, Nazir* 6:4 (42a).
75. See above, Tables 13:5-7.
76. *Zohar* 3:33a.
77. Ramban, *Torath HaAdam* 10b; *Chinukh* 364; *Yoreh Deah* 338:2; *Chokhmath Adam* 151:12; *Kitzur Shulchan Arukh* 193:14; *Sh'nei Luchoth HaB'rith, Mesekheth Pesachim* 2:27a.
78. *Yoreh Deah* 338:2 in *Hagah;* HaGra *ad. loc.* 338:6; *cf. Avodah Zarah* 8a.
79. *Chokhmath Adam* 151:12; *Maavar Yavok* 1:7, 9.
80. *Zohar* 2:119a, 2:454b, 3:33a; *Maavar Yavok* 1:39; *Sh'nei Luchoth HaB'rith, Mesekheth Pesachim* 2:27b; *Chokhmath Adam* 151:12. *Cf. Berakhoth* 61b; *Yerushalmi, Berakhoth* 9:5 (67b); *Yerushalmi, Sotah* 5:5 (25a); *Tanchuma, Ki Tavo* 2.
81. *Emunoth VeDeyoth* 5:6 (73a) adds this.
82. *Sanhedrin* 6:2 (43b); Maharsha, Rashash, *ad. loc.; Berakhoth* 60a; *Yad, Sanhedrin* 13:1; *Yoreh Deah* 338:1 in *Hagah; Kitzur Shulchan Arukh* 193:13.
83. *Cf. Beth Hillel, Yoreh Deah* 338:1.
84. See note 82; *Pirkey Rabbi Eliezer* 38 (90b).

SEVENTEEN

ATONEMENT

17:1　When a person repents out of love of God, all his sins are counted as virtues,[1] and no further atonement is required.[2] However, if he repents out of fear of God, his sins are counted as accidental, and still require some further atonement.[3]

17:2　As soon as a person repents in his heart,[4] he is immediately[5] considered a righteous person.[6] Even as far as judicial law is concerned, all he need do is completely abandon his sin.[7] Similarly, repentance alone helps to protect a person from judgment, both in this world[8] and the next.[9]

17:3　However, for a person to be perfectly cleansed and acceptable before God,[10] repentance alone may not be enough, and some

---

1. See above, 15:30, 15:63.
2. *Cheredim, Teshuvah* 3 (p. 211), citing Rabbi Meir of Toledula, from *Avoth* 4:11; *Minchath Chinukh* 364 (273d); Rabbi Yoshia Pinto (Riph) on *Eyn Yaakov, Yoma* 73.
3. See above, 15:29; below, 17:3, note 11.
4. *Kethuvoth* 49b; Rif 20b; *Shiltey Gibborim ad. loc.* no. 2; *Rosh* 2:14; *Yad, Ishuth* 8:5; *Lechem Mishneh ad. loc.; Evven HaEzer* 38:31; *Zohar* 1:41a, 2:150a, 3:129a; *Tikuney Zohar* 32 (76b); *Rokeach* 19; *Minchath Chinukh* 364 (270c); *Teshuvoth Ram Padua* 37; *Teshuvoth Mahari Mintz* 12. *Cf. Gittin* 57b; *Midrash Tehillim* 45:4; *Yalkut Shimoni* 2:749; *Or Zarua* 112. This is even true if he still has a stolen article in his possession; *Chelkath Mechokek* 38:44; *Beth Sh'muel* 38:35; *Beer Hetiv, Evven HaEzer* 38:40; *Shai LaMorah ibid.; cf. Bava Kama* 94b.
5. *Pesikta* 25 (163b), from Psalms 46:11; *cf. Shir HaShirim Rabbah* 5:3.
6. Whether he is considered perfectly righteous, see *Teshuvoth Kol Eliahu* 2; *Chasdey David* on *Tosefta, Yoma* 4:9.
7. *Sanhedrin* 25b; *Yad, Eduth* 12:4-6; *Choshen Mishpat* 34:29-33; *Beth Sh'muel* 38:35; *Likutey Amarim (Tanya), Iggereth HaTeshuvah* 1 (91a).
8. *Avoth* 4:11; *Tosefoth Yom Tov ad. loc.; Pesikta* 25 (160a); *VaYikra Rabbah* 10:5; Rabbenu Yonah, *Shaarey Teshuvah* 4:1; *Tosafoth, Shevuoth* 12b *s.v. Lo; Minchath Chinukh loc. cit.* (271d); *Asarah Maamaroth* 1:1:16.
9. *Likutey Amarim, Iggereth HaTeshuvah* 1 (91b); *Zohar,* cited in note 4; *Korban Nethanel, Yoma* (Rosh 8:17) no. 60.
10. *Likutey Amarim, Iggereth HaTeshuvah* 1 (91a).

further atonement may be necessary.[11] Until one's sin is completely atoned for, it leaves a stain on his soul preventing the complete acceptance of his good deeds, just as dirt on a cloth prevents it from accepting dye.[12] The damage done to his soul must be repaired by atonement, just as a broken vessel is repaired.[13] Furthermore, atonement may be necessary in order that the sin not constantly reinforce itself until repentance becomes almost impossible.[14]

17:4   There are four types of atonement given to us by God: repentance, *Yom Kippur,* suffering, and death. Repentance alone is enough to atone for violating a positive commandment; *Yom Kippur* is required for violations of negative commandments; suffering atones for sins incurring penalties of *Kareth* and death; and death atones for sins involving a desecration of God's name.[15] Repentance and confession are prerequisites for all these atonements.[16]

17:5   Concerning repentance, God calls to us through His prophet: "Return, you backsliding children, and I will heal your backslidings" (Jeremiah 3:22).[17] It is primarily for the violation of positive commandments that repentance atones.[18] When a person

11. *VaYikra Rabbah* 10:5; *Pesikta* 25 (160a), 28 (183a); *Tanchuma, Emor* 22; *Yalkut Shimoni* 1:551; Rabbenu Yonah, *Shaarey Teshuvah* 4:1; *Tosafoth, Zevachim* 12b *s.v. Sh'ma Mina; Piskey Recanti* 67, cited in *Makor Chesed* (on *Sefer Chasidim*) 203:1; *Teshuvoth Chaim Sha'al* 38:39; *Teshuvoth Chut HaShani* 65; *Sedey Chemed* 15:156 (46d); *Teshuvoth Mattah Levi* 2:5.
12. *Reshith Chokhmah, Shaar HaAhavah* 11 (91b), *Shaar HaTeshuvah* 2 (108c).
13. *Cf. Chagigah* 15a; *Yerushalmi* 2:1 (9b); *Avoth DeRabbi Nathan* 24:5; *Koheleth Rabbah* 7:18, from Job 28:17.
14. *Minchath Chinukh* 364 (272c). However, see *Emunoth VeDeyoth* 5:5 (82b), that repentance alone is enough for this.
15. *Yoma* 86a; *Yerushalmi* 8:7 (42a); *Yerushalmi, Shevuoth* 1:6 (7a-b); *Yerushalmi, Sanhedrin* 10:1 (49a); *Mekhilta* on Exodus 20:7 (69a); *Yalkut Shimoni* 2:269; Rif, *Yoma* 5a; Rosh 3:17; Rambam *Tosefoth Yom Tov,* on *Mishnah Yoma* 8:8; *Yad, Teshuvah* 1:4; *Chovoth HaLevavoth* 7:8; Rabbenu Yonah, *Shaarey Teshuvah* 4:6; *Sefer Chasidim* 20; *Menorath HaMaor* 1:end (29), 5:introduction (275); *Asarah Maamaroth* 1:1:16; *Cheredim, Teshuvah* 1 (p. 203); *Reshith Chokhmah, Shaar HaTeshuvah* 3 (108b); Maharal, *Nethivoth Olam, Nethiv HaTeshuvah* 3 (156b); *Likutey Amarim, Iggereth HaTeshuvah* 1 (90b); *Minchath Chinukh* 364 (271d).
16. See above, 16:4.
17. See note 15. *Chovoth HaLevavoth* 7:8 cites Malachi 3:7: "Return to Me, and I will return to you, says the God of hosts." *Cf. Bahir* 67.
18. *Ibid.; Shevuoth* 12b; *Zevachim* 7b. This refers only to positive commandments not punishable by *Kareth; cf. Chovoth HaLevavoth* 7:8; *Minchath Chinukh* 364 (271d).

violates a positive commandment, he distances himself from God. Repentance brings him close again. It atones for the sin of having neglected God's commandment,[19] although no repentance can make up the loss of merit incurred.[20]

17:6 Repentance alone can also atone for negative commandments where no great sin is involved.[21] Therefore, it atones for having transgressed a negative commandment connected to a positive commandment,[22] and for all prohibitive commandments violated out of ignorance.[23]

17:7 Concerning the atonement of *Yom Kippur*,[24] the Torah states, "[Each year] on the 10th day of the 7th month, you must afflict yourselves [through fasting] and not do any work... For on this day you shall have all your sins atoned, so that you will be cleansed. Before God you will be cleansed of all your sins. It is a Sabbath of Sabbaths to you, and [a day upon which] you must fast. This is a law for all time" (Leviticus 16:29-31).[25] *Yom Kippur,* together with repentance, is required to atone for violations of negative commandments.[26] In addition, it lightens the judgment for more severe sins.[27]

---

19. Maharal, *Nethivoth Olam, Nethiv HaTeshuvah* 3 (156a); *Likutey Amarim, Iggereth HaTeshuvah* 1 (90b).
20. See above, 13:37, 15:63.
21. *Yoma* 8:8 (85b).
22. *Yoma* 85b; Rambam, Bertenoro, *Yoma* 8:8; *Minchath Chinukh* 364 (271d); see above, 13:39. *Minchath Chinukh* also discusses a negative which does not involve action; see above, 13:39.
23. Rambam, Bertenoro, *Yoma* 8:8; *cf. Yerushalmi, Yoma* 8:6 (41b).
24. Even without the ancient service and sacrifices; *Sifra* on Leviticus 16:20 (83a), 23:28 (102a); *Yad, Teshuvah* 1:3. *Cf. Tosefta, Yoma* 4:15; *Yerushalmi, Yoma* 8:7 (42b); *Yerushalmi, Shevuoth* 1:6 (7b); *Yerushalmi, Sanhedrin* 10:1 (49b); *Tosafoth, Shevuoth* 13b *s.v. DeAvad;* HaGra, *Orach Chaim* 607:6 *s.v. Yom.*
25. See note 15; *Megillah* 20b; *Bereshith Rabbah* 65:10; *VaYikra Rabbah* 20:7, 21:10, 27:9; *BaMidbar Rabbah* 16:14; *Shir HaShirim Rabbah* 1:38, 6:17, 8:8; *Tanchuma, Ki Tissa* 31, *Pekudey* 11, *Acharey Moth* 7, *Emor* 22; *Pesikta* 2 (15b), 9 (78a), 27 (174b, 177b); *Midrash Tehillim* 15:5, 118:2; *Pirkey Rabbi Eliezer* 46 (111a); *Zohar* 2:135a, 3:15b, 3:62b, 3:69b, 3:102b; Rabbenu Yonah, *Shaarey Teshuvah* 4:3.
26. See note 15.
27. *Cf. Yerushalmi, Yoma* 8:7 (42b); *Yerushalmi, Shevuoth* 1:6 (7b); *Yerushalmi, Sanhedrin* 10:1 (49a); *Mekhilta* on Exodus 20:7 (69a). But see *Minchath Chinukh* 364 (272c), citing *Yeffeh Mareh,* that this might be disputed by *Yoma* 86a. From *Pirkey Rabbi Eliezer* 46 (111a), it appears that *Yom Kippur* atones for all sins; see Radal *ad. loc.* 46:49 for a complete discussion.

17:8 Out of God's goodness and love,[28] He gave Israel one day to cleanse themselves from their sins of the entire year.[29] God set this day on the 10th of the Hebrew month of Tishrei, at the end of the ten day period of judgment beginning with *Rosh HaShanah,*[30] in order that we may repent before our judgment is finalized.[31] This day is also the anniversary of Abraham's circumcision, and the merit of this act is recalled.[32] Furthermore, this day is also the anniversary of the day that God forgave the Jewish people for the sin of the Golden Calf, whereupon it was permanently set aside as a day of forgiveness.[33]

17:9 *Yom Kippur* is a day when the power of evil is diminished,[34] and God's light shines into every soul.[35] Therefore, since the violation of negative commandments blackens the soul,[36] the power of holiness on *Yom Kippur* is required to cleanse it and restore it to its pristine purity.[37]

17:10 It is a positive commandment to rest from work[38] and fast[39] on

28. *Bereshith Rabbah* 65:10; *VaYikra Rabbah* 21:10, 27:9; *Tanchuma, Emor* 22; *Pesikta* 9 (78a).
29. *Cf. Shir HaShirim Rabbah* 1:38, 6:17, 8:8; *Midrash Tehillim* 15:5; *Zohar* 3:62b.
30. See above, 15:40.
31. *Midrash Tehillim* 118:2; *Menorath HaMaor* 5:2:2:1 (295). *Cf. BaMidbar Rabbah* 16:14.
32. *Pirkey Rabbi Eliezer* 29 (64a). *Cf. Tosafoth, Rosh HaShanah* 11a *s.v.* *Ela; Baaley Tosafoth* on Genesis 17:26.
33. *Seder Olam* 6; *Tanchuma, Ki Tissa* 31, *Pekudey* 11; *Pirkey Rabbi Eliezer* 46 (110b); *Tana DeBei Eliahu Zuta* 4 (9b). *Cf.* Rashi, Bertenoro, *Taanith* 4:8 (26b) *s.v.* *Zeh;* Rashi, *Taanith* 30b *s.v.* *SheNithnu Bo;* Rashbam, *Bava Bathra* 121a *s.v.* *Yom;* Targum *Yonathan,* Rashi, *Baaley Tosafoth,* Ramban, on Exodus 18:13; Rashi on Exodus 31:18; *Tosafoth, Bava Kama* 82a *s.v.* *K'day;* Rosh, *Rosh HaShanah* 4:14; *Tur, Orach Chaim* 581; *Magen Avraham* 581:2; *Turey Zahav* 581:1.
34. *Yoma* 20a; *Nedarim* 32b, Ran *ad. loc. s.v.* *HaSatan; VaYikra Rabbah* 21:3; *BaMidbar Rabbah* 18:17; *Tanchuma, Korach* 12; *Pirkey Rabbi Eliezer* 46 (111a); *Zohar* 1:64a, 1:114b, 1:174b, 1:190a, 1:245a, 2:284b, 3:63a, 3:102a, 3:202b, 3:232b, 3:248b, 3:255a; *Tikuney Zohar* 69 (102a); *Zohar Chadash* 20c; *Sefer Chasidim* 258 (end); *Menorath HaMaor* 5:2:2:2 (296).
35. *Sh'nei Luchoth HaB'rith, Teshuvah* 2:180b, citing *Tolaath Yaakov, Sithrey Yom HaKippurim* (p. 39a). *Cf. Bereshith Rabbah* 2:4, 3:10.
36. *Nethivoth Olam, Nethiv HaTeshuvah* 3 (156a); *Likutey Amarim, Iggereth HaTeshuvah* 1 (90b). See above, 13:6; Volume 1, 5:51.
37. See note 29; *Zohar* 2:135a, 3:67a, 3:102b; *Derekh HaShem* 5:8:5; *Likutey Amarim, Iggereth HaTeshuvah* 1 (90b). See also *Shir HaShirim Rabbah* on Song of Songs 1:5: "I am blackened [by sin] all the days of the year, but I am comely on *Yom Kippur.*"
38. *Yad, Shevithath Assor* 1:1; *Sefer HaMitzvoth,* Positive Commandment 165; *Sefer Mitzvoth Gadol,* Positive Commandment 32; *Chinukh* 317. See above, Table 13:4, no. 12.
39. *Yad, Shevithath Assor* 1:4; *Sefer HaMitzvoth,* Positive Commandment 164; *Sefer*

Yom Kippur, as the Torah states, "The 10th day of this 7th month shall be the Day of Atonement *(Yom HaKippurim)* for you. It is a sacred holiday when you must fast... Do not do any work on this day; it is a day of atonement, when you gain atonement before God your Lord" (Leviticus 23:27-28).[40] By tradition, five things are forbidden on *Yom Kippur.* These are, eating and drinking, bathing, anointing, sexual intercourse, and wearing leather shoes.[41] All these "afflictions" serve to separate one from worldliness[42] and to reinforce the spiritual through which sin is erased.[43] In order to further symbolize the spirituality of this day, it is also a custom by some to wear white[44] and to stand during the entire *Yom Kippur* service.[45]

17:11 It is customary to make a feast on the day before *Yom Kippur*[46] to celebrate the fact that God is about to forgive one's sins.[47] It is also customary to buy a live chicken and to circle it around one's head,[48] symbolizing that its slaughter should atone for one's sins.[49] It is likewise customary by some to receive the 39 lashes

Mitzvoth Gadol, Positive Commandment 31; *Chinukh* 313. See above, Table 13:4, no. 11.

40. *Cf.* Leviticus 16:29; *Sifra ad. loc.* (83a); *Yoma* 74b.
41. *Yoma* 8:1 (83b); *Targum Yonathan* on Leviticus 23:27; *Yad, Shevithath Assor* 1:4; *Orach Chaim* 611:1. Some maintain that all five of these are Biblical; *Yad loc. cit.; She'ilthoth, Zoth HaBerakhah* 167; *Magen Avraham* 611:0; *Shaar HaTziun* (on *Mishnah Berurah*) 611:1. Others maintain that all except eating and drinking are rabbinical; Rashi, *Yoma* 74a *s.v. Shabbathon; Tosafoth, Yoma* 77a *s.v. DeTenan, Niddah* 32a *s.v. U'KeShemen;* Ran, *Yoma* (Rif 1a) *s.v. Yom; Tosafoth Yeshenim, Yoma* 73b *s.v. Yom;* Rosh 8:1; *Shaar HaTziun* 611:2. Also see *Pri Chadash* 611:1; *Chokhmath Shlomo ibid.; Mishnah Berurah* 611:3; *"Rav" Shulchan Arukh* 611:2.
42. *Chinukh* 312, 317.
43. *Tanchuma, Emor* 22; *Tana DeBei Eliahu Zuta* 4 (9b); *Pirkey Rabbi Eliezer* 46 (111b).
44. *Orach Chaim* 610:4 in *Hagah; Magen Avraham* 610:5; *Mishnah Berurah* 610:17; *Kitzur Shulchan Arukh* 131:15.
45. *Pirkey Rabbi Eliezer* 46 (111a); Rosh, *Yoma* 3:24; *Orach Chaim* 619:5; *Magen Avraham* 610:10; *Turey Zahav* 610:5; *Mishnah Berurah* 610:13; *Kitzur Shulchan Arukh* 132:4.
46. *Berakhoth* 8b; *Pesachim* 68b; *Rosh HaShanah* 9a; *Yoma* 81b; *Orach Chaim* 604:1; *Kitzur Shulchan Arukh* 131:4.
47. *Bereshith Rabbah* 11:5; *Pesikta Rabathai* 23 (119a); *Tosafoth, Kethuvoth* 5a *s.v. Ela; Shaarey Teshuvah* 4:8-10; Mordecai, *Yoma* 723; *Tur, Orach Chaim* 604; *Sh'nei Luchoth HaB'rith, Teshuvah* 2:180b; *Turey Zahav, Orach Chaim* 604:1; *Chayay Adam* 144:1. *Cf.* Rashi, *Kethuvoth* 5a *s.v. SheChal Lihioth; Tosafoth, Chullin* 133a *s.v. LeBar.*
48. *Cf.* Rashi, *Shabbath* 81b *s.v. Hai Parpissa; Korban Nethanel, Yoma* (Rosh 3:12) no. 80.
49. *Machzor Vitri,* p. 339; Rosh, *Yoma* 8:23; *Kol Bo* 48; *Orach Chaim* 605:1; *Magen*

administered by the courts[50] on the eve of *Yom Kippur* as a sign of repentance and atonement.[51]

17:12 *Yom Kippur* only atones if one repents and confesses.[52] If one does not believe in *Yom Kippur*,[53] or does not desire its atonement,[54] no atonement is obtained.[55]

17:13 If one sins and repents on *Yom Kippur* itself, he is still forgiven,[56] since atonement comes at the very end of the day.[57] This is one reason why the *Shofar* is sounded at the conclusion of *Yom Kippur*.[58]

17:14 Suffering atones for sin.[59] This is the intention of the verse, "If they profane My laws and do not keep My commandments, I will punish them with a rod for their defiance, and plagues for their sins" (Psalms 89:32-33).[60] This is the atonement required for sins punishable by *Kareth* or death,[61] as well as for false oaths.[62]

Avraham 605:1; *Chazay Adam* 144:4; *Kitzur Shulchan Arukh* 131:1. *Cf. Chullin* 95a, 110b. However, some opposed this custom; *Orach Chaim* 605:1; HaGra *ad. loc.; Teshuvoth Rashba* 395.

50. See above, 13:44.
51. *Machzor Vitri*, p. 334; Rosh, *Yoma* 8:25; *Kol Bo* 48; *Orach Chaim* 608:6; *Magen Avraham* 607:9; *Chazay Adam* 144:11; *Kitzur Shulchan Arukh* 131:11.
52. *Yoma* 8:8 (85b); *Shevuoth* 13a; *Kerithoth* 7a; *Targum Yonathan* on Leviticus 16:30; *Sifra* on Leviticus 23:28 (102a); *Yad, Teshuvah* 1:3; *Menorath HaMaor* 5:2:2:3 (297).
53. *Kerithoth* 7a; *Yerushalmi, Yoma* 8:6 (42a); *Yad, Shegagoth* 3:10; *Orach Chaim* 607:6 in *Hagah.*
54. *Kerithoth* 7a; *Yerushalmi, Yoma* 8:7 (42a); *Yerushalmi, Shevuoth* 1:6 (7a).
55. Also if one sins with the intent that *Yom Kippur* should atone; see above, 15:54, notes 195, 198.
56. *Shevuoth* 13a; *Kerithoth* 7a; *Yad, Shegagoth* 3:9.
57. *Cf. Yerushalmi, Yoma* 8:7 (42b); *Yerushalmi, Shevuoth* 1:6 (7b), where it is disputed whether the atonement is all day or at the end of the day. The latter opinion is that of *Tosefta, Yoma* 4:15, and this is the opinion of Rabbenu Chananel, *Yoma* 87b; *Shevuoth* 13b; *Sefer Halttur, Hilkhoth Yom Kippur; Rokeach* 217; *Tosafoth, Shevuoth* 13a *s.v. DeAvad;* Rashba, Ritva, *ibid.; Minchath Chinukh* 364 (272c). *Cf. Kerithoth* 6:4 (25a); *Megillah* 20b; *Yad, Shegagoth* 3:9; *Kethuvoth* 103b.
58. *Chokhmath Shlomo, Orach Chaim* 623:2; *Menorath HaMaor* 5:2:2:3 (297). *Cf. Tosafoth, Shabbath* 114b *s.v. VeAmai; Sefer Mitzvoth Gadol,* Negative Commandment 69 (24c); *Orach Chaim* 623:6; *Turey Zahav* 623:2; *Beer Hetiv* 623:6; "Rav" *Shulchan Arukh* 623:14; *Mishnah Berurah* 623:12; *Chazay Adam* 145:37; *Kitzur Shulchan Arukh* 133:26.
59. *Berakhoth* 5a; *Mekhilta* on Exodus 20:20 (72b); *Reshith Chokhmah, Shaar HaTeshuvah* 3 (111c); *Radak* on Jeremiah 2:22; *Menorath HaMaor* 5:3:1:2 (299).
60. *Cf. Radak ad. loc.;* 2 Samuel 7:14. See note 15.
61. *Ibid.;* Rabbenu Yonah, *Shaarey Teshuvah* 4:11. Sins punishable by death at the hand of God are also in this category; *cf. Mekhilta loc. cit.* (73a); *Asarah Maamaroth* 1:1:18; *Minchath Chinukh* 364 (272d).
62. *Chovoth HaLevavoth* 7:8; *Minchath Chinukh* 364 (271b). *Cf. Yoma* 86a; *Shevuoth* 13b; *Mekhilta loc. cit.; Yad, Teshuvah* 1:2; *Kesef Mishneh ad. loc.;* see below, note 91.

17:15 Sins punishable by *Kareth* and more severe penalties cause one's soul to be cut off from its spiritual source.[63] This kind of damage cannot be repaired without loosening the grasp of the material on the soul[64] through the weakening of the physical by suffering.[65] Suffering thereby frees the soul from its material bonds, and allows it to become rejoined to its spiritual source.[66] Like a sacrifice, suffering therefore reconciles the spiritual in man with the material.[67]

17:16 Suffering is sent by God as a sign that one's repentance has been accepted,[68] and for this reason a penitent may occasionally suffer an undue degree of anguish.[69] Suffering can also serve as a warning for one to repent.[70]

17:17 Suffering only serves to atone for sin when one repents[71] and accepts it as such.[72] Furthermore, if one repents, it helps to decrease the amount of suffering required for atonement.[73]

17:18 Suffering can take many forms, such as sickness,[74] poverty,[75] exile,[76] or the death of one's children.[77] It can also come as the death of religious leaders, which causes anguish for all mankind.[78]

17:19 A person can avert suffering by the hand of God by imposing it upon himself in the form of fasting and other self

63. See above, 13:48.
64. Just as salt removes the blood from meat (where salt represents suffering, meat represents the physical, and blood represents the soul); *cf. Berakhoth* 5a; *Zohar* 3:153a; *Reshith Chokhmah, Shaar HaTeshuvah* 3 (111c).
65. Maharal, *Nethivoth Olam, Nethiv HaTeshuvah* 3 (156b), *Nethiv HaYissurin* 1 (174a).
66. Like the breaking of a tooth which releases a slave from servitude; *Berakhoth* 5a; *Yalkut Shimoni* 1:339; *Nethivoth Olam ibid.* (175b).
67. *Mekhilta* on Exodus 20:20 (73a); *Reshith Chokhmah, Shaar HaTeshuvah* 3 (111c). See above, 13:25.
68. *Likutey Amarim, Iggereth HaTeshuvah* 1 (91a).
69. *Cf. Emunoth VeDeyoth* 5:6 (72b); *Sefer Chasidim* 613.
70. *Menorath HaMaor* 5:3:1:1 (298).
71. See above, 17:4.
72. *Berakhoth* 5a; *Yalkut Shimoni* 2:338.
73. *Tana DeBei Eliahu Rabbah* 18; *Reshith Chokhmah, Shaar HaTeshuvah* 3 (112a). *Cf. Avoth* 4:11; see above, 15:68.
74. *Berakhoth* 5b; *Mekhilta* on Exodus 20:20 (73a).
75. *Pesikta* 25 (165a).
76. *Sanhedrin* 37b.
77. *Berakhoth* 5b; Maharal, *Nethivoth Olam, Nethiv HaYissurin* 2 (176b f.). *Cf. Shabbath* 33b.
78. *Moed Katan* 25a, 28a; *Yerushalmi, Yoma* 1:1 (2a); *Shemoth Rabbah* 35:4; *VaYikra Rabbah* 27:7 (end); *Tanchuma, VeYakhel* 9; *Pesikta* 27 (174b); *Sh'nei Luchoth HaB'rith, Mesekheth Taanith* 2:137a; *Kli Yakar* on Numbers 20:1. *Cf. Sanhedrin* 39a.

mortification.[79] This is what the prophet meant when he said, "Yet even now, says God, you must return to Me with all your heart, with fasting, with weeping, and with lamentation. Tear your hearts, not your clothing, and return to God your Lord, for He is kind and merciful, slow to anger and great in love, forgiving evil" (Joel 2:12-13).[80] In a sense, fasting can take the place of sacrifice, where one's own flesh is offered in place of the animal's,[81] thereby strengthening the spiritual in man.[82] However, fasting alone, without repentance, is of no avail.[83]

17:20 One can similarly undertake other forms of self mortification[84] such as self exile.[85] In order to atone for a sin completely, one must undertake suffering equal to the enjoyment gained by the sin[86] and also equal to the punishment prescribed for it.[87]

17:21 There are other things that diminish a person materially, and which thereby can take the place of suffering. One such thing is charity, which is a good deed that diminishes one's material possessions.[88] Another is the study of Torah, in which one serves God while minimizing the amount of time spent on one's material wellbeing.[89]

17:22 There are four sins, however, which can only be forgiven

---

79. Rabbenu Yonah, *Shaarey Teshuvah* 4:12; *Likutey Amarim, Iggereth HaTeshuvah* 1 (91a); *Shivechey HaRan* 9; *Sichoth HaRan* 160-162.
80. *Ibid.; cf. Menorath HaMaor* 5:1:3:1 (285). *Cf. Sh'nei Luchoth HaB'rith, Mesekheth Rosh HaShanah, Amud HaDin* 2:158b, who writes that one should take account of one's physical condition before undertaking fasts; *cf.* 2 Samuel 12:16; 1 Kings 21:17. See also *Cheredim, Teshuvah* 3 (p. 214); *Likutey Amarim, Iggereth HaTeshuvah* 3 (92b); *Sefer Baal Shem Tov, Mishpatim* 17.
81. *Berakhoth* 17a; *Orach Chaim* 565:4; *Menorath HaMaor* 5:1:3:1 (285); *Zohar* 2:20b, 2:119b, 2:153a; *Zohar Chadash* 80a.
82. Maharal, *Nethivoth Olam, Nethiv HaTeshuvah* 7 (167a).
83. *Midrash Tehillim* 25:5 (end).
84. *Cf.* 1 Kings 21:27; Jonah 3:5; Nehemiah 9:1; *Reshith Chokhmah, Shaar HaTeshuvah* 5 (117d*f.*), quoting *Sefer HaKaneh*.
85. *Berakhoth* 56a; *Sanhedrin* 37b; *Zohar* 3:216a. *Cf. Yad, Teshuvah* 2:4; *Eduth* 12:9; *Yoreh Deah* 119:18 in *Hagah; Choshen Mishpat* 34:34.
86. This is called *Teshuvath HaMishkal,* literally "measured repentance"; *Rokeach* 6, 8; *Kol Bo* 67; *Sefer Chasidim* 167; *Sh'nei Luchoth HaB'rith, Mesekheth Rosh HaShanah, Amud HaDin* 2:158a.
87. This is *Teshuvath HaKathuv; Rokeach* 7, 11.
88. *Berakhoth* 5b; Rabbenu Yonah, *Shaarey Teshuvah* 4:11. See above, 15:25.
89. *Ibid. Cf. VaYikra Rabbah* 25:1; *Sanhedrin* 26b, 99b.

through suffering, no matter how completely one repents. All of these are derived from scripture.[90] They are, swearing falsely, bearing false witness, bloodshed, and adultery. Swearing falsely, as the Torah states: "God will not allow the one who takes His name in vain to go unpunished" (Exodus 20:7).[91] Bearing false witness: "A false witness will not go unpunished" (Proverbs 19:5).[92] Bloodshed: "Those guilty of bloodshed will not go unpunished" (Joel 4:21).[93] Adultery: "Anyone who goes in to his neighbor's wife — whoever touches her — will not go unpunished" (Proverbs 6:29).[94]

17:23 Some sins are not atoned except by death, as God told His prophet, "Surely they will not be forgiven for this sin until they die" (Isaiah 22:14).[95] This category includes anything that maligns our religion,[96] thereby diminishing God's glory and desecrating His name.[97]

17:24 Since all things were created for God's glory,[98] and one must be ready to give his life for this,[99] one who desecrates God's name is not even worthy of existence, much less so, of God's mercy.[100] Therefore, the spiritual damage done by this sin cannot be repaired as long as one has any relationship with the material world, and there can be no atonement except with death.[101]

---

90. *Emunoth VeDeyoth* 5:6 (72b); *Chovoth HaLevavoth* 7:4; *Sefer Chasidim* 613, where these scriptural sources are given. For others, see *Tana DeBei Eliahu Rabbah* 15 (76a).
91. See note 62; *Shevuoth* 39a.
92. *Cf.* Ralbag, *Metzudoth David, ad. loc. Cf. Zohar* 3:44b.
93. *Cf. Tosefta, Peah* 1:2; see above 14:13, note 40; *Sanhedrin* 7a.
94. *Ibid.; cf. Sanhedrin* 107a; *Shemoth Rabbah* 16:2; *Zohar* 3:44b; *Tosafoth, Sotah* 4b *s.v. Hee.* See above, 15:53.
95. *Cf.* Radak *ad. loc.* See above, note 15; *Zohar* 1:273a, 3:121a, 3:307b. *Cf. Tanchuma, VaYeshev* 2; *Pirkey Rabbi Eliezer* 38 (89b), who apply this to the selling of Joseph, but see Radal *ad. loc.* 38:89, that this was also considered a desecration of God's name. Some say that this passage refers to a second death in the future world; *cf. Targum Yonathan,* Rashi, Mahari Kara, Radak, *ad. loc.;* Radal *loc. cit.* 38:90. Also see *Zohar* 3:44b, where this is applied to adultery.
96. *Cf. Yoma* 86a, Rashi *ad. loc. s.v. Chillul HaShem, BeEmor Lahem;* see above, 2:19.
97. See above, 2:20; *Rokeach* 28; Rabbenu Yonah, *Shaarey Teshuvah* 4:4.
98. See Volume 1, 3:5.
99. See above, 3:2.
100. Maharal, *Nethivoth Olam, Nethiv HaTeshuvah* 3 (156b).
101. *Ibid.;* Rabbenu Yonah, *Shaarey Teshuvah* 4:4.

17:25   However, like all other sins, even the desecration of God's name can be atoned by doing the exact opposite of the sin.[102] Therefore, if a person sanctifies God's name, bringing many people to serve Him, this sin can be atoned even during one's lifetime.[103] Similarly, devoting oneself to the study of the Torah, which strengthens Godliness in the world generally,[104] can bring atonement even for the sin of desecrating God's name.[105]

17:26   If one repents[106] and confesses,[107] death atones for all his sins.[108] Therefore, even a very wicked person who repents before death is absolved from all suffering beyond death,[109] and is treated like the righteous with regard to mourning and burial.[110] If he does not repent, however, his sins are not atoned. Regarding this, it is written, "Their sins shall remain [engraved] on their bones" (Ezekiel 32:27).[111]

17:27   However, if a very wicked person is murdered[112] or executed by government authorities,[113] all his sins are atoned even without repentance and confession,[114] because of the anguish and terror of

---

102. See above, 15:24.
103. Rabbenu Yonah, *Shaarey Teshuvah* 4:5, 4:16.
104. *Cf. Likutey Amarim (Tanya), Sefer Shel Benonim* 6 (10b); see above, 15:25.
105. *Shaarey Teshuvah* 4:16. *Cf. Mekhilta* on Exodus 20:7 (69a), that the sin of Eli's sons, which involved the desecration of God's name, is not atoned except with death, while according to *Rosh HaShanah* 18a it is atoned through selfless devotion to the learning of Torah; see above, 15:25, note 89.
106. *Sifri, Yalkut Shimoni* (1:749), on Numbers 15:31. However, see above, 13:50, that sins punishable by premature death can be atoned even without repentance.
107. See above, 16:21, 16:25.
108. *Yoma* 8:8 (85b); *Avoth DeRabbi Nathan* 39:1; *Mekhilta loc. cit.; Shaarey Teshuvah* 4:20. *Cf.* Rashi, *Me'ilah* 3:1 (10b) *s.v. V'lad; Sefer Chasidim* 170, 1171. See above, 15:46, note 161, that for this reason no other atonement is needed after death. See *Minchath Chinukh* 364 (272d) for discussion whether only untimely death atones completely, and (273d) whether death atones for sins against man, and if forgiving a person helps after he dies. See *Sefer Chasidim* 167, that one should never tell a penitent to kill himself.
109. *Tosafoth, Shevuoth* 13a *s.v. BeOmed;* Rosh, *Rosh HaShanah* 1:5.
110. *Sifethey Cohen, Yoreh Deah* 345:8; *Chokhmath Adam* 156:3.
111. Rashi, Mahari Kara, *ad. loc.; Yalkut Shimoni* 1:749, quoting *Sifri loc. cit.*
112. *Sifri* on Numbers 15:31; *Kitzur Shulchan Arukh* 201:5; *Teshuvoth Chatham Sofer, Yoreh Deah* 333.
113. *Yoreh Deah* 345:2 in *Hagah;* HaGra *ad. loc.* 345:2; *Sifethey Cohen, Yoreh Deah* 345:8.
114. *Koheleth Rabbah* 4:2; Ramban, *Torath HaAdam* 10b; *Sifethey Cohen, Yoreh Deah* 345:8.

such a death.[115] Therefore, even an apostate[116] who meets such a death should be treated like the righteous.[117]

17:28 The first three times that a person commits a sin, his repentance is readily accepted. This is what the wise Elihu meant when he said to Job, "Yes, God does all these things with a man, twice, three times, in order to bring his soul back from destruction and illuminate him with the light of life" (Job 33:29-30).[118] However, after committing a sin[119] more than three times,[120] a person is considered a habitual sinner,[121] greatly reinforcing the spiritual damage of the sin,[122] and making both repentance[123] and atonement[124] more

115. *Sanhedrin* 47b (top); *Midrash Tehillim* 79:3; Rabbenu Yonah, *Shaarey Teshuvah* 4:20; Rashi on Psalms 79:2.

116. *Sifethey Cohen, Yoreh Deah* 340:9.

117. *Hagahoth Asheri,* cited in *Hagah, Yoreh Deah* 340:5; *Sifethey Cohen* 340:10; *Turey Zahav* 340:3; *Beer Hetiv* 340:7; *Yoreh Deah* 376:4 in *Hagah* (end); *Sifethey Cohen* 376:15; *Turey Zahav* 376:6; *Beer Hetiv* 376:12; *Chokhmath Adam* 156:3; *Kitzur Shulchan Arukh* 201:5.

118. *Yoma* 86b; *Tosefta, Yoma* 4:12; *Yalkut Shimoni* 2:519. However, others apply this to the exiles or reincarnations of the soul; *cf. Zohar* 2:114b, 3:178b; *Tikuney Zohar* 6 (22b), 26 (72a), 32 (76b), 69 (100b). For other interpretations, see *Yerushalmi, Peah* 1:1 (5b); *Yerushalmi, Kiddushin* 1:9 (23a); *Yerushalmi, Sanhedrin* 10:1 (49a); *Yerushalmi, Shevuoth* 1:6 (7b); *Moreh Nevukhim* 3:23.

119. For discussion whether this must be the same sin repeated; *cf. Sefer Tosefoth Yom HaKippurim,* cited in *Anaf Yosef* on *Eyn Yaakov, Yoma* 76. According to Maharsha, *Yoma* 86b *s.v. Paam,* it only refers to the same sin, and this appears to be the opinion of Rosh, *Yoma* 3:17. However, according to *Yad,* Raavad, *Teshuvah* 3:5, it appears to refer to all sins.

120. If one does not repent in between; *Emunoth VeDeyoth* 5:5 (72b); *Nitzotzey Oroth, Zohar* 3:101a no. 1. However, *Minchath Chinukh* 364 (272c) maintains that repentance is not enough, and that atonement is required in between. See above, 17:3.

121. Maharal, *Nethivoth Olam, Nethiv HaTeshuvah* 3 (155b); *Tana DeBei Eliahu Rabbah* 15 (76b). *Cf. Tur, Orach Chaim* 389, *Yoreh Deah* 119, quoting *Teshuvoth Rashba; Mishneh LeMelekh, Shegagoth* 3:7; see above, 13:56. See also *Yevamoth* 64b, *Tosafoth ibid.* 65a *s.v. VeShor HaMu'ad;* Rosh 6:14, that a presumption is established after three times.

122. *Cf. Pirkey Rabbi Eliezer* 15 (36a); *Yalkut Shimoni* 2:519; *Zohar* 1:73b, 3:101a; *Zohar Chadash* 69b; *Baaley Tosafoth* on Deuteronomy 30:3.

123. *Shemoth Rabbah* 13:3. *Cf. Avoth DeRabbi Nathan* 40:5, where this is related to sinning with the intent to repent.

124. There are two basic opinions regarding this. Rosh, *Yoma* 8:17, writes that this is harsher than above in our text (17:4), and that after three times, *Yom Kippur* is required to atone violations of positive commandments, and suffering for negatives. On the other hand, Raavad, *Teshuvah* 3:5, writes that this is more lenient than 17:4, and that suffering is not required until after three violations even for sins punishable by *Kareth* and death. However, there is a third opinion, that does not relate *Yoma* 86b to atonement at all, but to heavenly judgment; *cf.* Rif, *Rosh HaShanah* 4a; Ran *ad. loc. s.v. Nossey Avon; Yad, Teshuvah* 3:5; *Migdal Oz, Kesef Mishneh, Lechem Mishneh, ad. loc.;* Rosh, *Rosh HaShanah* 1:5. *Cf. Zohar* 3:216a; Radal (on *Pirkey Rabbi Eliezer*) 15:22. Also see *Korban Nethanel, Yoma* (Rosh 8:17) no. 80, from *Sanhedrin* 43b.

difficult.[125] Accordingly, the prophet says, "Thus says God: For three transgressions of Israel, I will reverse the punishment, but for the fourth, I will not reverse it" (Amos 2:4).[126] After three times, repentance no longer helps to spare one from punishment in this world.[127]

17:29 Many diseases can be cured painlessly by wonder drugs that only attack the cause of the illness without harming the body, rather than by general cures which may be both painful and drawn out. The same is true of atonement. Although many sins may ordinarily require difficult and painful atonements, there are some things which have the power to erase all sin completely and yet painlessly.[128]

17:30 Since sin tends to diminish Godliness, both in the world and in one's soul,[129] things which bear definite witness to God in this world tend to erase sin. Therefore, one who says the response to the *Kaddish,* "May His great Name be blessed for ever and ever,"[130] with all his strength and intention[131] is forgiven all his sins,[132] since this prayer was composed as an acknowledgment of God's absolute sovereignty.

17:31 Similarly, one who keeps the Sabbath with exemplary care is forgiven all his sins,[133] since this bears witness to God's act

125. And after three times, one is also judged for his previous sins; *Shemoth Rabbah* 7:2; *Binah LeItim* 12, quoted in *Anaf Yosef loc. cit.*
126. *Cf.* Rif, *Yoma* 5b; *Yad, Teshuvah* 3:5, who relate this only to a congregation, which is forgiven their first three sins, whereas an individual is only forgiven his first two. *Cf.* Maharsha, *Korban Nethanel,* Radal, *loc. cit.*
127. *Sanhedrin* 7a; Rashi *ad. loc. s.v. A'Trey; Shemoth Rabbah* 13:3; *Emunoth VeDeyoth* 5:5 (72b); Rosh, Raavad, *loc. cit.; Tanchuma, BeHar* 3.
128. *Cheredim, Teshuvah* 7 (p. 258); *Sh'nei Luchoth HaB'rith, Teshuvah* 2:189a, where all cases in 17:30-33 are given.
129. See Volume 1, 5:50-51.
130. *Cf. Berakhoth* 3a; *Targum Yonathan* on Genesis 49:1, Deuteronomy 6:4.
131. Rashi, *Shabbath* 119b *s.v. BeKol Kocho; Tosafoth ibid. Kol;* Maharsha *ibid.;* Rabbenu Yonah, *Berakhoth* (Rif 13b) *s.v. BeKol; Yad, Tefillin* 9:1; *Orach Chaim* 56:1; *Zohar* 1:38b, 1:62b, 2:129b; *Tikuney Zohar,* introduction (13a), 22 (68b); *Teshuvoth Yaskil Avdi, Orach Chaim* 1:4.
132. *Shabbath* 119b; *Yalkut Shimoni* 2:46; Rif, *Berakhoth* 13b; Rosh 3:19; *Tur, Orach Chaim* 26; *Kitzur Shulchan Arukh* 15:5; *Mishnah Berurah* 56:1; *Zohar* 3:20a; *Tikuney Zohar,* introduction (4b), 19 (40a); *Tikuney Zohar Chadash* 111c; *Cheredim, Teshuvah* 7 (p. 259 top).
133. *Shabbath* 118b; *Midrash Tehillim* 92:2; *Pirkey Rabbi Eliezer* 18 (44a); *Tur, Orach*

of creation.[134] Similarly, one who jubilantly praises God for his miracles, such as in the Song of the Red Sea,[135] is forgiven all his sins.[136]

17:32 God acts toward a person as he acts toward others,[137] and therefore one who is always ready and willing to forgive others is forgiven all his sins.[138]

17:33 One who establishes a particularly close relationship with God is forgiven just like a child. Therefore, one who secludes himself to commune with God[139] is forgiven his sins.[140] The heartfelt recital of King David's Psalms is particularly suited for this type of communion.[141] Similarly, one who listens attentively to sermons preaching the love and fear of God is granted forgiveness.[142]

17:34 One who changes his station in life is given a fresh start by God, and is forgiven all his sins. Therefore, one who is ordained or appointed to a position of leadership has complete atonement.[143] Similarly, a bride and bridegroom are forgiven all their sins on their wedding day,[144] and for this reason it is customary for them to fast on this auspicious day.[145]

17:35 While the Temple stood, the various sacrifices offered complete

Chaim 242; *Turey Zahav* 242:0; *Cheredim loc. cit. Cf. Mekhilta* on Exodus 16:28 (50b).

134. *Cf.* Exodus 3:13, 3:17; Ezekiel 20:12, 20:20; *Menachoth* 36b.
135. Exodus 15; Daily Prayer Book, Morning Service.
136. *Midrash Tehillim* 18:6; *Cheredim loc. cit. Cf. Shemoth Rabbah* 24:3; *Shir HaShirim Rabbah* 4:3; *Yalkut Shimoni* 1:254, 2:60; Rashi on Judges 6:1.
137. See below, note 205.
138. *Rosh HaShanah* 17a; *Megillah* 28a; *Yoma* 23a, 87b; *Menorath HaMaor* 5:1:2:3 (282); *Cheredim loc. cit.*
139. This is called *Hithbodeduth.* See Volume 1, 6:23, notes 60, 65. *Cf. Cheredim, Teshuvah* 3 (p. 215); Rabbi Nachman of Breslev, *Hishtap'khuth HaNefesh,* introduction (p. 13), 2 (p. 43); in English, Rabbi Kaplan's translation, *Outpouring of the Soul,* p. 20 *ff. Cf. Berakhoth* 5:1 (30b); Sforno on Genesis 35:1.
140. *Cheredim, Teshuvah* 7 (p. 260).
141. *Cf. Tikkun HaKelali* (Rabbi Nachman of Breslev), that an atonement for sin, especially sexual sins, is the reading of the ten Psalms: 16, 32, 41, 43, 59, 76, 90, 105, 137, 150.
142. *Cheredim loc. cit.*
143. *Sanhedrin* 14a; Maharsha, Maharatz Chajas, *ad. loc.; Yerushalmi, Bikkurim* 3:3 (11b); *Yalkut Shimoni* 2:117. *Cf. Yoma* 22a; *Targum Yonathan,* Radak, on 1 Samuel 13:1.
144. *Yerushalmi, Bikkurim loc. cit.; Magen Avraham* 573:0; *Beth Sh'muel (Bash)* 61:6; *Beer Hetiv, Evven HaEzer* 61:5; *Chokhmath Adam* 129:2; *Kitzur Shulchan Arukh* 146:1; *Mishnah Berurah* 573:8.
145. *Orach Chaim* 573:1 in *Hagah; Evven HaEzer* 61:1 in *Hagah.*

atonement, since it was for that reason that they were specified for particular sins.[146] Similarly, the *Yom Kippur* scapegoat completely atoned for the sins of all Israel, since it symbolized the destruction of all evil.[147] In a like manner, the punishments administered by the courts offered complete atonement, since they were ordained as such.[148] However, here too, the prerequisite for all these atonements was repentance and confession.[149]

17:36 When a person sins against God alone, God alone can forgive him. But when one sins against another human being, then he must first make the necessary restitution and gain forgiveness from the one he has wronged.[150] Neither repentance,[151] nor *Yom Kippur,*[152] nor death itself,[153] can wipe out a sin until forgiveness has been earnestly sought from the one against whom it was committed.

17:37 Every sin against man is also a sin against God.[154] However, even the sin against God is not forgiven until forgiveness has been gained for the sin against one's fellow.[155] Therefore, although one is required to confess such sins before God,[156] one's confession is not valid until restitution has been made and the victim's forgiveness obtained.[157]

17:38 If a person has hurt another in any way, he must seek

146. *Yoma* 8:8 (85b); *Minchath Chinukh* 364 (272a); *Likutey Amarim, Iggereth HaTeshuvah* 2 (91b). *Cf.* Leviticus 5:26, 5:31, 5:35, 5:10, 5:13, 5:16, 5:18, 15:30; Numbers 15:25, etc.
147. Leviticus 16:22; *Shevuoth* 1:6 (2b); *Yad, Teshuvah* 1:2; *Chinukh* 364; *Minchath Chinukh* 364 (272b, 273b).
148. See above, 13:52, note 181; *Minchath Chinukh loc. cit.* (272b).
149. See above, 16:4; Rashi, *Yoma* 8:8 (85b) *s.v. Chatath. Cf. Berakhoth* 23a; *Targum* on Ecclesiastes 4:17.
150. *Rosh HaShanah* 17b; Maharatz Chajas *ad. loc.; Emunoth VeDeyoth* 5:6 (73a); *Menorath HaMaor* 5:1:2:4 (283).
151. *Yad, Teshuvah* 2:9; *Sefer Chasidim* 23.
152. *Ibid.; Yoma* 8:8 (85b); *Sifra* on Leviticus 16:30 (83a); Rabbenu Yonah, *Shaarey Teshuvah* 4:18; *Orach Chaim* 606:1; *Chayay Adam* 144:5; *Kitzur Shulchan Arukh* 131:4.
153. *Minchath Chinukh* 364 (273).
154. *Pri Megadim, Eshel Avraham* 606:1. For a discussion whether rape and seduction are considered sins against man; *cf. Pri Chadash* 606:1, citing *Maharik Shoresh* 129; *Pri Megadim, Mishbetzoth Zahav* 606:1.
155. *Pri Chadash* 606:1, citing Rabbi Sh'muel Garmison; *Pri Megadim, Minchath Chinukh, loc. cit.*
156. See above, 16:3.
157. Rabbenu Yonah, *Shaarey Teshuvah* 1:45, 4:18. *Cf. Bava Kama* 9:12 (110a); *Yad, Gezelah* 8:13.

forgiveness even though he has made monetary restitution for the injury.[158] Similarly, if one robs another, besides making restitution, he must also seek forgiveness for the anguish caused by the robbery.[159] In the case of purely monetary damage, however, where there was no intent to hurt the victim, monetary restitution is a complete atonement.[160]

17:39 In order to repent, one must make complete restitution for any theft or damage.[161] If the injured person is not to be found, however, one need not seek him out,[162] but can leave the restitution money with a competent rabbinical court (*Beth Din,* בֵּית דִין),[163] and thus obtain complete atonement.[164]

17:40 For repentance to be complete, one must cleanse himself of the taint of any illegal gain, even where restitution is not required by law.[165] Therefore, if one has stolen from or hurt a number of persons, and does not know which, he must make restitution to all in order to repent completely.[166] Similarly, he must make good all loss, as well as any pain and shame, that may have resulted from his action.[167] He must also make restitution for all profits or any other benefits he may have accumulated as a result of the act.[168] Even if stolen land has been in one's family for many generations, one is considered responsible, and is required to return it.[169]

158. *Bava Kama* 8:7 (92a); *Yad, Chovel* 5:9; *Choshen Mishpat* 422:1; *Rokeach* 16; *Menorath HaMaor* 5:1:2:4 (283); *Sh'nei Luchoth HaB'rith, Mesekheth Rosh HaShanah, Amud HaDin* 2:160b.
159. *Yad, Teshuvah* 2:9; *Lechem Mishneh, Chovel* 5:9.
160. *Yad, Chovel* 5:9. *Cf. Sanhedrin* 4:5 (37a); *Yad, Sanhedrin* 12:3.
161. *Yoma* 87a; *Bava Metzia* 115a; *Bava Bathra* 173b.
162. *Bava Kama* 104a; *Yad, Gezelah* 7:9; *Choshen Mishpat* 367:1; *Sifethey Cohen* 367:1; *Beer Hetiv* 367:1; *Sefer Chasidim* 597. *Sefer Meirath Eynayim* (367:2) writes that this was legislated as an aid to repentance, but *Sifethey Cohen* (367:2) disputes this, and maintains that the Torah itself absolves one from this. It is only when one has sworn falsely that he must seek out his victim; *Bava Kama* 9:5 (103a); *Bava Metzia* 4:7 (55a).
163. *Bava Kama* 9:5 (103a); *Yad, Gezelah* 7:10; *Choshen Mishpat* 367:2.
164. *Ibid. Cf. Tosafoth, Bava Kama* 103a *s.v. Aval.*
165. *Sefer Chasidim* 599, 628.
166. See above, 15:52, note 187.
167. *Sefer Chasidim* 598. *Cf. Sanhedrin* 4:5 (37a); *Bereshith Rabbah* 22:21; Rashi on Genesis 4:10.
168. *Sefer Chasidim loc. cit.*
169. *Sefer Chasidim* 595. *Cf. Sukkah* 30b, 31a; *Bava Kama* 95a; *Bava Bathra* 44a; *Yad, Gezelah* 8:14; *Choshen Mishpat* 371:1.

17:41   If there is any question as to whether or not one is required to make restitution, or as to the amount, he should seek the advice of a rabbi. Since he may be tempted to act to his own advantage, he should not rely on his own subjective judgment.[170]

17:42   Even if a person was a professional thief or robber, the doors of repentance are not closed to him. In order to make it easier for such an individual to change his ways and repent, our sages legislated that one should not accept restitution from a professional[171] thief[172] or userer,[173] but forgive him without any repayment.[174] However, even they must return any article illegally in their possession,[175] unless its return would cause great expense or inconvenience.[176] Similarly, if they do not repent on their own, but are forced by the courts, all illegal monies in their possession must be returned.[177] Although the law frowns upon one who accepts restitution from them,[178] it is permitted to do so if one needs it to repay his own debts.[179]

17:43   Nevertheless, even a professional thief or userer must make full restitution in order to repent completely before God,[180] and therefore, if he insists upon making restitution, it may be accepted.[181]

17:44   If a thief wishes to repent and voluntarily returns a stolen

170. *Chayay Adam* 144:6; *Kitzur Shulchan Arukh* 131:4; *Mishnah Berurah* 606:1.
171. *Tosafoth, Bava Kama* 94b *s.v. BeYemey Rebbi;* Rosh 9:2; *Hagahoth Maimonioth, Malveh* 4:5 no. 4; *Yoreh Deah* 161:7; *Hagah, Choshen Mishpat* 366:1.
172. *Bava Kama* 94b; *Tosefta, Shevi'ith* 8:12; *Yerushalmi, Shevi'ith* 10:4 (30b); *Yad, Gezelah* 1:13; *Choshen Mishpat* 366:1.
173. *Ibid.; Yad, Malveh* 4:5; *Yoreh Deah* 161:7.
174. For other cases, see below, note 176; *Chullin* 5a; *Chovoth HaLevavoth* 7:9; *Yad, Gezelah* 2:2, *Nizkey Mamon* 5:10; *Teshuvoth Radbaz* 528. For a Biblical source for such legislation, see *Sefer Chasidim* 539.
175. *Rif, Bava Kama* 33b; Rosh 9:2; *Yad, Yoreh Deah, Choshen Mishpat, loc. cit.*
176. *Sefer Meirath Eynayim (Sema)* 366:2; *Beer Hetiv* 366:2. *Cf. Gittin* 5:5 (55a); *Eduyyoth* 7:9; *Bava Kama* 66b, 95a; *Yad, Gezelah* 1:5; *Choshen Mishpat* 360:1.
177. Rosh, *Yad, loc. cit.; Choshen Mishpat* 366:1 in *Hagah; Sifethey Cohen, Yoreh Deah* 161:12.
178. *Cf.* Rashi, *Bava Kama* 94b *s.v. Ein Ruach;* Rambam on *Mishnah Shevi'ith* 10:9; *Tosefoth Yom Tov* on *Avoth* 3:13; *Sefer Meirath Eynayim (Sema)* 366:3.
179. *Sefer Chasidim* 1082; *Makor Chesed ad. loc.* 1082:2; *Sifethey Cohen, Choshen Mishpat* 366:1; *Beer Hetiv* 366:3; *Mishneh LeMelekh, Malveh* 4:4 (end).
180. *Choshen Mishpat* 366:1; *Chokhmath Shlomo ad. loc.; Sifethey Cohen, Yoreh Deah* 161:13.
181. *Sefer Meirath Eynayim (Sema)* 366:4; *Beer Hetiv* 366:4. *Cf. Shevi'ith* 10:8; *Yad, Shemittah* 9:28; *Choshen Mishpat* 67:36.

article or money, his victim is advised not to reveal the name and identity of the guilty party in order to make his repentance easier.[182] However, if others are suspected, the thief himself should publicly confess in order to clear their names.[183]

17:45 One must seek forgiveness separately from each person whom he has wronged.[184] If he asks forgiveness from a group in general, and knows that he has wronged a member of the group in particular, he has not fulfilled his obligation.[185]

17:46 One should first attempt to seek forgiveness from the person wronged by himself.[186] In doing so, he should also specify the wrong,[187] unless it is likely that this would embarrass the other.[188] However, one should not attempt to gain forgiveness while the other is still angry at him.[189]

17:47 It is preferable to seek forgiveness by oneself rather than through an intermediary.[190] However, if it is difficult to do so alone, or if there is more likelihood in gaining forgiveness, one may request the assistance of an intermediary.[191]

17:48 If one is not successful in gaining forgiveness by himself,[192] he should return three times, bringing three friends each time.[193] In

---

182. *Sefer Chasidim* 630.
183. *Ibid.* See above, 16:15.
184. *Yoma* 87a; *Yad, Teshuvah* 2:9; *Orach Chaim* 606:1; Rabbenu Yonah, *Shaarey Teshuvah* 4:19.
185. *Mishnah Berurah* 606:3, quoting *Matteh Ephraim. Cf. Minchath Chinukh* 364 (273d).
186. See below, note 192.
187. *Kesef Mishneh, Teshuvah* 2:5; *cf.* Rashi, *Yoma* 86b *s.v. Averoth.*
188. *Magen Avraham* 606:0; *Machtzith HaShekel ad. loc.;* HaGra *ibid.; Beer Hetiv* 606:3; *"Rav" Shulchan Arukh* 606:1; *Mishnah Berurah* 606:3.
189. *Berakhoth* 7b.
190. *Sh'nei Luchoth HaB'rith* 2:160b, 2:166b, quoting Ibn Chaviv; *Machtzith HaShekel* 606:0; *Pri Chadash* 606:1.
191. *Kitzur Shulchan Arukh* 131:4; *Mishnah Berurah* 606:2.
192. Rabbenu Yonah, *Shaarey Teshuvah* 4:19; *Biur Halakhah* 601:1 *s.v. Yachzor,* both write that one should go the first time alone; *cf. Yerushalmi, Yoma* 8:7 (42b); *Yerushalmi, Bava Kama* 8:7 (36b); *Yad, Chovel* 5:10; *Choshen Mishpat* 422:1. *Cf. Sefer Chasidim* 44; *Makor Chesed ad. loc.* 44:7, that one should go twice alone before bringing friends, but see *Perush ad. loc.* 44:5, that "twice" may be a misprint. Still others maintain that one should bring three people along the first time; *"Rav" Shulchan Arukh* 606:2; *Reshith Chokhmah, Shaar HaTeshuvah* 7 (126c).
193. *Yoma* 87a; *Yad, Teshuvah* 2:9; *Orach Chaim* 606:1; *"Rav" Shulchan Arukh* 606:2; *Chayay Adam* 144:5; *Shaarey Teshuvah* 4:19; *Reshith Chokhmah, Shaar HaTéshuvah* 7 (126c).

order to gain forgiveness, a different approach may be used each time.[194]

17:49 If forgiveness is not obtained in this manner, he need do no more.[195] Since he has done all that the law requires, he need no longer seek forgiveness, and his sin is atoned by repentance and *Yom Kippur* alone.[196] Regarding this it is written, "He comes before men and declares, 'I have sinned and done wrong, and have gained no benefit therefrom.' Thus he redeems his soul from punishment, and his spirit shall behold the light" (Job 33:27).[197]

17:50 In such a case, one should make it known before ten men that forgiveness was sought according to the law and not granted,[198] so that he not be suspected of refusing to repent.[199] However, if one wishes to, he may seek forgiveness as many times as he wishes,[200] as long as it does not impinge on one's dignity as a scholar.[201]

17:51 However, if one has wronged one of his teachers or rabbis,[202] he is required to seek forgiveness as many times as necessary, until it is granted.[203]

17:52 When one is asked to forgive, he should not be stubborn and refuse,[204] as we are taught that one who readily forgives

194. *Magen Avraham* 606:1, quoting *Bayith Chadash; Beer Hetiv* 606:1; *Mishnah Berurah* 606:3.
195. *Yoma* 87a; *Yad, Teshuvah* 2:9; *Orach Chaim* 606:1.
196. *Pri Chadash* 606:1. *Cf. Tanchuma, VaYera* 30; *Pesikta Rabathai* 39 (165a); *Mordecai, Yoma* 723; *Marah HaPanim* on *Yerushalmi, Yoma* 8:7 (42b) s.v. *Kethiv.*
197. *Yerushalmi, Yoma* 8:7 (42b); *Korban Nethanel ad. loc. s.v. Im; Yerushalmi, Bava Kama* 8:7 (36b).
198. *Tanchuma, Pesikta Rabathai,* Mordecai, cited in note 196; *Orach Chaim* 606:1 in *Hagah;* HaGra *ad. loc. s.v. Mihu; "Rav" Shulchan Arukh* 606:2; *Chayay Adam* 144:5.
199. *"Rav" Shulchan Arukh* 606:2; *Mishnah Berurah* 606:6.
200. Rashi, *Yoma* 87b s.v. *Rav; Turey Zahav* 606:1; *Machtzith HaShekel* 606:2; HaGra, *Orach Chaim* 606:1 s.v. *Mihu; Chayay Adam* 144:5; *Shaar HaTziun* (on *Mishnah Berurah*) 606:6; see below, note 201. However, *Pri Chadash* 606:1, maintains that it is forbidden to go more than three times.
201. *Magen Avraham* 606:2; *Beer Hetiv* 606:2; *Mishnah Berurah* 606:5; *"Rav" Shulchan Arukh* 606:3.
202. Even if it is not his only rabbi; *Magen Avraham* 606:3, citing *Meil Tzedakah* 2:49; *Beer Hetiv* 606:3; *Mishnah Berurah* 606:7.
203. *Yoma* 87b; *Rabbenu Chananel ad. loc.;* Rif 6a; Rosh 8:17; *Yad, Teshuvah* 2:9; *Orach Chaim* 606:1; *"Rav" Shulchan Arukh* 606:3. However, *cf. Kesef Mishneh, Teshuvah* 2:9, that Rashi *ibid. s.v. Rav* explains it in a completely different manner.
204. *Bava Kama* 8:7 (92a); *Yoma* 87b; *Yad, Teshuvah* 2:10, *Chovel* 5:10; *Orach Chaim* 606:1 in *Hagah; Choshen Mishpat* 422:1; *"Rav" Shulchan Arukh* 606:4.

will himself be forgiven,[205] and have his prayers answered.[206] One should therefore forgive even if he was hurt out of spite.[207] It is an act of piety[208] and a true Jewish trait,[209] to forgive immediately, even before being asked.[210] For this reason, it is customary to forgive any hurt or insult before retiring each night.[211]

17:53   However, one may refuse to forgive if it is for the other's own good,[212] in order to cause him to repent more fully,[213] and never repeat the sin.[214] Similarly, one may refuse to forgive if he fears that he will incur a personal loss by doing so.[215] Even in these cases, however, one should forgive in his heart.[216]

17:54   One is not required to forgive a person who has slandered him,[217] since the damage is likely to affect others,[218] and many might hear the slander who will not hear its retraction.[219] Regarding this it is written, "Do not reveal the mystery of another, lest the one who hears betray you, and the slander you spoke not be retracted." (Proverbs 25:9-10).[220] However, even in such a case, it

205. *Yoma* 87b; *Tosefta, Bava Kama* 9:10; *Yerushalmi, Bava Kama* 8:7 (36b); *Mishnah Berurah* 606:8; *Kitzur Shulchan Arukh* 131:4. *Cf. Zohar* 1:71a, 1:229b; *Sefer Chasidim* 607; Maharal, *Nethivoth Olam, Nethiv HaTeshuvah* 7 (1167a); see above, note 137.
206. *Taanith* 25b; *Rokeach* 214; *Kitzur Shulchan Arukh* 131:4, citing *Eliahu Rabbah; cf. Bava Kama* 92a.
207. *Shaar HaTziun* (on *Mishnah Berurah*) 606:8.
208. *Sefer Chasidim* 11.
209. *Yevamoth* 79a; *Yad, Teshuvah* 2:1, *Chovel* 5:10; *Sefer Chasidim* 24; *Choshen Mishpat* 422:1; *Sefer Meirath Eynayim ad. loc.* 422:4.
210. *Tosefta, Bava Kama* 9:11.
211. *Zohar* 1:201b. See above, 16:17, note 64.
212. *Orach Chaim* 606:1 in *Hagah,* from *Yoma* 87b; *Magen Avraham* 606:4; *Turey Zahav* 606:2; *Pri Chadash* 606:1.
213. *Turey Zahav* 606:2; *"Rav" Shulchan Arukh* 606:4; *Mishnah Berurah* 606:9.
214. *Chayay Adam* 144:5.
215. *Magen Avraham* 606:4; *Turey Zahav* 606:2; *Beer Hetiv* 606:4; *"Rav" Shulchan Arukh* 606:4; *Mishnah Berurah* 606:10.
216. *Mishnah Berurah* 606:9; *Shaar HaTziun ad. loc.* 606:10.
217. *Yerushalmi, Bava Kama* 8:7 (36b); Mordecai, *Yoma* 723 (end); *Sefer Mitzvoth Gadol,* Positive Commandment 16 (end); *Hagahoth Maimonioth, Teshuvah* 2:10 no. 9; *Orach Chaim* 606:1 in *Hagah; Sefer Meirath Eynayim, Choshen Mishpat* 422:5; *Beer Hetiv, Choshen Mishpat* 422:1; *Pri Chadash, Orach Chaim* 606:1; *"Rav" Shulchan Arukh* 606:4; *Chayay Adam* 144:5; *Sefer Chasidim* 44; *Sh'nei Luchoth HaB'rith* 2:166b.
218. *Sefer Meirath Eynayim, Choshen Mishpat* 422:6; *Beer Hetiv* 422:1.
219. *Ibid.; Magen Avraham* 606:5, from *Yam Shel Shlomo, Bava Kama* 8:63, quoting Maharai 212; *Mishnah Berurah* 606:11; *"Rav" Shulchan Arukh* 606:4.
220. *Sefer Chasidim* 613, writes that there is no forgiveness for this sin. See Rashi, *Metzudoth David,* HaGra, Malbim, on Proverbs 25:10.

is an act of piety to forgive, and if one does not wish to forgive the other openly, he should at least do so in his heart.[221] One who has been forgiven for slandering should make every effort to publicize the falsehood of the slander.[222]

17:55 If the person against whom one has sinned has died, he should bring ten people[223] to the person's grave,[224] stand barefoot[225] as a sign of penitence,[226] and declare,[227] "I have sinned against the God of Israel, and against this person whom I have wronged."[228] He should also specify the sin,[229] unless it would shame the dead.[230] The people assembled then answer three times, "You are forgiven."[231]

17:56 If one is very far from the person's grave,[232] so that it is difficult to go there in person, one may send an agent, who then must bring ten persons[233] to the gravesite and declare, "I am the agent of X, publicly announcing that he sent me to say that he has sinned

221. *Magen Avraham* 606:5; *Mishnah Berurah* 606:11; *"Rav" Shulchan Arukh* 606:4; *Chayay Adam* 144:5.
222. *Sefer Chasidim* 631.
223. For the significance of the ten; *cf. Pri Chadash* 606:2; *Pri Megadim, Eshel Avraham* 606:7. Also see *Nedarim* 8a; Ran *ad. loc. s.v. Nidahu; Tosafoth,* Rosh, *ibid. s.v. Tzarikh Asarah; Sifethey Cohen, Yoreh Deah* 334:53.
224. *Chayay Adam* 144:5 writes that there is no atonement unless one goes to the grave. *Cf. Emunoth VeDeyoth* 7:6 (73a), however, who does not require this.
225. *Magen Avraham* 606:7; *Beer Hetiv* 606:7; *Mishnah Berurah* 606:14; *"Rav" Shulchan Arukh* 606:5; *Chayay Adam* 144:5; *Kitzur Shulchan Arukh* 131:5.
226. *Cf.* 2 Samuel 15:30; Isaiah 20:2-3; Jeremiah 2:25; *Yoma* 77a; *Moed Katan* 15b; *BaMidbar Rabbah* 3:2; *Orach Chaim* 554:1; *Yoreh Deah* 334:12, 382:1; *Sifethey Cohen* 334:13.
227. *Emunoth VeDeyoth* 7:6 (73a) writes that it should be said three times, because if he was alive and asked in a similar manner without answering, the petitioner would be forgiven automatically.
228. *Yoma* 87a; *Yad, Teshuvah* 2:10; *Orach Chaim* 606:2; *"Rav" Shulchan Arukh, Chayay Adam, Kitzur Shulchan Arukh, loc. cit.; Reshith Chokhmah, Shaar HaTeshuvah* 7 (126c). See *Machtzith HaShekel* 606:7, quoting *Yam Shel Shlomo, Bava Kama* 8:50, that a son may not forgive for his deceased father.
229. *Mishnah Berurah* 606:15, citing *Matteh Ephraim; Kitzur Shulchan Arukh* 131:5. This is also indicated by the wording of *Yad, Teshuvah* 2:11.
230. *Kitzur Shulchan Arukh loc. cit.*
231. *Mishnah Berurah* 606:15, quoting *Eliahu Rabbah; Chayay Adam, Kitzur Shulchan Arukh, loc. cit.*
232. *Choshen Mishpat* 420:38 in *Hagah.* In this case, far is usually considered to be more than 3 "parasangs" or 12 Hebrew miles; *Yam Shel Shlomo, Bava Kama* 8:50; *Magen Avraham* 606:7; *Mishnah Berurah* 607:14; *"Rav" Shulchan Arukh* 606:5; *Chayay Adam, Kitzur Shulchan Arukh, loc. cit.* For an indication of this, *cf. Eruvin* 55b; *Yoma* 75b; Rashi, *Sanhedrin* 5b *s.v. KeNeged; Sifethey Cohen, Yoreh Deah* 242:2.
233. *Ibid.; Machtzith HaShekel, Orach Chaim* 606:7; Rabbi Akiba Eiger *ibid.* However, *cf. Sefer Meirath Eynayim* 420:53, who writes that the agent need only bring two other people from the city; *cf. Shaar HaTziun* (on *Mishnah Berurah*) 606:15, citing *Matteh Ephraim,* that this is a misprint. However, see above, 10:56, note 162.

against the God of Israel and against this person whom he has wronged."[234]

17:57 Just as it is forbidden to slander or curse the living, so is it forbidden to do so to the dead.[235] Therefore, if one has maligned the dead, he must also ask forgiveness.[236] This can be done on the spot where one committed the wrong, and he need not go to the grave.[237]

17:58 Just as it helps to forgive the living, so it helps to forgive the dead.[238]

17:59 If one owes restitution to one who has died, he should give it to his heirs.[239] If there are no heirs, he should deposit the money with a proper rabbinical court,[240] where it will be given to charity,[241] and confess his sin.[242]

17:60 Even though one should always seek forgiveness as soon as practical, it is especially important to do so before *Yom Kippur*.[243] We thus begin the holy day cleansed of all sin,[244] in a spirit of peace and reconciliation.[245]

234. *Kitzur Shulchan Arukh* 131:5; *Mishnah Berurah* 606:14.
235. *Tanchuma, VaEthChanan* 6, cited in Mordecai, *Yoma* 724, *Bava Kama* 106; *Orach Chaim* 606:3; *Choshen Mishpat* 420:38 in *Hagah*; *Sifethey Cohen* 420:6; *Teshuvoth Aaron ibn Chaim* 90, 93, 111. *Cf. Eduyyoth* 5:6; *Berakhoth* 19a; *Yad, Talmud Torah* 6:14; *Yoreh Deah* 334:47.
236. *Choshen Mishpat loc. cit.*
237. *Shiltey Gibborim, Bava Metzia* (Rif 33a); *Magen Avraham* 606:7; *Beer Hetiv* 606:7; *Pri Chadash* 606:2; *Mishnah Berurah* 606:14; "*Rav*" *Shulchan Arukh* 606:7; *Chayay Adam, Kitzur Shulchan Arukh, loc. cit.* However, see Rabbi Akiba Eiger, on *Magen Avraham, Orach Chaim* 606:7, that according to *Yam Shel Shlomo, Bava Kama* 8:50, *Choshen Mishpat loc. cit.*, one must take the most stringent course and go to their gravesite with ten; *cf. Teshuvoth Mahari Weil*, p. 107; *Teshuvoth Rashban, Orach Chaim* 118. However, *cf. Matteh Ephraim* 606:7, that this is only true when one has slandered the dead.
238. *Minchath Chinukh* 364 (273d). See above, note 108.
239. *Bava Kama* 9:5 (103a); *Tosefta* 10:6; *Yad, Teshuvah* 2:11, *Gezelah* 8:1; *Choshen Mishpat* 367:4.
240. See above, note 163.
241. *Sefer Meirath Eynayim (Sema)* 367:18. *Cf. Bava Kama* 109a; *Yad, Gezelah* 8:4; *Choshen Mishpat* 367:6; *Pith'chey Teshuvah* 367:2; *Teshuvoth Rashba* 2:308; *Mishneh LeMelekh, Gezelah* 3:5.
242. *Yad, Teshuvah* 2:11.
243. *Yoma* 87a-b; *Rosh* 8:24; *Rokeach* 218; *Menorath HaMaor* 5:2:2:1 (295); *Sh'nei Luchoth HaB'rith* 2:166b; *Atereth Zekenin, Orach Chaim* 606:1; *Mishnah Berurah* 606:1; "*Rav*" *Shulchan Arukh* 606:1; *Chayay Adam* 144:5.
244. *Chayay Adam, Mishnah Berurah, loc. cit.*
245. *Pirkey Rabbi Eliezer* 46 (111b), *Radal ad. loc.* 46:58; *Rosh, "Rav" Shulchan Arukh, loc. cit.*

17:61 If a person wrongs another and cannot find him, or if he does
not recall against whom he has sinned, he should repent before
God with all his might. In all cases such as this, God will help him
find atonement, and forgive those sins which cannot otherwise be
rectified.[246]

246. *Chovoth HaLevavoth* 7:10. *Cf. Shemoth Rabbah* 31:1.

EIGHTEEN
REWARD AND PUNISHMENT

18:1 One of the foundations of our faith is the belief that God ultimately rewards good and punishes evil.[1] The Torah thus states, "All His ways are just; He is a faithful God, never unfair; righteous and moral is He" (Deuteronomy 32:4).[2]

18:2 However, since the present world (*Olam HaZeh,* עולם הזה), must serve as an environment of challenge and accomplishment, and therefore contain evil,[3] it could not serve as the place of reward.[4] God therefore created another dimension, the World to Come (*Olam HaBa,* עולם הבא),[5] far removed from this world in essence,[6] and completely good,[7] as the place of reward.[8] The present world is thus essentially a corridor or place of preparation[9] in which man earns his reward,[10] while the World to Come is the place of ultimate reward.[11]

18:3 Although the main reward for good is not in this world,[12] God

1. Thirteen Principles of Faith 11; see Table 14:1; *Ikkarim* 3:12. *Cf. Berakhoth* 5b; *Mekhilta* on Exodus 14:29 (33a); *Shir HaShirim Rabbah* 1:45; *Tanchuma, Shemoth* 18; *Zohar* 1:10b; *Menorath HaMaor* 5:3:1:1 (298).
2. *Emunoth VeDeyoth* 9:3; *Moreh Nevukhim* 3:17. *Cf. Taanith* 11a; *Bava Kama* 50a; *Avodah Zarah* 18a; Psalms 92:16.
3. See Volume 1, 3:27-29.
4. *Emunoth VeDeyoth* 9:1 (93a); *Derekh HaShem* 1:3:4. *Cf.* Maharal, *Tifereth Yisrael* 60.
5. *Cf. Menachoth* 29b; *Yerushalmi, Chagigah* 2:1 (10a); *Bereshith Rabbah* 1:14, 12:9; Rashi on Genesis 2:4; *Or HaChaim* on Genesis 1:1 (no. 15).
6. *Cf. Bereshith Rabbah* 41:1; *BaMidbar Rabbah* 3:1; *Tanchuma, BaMidbar* 15; *Midrash Tehillim* 92:11.
7. *Kiddushin* 39b; *Chullin* 142a; *Yad, Teshuvah* 8:1.
8. *Cf. Targum, Targum Yonathan,* Rashi, on Leviticus 18:5; *Bereshith Rabbah* 62:3, 67:2; *Shemoth Rabbah* 52:3; *Yad, Teshuvah* 9:1; *Sefer Chasidim* 301, 608; *Menorath HaMaor* 3:10:2:3 (236); *Derekh HaShem* 2:2:3.
9. *Avoth* 4:16; *Emunoth VeDeyoth* 9:4 (95a).
10. *Cf. Midrash Tehillim* 25:1; *Yalkut Shimoni* 2:701.
11. *Avoth* 2:16; *Eruvin* 22a; *Avodah Zarah* 3a, 4b; *Tanchuma, Bereshith* 1; *Sefer Chasidim* 604.
12. Rabbi Yaakov, *Kiddushin* 39b and *Chullin* 142a; *cf. Zohar* 3:33b; *Yad, Teshuvah* 9:1.

does give some compensation here[13] in order to encourage the righteous[14] by showing them that good is rewarded.[15] The Psalmist prayed for such encouragement when he said, "Show me a sign of favor so that my enemies will realize [that You are still with me] and be ashamed" (Psalms 86:17).[16] Similarly, God punishes the wicked in this world as a warning to themselves as well as to others who would be tempted to follow after them.[17]

18:4 Often, God rewards a person for his good deeds by putting him in a position to be able to do more good.[18] Sometimes this is accomplished by increasing his material wellbeing.[19] If a person then makes good use of his worldly gifts, they can be increased[20] until he has the good fortune to attain good both in this world and the next.[21]

18:5 It is for this reason that good deeds often protect one from sin[22] and evil,[23] as the scripture states, "One who keeps a commandment will not know any evil thing" (Ecclesiastes

Many authorities maintain that Rabbi Yaakov disputes the *Mishnah, Peah* 1:1; see below, note 43. *Cf.* Maharsha, *Kiddushin* 40a *s.v.* BeShalach; Radal, *Kiddushin* 39b *s.v.* S'khar Mitzvah; Maharsha, Maharshal, Maharam, on *Tosafoth, Shabbath* 127a *s.v.* Okhel MiPerothehen. Other authorities dispute this; *cf.* Marginal Note *ibid.* *Cf.* Tosefoth Yom Tov, *Kiddushin* 1:10.

13. *Menachoth* 44a. *Cf. Iyun Yaakov* (on *Eyn Yaakov*) *Menachoth* 10, who maintains that this disputes both Rabbi Yaakov and *Peah* 1:1. But Maharsha *ibid.* disagrees and maintains that, though the future reward for certain commandments may be diminished by sin, it is not diminished for the commandments listed in *Peah* 1:1. See below, notes 22, 56.

14. *Cf. Megillah* 11a; *Esther Rabbah,* introduction:6; *Aggadath Bereshith* 35.

15. *Emunoth VeDeyoth* 5:1 (69b). *Cf. Yerushalmi, Avodah Zarah* 3:1 (18b); *Bereshith Rabbah* 62:3; *Ruth Rabbah,* introduction:3; *Bereshith Rabbah* 49:16; Ibn Ezra, Rashbam, *Or HaChaim,* on *Shemoth* 32:12; *BaMidbar Rabbah* 1:1; *Tanchuma, BaMidbar* 1. This is also a possible interpretation of *Yerushalmi, Peah* 1:1 (3b); *Midrash Tehillim* 9:3; *Pesikta Rabathai* 23 (121b), although the commentators interpret it differently.

16. *Emunoth VeDeyoth* 5:1 (69b).

17. *Ibid.,* from Deuteronomy 28:46; *cf.* Ibn Ezra *ad. loc.*

18. *Cf. Avoth* 4:2; *Yoma* 29a; *Bava Bathra* 9b; *Makkoth* 10b; *Devarim Rabbah* 6:3; *Tana DeBei Eliahu Zuta* 3; *Zohar* 1:198b, 2:50a, 3:47a, 3:167a; *Zohar Chadash* 85a; *Shabbath* 32a; *Bava Bathra* 119b; *Sanhedrin* 8a; *Tosefta, Yoma* 4:11; *BaMidbar Rabbah* 13:17; *Ikkarim* 4:6. See Volume 1, 3:47.

19. *Yad, Teshuvah* 9:1; *Derekh HaShem* 2:3:4.

20. *Shemoth Rabbah* 31:2; *Tanchuma, Mishpatim* 8.

21. *Bereshith Rabbah* 8:1; *VaYikra Rabbah* 14:5; *Midrash Tehillim* 139:5; *Yalkut Shimoni* 2:887; *Tosafoth, Berakhoth* 5b *s.v.* Lo; *Sefer Chasidim* 367; *Menorath HaMaor* 3:10:2:3 (236). *Cf. Berakhoth* 7a; *Horayoth* 10b.

22. *Menachoth* 44a. *Cf. Yevamoth* 99b; *Kethuvoth* 28b; *Chullin* 5b.

23. *Sotah* 3:4 (20a), 21a; *Yerushalmi, Sotah* 3:4 (15b); *Tanchuma, Naso* 1; *Tikuney Zohar* 50

8:5).[24] Our sages thus teach us that one who is in the process of performing a good deed is protected by God,[25] unless danger is imminently present.[26] Under some conditions, virtue can even protect one from death,[27] thereby prolonging one's life,[28] as it is written, "Keep My commandments and live" (Proverbs 7:2).[29]

18:6 This is especially true of the study of God's Torah,[30] as it is written, "For it is your life and the length of your days" (Deuteronomy 30:20).[31] Those who devote themselves to studying the Torah are often protected[32] from the vicissitudes of life,[33] as well as from sickness[34] and troubles,[35] so that they can be free[36] to pursue their studies.[37] Such study provides an environment of grace[38] whereby a person can even be protected from imminent death.[39]

18:7 Although the main reward of good is reserved for the Ultimate Future, the good brought about incidently by one's deeds is rewarded here.[40] God thus told His prophet, "Say to the righteous that it shall be good, for he shall eat the *fruit* of his deeds"

(143a); *Menorath HaMaor* 3:10:2:1 (234); *Derekh HaShem* 2:3:4. *Cf. Shabbath* 139a; *Rosh HaShanah* 16a; *Bava Kama* 50a; *Menorath HaMaor* 5:2:1:2 (191).

24. *Shabbath* 63a; *Shemoth Rabbah* 30:16; *Koheleth Rabbah* 8:9.
25. *Pesachim* 8b; *Yoma* 11a; *Kiddushin* 39b; *Chullin* 142a; *Zohar* 3:273a, 3:298a; *Menorath HaMaor* loc. cit. *Cf. BaMidbar Rabbah* 16:1; *Tanchuma, Shelach* 1.
26. *Ibid.; Zohar* 1:111b, 1:112b, 1:209a, 1:230b; *Zohar Chadash* 22a.
27. *Cf.* Proverbs 10:2, 11:4; *Shabbath* 156b; *Rosh HaShanah* 16b; *Bava Bathra* 10a; *Yoreh Deah* 247:4; *Menorath HaMaor* 3:7:2:4 (192).
28. *Kiddushin* 1:10 (39b); *Menorath HaMaor* 3:10:1:3 (232). *Cf. Berakhoth* 8a, 28b, 54b; *Megillah* 27b; *Yoma* 9a; *Menorath HaMaor* 1:1:1:4 (5), 3:1:1:1 (91), 3:3:1:19 (109).
29. *Shemoth Rabbah* 30:18, 31:16; *Tanchuma, Mishpatim* 12, *Ekev* 4.
30. *Avoth* 6:7; *Kethuvoth* 111b; *VaYikra Rabbah* 25:1; *Tanchuma, Ekev* 5; *Midrash Tehillim* 1:19, 16:12, 17:5; *Menorath HaMaor* 4:2:1:1 (253), 4:2:1:2 (254).
31. *Berakhoth* 55a, 61b; *Shabbath* 13a; *Pesachim* 49a; *Kethuvoth* 111b; *Kiddushin* 40a.
32. *Cf. Eruvin* 54a.
33. Rabbi Nehuniah ben HaKana, *Avoth* 3:5.
34. *Mekhilta* on Exodus 15:26.
35. *Berakhoth* 5a, 14a.
36. *Avoth* 6:2; *Eruvin* 54a; *Shemoth Rabbah* 32:1, 41:9; *VaYikra Rabbah* 18:3; *BaMidbar Rabbah* 16:15; *Tanchuma, Shelach* 13, *Ekev* 8.
37. *Cf. Avodah Zarah* 19a; *Shabbath* 114a; *Midrash Tehillim* 1:17; *Or Zarua, Tefillin* 594.
38. *Berakhoth* 61b; *Chagigah* 3b, 12b; *Avodah Zarah* 3b; *Yad, Talmud Torah* 3:13.
39. *Shabbath* 30b, Rashi *ad. loc. s.v. Hu; Bava Metzia* 86a; *Makkoth* 10a; *Zohar* 1:131a, 2:200a; *Menorath HaMaor* 4:2:1:1 (253). *Cf. Sotah* 21a; *Yerushalmi* 3:4 (15b).
40. *Kiddushin* 40a, Maharsha *ad. loc. s.v. VeEleh.*

(Isaiah 3:10).[41] Actions which result in good for others,[42] such as[43] honoring parents,[44] kindness to fellow human beings[45] and animals,[46] honesty in business,[47] and bringing about peace,[48] are therefore rewarded in this world.[49]

18:8 Likewise, since the study of the Torah brings a person to do good,[50] it is rewarded both in this world and the next.[51] To a lesser degree, the same is true of prayer.[52]

18:9 The commandments themselves are essentially spiritual, and for this reason, not rewarded in this world. Since the enhancement of their observance pertains to this world, however, it is also rewarded here.[53]

18:10 All the reward that the righteous receive in this world is a free gift[54] given as interest for their deeds.[55] It therefore does not in

---

41. "Fruits" represent the "dividends" or "interest" that one can draw from while living in this world, while the "principal" or "capital" remains for the next world; *ibid., Tosefta, Peah* 1:3; *Yerushalmi* 1:1 (3a, 5a); *Avoth DeRabbi Nathan* 40:2; *Bereshith Rabbah* 33:1; *Midrash Tehillim* 62:4, 114:1. See below, 18:10, note 55.

42. *Kiddushin* 40a; Rosh, *Tosefoth Yom Tov, Peah* 1:1.

43. *Peah* 1:1; *Shabbath* 127a; *Kiddushin* 39b, 40a; *Avoth DeRabbi Nathan* 40:1; *Tanchuma, Yithro* 14; *Sefer Mitzvoth Gadol,* Positive Commandment 12 (98a); *Menorath HaMaor* 3:8:5:1 (220).

44. See note 43; *Yerushalmi, Peah* 1:1 (3b); *Devarim Rabbah* 1:14; *Tanchuma, Ekev* 2; *Pesikta Rabathai* 23 (121b); *Emunoth VeDeyoth* 5:6 (73a).

45. See note 43; *Tana DeBei Eliahu Rabbah* 12 (89a). *Cf. Shabbath* 127a, where Rabbi Yochanan includes in this category: hospitality, visiting the sick, prayer, coming early to the house of study, teaching one's children religion, and judging one's fellow on the scale of merit; *cf.* Rashi *ad. loc.* 127b *s.v. Hakhi Garsinan; Menorath HaMaor* 3:7:1:1 (187).

46. See note 44, where all these sources include the commandment of sending off the mother bird (Deuteronomy 22:6-7), although in *Kiddushin* 40a it is specifically excluded. *Emunoth VeDeyoth loc. cit.* extends this to all kindness to animals.

47. *Emunoth VeDeyoth loc. cit.,* from Deuteronomy 25:15; *cf. Yerushalmi, Bava Bathra* 5:5 (18a); *VaYikra Rabbah* 15:7.

48. See note 43.

49. *Cf.* Rashash, *Kiddushin* 39b; see above, note 12.

50. Rambam, *Tosefoth Yom Tov,* on *Peah* 1:1; Maharal, *Tifereth Yisrael* 62.

51. See note 43; *Menorath HaMaor* 4:2:1:1 (253). *Cf. Tanchuma, Noah* 3, that the reward for studying the written Torah is given in this world, while the reward for studying the unwritten Torah is reserved for the next.

52. *Shabbath* 127a; *Sefer Mitzvoth Gadol,* Positive Commandment 12. *Cf. Shabbath* 10b.

53. *Bava Kama* 9a, Rashi *ad. loc. s.v. Ad; Tosafoth ibid. s.v. Mishel; Etz Yosef, Devarim Rabbah* 3:1; Maharal, *Tifereth Yisrael* 60; see above, 6:13.

54. *Bereshith Rabbah* 4:5; *Targum Yonathan* on Genesis 15:1; *Midrash Tehillim* 119:8; *Tifereth Yisrael loc. cit.*

55. See note 41; *Shemoth Rabbah* 47:4; *Devarim Rabbah* 3:1; *Zohar* 1:196b, 3:253a; *Tosafoth, Yevamoth* 109a *s.v. Asya; Sefer Chasidim* 604, 608.

any way diminish from their future reward.[56] The true reward of the righteous is in the Future World, and no power on earth can diminish it.[57]

18:11 A wicked person, on the other hand, is by definition completely immersed and trapped in his own evil.[58] This prevents him from being able to receive any future spiritual reward.[59] Since God does not deny even the wicked[60] any part of their reward,[61] He gives them their complete reward in this world,[62] granting them a good and carefree life,[63] but denying them any future good.[64] Regarding this it is written, "There is a path that seems right to a man, but at its ends are the paths of death" (Proverbs 14:12, 16:25).[65] Similarly, any good that is done for an ulterior motive is rewarded only in this world.[66]

18:12 One cannot determine whether he will receive his reward for good in this world or the next, since this decision is completely in God's hands.[67] Similarly, one cannot ask for his reward on the basis of justice,[68] since God owes no debt to any man for the good he does.[69] All of a man's good deeds are sufficiently rewarded by the mere fact that God gives him life[70] and causes the sun to shine on him.[71]

56. *Sifri* on Deuteronomy 32:4, 32:34; *Yalkut Shimoni* 1:942 (336b), 1:946 (339a); *Emunoth VeDeyoth* 5:1 (69b), *Shevil Emunah ad. loc.* 5:1:18; *Sefer Chasidim* 604. *Cf. Shemoth Rabbah* 36:3.
57. *Sefer Chasidim* 605.
58. *Kiddushin* 40b. See Proverbs 5:22, note 101 below. See also Kaplan, *Torah Anthology*, Volume 8, p. 82.
59. *Zohar* 1:180b; Maharal, *Tifereth Yisrael* 60.
60. *Cf. Emunoth VeDeyoth* 5:2 (70a); Rambam, *Iggereth HaShmad*, pp. 10-11; *Sefer Chasidim* 164, 353; *Sotah* 21a; see below, note 94.
61. *Pesachim* 118a; *Nazir* 23b; *Bava Kama* 38b; *Horayoth* 10b; *Tanchuma, Naso* 13; *Moreh Nevukhim* 3:17.
62. *Cf. Sanhedrin* 101a; *Menorath HaMaor* 3:10:2:3 (236); *Midrash Tehillim* 17:11; *Yalkut Shimoni* 2:671.
63. *Cf. Arakhin* 16b; *Menorath HaMaor* 5:3:1:3 (300).
64. See below, 20:3.
65. *Kiddushin* 40b.
66. *Midrash Tehillim* 31:9; Ramban, *Or HaChaim*, on Leviticus 18:5. *Cf. Nitzotzey Oroth, Zohar* 2:11a.
67. *Sefer Chasidim* 366. But see *Sotah* 10a, Rashi *ad. loc. s.v. Nakam; Devarim Rabbah* 11:6.
68. *Sefer Chasidim* 164. *Cf. Bereshith Rabbah* 45:7.
69. *Devarim Rabbah* 2:1; *Tanchuma, VaEthChanan* 3.
70. *Eikhah Rabbah* 3:32; *Aggadath Bereshith* 61.
71. *VaYikra Rabbah* 28:1; *Koheleth Rabbah* 1:4.

18:13 Since a person must serve God primarily for His own sake, and not for any reward,[72] one is obliged to keep God's commandments even if he does not wish any reward for them.[73] Neglecting to observe any commandment is therefore a sin insofar as it is a rebellion against God's expressed will.[74]

18:14 The main punishment of the wicked is in the Future World.[75] Still, God often punishes them here so that people will fear and respect His teachings.[76] Similarly, God may prevent a person from doing any good in this world which might detract from his ultimate punishment,[77] the fruit of sin being evil in both worlds.[78]

18:15 If a sin is committed against God alone, and does not have any far reaching effects, any punishment received in this world reduces one's future punishment.[79] However, when a person's sin results in other evil, he may be punished for the fruits of his deed in this world, while the complete punishment for the act itself is reserved for the Future World.[80]

18:16 Therefore, for example, the three cardinal sins — idolatry, sexual crimes, and murder — are punished both in this world and the next, since they are certain to have far reaching effects. The same is true for malicious gossip which causes another to have a bad name.[81] Likewise, atheism and blasphemy, as well as gross disrespect for our religious teachers,[82] result in a person being cut off from God both in this world and the next.[83]

18:17 In a similar manner, any sin which causes others to despise God and His teachings is punishable in this world for the sins

72. *Avoth* 1:3; *Avodah Zarah* 19a; *Yad, Teshuvah* 10:4.
73. *Sefer Chasidim* 301. *Cf. Avoth* 2:16, Bertenoro *ad. loc.; Yad, Talmud Torah* 3:6.
74. See above, 17:5, note 19. *Cf. Berakhoth* 47a; *Shabbath* 32b; *Pesachim* 113b; *Sotah* 22a; *Menachoth* 43b; *Orach Chaim* 24:6; *Kitzur Shulchan Arukh* 9:21.
75. *Yad, Teshuvah* 9:1.
76. *Cf. Shemoth Rabbah* 30:1; *VaYikra Rabbah* 24:1; *Tanchuma, Tetzaveh* 10, *Kedoshim* 1.
77. *Yad, Teshuvah* 9:1 (end).
78. *Koheleth Rabbah* on Ecclesiastes 5:2.
79. *Sefer Chasidim* 164.
80. *Kiddushin* 40a; *Sefer Chasidim* 605.
81. *Tosefta, Peah* 1:2; *Yerushalmi* 1:1 (4a); *Avoth DeRabbi Nathan* 40:1; Rambam, *Avoth* 1:17; *Yad, Deyoth* 7:3; *Sefer Mitzvoth Gadol,* Negative Commandment 9; *Menorath HaMaor* 2:4:2:2 (52).
82. *Tanchuma, BaMidbar* 15. *Cf. BaMidbar Rabbah* 3:1. See above, 14:21.
83. *Cf. Sanhedrin* 64b, 90b; *Shevuoth* 13a; *Yad, Teshuvah* 8:1.

of others brought about by this disrespect, and in the next world for the sin itself.[84] For such sins, God punishes immediately and without mercy.[85]

18:18   When one sins against another, he is not only punished for the sin itself, but for all the additional suffering that it causes others.[86] When the sin causes others to cry out, the punishment is all the more immediate and severe.[87]

18:19   The ultimate reward for good is infinite, while the punishment for evil is temporary. Because of this disparity, the good that a person does is never used to cancel out the punishment that he deserves for his evil deeds.[88] Rather, God first punishes the individual for the evil he did, and then rewards the good.[89] We are thus taught that God does not even accept the bribery of one's good deeds to lessen his punishment.[90] Even if a person causes many to do good, he is still punished for his sins.[91] Nevertheless, a person's good deeds may delay his punishment in order to give him a chance to repent,[92] or decrease his suffering if he has already repented.[93]

18:20   Conversely, evil does not cancel out good, and though a person may be very wicked, he is still rewarded for any good he may have done.[94] One only loses his reward for good when he regrets having done it,[95] as we are taught, "But when the righteous man turns

---

84. Rashi, *Kiddushin* 40a *s.v. Averoth.*
85. *Kiddushin* 40a, *Tosafoth ad. loc. s.v. Ein;* Maharsha *ibid.;* Rambam, *Iggereth HaShmad,* p. 14; *Sefer Mitzvoth Gadol,* Negative Commandment 2.
86. *Sefer Chasidim* 659. *Cf. Bereshith Rabbah* 91:10; Rashi on Genesis 42:22; see above, 17:40.
87. *Mekhilta* on Exodus 22:21 (95b); *Tosafoth, Rosh HaShanah* 17b *s.v. Shalosh,* in *Hagah; Sefer Chasidim* 658. *Cf. Bereshith Rabbah* 49:10; *Sanhedrin* 109b.
88. *Midrash Tehillim* 62:13.
89. *Ibid.; Midrash Tehillim* 30:4; *Sifri* on Deuteronomy 33:6; *Yalkut Shimoni* 1:953, 2:947; Sforno on Ecclesiastes 15:7. *Cf. Yerushalmi, Berakhoth* 9:5 (67a); *Peney Moshe ad. loc. s.v. U'MeKazez; Sanhedrin* 101b. However, *cf. Midrash Sh'muel* on *Avoth* 4:22; *Makor Chesed* (on *Sefer Chasidim*) 605:8, where this is disputed.
90. See above, 13:9.
91. *Sefer Chasidim* 352.
92. *Cf. Arukh s.v. Kaf,* cited in Maharsha, *Kiddushin* 40a *s.v. Ain.*
93. *Sefer Chasidim* 589. *Cf. Midrash Tehillim* 17:5; *Zohar* 3:123b; *Tikuney Zohar* 50 (142b). Also see *Chagigah* 15a; *Kiddushin* 40b; *Sanhedrin* 102, 103b.
94. See above, note 60; *Zohar* 3:101a; *Sefer Chasidim* 354, 355.
95. *Kiddushin* 40b; *Sefer Chasidim* 354, 355.

away from his righteousness... none of his good deeds shall be remembered" (Ezekiel 18:24).[96]

18:21   Just as God created a self-sustaining system of physical law, so He created a self-sustaining system of spiritual law. God conceived creation so that man's good comes, not as a *reward* for his action, but as a *direct result* of his action. The same is true of the evil that overtakes a person. It is thus written, "Righteousness guards the one who is upright in his ways, but wickedness overthrows the sinner" (Proverbs 13:6).[97] Punishment is thus not an act of divine retaliation, but the direct consequence of one's sin.[98] It is thus written, "Evil and good come not from the mouth of the Most High. Why then should a living man complain, a strong man for [the punishment] of his sins?" (Lamentations 3:38-39).[99] One's own deeds set up the mechanism whereby he is rewarded and punished,[100] as it is written, "A wicked man's sins shall ensnare him; he shall be bound with the cords of his own wrongdoing" (Proverbs 5:22).[101] A person must live with the baggage he carries,[102] and exit through the door he entered.[103] The system exists, and it is up to the individual to avoid being trapped by it.[104] Just as God does not tamper with physical law, neither does He abrogate His moral law.[105]

18:22   In order to demonstrate His moral law,[106] and magnify His name,[107] God often makes the punishment fit the crime.[108] We are thus taught, "God is known by the judgment He executes, when

96.   *Sefer Chasidim* 37; *Emunoth VeDeyoth* 5:2 (70a). *Cf.* Ezekiel 3:20, 33:12-13, 33:18.
97.   See Volume 1, 5:52.
98.   *Nefesh HaChaim* 1:12; *cf. Moreh Nevukhim* 3:17.
99.   See Volume 1, 3:31, note 38. *Cf. Tana DeBei Eliahu Zuta* 3; *Midrash Tehillim* 119:8.
100. *Cf. Avoth* 4:11; see below, 21:16.
101. *Zohar* 1:119a; *Tikuney Zohar* 40 (81a); Rambam, *Avoth* 2:6.
102. *Koheleth Rabbah* 3:11.
103. *VaYikra Rabbah* 19:6.
104. *Yalkut Shimoni* 2:938.
105. *Yerushalmi, Rosh HaShanah* 1:3 (7b); *Shemoth Rabbah* 30:6; *VaYikra Rabbah* 35:3. *Cf. Tanchuma, Noah* 18; Rashi on Genesis 11:5.
106. *Or HaShem* (Crescas) 3:3:1 (72b); *Ikkarim* 4:9. *Cf. Moreh Nevukhim* 3:17. This is also because the deed itself brings on the punishment; *Tanchuma, Tazria* 6; Rambam on *Avoth* 2:6.
107. *Mekhilta* on Exodus 18:11 (59a).
108. *Shabbath* 105b; *Sanhedrin* 90a; *Nedarim* 32a; *Mekhilta* on Exodus 14:26 (32b), 18:11

the wicked man becomes snared in the work of his own hands" (Psalms 9:17).[109] We are also taught, "According to the gauge with which one measures, so is he measured,"[110] and similarly, "He who digs a pit, shall himself fall into it" (Proverbs 6:27).[111] The prophet likewise said, "As you have done, so will it be done to you; your deeds will return on your own head" (Obadiah 1:15).[112]

18:23 Just as God makes the punishment fit the crime, so does He make the reward fit the good deed.[113] King David thus sang, "God, [You have] rewarded me according to my righteousness... With the merciful, You are merciful; with the upright, You are upright" (Psalms 18:25-26).[114] The only difference is that reward is bestowed plentifully rather than measured out exactly.[115] King Solomon expressed this metaphorically as, "Cast your bread upon the waters, for after many days you will surely find it" (Ecclesiastes 11:1). That is, long after one has forgotten a simple act of kindness or charity performed for someone else in need, tremendous good can result which is totally disproportionate to the initial deed.[116]

(59a); *Targum*, Rashi, on Exodus 18:11; *Shemoth Rabbah* 1:22, 9:9, 22:1; *BaMidbar Rabbah* 10:5; *Shir HaShirim Rabbah* 2:33, 3:3; *Eikhah Rabbah* 0:21; *Tanchuma, VaEra* 14; *Midrash Tehillim* 10:2, 13:1; *Tana DeBei Eliahu Rabbah* 11; *Yalkut Shimoni* 2:103; *Zohar* 1:108a, 3:92b, 3:123a, 3:161b, 3:299a; *Tikuney Zohar* 6 (23b); *Sefer Chasidim* 53, 155, 217, 698; *Reshith Chokhmah, Shaar HaYirah* 11 (30d). For examples, see Numbers 14:24; Isaiah 30:10; *Sotah* 1:8 (9b); *Taanith* 21a; *Bereshith Rabbah* 31:5, 32:7, 32:11, 85:11; *BaMidbar Rabbah* 9:30; *Eikhah Rabbah* 0:14, 2:12; *Midrash Tehillim* 81:2; *Pirkey Rabbi Eliezer* 42 (99b). A good example of this is *Tisha B'Av; cf. Taanith* 29a; *Sotah* 35a; *Sanhedrin* 104b; *Yerushalmi, Taanith* 4:5 (23b); *Targum* on Numbers 14:1; Lamentations 1:2; *BaMidbar Rabbah* 16:11; *Tanchuma, Shelach* 12.
109. *Cf. Mekhilta* on Exodus 14:26 (32b).
110. *Sotah* 1:7 (8b); *Megillah* 12b; *Sanhedrin* 100a; *Tosefta, Sotah* 3:1; *Mekhilta* on Exodus 13:21 (25a), 14:25 (32a), 15:4 (38a), 15:5 (38b), 15:8 (40a), 17:14 (55a); *Shemoth Rabbah* 25:13; *BaMidbar Rabbah* 9:23; *Tanchuma, BeShalach* 4; *Midrash Tehillim* 81:2; *Tana DeBei Eliahu Rabbah* 9 (64a); *Zohar* 3:2b, 3:123a, 3:161b, 3:239b; *Tikuney Zohar* 6 (23b); *Tikuney Zohar Chadash* 97a; Rashi on Exodus 14:25, 15:4; *Moreh Nevukhim* 3:17; *Reshith Chokhmah, Shaar HaYirah* 11 (30c). *Cf.* Rashi, Radak, Ibn Ezra, on Isaiah 27:8.
111. *Cf.* Psalms 7:16, 10:16; Proverbs 12:14; Isaiah 59:18; *Mekhilta* on Exodus 14:26 (32b); *Koheleth Rabbah* 10:10. Also see *Avoth* 2:6; *Sukkah* 53a.
112. *Cf. BaMidbar Rabbah* 11:1.
113. *Sotah* 1:8 (9b); *Tosefta* 4:1; *Mekhilta* on Exodus 13:21 (25a); *Tana DeBei Eliahu Rabbah* 9 (64a); *Sefer Chasidim* 53. For examples, see *Bava Metzia* 86b; *Sotah* 17a; *Chullin* 89a; *Bereshith Rabbah* 36:9, 43:13; *Koheleth Rabbah* 11:4; *Midrash Tehillim* 108:2.
114. *VaYikra Rabbah* 11:5; *Midrash Tehillim* 18:22.
115. *Sotah* 9b; *Tosafoth, Sotah* 11a *s.v. Miriam; Sefer Chasidim* 698; *Tosefoth Yom Tov, Mishnah Sotah* 1:8.
116. *Targun ad. loc.; Koheleth Rabbah* 11:1; *Radal ad. loc.*

18:24 God generally makes the result fit the act in an equal and opposite manner.[117] Thus, for example, a person who seeks honor is often denied it, while one who shuns recognition is honored by his fellows.[118] It is thus written, "A man's pride shall bring him low, but the humble in spirit shall attain honor" (Proverbs 29:23).[119]

18:25 Just as God punishes a person according to his sin, so does He show mercy to match His punishment,[120] thereby setting an example of how one should make good all damage.[121] Our sages therefore teach us that God heals with the same thing with which He strikes.[122]

18:26 As a symbol of God's judgment, the first to sin are often the first to be punished.[123] Similarly, when an individual is punished, he may suffer pain with the part of his body that sinned, thus pointing directly to the divine origin of the punishment.[124] In an equal and opposite manner, the divine origin of reward is underscored when it can be traced back to some merit on the part of the individual.[125]

18:27 There are numerous traditions that specific punishments come for specific sins, and these punishments are a particular sign of divine retribution.[126] Thus, for example, loathsome diseases,[127] death in childbirth,[128] and death in the family,[129] are

117. *Cf.* 1 Kings 3:11; *Eruvin* 54b; *Sefer Chasidim* 53.
118. *Yerushalmi, Avodah Zarah* 3:1 (18b); *Tanchuma, VaYikra* 3; *Bereshith Rabbah* 6:6, 37:10; *Pesikta Rabathai* 3 (12b); *Rashi* on Genesis 10:25; *Shevet Mussar* 17. *Cf.* *Bereshith Rabbah* 19:1.
119. *Tanchuma loc. cit.*
120. *Eikhah Rabbah* 1:65; *Pesikta Rabathai* 33 (157a); *Yalkut Shimoni* 1:743, 2:308; *Menorath HaMaor* 5:3:2:3 (304).
121. *Cf.* *Shemoth Rabbah* 23:3.
122. *Mekhilta* on Exodus 1:24 (32a); *Shemoth Rabbah* 23:3, 26:2, 50:3; *VaYikra Rabbah* 18:5; *Tanchuma, VaYeshev* 9, *BeShalach* 23-24; *Pesikta Rabathai* 33 (156b); *Zohar* 3:173b. *Cf.* *Mekhilta* on Exodus 15:25 (45b).
123. *Mekhilta* on Exodus 12:12 (7b), 14:4 (26a); *Bereshith Rabbah* 50:11; *BaMidbar Rabbah* 9:17; *Tanchuma, BeShalach* 6; *Rashi* on Exodus 12:12, 14:4.
124. *Ibid.; Sotah* 1:7 (8b); *Tosefta, Sota* 4:4.
125. *Ibid.*
126. *Cf.* *Shabbath* 32-33.
127. *I.e.* Leprosy; *cf.* *Arakhin* 15b; *VaYikra Rabbah* 15:5, 16:1, 17:3, 18:4; *BaMidbar Rabbah* 7:5; *Koheleth Rabbah* 12:7; *Tanchuma, Tazria* 11, *Metzorah* 1, 4. *Cf.* *Berakhoth* 5b.
128. *Shabbath* 2:6 (31b); *Koheleth Rabbah* 3:2; *Tanchuma, Noah* 1, *VaYigash* 1, *Metzorah* 9.
129. *Shabbath* 32a.

seen as punishments for specific categories of sin. Similarly, in the case of a nation, exile, famine, and plague, are seen as punishments for certain sinful behavioral patterns.[130]

18:28 If a person knows something to be wrong, he can be punished for it,[131] even though it is not expressly forbidden by the Torah.[132] In certain instances, a punishment not specified by the Torah can be worse than one which is.[133]

18:29 For example, a person can be punished for speech without action. In such a case, the punishment can be greater, since speech involves one of man's highest faculties. This is alluded to in the verse, "A grievous word stirs up anger" (Proverbs 15:1).[134] Similarly, one can be punished even for thought, especially if the thought brings one to sin in deed.[135]

18:30 The study of God's Torah is essential to the survival of the Jewish people.[136] Its neglect can spell ruin. God therefore told His prophet, "Why was the land destroyed? ...Because they abandoned My Torah" (Jeremiah 9:11-12).[137] On the other hand, Torah study serves to protect the Jewish people, both individually[138] and collectively,[139] as it is written, "It is a tree of life to all who grasp on to it" (Proverbs 3:18).[140]

18:31 If one desecrates God's name through his sin, thereby giving our religion a bad name,[141] his punishment is all the more swift and unmitigated.[142] Similarly, if one causes others to suffer, and they cry out to God, his punishment is hastened. God thus said,

130. *Avoth* 5:8-9; *Avoth DeRabbi Nathan* 38; *Shabbath* 33a; *BaMidbar Rabbah* 7:10; *Zohar* 3:183b.
131. *Sefer Chasidim* 153. *Cf. Moreh Nevukhim* 3:17.
132. *Sefer Chasidim* 378. *Cf. Eruvin* 21b; *Kiddushin* 21a.
133. *Sefer Chasidim* 406, 591. See above, 13:30, note 103.
134. *Cf. Midrash Tehillim* 39:1; *Yalkut Shimoni* 2:721.
135. See above, 13:13-14; *Emunoth VeDeyoth* 5:8 (74a).
136. *Cf. Tanchuma, BeChukothai* 5.
137. God therefore says, "If only they had abandoned Me, but kept My Torah, the land would have been protected"; *Yerushalmi, Chagigah* 1:7 (6a); *Eikhah Rabbah* 0:2; *Pesikta* 15 (120b); *Zohar* 1:185a. *Cf. Nedarim* 81a; *Bava Metzia* 85a.
138. *Sotah* 21a. *Cf. Midrash Tehillim* 1:17; *Or Zarua, Tefillah* 595.
139. *Bereshith Rabbah* 65:16; *VaYikra Rabbah* 25:1; *Zohar* 2:58b.
140. *Cf. Berakhoth* 32b; *Taanith* 7a; *Nedarim* 62a; *Avoth* 6:7; *Arakhin* 15b.
141. See above, 2:19.
142. *Kiddushin* 40a; Rambam, *Iggereth HaShmad*, p. 14; *Sefer Mitzvoth Gadol*, Negative Commandment 2.

"Do not mistreat a widow or an orphan. If you mistreat them, and they cry out to Me, I will hear their cry. I will [then] display My anger and kill you by the sword, so that your wives will be widows, and your children, orphans" (Exodus 22:21-23).[143] In such cases, one's punishment is not for the sin alone but also for all the suffering that it causes others.[144]

18:32 Since God punishes even for minor sins, any transgression should cause a person to fear.[145] Even a promise of good can be annulled by sin,[146] since one thereby waives God's protection.[147]

18:33 If a person is punished for sin in this world, he may be punished by death,[148] by pain, by sickness,[149] or by loss of property.[150] Often, God warns a person to repent by chastising him through his possessions, and only then by sickness and pain.[151] Those close to Him are first chastised through their property, while those far from Him are immediately stricken in their bodies.[152]

18:34 Even if a person is worthy of death, God in His mercy often brings about his punishment little by little, through pain,[153] sickness, and loss of property.[154] In such a way, "He adds one to another to finish the accounting" (Ecclesiastes 7:27).[155] God would rather expend His wrath on wood and stone than on human beings.[156]

18:35 Occasionally, God[157] may punish a person by taking the lives

---

143. *Mekhilta* (95b) *ad. loc.; Tosafoth, Rosh HaShanah* 17b (note); *Sefer Chasidim* 658.
144. *Sefer Chasidim* 659, 666. See note 86.
145. *BaMidbar Rabbah* 11:5; *Pesikta Rabathai* 15 (68b). *Cf. Sotah* 8:5 (44a); *Tosefta* 7:14; *Targum Yonathan*, Rashi, Ramban, on Deuteronomy 20:8; *Zohar* 1:202a.
146. *Berakhoth* 4a; see Volume 1, 8:17, note 30.
147. *Tanchuma, BeShalach* 28.
148. See above, 13:47-51.
149. *Cf. Tanchuma, Tazria* 8.
150. *Yad, Teshuvah* 6:1.
151. *VaYikra Rabbah* 17:4; *Ruth Rabbah* 2:10; *Pesikta* 7 (65b); *Pesikta Rabathai* 17 (88b); *Yalkut Shimoni* 2:601, 2:892; *Zohar* 3:86a. *Cf. Tanchuma, BeHar* 3.
152. *Tanchuma, Metzorah* 4.
153. *Tanchuma, VaEthChanan* 6.
154. *Yerushalmi, Sotah* 1:7 (6b); *BaMidbar Rabbah* 9:23; *Koheleth Rabbah* 7:48; *Pesikta* 25 (165a); *Yalkut Shimoni* 2:533; *Menorath HaMaor* 5:3:1:2 (299). See below, note 200. However, see Rabbenu Yonah, *Shaarey Teshuvah* 3:107.
155. *Ibid.; Sotah* 8b; *Tosefta* 3:1; *Midrash Tehillim* 81:2.
156. *Eikhah Rabbah* 4:15; *Midrash Tehillim* 79:3; *Yalkut Shimoni* 2:824.
157. Whether a human court is required to punish young children for their parents' sins, see *Tosefta, Sanhedrin* 14:1. Regarding children of an apostate city, see above, Chapter 12, note 139. Regarding Akhan's children mentioned in Joshua 7:24, see Ralbag *ad.*

of his minor[158] children.[159] Indeed, the death of one's child may serve as a ransom for his own life,[160] making him acceptable again in God's eyes.[161] Since young children do not have a well developed concept of death, their demise is more of a trauma to their parents than to themselves, making it a legitimate vehicle of divine punishment.[162] It is for this reason also that children sometimes die for the sins of their generation.[163]

18:36 Similarly, a person may also be punished by the death of adult members of his family,[164] as we find in the Torah, "I [God] will direct My anger against that person and his family" (Leviticus 20:5).[165] However, in such a case, the other adults must also bear responsibility for the sin by condoning it,[166] and not trying to prevent it.[167] Although even a stranger would bear responsibility in such a case, the punishment for one's family is more immediate and severe.[168]

18:37 Virtue is it own reward, and sin its own punishment.[169] God may therefore arrange to reward a person by giving him the opportunity to do good.[170] Conversely, He may punish him by removing such an opportunity,[171] thereby making repentance difficult.[172]

loc.; Sanhedrin 44a; *Tanchuma, Masai* 5, that they were not killed. However, in *Pirkey Rabbi Eliezer* 38 (90b), Radal *ad. loc.* 38:114, we find an opinion that they were killed, and here Rabbi Eliezer follows his own opinion in the above *Tosefta* that young children are put to death for their parents' sins.

158. *Cf. Yalkut Shimoni* 2:600; *Zohar* 1:118b; see above, 13:49, note 170; 13:51, note 178.
159. *Cf. Koheleth Rabbah* 4:1; *Zohar* 1:19b, 2:96a, 2:113a, 3:234a; Rashi on Deuteronomy 24:16.
160. *Cf. Sotah* 49a; *Tana DeBei Eliahu Rabbah* 10; *Midrash Tehillim* 62:13; *Zohar* 2:113b; *Or HaChaim* on Exodus 22:5, 22:14.
161. *Tanchuma, Ki Tetze* 2.
162. *Yad, Teshuvah* 6:1; Ralbag on Joshua 7:24.
163. *Shabbath* 33b; *Zohar* 3:17b. *Cf.* Rashi, *Shabbath* 106a *s.v. DeAmri Leh D'Meth Katan; Berakhoth* 61a.
164. *Cf. Sotah* 13b; see above, Chapter 10, note 114; *Shabbath* 32b; *Rosh HaShanah* 6a; *Zevachim* 29b, *Tosafoth ad. loc. s.v. Ela; Sanhedrin* 22a; *Tosafoth, Shevuoth* 39a *s.v. VeEin; VaYikra Rabbah* 37:1; *Zohar* 1:175a; *Nitzotzey Oroth ad. loc.* no. 1.
165. *Targum Yonathan, Sifra* (91c), Rashi, Sforno, *ad. loc.; Shevuoth* 39a.
166. *Ibid. Cf.* Maharsha, *Sotah* 13b *s.v. Af.*
167. *Shevuoth* 39a, Maharsha *ad. loc. s.v. Ein Lekha Mishpachah; Tosafoth, Shevuoth* 39b *s.v. Hatham.*
168. *Shevuoth* 39a.
169. *Avoth* 4:2; Bertenoro, *Tosefoth Yom Tov, ad. loc.; cf. Koheleth Rabbah* 5:2; *Sefer Chasidim* 177.
170. *Shabbath* 32a; see Volume 1, 3:48, note 70.
171. *Cf. Bava Kama* 16b.

18:38   God's purpose in creation was purely altruistic, to give freely of His infinite good.[173] Indeed, since no finite being can be worthy of such goodness on the basis of his own merit, this was entirely an act of love and mercy.[174] It is thus written, "The world is built on love" (Psalms 89:3).[175] Still, God's plan of giving of His goodness freely is balanced by His desire that man enjoy this goodness through the pleasure of his own accomplishment, and therefore, as a reward for good deeds.[176] God therefore established the world on the basis of justice,[177] as it is written, "The King maintains the world with justice" (Proverbs 29:4).[178]

18:39   Since unmitigated mercy would make God's goodness meaningless,[179] while unabated justice would make its attainment impossible,[180] God established His universe under a rule of both justice and mercy.[181] Still, in all cases, His mercy takes precedence over His justice, as we find, "Righteousness and justice are the foundation of Your throne; mercy and truth go before You" (Psalms 89:15).[182]

18:40   Even God's punishment is for the ultimate good of the individual as well as humanity. His punishment is thus never administered in anger,[183] as the Psalmist said, "But He is merciful; He pardons sin and does not destroy; He frequently turns His anger away

---

172. *Yad, Teshuvah* 6:2; see Volume 1, 3:49.
173. See Volume 1, 3:5.
174. *Cf. Zohar* 1:156b.
175. *Targum,* Rashi, *ad. loc.; Midrash Tehillim* 89:2; *Zohar* 1:10b, 1:130b, 1:152b, 2:79a, 2:166b, 3:77a, 3:133b, 3:145b, 3:257a, 3:359b; *Likutey Amarim (Tanya), Shaar HaYichud VeHaEmunah* 6 (80a).
176. See Volume 1, 3:13, 3:17.
177. *Derekh HaShem* 2:8:1. *Cf. Berakhoth* 58b; *Raya Mehemna, Zohar* 1:134b. See also *Bereshith Rabbah* 35:4; *Zohar* 1:157a, 2:175b, 3:30b.
178. *Bereshith Rabbah* 14:1; *Shemoth Rabbah* 30:10; *Tanchuma, Mishpatim* 2; *Zohar* 1:180b; *Derekh HaShem* 2:8:1. *Cf.* Psalms 45:7, Rashi *ad. loc.*
179. *Likutey Amarim, Shaar HaYichud VeHaEmunah* 6 (80b); see Volume 1, 3:9.
180. *Bereshith Rabbah* 12:14; *Pesikta Rabathai* 40 (166b); *Zohar* 1:180b; *cf. Bereshith Rabbah* 39:6.
181. *Bereshith Rabbah* 21:8, 26:4; *Tanchuma, VaEthChanan* 6; *Zohar* 1:58b, 1:114b, 1:180b, 1:230b, 2:113b, 3:32a; *Tikuney Zohar,* introduction (16a), 50 (86a); Rashi on Genesis 1:1; *Derekh HaShem* 2:8:1; *Likutey Amarim, Shaar HaYichud VeHaEmunah* 4 (79b). *Cf. Taanith* 8a; *Zohar* 3:85b; *Shaarey Zohar* 55c.
182. *Tanchuma, VaYera* 1.
183. *Midrash Tehillim* 6:3, 94:1; *Yalkut Shimoni* 2:635. *Cf. Eikhah Rabbah* 1:3, 2:10, 1:12; *Yalkut Shimoni* 2:521, that if one does not seek strict justice against others, God's justice with him is likewise not as severe. Also see *Derekh HaShem* 2:8:1.

and never arouses all His wrath" (Psalms 78:38).[184] God also does not exact all the punishment that a sin may warrant,[185] as we find, "For You are our God — You have therefore punished us less than our sins deserve" (Ezra 9:13).[186] Finally, whatever punishment God does inflict is brought about with wisdom and love, as the prophet declared, "He is also wise when He brings evil" (Isaiah 31:2).[187]

18:41 Like physical law, moral law would normally require that punishment be immediate, similar to any effect that follows directly after its cause.[188] However, God in His mercy does not punish immediately,[189] but warns the sinner,[190] and gives him a chance to repent[191] and mitigate his punishment.[192] Even the completely wicked are given time, since they may repent, or have worthy children,[193] or do good for others.[194] Just as God sustains evil in His world, so does He sustain the sinner,[195] even while he is in the process of sinning.[196]

18:42 Therefore, even when God's justice does decree punishment, it is often mitigated by His mercy.[197] At times, God Himself may

184. *Cf. Pirkey Rabbi Eliezer* 45 (108b); *Zohar* 1:23b.
185. *Midrash Tehillim* 94:1; *Ikkarim* 4:38, from Micah 7:18.
186. *Midrash Tehillim* 30:4, 63:4; *Yalkut Shimoni* 2:784; Rashi on Psalms 62:13.
187. *Yerushalmi, Yevamoth* 8:3 (49b); *Yerushalmi, Kiddushin* 4:1 (43b); *VaYikra Rabbah* 32:6; *BaMidbar Rabbah* 9:4.
188. See above, 15:9.
189. *Eruvin* 22a; *Bava Kama* 50b; *Sanhedrin* 111b.
190. *Shemoth Rabbah* 9:8; *Tanchuma, VaEra* 13; *Zohar* 1:58a.
191. *Tanchuma, Tazria* 9; *Midrash Tehillim* 77:1; *Tosafoth, Eruvin* 22a, *Bava Kama* 50b, *s.v. Erekh Apayim;* see above, 15:9.
192. *Sefer Chasidim* 1168; *Tosefoth Yom Tov* on *Avoth* 4:11.
193. *Cf. Bava Kama* 39b; *Targum Yonathan,* Rashi, on Exodus 2:12; *VaYikra Rabbah* 32:4; *Zohar* 2:12b.
194. All three reasons are given in *Koheleth Rabbah* 7:32; *Zohar* 1:56b; *Emunoth VeDeyoth* 5:3 (71a); *Rabbenu Yonah, Shaarey Teshuvah* 3:123. The wording for the last reason in *Koheleth Rabbah* is, "so that they may do good and be rewarded in this world"; but see *Derekh Emeth, Zohar* 1:56b no. 2, that this means, "so that they may do good to others." Also see *Zohar* 1:118a, 1:140a, 1:227a.
195. *Yerushalmi, Berakhoth* 9:2 (64a); *Midrash Tehillim* 18:12.
196. *Shemoth Rabbah* 41:1; *BaMidbar Rabbah* 20:16; *Midrash Tehillim* 3:3, from Nehemiah 9:18-20; Rabbi Moshe Cordevero (Ramak), *Tomer Devorah* 1:1 *s.v. Mi El Kamokha, Sovel Alvon.*
197. *Cf. Rosh HaShanah* 17a; *Yerushalmi, Peah* 1:1 (5a); *Yerushalmi, Sanhedrin* 10:1 (49a); *Midrash Tehillim* 30:4, 103:15. Also see *Shir HaShirim Rabbah* 7:11; *Koheleth Rabbah* 11:5, that God has mercy on Israel in the merit of Sabbath and Circumcision.

protect a person from His decree and render it comparatively harmless,[198] as when He makes a means of healing available before an actual blow.[199] Similarly, God will often mete out the punishment little by little rather than all at once,[200] thus reducing its overall hurt.[201] On the other hand, He may reduce the pain of His punishment by gently administering it all at once, rather than protracting it.[202]

18:43 Since God desires to benefit man, evil comes to the righteous slowly, while good comes quickly.[203] It is only those whom God hates that He punishes all at once,[204] since the wicked turn even His mercy into harsh judgment.[205]

18:44 However, even the punishment of the wicked, while serving God's secondary purpose in creation, goes against His primary purpose of altruism. Accordingly, we are taught that God regrets when He must punish the wicked.[206] This is what the Torah means when it states, "God regretted that He had made man on earth, and He was pained to His very core" (Genesis 6:6).[207] We are thus taught that while God openly proclaims His mercy, He suppresses His judgment,[208] with the hope that He will find some pretense for His attribute of mercy to overcome His attribute of strict justice.[209]

18:45 However, God can rise above His own moral law, and sometimes

---

198. *Cf. Midrash Tehillim* 6:3; *Yalkut Shimoni* 2:635, where this is likened to a king who swears that he will smite his son with his sword, but who later has compassion on the boy. In order to fulfill his oath, he places the sword in its scabard to render it comparatively harmless, and then strikes his son with it.

199. See above, 18:25, note 122; below, 21:28, note 133. *Cf. Zohar* 3:199b.

200. *Yerushalmi, Taanith* 2:1 (9a); *Midrash Tehillim* 103:11; *Pesikta* 25 (161b); *Tanchuma, Tazria* 6. See above, notes 154, 155.

201. See note 198. This is likened to a king who swears that he will hurl a large rock at his son, but ends up breaking it into small pebbles and throwing them at him one at a time.

202. *Ibid.* This is likened to a king who decrees a punishment of 100 lashes on his son, but reduces its severity by doubling the rope 100 times and striking with it once.

203. *Shabbath* 97a; *Shemoth Rabbah* 3:18.

204. *Avodah Zarah* 4a; *Reshith Chokhmah, Shaar HaTeshuvah* 3 (112b), from Amos 3:2.

205. *Bereshith Rabbah* 33:3 (end), 73:3.

206. *Sanhedrin* 6:5 (46a); *Bereshith Rabbah* 8:3. Also see *Avodah Zarah* 64b; *Zohar* 2:113a, 3:44b.

207. *Targum,* Rashi, Ramban, *ad. loc.; Bereshith Rabbah* 27:6; *Avodath HaKodesh* 3:60.

208. *BaMidbar Rabbah* 1:1; *Tanchuma, BaMidbar* 1.

209. *Berakhoth* 7a; Maharal, *Beer HaGolah* 4 (23d).

He overrides justice completely for some ultimate good known only to Himself.[210] Thus, He told Moses, "I will be gracious to whom I will be gracious and I will be merciful to whom I will be merciful" (Exodus 33:19).[211] Accordingly, God may eliminate deserved punishment completely[212] or grant a person completely undeserved reward.[213] God thus proclaimed the Thirteen Attributes of His Mercy to Israel: "God (1), merciful (2) and gracious (3), slow (4) to anger (5), with tremendous love (6) and truth (7). Safeguarding deeds of love (8) for thousands [of generations] (9), forgiving sin (10), rebellion (11) and error (12), and cleansing (13)" (Exodus 34:6-7).[214]

18:46 As a result of accepting God's Torah at Sinai, Israel merited a special relationship with God,[215] and they are destined to receive God's reward in the Ultimate Future. Still, in order to be worthy of this privilege, they are judged more harshly in this world for their sins. God thus tells us through His prophet, "Only you have I known of all the families of the earth, therefore I will keep an account of all your sins" (Amos 3:2).[216] The gentile nations,

---

210. *Derekh HaShem* 2:8:1. *Cf. Zohar* 1:119a, 1:180b.
211. Or, "I will be kind and show mercy to whomever I desire"; *ibid., Targum Yonathan,* Rashi, *ad. loc.; Berakhoth* 7a.
212. *Ibid.*
213. *Shemoth Rabbah* 45:6; *Devarim Rabbah* 2:1; Rashi on Deuteronomy 3:23; *Moreh Nevukhim* 1:54. See also *Pesachim* 118a; *BaMidbar Rabbah* 12:14; *Tanchuma, Naso* 19; *Midrash Tehillim* 136:1.
214. *Cf.* Ibn Ezra *ad. loc.;* also *Targum,* Rashi, Ramban, *Baaley Tosafoth,* Sforno. See *Midrash Tehillim* 93:8, where the number of Attributes is discussed; *Rosh HaShanah* 17b, *Tosafoth ad. loc. s.v. Shalosh;* Ran (Rif 4b) *s.v. VeKathav;* Rosh 1:5; *Yoma* 36b, 88a; *Pirkey Rabbi Eliezer* 46, Radal *ad. loc.* 46:76; *Zohar* 3:128a, 3:185b; *Zohar Chadash* 24c; *Teshuvoth HaRambam* (Jerusalem, 1934) 45; *Sefer Chasidim* 250; *Makor Chesed ad. loc.* 250:3; Maharal, *Nethivoth Olam, Teshuvah* 6 (163*ff.*); *Arugath HaBosem* 2:103-105; *Nefutzoth Yehudah* 47; *Otzar HaKavod, Rosh HaShanah loc. cit.* (35a); *Nitzotzey Zohar* 2:4b no. 3, 3:130b no. 7. For a general discussion of the Thirteen Attributes, see *Etz Chaim, Shaar Arikh Anpin* 9; *Zohar* 1:1a, 1:20b, 2:91a, 2:180b, 2:202b, 3:66b, 3:147a, 3:161b, 3:228a, 3:233b, 3:246b, 3:276; *Tikuney Zohar* 22 (67a); *Livnath HaSapir, Lekh Lekha* (19d); *HaEmunoth* 4:4 (38b); *Magen David* (Radbaz) 5 (14d); *Pardes Rimonim* 1:7; *Meah Keshitah* (Rabbi Moshe of Pano) 58; *Bahir* 137. *Cf. Zohar* 3:130b, that the Thirteen Attributes are also found in Micah 7:18-20; see below, note 221.
215. *Shemoth Rabbah* 30:10.
216. Ibn Ezra, Radak, *ad. loc.; Avodah Zarah* 4a; *Tana DeBei Eliahu Rabbah* 15 (75b); *Zohar* 2:17b; *Chovoth HaLevavoth* 3:6, 5:5; *Kuzari* 2:44 (53b). *Cf.* Leviticus 10:3. See Volume 1, 4:50; below, 19:11.

on the other hand, play a secondary role in God's ultimate plan and reward,[217] and are therefore punished in this world only for gross immorality.[218] God may also punish them when they oppress Israel or cause Israel to sin,[219] as He commanded Moses before his death, "Take revenge for the Israelites against the Midianites" (Numbers 31:2). It is also written, "God takes revenge against His adversaries; He bears a grudge against His enemies" (Nahum 1:2).[220]

18:47 God's Thirteen Attributes of Mercy thus pertain primarily to Israel, as the prophet declares, "Who is a God like You (1), who pardons sin (2) and overlooks the rebellion (3) of the remnant of His heritage (4)? He does not retain His anger forever (5), for He desires mercy (6). He will again have mercy on us (7). He will subdue our sins (8), and cast all our errors in the depths of the sea (9). You will show truth to Jacob (10), love to Abraham (11), as sworn to our fathers (12) from days of old (13)" (Micah 7:18-20).[221] On the other hand, God is exacting,[222] wrathful and without mercy[223] in the final judgment of the nations.[224] An essential part of Israel's original covenantal relationship with God was that they would accept God's punishment. He therefore sends them suffering to cleanse them of sin.[225] Those nations which do not accept God's punishment end up being destroyed and disappearing from the stage of history.[226]

18:48 Likewise, God often decrees large scale suffering on the nations in order to warn Israel to repent. He thus told His prophet, "I have cut off nations, their corners are desolate... I have said,

---

217. *Shemoth Rabbah* 30:18; *Tanchuma, Mishpatim* 3. *Cf. Shir HaShirim Rabbah* 7:7; *Midrash Tehillim* 2:14.
218. Radak on Jonah 1:2, Amos 3:2.
219. Mahari Kara on Jonah 1:2.
220. *Bereshith Rabbah* 55:3; *Koheleth Rabbah* 8:8.
221. *Cf. Rosh HaShanah* 17a (end); *Ikkarim* 4:38; *Kuzari* 2:44 (53b); *Zohar* 3:131b; *Tomer Devorah* (Ramak) 1; *Etz Chaim, Shaar Arikh Anpin* 9.
222. *Bereshith Rabbah* 82:9; *Yalkut Shimoni* 1:126, 2:396; Rashi, *Avodah Zarah* 4a *s.v. VeHayinu. Cf. Tanchuma, Kedoshim* 1; Rashi on Isaiah 3:13.
223. *Avodah Zarah* 4a; *cf. Tosafoth, Shabbath* 44a *s.v. Ketzef.*
224. Rashi, *Avodah Zarah* 4a *s.v. Nifra.*
225. *Tanchuma, VaYetze* 2.
226. *Tanchuma, Nitzavim* 1.

'Surely you will fear Me [Israel]. You will accept correction'" (Zephaniah 3:6-7).[227]

18:49 Until the Torah was given to Israel, God judged the world collectively rather than holding each person responsible only for his own individual deeds.[228] Though the Jewish people are judged on an individual basis after the giving of the Torah, every Jew retains a measure of responsibility for his fellow Jew and is punished for not preventing the other from sinning.[229] Complete responsibility for each other's secret sins did not take effect until the Israelites crossed the Jordan under the leadership of Joshua,[230] and swore mutual responsibility on Mount Gerezim and Mount Eval.[231]

18:50 Even today, the world is judged collectively according to the deeds of the majority of humanity.[232] Similarly, each nation and community is judged as a whole.[233] Large scale disasters are often signs that God deems certain areas worthy of complete destruction, but withholds it in His mercy.[234] However, God does not wantonly destroy His creation merely because fools use it for idolatry or other sinful puposes.[235]

18:51 When God sends a large scale judgment to the world, even innocent children are not spared.[236] In such cases, one's merit may be great enough to save himself,[237] but it cannot save his children. God thus warned through His prophet, "Or I may send a pestilence to that land, and pour out My fury upon it in blood, to cut off from it man and beast. Though Noah, Daniel, and Job were in it... they shall save neither son nor daughter. They

227. *Yevamoth* 63a; *Tanchuma, Metzorah* 4, *BeHar* 3; Rashi on Exodus 7:3.
228. *Tanchuma, Reeh* 3. *Cf. Devarim Rabbah* 4:3; *Eikhah Rabbah* 3:31.
229. See above, 12:2, 12:57, 18:36.
230. *Sanhedrin* 43b; *Mekhilta* on Exodus 20:1 (66b); *Tanchuma, Yithro* 13; *Targum Yonathan*, Rashi, Ramban, Ibn Ezra, *Baaley Tosafoth*, on Deuteronomy 29:28.
231. Deuteronomy 11:29, 27:11; Joshua 8:33. *Cf.* Rashi *loc. cit.;* Rashi on *Sanhedrin* 43b *s.v. Harei K'var Neemar.*
232. *Kiddushin* 40b; *Tosefta* 1:11; *Koheleth Rabbah* 10:1; *Zohar* 1:53a, 2:42a, 2:194a; *Yad, Teshuvah* 3:2.
233. *Yerushalmi, Taanith* 3:4 (15a); *Yad loc. cit. Cf. Zohar* 3:29b.
234. *Yerushalmi, Berakhoth* 9:2 (64a); *Midrash Tehillim* 18:12, 104:25.
235. *Avodah Zarah* 54b; *Mekhilta* on Exodus 20:5 (68b); *Zohar* 2:188a; *Zohar Chadash* 22d.
236. See below, 20:36.
237. See below, 20:25.

shall only save their own souls by their righteousness" (Ezekiel 14:19-20).[238]

18:52   The punishment for certain sins may have a long term impact on a person's offspring, as we find, "Our ancestors erred and are no longer here, but we bear their sins" (Lamentations 5:7).[239] The very fact that a person is wicked can influence the behavior of his children, causing them to inherit a propensity for sin. Regarding this it is written, "From serpentine origins, a cobra shall come forth" (Isaiah 14:29).[240] If a wicked person's descendants continue his sin[241] in an unbroken line,[242] his punishment will continue to affect them as well, as the Torah states in the Ten Commandments, "Where My enemies are concerned, I keep in mind the sin of the fathers for [their] descendants to the third and fourth generation" (Exodus 20:5).[243]

18:53   Generally, the punishment for an isolated sin will last a maximum of four generations, as indicated in the above passage.[244] However, if the sin is repeated, its effects are reinforced, and can last for many more generations.[245] Similarly, if the sin results in a decree against one's descendants, it can last forever.[246]

18:54   One is only punished for his parents' sins if he continues in their evil ways.[247] A righteous individual, on the other hand, is not responsible for his parents' evil, as the prophet taught us, "The soul that sins shall die. The child shall not bear the sin of the father, nor shall the father bear the sin of the child" (Ezekiel

238. See also Ezekiel 14:12-20; Rashi, Mahari Kara, Radak, on Ezekiel 14:14; *Sefer Chasidim* 164. *Cf.* Jeremiah 15:1.
239. *VaYikra Rabbah* 15:5; *Eikhah Rabbah* 5:8. *Cf.* Jeremiah 31:29.
240. *Sefer Chasidim* 196.
241. *Berakhoth* 7a; *Sanhedrin* 27b; *Targum Yonathan,* Rashi, on Exodus 20:5; *Targum Yonathan,* Rashi, *Sifra* (112b), on Leviticus 26:39; *Yalkut Shimoni* 1:290; *Zohar* 2:116b; *Tikuney Zohar* 69 (102a, 112a, 118b); *Tikuney Zohar Chadash* 121c.
242. *Mekhilta* on Exodus 20:5 (68b); *Pesikta* 26 (167b); *Yalkut Shimoni* 1:292, 1:744. *Cf. Sifra loc. cit.*
243. *Cf.* Ibn Ezra, Ramban, *ad. loc.;* Exodus 34:7; Numbers 14:18; Isaiah 14:21; Jeremiah 2:9; Psalms 109:14.
244. *Or HaChaim* on Exodus 20:5; *Sefer Chasidim* 164.
245. *Sefer Chasidim* 196.
246. *Ibid. Cf. Rosh HaShanah* 18a.
247. See note 241.

18:20).[248] However, if the father rejoices in his own wickedness, the child may also bear its consequences, even if he is innocent.[249]

18:55 God's desire to bestow goodness is vastly greater that His desire to punish.[250] The effects of one's good deeds therefore help his children for all generations,[251] as the Torah continues, "But for those who love Me and keep My commandments, I show love for thousands of generations" (Exodus 20:6).[252] Even the dead are aware of what happens to their descendants,[253] and therefore this good is an actual part of their eternal reward.[254]

18:56 The merit of one's parents[255] and personal ancestors[256] can therefore help him[257] and protect him.[258] Similarly, the merit of the Patriarchs[259] and Matriarchs[260] helps Israel[261] and saves them from destruction.[262] It is thus written, "I will remember My covenant with Jacob as well as My covenant with Isaac and My covenant with Abraham" (Leviticus 26:42).[263] It is for this reason that the merit of the Patriarchs is often recalled in prayer,[264] as

248. *Cf.* Ezekiel 18:14-19; *Shabbath* 55a; *Shemoth Rabbah* 31:6. See also *Makkoth* 24a, Maharsha *ad. loc.*, that Ezekiel annuled the rule that children die for their parents' sins; but see *BaMidbar Rabbah* 19:20 that it was Moses himself who annulled it; *cf.* Deuteronomy 24:16; Ibn Ezra *ad. loc.*
249. *Sefer Chasidim* 164; *B'rith Olam ad. loc.* 164:3. *Cf. Shabbath* 23b.
250. Some say that it is 500 times as great, from Exodus 20:5-6; *cf.* Rashi on Exodus 20:6; *Makkoth* 3:15 (23a), Rashi *ad. loc. s.v. Al;* Bertenoro, *Tosefoth Yom Tov, ibid.*
251. *Mekhilta* on Exodus 20:5 (68b); *Yalkut Shimoni* 1:292; Rashi, *Makkoth loc. cit.,* that "thousands of generations" means forever. *Cf.* Psalms 89:34.
252. Ibn Ezra *ad. loc.; Shemoth Rabbah* 44:7; *BaMidbar Rabbah* 9:54. *Cf. Sotah* 31a; *Or HaChaim ad. loc.,* that merit from love lasts two thousand generations, while merit from fear lasts one thousand.
253. See below, Chapter 23, note 18.
254. *Cf. Eikhah Rabbah* 2:9; *Midrash Tehillim* 14:7; *Pesikta Rabathai* 41 (174b).
255. *Bereshith Rabbah* 29:5; *Tanchuma, Noah* 2. *Cf. Midrash Tehillim* 103:15.
256. *Cf. Berakhoth* 27b. *Menachoth* 53a; *Bava Metzia* 85a.
257. *Derekh HaShem* 2:3:7.
258. *Shabbath* 129b.
259. *Bereshith Rabbah* 50:18; *Shemoth Rabbah* 29:8; *Shir HaShirim Rabbah* 2:16.
260. *Sifra* (112c) on Leviticus 26:42; *VaYikra Rabbah* 36:4; *Yalkut Shimoni* 1:675.
261. *Mekhilta* (48a) on Exodus 16:10; *Bereshith Rabbah* 56:4; *Shemoth Rabbah* 1:43. For discussion on whether the merit of the Patriarchs is still in force, see *Shabbath* 55a, *Tosafoth ad. loc. s.v. U'Sh'muel; Yerushalmi, Sanhedrin* 10:1 (50a); *VaYikra Rabbah* 36:5; *Zohar* 1:168a; *Tikuney Zohar Chadash* 113d. See below, note 271.
262. *Shemoth Rabbah* 1:36.
263. *Cf. Tosafoth loc. cit.* that even those who maintain that the merit of the Patriarchs is no longer in force, agree that the merit of their covenant is. *Cf.* Exodus 2:24, 6:5; Ezekiel 16:60; Psalms 106:45.
264. *Mekhilta* (54a), *Targum Yonathan,* on Exodus 17:9; *Shemoth Rabbah* 44:1.

we see from Moses' plea to God, "Remember Your servants, Abraham, Isaac, and Israel!" (Exodus 32:13).[265]

18:57 Although parental merit helps,[266] one should not depend on ancestry alone,[267] since one's own effort is also required.[268] If a person is wicked, even his parents cannot save him,[269] as the Psalmist said, "No man can by any means save his brother, nor give God a ransom for him" (Psalms 49:8).[270] Therefore, even the merit of the Patriarchs does not help for the wicked[271] who must rely entirely upon God's mercy.[272] Conversely, the merit of one's own effort can help him even when that of his ancestors cannot.[273]

18:58 The fundamental principle in understanding all reward and punishment in this world is that God is just to all. The Psalmist expressed this when he said, "He will judge the world with righteousness, and the nations with equity" (Psalms 98:9).[274] God judges every man,[275] and judges all with the same justice.[276] One should therefore never suspect God of being in any way unjust.[277] The prophet warned about this when he said in God's name, "For I, God, love justice" (Isaiah 61:8).[278]

18:59 It is only a nonbeliever who says that there is no Judge and no ultimate justice.[279] The Psalmist described such a person when he wrote, "He says in his heart, 'God is oblivious, He hides His face, He will never see'" (Psalms 10:11).[280] If one is indifferent to divine retribution and considers it to be mere accident, then God

265. *Tanchuma, Ki Tissa* 23.
266. *Midrash Tehillim* 59:1; *Yalkut Shimoni* 2:971.
267. *Midrash Tehillim* 146:2.
268. *Avoth* 2:12, Bertenoro, *Tosefoth Yom Tov, ad. loc.*
269. *Sanhedrin* 104a, from Deuteronomy 32:29; *Tosafoth, Sotah* 10b *s.v. DeAeiteh LeAlma DeAtei.*
270. *Midrash Tehillim* 46:1, 146:2.
271. *Raya Mehemna, Zohar* 3:174a. *Cf. Tikuney Zohar* 21 (54b), that even for intermediates the merit of the Patriarchs is no longer in effect. However, see *Sefer Chasidim* 549; below, 20:13.
272. *VaYikra Rabbah* 36:5; *Midrash Tehillim* 121:1; *Aggadath Bereshith* 83.
273. *Tanchuma, VaYetze* 13.
274. *Cf.* Psalms 99:4; *Shemoth Rabbah* 30:1; *Tanchuma, Mishpatim* 1.
275. *Tanchuma, Misphatim* 15.
276. *Tanchuma, VaEthChanan* 1. *Cf. Midrash Tehillim* 3:1.
277. *Berakhoth* 5b, *Tosafoth ad. loc. s.v. Dina; Zohar* 1:180b.
278. *Midrash Tehillim* 99:2.
279. *Targum Yonathan* to Genesis 4:8; *Bereshith Rabbah* 26:14.
280. *Bereshith Rabbah loc. cit. Cf.* Job 22:13.

continues to punish him with "accidents" of a more serious and troublesome nature. This is what the Torah means when it warns, "If you still do not obey Me and continue to remain indifferent to Me, then I will be indifferent to you with a vengeance" (Leviticus 26:27-28).[281] If one does not trust in God, he is no longer worthy of His protection.[282]

18:60 One should realize that all that God does is for his own benefit,[283] and should accustom himself to say, "All that God does is for the best."[284] Even the prosperity of the wicked and the suffering of the righteous[285] is part of God's ultimate plan for good.[286] God does not desire the guilt of any creature.[287] He only judges the world for good at the same time that He judges according to what mankind does.[288]

18:61 Therefore, one should bless God for evil just as one blesses Him for good,[189] as we find by Job, "God has given, God has taken, blessed be the name of God" (Job 1:21).[290] One should not be like the heathens who only praise their gods when things are good,[291] but like our saints who accepted even suffering with joy.[292] It is thus a positive commandment to acknowledge God's righteousness in judgment, as the Torah commands, "You must contemplate the fact that just as a man corrects his child, so God your Lord is correcting you" (Deuteronomy 8:5).[293]

281. *Yad, Taanith* 1:3; *Moreh Nevukhim* 3:36; *Iggereth Teiman*, p. 27; *Menorath HaMaor* 5:3:1:1 (298). Cf. *Tosafoth, Rosh HaShanah* 17a s.v. *Shelrah*.
282. *Shemoth Rabbah* 26:3; *Pesikta* 3 (21b); *Pesikta Rabathai* 13 (55b); Rashi on Exodus 17:8.
283. *Taanith* 21a; *Sanhedrin* 108b; *Kuzari* 3:11 (20b).
284. *Berakhoth* 60b; *Yalkut Shimoni* 2:893; *Orach Chaim* 230:5.
285. *Bereshith Rabbah* 65:4; *Midrash Tehillim* 119:8; *Mishnah Berurah* 222:4.
286. *Derekh HaShem* 2:2:8.
287. *Shemoth Rabbah* 9:1; *Tanchuma, VaYishlach* 9, *VaEra* 11, *Tazria* 7, 9, from Ezekiel 33:11; Isaiah 42:21.
288. *Avoth* 3:21.
289. *Berakhoth* 9:5 (54a), 33b, 48b; *Yad, Berakhoth* 10:3; *Orach Chaim* 222:3; *Kitzur Shulchan Arukh* 59:2; *Menorath HaMaor* 5:3:1:2 (299).
290. *Berakhoth* 60b; *Bava Bathra* 16a; *Yerushlmi, Berakhoth* 9:5 (67a); *Avoth DeRabbi Nathan* 14:6; *Mekhilta* on Exodus 20:20 (72b); *VaYikra Rabbah* 24:2; *Tanchuma, Yithro* 16; *Kuzari* 3:17 (22a).
291. *Mekhilta loc. cit.; Yalkut Shimoni* 1:302; *Reshith Chokhmah, Shaar HaTeshuvah* 3 (111b).
292. *Menorath HaMaor* 5:3:1:4 (301), from *Shabbath* 33b; *Sanhedrin* 101a, 107a.
293. *Sefer Mitzvoth Gadol*, Positive Commandment 17; *Reshith Chokhmah, Shaar HaAhavah* 12 (100b). Cf. *Mekhilta, Tanchuma, loc. cit.*

NINETEEN

DIVINE PROVIDENCE

19:1   God created the world for a purpose.[1] As Omnipotent[2] and Omniscient[3] ruler of the universe, He therefore extends His providence to all things,[4] overseeing them and maintaining them in a condition to fulfill His ultimate purpose.[5]

19:2   God therefore created the present world as a perfect place to fulfill His purpose,[6] with all nature under His command.[7] The acausality resulting from the quantum nature of matter gives God the power to control events without altering His laws of nature.[8] Therefore, even when God does not miraculously intervene in worldly happenings, as when things occur through the laws of

1.   "God created the world in order to bestow good to it"; *Derekh HaShem* 1:2:1. In his article, *A World of Love — The Purpose of Creation* (in *If You Were God*, pp. 41, 43), Rabbi Kaplan elaborates on this concept. He asks, "Why did God create the world? The question is both very simple, and yet, at the same time involves some of the most sublime mysteries. For the truth is that we do not have the power to understand God, and just as we cannot understand Him, so can we not understand His reasons. But if we cannot understand God, we can try to understand the world, and ask why it exists... Of course, there is a limit beyond which we cannot ask. We cannot ultimately understand God's motive in creation, any more than we can understand anything else about His being. Ultimately, He created for His own purpose, unknown to any other than Himself... With relation to ourselves, we call God's motives 'good.' But in relation to God Himself, it is totally beyond our understanding. But God had a plan for the world, and this plan was ultimate Good... It was this plan that ultimately led God to create the world. Good cannot be given unless there is someone to receive it..." See below, note 12.

2.   See Volume 1, 2:13; *cf. Shemoth Rabbah* 28:3; *Tanchuma, Shemoth* 18.

3.   See Volume 1, 2:45; *Moreh Nevukhim* 3:16; *Ikkarim* 4:1; *Menorath HaMaor* 5:3:1:2 (298). *Cf. Tanchuma, Yithro* 1.

4.   *Moreh Nevukhim* 3:17; *Milchamoth HaShem* 3:2, 4:4-5; *Kuzari* 3:11 (19b), *Kol Yehudah ad. loc.; Ikkarim* 4:1; *Shomer Emunim (HaKadmon)* 2:81; *Likutey Amarim, Shaar HaYichud VeHaEmunah* 2 (77a).

5.   *Derekh HaShem* 2:1:1.

6.   *Chovoth HaLevavoth* 2:1; *Sefer Mitzvoth Gadol,* Positive Commandment 3.

7.   *Cf.* Jeremiah 33:31; Psalms 46:8, 147:14; Job 36:27, 38:25.

8.   *Cf. Chinukh* 546; see Volume 1, 3:33.

nature, by accident, or as a result of man's free will,[9] all happenings ultimately result from God's will.[10]

19:3   God created this planet and all that is on it[11] for the sake of man.[12] As a result, His providence extends to man in a very particular and individual manner.[13] Every deed of man is weighed,[14] every hair measured,[15] and every bruise counted,[16] leading each man toward the destiny for which he was born.[17] The prophet thus said, "Great in counsel, mighty in deeds, Your eyes are open to all the ways of men, giving every one according to his ways, and according to the fruit of his actions" (Jeremiah 32:19).[18]

19:4   Everything God created has a purpose to fulfill.[19] Although God is omnipotent and has no need of messengers,[20] He decreed that the world should run according to natural laws.[21] In this way, He makes use of all things to fulfill His will and to guide man towards his destiny.[22] Therefore, every thing that may affect man, be it a drop of rain,[23] or a thunderclap,[24] is under God's direct control.[25]

9.   *Kuzari* 5:20 (50a).
10. *Ibid.* 50b, 51b. *Cf. Ikkarim* 4:21.
11. *Menorath HaMaor* 5:3:2:1 (302). *Cf. Sanhedrin* 108a; *Bereshith Rabbah* 28:6.
12. *Derekh HaShem* 1:2:5. See *Koheleth Rabbah* on Ecclesiastes 7:13; *Sanhedrin* 37a; *Zohar* 1:134b; *Emunoth VeDeyoth* 4:0; *Ikkarim* 1:11. See Kaplan, *Moreh Or* (Jerusalem, 1992) 3:1; *Innerspace*, p. 14, note 36.
13. *Moreh Nevukhim* 3:17 (25b); *Ikkarim* 4:7; *Sheveiley Emunah* 1 (10a); *Derekh HaShem* 2:1:3.
14. *Sheveiley Emunah* 9 (85d).
15. *Bava Bathra* 16a; *Maharsha ad. loc.; Niddah* 52b; *VaYikra Rabbah* 15:3; *Tanchuma, Tazria* 6; *Zohar* 3:129a, 3:131; *Tikuney Zohar* 70 (122a); *Divrey Shaul, Chukath.*
16. *Chullin* 7b; *Yalkut Shimoni* 2:730; *Zohar* 2:151b, 3:274b; *Chinukh* 546.
17. *Cf.* Psalms 22:10-11.
18. *Moreh Nevukhim* 3:17 (25b). *Cf. Mekhilta* on Exodus 14:26 (32b); *Yalkut Shimoni* 2:236, 1:942, 2:319, 2:758; *Zohar* 3:129b; *Chovoth HaLevavoth* 4:3.
19. *Shabbath* 77b; *Yerushalmi, Berakhoth* 9:2 (64a); *Bereshith Rabbah* 10:8; *Shemoth Rabbah* 10:1; *VaYikra Rabbah* 22:1-2; *BaMidbar Rabbah* 18:18; *Koheleth Rabbah* 5:8; *Tanchuma, Chukath* 1; *Midrash Tehillim* 18:12; *Yalkut Shimoni* 1:25, 1:759.
20. *Bereshith Rabbah* 28:2.
21. *Chinukh* 546.
22. *Bereshith Rabbah* 10:8; *Shemoth Rabbah* 10:1; *Koheleth Rabbah* 3:22, 5:9-10; *Tanchuma loc. cit. Cf. Gittin* 56b; *Pirkey Rabbi Eliezer* 49 (117b). God is also said to have many armies; *Esther Rabbah* 7:21; *Midrash Tehillim* 2:4; *cf. VaYikra Rabbah* 27:11; *Tanchuma, Emor* 13; *Pesikta* 9 (79a).
23. *Bava Bathra* 16a; *Bereshith Rabbah* 13:9; *Devarim Rabbah* 7:7. *Cf. Berakhoth* 59b; *Yerushalmi, Berakhoth* 9:2 (65b); *Yerushalmi, Taanith* 1:3 (4b); *Yad, Berakhoth* 10:10; *Orach Chaim* 221:2.
24. *Bava Bathra* 16a; *VaYikra Rabbah* 15:3.

19:5   Even apparent accidents ultimately come from God. God will set up a chain of events, taking account of all possible human decisions, which will place a person in a predicament from which his destiny will ensue.[26] This is what the Psalmist meant when he said, "A man's very steps are established by God" (Psalms 37:23).[27] Nevertheless, God has also given man wisdom to safeguard his own well-being, and has therefore commanded us to avoid needless dangers.[28]

19:6   Although animals have a measure of free will,[29] they do not have a highly developed intellect[30] and are therefore not responsible for their actions.[31] Still, God has mercy even on dumb animals, as it is written, "God is good to all; His love is on all His works" (Psalms 145:9).[32] Indeed, there are times when men do not deserve to be saved, but are spared because of God's mercy toward their livestock.[33]

19:7   God certainly does not guide the destiny of individual animals the same as He guides man's.[34] He therefore does not extend the same protection to beasts as He does to man.[35] It is only entire species of animals that have a destiny decreed by God,

25. Cf. Isaiah 10:5-10; Jeremiah 5:24, 18:7-8; Amos 4:7; Psalms 19:1-7, 37:5, 46:7, 10; Proverbs 16:4; Job 37:2-7; Daniel 2:21, 4:14.
26. Moreh Nevukhim 3:17 (25b); cf. Tanchuma, Reeh 12; Pesikta 11 (97b).
27. Chullin 7b; Yalkut Shimoni 2:730. Cf. Proverbs 20:24.
28. Tosafoth, Niddah 16b s.v. HaKol; Chinukh 546. See above, 5:40; below, 19:42, 20:21.
29. Moreh Nevukhim 3:17 (25b).
30. Cf. VaYikra Rabbah 32:2; Koheleth Rabbah 10:22.
31. Moreh Nevukhim 3:17 (25b); Ramban on Genesis 8:1.
32. Tanchuma, Noah 6. Cf. Berakhoth 7b; Bava Metzia 85a; Sanhedrin 39b; Avodah Zarah 4b; Menachoth 53b; Yerushalmi, Kilayim 9:3 (42a); Yerushalmi, Kethuvoth 12:3 (65b); Bereshith Rabbah 33:3.
33. Yerushalmi, Bava Metzia 2:5 (8b); Bereshith Rabbah 33:1; VaYikra Rabbah 27:1; Tanchuma, Emor 5; Yalkut Shimoni 2:727, from Psalms 36:7. Cf. Radak on Jonah 4:11.
34. Moreh Nevukhim 3:17 (25b); Shem Tov ad. loc.; Ikkarim 4:10; Milchamoth HaShem 4:4-5; Kol Yehudah, Kuzari 3:11 (19b). Cf. Moreh Nevukhim 3:51 (67a); Menorath HaMaor 3:end (237).
35. Shabbath 53b; Bava Kama 2b; Maharatz Chajas ad. loc.; Tosafoth, Zevachim 116a s.v. Dilma, Bekhoroth 37b s.v. Keday, Chullin 42b s.v. VeAmar, Eruvin 7a s.v. KeGon, Gittin 56b s.v. NeNiker, Bava Kama 51a s.v. Naavid; Tosefoth Yom Tov, Yevamoth 16:4; Kesef Mishneh, Gerushin 13:16; Beth Sh'muel, Evven HaEzer 17:97; HaGra ibid. 17:104; Beer Hetiv 17:103; Shiurey Korban, Yerushalmi, Yevamoth 16:4 (83b). Cf. Tosafoth, Bava Kama 23b s.v. SheYehu.

who guides their evolution, maintains their numbers, or decrees their extinction.[36] In general, God has established nature in such a manner that every species is sustained.[37] Regarding this the Psalmist sang, "He provides animals with their food, [sustaining] the young ravens when they cry out" (Psalms 147:9).[38]

19:8 Nevertheless, when the destiny of any living creature is linked to that of men, it is also individually judged[39] and guided by God.[40] Therefore, when a snake bites[41] or a bird is captured,[42] it happens only through God's decree. Similarly, the destinies of domestic animals are linked to their owners, as are all their possessions.[43] Indeed, God watches the animals of the righteous to such an extent as to prevent them from doing anything embarrassing to their owners.[44]

19:9 Since Israel has a special relationship to God[45] and His purpose in creation,[46] the Jewish people enjoy a special degree of Divine Providence. It is thus written, "They shall know that I, God their Lord, am with them, and they, the house of Israel, are My people" (Ezekiel 34:30).[47] God is therefore seen as Israel's Shepherd, as the prophet continues, "You are My sheep, the sheep of My pasture; you are [the quintessence of] Man (Adam), and I am your God" (*ibid.* 34:31).[48]

36. *Ikkarim* 4:11. *Cf. Sanhedrin* 108a; *Bereshith Rabbah* 28:8; *Tanchuma, Noah* 5, 12; *Zohar* 1:68a; Rashi on Genesis 6:12; Maharal, *Gur Aryeh* 23d.
37. *Shabbath* 107b; *Avodah Zarah* 3b; *Zohar* 2:170a, 3:252b; *Zohar Chadash* 86d; *Moreh Nevukhim* 3:17. *Cf. Kethuvoth* 63b; *Shabbath* 155b; *Ikkarim loc. cit.*
38. *Moreh Nevukhim* 3:17. *Cf.* Psalms 104:21, 145:16.
39. *Cf.* Rashi on Genesis 8:1.
40. *Derekh HaShem* 2:1:3.
41. *Koheleth Rabbah* 10:14.
42. *Yerushalmi, Shevi'ith* 9:1 (25b); *Bereshith Rabbah* 70:6; *Esther Rabbah* 3:7; *Etz Yosef ad. loc. s.v. Afilu; Koheleth Rabbah* 10:11; *Midrash Tehillim* 17:13; *Pesikta* 10 (89a); *Tosafoth, Avodah Zarah* 16b *s.v. Dimus.*
43. *Menachoth* 76a; see above, 6:15, note 44.
44. *Yevamoth* 99b; *Kethuvoth* 28b; *Gittin* 7a; *Chullin* 5b, 6a, 7a; *Tosafoth, Shabbath* 12b *s.v. Rabbi, Pesachim* 106b *s.v. Ishteli, Yevamoth* 99b *s.v. Salka Daatakh, Gittin* 7a *s.v. Hashta, Chullin* 5b *s.v. Tzadikim.*
45. *Berakhoth* 6a. *Cf. Mekhilta* 28a, 29b, 41b, 43b, 44a, 57a, 62b; *Sifra* 44c; *Pesikta* 1 (1a-b, 4a-b), 5 (47a-b, 50a), 12 (104a), 25 (157a).
46. See Volume 1, 4:54; *VaYikra Rabbah* 26:4; *Tanchuma, Bereshith* 1; *Yalkut Shimoni* 1:2; Rashi on Genesis 1:1; *Menorath HaMaor* 5:3:2:1 (302).
47. *Cf.* Ezekiel 37:27.
48. *Shemoth Rabbah* 34:3. *Cf. Bava Metzia* 114b.

19:10 Although the Jewish people are a persecuted minority among the nations, God's providence constantly protects them and allows them to survive[49] and maintain their numbers.[50] God also fights Israel's battles, as the Torah declares, "Happy are you Israel! Who is like you? [You are] a nation delivered by God, the Shield who helps you and your triumphant Sword" (Deuteronomy 33:29).[51]

19:11 Through God's love for Israel, He frequently brings suffering upon them[52] in order that they may repent and return to Him.[53] He similarly causes them to be persecuted in order to prevent them from becoming assimilated among the nations of the world and as a reminder to maintain their high moral standards undiluted.[54]

19:12 Of course, God loves every Jew,[55] and does not wish to see a single one harmed.[56] Our sages thus teach us that even when Israel sins, they are still God's children.[57] Therefore, though rulers and governments who rise up against Israel may initially achieve greatness,[58] in order that she not fall before the puny,[59] all her enemies are eventually broken before her.[60] Like a wave which rises before striking the shore, and then breaks and is dissipated, so are Israel's enemies eventually destroyed.[61] Similarly, one who speaks well about Israel is rewarded,[62] while he who speaks against her is punished.[63]

19:13 The closer a person is to God, the greater the providence he

49. *Tanchuma, Toldoth* 5; *Ikkarim* 4:9.
50. *BaMidbar Rabbah* 2:17; *Pesikta Rabathai* 11 (45a); *Aggadath Shemoth* 32.
51. *Midrash Tehillim* 36:1; *Yalkut Shimoni* 1:963, 2:724.
52. *Shemoth Rabbah* 1:1. *Cf. ibid.* 30:30.
53. *Shemoth Rabbah* 36:1. *Cf. Tanchuma, BaHar* 3.
54. *Shemoth Rabbah loc. cit.*
55. *Midrash Tehillim* 119:21.
56. *Tanchuma, BaMidbar* 25, from 2 Kings 14:27.
57. *Taanith* 26b. This is disputed in *Kiddushin* 36a; *Yerushalmi, Kiddushin* 7:1 (21b); *Sifri* 2:96, 2:306, and the exact opinion is found in *Shemoth Rabbah* 46:4, from Hosea 2:7.
58. *Gittin* 56b; *Sanhedrin* 104b; *Eikhah Rabbah* 1:32.
59. *Chagigah* 13b; *Tosafoth ad. loc. s.v. Shelo.*
60. *Esther Rabbah* 7:2. See below, 20:6
61. *Midrash Tehillim* 2:2; *Yalkut Shimoni* 2:350.
62. *Pesikta* 23 (196a); *Yalkut Shimoni* 1:906, 2:151; *Zohar* 1:23a; *Zohar Chadash* 23b; *Mesilath Yesharim* 19 (29b).
63. *Mekhilta* on Exodus 12:1 (2a); *Shir HaShirim Rabbah* 1:39; *Tana DeBei Eliahu Zuta* 8; *Zohar* 1:93a.

enjoys, and the more the laws of chance are violated for his benefit.[64] God thus told the Patriarch Jacob, "I am with you. I will protect you wherever you go" (Genesis 28:15).[65] It is also written, "He protects the feet of His pious ones" (I Samuel 2:9),[66] and "He does not remove His gaze from the righteous" (Job 36:7).[67] On the other hand, the ungodly are abandoned by God,[68] deprived of His providence, and left to the vicissitudes of chance.[69] Regarding them the Psalmist said, "But man does not abide in honor [when] he is like the beasts that perish" (Psalms 49:13).[70]

19:14 Because of the quantum nature of matter, all the laws of nature are statistical in character, and are binding because the laws of chance are not violated for ordinary persons.[71] However, the perfectly righteous,[72] who enjoy the highest degree of Divine Providence, can experience violations of the laws of nature.[73] Therefore, the righteous are sometimes protected and guided by miracles.[74]

19:15 Although God created the laws of nature for a purpose, He often overrides this purpose in order to fulfill the destiny of the righteous.[75] As a person approaches closer to God,[76] and his will approaches God's will,[77] he becomes more and more closely related

64. *Moreh Nevukhim* 3:18 (26b), 3:51 (67b); *Ikkarim* 4:10; *Menorath HaMaor* 3:end (237); *Sheveiley Emunah* 1 (9d).
65. God told Abraham, "Fear not, Abram, I am your shield"; Genesis 15:1. He told Isaac, "I will be with you and bless you"; Genesis 26:3. He told Moses, "I will be with you"; Exodus 3:12. He told Joshua, "As I was with Moses, I will be with you. I will not fail you or forsake you"; Joshua 1:5. See *Moreh Nevukhim* 3:18.
66. *Moreh Nevukhim* 3:18; *Derekh HaShem* 2:3:4. *Cf.* *Yoma* 38b; *Shabbath* 104a; *Bava Bathra* 119a; *Makkoth* 10b; *Yerushalmi, Peah* 1:1 (5b).
67. *Cf.* Radak *ad. loc.*
68. *Menorath HaMaor* 3:10:2:1 (234), from *Pesachim* 113b; *Yoreh Deah* 265:12.
69. *Moreh Nevukhim loc. cit.; Menorath HaMaor* 3:end (237); *Sheveiley Emunah* 1 (10a).
70. *Cf.* Psalms 49:21; *Moreh Nevukhim loc. cit.; Shabbath* 151b; *Sanhedrin* 38b.
71. Ramban on Deuteronomy 11:13.
72. *Cf. Avodah Zarah* 18a; Ramban on Leviticus 27:29; *Teshuvoth Rashba* 4:296; *Teshuvoth Rivash* 171, from 1 Samuel 14:45; *cf.* Radak *ad. loc.*
73. *Cf. Koheleth Rabbah* 3:17; *Yalkut Shimoni* 2:21.
74. *Chinukh* 546.
75. *Derekh HaShem* 2:5:6. See below, note 87, that the righteous are therefore able to nullify God's decrees through their prayers.
76. *Avodath HaKodesh* 3:9 (66d); Radal, *Pirkey Rabbi Eliezer* 11:2 (28a).
77. *Avoth* 2:4; Bertenoro, *Tosefoth Yom Tov, ad. loc.; Avoth DeRabbi Nathan (B)* 32 (36a); *Chovoth HaLevavoth* 4:3 (108a).

to God's purpose in creation.[78] At such a point, the fulfillment of his desires becomes essential for God's purpose,[79] and therefore, he is allowed to have a share in God's rule over nature.[80] The more a man begins to resemble his Creator and become one with Him, the more he begins to partake of His power.[81] It is almost as if God places His hand over that of the righteous,[82] and allows them to control the elements[83] even as He does.[84] As in the case of the patriarchs and the prophets, God often reveals His plans and acts of providence to the righteous.[85]

19:16   It is for this reason that the righteous can often[86] nullify decrees set forth by God Himself.[87] So great is the power of the righteous that they can kill with a mere word[88] or glance.[89] Sometimes this can even happen without their intending it,[90] "Like a ruler who utters something inadvertantly" (Ecclesiastes 10:5).[91] With regard to the truly righteous, we are therefore taught, "Warm yourself by the fire of the sages, but be careful of their coals that you not be burned. For their bite is the bite of a fox, their sting

78. God therefore honors the righteous; *Tanchuma, Shemini* 11.
79. *Avoth loc. cit.;* Rabbenu Yonah, *Magen Avoth, ad. loc. Cf. Avodah Zarah* 19a; *Midrash Tehillim* 1:17; *Or Zarua, Tefillin* 594, that God does the will of those who study Torah. *Cf. BaMidbar Rabbah* 22:5; *Tanchuma, Mattoth* 4, that he allows the righteous to see what they desire. *Cf. Avoth DeRabbi Nathan* 2:3; *Tanchuma, Shoftim* 19, that God agrees with the righteous.
80. *Shabbath* 59b, from Job 22:28. *Cf. Avoth* 6:1; *Bereshith Rabbah* 6:14; *Chinukh* 546; *Avodath HaKodesh* 3:9 (67b). See also *Pirkey Rabbi Eliezer* 11 (28a); *Radal ad. loc.* 11:43; *Zohar* 1:221b, 2:55a, 3:107b; *Tikuney Zohar* 56 (93b), that all creation wished to worship Adam.
81. *Avodath HaKodesh* 3:10 (68a).
82. *Ibid.; Shemoth Rabbah* 21:6.
83. *BaMidbar Rabbah* 2:12.
84. *Bereshith Rabbah* 76:1; *Devarim Rabbah* 10:3; *Aggadath Shemoth* 29; *Yalkut Shimoni* 2:165.
85. *Ikkarim* 4:11.
86. But not always; *cf. Eikhah Rabbah* 0:24.
87. *Moed Katan* 16b; *Bereshith Rabbah* 78:3; *BaMidbar Rabbah* 14:17; *Tanchuma, VaYera* 19, *Ki Tavo* 1; *Aggadath Bereshith* 22; *Tana DeBei Eliahu Rabbah* 2. *Cf. Taanith* 3:8 (19a), 23a; *Shabbath* 63a; *Bava Metzia* 59b, 85a; *Zohar* 1:10a, 1:45b.
88. *Cf. Bava Metzia* 59b; *Shemoth Rabbah* 1:29; *VaYikra Rabbah* 32:4; *Rashi* on Exodus 2:14.
89. *Cf. Berakhoth* 58a; *Shabbath* 34a; *Bava Bathra* 75a; *Sanhedrin* 100a.
90. *Makkoth* 11a; *Zohar* 1:175a; *Zohar Chadash* 73. *Cf. Bereshith Rabbah* 74:3; *Pirkey Rabbi Eliezer* 36 (84b); *Rashi* on Genesis 31:32.
91. *Moed Katan* 18a; *Bereshith Rabbah* 74:6; *Koheleth Rabbah* 10:7; *Tanchuma, VaYetze* 12; *Aggadath Bereshith* 51.

is the sting of a scorpion, their hiss is the hiss of a venomous snake, and all their words are like coals of fire."[92]

19:17 Nevertheless, righteous individuals never depended upon,[93] prayed for,[94] or sought miracles.[95] They fully realized that miracles do not happen every day,[96] and that those which do occur can diminish one's merit.[97] They also knew that there is no guarantee of assistance to the righteous in this world.[98] On the contrary, God is extremely exacting with them.[99] It was only when all Israel was involved that they did pray for[100] and expect miracles.[101]

19:18 Miracles are dramatic evidence of God's providence. We thus find that God warned Pharaoh before the fourth plague, "On that day, I will miraculously set apart the land of Goshen where My people remain, so that no harmful creatures will be found there. You will then know that I am God, right here on earth" (Exodus 8:18).[102] Similarly, providence is evidenced[103] by the fact that good and Godly concepts endure[104] and bear fruit,[105] while evil is ultimately destroyed.[106] We are thus taught, "There are many thoughts in man's heart, but it is God's counsel that shall endure" (Proverbs 19:21).[107]

19:19 Though man was created for the sake of his ultimate future existence, he is still part of this world,[108] and subject to its natural

92. *Avoth* 2:15; *Tosefoth Yom Tov ad. loc; Pesikta Rabathai* 3 (9b).
93. See above, 1:35; *Chinukh* 546.
94. *Yerushalmi, Taanith* 3:2 (14a).
95. *Berakhoth* 60a.
96. *Pesachim* 50b; *Megillah* 7b; *Zohar* 1:111b, 1:230b.
97. *Shabbath* 32a; *Taanith* 20a; *Zohar* 1:111b, 1:230b, 1:209a.
98. *Bereshith Rabbah* 76:2.
99. *Etz Yosef ad. loc.; cf. Berakhoth* 4a; *Sanhedrin* 98b.
100. *Cf. Taanith* 3:8 (19a), 23a; *Tanchuma, Ki Tavo* 1.
101. *Cf. Pesachim* 64b; *Horayoth* 11b; Rashi, *Megillah* 3b *s.v. Hah.*
102. Ramban *ad. loc.; Sheveiley Emunah* 1 (9c). *Cf.* Exodus 8:6, 9:14, 10:2.
103. *Ikkarim* 4:9.
104. See Volume 1, 1:11; *Zohar* 1:17b, 1:33a, 1:252b; *Tikuney Zohar* 5 (19b); *Tikuney Zohar Chadash* 116a.
105. *Tosefta, Peah* 1:3; *Kiddushin* 40a; *Midrash Tehillim* 62:4.
106. *Cf.* Psalms 92:8.
107. *Cf. Sanhedrin* 26b.
108. *Derekh HaShem* 2:2:1.

laws.[109] However, the laws of nature themselves were ordained by God to accomplish His purpose, and therefore, behind each natural law is a reason founded in moral law.[110] Furthermore, although events are brought about in a natural manner, the fact that they occur to certain individuals is determined by Divine Providence.[111]

19:20 In order to fulfill His purpose, God decreed that both good and evil exist in the world, and that each man fulfill his task in life by striving to acquire good traits and overcome evil traits in himself. For example, pride is a bad trait, while its opposite, humility, is a good one. Mercy is a good trait, while callousness is its opposite. The quality of being happy with what one has is a good one, while its opposite is bad. The same is true of all other traits. In order to provide an environment for these traits to exist, God divided individuals into different stations in life. Each of these stations is then a test for a particular individual, allowing all these bad qualities to exist, while giving him the opportunity to strive against them and embrace the good.[112] The fulfillment of God's Torah also requires the social intercourse that results from these variations of station.[113] Thus, for example, if wealth and poverty did not exist, there would be no opportunity for the rich to demonstrate either generosity or indifference to the poor who need their help. The poor likewise could not be tested to determine whether or not they would be satisfied and thank God for the little that they do have.[114]

19:21 The main task of Divine Providence in this world is therefore to set each person in his station in life in order that he may serve God according to his destiny.[115] All things that God does in this world are directed toward this purpose.[116] Some things directly

---

109. *Chinukh* 546. *Cf. Avodah Zarah* 54b.
110. Maharal, *Beer HaGolah* 6 (52b).
111. *Moreh Nevukhim* 3:17. *Cf. Ikkarim* 4:5.
112. *Derekh HaShem* 2:3:1. See Volume 1, 3:21.
113. *Cf. Pesachim* 65a; *Kiddushin* 82b; *Bava Bathra* 16a; *Sanhedrin* 100b.
114. *Derekh HaShem ibid. Cf. Bava Bathra* 10a.
115. *Ibid.* 2:3:3. *Cf. Sefer Chasidim* 748; *Berakhoth* 33b; *Kethuvoth* 3b; *Ner LaMaor* on *Or HaChaim,* Exodus 15:26.
116. *Derekh HaShem* 2:3:2.

effect the person involved, while others are used to set up chains of events to direct him toward his destiny.[117]

19:22 Every man's station in life is a test, wherein he can choose either to serve God to the best of his ability or not.[118] Whether a person is rich or poor, healthy or sickly, intelligent or dull, he can always make use of his qualities for good or for bad.[119] Regarding this important principle, God told us through His prophet, "Let the wise man not glory in his wisdom, let the strong man not glory in his strength, and let the rich man not glory in his wealth. But if one would glory, let him glory in this: that he has intelligence and that he knows Me, that I am God, performing lovingkindness, justice and righteousness on the earth, for in these things I delight" (Jeremiah 9:22-23).[120]

19:23 Though a person's station in life might make it more difficult for him to do good, he is still required to use all his resources to serve God.[121] For this reason, it is taught, "In all your ways know Him, and He will straighten your paths" (Proverbs 3:6).[122] If a person's nature[123] or environment[124] tend to make it more difficult for him to serve God, then his reward will be that much greater,[125] since reward is always gauged according to the effort expended.[126] Similarly, in such a case, his punishment for disobeying God's commandments will be reduced, since God takes extenuating circumstances into consideration.[127] On the other hand, one whose station in life makes it easy to serve God, is

---

117. *Ibid.* 2:3:12. *Cf. Niddah* 31a, from Isaiah 12:1; *Ikkarim* 4:5.
118. *Shemoth Rabbah* 31:2; *Tanchuma, Mishpatim* 8; Maharal, *Nethivoth Olam, Yesurin* 3 (180b); *Derekh HaShem* 2:3:1.
119. *Ibid.; BaMidbar Rabbah* 22:6; *Tanchuma, Mattoth* 5.
120. *Ibid. Cf. Midrash Tehillim* 112:1.
121. *Akedath Yitzchak* 22 (1:158b). *Cf. Shabbath* 156a; Maharsha *ad. loc. s.v. Iy; Yad, Deyoth* 1:2.
122. *Berakhoth* 63a; Rambam, *Shemonah Perakim* 6; *Akedath Yitzchak* 72 (4:2b). *Cf. Avoth DeRabbi Nathan* 17:1; *Midrash Tehillim* 119:5.
123. *Cf.* Rashi, *Sukkah* 52b *s.v. VaAsher; Tosafoth, Sanhedrin* 26b *s.v. HaChashud.*
124. *Shemoth Rabbah* 43:8; *Sefer Chasidim* 525, 1167. *Cf. Sanhedrin* 102a.
125. *Emunoth VeDeyoth* 5:7 (73b); *Sefer Chasidim* 59a; *Afukey Yehudah* 2:25; *Derekh HaShem* 2:3:4. *Cf. Taanith* 25a.
126. *Avoth* 5:23.
127. *Shemoth Rabbah* 43:8; *Sefer Chasidim* 591, 1167.

punished all the more for failing to do so.[128] Though providence makes it easier for some to serve God, and more difficult for others, the truth is that it all balances out fairly in the end.[129]

19:24 This underscores the fact that, while it is true that God decrees a person's station, this does not excuse him from doing his best to serve God. Similarly, the fact that God decrees that a person should be poor is no excuse for the rich to withhold charity from him, since it was for this very reason that God created a world of contrasts.[130] Likewise, although it may have been decreed that a person should be murdered, this does not excuse the killer, since God has many messengers.[131]

19:25 A person's circumstances are determined by an extremely large number of variables, depending on the laws of nature, his own effort, his merit, and his fortune or *mazal.*[132] The most important of these is a person's fortune, since this generally acts as a limiting factor on both his merit and his effort.[133] A person's fortune, in turn, is largely determined by his parentage,[134] the time[135] and place[136] in which he lives, his society,[137] his habits,[138] and his occupation.[139]

128. *Emunoth VeDeyoth loc. cit. Cf. Horayoth* 11a.
129. *Derekh HaShem* 2:3:4.
130. *Bava Bathra* 10a; *Tanchuma, BeHar* 2. *Cf. Yad, Matnoth Ani'im* 10:3; *Yoreh Deah* 247:1.
131. *Taanith* 18b; *Koheleth Rabbah* 3:22; Ramban on Genesis 15:13.
132. *Tifereth Yisrael, Kiddushin* 4:14, *Boaz* no. 1. The Jewish concept of *Mazal,* "destiny" or "fortune," is never used in the sense of "luck" or "chance," on the one hand, or "inevitable fate," on the other. Rather, *Mazal* is part of God's system of Divine Providence. As the Kabbalists define it, at its highest level, *Mazal* is a completely spiritual concept through which God interacts with and brings about His ultimate purpose for creation. At lower levels, *Mazal* involves the planets and constellations *(Mazaloth).* These are the most physical aspect of God's system of Divine Providence. Like the hardware of a huge computer, they are like wires and electrodes through which extremely subtle spiritual forces are transmitted to the terrestrial world. The main thing is that God set up the entire system of spiritual and physical universes in order to interact with man, and to fulfill His purpose for creation through man. *Mazal* is the mechanism that God uses to affect circumstances and create test situations. It is never used to determine what a person will do with his free will; see below, note 142.
133. *Ibid. Cf. Sefer Chasidim* 550.
134. *Ibid.,* from Proverbs 19:14; *Eduyyoth* 2:9; see below, 19:32.
135. *Ibid.,* from *Shabbath* 147b; *Eruvin* 65a; *Yad, Talmud Torah* 3:13; *Yoreh Deah* 156:23; *Bava Bathra* 16b.
136. *Ibid.,* from *BaMidbar Rabbah* 16:9; *Makkoth* 9b; *Bava Bathra* 158b; *Kiddushin* 49b.
137. *Ibid.,* from Proverbs 13:29, 22:25; *Bava Bathra* 22a; *Pesachim* 112a; *Avoth* 1:4, 1:6, 2:9; Psalms 119:3; Ecclesiastes 5:10; *Bava Kama* 93a; Isaiah 41:1.

19:26   As an individual, a person is also part of his society. His fortune will therefore necessarily effect the entire group of which he is a part, and set up chains of events which may even affect all humanity.[140] It is for this reason that a person's fortune cannot depend entirely on his own merit,[141] but is rather determined largely by his place in God's overall plan.[142] Accordingly, we are taught that a person's lifespan, his children, and his livelihood, do not depend as much upon his merit as upon his fortune.[143] God does not reorder His universal plan for the sake of a single individual.[144]

138. *Ibid.,* from *Kethuvoth* 59b; *Moed Katan* 9b; *Yoma* 76b; *Horayoth* 13b; *Pesachim* 42b, 114a; Proverbs 21:17.
139. *Ibid.,* from *Kiddushin* 4:14 (82a). Regarding Torah scholars; *cf. Bava Metzia* 84b; *Rosh HaShanah* 15a; *Taanith* 7a; *Gittin* 41a; *Avodah Zarah* 16b; *Megillah* 14b; *Nedarim* 49b.
140. *Derekh HaShem* 2:3:7. *Cf. Anaf Yosef, Esther Rabbah* 0:1.
141. Ran, *Moed Katan* 28a, quoted in *HaKothev, Eyn Yaakov* 19; *Or HaShem* (Crescas) 3:3:3 (74a). See below, note 153.
142. This is actually the definition of *Mazal; cf. Damesek Eliezer, Zohar* 3:134a, quoted in *Nitzotzey Zohar ibid.* no. 5. See *Tifereth Yisrael, Kiddushin* 4:14, who defines two levels of *Mazal,* one lower and one hidden or higher fortune; *cf. Tosefoth Yom Tov ibid.* See also *Zohar* 3:25b; *Tikuney Zohar* 10 (25b), 70 (127a). Also see *Derekh HaShem* 2:7:2-3, who writes, "Every process that occurs among physical things, as well as all that happens to them, is initiated on high, and then transmitted by the stars to the terrestrial world in its necessary form. Thus, for example, life, wealth, wisdom, children, and similar matters are all initiated on high among the Root forces. They are then reflected to the terrestrial world... [so that] every event that takes place in the terrestrial world is allocated to a particular star... Every human being is also subjugated to this system, and whatever happens to him is a result of this astrological influence. It is also possible, however, that this stellar influence be overridden by a higher power. [This is normally true in the case of the Jewish people, and accordingly] our sages teach us, 'There is no *Mazal* for Israel' (*Shabbath* 156a). The power of God's decree and influence dominates over the power which is transmitted through the stars, and what results is therefore dependent on this higher influence rather than on the astrological"; see below, notes 153, 154. *Cf.* Rambam, Letter to Marseilles Congregation *(Iggereth LeKahal Marsilia),* p. 27; *Kuzari* 1:75 (46a).
143. *Moed Katan* 28a; *Tosafoth ad. loc. s.v. Eleh; Tosafoth, Shabbath* 156a *s.v. Ein Mazal L'Yisrael; Zohar* 1:24a, 1:43b, 1:115a, 1:137a, 1:159b, 1:160b, 1:181a, 1:207b, 2:6a, 2:252b, 2:247b, 3:25b, 3:77b, 3:79b, 3:116b, 3:137b, 3:289a, 3:292b, 3:295b: *Tikuney Zohar,* introduction (15b), 10 (25b), 22 (67b), 50 (86b), 69 (100a), 70 (127a); *Zohar Chadash* 36c, from 1 Samuel 1:10; Isaiah 38:5; Psalms 55:23; *Sefer Chasidim* 321; *Makor Chesed ad. loc.* 321:5; *Menorath HaMaor* 5:1:1:3 (300); *Or HaShem* (Crescas) 3:3:3 (73b); *Asarah Maamaroth* 1:2:30; *Akedath Yitzchak* 22 (1:148a); *Derekh HaShem* 2:3:7. See below, 19:36, note 193.
144. *Taanith* 25a; Maharsha *ad. loc.; Tosafoth, Moed Katan* 28a *s.v. Eleh; Tikuney Zohar* 69 (100b); *Tikuney Zohar Chadash* 114a; *Akedath Yitzchak* 22 (1:148b); *Sefer HaB'rith* 1:2:7, quoted in *Yad Yosef* on *Eyn Yaakov, Taanith* 67.

19:27 Our sages thus enumerated many things which depend upon fortune,[145] even a Torah scroll in its ark.[146] Although such things as life,[147] livelihood[148] and children[149] are to some extent influenced by merit[150] and prayer,[151] in the majority of cases, they too are still circumscribed by one's fortune.[152]

19:28 As a person draws himself closer and closer to God, however, and thereby enjoys a greater degree of providence, he can rise above his fortune.[153] We are thus taught that fortune does not completely[154] dominate Israel.[155] The important thing to remember is that all is ultimately in God's hands,[156] and no man really knows the extent to which God is protecting and guiding him in all his affairs.[157]

19:29 Though a person's fortune may be largely determined

145. *Targum* on Ecclesiastes 9:2; *Tifereth Yisrael, Kiddushin* 4:14. *Cf. Pilpula Charifta, Sanhedrin* (Rosh 4:5) no. 90.

146. Which symbolizes the opposite of "chance"; *Zohar* 3:134a; *Tikuney Zohar* 69 (100a); *Maharam Shif, Derushim* (end of *Chullin*) beginning, *s.v. HaKol.*

147. *Sefer Chasidim* 321, from Exodus 23:26, 20:12; Deuteronomy 11:21; Proverbs 11:4; *Sotah* 3:4 (20a).

148. *Ibid.*, from *Shabbath* 119a. *Cf. Moed Katan* 28a; *Shabbath* 151b; *Eruvin* 41b; *Temurah* 16a.

149. *Ibid.*, from *Berakhoth* 31b.

150. *Cf.* Rashi, *Tosafoth, Shabbath* 156a *s.v. Ein Mazal L'Yisrael; Tosafoth, Moed Katan* 28a *s.v. Eleh; Tosefoth Yom Tov, Kiddushin* 4:14; Maharsha, *Moed Katan* 28a *s.v. BeMazala; Ikkarim* 4:4; *Derekh HaShem* 2:3:4. Many write that while fortune plays a role for the individual, an entire community is judged more on the basis of merit alone; *cf. Teshuvoth Rashba* 1:19, 1:148, 1:409; *Teshuvoth Zikhron Yehudah* 91; *Teshuvoth Tashbatz* 2:1; Maharsha, *Shabbath* 156a *s.v. Ein;* Maharatz Chajas, *Sotah* 2a. Also see *Tanchuma, MiKetz* 1, that while the amount of rain may be predetermined, where and when it falls depends on merit.

151. *Cf. Niddah* 70b; *Bava Kama* 80b; *Moed Katan* 28a; *Shabbath* 151b; *Eruvin* 41b; *Temurah* 16a; Rashi, *Shabbath* 156a *s.v. Ein; Tosefoth Yom Tov, Kiddushin* 4:14. See *Makkoth* 11b, that prayer can even help by judgment in earthly courts; *cf. Pilpula Charifta loc. cit.*

152. *Tifereth Yisrael, Kiddushin* 4:14.

153. *Zohar Chadash* 32a; *Or HaShem* 3:3:3 (74a); *Akedath Yitzchak* 22 (1:148a). *Cf. Avoth* 3:5; *Nedarim* 32a; *Sanhedrin* 65a.

154. *Bereshith Rabbah* 85:3, from Isaiah 47:13; *Derekh HaShem* 2:7:3.

155. *Shabbath* 156a; *Sukkah* 29a; *Nedarim* 32a; *Shemoth Rabbah* 38:7; *Zohar* 3:116b; *Tikuney Zohar* 59 (86b), 69 (100a); *Zohar Chadash* 32a; *Tosafoth, Moed Katan* 28a *s.v. Eleh; Sefer Chasidim* 321; *Makor Chesed ad. loc.* 321:12; *Ikkarim* 4:4; *Or Hashem* 3:3:3 (63b); *Derekh HaShem* 2:7:3; *Teshuvoth Zikhron Yehudah* 91.

156. "All is in the hand of Heaven, except for the fear of heaven"; *Berakhoth* 33b; *Megillah* 25a; *Niddah* 16b; see Volume 1, 3:32. *Cf. Kethuvoth* 30b; *Sefer Chasidim* 748; *Tifereth Yisrael loc. cit.* See *Akedath Yitzchak* 22 (1:148a); see below, 20:53.

157. *Yoma* 22b; *Bava Kama* 20b; *Menorath HaMaor* 5:3:1:3 (300).

from birth,[158] one can always change it by altering his circumstances.[159] Sincere effort and hard work can also change a person's fortune,[160] both in terms of his material as well as his spiritual standing.[161] The Psalmist alluded to this when he sang, "A Song of Ascents. Happy [are you,] every one who fears God and walks in His ways. You shall eat the fruit of your effort. Happy are you, and goodness [is reserved] for you" (Psalms 128:1-2). "Happy are you" — in this world, and "goodness is reserved for you" — in the World to Come.[162]

19:30 Likewise, though God may have decreed good for a person, he still has to work to obtain it, as the Torah tells us, "God your Lord has blessed you in all the *work* of your hands" (Deuteronomy 2:7).[163] The greatest blessing is that of the righteous, who find none of their efforts wasted. Regarding them the prophet said, "They shall not labor in vain nor bring forth for chaos, for they are the seed of God's blessed" (Isaiah 65:23).[164]

19:31 However, there are certain areas in which all the effort in the world cannot bring one beyond the limits that God's plan has set for him.[165] Scripture alludes to this when it states, "The blessing of God is what makes a person rich, and toil adds nothing to it" (Proverbs 10:22).[166] For this reason we are taught that if one does not see a sign of success in an endeavor for five years, it is probable that he will never be successful in it.[167] Likewise, we

---

158. Maharsha, *Moed Katan* 28a *s.v. BeMazala;* see below, note 196.
159. *Rosh HaShanah* 16b; *Yerushalmi, Shabbath* 6:9 (39a); *Zohar* 1:133b; *Sefer Chasidim* 321; *Makor Chesed ad. loc.* 321:12.
160. *Ikkarim* 4:6.
161. *Ibid.* Even when the merit of one's good deeds is not sufficient to offset a particularly difficult life test which has been decreed because of one's own sins or those of his ancestors, sincere repentence can help; *cf. Berakhoth* 5a. See also *Shorashim* on *Ikkarim* 4:5, note 7.
162. *Avoth* 4:1; *Berakhoth* 8a; *Chullin* 44b; *BaMidbar Rabbah* 8:10; *Ikkarim* 4:6.
163. Deuteronomy 14:29; *Midrash Tehillim* 23:3, 136:10; *Tana DeBei Eliahu Rabbah* 14 (73a); *Yalkut Shimoni* 1:808, 2:690; *Ikkarim* 4:6; *Tifereth Yisrael loc. cit.*
164. *Ikkarim* 4:6. *Cf. Mekhilta* on Exodus 22:23 (96a); *Tanchuma, Kedoshim* 14.
165. *Ikkarim* 4:5.
166. Rashi, *Metzudoth David ad. loc.; Tifereth Yisrael, Kiddushin* 4:14.
167. *Chullin* 24a; *Tosefta, Shekalim* 3:16; *Sifri* 1:63; *BaMidbar Rabbah* 6:3; Rashi on Numbers 8:24.

are taught that one should not be too forceful or headstrong in getting one's way,[168] since all things have a time and place.[169]

19:32 God judges every individual with respect to his forebears who preceded him, his descendants who follow him, and the people of his generation, city and community who are associated with him.[170] Of these, a person's fortune and destiny is influenced most strongly by his parentage. This is true both because of the effects of heredity and environment,[171] as well as due to the moral values which people internalize through their parents.[172] A very special providence is therefore bestowed on a child when he is conceived, at which time his hereditary traits and much[173] of his fortune is determined.[174] Similarly, an extra degree of providence is evidenced at childbirth.[175]

19:33 Each marriage sets up such an extremely complex chain of events as to be almost a world in itself.[176] Therefore, the degree of providence required to bring about a marriage is as great as that required for a miracle.[177] We are thus taught that one of the main tasks[178] of providence is the making of matches,[179] even to

---

168. Literally, "push the hour" *(lid'chok ha'shaah); Berakhoth* 64a; *Eruvin* 13b; *Tikuney Zohar* 69 (100b).

169. *Avoth* 4:3; *Shabbath* 156a; *Zohar* 3:58b, 3:251a; *Tikuney Zohar,* introduction (4a), 18 (36a), 69 (100a).

170. *Derekh HaShem* 2:3:7.

171. *Eduyyoth* 2:9; *Tosefta, Eduyyoth* 1:10; *Yerushalmi, Kiddushin* 1:7 (19b). *Cf. Tanchuma, Toldoth* (Buber) 64b; *Aggadath Bereshith* 40:6; *Yalkut Shimoni* 2:142; *Reshith Chokhmah, Perek Gidul Banim* 248c; *Avoth DeRabbi Nathan* 37:9.

172. *Cf. Koheleth Rabbah* 4:15; *Midrash Tehillim* 59:1; *Yalkut Shimoni* 2:971. See also *Bava Metzia* 85a; *Tosefta, Bava Metzia* 3:14.

173. But not all of his fortune, since a person still has free will to overcome his inborn traits; *cf. Tosafoth, Tosafoth HaRosh, Niddah* 16b *s.v. HaKol;* Maharatz Chajas *ad. loc.* See Rambam, *Shemonah Perakim* 8; Volume 1, 3:41.

174. *Niddah* 16b; *Tanchuma, Pekudey* 3; *Tifereth Yisrael, Kiddushin* 4:14.

175. *VaYikra Rabbah* 27:7; *Tanchuma, Tazria* 4, *Emor* 11; *Pesikta* 9 (77b); *Yalkut Shimoni* 1:643, 2:314, from Isaiah 41:24; *HaManhig, Rosh HaShanah* 21. These sources also indicate that providence is evidenced by violations of the laws of probability.

176. *Zohar* 1:89a.

177. *Sotah* 2a; *Sanhedrin* 22a; *Bereshith Rabbah* 68:4; *VaYikra Rabbah* 8:1; *Midrash Tehillim* 59:2; *Zohar* 1:21b, 1:207b, 2:170b, 3:283b; Maharal, *Beer HaGolah* 4 (40b).

178. *Bereshith Rabbah* 68:4; *VaYikra Rabbah* 8:1; *BaMidbar Rabbah* 3:4; *Tanchuma, Ki Tissa* 5; *Zohar* 1:89a; *Beer HaGolah loc. cit.*

179. *Moed Katan* 18b; *Yerushalmi, Betza* 5:2 (20b); *Yerushalmi, Taanith* 1:8 (7b), 4:6 (25b); *Yerushalmi, Kethuvoth* 1:1 (2a); *Targum* on Psalms 68:7; *Bereshith Rabbah* 68:3; *Zohar* 1:85a, 1:90b, 2:109a. *Cf. Orach Chaim* 551:2.

the extent of bringing people together from opposite ends of the earth.[180]

19:34 Therefore, as soon as a child is conceived, God proceeds to set up a chain of events that will lead to his eventual marriage.[181] Nevertheless, this may be constantly revised,[182] since each person has free will, and one's choice of a wife will be affected by his moral values.[183] Furthermore, like all other aspects of a person's destiny, this can be altered by merit[184] and prayer.[185] But after all is said and done, no matter what a person does, the making of a marriage is in God's hands. For a marriage to be successful, it must be made in heaven.[186] It is therefore written, "House and riches are bequeathed by one's parents, but a discriminating wife is from the Lord" (Proverbs 19:14).[187]

19:35 As important to the historic process as His control of human populations, is God's regulation of the world's economic life.[188] Here again, we are taught that a major task of Divine Providence is determining each man's economic fortune and fitting it into God's overall plan.[189] It is thus written, "God makes poor and makes rich; He brings low and lifts up high" (1 Samuel 2:7).[190] Similarly, the Psalmist said, "For God is the Judge: He lowers one person down and raises up another" (Psalms 75:8).[191]

180. *Yerushalmi, Kiddushin* 3:12 (40a); *Bereshith Rabbah* 65:2, from Psalms 68:7; *Bereshith Rabbah* 68:3; *BaMidbar Rabbah* 3:4; *Tanchuma, Ki Tissa* 5. See Kaplan, *Made in Heaven* (Moznaim, 1983), Chapter 1.
181. *Sotah* 2a; Maharsha, Maharatz Chajas, *ad. loc.; Sanhedrin* 22a; *Zohar* 1:89a, 1:91b; *Sheveiley Emunah* 3 (26c). *Cf. Sanhedrin* 107a; *Midrash Tehillim* 3:3; *Zohar* 1:8b, 1:73b, 2:107a, 3:38b, 3:71b, 3:78b; *Tikuney Zohar* 14 (30a); *Tikuney Zohar Chadash* 121c.
182. *Cf. Moed Katan* 18b; Maharsha *ad. loc.,* that this is decreed every day.
183. *Sotah* 2a; Maharsha, Maharatz Chajas, *ad. loc.; Sanhedrin* 22a; *Midrash Tehillim* 125:2; *Zohar* 1:91a, 1:229a; *Tikuney Zohar* 14 (30a); *Teshuvoth HaRambam* (Lipsia) 119; *Sheveiley Emunah* 3 (26c); *Akedath Yitzchak* 8 (1:60a), 22 (1:159a); *Teshuvoth Tashbatz* 2:1. *Cf. Bava Bathra* 110; *Sefer Chasidim* 1092, 1099, 1100.
184. *Akedath Yitzchak* 22 (1:159a).
185. See references in note 179. Also see *Tosafoth, Sanhedrin* 22a *s.v. Arba'im; Zohar* 1:91a-b, 2:101a; *Sefer Chasidim* 383.
186. See *Yerushalmi, Kiddushin* 3:12 (40a); *Sefer Chasidim* 383, that other marriages are likely to fail.
187. *Moed Katan* 18b; *Bereshith Rabbah* 68:3; *Midrash Tehillim* 59:2; *Zohar* 1:229a.
188. *Pesachim* 118a; *Bereshith Rabbah* 20:33, 97:3.
189. *VaYikra Rabbah* 8:1; *BaMidbar Rabbah* 3:4, 22:7; *Tanchuma, VaYishlach* 10, *Ki Tissa* 5, *Mattoth* 6. *Cf. Temurah* 16a; *Ruth Rabbah* 3:1, from Ezekiel 21:31.
190. *Ibid.*
191. *Ibid.; Tanchuma, Tazria* 6.

19:36 The degree of providence required to set each individual in his economic station is as great as that required to produce a miracle.[192] This is especially true since wealth affects different people in different ways, and therefore cannot be granted on the basis of merit alone.[193] For this reason, the key to wealth remains in God's hand alone,[194] and even the righteous have no promise of livelihood.[195]

19:37 In general, the chain of events governing a person's economic fortunes is largely determined from the time of his conception.[196] Besides this, however, each person is constantly judged,[197] and his financial fortunes determined over periods of time.[198] God tries to satisfy the needs and wants of every creature,[199] as the Psalmist said, "You open Your hand, and satisfy the desires of all living things" (Psalms 145:16).[200] However, God also knows what is ultimately best for each person, and He measures out their livelihoods accordingly.[201] King Solomon thus prayed, "Allot to every man according to all his ways — for You know the heart of each — for You alone know the hearts of men" (2 Chronicles 6:30).[202]

19:38 One should have trust in God, and know that just as He gives life, so will He give sustenance.[203] Nevertheless, one must also

192. *Pesachim* 118a; *Bereshith Rabbah* 20:22, 97:3; *Midrash Tehillim* 80:2, 89:2, 106:1, 136:9; *Yalkut Shimoni* 2:864; *Zohar* 1:207b, 2:170a, 2:218a, 3:273a, 3:278a, 3:292b; *Tikuney Zohar* 21 (59a), 69 (102a); *Zohar Chadash* 86d; *Nitzotzey Oroth, Zohar* 2:178b no. 3.
193. *Zohar* 2:170a. See above, note 143.
194. *Taanith* 2a-b; *Bereshith Rabbah* 73:3. *Cf. Sanhedrin* 113a; *BaMidbar Rabbah* 7:6; *Midrash Tehillim* 78:5; *Zohar* 1:116b.
195. *Bereshith Rabbah* 69:4; *VaYikra Rabbah* 35:2; *Tanchuma, VaYetze* 3; *Yalkut Shimoni* 2:831.
196. *Sotah* 2a; *Sanhedrin* 22a.
197. *Tanchuma, Tazria* 6.
198. *Betza* 16a; *Tosafoth ad. loc. s.v. Kol; VaYikra Rabbah* 30:1; *Anaf Yosef ad. loc.; Pesikta* 28 (178b); *Rokeach* 228, 307; *Or Zarua, Rosh Chodesh* 453; *Tur, Orach Chaim* 242, 419; *Magen Avraham, Turey Zahav, Mishnah Berurah,* 419:1. *Cf. Bereshith Rabbah* 97:3; *Midrash Tehillim* 89:2.
199. *VaYikra Rabbah* 14:2.
200. *Taanith* 8b; *Shemoth Rabbah* 25:3; *Esther Rabbah* 2:14; *Zohar* 2:62a. *Cf. Shemoth Rabbah* 25:16. See Rabbi Abraham Yehoshua Heschel of Opt, *Ohev Yisrael, Shemini* 61a.
201. *Tanchuma, MiKetz* 1; *Zohar* 1:194a. *Cf. Avodah Zarah* 54b; *Zohar* 1:127a, 3:2a, 3:306a; *Zohar Chadash* 10b.
202. *Shemoth Rabbah* 31:4; *Tanchuma, Terumah* 9. *Cf. Sefer Chasidim* 530.
203. *Mekhilta* to Exodus 16:4 (47b). *Cf. Taanith* 8b.

do one's share in planning for the future, in order not to be in the category of "Your life will hang in suspense" (Deuteronomy 28:66).²⁰⁴ One who has complete trust in God is assured that he will be successful in all his endeavors.²⁰⁵

19:39 Though a person's total lifespan is determined by heredity and environment,²⁰⁶ his days are largely predetermined from the time of his conception,²⁰⁷ and perhaps even generations earlier.²⁰⁸ It is thus written, "The days of a human being are few and full of trouble. He comes forth like a flower and is cut down; [his life] flees like a shadow and does not endure... His days are determined, the number of his months is with You. You have appointed his limits, beyond which he cannot pass" (Job 14:1-5).²⁰⁹

19:40 When one lives out his appointed days, he dies without terror or suffering, like a lamp that goes out when its oil is depleted.²¹⁰ Such a person is likened to a fruit which is harvested in its proper time,²¹¹ as it is written, "You shall come to your grave in ripe old age, like a full sheath of corn comes up in its season" (Job 5:26).²¹² It is a blessing to live out one's appointed time, as God promised, "I will make you live out full lives" (Exodus 23:26).²¹³

19:41 However, a person's days may be increased because of great²¹⁴ merit,²¹⁵ or decreased because of sin.²¹⁶ It is thus written,

204. *Menachoth* 103b; *Yerushalmi, Shabbath* 8:1 (54b); *Yerushalmi, Shekalim* 3:2 (13b), 8:1 (32a); *Esther Rabbah* 0:1.
205. *Midrash Tehillim* 119:3.
206. *Bereshith Rabbah* 65:7; Rashi on Genesis 27:1; see above, note 171.
207. *Koheleth Rabbah* 3:4; Rashi, *Yevamoth* 50a *s.v. Sh'nei; Emunoth VeDeyoth* 6:6 (79b); Ibn Ezra on Exodus 23:26. *Cf. Tanchuma, Pekudey* 3; *Zohar* 2:252b.
208. *Tanchuma, BeChukothai* 1.
209. *Ibid.;* Rashi, Ibn Ezra, *ad. loc.; Yalkut Shimoni* 1:671, 2:175, 2:906.
210. *Bereshith Rabbah* 62:5; *Shir HaShirim Rabbah* 6:6; *Koheleth Rabbah* 5:15; Sforno on Exodus 23:26.
211. *Ibid.; Yerushalmi, Berakhoth* 2:8 (20a).
212. "Ripe old age" is *BeKhelach* (בְּכֶלַח) in Hebrew, which has a numerical value of 60. This means that when a person who is more than 60 years old dies, it is considered a good, natural death, not death by Divine Punishment; Rashi *ad. loc.; cf. Moed Katan* 28a; *Tosafoth ad. loc. s.v. U'Mithah;* Rashbam, Exodus 23:26.
213. *Yevamoth* 50a; *Emunoth VeDeyoth* 6:6 (79b).
214. *Tosafoth, Yevamoth* 50a *s.v. Mosifin. Cf.* Maharsha *ibid.*
215. According to the sages; *Yevamoth* 50a; *Koheleth Rabbah* 3:4; *Emunoth VeDeyoth* 6:6 (79b); Ibn Ezra on Exodus 23:26. However, Rabbi Akiba maintains that even for great merit, one can only fulfill one's days, but not increase them; *cf.* Maharsha *loc. cit.; Asarah Maamaroth* 1:2:28.

"The fear of God prolongs one's days, but the years of the wicked shall be shortened" (Proverbs 10:27).[217] A person can die before his time because of his wickedness[218] or folly,[219] as we are warned, "Do not be overly wicked or foolish; why should you die before your time?" (Ecclesiastes 7:17).[220]

19:42   Ordinarily, a person is not punished by death except for his sins.[221] There are times, however, that a person is punished by God removing His providence from him, leaving him to die by worldly accidents.[222] Regarding this it is written, "One can be gathered up without [apparent] justice" (Proverbs 13:23).[223] This is also true in times of universal judgment, when both the righteous and wicked are swept away together.[224] Similarly, in a great majority of cases, early death is not caused by God's decree, but by the individual's own carelessness[225] and sexual intemperance.[226]

19:43   Notwithstanding all this, every life that is taken by God is taken in judgment.[227] In general, God tries to plan each person's death so that it will do him the most spiritual good.[228] Thus, God might take the life of a wicked person to stop him from sinning further, or that of a righteous individual so that he need no longer battle

---

216. Maharsha *loc. cit.* See above, 13:47, 13:49.
217. *Devarim Rabbah* 9:1; *Emunoth VeDeyoth,* Ibn Ezra, *loc. cit.*
218. *Yevamoth* 50a; *Tosafoth, Shabbath* 25a *s.v. Kareth. Cf. Berakhoth* 55a.
219. *Cf.* Ibn Ezra on Deuteronomy 20:7; *Avi Ezer ad. loc.*
220. Ibn Ezra on Exodus 23:26. *Cf. Shabbath* 31b; *Yoma* 22b.
221. Rav Ami, *Shabbath* 55a, although on *Shabbath* 55b this is refuted as a general rule since there are some exceptions; *cf. Tosafoth ad. loc. s.v. U'Shema Mina; Zohar* 1:57b. *Cf. VaYikra Rabbah* 37:1; *Koheleth Rabbah* 5:2; *Yalkut Shimoni* 2:151, 2:840; *Moreh Nevukhim* 3:17 (25a); *Shem Tov ad. loc.;* Ramban, *Torath HaAdam* 73a; Rabbenu Yonah, *Berakhoth* (Rif 34b); Rosh, *Berakhoth* 7:13. Also see *Berakhoth* 33a; *Tosefta* 3:30; *Yerushalmi* 5:1 (38a).
222. *Sheveiley Emunah* 1 (10a). *Cf. Sotah* 11a.
223. Rashi, Ralbag, *ad. loc.; Chagigah* 4b; *Bereshith Rabbah* 49:15; *Yalkut Shimoni* 2:550; *Zohar* 1:113a, 2:139a, 2:196a, 2:249a, 3:40b, 3:54b, 3:59b, 3:283, 3:291b; *Sefer Chasidim* 213; *Chidushey Anshey Shem, Berakhoth* (Rif 34b).
224. *Bava Kama* 60a; *Zohar* 1:113a, 2:182b; see below, 20:36.
225. *VaYikra Rabbah* 16:8. *Cf. Zohar* 2:196a; *Koheleth Rabbah* 3:2. See below....
226. Rashi, *Bava Metzia* 97a *s.v. DeNashei Katluhu, Baal BeIyloth Harbe; Yad, Deyoth* 4:19; *Orach Chaim* 240:14; *Kitzur Shulchan Arukh* 151:17. *Cf. Gittin* 70a.
227. *Cf. Berakhoth* 46b; Rosh 7:13; *Maadney Yom Tov ad. loc.* no. 200; Rabbenu Yonah, *Chidushey Anshey Shem, ad. loc.; Yoreh Deah* 379:1 in *Hagah.* However, this reading is omitted in Rif, *Berakhoth* 34b; *Yad, Berakhoth* 2:8; *cf. Hagahoth Maimonioth, Kesef Mishneh, ad. loc.*
228. *Yerushalmi, Berakhoth* 2:8 (20a); *Bereshith Rabbah* 62:5; *Shir HaShirim Rabbah* 6:6; *Koheleth Rabbah* 5:15.

the evil in himself.[229] On the other hand, God may give the wicked additional years to repent,[230] or take away years from the righteous lest they turn to evil.[231] King Solomon thus wrote, "I have seen all kinds of things in the fleeting days: There was the righteous man who perished in his righteousness, and there was the wicked man who lived long in his evildoing" (Ecclesiastes 7:15).[232]

19:44   God does not desire the death of the righteous, as it is written, "Precious in God's eyes is the death of His saints" (Psalms 116:15).[233] When a good person dies before his time, he often receives the same reward that he would have had for his full lifetime.[234] Similarly, by making efficient use of their time, many righteous people have accomplished in a short time what others cannot accomplish in a long lifetime.[235]

19:45   God created this world as a place of maximum challenge,[236] and therefore, man must be inherently imperfect and die.[237] The sin of Adam revealed this imperfection[238] because of which man must make the transition of death.[239] Accordingly, God told Adam, "But from the Tree of Knowledge of Good and Evil, do not eat, for on the day you eat from it, you will definitely die" (Genesis 2:17).[240] Since we are all descendants of Adam, all men must share this fate.[241]

19:46   Therefore, death is the destiny of every man, and none can escape it. We are thus taught, "[Just as] no man can control the

---

229. *Bereshith Rabbah* 9:5.
230. *Koheleth Rabbah* 7:32; *Zohar* 2:10b.
231. *Ibid. Cf. Bereshith Rabbah* 25:1; Rashi on Genesis 5:24; *Maadney Yom Tov loc. cit.*
232. *Koheleth Rabbah* 7:32.
233. Or, "It is difficult for God to decree the death of His saints"; *Devarim Rabbah* 9:1.
234. *Tanchuma, Ki Tissa* 3. *Cf. Sefer Chasidim* 222.
235. *Yerushalmi, Berakhoth* 2:8 (20a); *Koheleth Rabbah* 5:18; *Shir HaShirim Rabbah* 6:8. [The author was one of these remarkable people. *Ed.*]
236. See Volume 1, 3:22-27.
237. *Koheleth Rabbah* 1:9.
238. *Cf. Tanchuma, VaYeshev* 4, that God created death before He created Adam, knowing that he would sin and die.
239. *Avodah Zarah* 5a; *Sanhedrin* 102a; *Avodath HaKodesh* 2:21 (41d).
240. *Cf.* Rashi *ad. loc.; Bereshith Rabbah* 16:10.
241. *Sifra* 27a; *Bereshith Rabbah* 16:10, 21:1. *Cf. Devarim Rabbah* 9:4; *Koheleth Rabbah* 7:28, where the example given is that a child born in prison must suffer, though it is the fault of its mother that it is there at all.

wind or stop it from blowing, neither is there any control over the day of death" (Ecclesiastes 8:8).[242] No matter what a person may attain in life, he cannot conquer death. It is thus written, "The triumph of the wicked is shortlived, and the rejoicing of the hypocrite is but for a moment. Though he be elevated to the heavens in his eminence, and his head reach the clouds, he shall perish forever like his own dung. Those who see him shall ask, 'Where has he gone?'" (Job 20:5-7).[243] Even the perfectly righteous must die,[244] since no distinctions can be made in this world which might tend to destroy or diminish man's choice between good and evil.[245]

19:47 Because of man's inherent imperfection, death is for his own good,[246] since it reminds him that he is below God[247] and that he must repent each day.[248] Since man must constantly be in a state of repentance,[249] no man is allowed to know the time of his death.[250] Regarding this it is written, "For no man knows his time. Like fish caught in a net of evil, and birds caught in a trap, so are men trapped when a time of evil suddenly descends upon them" (Ecclesiastes 9:12).[251] However, God makes man forget his death, so that he may also flourish in this world.[252]

242. *Devarim Rabbah* 9:3; *Koheleth Rabbah* 8:11. *Cf. Bereshith Rabbah* 96:3; *BaMidbar Rabbah* 15:12; *Tanchuma, BeHa'alothekha* 10.
243. *Tanchuma, VaEthChanan* 6. *Cf. Avoth* 4:22; *Tanchuma, Pekudey* 3; *Midrash Tehillim* 38:1.
244. *Shabbath* 55b; *Zohar* 1:53a, 1:57b, 2:194b. *Cf. Sanhedrin* 48b, 101a; *Zohar* 3:276a; *Mitzpeh Eithan* on *Shabbath* 55b.
245. *Bereshith Rabbah* 9:6. See Volume 1, 3:36.
246. *Bereshith Rabbah* 9:5; *Zohar* 1:47a, 1:144b.
247. *Bereshith Rabbah* 9:6. *Cf. Bava Bathra* 75a (end).
248. *Zohar* 2:149b, 2:209a. See above, 15:38.
249. Maharsha, *Shabbath* 30a.
250. *Shabbath* 30a; *Ruth Rabbah* 3:2; *Koheleth Rabbah* 5:13; *Yalkut Shimoni* 2:735; *Zohar* 1:218a. *Cf. Nitzotzey Oroth, Zohar* 3:205a no. 1, that although a person does not know his day of death, he may know when years have been added to his life; *cf. Bava Bathra* 11a. Also see *Etz HaDa'ath* (Rabbi Chaim Vital) on Genesis 27:2, that some righteous individuals know when they are about to die, but not the exact hour or day.
251. *Bereshith Rabbah* 65:7; *Koheleth Rabbah* 11:9. *Cf.* Psalms 54b; *Sanhedrin* 81b; *Mekhilta* on Exodus 16:32 (51a).
252. "If God had not made men's hearts oblivious to their imminent death, they would not build and plant, but say, 'Tomorrow I am going to die, why should I stand and toil for the benefit of others'"; *Tanchuma, Kedoshim* 8; *Midrash Tehillim* 9:1.

19:48 When a person becomes sick and bedridden, he is judged whether he is worthy of recuperating,[253] and therefore whether he is worthy of experiencing a special degree of providence.[254] We are thus taught that God pays special attention to the sick, as the Psalmist said, "God strengthens the sick man on his bed" (Psalms 41:4).[255] Therefore, although a sick person must seek out the best possible medical treatment, he should still pray to God for divine aid.[256]

19:49 Life, children and economic prosperity, form the basis of God's control of the historical process. Power over these things therefore remains in His hands alone.[257] God makes His long term plans for humanity on the assumption that man will do good.[258] As such, any sin affecting life, children, or property, causes God to revise His plans.[259] It is for this reason that God strongly forbade such sins in the Ten Commandments, "Do not commit murder. Do not commit adultery. Do not steal. Do not testify as a false witness against your neighbor" (Exodus 20:13).[260] These sins are even worse than idolatry, since idol worship only affects God's honor, while these pervert His very control of history.[261]

19:50 Murder is one of the very worst of sins,[262] since its effects can be felt for all future generations.[263] Since the offspring of a single person can comprise a significant portion of humanity after a

253. *Shabbath* 32a; *Zohar* 3:309a; *Zohar Chadash* 14c, 18d; *Kitzur Shulchan Arukh* 192:1.
254. *Shabbath* 12b; *Nedarim* 40a; *Zohar* 3:234b; *Tikuney Zohar* 18 (33b); *She'iltoth, Acharey Moth* 93; Rashi on Genesis 47:31; Rosh, *Shabbath* 1:30; *Yad, Avel* 14:6; *Yoreh Deah* 335:3.
255. *Shabbath* 12b; *VaYikra Rabbah* 34:1.
256. See above, 5:3, note 7.
257. *Akedath Yitzchak* 22 (1:158b), from *Taanith* 2a; *Sanhedrin* 113a; *Bereshith Rabbah* 73:3; *BaMidbar Rabbah* 7:6; *Midrash Tehillim* 78:5; *Zohar* 1:10a, 1:102b, 1:116b, 1:117b; *Tosafoth, Niddah* 16b *s.v. Malakh; Ikkarim* 4:8 (149b). *Cf. VaYikra Rabbah* 14:2; *Taanith* 10a; *Zohar* 3:244a.
258. See Volume 1, 3:39, note 59. *Cf. Avoth* 3:15.
259. *Sh'nei Luchoth HaB'rith, Beth HaBechirah* 1:44b *s.v. VeAtah.* See below, note 282.
260. *Cf.* Ramban, *Torath HaAdam* 73a.
261. *Shemoth Rabbah* 30:17.
262. See above, 14:13.
263. *Cf. Sanhedrin* 4:5 (37a); *Bereshith Rabbah* 22:21; *Avoth DeRabbi Nathan* 31:2; *Targum Yerushalmi,* Rashi, on Genesis 4:10. Also *Shemoth Rabbah* 1:33; *VaYikra Rabbah* 32:4; *Midrash Tehillim* 24:7; *Zohar* 2:12b; *Targum Yonathan,* Rashi, on Exodus 2:12.

sufficient number of generations,[264] we are taught that one who kills a single human being is like one who destroys an entire world.[265] Since, unlike animals, man enjoys individual providence, every murder forces God to set up new chains of events to assure the birth of those persons upon whom history depends.[266]

19:51 Similarly, sexual crimes upset God's plans of matching individuals to produce special traits in their children. The illegitimate children of such contacts are not anticipated by providence and therefore have no status in God's plans.[267] When such a child is not known to be illegitimate, God therefore causes him to die at an early age[268] before he can marry and have children of his own.[269] Similarly, when a child is known to be illegitimate, he is forbidden by Torah law from the normal channels of marriage in order that he not affect a large segment of the population.[270] Nevertheless, a bastard who becomes pious and learned can take precedence over the High Priest.[271]

19:52 When general immorality and a high rate of illegitimacy prevail, God may have to take action to destroy all illegitimate offspring before they are forgotten and mix with the general populace. Since most family details are forgotten after three generations,[272] or approximately seventy years,[273] God may bring about a general

264. If we assume that a certain couple have a "small" family of only two children, and that each of their descendants also has a similar family, averaging two children, the number of descendants will double in each generation. Thus, the couple has two children, four grandchildren, eight great-grandchildren, and sixteen great-great-grandchildren. After 10 generations, this couple has 1024 descendants, after 20 generations, they have 1,048,576 descendants, and after only 24 generations — a mere 600 years — there will be 16,777,216 descendants. This is very close to the current world Jewish population. See Kaplan, *Made in Heaven* (Moznaim, 1983), p. 4.
265. *Sanhedrin, Avoth DeRabbi Nathan, loc. cit.*
266. *Sheveiley Emunah* 1 (10a). Cf. *Pesikta Rabathai* 21 (108a); *Zohar* 3:12a, from Habakkuk 1:14; also *Avodah Zarah* 4a; *Yalkut Shimoni* 2:562.
267. *BaMidbar Rabbah* 9:4.
268. *Yevamoth* 78b; *Kiddushin* 71a; *Yerushalmi* 3:12 (40b); *VaYikra Rabbah* 32:6; *BaMidbar Rabbah* 9:4.
269. Cf. *Baal HaTurim* on Deuteronomy 23:3.
270. Deuteronomy 23:3; *Targum Yonathan*, Rashi, *ad. loc.; Yevamoth* 8:3 (78b); *Yad, Issurey Biyah* 15:1; *Evven HaEzer* 4:1; *Chinukh* 560.
271. *Horayoth* 3:8 (13a); *Yerushalmi, Shabbath* 12:3 (69b); *BaMidbar Rabbah* 6:1; *Yad, Talmud Torah* 3:2, *Matnoth Ani'im* 8:18; *Yoreh Deah* 246:15 in *Hagah*, 251:9; *Sifethey Cohen* 246:14, 251:15; *Beer Sheva* 53c.
272. *Yevamoth* 78b.
273. Cf. *Kethuvoth* 20b; *Ohaloth* 16:2; Rambam, Bertenoro, *ad. loc.;* Mordecai, *Bava*

catastrophe to wipe out all illegitimate offspring within this period.[274] Since this general immorality will badly upset God's ultimate plans, He may have to destroy a large segment of the population, both innocent and guilty alike, through famine, war, or plague, in order to set His plans in order again.[275] It is for this reason that God shows little mercy in the case of sexual crimes,[276] causing the person tempted by fleshpots to eat his own flesh in remorse.[277]

19:53 Robbery also upsets God's plans for the world, causing redistribution of property contrary to His will.[278] Since this crime also causes much suffering,[279] it is the one sin for which the judgment of a city or nation may be sealed.[280] The punishment for corruption is most severe, since only a major catastrophe can set things right, and accordingly the prophet said, "The people of the land have oppressed and robbed one another... I have therefore poured out My indignation upon them" (Ezekiel 22:29-31).[281]

19:54 Similarly, the miscarriage of justice is a sin that can upset God's plans,[282] and therefore cause general disaster.[283] Like robbery, it can seal the doom of a country.[284] All judges are therefore warned that their decisions not only involve other human beings, but have an effect on God's own plans, as it is written, "Consider what you do, for you judge not [only] for man, but for God who is with you in judgment" (2 Chronicles 19:6).[285]

Bathra 521; *Tosefoth Yom Tov, Bava Bathra* 2:4; *Choshen Mishpat* 155:13; *Sifethey Cohen* 155:9; *Sefer Meirath Eynayim (Sema)* 155:33. *Cf. Shabbath* 10b; Rashi on Genesis 19:20; *Makkoth* 1:10 (7a); *Zohar* 2:27b, 2:34b.

274. *Yerushalmi, Yevamoth* 8:3 (49b); *Yerushalmi, Kiddushin* 4:1 (43b); *VaYikra Rabbah* 32:6; *BaMidbar Rabbah* 9:4; *Sefer Chasidim* 213.

275. *Yerushalmi, Sotah* 1:5 (6a); *Bereshith Rabbah* 26:10; *VaYikra Rabbah* 23:9; *Tanchuma, Bereshith* 12; Rashi on Genesis 19:20.

276. *Bereshith Rabbah* 26:10; *BaMidbar Rabbah* 9:4; *Tanchuma, VaYera* 9; *Zohar* 2:3b. *Cf. Shaarey Zohar* 136c.

277. *Bereshith Rabbah* 41:9; *Tanchuma, VaYera* 12; *Pesikta Rabathai* 12.

278. See below, note 282.

279. *VaYikra Rabbah* 33:3; *Koheleth Rabbah* 1:34; *Yalkut Shimoni* 2:362, 2:546.

280. *Sanhedrin* 108a; *Bereshith Rabbah* 31:4; *Tanchuma, Noah* 4; *Zohar* 1:67a; *Zohar Chadash* 21d; Rashi on Genesis 6:13; *Sifethey Chakhamim (Mem) ad. loc.;* Maharal, *Gur Aryeh* 21a *ad. loc.;* Ramban *ibid.;* Radak on Jonah 1:2.

281. *VaYikra Rabbah* 33:3; *Koheleth Rabbah* 1:34.

282. *Yerushalmi, Sanhedrin* 1:1 (2b end); *Tanchuma, Shoftim* 7.

283. *Cf. Shemoth Rabbah* 31:8.

284. *Shemoth Rabbah* 30:15.

285. See above, note 282; *cf. Sanhedrin* 6b; *Tosefta* 1:4.

19:55 One of the important tasks of Divine Providence is maintaining a certain number[286] of righteous individuals in each generation.[287] By their merit[288] and example, these invidivuals offer spiritual support to all humanity.[289] In order to assure that individuals will be born with both the heredity and environment,[290] as well as the spiritual traits[291] needed to be great spiritual leaders, God sets up chains of events, sometimes dating all the way back to Adam.[292] Providence also arranges that before one saint dies, another is born.[293]

19:56 Although man has free will, certain individuals are predisposed by birth to be good.[294] Accordingly, God told His prophet, "Before I formed you in the womb, I knew you, and before you were born, I sanctified you. I appointed you a prophet to the nations" (Jeremiah 1:5).[295] Similarly, when God needs avengers, He causes

---

286. Some sources give this number as 36; *cf. Sukkah* 45b; *Sanhedrin* 97b. In *Tikuney Zohar* 21 (50b), we find a total of 72 righteous individuals, 36 in Israel, and 36 in other lands. However, the majority of sources give this number as 30; *cf. Yerushalmi, Avodah Zarah* 2:1 (9a); *Bereshith Rabbah* 35:2, 49:7, 98:14; *Tanchuma, VaYera* 13, *MiKetz* 6; *Midrash Tehillim* 5:5; *Pesikta* 10 (88a); *Midrash Lekach Tov, Lekh Lekha* 15:5, *VaYera* 18:18; *Zohar* 1:105b, 1:255a; *Zohar Chadash* 26a; *Bahir* 101; *Baal HaTurim* on Deuteronomy 26:1. According to *Midrash Tehillim* 5:5, 18 of these are in Israel, and 12 in other lands; *cf. Yerushalmi loc. cit.; Bereshith Rabbah* 98:14. According to *Chullin* 92a, there are 45 righteous individuals in the world, 30 in Israel and 15 in other lands, as well as 30 righteous gentiles. Other sources give 50; *cf. Pirkey Rabbi Eliezer* 25 (58b); *Radal ad. loc.* 25:13. In *Bereshith Rabbah* 56:9, we find that each generation must have righteous men like Abraham, Jacob, Moses and Samuel, based on the fact that the name of each is doubled in scripture; *cf. Etz Yosef ad. loc.;* Genesis 22:11, 46:2; Exodus 3:4; 1 Samuel 3:10. Still another source requires three righteous individuals in each generation; *BaMidbar Rabbah* 3:1; *Midrash Tehillim* 92:11.
287. *Yoma* 38b, from 1 Samuel 2:8; *Likutey Amarim, Sefer Shel Benonim* 1 (5b).
288. *Berakhoth* 17b; *Taanith* 24b; *Chullin* 86a.
289. *Yoma* 38b; *Chagigah* 12b; *Mekhilta* on Exodus 15:1 (34b); *Bereshith Rabbah* 75:11; *Tanchuma, BeShalach* 10, *Nitzavim* 2; *Midrash Tehillim* 136:5; *Yalkut Shimoni* 2:633, from Proverbs 10:25. *Cf. Midrash Tehillim* 116:6, 117:2.
290. Rabbi Yaakov Emdin (Maharibatz) on *Yoma* 38b.
291. *Bava Bathra* 16a; Maharsha *ad. loc.; Yalkut Shimoni* 2:904, from Job 10:7; *Likutey Amarim, Sefer Shel Benonim* 1 (5a), 1:14 (20a).
292. *Cf. Sanhedrin* 38b; *Avodah Zarah* 4a; *Bereshith Rabbah* 24:2; *Shemoth Rabbah* 40:2; *Tanchuma, Ki Tissa* 12; *Pesikta Rabathai* 28; *Zohar* 1:55a, 1:90b, 1:227b, 2:70b; Rashi on Jeremiah 1:5. *Cf. Menachoth* 28b; *VaYikra Rabbah* 26:7; *Tana DeBei Eliahu Zuta* 10; *Zohar* 3:157a.
193. *Yoma* 38b; *Kiddushin* 72b; *Bereshith Rabbah* 58:2; *Koheleth Rabbah* 1:10; *Aggadath Shemoth* 8.
294. *Chullin* 139b; *Pirkey Rabbi Eliezer* 32 (72a).
295. Rashi, Radak, *ad. loc.; Yoma* 82b; *Yerushalmi, Berakhoth* 1:6 (11b); *Mekhilta* on Exodus 13:2 (19a); *Midrash Tehillim* 9:7, 139:4; *Zohar* 1:53b; *Tosafoth, Menachoth* 53b

individuals predisposed toward evil to be born. Regarding these, the Psalmist said, "The wicked are estranged from conception; speakers of falsehood err from birth" (Psalms 58:4).[296]

19:57 Although many acts of providence are miraculous, their supermundane nature is kept hidden from man.[297] It is for this reason that God only bestows His blessing upon that which is hidden from the eye,[298] and never upon that which can be measured.[299]

19:58 God has a special love for messengers of good,[300] and therefore protects them with a special degree of providence,[301] except where danger is imminent.[302] Similarly, God pays particular attention to a person who is being pursued.[303]

19:59 Although each individual enjoys particular providence, that extended to groups, institutions[304] and governments is much more exacting. Accordingly, we are taught that the chains of events leading to changes in government[305] are so precisely ordained by providence, that the time of succession is determined to a hairsbreadth.[306]

19:60 Although war sometimes fulfills God's purpose, He constantly strives for peace in the world.[307] The ultimate blessing[308] which God wishes to bestow is that of peace, as the Psalmist said, "God will give strength to His people; God will bless His people with peace" (Psalms 29:11).[309]

s.v. Ben; Moreh Nevukhim 2:32 (68b). *Cf. Bereshith Rabbah* 63:6; *Midrash Tehillim* 58:2; *Zohar* 1:139a; Rashi on Genesis 25:22.
296. *Ibid.*
297. *Niddah* 31a; *Shemoth Rabbah* 24:1; *Midrash Tehillim* 106:1, 136:2; *Yalkut Shimoni* 2:864.
298. *Taanith* 8b; *Bava Metzia* 42a; *Orach Chaim* 230:2.
299. *Ibid.; Bereshith Rabbah* 64:6.
300. *BaMidbar Rabbah* 16:1.
301. *Pesachim* 8a; *Yoma* 11a; *Kiddushin* 39b; *Chullin* 142a; *Zohar* 3:273a, 3:298a.
302. *Ibid.; cf. Zohar* 1:111b, 1:209a, 1:230b; *Zohar Chadash* 22a.
303. *VaYikra Rabbah* 27:5; *Koheleth Rabbah* 3:19; *Ikkarim* 4:9.
304. *Cf. Moed Katan* 28a.
305. *Zohar* 1:177a.
306. *Berakhoth* 48b; *Shabbath* 30a; *Moed Katan* 28a; *Yoma* 38b; *Taanith* 5b; *Shir HaShirim Rabbah* 3:8; *Ruth Rabbah* 3:2; *Koheleth Rabbah* 5:13; *Zohar* 3:284a; *Tikuney Zohar* 19 (38a). See Rashi, *Yoma* 38b *s.v. VeEin Malkhuth Nogaath BeChaverthah*, from Daniel 5:20; Ezekiel 30:18.
307. *Bereshith Rabbah* 38:6, 48:21, 100:9; *BaMidbar Rabbah* 11:16; *Devarim Rabbah* 5:14.
308. *VaYikra Rabbah* 9:9.
309. *Uktzin* 3:11.

TWENTY

APPARENT INJUSTICE

20:1   Although belief in God's justice is a foundation of our faith, we often find apparent injustice when the wicked prosper and the righteous suffer.[1] King Solomon spoke of this when he said, "There is a vanity which transpires upon the earth. There are righteous men who get what the wicked deserve, and there are wicked men who get what the righteous deserve" (Ecclesiastes 8:14).[2] The Psalmist similarly complained, "Behold these wicked people, their world is peaceful; they attain great wealth. Have I then purified my heart in vain and cleansed my hands [for naught]? For I am plagued all [my] days and my chastisement [is renewed] each morning" (Psalms 73:12-14).[3] Nevertheless, we believe that even in such cases God's justice is manifest, and it is either for the ultimate benefit of the individual or for all mankind.[4]

20:2   The first apparent injustice — why the wicked prosper — is the more pressing question. The prophet therefore asks, "Why do the wicked prosper in their ways? Why are those who deal treacherously at peace?" (Jeremiah 12:1).[5] Why is it that, "Robbers prosper in their tents, and those who provoke God are secure" (Job 12:6)?[6] Why do, "Those who do evil prosper, and those who put God to the test escape" (Malachi 3:15)?[7]

1.   *Berakhoth* 7a; *Shemoth Rabbah* 45:6; *Zohar* 2:117b, 3:168a, 3:231a, 3:276a. *Cf.* Rabbi Yanai, *Avoth* 4:14; *Midrash Sh'muel ad. loc* 4:19.
2.   *Ikkarim* 4:14. *Cf. BaMidbar Rabbah* 19:6; *Tanchuma, Chukath* 10; *Likutey Moharan* 31:8.
3.   *Chovoth HaLevavoth* 4:3 (110a); *Moreh Nevukhim* 3:19 (28a); *Ikkarim* 4:14.
4.   *Horayoth* 10b; *Yerushalmi, Horayoth* 3:2 (15b); *Koheleth Rabbah* 8:15.
5.   *Chovoth HaLevavoth* 4:3 (110a); *Moreh Nevukhim* 3:19 (28a); *Ikkarim* 4:14; *Menorath HaMaor* 5:2:1:3 (292). *Cf. Sanhedrin* 96a; *Devarim Rabbah* 1:16. Also see *Koheleth Rabbah* 3:24.
6.   *Ikkarim* 4:14. *Cf. Yerushalmi, Taanith* 3:4 (15a).
7.   *Chovoth HaLevavoth* 4:3 (110a); *Ikkarim* 4:14. *Cf. BaMidbar Rabbah* 11:1.

20:3   One answer to this is that the visible world represents only half a picture, the other half being man's ultimate future. Therefore, since God does not deny any creature his reward,[8] and because a person immersed in evil is unable to benefit from anything spiritual,[9] God gives the wicked their reward in this world, allowing them to prosper.[10] The only reason they are rewarded here, however, is because they have no spiritual future.[11] The Torah thus states, "But [God] rewards His enemies to their face to destroy them" (Deuteronomy 7:10). That is, He rewards them in this world in order to destroy them in the next.[12] Indeed, we are taught that many pleasures were created solely in order to reward the wicked in this world.[13]

20:4   Hence, the good that the wicked receive in this world is to their detriment.[14] King David thus wrote, "When the lawless thrive like grass and the wicked prosper, it is so that they may be destroyed forever" (Psalms 92:8).[15] It is also written, "There is a path that seems right to a man, but at its ends are the paths of death" (Proverbs 14:12, 16:25).[16] We are thus taught that if a person finds himself inordinately free of suffering and troubles, he should

---

8.   See above, 18:11, note 61. *Cf.* 1 Kings 14:13; Ralbag *ad. loc.; Sefer Chasidim* 606. Also *Taanith* 11a, from Deuteronomy 32:4.
9.   *Kiddushin* 40a; *Rosh David* (Chida) *ad. loc.; Avoth DeRabbi Nathan* 39:1; *Zohar* 1:180b; Maharal, *Tifereth Yisrael* 60; *B'rith Olam* on *Sefer Chasidim* 606; see above, 18:11.
10.   *Kiddushin* 39b; *Sanhedrin* 111a; *Yerushalmi, Peah* 1:1 (5a); *Yerushalmi, Kiddushin* 1:9 (23a); *Yerushalmi, Sanhedrin* 10:1 (49a); *Avoth DeRabbi Nathan* 25:1; *Bereshith Rabbah* 33:1; *VaYikra Rabbah* 27:1; *Tanchuma, Kedoshim* 1, *Emor* 5; *Midrash Tehillim* 17:11, 86:7, 103:11, 119:8; *Pesikta* 9 (73a); *Yalkut Shimoni* 2:726; *Zohar* 3:9a, 3:231a; *Tikuney Zohar* 69 (111a); *Emunoth VeDeyoth* 5:2 (70a); Ramban, *Torath HaAdam* 73a; *Sefer Chasidim* 342, 408, 530, 605, 606, 695, 696; *Ikkarim* 4:14; *Derekh HaShem* 2:2:6. *Cf. Yerushalmi, Chagigah* 2:2 (11a); *Yerushalmi, Sanhedrin* 606 (28b).
11.   *Midrash Tehillim* 73:1; *Yalkut Shimoni* 2:808; Rashi on Psalms 73:4. *Cf. Shemoth Rabbah* 30:18; *Tanchuma, Mishpatim* 3.
12.   Targum, *Targum Yonathan,* Rashi, Ibn Ezra, Ramban, *ad. loc.; Shemoth Rabbah* 45:6; *Tanchuma, Mishpatim* 9, *Ki Tissa* 27; *Midrash Tehillim* 7:17, 94:4; *Pesikta* 25 (161b); *Zohar* 1:25b, 1:180b, 3:277b; *Chovoth HaLevavoth* 3:6 (87b); *Tosafoth, Rosh HaShanah* 16b *s.v. VeNechtamim; Sefer Mitzvoth Gadol,* Positive Commandment 17; *Sefer Chasidim* 605, 606; *Ikkarim* 4:12. *Cf. Eruvin* 22a.
13.   *Eruvin* 65a; *BaMidbar Rabbah* 10:8.
14.   *Yoma* 87a, from Proverbs 18:5. See note 4.
15.   *Tanchuma, Mishpatim* 9; *Pirkey Rabbi Eliezer* 19 (45a); *Ikkarim* 4:12. *Cf. Esther Rabbah* 7:2; *Midrash Tehillim* 37:2; *Zohar* 3:76a.
16.   See above, 18:11.

examine his ways. He may be receiving his just reward entirely in this world.[17]

20:5 Likewise, a person who regrets any good that he has done is denied all future reward for it, but may be given some reward in this world. It is for this reason that an apostate may prosper greatly after abandoning the Jewish faith.[18]

20:6 God often inflates and elevates the wicked before casting them down in order that their punishment be greater[19] and more publicized.[20] We are taught that the wicked are like grasshoppers who jump high and then fall.[21] Regarding this it is written, "Conceit precedes destruction" (Proverbs 16:18).[22]

20:7 At times, God has mercy on the wicked[23] and gives them good in order that they may be thankful to Him and repent.[24] On the other hand, there are times that God grants them prosperity in order to harden their hearts and prevent them from repenting. All depends on a person's individual nature, and the extent of his wickedness.[25]

20:8 Prosperity may have been decreed for a person while he was still righteous, and the effects of this good might remain even after he turns to evil.[26] This is because a person is not judged for any sins he may do in the future,[27] as it is written, "[God] knows the corrupt man, and though He foresees [the latter's] vice, He does not consider it" (Job 11:11).[28]

17. *Arakhin* 16b; Maharsha *ad. loc.;* Ramban, *Torath HaAdam* 72a; *Menorath HaMaor* 5:3:1:3 (300).
18. *Emunoth VeDeyoth* 5:2 (70b).
19. *Ibid.* 5:3 (71a); *Chovoth HaLevavoth* 4:3 (111a); *Sefer Chasidim* 695.
20. *Esther Rabbah* 7:2. See above, 19:12.
21. *Midrash Tehillim* 2:2
22. Rashi on *Avoth* 1:13; *Sefer Chasidim* 695. Cf. *Megillah* 15b.
23. *Yerushalmi, Berakhoth* 9:2 (64a); *Koheleth Rabbah* 7:32; *Tanchuma, Tazria* 9; *Midrash Tehillim* 7:1; *Tosafoth, Eruvin* 22a *s.v. Erekh Apayim; Emunoth VeDeyoth* 5:3 (71a); Rabbenu Yonah, *Shaarey Teshuvah* 3:123. See above, 15:9, 18:41.
24. *Ikkarim* 4:12; *Tifereth Yisrael, Kiddushin* 4:14; *cf.* Isaiah 26:10; *Targum,* Ibn Ezra, Radak, *ad. loc.; Megillah* 6a.
25. Ramban, *Torath HaAdam* 73a; *Ikkarim* 4:14. See Volume 1, 3:49; above, 15:55.
26. *Ikkarim* 4:14.
27. *Rosh HaShanah* 16b; *Yerushalmi, Rosh HaShanah* 1:3 (7b); *Bereshith Rabbah* 53:19; *Shemoth Rabbah* 3:3; *Tanchuma, VaYetze* 5; *Midrash Tehillim* 5:5; *Targum Yonathan,* Rashi, Ramban, on Genesis 21:17; *Zohar* 1:121b; *Zohar Chadash* 20a.
28. Rashi *ad. loc.; Yerushalmi, Shemoth Rabbah, Tanchuma, loc. cit.*

20:9   God may also grant good to a wicked person knowing that he will later repent.[29] Though God does not punish a person for his future sins, He does reward one for his future good deeds.[30]

20:10   Since God judges cities, nations, and the entire world collectively,[31] the wicked may prosper because of the place where they live or because of the group with which they are associated.[32] This is especially true when they live among the righteous and partake of their blessing.[33]

20:11   Thus, a wicked individual may be given good because of his association with a good man.[34] This is what Laban meant when he said to Jacob, "Through divination I have learned that it is because of you that God has blessed me" (Genesis 30:27).[35] Regarding Joseph, it is also written, "As soon as [his master] had placed him in charge of his household and possessions, God blessed the Egyptian because of Joseph" (Genesis 39:5).[36] In a similar manner, God may grant a wicked person good because of the prayer of a righteous man.[37]

20:12   There are times when God brings good to an entire undeserving city or nation for the sake of one righteous individual,[38] as God's angel promised Lot, "I will not overturn the city you mentioned" (Genesis 19:21).[39] Countless people may be benefitted for the sake of one man, as God promised Abraham, "All the families of

29. *Chovoth HaLevavoth* 4:3 (111a); *Sheveiley Emunah* 9 (87c); *cf. Emunoth VeDeyoth* 5:3 (71a). See note 23.
30. *Zohar* 1:121b, 1:227a.
31. *Cf. Kiddushin* 40b; *Yad, Teshuvah* 3:2, 3:4; Ramban on Deuteronomy 11:13.
32. *Ikkarim* 4:14; *Derekh HaShem* 2:3:7.
33. *Sukkah* 56b.
34. *Avoth DeRabbi Nathan* 30:3; *Zohar* 1:189a; *Ikkarim* 4:14. *Cf.* Genesis 13:5; *Targum Yonathan,* Rashi, *ad. loc.;* Genesis 19:29; *Bava Kama* 93a; *Bereshith Rabbah* 41:4; *Eikhah Rabbah* 1:40.
35. *Berakhoth* 42a; *Sanhedrin* 39b; *Tosefta, Sotah* 10:3; *Yerushalmi, Avodah Zarah* 3:2 (19a); *Bereshith Rabbah* 73:6.
36. *Ibid.*
37. *Emunoth VeDeyoth* 5:3 (70a), from Genesis 19:21.
38. *Cf. Taanith* 9b, 21b; *Yerushalmi, Taanith* 3:2 (14a); *VaYikra Rabbah* 35:9.
39. Rashi *ad. loc.* Whereas Lot is here considered righteous, this was in relation to the people of Sodom; in relation to Abraham, he was considered wicked, and it was only in Abraham's merit that both he and the people of Tzoar were saved; Rashi, Genesis 19:19; *Sifethey Chakhamim ad. loc. Peh;* Also see *Zohar* 1:104a, on Genesis 19:29.

the earth will be blessed through you" (Genesis 12:3).[40] Indeed, there are times when the entire world may be sustained by the merit of a single saint.[41] It is thus written, "The righteous man is the foundation of the world" (Proverbs 10:25).[42]

20:13 Our sages teach us that a parent can endow his children with five things.[43] It is thus possible that one be born affluent as a result of his parentage, or that he later attain wealth as a result of his parents' merit.[44] In order to save oneself and avoid ultimate destruction, on the other hand, one cannot rely upon parental merit. Without some merit of his own,[45] even the merit of the Patriarchs cannot help him.[46]

20:14 Similarly, success and other good may be granted to an individual in order that his children be born with these advantages.[47] There are times when the merit of a good child helps even where parental merit does not.[48] God may cause one to prosper so that his righteous children may have plenty. It is thus written, "The wealth of the sinner is laid up for the righteous" (Proverbs 13:22).[49] Similarly, "[The wicked] may prepare [a garment], but the righteous will wear it and the innocent will divide his silver" (Job 27:17).[50] Since God sets up chains of events well in advance to fulfill His goals, He may even grant a wicked man prosperity for the sake of a descendant many generations removed.[51]

40. *Cf.* Genesis 22:18, 26:4, 26:24.
41. *Tanchuma, Noah* 3; *Berakhoth* 17b; *Taanith* 24b; *Chullin* 86a; *Yerushalmi, Maaser Sheni* 5:5 (33a). *Cf. Taanith* 21b; *Bava Metzia* 85a; *Sanhedrin* 114a.
42. See above, 19:55, note 289.
43. *Eduyyoth* 2:9. These five things are, looks, strength, wealth, intelligence, and longevity.
44. Ramban, *Torath HaAdam* 73; *Ikkarim* 4:12; *Derekh HaShem* 2:3:7. *Cf. Berakhoth* 7a; *Bereshith Rabbah* 29:5; *Tanchuma, Noah* 2; *Chovoth HaLevavoth* 4:3 (111a); *Sefer Chasidim* 549, 695; see above, 18:56. See also *Berakhoth* 18b (end).
45. *Tosafoth, Sotah* 10b *s.v. DeIythey;* Rabbi Yaakov Emden (Maharibatz) *ad. loc.*
46. See above, 18:57.
47. *Bereshith Rabbah* 29:5; *Tanchuma, Noah* 5; *Zohar* 1:115a, 2:273b, 3:57a; *Zohar Chadash* 35d; *Sefer Chasidim* 501, 1171; *Chasdey Olam ad. loc.* 605; *Sheveiley Emunah* 9 (87b). *Cf. Sanhedrin* 19a; *Bereshith Rabbah* 62:2; *VaYikra Rabbah* 26:4; *Tanchuma, Toldoth* 4, *Shemoth* 4, that Jacob redeemed Abraham.
48. *Sanhedrin* 104a; *Tosafoth, Sotah* 10b *s.v. DeIythey. Cf. Yevamoth* 26a.
49. *Ikkarim* 4:12. *Cf. Bava Kama* 119a.
50. *Ibid. Cf. Pesachim* 49b; *Bava Metzia* 61b; *Yerushalmi, Bava Kama* 10:1 (42b); *Chovoth HaLevavoth* 4:3 (111a). See *Tosafoth, Avodah Zarah* 26b *s.v. Ani,* that for this reason even where it is permissible to kill a person, it is forbidden to destroy his property.
51. *Sefer Chasidim* 549. *Cf. Bava Kama* 38a. Also see *Bereshith Rabbah* 26:15, that Noah was saved primarily for the sake of his descendant Moses; *cf. Zohar* 1:68a, 1:67b.

20:15 Occasionally, God will grant the wicked prosperity and strength in order that He may use them as instruments of His punishment.[52] Thus, for example, God told His prophet, "I will strengthen the arms of the king of Babylon and put My sword in his hand" (Ezekiel 30:24).[53] He also warned, "Woe to Assyria, the rod of My anger, for I have placed the staff of My indignation in their hands" (Isaiah 10:5).[54] Knowing this, the Psalmist therefore prayed, "O God, rise up before [my enemies], cast them down! Rescue my soul from the wicked who serve as Your sword" (Psalms 17:13).[55]

20:16 Another reason why the wicked prosper is to preserve free will, since if they were immediately punished, no man would sin.[56] King Solomon thus wrote, "Because the sentence for an evil act is not executed speedily, men become fully set in their hearts on doing evil" (Ecclesiastes 8:11).[57] Since the prosperity of the wicked represents another challenge in this world, it tends to increase the rewards of the righteous who overcome it.[58]

20:17 Moreover, a wise person understands that the prosperity of the wicked is an indication of the even greater ultimate reward of the righteous.[59] King Solomon thus continues, "Yet because a sinner does evil a hundred times and lives long, therefore I also know that it shall be well with those who fear God" (*ibid.* 8:12).[60] If God grants prosperity to evildoers, how much more so will He grant ultimate prosperity to the righteous.[61]

52. *Emunoth VeDeyoth* 5:3 (71a); *Sheveiley Emunah* 9 (87c); *Ikkarim* 4:12. *Cf. Koheleth Rabbah* 3:22.
53. *Sheveiley Emunah* 9 (87c).
54. *Midrash Tehillim* 17:10; Radak on Psalms 17:13; *Ikkarim* 4:12. *Cf.* Jeremiah 51:20.
55. Rashi, Ibn Ezra, Radak, *ad. loc.; Sheveiley Emunah* 9 (87c); *Midrash Tehillim* 17:10. Others, however, read this "by Your sword," as in the *Targum ad. loc.* and most English translations; this is also an alternate interpretation in *Midrash Tehillim.*
56. *Shaar HaShamayim* 1:22, cited in *Menorath HaMaor* 3:end (237), 5:2:1:3 (292). See Volume 1, 3:26; above, 19:46, note 245.
57. *Ikkarim* 4:12. *Cf. Koheleth Rabbah* 8:14; *Chovoth HaLevavoth* 7:3.
58. *Ikkarim* 4:12; *Chovoth HaLevavoth* 4:3 (111a). *Cf.* Ramban, *Torath HaAdam* 73a. See Volume 1, 3:31.
59. *Sanhedrin* 96a; *Midrash Tehillim* 37:3; *Menorath HaMaor* 5:3:2:4 (304). Also *Esther Rabbah* 3:9; *Midrash Tehillim* 4:11; *Tana DeBei Eliahu Rabbah* 22 (96a); *Yalkut Shimoni* 2:628; *Sefer Chasidim* 342, 1109.
60. *Cf. Targum*, Rashi, Sforno, *ad. loc.; Akedath Yitzchak* 3 (1:22a).
61. *Nedarim* 50b; Maharatz Chajas *ad. loc.; Makkoth* 24b; *Bereshith Rabbah* 65:18;

20:18 Although God gives the wicked prosperity and an opportunity to repent, there is a limit to the evil that can remain unpunished. When this limit is reached, punishment is swift and thorough.[62] Regarding this it is written, "When his measure is filled, he shall suffer, the full force of misery shall come upon him" (Job 20:22).[63] It is also written, "For every matter there is a time and a judgment; [it is] when a man's evil becomes unbearable" (Ecclesiastes 8:6).[64]

20:19 The second apparent injustice — why the innocent suffer — is not as pressing,[65] since it is impossible for us to know what is in another man's heart, that is, whether he is a saint or a sinner.[66] For this reason, the prophet Samuel was told, "Man looks at appearances, but God looks at the heart" (1 Samuel 16:7).[67] Similarly, God told Jeremiah, "I, God, search the heart, I examine a man's motives, and thus allot each according to his way" (Jeremiah 17:10). God not only knows our conscious motives, but the depths of our unconscious. King Solomon thus taught us, "A man's ways may strike him as pure, but God weighs the spirit" (Proverbs 16:2). One cannot even hide his most secret thoughts from God, as King David said, "God searches every heart and knows every plan it devises" (1 Chronicles 28:9).

20:20 Still, the apparent injustice of the sum total of suffering in the world makes this too a question of great importance since it can undermine one's faith. The Psalmist thus admitted, "But as for me, my feet almost strayed [from the path of righteousness]; in

---

Mekhilta on Exodus 15:1; *Tanchuma, BeShalach* 12; *Teshuvoth Shevuth Yaakov* 1:182. *Cf. Yerushalmi, Moed Katan* 3:1 (10a); *Shiurey Korban ad. loc.*

62. *Derekh HaShem* 2:3:6; *Sotah* 9a; Maharsha *ad. loc.; Arakhin* 15a; *BaMidbar Rabbah* 14:17; *Midrash Tehillim* 10:5; *Zohar* 1:61b, 1:113b, 1:121b; Rashi on Genesis 15:16; *Kuzari* 2:44 (53b). *Cf.* Isaiah 27:8; *Shemoth Rabbah* 30:1. Also see above, 18:43, note 204. See also *Tanchuma, Netzavim* 1, that when God merely turns His attention to the deeds of the wicked, they are destroyed; *cf.* Maharal, *Nethivoth Olam, Yesurin* 3 (180a). Also *Midrash Tehillim* 36:2, that God waits until the wicked have lost the last vestiges of fear of Him; only then does He punish them. When David thus saw that Goliath was swearing and cursing God, he knew that his time had come.

63. *Cf. Targum*, Rashi, Ibn Ezra, *ad. loc.; Arakhin* 15a; *BaMidbar Rabbah* 14:17; *Midrash Tehillim* 10:5.

64. *BaMidbar Rabbah* 14:17.

65. *Ikkarim* 4:12; *Menorath HaMaor* 5:2:1:3 (292).

66. *Cf. Kiddushin* 39b.

67. *Cf. Sanhedrin* 106b; *Zohar* 3:144a; *Ikkarim* 4:13.

an instant, my steps would have slipped altogether, for I envied the arrogant when I beheld the prosperity of the wicked" (Psalms 73:2-3).[68]

20:21 Much of the evil that an innocent person may suffer, however, is brought about by his own[69] folly,[70] as the prophet said, "This has been of your own doing" (Malachi 1:9).[71] It is up to each individual to keep himself from injury, as we find, "Thorns and snares are in the way of the crooked man; he who watches his soul keeps far from them" (Proverbs 22:5).[72] One should not blame God for things brought about by one's own foolishness, as we are told, "A man's foolishness perverts his way; in his heart he ends up blaming [his misfortune on] God" (Proverbs 19:3).[73]

20:22 At times, what appears to be evil may actually prevent a much greater evil or bring about a much greater good.[74] It is thus written, "He rescues the poor man by afflicting him" (Job 36:15).[75] The Psalmist also said, "I will thank You, for You afflicted me, and [thereby] became my salvation" (Psalms 118:21).[76] Thus, for example, a person who wishes to embark on an ocean voyage may be injured and detained and miss his ship, only to find that his ship sank. As a result of this slight inconvenience, his life was saved.[77]

68. *Ikkarim* 4:14.
69. Of course, a person may also suffer at the hand of another; *cf. Moreh Nevukhim* 3:12 no. 2, but see *Kethuvoth* 30b, that this is also from God.
70. See above, 19:42, notes 225, 226.
71. *Moreh Nevukhim* 3:12 (15b); Ramban, *Torath HaAdam* 75b; *Chovoth HaLevavoth* 5:5 (14b); *Ikkarim* 4:13.
72. *Ibid.; Kethuvoth* 30a; *Bava Metzia* 107b; *Bava Bathra* 144b; *Avodah Zarah* 3b.
73. *Ibid. Cf. Taanith* 9a; Genesis 42:28.
74. *Ikkarim* 4:13; *Sheveiley Emunah* 9 (87b); *Tifereth Yisrael, Kiddushin* 4:14. *Cf.* Hosea 7:15; Rashi, Radak, *ad. loc.; Avodah Zarah* 4a.
75. *Ikkarim* 4:13. *Cf. Yevamoth* 103b.
76. *Midrash Tehillim* 118:19, although most other commentaries interpret it, "I will thank You for You answered me..." *Cf. Derekh HaShem* 2:3:12 (note 41), who cites a similar verse from Isaiah, "I will thank You, God, though You showed me anger" (Isaiah 12:1), and explains that this refers to a situation in which a farmer's cow falls into a ditch and breaks its foot while plowing. As a result of this inconvenience, however, the farmer finds a buried treasure; *Niddah* 31a; *VaYikra Rabbah* 5:4; *Yerushalmi, Horayoth* 3:4; *Bereshith Rabbah* 42:1; *Tana DeBei Eliahu Rabbah* 22; *Tana DeBei Eliahu Zuta* 4.
77. *Niddah* 31a; *Midrash Tehillim* 118:19, 136:3; *Ikkarim* 4:13; *Sheveiley Emunah* 9 (87b); *Sh'nei Luchoth HaB'rith, BeAsarah Maamaroth* 1:85b. *Cf. Yevamoth* 102b.

20:23   Even when real evil comes to the righteous, however, it can be understood if we remember that this world is only a preparation for the Future World.[78] Since every unrepented sin must be reckoned,[79] God therefore punishes the righteous for their few sins in this world so that they may enter the Future World with a clean slate.[80] The temporary suffering of the righteous in this world[81] is for their ultimate prosperity.[82] It is thus written, "Though your beginning was in pain, your end shall be greatly increased" (Job 8:7).[83]

20:24   The righteous are therefore punished for unrepented sins that they may have forgotten[84] or never considered wrong.[85] God may delay punishment for a sin in order to give a person an opportunity to repent. Still, one should never think that God will overlook his sins.[86] Such a thought misses the whole point that God desires justice and must therefore take everything a person does into account.[87] Every sin, no matter how minor, is judged by God, as we find, "For God will scrutinize every action; He will judge every hidden thing, whether it be for good or for bad" (Ecclesiastes 12:14).[88] We are taught that if suffering comes to a person, he

78.   "This world is like an antechamber before the World to Come. Prepare yourself in the antechamber so that you will be able to enter the banquet hall"; *Avoth* 4:16.
79.   *Taanith* 11a; *Ikkarim* 4:13; *Tifereth Yisrael, Kiddushin* 4:14. See below, note 87.
80.   *Kiddushin* 40b; *Bereshith Rabbah* 33:1; *Shemoth Rabbah* 31:4; *VaYikra Rabbah* 27:1, 33:2; *Tanchuma, Emor* 5; *Midrash Tehillim* 103:11; *Pesikta* 9 (73a); *Zohar* 1:180b; Ramban, *Torath HaAdam* 71b; *Chovoth HaLevavoth* 4:3 (110b); *Sefer Chasidim* 605; *Ikkarim* 4:13; *Sheveiley Emunah* 9 (87a); *Tifereth Yisrael, Kiddushin* 4:14.
81.   *Midrash Tehillim* 17:14, 75:1; *Pesikta* 27 (170a). Cf. *Midrash Tehillim* 1:20, that the righteous in this world are like precious stones covered with filth.
82.   *Bereshith Rabbah* 66:5.
83.   *Kiddushin* 40b; *Moreh Nevukhim* 3:23. Cf. *Devarim Rabbah* 7:3.
84.   *Ikkarim* 4:13. Cf. *Eikhah Rabbah* 1:44.
85.   *Avodah Zarah* 18a; *Zohar* 1:199a; *Sefer Chasidim* 31; *Ikkarim* 4:13; *Mesilath Yesharim* 10 (13a).
86.   *BaMidbar Rabbah* 14:17; *Ikkarim* 4:13.
87.   "Whoever says that God overlooks things, will have his life 'overlooked'"; *Bava Kama* 50b; *Yerushalmi, Betza* 3:8 (16b); *Yerushalmi, Shekalim* 5:1 (21b); *Yerushalmi, Taanith* 2:1 (9a); *Bereshith Rabbah* 67:4; *Esther Rabbah* 7:25, 8:1; *Tanchuma, Ki Tissa* 26; *Midrash Tehillim* 10:3; *Pesikta* 25 (161b); *Yalkut Shimoni* 2:535; *Moreh Nevukhim* 3:17; *Ikkarim* 4:13; *Magen Avoth* on *Avoth* 76b; *Mesilath Yesharim* 4 (7b); *Nefesh HaChaim* 1:12.
88.   *Chagigah* 5a. "Since God desires justice, ignoring the bad would be as much an injustice as ignoring the good. If He desires justice, He must deal with each individual according to his actions, with the most minute discrimination, for good or for bad; *Mesilath Yesharim* 4 (7b).

should first examine his deeds. It is thus written, "Let us search and examine our ways, and return to God" (Lamentations 3:40).[89]

20:25 Even if a person is good, he must pay for all his sins.[90] Indeed, God is more exacting with the righteous in this world[91] since they are closer to Him.[92] God thus told Moses and Aaron, "I will be sanctified among those who are close to Me" (Leviticus 10:3).[93] We are taught that God is exacting with the righteous to the hairsbreadth, as the Psalmist wrote, "With those who stand round about Him, He is very demanding" (Psalms 50:3).[94] It is also written, "God is dreaded in the assembly of His holy ones, and feared by all those who are round about Him" (Psalms 89:8).[95]

20:26 It is for this reason that the righteous are even punished for accidental sins.[96] They may also be punished in this world for not keeping the commandments in a way which is suitable to their rank.[97] Ultimately, however, God's justice is equal to all.[98] King Solomon declared this when he said, "There is only one judgment for the righteous and for the wicked" (Ecclesiastes 9:2).[99]

20:27 Many sins require suffering for a complete atonement, even after repentance.[100] It is for this reason that one who has repented may experience an undue degree of suffering.[101] The suffering of the righteous in this world is thus one of God's great kindnesses.[102] Through suffering, a person acquires his portion in

89. *Berakhoth* 5a; Ramban, *Torath HaAdam* 71b; *Menorath HaMaor* 5:3:1:1 (298).
90. *Taanith* 11a; *Chovoth HaLevavoth* 4:3 (110b).
91. *Cf. Shemoth Rabbah* 40:3, that Abraham was punished for uttering a single word.
92. *Tana DeBei Eliahu Rabbah* 2 (19a).
93. After Aaron's two sons died on the day the Tabernacle was dedicated; *Yalkut Shimoni* 1:250, 2:760; *Menorath HaMaor* 5:3:1:1 (298).
94. *Yevamoth* 121b; *Bava Kama* 50a; *Yerushalmi, Shekalim* 5:1 (22a); *Yerushalmi, Betza* 2:9 (16a); *Mekhilta* on Exodus 15:11 (41b); *Mesilath Yesharim* 4 (7a). *Cf. Tanchuma, Balak* 20.
95. *Ibid.*
96. *Bava Metzia* 33b; *Tanchuma, Shemini* 11; Ramban, *Torath HaAdam* 71b.
97. *Torath HaAdam* 71b, from *Berakhoth* 5a; *Menachoth* 41a.
98. *Bereshith Rabbah* 33:1; *VaYikra Rabbah* 27:1; *Tanchuma, Emor* 5; *Pesikta* 9 (73a).
99. *Tanchuma, Acharey Moth* 1, *VaEthChanan* 1. *Cf.* Job 9:22; *VaYikra Rabbah* 20:1; *Pesikta* 27 (167b); *Yalkut Shimoni* 1:811, 2:989.
100. See above, 17:1, 17:3, 17:14, 17:22.
101. *Emunoth VeDeyoth* 5:6 (72b); *Sefer Chasidim* 613. See above, 17:16. *Cf. Yevamoth* 48b; Rashi *ad. loc. s.v. Shelo.*
102. *Shemoth Rabbah* 1:1; *Likutey Amarim, Iggereth HaTeshuvah* 12 (101a). *Cf. Tanchuma, VaYetze* 2.

the Eternal Future.[103] Suffering also cleanses a person and eases his judgment in the next world.[104] All the suffering in the world is better than a moment of future punishment or the reduction of one's future rewards.[105] However, even when one receives punishment in this world, some future spiritual punishment may be required.[106]

20:28   Since God knew that man created with free will would sin, He created evil and suffering in the world as a means of atonement. This is the meaning of, "Judgments are ready for scorners, and lashes for the backs of fools" (Proverbs 19:29).[107] Furthermore, suffering serves as a warning to the naive not to sin, as we find, "By smiting the scorner, you cause the simple man to become wise" (Proverbs 19:25).[108]

20:29   Suffering was therefore created specifically as an antidote and atonement for sin.[109] First, suffering atones[110] because it weakens a person's desires for purely physical pleasures which are the primary cause of sin.[111] By loosening the grip of the material world on the soul,[112] suffering also enables a person to reconnect with his spiritual source.[113] By weakening the material,[114] it unplugs the

---

103. *Avodah Zarah* 4a; *Midrash Tehillim* 90:16.
104. *Yevamoth* 102b; *Bereshith Rabbah* 65:4; *VaYikra Rabbah* 29:2; *Ruth Rabbah* 0:3; *Mishnah Berurah* 222:4. *Cf. Eruvin* 41b; *Menorath HaMaor* 5:3:1:2 (299). *Derekh HaShem* 2:2:5.
105. Ramban, introduction to Job; *Reshith Chokhmah, Shaar HaKedushah* 12 (176c); *Likutey Amarim, Iggereth HaTeshuvah* 12 (101a). *Cf. Bereshith Rabbah* 44:24; *Shemoth Rabbah* 51:5; *Midrash Tehillim* 52:8; *Zohar* 2:83b; *Menorath HaMaor* 3:4:4:1 (138), 5:3:2:1 (302); *Sh'nei Luchoth HaB'rith, BeAsarah Maamaroth* 1:85a, that exile is better than *Gehinnom.* For counterpart of this, see Rabbi Yaakov, *Avoth* 4:17, "Better one hour in repentance and good deeds in this world than all the life of the World to Come."
106. *Cf.* Ramban, *Torath HaAdam* 71b; *Derekh HaShem* 2:2:5.
107. *VaYikra Rabbah* 15:4; *BaMidbar Rabbah* 13:6; *Tanchuma, Metzorah* 4.
108. *Cf.* Proverbs 21:11; *Shemoth Rabbah* 27:5; *Tanchuma, Yithro* 3; *Pesikta* 3 (22a).
109. *Derekh HaShem* 2:2:5, 2:3:9; *Reshith Chokhmah, Shaar HaTeshuvah* 3 (112b), from Psalms 139:10. *Cf. Eikhah Rabbah* 4:27.
110. *Mekhilta* on Exodus 20:20 (72b); *Tanchuma, Ki Tetze* 2; *Zohar* 3:57b.
111. *Sh'nei Luchoth HaB'rith, BeAsarah Maamaroth* 1:85a, citing *Derashoth HaRan.*
112. See above, 17:15, notes 64, 65, from *Berakhoth* 5a. *Cf. Menorath HaMaor* 5:3:1:1 (298).
113. See above, 17:15, note 66, from *Berakhoth* 5a; *Bereshith Rabbah* 92:1; *Tanchuma, Ki Tetze* 2; *Menorath HaMaor* 5:3:1:1 (298).
114. *Cf. Bereshith Rabbah* 69:3, from Psalms 65:11.

spiritual sources stopped up by sin.[115] Like a sacrifice, suffering atones by reconciling the material in man with the spiritual.[116]

20:30 Suffering therefore brings a person back to God,[117] and prepares the way for eternal life.[118] It is thus written, "The path of life is attained through ethical correction" (Proverbs 6:23).[119] A person should not complain when he is beset by suffering.[120] He should rather rejoice[121] in the realization that it is for his ultimate good.[122] Concerning this, the Psalmist declared, "Happy is the man whom You correct, O God!" (Psalms 94:12).[123] It is thus taught that in the Ultimate Future people will thank God for all the suffering that they experienced in this world.[124]

20:31 The righteous often live in poverty.[125] Since this is the worst form of suffering,[126] being equivalent to death itself,[127] it therefore saves one from all future judgment.[128] Similarly, the righteous

---

115. "If your sieve is clogged, beat upon it"; *Cf. Bereshith Rabbah* 81:2. See Volume 1, 4:49.

116. See above, 17:15, note 67; *Mekhilta* on Exodus 20:20 (73a); *Tanchuma, Yithro* 16; *Midrash Tehillim* 94:2, 118:16.

117. *Tanchuma, Ki Tetze* 2; *Midrash Tehillim* 94:2; *Menorath HaMaor* 5:3:1:1 (298). *Cf. Bereshith Rabbah* 94:5, that God only places His name on a living person who has undergone great suffering. Also *Chagigah* 5a (end), that one who does not suffer is not a true Jew.

118. *Cf. Pesikta* 25 (157a); *Yalkut Shimoni* 2:789; *Menorath HaMaor* 5:3:1:2 (299).

119. *Berakhoth* 5a; *Bereshith Rabbah* 9:10; *VaYikra Rabbah* 29:3, 30:2; *Midrash Tehillim* 16:12; *Pesikta* 28 (179b); *Yalkut Shimoni* 2:651, 2:670; *Menorath HaMaor* 5:3:1:2 (299), 5:3:2:1 (302); *Reshith Chokhmah, Shaar HaTeshuvah* 6 (122b).

120. *Bereshith Rabbah* 40:2, 92:1.

121. *Berakhoth* 5a; *Eruvin* 41b; *Tanchuma, Ki Tetze* 2; *Midrash Tehillim* 3:1, 72:3; *Yalkut Shimoni* 2:805; *Zohar* 1:151b; Rashi on Psalms 72:1; *Menorath HaMaor* 5:3:1:4 (301). See above, 18:61, note 292.

122. *Bereshith Rabbah* 9:10; *Menorath HaMaor* 5:3:2:1 (302); *Sh'nei Luchoth HaB'rith, BeAsarah Maamaroth* 1:85a.

123. *Berakhoth* 5a; *Bereshith Rabbah* 40:1, 92:1; *Shemoth Rabbah* 1:1; *Tanchuma, Shemoth* 1, *Ki Tetze* 2.

124. *VaYikra Rabbah* 32:1; see above, note 76.

125. *Sefer Chasidim* 530. *Cf. Kethuvoth* 77b; *Shemoth Rabbah* 31:4.

126. *Bava Bathra* 116a; *Shemoth Rabbah* 31:11, 31:14; *Tanchuma, Mishpatim* 11; *Zohar* 3:273b; Ran, *Shabbath* (Rif 11b); Maharal, *Nethivoth Olam, Yesurin* 3 (180b top).

127. *Nedarim* 7b, 64b; *Avodah Zarah* 5a; *Bereshith Rabbah* 71:9; *Shemoth Rabbah* 5:4; *Eikhah Rabbah* 3:6; *Tanchuma, Tzav* 13; *Pirkey Rabbi Eliezer* 40 (94b); *Yalkut Shimoni* 1:127, 1:742; *Zohar* 2:119a, 2:158b, 3:53b, 3:153b, 3:219a; *Tikuney Zohar* 22 (66b), 69 (101b); *Tikuney Zohar Chadash* 97d, 98b, 114a. *Cf. Bereshith Rabbah* 96:3, that death is a lowering, and *Zohar* 3:135b, that one who is lowered from his station is considered dead; also *Zohar* 1:63b.

128. *Eruvin* 41b; *Menorath HaMaor* 5:3:1:2 (299).

often suffer from chronic diseases,[129] since this suffering also helps them avoid future judgment.[130] Nevertheless, there is a tradition that God does not allow the perfectly righteous to suffer badly for more than three days.[131]

20:32 At times, God decrees poverty and suffering on a person to prevent him from sinning or being tempted to forsake God.[132] This is because prosperity tends to make a person forget the spiritual, as God told Israel, "You grew fat, thick and gross; you abandoned the God who made you and ignored the Mighty One who was your support" (Deuteronomy 32:15).[133] We are thus taught that God could find nothing as suitable as poverty to refine His people.[134]

20:33 At times, an otherwise innocent person suffers because he has money that he is legally or morally obligated to give to another or to charity. In such cases, God merely sends suffering and sickness so that this money is spent on physicians and medicines.[135] Similarly, this money may be lost to taxes, thieves[136] or other calamities.[137]

20:34 At times, an otherwise innocent person is punished because he is insensitive to the suffering of others. Regarding this it is written, "One who mocks the poor insults his Maker; and one who rejoices at calamity will not go unpunished" (Proverbs 17:5).[138] We are also warned, "When your enemy falls, do not rejoice. When he stumbles, do not be glad. For God will know; it will be evil in His eyes; and He will divert His anger from him" (Proverbs 24:17-18).[139]

129. *Shabbath* 118b; Rashi *ad. loc. s.v. MiMethey; Tosafoth ibid. s.v. Ruban; Kethuvoth* 103b; *Bereshith Rabbah* 62:2.
130. See above, note 128.
131. *Bereshith Rabbah* 91:9; *Esther Rabbah* 9:3; *Midrash Tehillim* 22:5. *Cf. Bereshith Rabbah* 56:1.
132. Rashi, *Yevamoth* 47b *s.v. Lo*, from *Sukkah* 52b; *Sefer Chasidim* 530; *Ikkarim* 4:13. *Cf. Shemoth Rabbah* 31:4; *Tanchuma, Terumah* 9. See above, 19:37, note 202.
133. *Ikkarim* 4:13; *cf.* Ralbag, *Living Torah, ad. loc.;* Deuteronomy 8:14, 31:20; Hosea 2:10; *Berakhoth* 32a; *Chovoth HaLevavoth* 4:3 (109b); *Moreh Nevukhim* 3:39; *Yad, Teshuvah* 9:1, *Issurey Biyah* 14:4; *Yoreh Deah* 268:2. *Cf. Sifri, Ekev* 43, *HaAzinu* 318.
134. *Chagigah* 9b; *Tosafoth ad. loc. s.v. KeBizra; VaYikra Rabbah* 13:4, 35:5; *Shir HaShirim Rabbah* 1:27; *Pesikta* 14 (117a); *Tana DeBei Eliahu Zuta* 5 (10a); *Yalkut Shimoni* 1:670, 2:256; *Zohar* 3:273b; *Ikkarim* 4:13.
135. *Shir HaShirim Rabbah* 6:17; *Sefer Chasidim* 530.
136. *Bava Bathra* 9a; *VaYikra Rabbah* 34:13; *Yalkut Shimoni* 2:352; *Sefer Chasidim* 211.
137. *Cf. Tanchuma, Reeh* 12; *Pesikta* 11 (97a); *Yalkut Shimoni* 1:892, 2:932.
138. *Sefer Chasidim* 530.
139. *Ibid.;* Sh'muel HaKatan, *Avoth* 4:19.

20:35 There are times when the innocent suffer because of the frailties of human nature which expose them to sickness and pain.[140] Similarly, they may suffer because of their heredity and environment,[141] or because of the station in life that is destined for them.[142] The world goes according to its way,[143] and no exception is made for the innocent.[144]

20:36 At times, the innocent suffer along with the guilty when judgment is brought upon a city or nation.[145] Job lamented this when he said, "If the plague shall suddenly strike, He disdains the misfortune of the innocent" (Job 9:23).[146] Accordingly, we are taught that once destruction is released, no distinction is made between the righteous and the wicked.[147] God thus told His prophet, "I will draw My sword out of its sheath and cut off from among you the righteous and the wicked" (Ezekiel 21:8).[148] In such cases, the righteous are often taken first in order to spare them the extra pain of seeing others suffer. In this sense, the death of the righteous is meant to serve as a warning of impending doom. The prophet thus complained bitterly, "The righteous perishes, and no man takes it to heart... Not one considers that the righteous is being taken away before the evil comes" (Isaiah 57:1).[149]

20:37 However, the perfectly righteous[150] may be saved even from

140. *Moreh Nevukhim* 3:12 no. 1.
141. Ramban, *Torath HaAdam* 73b; *Ikkarim* 4:13.
142. *Tifereth Yisrael, Kiddushin* 4:14. *Cf. Taanith* 25a; see above, 19:26, note 144.
143. *Avodah Zarah* 54b.
144. *Menorath HaMaor* 5:2:1:3 (292).
145. *Bereshith Rabbah* 49:14-15; *Sotah* 11a; *Ikkarim* 4:13; *Or HaChaim* on Genesis 9:11; *Anaf Yosef* on *Esther Rabbah* 0:1; see above, note 31; 18:51, note 238.
146. *Moreh Nevukhim* 3:23; *Zohar* 2:53a.
147. *Bava Kama* 60a; *Mekhilta* (11b); Rashi, Ramban, on Exodus 12:22; *Zohar* 1:63a, 1:68b, 1:69a, 1:71a, 1:102a, 1:107b, 1:113a, 1:182b, 1:197b, 1:204b, 2:36a, 2:197a, 2:264b, 3:38b, 3:54a, 2:92b; *Tikuney Zohar* 40 (81a), 62 (94b); *Zohar Chadash* 77a; *Tikuney Zohar Chadash* 118c. *Cf.* Isaiah 26:20; *Menachoth* 41a; *Devarim Rabbah* 4:4; *Sefer Chasidim* 1124.
148. *Bava Kama, Mekhilta, loc. cit.; Avodah Zarah* 4a; *Tanchuma, Mishpatim* 7.
149. Rashi, Ibn Ezra, *ad. loc.; Taanith* 11a; *Bava Kama* 60a; *Sanhedrin* 113b; *Tosefta, Sotah* 10:1; *Mekhilta* on Exodus 22:22 (95b).
150. *Avodah Zarah* 4a; *Nazir HaKodesh* 252a; *Iyay HaYam, Kesheth Yehonathan,* quoted in *Anaf Yosef* on *Taanith* 21b (*Eyn Yaakov* 50); *Iyun Yaakov ibid.;* Maharatz Chajas, *Shabbath* 55a. *Cf. Berakhoth* 7b; *Megillah* 6b; *Bereshith Rabbah* 49:18; *Sefer Chasidim* 164; see above, 2:24, note 46.

such unmitigated judgment.[151] It is thus written, "A thousand may fall at your [left] side, and ten thousand at your right, but [danger] shall not come near you" (Psalms 91:7).[152] Similarly, when Abraham pleaded for the people of Sodom, he said, "It would be a sacrilege even to ascribe such an act to You — to kill the innocent with the guilty, letting the righteous and the wicked fare alike. It would be a sacrilege to ascribe this to You! Shall the whole world's Judge not act justly?" (Genesis 18:25).[153] Those who have perfect trust in God may also be saved,[154] as it is written, "God is good, a stronghold in times of distress; He knows those who take refuge in Him" (Nahum 1:7).[155]

20:38   However, if an otherwise perfectly good person has the power to correct others and prevent their evil and does not do so, then he is no longer considered perfect.[156] In such a case, he shares the punishment of the others,[157] and is even punished first.[158] God thus instructed His destroying angels, "Slay utterly, the old people, boys and girls, women and children... and begin with My sanctified ones" (Ezekiel 9:6).[159] He also warned His prophet, "Son of man, I have appointed you as a sentry to the house of Israel. When you hear a word from Me, warn them in My name. When I say to a wicked man, 'You must die,' and you do not warn him... then that wicked man shall die with his sin, but I will seek his blood from your hands" (Ezekiel 3:17-18).[160]

151. *BaMidbar Rabbah* 5:4; *Tanchuma, BaMidbar* 26; *BaMidbar Rabbah* 18:9; Rashi on Numbers 16:22. *Cf. Lechem Mishneh, Teshuvah* 3:1.

152. Radak, Ibn Ezra, *ad. loc.; Anaf Yosef* on Taanith 21b (*Eyn Yaakov* 50).

153. *Avodah Zarah* 4a; *Or HaChaim* on Genesis 9:11.

154. *VaYikra Rabbah* 17:1; *Tanchuma, Noah* 7; *Midrash Tehillim* 4:5.

155. *Ibid.; Targum,* Rashi, Ibn Ezra, *ad. loc.; BaMidbar Rabbah* 5:4; *Tanchuma, BaMidbar* 26. *Cf. Zohar* 1:67b; *Derekh Emeth ad. loc.* no. 1; *Zohar* 2:38b, that when the righteous are hidden from the public eye, they can be saved.

156. *Avodah Zarah* 4a.

157. *Shabbath* 54b-55a; *Shemoth Rabbah* 27:8; *Eikhah Rabbah* 2:4; *Tanchuma, Mishpatim* 7, *Tazria* 9; *Zohar* 3:46a, 3:118a; *Zohar Chadash* 78a; *Chovoth HaLevavoth* 4:3 (110b); *Sefer Chasidim* 530; *Sheveiley Emunah* 9 (87b). *Cf. Yerushalmi, Sotah* 7:4 (31a); *BaMidbar Rabbah* 9:46; see above, 12:57.

158. *Zohar* 1:68a; *Tanchuma, Mishpatim* 7.

159. "Rav Yosef taught: Do not read 'My sanctuary' *(Mikdashai),* but 'My sanctified ones' *(MeKudeshai).* These are the people who kept the entire Torah from A to Z. [Even these people perished because they did not correct the wicked.]"; *Shabbath* 54b-55a; see note 157.

160. See above, 12:57.

20:39   Similarly, an otherwise perfectly good person may be punished for not praying and pleading mercy for his generation.[161] If one has the opportunity to pray for another and does not do so, he is called a sinner. It is thus written, "Far be it for me that I sin against God by not praying for you" (1 Samuel 12:23).[162] There are times, however, when God does not want the righteous to intercede for their generation. He therefore takes them away before they are able to do so.[163]

20:40   Since one who truly mourns the righteous is forgiven all his sins,[164] the death of the righteous is an atonement for their entire generation.[165] Many righteous individuals therefore voluntarily[166] accepted suffering and death for the sins of their generation.[167] In doing so, they followed the example of Moses himself who pleaded for his people after the sin of the Golden Calf, "Now, if You would, please forgive their sin. If not, You can blot me out from the book that You have written" (Exodus 32:32).[168] It was in this spirit that God told His prophet, "You shall

---

161. *Bava Bathra* 91b; *Makkoth* 11a; *Sefer Chasidim* 211, 530; *Ikkarim* 4:13; *Mesilath Yesharim* 19 (29b).

162. *Berakhoth* 12b. *Cf. BaMidbar Rabbah* 19:13; *Tanchuma, Chukath* 19.

163. *Zohar* 1:180a; Rashi, *Taanith* 11a s.v. *HaTzadik. Cf. Sefer Chasidim* 530.

164. *Moed Katan* 25a; *Zohar* 3:57b; *Magen Avraham, Orach Chaim* 621:0; *Beer Hetiv ad. loc.* 621:1.

165. *Shabbath* 33b; *Moed Katan* 28a; *Shemoth Rabbah* 35:4; Rashi, *Kethuvoth* 8b s.v. *Chashiv; Ikkarim* 4:13; see above, 17:18, note 78.

166. *Negaim* 2:1; Bertenoro *ad. loc. s.v.* Bayith; *Bava Metzia* 84b; *Tana DeBei Eliahu Rabbah* 27 (105b); *Yeshuoth Yaakov ad. loc.* no. 9; *Tana DeBei Eliahu Zuta* 2 (5a); *Zohar* 2:212a; *Sefer Chasidim* 528; *Derekh HaShem* 2:3:8.

167. *Yerushalmi, Berakhoth* 2:8 (20a); *Bereshith Rabbah* 33:1, 44:6; *VaYikra Rabbah* 2:5; *Shir HaShirim Rabbah* 6:6; *Koheleth Rabbah* 5:14; *Pesikta* 30 (191a); *Zohar* 1:65a, 1:67b, 1:180a, 2:10b, 2:36b, 2:38b, 2:53a, 2:195a, 2:269a, 2:257a, 3:17b, 3:38a, 3:46b, 3:118a. *Cf. Shabbath* 139; *Zohar* 3:20b, 3:155a. Also see *Tosafoth, Menachoth* 110a *s.v. U'Michael.*

168. Ramban *ad. loc.; Shemoth Rabbah* 46:1; *Zohar* 1:67b. "Blot me out from Your book" is an allegorical expression which means "erase me from Your memory" (*Moreh Nevukhim* 2:47), or "blot me out from all creation" (Ralbag). Others see it as meaning, "blot me out from the book of life," that is, "kill me" (Ramban; Abarbanel; *cf. Targum Yonathan; Rosh HaShanah* 16b). "Your book" could also allude to the supernal Torah which preceded creation and which God Himself "wrote" (Maharal, *Gur Aryeh; Sifethey Chakhamim*). Alternatively, "Your book" denotes the Torah itself which Moses still had not completed writing (Rashi). This explains the fact that the portion of *Tetzaveh* which precedes the account of the Golden Calf is the only one in which God speaks directly to Moses without, however, mentioning his name once (*Zohar* 3:246a; *Baal HaTurim* on Exodus 27:20; *cf. Makkoth* 11a).

bear their sin" (Ezekiel 4:4).[169] Regarding the type of righteous individual who gives his life for his generation, it is also written, "Surely he bore our sickness and suffered our anguish... he was wounded because of our transgressions, crushed because of our sins... his injury was a healing for us" (Isaiah 53:4).[170] When the innocent joyfully accept suffering, they hasten the redemption, as it is written, "You struck the one who rejoiced in doing righteousness... and now we are delivered" (Isaiah 64:4).[171]

20:41 The innocent are sometimes punished because of their association with the wicked.[172] God's prophet thus told King Jehoshaphat before his death, "Because you joined yourself with Achaziah, God has destroyed your efforts" (2 Chronicles 20:37).[173] The closer one is associated with the wicked, the more one partakes of their punishment.[174] The wise King Solomon therefore said, "He who goes with the wise shall become wise, but he who associates with fools shall suffer" (Proverbs 13:20). And the sages likewise warned, "Woe to the wicked, and woe to his neighbor."[175] We are thus admonished to avoid wicked friends and neighbors.[176] Concerning this, Jehoshaphat was confronted by another of God's prophets: "Should you then help the wicked and befriend those who hate God? Because of this, God's anger is directed against you" (2 Chronicles 19:2).[177] Likewise, when Jeremiah sought to escape his wicked environment, he cried out,

---

169. *Sanhedrin* 39a; *Ikkarim* 4:13.
170. Ramban on Exodus 32:32; *Ikkarim* 4:13; *Tana DeBei Eliahu Rabbah* 27 (105b); *Chovoth HaLevavoth* 4:3 (110b); *Sheveiley Emunah* 9 (87b). Some sources apply this to the Messiah; cf. *Sanhedrin* 98b; *Zohar* 2:212a. However, other commentaries write that it speaks about Israel as a whole, who suffer for the sins of the world; cf. Rashi, Radak, *ad. loc.;* *Kuzari* 2:35 (51b), 2:44 (54a).
171. *Taanith* 8a; *Menorath HaMaor* 5:3:1:2 (299).
172. *Avoth DeRabbi Nathan* 30:3; *Zohar* 2:36b; *Sefer Chasidim* 211; *Ikkarim* 4:13. Cf. *BaMidbar Rabbah* 19:9; *Tanchuma, Chukath* 1; Rashi on Numbers 20:23.
173. *Ibid.;* *Avoth DeRabbi Nathan* 9:4.
174. See above, 18:36.
175. *Negaim* 12:6; *Sukkah* 56b; *Sifra* on Leviticus 14:40 (73c); *Avoth DeRabbi Nathan* 9:1; *Zohar* 1:84a, 1:291b, 3:122b; Rabbenu Yonah, Bertenoro, on *Avoth* 1:7. Cf. *Bava Kama* 92a.
176. *Avoth* 1:7, 2:9 *s.v. Chaver Ra; Avoth DeRabbi Nathan* 9:4; *Tana DeBei Eliahu Zuta* 1 (2b); *Zohar* 1:38b, 1:84a, 3:218a; *Yad, Deyoth* 6:1; *Sefer Chasidim* 213; *Or HaChaim* on Genesis 12:1.
177. Rabbenu Yonah on *Avoth* 1:7. Cf. Proverbs 24:21-22.

"O that I were in the wilderness, in a wayfarers' lodge. O that I might leave my people and go from them! For they are all adulterers, an assembly of treacherous men" (Jeremiah 9:1).[178]

20:42 Though an innocent person is usually not punished for his parents' sins,[179] there are times when an evil decree may affect many later generations.[180] Such was the case concerning the decree of death for Adam which affected all mankind.[181] Similarly, the effects of the parents' punishment may be felt by their children for many generations.[182] A parent, on the other hand, is not normally punished for the sins of his grown[183] children.[184]

20:43 Likewise, an otherwise innocent person may suffer because he has acquired dishonest money from his parents. Regarding this it is written, "His children shall seek to appease the poor; they will restore what [their father] stole with his hands" (Job 20:10).[185] The Psalmist also said, "May the creditor seize all that he has, may strangers plunder his toil... and may none be gracious to his orphans" (Psalms 109:11-12).[186]

20:44 There are times when God afflicts a person who is completely blameless and undeserving.[187] Such afflictions are intended to

178. *Yad, Deyoth* 6:1.
179. See above, 18:54.
180. *Rosh HaShanah* 18a; *Yevamoth* 105a; *Bereshith Rabbah* 59:1; *Sefer Chasidim* 164; *Ikkarim* 4:13; see above, 18:53, note 245. Also see *Sanhedrin* 102a; *Shemoth Rabbah* 40:3; *Eikhah Rabbah* 2:4.
181. *Shabbath* 55b; *Bava Bathra* 17a; *Zohar* 1:53a, 2:54a; *Shaarey Zohar* 29b; see above, 18:52, note 241.
182. See above, 18:52.
183. *Bereshith Rabbah* 63:14; *Magen Avraham, Orach Chaim* 225:5; *Chokhmath Shlomo ibid.; Evven HaShoham* 26.
184. See above, note 27. Also see *Shir HaShirim Rabbah* 1:6, that the righteous can have wicked children.
185. Rashi on Ecclesiastes 1:4; *Sefer Chasidim* 530.
186. *Sefer Chasidim* 530. Cf. *Yerushalmi, Chagigah* 2:1 (9b); *Ruth Rabbah* 6:6; *Koheleth Rabbah* 7:18.
187. In the opinion of many authorities, God sends suffering even without sin; cf. *Shabbath* 55b; *Tosafoth ad. loc. s.v. U'Shema Minah; Emunoth VeDeyoth* 5:3 (70b); *Sefer Chasidim* 605, citing Rav Nissim Gaon; Rashi, *Berakhoth* 5a *s.v. Yesurin Shel Ahavah;* HaKothev (on *Eyn Yaakov* 12) *ibid.; Tosafoth, Berakhoth* 5b *s.v. DeAvad.* Other authorities maintained, however, that even according to its final conclusion *Shabbath* 55b does not allow suffering without sin; cf. Ramban, *Torath HaAdam* 73b; *Ikkarim* 4:13; *Tosefoth Yom Tov* on *Avoth* 4:11. Also see *Berakhoth* 5b; *Sanhedrin* 101a; *VaYikra Rabbah* 37:1; *Zohar* 3:57b; *Moreh Nevukhim* 3:17; *Torath HaAdam* 72a; *Menorath HaMaor* 5:3:1:1 (298); *Ikkarim* 4:5; *Sh'nei Luchoth HaB'rith,*

attenuate the material barriers that obscure his light[188] and strengthen him spiritually.[189] He can then attain moral and spiritual heights beyond anything he was capable of realizing by his own efforts.[190] These afflictions are called "sufferings of love" (*yisurin shel ahavah,* יִסּוּרִין שֶׁל אַהֲבָה),[191] regarding which it is written, "God corrects those whom He loves, just like a father [corrects] a child whom he cherishes" (Proverbs 3:12).[192] If accepted with love,[193] such suffering can bring a person to the loftiest spiritual heights,[194] as the prophet said, "But God preferred to crush him with disease, [to see] if he would offer his soul as compensation... Surely, He will grant him a portion among the great" (Isaiah 53:10, 12).[195]

20:45   Since sufferings of love are intended to bring a person closer to God, they do not generally interfere with his studies or prayers,[196] though they can do so and still be sufferings of love.[197] In any case, when suffering does interfere, one may pray to God to take it away.[198] Similarly, sufferings of love can involve afflictions which break a person's spirit, such as noxious diseases or the loss of children.[199]

    BeAsarah Maamaroth 1:85a, where it is indicated that all suffering is atonement for sin.

188. *Cf. Zohar* 1:187a, 3:168a, that when a coal has become all but completely extinguished, one must strike it to remove the ashes and make it burn brightly. Also see *Midrash Tehillim* 73:1.

189. *Zohar* 1:140b, 1:180b; *Sh'nei Luchoth HaB'rith, BeAsarah Maamaroth* 1:85a, quoting *Derashoth HaRan;* Maharal, *Nethivoth Olam, Yesurin* 1 (174f.).

190. *Tanchuma, Ki Tetze* 2; Rashi, *Berakhoth* 5a *s.v. Yesurin Shel Ahavah;* *HaKothev ibid.* on *Eyn Yaakov* 12; *Sh'nei Luchoth HaB'rith, BeAsarah Maamaroth* 1:86a.

191. *Berakhoth* 5a; *Bereshith Rabbah* 92:1; *Sheveiley Emunah* 9 (87b); *Menorath HaMaor* 5:3:1:3 (300). However, in *Torath HaAdam* 71b, we find that even the sufferings of love come to atone for some minor sins. *Ikkarim* 4:13 brings an opinion that sufferings of love are tests to show one's love of God; *cf. Menorath HaMaor loc. cit.* Also see *Moreh Nevukhim* 3:17, who dismisses this concept entirely as a minority opinion.

192. *Berakhoth* 5a; *Bereshith Rabbah* 92:1; *Tanchuma, Ki Tetze* 2; *Zohar* 3:114b.

193. *Cf. Taanith* 8a; *Eruvin* 41b. Also see *Mekhilta* on Exodus 19:9 (63b).

194. *Tanchuma, Ki Tetze* 2.

195. *Berakhoth* 5a. *Cf.* Maharsha *ad. loc. s.v. SheNeEmar;* *Bava Metzia* 85a; *Zohar* 1:180b; *Sefer Chasidim* 529, that such suffering also benefits all mankind; compare *Taanith* 8a.

196. *Berakhoth* 5a; *Bereshith Rabbah* 92:1.

197. Rabbi Yochanan *ibid.; Sh'nei Luchoth HaB'rith, BeAsarah Maamaroth* 1:85b; Maharal, *Nethivoth Olam, Yesurin* 1 (174b); *Menorath HaMaor* 5:3:1:3 (300).

198. *Sefer Chasidim* 529.

199. *Berakhoth* 5b; *Kesef MeZukak,* p. 166; *Menorath HaMaor* 5:3:1:3 (300); Maharal, *Nethivoth Olam, Yesurin* 2 (176a).

20:46 A person can voluntarily accept sufferings of love upon himself,[200] but in such a case also, it should not interfere with his studies or prayers.[201]

20:47 At times, God brings undeserved suffering to the righteous to test them and make them realize their true potential.[202] Similarly, it may be to demonstrate their greatness to others[203] and thereby sanctify God's name[204] by showing how the righteous do not serve God out of any thought of reward[205] but accept suffering and still do not depart from Him.[206] However, in all such cases, such suffering brings about a greater future reward, as we find, "He may have sent hardships to test you, but it was so that He would eventually do [all the more] good for you" (Deuteronomy 8:16).[207]

20:48 The suffering of the righteous also serves to preserve free will, since if only the wicked suffered, it would no longer be any challenge to be good.[208] Still, by virtue of the fact that the righteous suffer in this world, a sensible person should be able to infer the even greater future suffering of the wicked.[209]

20:49 Whenever a person receives undeserved suffering, whether he be a righteous adult or an innocent child,[210] God makes up his suffering in the future world.[211] The prophet alluded to this when he said, "Instead of your shame, you shall have a double portion... you shall inherit a double portion in your land and everlasting joy will be yours" (Isaiah 61:7).[212]

20:50 Innocent children[213] sometimes die for the sins of

200. *Reshith Chokhmah, Shaar HaTeshuvah* 4 (112c). *Cf. Bava Metzia* 85a.
201. *Cf. Bava Metzia* 84b.
202. *Ikkarim* 4:13; *Menorath HaMaor* 5:3:1:3 (300); see Volume 1, 3:52.
203. *Ibid.; Sefer Chasidim* 605; see Volume 1, 3:54.
204. *Midrash Tehillim* 17:14.
205. *Sefer Chasidim* 322, from Job 1:9. *Cf. Zohar* 2:33a; *Chovoth HaLevavoth* 10:4 (79b).
206. *Koheleth Rabbah* 3:24; *Chovoth HaLevavoth* 4:2 (110b).
207. *Sefer Chasidim* 605; *Ikkarim* 4:13. *Cf. Moreh Nevukhim* 3:17.
208. *Bereshith Rabbah* 9:6; see above, 19:46, note 245.
209. *Bereshith Rabbah* 65:18; *Midrash Tehillim* 11:7. *Cf. Ikkarim* 4:13 from Exodus 20:17; *Yoma* 38b.
210. *Emunoth VeDeyoth* 5:3 (70b); *Sefer Chasidim* 605.
211. *Ibid.;* Rashi, *Berakhoth* 5a *s.v. Yesurin Shel Ahavah; Menorath HaMaor* 3:end (237). *Cf. VaYikra Rabbah* 13:3.
212. *Cf. Bereshith Rabbah* 9:7.
213. It is only before the age of 13 that children die for the sins of their parents; *cf. Zohar* 1:118b; *Tikuney Zohar* 40 (81a); Rashi on Deuteronomy 24:16; *Yad, Teshuvah* 6:1; *Asarah Maamaroth* 1:2:23; *Levush, Orach Chaim* 225; *Magen Avraham* 225:5.

their[214] parents,[215] as it is written, "He repays the sins of the fathers [by striking] at the heart of their children after them" (Jeremiah 32:18).[216] Similarly, when there are no righteous individuals whose death can atone for the sins of the generation, young children are taken instead.[217] Children were given in trust for the continuance of God's teachings, and when this trust is broken, the children are taken. The prophet thus said, "Because you have forgotten the Torah of your God, I will also forget your children" (Hosea 4:6).[218]

20:51 Similarly, young children may die in order to prevent them from growing up to be wicked.[219] This is especially true of the children of the wicked who harden as they grow older[220] and tend to follow the ways of their parents.[221] Nevertheless, all children who die before their time have a portion in the World to Come.[222]

20:52 It is extremely difficult to understand why innocent children are born blind or crippled, and are thereby condemned to suffer throughout their lives.[223] It is also difficult to understand why unborn children are taken, or why orphans or the children of the righteous die when there is no parental sin.[224] Likewise, the tortures and brutal deaths of absolute saints are not sufficiently

214. In *Zivchey Shelemim* 30, we find that children only die for the sins of their father and not for those of their mother; but see *Shaarey Zohar* 27c where this is rejected on the basis of 1 Kings 17:18; *Kethuvoth* 72a; *Gittin* 35a. Also see *Pri Megadim, Eshel Avraham* 225:5.

215. See above, 18:35; 13:49, note 170; *Kethuvoth* 8b; *Tanchuma, Ki Tetze* 2; *Zohar* 3:17b, 3:87a, 3:203a. Cf. *Koheleth Rabbah* 4:13; *Tanchuma, Kedoshim* 14; *Tikuney Zohar* 24 (69a). Children who die for their parents' sins are called "oppressed"; cf. *Sotah* 49a; *Koheleth Rabbah* 4:1; *Zohar* 1:19b, 2:113a, 3:234a.

216. *Berakhoth* 5b.

217. *Shabbath* 33b; *Zohar* 3:17b. Cf. *Migdal Oz* on *Yad, Avodath Kokhavim* 4:6.

218. Rashi *ad. loc.; Shir HaShirim Rabbah* 1:24; *Tanchuma, VaYigash* 2; *Midrash Tehillim* 8:4; *Or HaChaim* on Exodus 22:5. For meaning of "forgotten"; cf. Radak *ad. loc.; Tikuney Zohar* 49 (81a).

219. See above, 13:51, note 178; *Tikuney Zohar* 49 (81). See *Teshuvoth Noda BeYehudah, Yoreh Deah* 2:164; *Teshuvoth Chatham Sofer* 155.

220. *Tana DeBei Eliahu Rabbah* 3 (27a); *Yalkut Shimoni* 2:165.

221. *Sanhedrin* 63b; *Menorath HaMaor* 5:3:2:3 (304).

222. *Sotah* 48b; *Koheleth Rabbah* 4:1; *Zohar* 2:113a. Also see *Sanhedrin* 110b; *Tosefta, Sanhedrin* 13:1; *Chasdey David ad. loc. Cf. Zohar* 2:96a, 2:234a.

223. Ramban, *Torath HaAdam* 26a; *Nishmath Chaim* 4:11 no. 2.

224. *Nishmath Chaim loc. cit.* no. 3.

explained by the above reasons.[225] However, all of these cases
must be considered in terms of the overall plan for creation.
According to this masterplan, every soul that has ever been born
in this world must reach a minimum degree of perfection before
God.[226] In order to achieve this, many souls must be born or
reincarnated more than once.[227]

20:53 Above and beyond this, God's justice is hidden from
man.[228] Though we can begin to understand some general rules
regarding God's justice, the details are far beyond human
understanding[229] and everything is ultimately in the hand of God
alone.[230] We must only realize that God desires the best for all,
that all is just, and that nothing can prevent the realization of His
will.[231] It is thus written, "For He is in Unity, who can hold Him
back? He does what His own will desires" (Job 23:13).[232] Since
no man shares God's absolute knowledge, none can question His
judgment.[233] In recognition of this, it is written, "Who can say to
Him, 'What have You done?'" (Job 9:12).[234] The prophet likewise
said, "Woe to he who strives with his Maker... Shall the clay say
to the One who fashioned it, 'What have You done?'" (Isaiah
45:9).[235]

225. *Ibid.* no. 1; *Torath HaAdam* 76a. *Cf. Menachoth* 29b; *Zohar* 1:131b; *Torath HaAdam* 73b;
     Shaar HaGilgulim 28; Maharal, *Tifereth Yisrael* 63.
226. *Shaar HaGilgulim loc. cit.*
227. *Torath HaAdam* 73b, 74b; *Sheveiley Emunah* 9 (86b); *Nishmath Chaim loc. cit.* Also
     see below, Chapter 23.
228. Rabbi Yanai, *Avoth* 4:14; Rashi, Rabbenu Yonah, Bertenoro, *Tosefoth Yom Tov,*
     ad. loc.; Berakhoth 7a; *Torath HaAdam* 73b; *Kuzari* 5:21 (55a). *Cf. Pesachim* 54b;
     Bereshith Rabbah 65:7; *Koheleth Rabbah* 11:9.
229. *Derekh HaShem* 2:2:4.
230. *Ibid.* 2:3:11.
231. *Moreh Nevukhim* 3:25.
232. *Mekhilta* on Exodus 14:28 (33a); *Shemoth Rabbah* 4:3; *Shir HaShirim Rabbah* 1:45;
     Tanchuma, Shemoth 18; *Moreh Nevukhim* 3:25.
233. *Shemoth Rabbah* 6:1; Rashi on Job 23:13.
234. *Cf.* Ecclesiastes 8:4; *Tanchuma, Tazria* 7; *Moreh Nevukhim* 3:25.
235. Rashi *ad. loc.; Midrash Tehillim* 7:17. *Cf.* Jeremiah 18:6.

TWENTY ONE

JUDGMENT

21:1 God constantly reviews each man's actions[1] and judges him accordingly[2] with regard to all his everyday affairs.[3] Regarding this type of judgment, it is written, "What is man that You... pay attention to him, that You remember him every morning, and test him each moment" (Job 7:17-18).[4]

21:2 However, this daily judgment only involves matters that have no long term effects.[5] Life and death,[6] children,[7] war and peace,[8] and poverty and wealth,[9] on the other hand, are judged once a year, on *Rosh HaShanah,* the Jewish New Year.[10]

1. *Cf. Rosh HaShanah* 16a, that the majority opinion is that man is recalled, but not judged each day; *cf. Magen Avraham* 591:9; *Mishnah Berurah* 591:4. Also see *Yad, Teshuvah* 3:2; *Menorath HaMaor* 5:2:1:3 (292).
2. *Tanchuma, VaYelekh* 2; *Zohar* 2:99b, 3:30b, 3:177a; *Reshith Chokhmah, Shaar HaYirah* 11 (30b-c). *Cf. Avodah Zarah* 3b; *Tosafoth ad. loc. s.v. Shenioth;* Maharsha *ibid.;* see below, note 36. In *Rosh HaShanah* 16a, *Tosefta* 1:12, *Yerushalmi* 1:3 (7a), we find the minority opinions of Rabbi Yosi and Rabbi Nathan that man is only judged each day or each hour, with no special judgment on *Rosh HaShanah.*
3. *Sefer Chasidim* 763; *Magen Avraham* 591:9. *Cf. Levushey Serad ad. loc.,* that *Sefer Chasidim loc. cit.* refutes the opinion given in note 2. According to note 2, however, this may be the interpretation that *Sefer Chasidim* attributes to the majority opinion. *Cf. Yerushalmi, Rosh HaShanah* 1:3 (7a), that the passage refers to everyday things like food and livelihood.
4. *Rosh HaShanah* 16a; *Yerushalmi, Tosefta, loc. cit.; Midrash Tehillim* 72:4.
5. See note 3.
6. *Rosh HaShanah* 16b; *Yerushalmi loc. cit.; Pesikta* 23 (150b), 24 (156b); *Yalkut Shimoni* 1:782; *Zohar* 2:265b; *Yad, Teshuvah* 3:3; *Rokeach* 200; *Menorath HaMaor* 5:2:1:2 (291); Abudarham, p. 273.
7. *Zohar* 2:44a; *Sefer Chasidim* 763. *Cf. Rosh HaShanah* 10b; *Berakhoth* 29a; *Yevamoth* 64a.
8. See note 6.
9. *Ibid. Cf. Betza* 16a; *VaYikra Rabbah* 30:1; *Pesikta Rabathai* 46 (187a); *Mesilath Yesharim* 21 (31a).
10. *Rosh HaShanah* 1:2 (16a); Rambam, Bertenoro, *Tosefoth Yom Tov, ad. loc.; Tanchuma, VaYishlach* 2; *Zohar* 1:69b, 1:160b, 2:44a; *Yad, Teshuvah* 3:3; *Sefer Chasidim* 258; *Asarah Maamaroth* 1:102; *Derekh HaShem* 2:6:5. On *Rosh HaShanah,* the world is

21:3   Since Adam was created on *Rosh HaShanah*,[11] and also sinned and was forgiven on that day,[12] God set aside the New Year as a time to weigh every man's actions and judge him accordingly.[13] God proclaimed a single day of judgment in order to give man a chance to repent and pray for a good year.[14]

21:4   The judgment of the perfectly righteous and absolutely wicked is sealed on *Rosh HaShanah.* The judgment of the average person, however, remains open until *Yom Kippur,* the Day of Atonement, in order to give him a chance to repent and change his judgment from bad to good.[15] The final judgment of all men is therefore sealed by the end of the day,[16] on *Yom Kippur.*[17]

21:5   Just as a person is judged for material things each year, so is he judged spiritually.[18] Those judged to be wicked are given

judged by the heavenly court; *cf. Yerushalmi, Rosh HaShanah* 1:3 (7b); *Pesikta* 5 (54a); *Targum,* Rashi, Ibn Ezra, on Job 1:6; *Zohar* 1:64a, 2:33b, 3:231a, 3:258b. *Cf. Chayay Adam* 144:5, that while the heavenly court judges on *Rosh HaShanah,* God alone judges on *Yom Kippur.*

11.   *Pesikta* 23 (150b); *Yalkut Shimoni* 1:782; *Rosh HaShanah* 10b; Maharsha, Rashash, *ad. loc.; Yerushalmi, Avodah Zarah* 1:23 (3a); *VaYikra Rabbah* 29:1; *Pirkey Rabbi Eliezer* 8 (18a); *Tosafoth, Rosh HaShanah* 8a *s.v. LeTekufoth;* Ran, *Rosh HaShanah* (Rif 3a) *s.v. BeRosh; Tosefoth Yom Tov, Rosh HaShanah* 1:2 *s.v. BeRosh; Rokeach* 200. According to a simple calculation based on the Biblical narrative, this took place almost six thousand years ago, on September 9, 3761 b.c.e.; *cf.* Rashi, *Sanhedrin* 97a *s.v. BeAlephim; Yad, Kiddush HaChodesh* 11:16; *Avodah Zarah* 8a.

12.   *Cf. Sanhedrin* 38b; *Avoth DeRabbi Nathan* 1:8; *Tanchuma, Shemini* 8; *Pirkey Rabbi Eliezer* 11 (28a); *Midrash Tehillim* 92:3; *Seder HaDoroth,* p. 16a.

13.   *VaYikra Rabbah* 29:1; *Pesikta* 23 (150b); Ran, *Rosh HaShanah* (Rif 3a) *s.v. BeRosh;* Maharsha, *Rosh HaShanah* 16a *s.v. Tana; Tosefoth Yom Tov, Rosh HaShanah* 1:2; *Menorath HaMaor* 5:2:1:2 (291).

14.   *Tanchuma, HaAzinu* 4; *Pesikta* 24 (156b). *Cf. Midrash Tehillim* 130:2; *Pesikta* 28 (183b).

15.   *Rosh HaShanah* 16b; *Yerushalmi* 1:3 (7a); *Zohar* 1:37a, 1:220b; *Yad, Teshuvah* 3:3. The majority of commentators write that the righteous who are judged worthy on *Rosh HaShanah* are inscribed immediately for a good life in this world; *cf.* Raavad, *Teshuvah* 3:2; *Lechem Mishneh ibid.;* Ramban, *Torath HaAdam,* "*Shaar HaGamul*" 70a; Mordecai, *Rosh HaShanah* 709; Ran, *Rosh HaShanah* (Rif 3b) *s.v. Tzadikim; Hagahoth Maimonioth, Teshuvah* 3:3 no. 1; *Menorath HaMaor* 5:2:1:3 (292). Another opinion is that "life" refers to everlasting life; see below, note 18. Also see *Asarah Maamaroth* 1:2:4; *Akedath Yitzchak* 76 (114a).

16.   *Mishnah Berurah* 623:3. *Cf. Orach Chaim* 232:2 in *Hagah;* "*Rav*" *Shulchan Arukh* 623:5. See above, 17:13, notes 57, 58.

17.   *Rosh HaShanah* 16a; *Yerushalmi loc. cit.; Tanchuma, VaYishlach* 2; *Menorath HaMaor* 5:2:2:1 (295). *Cf. Midrash Tehillim* 27:4, 118:3, 130:2.

18.   *Tosafoth, Rosh HaShanah* 16b *s.v. VeNechtamim,* that life and death refer to everlasting life; *cf. Lechem Mishneh, Hagahoth Maimonioth, loc. cit.; Korban Nethanel, Rosh HaShanah* (Rosh 1:4) no. 3. *Cf. Zohar* 2:33b, 2:265b; Bachya on Exodus 32:32.

all the reward for their good deeds in this world, and since they receive no future reward during that year,[19] they are considered spiritually dead.[20] Likewise, those judged to be righteous receive all their wordly reward as a free gift,[21] while the total reward for their good deeds during the year is set aside for their future life.[22]

21:6   Similarly, each person is judged whether or not he will be protected by providence during the coming year. The righteous are protected by providence, while the wicked are left to the forces of chance.[23]

21:7   *Rosh HaShanah* is the time when men are judged individually,[24] and communitites and nations are judged regarding matters of life and death.[25] However, God also decreed special judgments at other times in order that man should fix these as times of prayer and repentance.[26] Thus, we are taught that grain is judged on *Pesach* (Passover),[27] fruit trees on *Shavuoth* (Weeks),[28] and water on *Sukkoth* (Booths).[29] Nevertheless, even the judgment of these days is reviewed on *Rosh HaShanah*[30] in order that each individual be judged in relation to his environment.[31]

21:8   The judgment of communities and their leaders is reviewed each day, as King Solomon prayed, "May my words... be near to God our Lord day and night, to provide the needs of His servant, and the needs of His people Israel, according to the requirements of

19. Maharsha, *Rosh HaShanah* 16b. See above, 18:11.
20. *Ibid.,* since the wicked are so anesthetized to Godliness that they are considered dead even during their lifetimes; *cf. Berakhoth* 18b; *Yerushalmi* 2:3 (15b); *Bereshith Rabbah* 39:7.
21. See above, 18:10.
22. Maharsha *loc. cit.*
23. *Akedath Yitzchak* 76 (115a). See above, 18:59, 19:42.
24. Ran, *Rosh HaShanah* (Rif 3a) *s.v. BeArba; Tosefoth Yom Tov* 1:2.
25. *Tanchuma, HaAzinu* 4; *Pesikta* 24 (156b). *Cf. Menorath HaMaor* 5:2:1:2 (291).
26. *Rosh HaShanah* 16a.
27. *Rosh HaShanah* 1:2 (16a).
28. *Ibid.; Taanith* 2a; *Megillah* 31b.
29. *Ibid. Cf. Orach Chaim* 664:1; *Turey Zahav* 664:1; *Mishnah Berurah* 664:7; *Zohar* 1:220a; *Nitzotzey Oroth ad. loc.* no. 2. Also see *Tosafoth, Sukkah* 37b, *Menachoth* 62a, *s.v. Keday.*
30. *Tosafoth, Rosh HaShanah* 16a *s.v. BePesach,* from *Berakhoth* 18b.
31. *Mishneh LeMelekh, Teshuvah* 3:3.

each day" (1 Kings 8:59).[32] If good is decreed for a nation, and they are later found undeserving, God grants it in such a way that they cannot enjoy it. It is thus written, "He causes it to rain on uninhabited land, in a desert waste where there is no man" (Job 38:26).[33] Conversely, if they are later found more deserving, bounty is granted in such a way as to increase its usefulness and enjoyment.[34]

21:9 Though God's purpose in creation requires justice, He also desires to set up that justice in such a way as to give the maximum benefit to each man.[35] Therefore, those close to God are judged by day,[36] when they are involved in good deeds, while those far from Him are judged by night, while they are sleeping and not sinning.[37]

21:10 Knowing that we human beings are fallible creatures who cannot stand up under the scrutiny of absolute justice,[38] God constantly deals with us in mercy. The Psalmist spoke about this when he sang, "God's lovingkindness [surrounds me] the entire day" (Psalms 52:3).[39] Nevertheless, the evil in the world requires that there be times of absolute justice when the punishment of the wicked is decreed. Regarding this it is written, "God is a righteous judge, and therefore, He is angry every day" (Psalms 7:12).[40] Judgment is especially pronounced when world leaders reject God.[41] This judgment is said to last but a moment,[42] as it is written, "His anger lasts a moment; His favor a lifetime"

---

32. *Yerushalmi, Rosh HaShanah* 1:3 (7a); *Yerushalmi, Sanhedrin* 2:3 (11a). *Cf. Rosh HaShanah* 8b, 16a; *Avodah Zarah* 2b. However, *cf. Zohar* 3:233b, that these refer to the two days of *Rosh HaShanah*.

33. *Yerushalmi, Rosh HaShanah* 1:3 (8a).

34. *Ibid.; Rosh HaShanah* 17b; *Tanchuma, MiKetz* 1.

35. *Pesikta Rabathai* 49 (167b). See above, 18:38.

36. *Avodah Zarah* 3b, 4b; Maharal, *Beer HaGolah* 4 (33a). *Cf. Sefer Chasidim* 763.

37. *Yerushalmi, Rosh HaShanah* 1:3 (7a); *Bereshith Rabbah* 50:5; *Midrash Tehillim* 9:11; *Pesikta Rabathai* 49 (167b); *Yalkut Shimoni* 2:642; *Sefer Chasidim* 763. *Cf. Menorath HaMaor* 5:2:1:2 (291); *Rosh HaShanah* 8b.

38. See above, 18:39*ff.*

39. *Cf.* Rashi *ad. loc.; Zohar* 1:156b, 3:31a.

40. *Berakhoth* 7a; *Sanhedrin* 105a; *Avodah Zarah* 4a; *Yerushalmi, Sotah* 9:14 (46a); *Zohar* 1:8a, 2:1478a, 2:251a, 3:30b; *Tikuney Zohar* 70 (129b); *Reshith Chokhmah, Shaar HaYirah* 11 (30b).

41. "When the kings of east and west... bow down to their idols"; *Berakhoth loc. cit.* and parallels.

42. *Ibid.*

(Psalms 30:6).[43] Nevertheless, during this instant of anger, one who sins[44] or is cursed[45] can suffer greatly.

21:11 God's judgment is more acute during a time of danger,[46] especially if a person is careless.[47] Whenever an individual depends heavily upon his own merit, he is judged to see if such merit exists.[48]

21:12 In His mercy, God decreed that Israel's judgment be during the warm summer months, when such misfortunes as exile and homelessness would not be completely disastrous.[49] The Hebrew summer months of Tammuz and Av[50] are known particularly as times of punishment for the Jewish people,[51] since they sinned with the Golden Calf on the 17th of Tammuz,[52] and with the report of the spies on the 9th of Av.[53]

21:13 The months of Tammuz and Av are therefore called *Ben HaMetzarim,* literally "between the straits,"[54] and are times of suffering for Israel.[55] This is especially true[56] of the first nine days[57] of the month of Av.[58] One should avoid anything that may

43. *Ibid. Cf.* Isaiah 25:21.
44. *Zohar* 3:30b, 3:177b.
45. *Berakhoth loc. cit.* and parallels; Bachya on Numbers 22:20.
46. *Yerushalmi, Shabbath* 2:6 (19b); *Bereshith Rabbah* 91:12; *Zohar* 1:73b, 1:113a, 1:174b, 1:175a; *Derekh HaShem* 2:6:4. *Cf. Shabbath* 32a.
47. *Berakhoth* 55a; *Rosh HaShanah* 16b; Maharsha *ad. loc. s.v. Gimel.*
48. Rashi, *Berakhoth* 55a *s.v. Mazkirin.*
49. *Eikhah Rabbah* 1:44.
50. *Zohar* 2:12a, 3:259a; *Zohar Chadash* 36d, 32b. *Cf. Pesachim* 111b; *Eikhah Rabbah* 1:30. Some opinions also consider Shevat and Teveth to be particularly ominous months; *cf. Zohar loc. cit.; Tzavaath Rabbi Yehudah HaChasid* 41; *Teshuvoth Tashbatz* 558; *Yoreh Deah* 11:4 in *Hagah.*
51. *Taanith* 29a; *Arakhin* 11b; *Tosafoth, Taanith* 29b *s.v. Amara.*
52. *Taanith* 4:6 (26b); *Yoma* 4b; *Yad, Taanith* 5:2; *Orach Chaim* 549:1. See above, 17:8, note 33.
53. *Ibid. Cf. Taanith* 29a; *Targum Yonathan* on Numbers 13:20, 25, that the spies left on the 29th of Sivan and returned on the 8th of Av.
54. Lamentations 1:3.
55. *Eikhah Rabbah* 1:30; *Yalkut Shimoni* 1:545. This term is also sometimes applied to the time between the 17th of Tammuz and the 9th of Av; *cf. Orach Chaim* 551:2, 4 in *Hagah,* 551:16; *Chayay Adam* 133:8.
56. We therefore reduce happiness in Av; *Taanith* 4:6 (26b); *Yad, Taanith* 5:6; *Orach Chaim* 551:1; *Magen Avraham* 555:1, from *Tosafoth, Megillah* 5b *s.v. MeMaatin; cf. Pesachim* 55a; *Mishnah Berurah* 551:1; *Shaar HaTziun ad. loc.; Chayay Adam* 133:9.
57. *Korban Nethanel, Taanith* (Rosh 4:32) no. 5, from *Zohar* 2:78b; *cf. Nitzotzey Oroth ad. loc.* no. 3, and on *Zohar* 2:12a no. 4; *Megalleh Amukoth* 107; *Machzik Berakhah, Orach Chaim* 55a; *Mishnah Berurah* 551:2; *Chayay Adam* 133:9; *Kitzur Shulchan Arukh* 122:7.
58. *Magen Avraham* 551:2; *Teshuvoth Shevuth Yaakov* 3:55.

place him in jeopardy during this time.[59] Conversely, the month of Adar begins a time of prosperity for Israel, and one may expect an undue degree of success at this time.[60] Although considering certain times good or bad is forbidden as superstition,[61] this is not true when there is a firm tradition which must be respected.[62]

21:14 The 9th of Av, or *Tisha B'Av,* is a day of general calamity for the Jewish people.[63] When the Israelites heard the report of the spies and wept at their fate, they demonstrated a lack of faith in God's ability to bring them into the Promised Land.[64] As a result, God decreed that, since they had wept without cause on this day, it would become a day of suffering and weeping for future generations.[65] Regarding this the Psalmist said, "They scorned the desirable land and had no faith in His word... He therefore swore concerning them that He would cause them to fall in the wilderness,[66] cast their seed among the nations and scatter them on [distant] continents" (Psalms 106:24-27).[67]

21:15 *Tisha B'Av* has therefore been a day of evil for Israel. It was on *Tisha B'Av* that both the first and second Temples were destroyed, Betar was captured, and Jerusalem plowed over by the Romans.[68] This was also the day on which the Jews were

---

59. *Taanith* 29b; *Orach Chaim* 551:1.
60. *Taanith* 29b; *Magen Avraham* 686:4; *Mishnah Berurah* 686:8; *Chayay Adam* 155:1; *Kitzur Shulchan Arukh* 141:1.
61. Leviticus 19:26; *cf. Sanhedrin* 65b; *Yad, Avodath Kokhavim* 11:4; *Sefer HaMitzvoth,* Negative Commandment 32; *Sefer Mitzvoth Gadol,* Negative Commandment 53; *Chinukh* 250; *Yoreh Deah* 179:3. See above, 1:38.
62. *Yoreh Deah* 179:1 in *Hagah;* HaGra *ad. loc.* 179:7, from *Shabbath* 156a, *Gittin* 45a, *Tikuney Zohar* 70 (124b); *Teshuvoth Ramban* 286; *Teshuvoth Rashba* 413; *Teshuvoth Chatham Sofer, Orach Chaim* 551:1.
63. *Taanith* 4:6 (26b); *Yad, Taanith* 5:7ff.; *Orach Chaim* 552ff. *Cf. Eikhah Rabbah* 0:18, 3:13.
64. Numbers 14:1.
65. *Taanith* 29a; *Sotah* 35a; *Sanhedrin* 104b; *Yerushalmi, Taanith* 4:5 (23b); *Targum* on Numbers 14:1; Lamentations 1:2; *BaMidbar Rabbah* 16:12; *Tanchuma, Shelach* 12; *Tana DeBei Eliahu Rabbah* 29; *Zohar* 3:161a, 3:157a; Ramban on Numbers 14:1.
66. That is, they died in the desert on *Tisha B'Av* more than any other day; *cf. Taanith* 30b; *Bava Bathra* 121a; Rashi *ad. loc. s.v. SheKhalu; Tosafoth ibid. s.v. Yom; Yerushalmi, Taanith* 4:7 (26b); *Eikhah Rabbah* 0:33; *Midrash Tehillim* 78:7; *Aggadath Shemoth* 32.
67. Rashi *ad. loc.; BaMidbar Rabbah* 16:12; *Tanchuma, Shelach* 12; Ramban on Numbers 14:1.
68. See above, note 52.

expelled from Spain,[69] and the day the gas chambers of Treblinka began to operate.[70] It is the one day that God expresses His anger to Israel, regarding which it is written, "God has afflicted me on the day of His fierce anger" (Lamentations 1:12).[71]

21:16 Once God judges a person, He pronounces his sentence and sets up chains of events both in the physical and spiritual worlds in order to bring about his reward or punishment.[72] It is to such a sentence that our sages refer when they differentiate between "before the decree is sealed and after the decree is sealed."[73] Regarding the latter it is written, "It is a decree of the Most High" (Daniel 4:21).[74] We are taught that the effects of one of God's decrees can last 70 years.[75]

21:17 A heavenly decree makes a permanent mark[76] on the fabric of both the physical[77] and spiritual worlds.[78] It is therefore said that such a decree is written and sealed in a book.[79] Regarding this it is written, "The judgment was set, and the books were opened" (Daniel 7:10).[80] Since man's actions affect both the physical[81] and spiritual worlds,[82] they too are said to be written in a book.[83] It is thus allegorically written, "God listened and heard, and it

---

69. July 31, 1492; *cf. Universal Jewish Encyclopedia* 9:692.
70. July 23, 1942; *ibid.* 10:464. This was preceded by the mass expulsions from the Warsaw Ghetto which began on July 22, 1942. The organization of these actions on a somber Jewish holiday was no coincidence. The Nazis studied the Jewish calendar and frequently scheduled the most destructive actions while Jews were preoccupied; Levin, *The Holocaust* (Schocken, 1973), p. 318.
71. *Eikhah Rabbah* 1:42.
72. See above, 18:21.
73. *Cf. Derekh HaShem* 2:6:5.
74. *Cf.* Zephaniah 2:2; *Targum,* Rashi, Radak, *ad. loc.*
75. *Shabbath* 33a; *Zohar* 2:207b, 3:89b, 3:105a.
76. Radak on Psalms 56:9; Rabbenu Yonah, *Tosefoth Yom Tov,* on *Avoth* 2:1; *Menorath HaMaor* 5:2:1:3 (292).
77. Ibn Ezra on Exodus 32:32, Malachi 3:16, Psalms 69:29; Ramban on Exodus 32:22; Maharal, *Derekh Chaim* on *Avoth* 2:1.
78. Bachya on Exodus 32:32; Rabbi Chaim Vital on *Zohar* 2:200a; Maharal, *Derekh Chaim* on *Avoth* 2:1.
79. *Rosh HaShanah* 16b; Rashi *ad. loc. s.v. Shelosha; Bereshith Rabbah* 24:3; *Zohar* 1:57b, 2:790a, 2:246a; *Kuzari* 4:23 (43a); Raavad, introduction to *Sefer Yetzirah; Pardes Rimonim* 12:1, 23:16; *Asarah Maamaroth* 1:2:4, 1:2:26.
80. *Tikuney Zohar,* introduction (4a); Ibn Ezra on Exodus 32:32; *Sefer Chasidim* 605.
81. *Mesilath Yesharim* 1 (4a).
82. *Cf. Nefesh HaChaim* 1:3.
83. *Avoth* 2:1; *Zohar* 1:222b, 2:126b; *Tosafoth, Berakhoth* 6a *s.v. Chad.*

was written in a record book before Him" (Malachi 3:16).[84] It is this "book" which contains much of what is in store for man, as it is written, "In Your book all things are written" (Psalms 139:16).[85] It is the wise individual who can read God's writing, as the prophet said, "Seek out God's book and read" (Isaiah 34:16).[86]

21:18 Since the sealing of a decree may set up chains of events involving many persons, prayer and repentance essentially only help before the decree is sealed.[87] However, even after an evil decree is sealed, repentance and prayer can help[88] to delay its effects[89] and reduce its harm.[90]

21:19 Crying out to God with all one's heart can help divert an evil decree completely,[91] as it is written, "They cried out to God in their trouble, and He rescued them from their distress" (Psalms 107:6).[92] Similarly, tears of anguish can change a decree,[93] since the gates of tears are never shut.[94] The Psalmist thus prayed, "Hear my prayer, O God, listen to my cry and do not ignore my tears" (Psalms 39:13).[95] In such a case, one becomes like the righteous whose prayers can alter the destinies of those around them.[96]

21:20 When God seals a decree, He does so by setting up a chain of events based upon an individual's most probable course of action.[97] However, each person still has free will, and can therefore

84. *Cf. Berakhoth* 6a; *Zohar* 2:200a.
85. *Cf.* Radak, Ibn Ezra, *ad. loc.*
86. Ibn Ezra *ad. loc.; Zohar* 2:56a.
87. *Rosh HaShanah* 17b, 18a; *Yevamoth* 49b, 105a; *Avodah Zarah* 17b; *Niddah* 70b; *Yerushalmi, Yevamoth* 12:6 (69a); *Sifri* 142; *Bereshith Rabbah* 81:2; *BaMidbar Rabbah* 11:15; *Tanchuma, VaYikra* 5, *Tzav* 5; *Zohar* 1:57a; *Yad, Teshuvah* 2:6.
88. *Zohar* 2:107a; Radak on 1 Chronicles 3:17; *Sefer Chasidim* 605; *Menorath HaMaor* 5:3:2:5 (306). *Cf. VaYikra Rabbah* 10:5; *Pesikta Rabathai* 47 (199b), where it is disputed whether repentance accomplishes half and prayer all, or vice versa; *cf. Sanhedrin* 37b.
89. *Sefer Chasidim* 1168.
90. *Midrash Tehillim* 6:3; see above, 18:42. *Cf. Tosefoth Yom Tov* on *Avoth* 4:11.
91. See above, 15:68, notes 249, 250; *Rosh HaShanah* 16a, 18a.
92. *Rosh HaShanah* 16b; *Zohar* 2:20a. *Cf. Yerushalmi, Berakhoth* 4:3 (33b); *Yerushalmi, Taanith* 2:2 (9b).
93. *Zohar* 1:123a.
94. *Berakhoth* 32b; *Bava Metzia* 59a.
95. *Ibid. Cf. Bereshith Rabbah* 53:18.
96. See above, 19:13, 20:12.
97. See Volume 1, 3:40, 3:41.

offset the effects of the decree by changing his habits and way of life.[98] Similarly, the difficulties of moving to another location can often offset the effects of an evil decree.[99] All this must be accompanied by repentance,[100] which can offset the effects of a decree spiritually as well as materially.[101]

21:21 Since a person's destiny is largely affected by his economic status,[102] the change brought about by charitable donations can be enough to offset the effects of an evil decree.[103] Regarding this it is written, "Charity saves from death" (Proverbs 10:2, 11:4).[104] Likewise, we are taught that tithes have the power to change a curse to a blessing.[105]

21:22 God grants special inspiration to parents in the selection of a name for their children which will somehow hint to each child's destiny.[106] Based on this, our great sages could learn much from a person's name.[107] It is thus written, "As is his name, so is he" (1 Samuel 25:25).[108] A person's name can greatly affect his life,[109] and therefore, we are warned not to give a child an evil sounding

98. *Rosh HaShanah* 16b; *Bereshith Rabbah* 33:15; *Koheleth Rabbah* 5:4; *Pesikta* 39 (191a); *Zohar* 3:121b. *Cf. Zohar* 3:217b; Rashi, *Rosh HaShanah* 16b *s.v. Shinuy,* that changing deeds refers to repentance, but in the above Midrashim, changing deeds and repentance are both counted separately. Also see *Tanchuma, Noah* 8.

99. *Ibid.; Yerushalmi, Shabbath* 6:9 (39a); *Ikkarim* 4:4, 4:18. *Cf.* Rashi on Genesis 12:1. Also see *Bava Metzia* 75b; *Zohar* 1:187a, 3:166b; *Sefer Chasidim* 246.

100. *Yad, Teshuvah* 2:4; *Sefer Mitzvoth Gadol,* Positive Commandment 17; Ran, *Rosh HaShanah* (Rif 3b) *s.v. Shinuy;* Maharsha, *Rosh HaShanah* 16b *s.v. Arba Devarim.* See above, 17:20, note 85.

101. See above, 15:11.

102. See above, 19:35.

103. See above, 15:68, notes 249, 250; *Rosh HaShanah* 16b.

104. *Shabbath* 156b; *Rosh HaShanah* 16b; *Bava Bathra* 10a; *Avoth DeRabbi Nathan* 3:9; *Tana DeBei Eliahu Rabbah* 10 (65a); *Zohar* 1:199a, 3:111a, 3:113b, 3:273b; *Sefer Chasidim* 1172. *Cf. Yoreh Deah* 147:4; *Sifethey Cohen ad. loc.* 147:2.

105. *Shemoth Rabbah* 41:1; *Tanchuma, Ki Tissa* 14. *Cf. Yerushalmi, Maaser Sheni* 5:5 (32b).

106. *Shulchan Arukh HaAri,* cited in *Taamey HaMinhagim* 2:115 (p. 534). *Chafetz HaShem, Berakhoth* 13a; *Beer Mayim Chaim* on Genesis 2:19. *Cf. Zohar* 1:58a, 2:279b, 2:223a; *Tosafoth, Bava Bathra* 143b *s.v. SheHayu.*

107. *Yoma* 83b; *Yerushalmi, Rosh HaShanah* 3:9 (18a); *Bereshith Rabbah* 42:8; *Ruth Rabbah* 2:5. *Cf. Eruvin* 13b; *Megillah* 14a; *Sotah* 13a; *Bava Bathra* 91a; *Targum Yonathan* on Genesis 14:1-2.

108. *Cf. Midrash Tehillim* 53:1.

109. *Berakhoth* 7b; *Zohar* 1:58b, 1:60a, 1:156b, 2:179b, 2:223a, 3:75b; *Sefer Chasidim* 72c; *Bahir* 80; *Sefer Chasidim* 244; *Kav BeShamayim* 59; *Sefer HaRikmah* 180; *Emunah U'Bitachon* 19; *Teshuvoth Rashba* 4:30; *Asarah Maamaroth* 2:2:33; *Or HaChaim* on Deuteronomy 29:17, 31:1. However, sometimes a good person can have an ugly name, and vice versa; *BaMidbar Rabbah* 16:7; *Tanchuma, Shemoth* 2, *Shelach* 6.

name,[110] nor to name him after a person who has experienced calamity.[111] Changing one's name can thus offset the effects of an evil decree,[112] especially if it is done as an act of repentance.[113] For this reason, it is customary to change or add to the name of one who is seriously ill in a special synagogue service.[114]

21:23 Since the chains of events involved in a decree usually need not cross community lines, the prayers and repentance of an entire community can change a decree completely.[115] Regarding this, God told His prophet, "At one instant I may speak concerning a nation and concerning a kingdom, to pluck up, to pull down, and to destroy it. But if that nation will only turn away from its evil... then I will retract the evil that I thought to execute upon it" (Jeremiah 18:7-8).[116]

21:24 At times, God would reveal a decree to His prophets in the form of an oath. This was a sign that it involved such far reaching consequences that it could not be changed even by the prayer and repentance of an entire community or nation.[117] Even in such a case, however, it could be annulled by a sage.[118] Nevertheless, there are some decrees that involve so many lives and such far reaching consequences, that they cannot be changed by any means. Such decrees are said to be "written in blood."[119]

---

110. *Yoma* 38b; *Tanchuma, HaAzinu* 7. *Cf. Tosafoth, Kethuvoth* 104b *s.v. Shnei, Shabbath* 12b *s.v. Shavna, Megillah* 10b *s.v. Rabbah; Beth Sh'muel, Evven HaEzer* 129; *Shemoth Anashim s.v. Avishalom; Tiv Gittin ad. loc.* no. 17; *Teshuvoth Besamim Rosh* 190.

112. See above, note 98; *Yerushalmi, Shabbath* 6:9 (39a); *Tanchuma, Shoftim* 11; *Zohar* 1:133b, 3:111b, 3:217b; *Tikuney Zohar Chadash* 118a.

113. *Yad, Teshuvah* 2:4. *Cf. Zohar* 3:9a, 3:76b; *Targum* on 2 Chronicles 15:16, 13:2.

114. *Sefer Chasidim* 245; *Yoreh Deah* 335:10 in *Hagah; Teshuvoth Mahari Bruno* 101; *Devash LePhi, Shin* 14; *Taamey HaMinhagim (Kuntres Acharon)* 216 (p. 105). Also see Mordecai, *Gittin* 369; *Evven HaEzer* 129:18; *Chelkath Mechokek ad. loc.; Teshuvoth Maharik* 398.

115. *Rosh HaShanah* 17b, 18a; *Yevamoth* 49b, 105a; *Yerushalmi, Taanith* 2:1 (9a); *Midrash Tehillim* 13:1; *Zohar* 1:105b; *Yad, Teshuvah* 2:6.

116. *Shemoth Rabbah* 45:1. *Cf.* Jeremiah 36:3; Jonah 1:10.

117. *Rosh HaShanah* 18a; *Yevamoth* 105a.

118. *Berakhoth* 32a; *Yerushalmi, Nedarim* 3:1 (8a); *Shemoth Rabbah* 43:5; *Midrash Tehillim* 90:5. *Cf. Bava Bathra* 74a; *Tosafoth ad. loc. s.v. VeAkhshav; Sanhedrin* 38b; *Zohar* 1:236b. Also see *Chagigah* 10a; *Sanhedrin* 110b; *Yerushalmi, Chagigah* 1:8 (6b); *VaYikra Rabbah* 32:2; *Koheleth Rabbah* 10:23. See *VaYikra Rabbah* 10:5, however, that the heavenly court annuls God's oath when one repents.

119. *Esther Rabbah* 7:18; *Etz Yosef, Anaf Yosef, ad. loc. Cf.* Jeremiah 17:1; Rashi, Radak, *ad. loc.;* Job 19:24.

21:25   In general, God does not retract a good decree,[120] as the Torah states, "God is not human that He should be false, nor mortal that He should change His mind. Shall He say something and not do it, or speak and not fulfill?" (Numbers 23:19).[121] Though God never retracts a good decree, even because of sin,[122] a person's sins[123] can cause Him to bring the good in such a way that no benefit is derived from it,[124] thus effectively annulling the good. Regarding this, God told His prophet, "At another instant I may speak concerning a nation and concerning a kingdom, to build and to plant it. But if it does evil in My sight by not obeying Me, I will retract the good with which I promised to benefit it" (Jeremiah 18:9-10).[125]

21:26   When God decrees evil upon the wicked, He causes it to materialize slowly and in increments, thereby giving them a chance to repent. When He decrees good for the righteous, He causes it to materialize as quickly as possible.[126]

21:27   Though God may have decreed that a person must die, this does not excuse his murderer,[127] since God has many other messengers.[128] Similarly, though God may have decreed that a person suffer poverty and destitution, this does not excuse one from giving him charity, since his poverty may have been decreed

---

120. *Berakhoth* 7a; *Shabbath* 55a; Maharatz Chajas *ad. loc.; Yerushalmi, Taanith* 2:1 (9a); *Bereshith Rabbah* 53:5; *Eikhah Rabbah* 2:4; *Tanchuma, VaYera* 13; *Midrash Tehillim* 13:1; see Volume 1, 8:15.
121. *Yerushalmi, Taanith* 2:1 (9a); *Midrash Tehillim* 13:1.
122. *Tanchuma, VaYera* 13.
123. *Berakhoth* 4a; *Midrash Tehillim* 27:7; *Akedath Yitzchak* 96 (5:56a). *Cf. Bereshith Rabbah* 76:2, that there is no guarantee that the righteous will be rewarded in this world.
124. See above, 21:8.
125. Radak *ad. loc.* See *Or HaShem* (Crescas) 2:4:2, that according to Rambam in his introduction to the Mishnah this refers to a case where the prophet does not reveal the good to others, since this can be changed; see Volume 1, 8:16. Also quoted is the opinion of Ralbag, *Milchamoth HaShem,* that good depending on nature can be changed, but that depending on providence cannot. The opinion of *Or HaShem* is that Jeremiah refers to a case in which the good is not revealed to the prophet at all. *Cf. Akedath Yitzchak* 96 (5:56a), that sin can change good, even where there is a decree. Also see Abarbanel on Jeremiah 18:12; Maharsha, *Berakhoth* 4a *s.v. Sh'ma.*
126. *Shabbath* 97a; *Shemoth Rabbah* 3:18.
127. Ramban on Genesis 15:13.
128. *Taanith* 18b; *Koheleth Rabbah* 3:22; *Semachoth* 8; *Megillath Taanith* 12.

for this specific reason, to give others the opportunity to acheive merit through charity.[129]

21:28 God judges the world and makes plans taking future events into account,[130] as He said through His prophet, "I declare the end from the beginning. From ancient times, I reveal what is to be" (Isaiah 46:10).[131] Nevertheless, God does not judge a person for his future sins.[132] In addition, when God must bring evil upon the righteous, He often prepares its healing in advance.[133]

129. *Bava Bathra* 10a. *Cf. Tanchuma, BeHar* 2.
130. *Cf. Pirkey Rabbi Eliezer* 26 (61b), 36 (83a), 38 (88a), 48 (114b); *Sefer Chasidim* 549; *Menorath HaMaor* 5:3:2:4 (305).
131. *Cf.* Malbim *ad. loc.; Sifri* 2:22; *BaMidbar Rabbah* 16:11; *Tanchuma, Shelach* 9.
132. See above, 20:8.
133. *Megillah* 13b; *Shir HaShirim Rabbah* 4:12; see above, 18:25,18:42, 21:28. *Cf. Shemoth Rabbah* 21:7.

TWENTY TWO

PRAYER

22:1 We are commanded[1] to serve God every day, as the Torah states, "Serve God your Lord, and He will bless your bread and your water" (Exodus 23:25).[2] Just as bread and water are daily necessities,[3] so is the service of God.[4]

1. According to many authorities, the essence of prayer, i.e. non-formal daily worship, is a Biblical commandment; *cf. Yad, Tefillah* 1:1; *Sefer HaMitzvoth,* Positive Commandment 5; *Sefer Mitzvoth Gadol,* Positive Commandment 19; *Ikkarim* 4:20; Abudarham 2 (p. 5); *Magen Abraham, Orach Chaim* 106:2; *Cheredim,* Positive Commandments 1:17 (p. 56). See also *Zohar* 3:257a (no. 11), 2:91a. Other authorities, however, maintain that even the essence of prayer is not a Biblical commandment. As Ramban says, prayer is a means of approaching God and calling out to Him. Prayer must originate from below. Therefore, even the essence of prayer is only required by rabbinical legislation; *cf.* Ramban on *Sefer HaMitzvoth loc. cit.,* quoted in *Kesef Mishneh* on *Yad loc. cit.;* Rashi, *Berakhoth* 17b *s.v. Elu,* 20b *s.v. VeChayavin; Tosafoth loc. cit.* 17b *s.v. Elu,* 20b *s.v. BeTefillah;* Bertenoro, *Berakhoth* 3:1, 3:3; *Turey Zahav, Orach Chaim* 106:1-2; *Pri Chadash, Orach Chaim* 89:1. We find a Talmudic statement that prayer is rabbinical in *Berakhoth* 21a and *Sukkah* 38a; *cf.* Ramban *loc. cit.;* but see *Megillath Esther ibid.* and *Kesef Mishneh loc. cit.,* that this refers to formal prayer at a given time. There is also evidence that this was the dispute between Rabbi Eleazar and Rabbi Yochanan recorded in *Berakhoth* 21a; *cf. Yerushalmi, Shabbath* 1:2 (7a); *Pri Chadash loc. cit.,* and also see *Marah HaPanim* on *Yerushalmi, Berakhoth* 4:1 (29a). For further discussion, see *Chinukh* 433; *Eliah Rabbah* 106:2; *Beer Hetiv, Shaarey Teshuvah, Orach Chaim* 106:1; *Teshuvoth Shaagath Aryeh* 2:14; *Pri Megadim,* introduction to Laws of Prayer; *Mishnah Berurah* 106:4; *"Rav" Shulchan Arukh* 106:2; *Chayay Adam* 16:1; *Teshuvoth Tzemach Tzedek* 64 (3:3a). Also see *Magen Abraham* 55:7 and *Beer Hetiv* 55:8, where it appears that prayer is rabbinical in origin. But see *Pri Megadim ad. loc.,* that this refers to praying with a *minyan* of ten; *cf. Mishnah Berurah* 55:31. For the reason why we do not say a blessing over prayer, see *Pri Megadim, Eshel Avraham* 106:4; *Taamey HaMinhagim* 67 (p. 38) quoting Abudarham 93a.
2. *Yad, Tefillah* 1:1; *cf. Kesef Mishneh ad. loc.; Moreh Nevukhim* 1:36; *Sefer HaMitzvoth, Sefer Mitzvoth Gadol, loc. cit.; Ikkarim* 4:30. See *Bava Kama* 92b; *Bava Metzia* 107b; *Pri Chadash* 89:1, that this passage refers to the *Sh'ma* as well as to prayer. This implies that even though saying the *Sh'ma* is a Biblical command in its own right, it is also counted as worship and serving God. See also Deuteronomy 6:13, 10:12, 10:20, 13:5.
3. *Cf. Yoma* 76a; *Lev Sameach* on *Sefer HaMitzvoth,* Positive Commandment 5.
4. *Kiryath Sefer* (Mabit), quoted in *Lechem Mishneh, Tefillah* 1:1 and *Pri*

22:2   Although one serves God in many ways,[5] the main way an individual serves God is in worship,[6] where he can commune with God with his every thought and emotion. Regarding this the Torah states, "Love God your Lord and serve Him with all your heart and soul" (Deuteronomy 11:13).[7]

22:3   We are therefore commanded to worship God every day,[8] and this commandment applies to men and women alike.[9] However, neither the number of prayers, nor their time,[10] nor their form,[11] is prescribed by the Torah.

22:4   Worship can take many forms[12] as long as it provides a

Megadim, introduction to the Laws of Prayer. However, *Kesef Mishneh ibid.* and *Megillath Esther* on *Sefer HaMitzvoth,* Positive Commandment 5, give the reason that if it were not a daily commandment, it could not be obligatory, unless it were to be fulfilled by a single prayer in one's lifetime.

5.   *Sefer HaMitzvoth,* Postive Commandment 5; *Cheredim,* Positive Commandments 1:17 (p. 56). *Cf. Zohar* 3:111b.

6.   *Pirkey Rabbi Eliezer* 16 (37a); Rabbenu Yonah, *Avoth* 1:2. *Cf.* Maharshal on *Sefer Mitzvoth Gadol,* Positive Commandment 19. See *Berakhoth* 32b.

7.   *Cf. Sifri, Ekev ad. loc.* (41); *Yalkut Shimoni* (1:863); Rashi *ad. loc.; Taanith* 2a; *Yerushalmi, Berakhoth* 4:1 (29a); *Yad, Tefillah* 1:1; *Sefer HaMitzvoth,* Positive 5; *Sefer Mitzvoth Gadol,* Positive 19; *Magen Avraham* 106:2.

8.   *Yad, Tefillah* 1:1; *Chinukh* 433; see above, note 4. However, the necessity of praying every day is not mentioned in *Sefer HaMitzvoth* nor in Abudarham 2 (p. 5). See note 1, that Ramban disputes this and maintains that prayer is only a Biblical obligation in time of trouble; see below, note 22; *Kinath Sofrim* on *Sefer HaMitzvoth,* Positive 5.

9.   *Berakhoth* 3:3 (20b); *Yad, Tefillah* 1:2; *Orach Chaim* 106:2. According to those who maintain that prayer is Biblical, the rabbinical legislation regarding formal prayer does not apply to women and they need only say a short daily prayer. According to those who maintain that prayer is a rabbinical commandment, however, it was legislated for men and women alike; *cf. Magen Avraham* 106:2; *Pri Chadash* 89:1; *Pri Megadim, Eshel Avraham* 89:1; *"Rav" Shulchan Arukh* 106:2; *Mishnah Berurah* 106:4. *Cf. Magen Avraham* 70:1. Also *Sh'nei Luchoth HaB'rith, Inyanay Tefillah* 2:212b, who requires that women recite the entire service. Also see *Sotah* 22a, that a young girl should not pray too much.

10.   Rif, *Berakhoth* 11b; Rabbenu Yonah *ad. loc. s.v. Tefillah; Yad, Tefillah* 1:1-2; *Orach Chaim* 106:2. *Cf. Berakhoth* 21a; *Pesachim* 54b; *Yad, Tefillah* 10:6; *Megillath Esther* on *Sefer HaMitzvoth,* Positive 5; also *Tosefta, Berakhoth* 3:1, cited in *Sefer HaMitzvoth,* Positive 10; *Kesef Mishneh, Tefillah* 1:1; *Korban HaEdah, Yerushalmi, Shabbath* 1:2 (7a) *s.v. Lishna.* See also *Yad, Tefillah* 3:1, from *Berakhoth* 26a. However, from *Taanith* 28a, *Tosafoth ad. loc. s.v. Hallelu,* it appears that even the time and number of daily prayers is Biblical; *cf.* Rashi *ibid. s.v. Hallelu; Binyan Shlomo, Tefillah* 1:1; *Pri Chadash* 89:1, but see Maharatz Chajas *ibid.,* that in this case "Biblical" means mentioned in the Torah, and not necessarily a Biblical command. Also see Rabbenu Chananel, Rabbenu Gershon, *ibid.,* who interpret this entire discussion differently. However, see *Zohar* 3:257a (no. 1).

11.   *Yad, Tefillah* 1:1; *Kesef Mishneh ad. loc.; Magen Avraham* 106:2; see above, note 9.

12.   *Sifri, Ekev* 26; *Devarim Rabbah* 2:1; *Tanchuma, VaEthChanan* 3. *Cf. Pesachim* 117a; *Zohar* 1:23b, 2:19b.

strong communion between man and God.[13] It can consist of praising God, of asking Him to fulfill our basic needs, or of thanking Him for past good. Our tradition[14] teaches that we should praise God before asking Him to satisfy our needs,[15] just as one engages in pleasant conversation with a friend before discussing business.[16] King Solomon therefore said, "Hearken to the song and to the prayer which Your servant prays before You today" (1 Kings 8:28).[17] Likewise, we are taught to thank God for past good after asking for our needs,[18] just as a servant thanks his master after receiving his portion.[19]

22:5   It is proper to ask God for small things before asking for greater ones.[20] Even if a person feels he has everything he needs, he must always pray to God for the future.[21]

22:6   There is a particular obligation to pray in time of trouble,[22] as the Torah states, "When... an enemy attacks you in your land, you shall sound the alarm" (Numbers 10:9).[23] For this reason it was legislated that the community fast and pray whenever

13. *Cf. Hishtap'khuth HaNefesh* 72 (p. 92b), from Genesis 30:8, citing *Likutey Halakhoth, Tefillah* 5.
14. Rashi, *Avodah Zarah* 8a *s.v. Rabbi Yehoshua; Kesef Mishneh, Tefillah* 1:2.
15. *Berakhoth* 32a; *Avodah Zarah* 7b; *Sifri, Ekev* 343; *Midrash Tehillim* 102:2; *Yalkut Shimoni* 1:951, 2:192; *Zohar* 1:169a, 1:244a, 3:360b, 3:365a, 3:285a; *Zohar Chadash* 91a; *Tikuney Zohar Chadash* 106b; *Yad, Tefillah* 1:2; *Kesef Mishneh, Lechem Mishneh, ad. loc.; Yad, Tefillah* 1:4; Abudarham 2 (p. 9); *Menorath HaMaor* 3:3:1:17 (107); *Pri Megadim,* introduction to the Laws of Prayer.
16. *Berakhoth* 34a; *VaYikra Rabbah* 5:7; *Midrash Tehillim* 19:17; *Tur, Orach Chaim* 582; *Chokhmath Shlomo, Orach Chaim* 112:1.
17. "Song *(Rinah)* is the praise of God, while prayer *(Tefillah)* relates to the needs of man"; Ralbag *ad. loc.; Devarim Rabbah* 2:1; *Berakhoth* 31a; Rashi *ad. loc. s.v. Rina; Tosefta, Berakhoth* 3:9; *Shaarey Orah* 1 (4a). However, see *Yerushalmi, Berakhoth* 4:4 (34b), where the exact opposite is derived from this passage. Also see *Berakhoth* 6a; Rashi *ad. loc. s.v. BiM'kom.*
18. *Sifri, Ekev* 343; *Yalkut Shimoni* 1:951; *Yad, Tefillah* 1:2; *Pri Megadim,* introduction to Laws of Prayer. *Cf. Akedath Yitzchak* 58 (3:15b); *Avodath HaKodesh* 2:10.
19. *Berakhoth* 34a; *Tur, Orach Chaim* 112; *Machtzith HaShekel* 112:1; *Mishnah Berurah* 112:1.
20. *VaYikra Rabbah* 5:7; *Midrash Tehillim* 19:17; *Yalkut Shimoni* 2:677; Rashi on Psalms 19:14. See above, 16:9, note 29.
21. *Pri Megadim,* introduction to Laws of Prayer. *Cf. Zohar* 2:62b, 1:199b.
22. Ramban on *Sefer HaMitzvoth,* Positive 5; *Megillath Esther, Kinath Sofrim, ibid.; Chinukh* 433; *Magen Avraham* 106:2.
23. *Sifri* 1:76; *Yalkut Shimoni* 1:725; *Yad, Taanith* 1:1; *Maggid Mishneh ad. loc.; Sefer*

calamity threatens.[24] It is thus written, "In the land, there may be famine or plague, blight, mildew, locust or weevil, their enemies may besiege them in their cities, there may be some epidemic or sickness. Some prayer, some supplication may be made by any man, by any of Your people Israel — each one knowing the anguish of his own heart — and he shall spread his hands toward this Temple. And You shall hear from heaven, the place of Your abode, and forgive" (1 Kings 8:37-39).[25]

22:7 We pray, not to remind God of our needs, but to remind ourselves of our dependence upon Him.[26] We are therefore commanded to pray to God for everything, though it is understood that He knows our deepest thoughts and needs,[27] since the very act of praying heightens a person's awareness of God and His providence,[28] and thus makes one worthy of the good that God wants to give.[29] It was for this reason that prayer was the way of the Patriarchs,[30] as well as of all the great men and women of Israel, from the earliest times.[31]

22:8 Although all the commandments benefit a person in this world and the next, prayer is the universal remedy that helps for all things.[32] It helps to cure the sick, as we find, "I have heard your prayer, I have seen your tears. Behold I will heal you" (2 Kings 20:5).[33] Similarly, prayer can help for children,[34] for rain,[35] for victory in war,[36] and even to save from imminent death.[37] Prayer

HaMitzvoth, Positive 59; *Moreh Nevukhim* 3:36 (49a); *Chinukh* 384. However, this concept is omitted in *Sefer Mitzvoth Gadol,* Positive 170.
24. *Taanith* 3:5 (19a); *Yad, Taanith* 1:4; *Lechem Mishneh* 1:1.
25. Radak *ad. loc.;* Ramban on *Sefer HaMitzvoth,* Positive 5.
26. *Chovoth HaLevavoth* 8:3 no. 18.
27. See Volume 1, 2:46; Maharal, *Nethivoth Olam, Avodah* 3 (82a).
28. *Moreh Nevukhim* 3:36 (49a), 3:44 (56a), 3:51 (65b).
29. Maharal, *Nethivoth Olam, Avodah* 3 (82a); *Chinukh* 433; *Akedath Yitzchak* 96 (3:13a).
30. *Bereshith Rabbah* 52:14, 60:14; *Shemoth Rabbah* 21:1; *Tanchuma, BeShalach* 9.
31. *Hishtap'khuth HaNefesh,* introduction (p. 3*ff.*). *Cf.* Rashi on Genesis 2:5. Some say that it is for this reason that the Yiddish word for "worship" is *Davenin,* taken from the Aramaic *DeAv Inun,* "they are from the Fathers"; *Taamey HaMinhagim* 161 (p. 69), quoting *Maggid Taalumah.*
32. *Ikkarim* 4:16, 4:20. See Kaplan, *A Call to the Infinite* (Moznaim, 1986), pp. 31-33.
33. *Ibid.*
34. *Cf.* Genesis 25:21.
35. *Cf.* 2 Samuel 21:1; *Targum ad. loc.*
36. *Cf.* 2 Chronicles 32:20.
37. *Cf.* Deuteronomy 9:19.

helps for Jew and non-Jew alike, as King Solomon requested, "There may also be strangers, not from Your people Israel, who come from faraway lands for the sake of Your Name. For they hear of Your great Name, Your mighty hand and outstretched arm, and they come and pray toward this Temple. And You shall hearken from heaven, the place of Your abode, and You shall do all that the stranger calls You to do" (1 Kings 8:41- 43).[38]

22:9   Prayer can also bring a person to the highest levels of spiritual perfection and Godly gifts.[39] It is the way of the saints,[40] and the path by which they achieved greatness.[41]

22:10   Prayer is the primary way that one seeks God, as the Psalmist said, "Praise God, all you who seek Him" (Psalms 22:37).[42] Prayer that issues from the depths of the human heart calls God forth from the depths of His concealment, as the Psalmist said, "From the depths I call You, O God" (Psalms 130:1).[43] It is therefore through prayer that we literally bind ourselves to God,[44] as it is written, "Cleave to Him and serve Him with all your heart and soul" (Joshua 22:5).[45] In true prayer, we bare our soul before God, as it is written, "I poured out my soul before God" (1 Samuel 1:15).[46]

22:11   Since God is inherently perfect, no man can do anything for Him.[47] Serving God therefore involves fulfilling the purpose for which He created us.[48] Since this purpose is to come close to

38. *Cf.* Rashi, Radak, Ralbag, *ad. loc.; Ikkarim* 4:20; *BaMidbar Rabbah* 1:3; *Tanchuma, Terumah* 9, *BaMidbar* 3.
39. *Likutey Moharan Tinyana* 111; *Hishtap'khuth HaNefesh* 12 (p. 51).
40. *Likutey Moharan Tinyana* 100; *Histhtap'khuth HaNefesh* 8 (p. 48).
41. *Ibid. Cf. Shemoth Rabbah* 38:5.
42. *Cf.* Ramban on Genesis 25:22, from Psalms 34:5, Amos 5:4; Ibn Ezra on Psalms 34:11.
43. *Zohar* 2:63a-b, 3:26a, 3:70a; *Shaarey Orah* 3-4 (37b end). *Cf. Likutey Amarim, Iggereth HaKodesh* 12 (118b).
44. *Zohar* 2:213b; Maharal, *Nethivoth Olam* 4 (86a); *Likutey Moharan Tinyana* 120; *Hishtap'khuth HaNefesh* 13 (p. 52).
45. *Cf.* Deuteronomy 10:20, 11:22, 30:20; Ibn Ezra on Psalms 1:3; Ramban on Deuteronomy 1:22, Song of Songs 1:2.
46. Radak, Abarbanel, *ad. loc.;* Rashi, *Berakhoth* 5b *s.v. Toref; Nefesh HaChaim* 2:14. *Cf.* Psalms 62:9, 102:1.
47. See Volume 1, 2:35, 3:4.
48. See Volume 1, 5:54*ff.*

Him,[49] anything that brings man closer to God is considered
His service.[50] Therefore, since prayer causes one to acknowledge
one's dependence upon God, and thereby brings one close to
Him, it is the primary service of God.[51] Prayer is the service of
the heart.[52] Without sincere intent it is like a body without a
soul[53] and like a shell without fruit.[54]

22:12   Prayer is considered the service of God similar to the sacrifices
of the Holy Temple.[55] The Psalmist thus said, "Let my prayer
be set forth as incense before You, the lifting of my hands
as the evening sacrifice" (Psalms 141:2).[56] Just as a sacrifice
unites[57] the spiritual and material,[58] by making a lowly animal
the object of serving God,[59] so does prayer unite the spiritual
and material,[60] by making the request of our material needs a
service of God.[61] It is for this reason that, when it is impossible
to bring sacrifices,[62] prayer can be offered in their stead,[63] as the
prophet exclaimed, "We will offer the words of our lips instead
of calves" (Hosea 14:3).[64] Thus, formal prayers were ordained in

49. See Volume 1, 3:12.
50. See Volume 1, 3:15.
51. Maharal, *Nethivoth Olam, Avodah* 3 (84a); *Midrash Tehillim* 66:1; *Zohar* 2:59b, 2:115b, 3:111b, 3:223a; *Tikuney Zohar* 51 (87a); *Tikuney Zohar Chadash* 96a, 106c; *Likutey Amarim, Iggereth HaKodesh* 12 (118b).
52. See above, note 7; *Nefesh HaChaim* 2:1.
53. *Chovoth HaLevavoth* 8:3:9 (46a); *Asarah Maamaroth* 1:3; *Akedath Yitzchak* 38 (3:13a); *Sh'nei Luchoth HaB'rith, Inyanay Tefillah* 2:202b.
54. *Chovoth HaLevavoth* 8:3:9 (46a).
55. *Sifri, Ekev* 41; Rashi on Deuteronomy 11:13; *Orach Chaim* 98:4; Abudarham 2 (p. 5); *Avodath HaKodesh* 2:14; *Sh'nei Luchoth HaB'rith, Amud HaShalom* 2:204a (note). *Cf. Berakhoth* 15a.
56. *Berakhoth* 6b; *Sifri, Ekev* 41; Rashi on Deuteronomy 11:13; Abudarham 2 (p. 5); *Tanchuma, Ki Thavo* 1; *Midrash Tehillim* 108:2, 141:2; *Zohar* 1:230a.
57. *Zohar* 1:164a, 1:246b, 1:248b, 2:37b, 3:4a, 3;7a, 3:202a, 3:252b, 3:240b; *Nefesh HaChaim* 2:9 (note).
58. *Zohar* 1:45b, 1:65a, 1:89b, 1:206b, 1:244a, 2:259b, 3:5b; *Zohar Chadash* 38a, 51b; *Pri Etz Chaim* 5, 7.
59. See above, 13:25, note 86.
60. *Zohar* 1:230a, 2:213b.
61. *Nefesh HaChaim* 2:14.
62. *Tanchuma, Tzav* 6.
63. *Taanith* 27b; *BaMidbar Rabbah* 18:17; *Tanchuma, VaYishlach* 9, *Korach* 12; *Midrash Tehillim* 5:7, 141:2.
64. *Ibid.;* Rashi, Mahari Kara, Ibn Ezra, *ad. loc.; Sefer Mitzvoth Gadol,* Positive 19; *Menorath HaMaor* 3:3:1:2 (92).

place of the regular daily sacrifices performed in the Temple in Jerusalem — which themselves were accompanied by prayer and song.[65] Moreover, the prayer of a sincere heart[66] is better than any sacrifice,[67] as the Psalmist exclaimed, "I will praise the name of God with a song, I will exalt Him with thanksgiving, and it shall please God more than the offering of a bullock" (Psalms 69:31-32).[68]

22:13 Since the object of prayer is to ask God to make changes in the physical world, it serves to enhance His relationship to the world and thereby unify the spiritual and material planes.[69] This is the meaning of the teaching that prayer must rise up and penetrate all the spiritual worlds[70] in order to cause God's goodness to flow down and unify[71] and nourish them.[72] Each prayer can set up chains of events that involve the creation of many spiritual worlds,[73] and even similar prayers will have different effects because of the different circumstances under which they are uttered.[74]

22:14 It is for this reason that prayer is so important before God,[75] and is said to stand in the highest spiritual realms.[76] It is also for this reason that the prayers and praises of mortal humans take preference over those of even the highest celestial beings.[77] The prayers of Israel are particularly desired by God. Regarding Israel, God declared, "I fashioned this people for Myself, that they might declare My praise" (Isaiah 43:21).[78] The Psalmist also proclaimed, "[God's] praise is reflected in the assembly of His devoted servants.

---

65. *Berakhoth* 26b.
66. Maharshal on *Sefer Mitzvoth Gadol,* Positive 19.
67. *Berakhoth* 32b; *Tanchuma, Ki Tavo* 1; *Sefer Mitzvoth Gadol,* Positive 19.
68. *Midrash Tehillim* 39:3.
69. *Likutey Amarim, Kuntres Acharon* (155a).
70. *Zohar* 3:201a, 3;260b; *Nefesh HaChaim* 2:10.
71. *Zohar* 2:213b, 1:230a, 2:200b; *Etz Chaim* 36:3 (192b); *Reshith Chokhmah, Shaar HaAhavah* 8 (80c); *Nefesh HaChaim* 2:14 (note); see above, note 60.
72. *Zohar* 1:24a, 3:226a, 3:235a, 2:244a; *Nefesh HaChaim* 2:9.
73. *Tikuney Zohar* 18 (35b), 69 (106b); *Nefesh HaChaim* 2:10.
74. *Tikuney Zohar* 22 (65a); *Nefesh HaChaim* 2:13. See Kaplan, *Torah Anthology,* Volume 4, pp. 115-120.
75. *Devarim Rabbah* 8:1.
76. *Berakhoth* 6b; Rashi *ad. loc. s.v. Devarim; Nefesh HaChaim* 2:10; *Keter Shem Tov* 138.
77. *Chullin* 91b; *Yalkut Shimoni* 1:890, 2:951.
78. *Midrash Tehillim* 104:1.

Let Israel therefore rejoice in their Maker; let the inhabitants of Zion delight in their King. Let them praise His Name... for God desires His people and He will adorn the humble with deliverance" (Psalms 149:1-4).[79]

22:15 Even if God desires our good, prayer is still necessary, since all good is granted on the condition that one be worthy of it and work for it. Thus, for example, even if God were to decree that a particular farmer should enjoy a good season, he would have to plow and plant in order to harvest a good crop.[80] Similarly, the effort that a person puts into praying is often prerequisite to realizing whatever good God has decreed.[81]

22:16 By praying, we acknowledge our utter dependence upon God. We can then come closer to Him and remove all the barriers that might have prevented us from receiving the good He wishes to bestow upon us.[82] Evil, on the other hand, is the greatest barrier between man and God, and is actually the result of man's separation from God. Evil thus prevents us from receiving the good that God wishes to bestow. Prayer is the most efficacious means at our disposal to remove evil and alleviate its effects.[83]

---

79. Ibn Ezra *ad. loc.; Midrash Tehillim* 149:4.
80. *Ikkarim* 4:18. See also *Or HaShem* (Crescas) 3b:1:1 (83a); *Chinukh* 433.
81. *Ibid. Cf. Tanchuma, MiKetz* 10.
82. *Sheveiley Emunah* 1 (8a). *Cf. Sanhedrin* 44a.
83. *Cf. Sefer Chasidim* 651.

TWENTY THREE

IMMORTALITY AND THE SOUL

23:1   One of the foundations of our faith is the belief in the immortality of the soul, and in life after death.

23:2   If one believes in God's justice, one must also believe in the immortality of the soul. How can we otherwise reconcile the fact that many righteous individuals suffer in this life?

23:3   Just as the unborn child has many endowments which are of no use to it in the womb, but demonstrate that it will be born into a world where they will be used, so does a human being have many endowments which are of little value in this life, which indicate that man will be reborn into a higher dimension after death.[1]

23:4   Details of immortality are not mentioned in the Torah since revelation only deals with the present world. The prophet therefore says when speaking of the World to Come, "Never has the ear heard it — no eye has seen it — other than God: That which He will do for those who hope in Him" (Isaiah 64:3). That is, not even the great prophets were allowed to envision the reward of the righteous in the Ultimate Future.[2]

23:5   Man shares physio-chemical life processes with animals, and on the physical plane is indistinguishable from them. We therefore speak of man having an "animal soul" *(Nefesh HaBahamith)*[3] which

---

1.   *Sh'nei Luchoth HaB'rith, BeAsarah Maamaroth* 1:63b, note. See *Gesher HaChaim* 3:1-2.
2.   *Berakhoth* 34b; *Shabbath* 63a; *Sanhedrin* 99a; Rashi *ad. loc.;* *Yad, Teshuvah* 8:7; *Emunoth VeDeyoth* 9:2; Maharal, *Tifereth Yisrael* 57-58.
3.   *Etz Chaim* 49:3; *Mevo Shearim* 6:2:7; *Shaarey Kedushah* 1; *Derekh HaShem* 3:1:1; *Likutey Amarim (Tanya), Sefer Shel Benonim* 1 (5b), 9 (13b). See also *Zohar* 2:94b, 3:33b; Ramban on Genesis 1:20, Leviticus 17:14; *Or HaChaim* on Genesis 1:21. *Cf. Yad, Teshuvah* 8:3; Ralbag on Proverbs 12:10; *Tanchuma, VaYikra* 8. This animal soul can most probably be identified with the information contained in the human brain

is contained in the blood, *i.e.* in the physio-chemical life processes.[4] Regarding this soul, the Torah says, "The life-force of the flesh is in the blood" (Leviticus 17:11).[5]

23:6 Since this animal soul is what draws man away from the spiritual, it is commonly called the "Evil Urge" *(Yetzer HaRa)* in the Talmud.[6]

23:7 In addition to his material self, however, man possesses a soul which is unique among all of God's creations. In describing the creation of Adam, the Torah says, "God formed man out of the dust of the ground, and breathed into his nostrils a soul-breath of life *(Nishmath Chaim)*. Man [thus] became a living creature *(Nefesh Chayah)*" (Genesis 2:7). The Torah is teaching us that the human soul came directly from God's innermost Essence in the same way that a breath issues forth from a person's lungs and chest cavity. The rest of creation, on the other hand, was created with speech, which is a lower level, for just as sound waves are generated by a person but do not contain any air from the lungs, so the rest of creation emanates from God's Power but not from His Essence.[7]

23:8 The soul consists of three parts which are called by the Hebrew names, *Nefesh, Ruach* and *Neshamah*. The word *Neshamah* is a cognate of *Neshimah,* which means literally "breath." *Ruach* means "wind." *Nefesh* comes from the root *Nafash,* meaning "rest," as in the verse, "On the seventh day, [God] ceased work and rested *(Nafash)*." (Exodus 31:17). God's exhaling a soul can be compared to a glassblower forming a vessel. The breath *(Neshamah)* first leaves his lips, travels as a wind *(Ruach)* and finally comes to rest *(Nefesh)* in the vessel. Of these three levels of the soul, *Neshamah* is therefore the highest and closest to God, while *Nefesh* is that aspect of the soul residing in the body. *Ruach* stands between the

and body, as well as with its ability to function. However, this interacts with the higher parts of the soul, *Nefesh, Ruach,* and *Neshamah;* see note 8.

4.   *Cf. Derekh HaShem* 3:1:2.
5.   *Targum ad. loc.; Emunoth VeDeyoth* 6:1 (end).
6.   *Cf. Berakhoth* 5a, 54a, 60b, 61b; *Sanhedrin* 91b, on Genesis 4:7; *Moreh Nevukhim* 3:8; *Derekh HaShem* 1:3:1, 2:2:2.
7.   See *Likutey Amarim, Sefer Shel Benonim* 2 (6a); *Nefesh HaChaim* 1:15. This is the

two, binding man to his spiritual Source. It is for this reason that Divine Inspiration is called *Ruach HaKodesh* in Hebrew.[8]

23:9   The *Neshamah* is affected only by thought, the *Ruach* by speech, and the *Nefesh* by action.[9]

23:10   All souls were created at the beginning of time, and are stored in a celestial treasury until the time of birth.[10]

23:11   The soul has its first attachment to the body from the moment of conception,[11] and remains with it until the moment of death. Death is thus often referred to in Hebrew as "departure of the soul" *(Yetziath HaNeshamah).*[12]

23:12   We are taught that immediately after death the soul is in a state of great confusion.[13] It is therefore customary to stay near a dying person, so that he not die alone.[14]

Kabbalistic view. For the philosophical view, see *Emunoth VeDeyoth* 6:2; Rambam, *Shemonah Perakim* 1; *Yad, Teshuvah* 8:3.

8.   *Nefesh HaChaim* 1:15; *Etz Chaim* 5:5, from Psalms 23:31. On the verse, "Who knows the soul of an animal if it goes up, or the soul of man if it goes down" (Ecclesiastes 3:21), the Midrash states that the *Nefesh* is in the blood, while the *Ruach* goes up and down. The *Neshamah* is said to be man's essence; *Bereshith Rabbah* 14:9; Rashi *ad. loc.* In the *Zohar* (3:25a top), we find that, "The *Nefesh* is bound to the *Ruach,* the *Ruach* to the *Neshamah,* and the *Neshamah* to the Blessed Holy One." The three thus form a sort of chain, linking man to God. The Midrash *ibid.* mentions five parts of the soul, *Nefesh, Ruach, Neshamah, Chayah* (Living Essence) and *Yechidah* (Unique Essence). See *Nefesh HaChaim* 2:17 where it is explained that *Chayah* is the root of the soul and *Yechidah* is the highest part of this. See also *Moreh Nevukhim* 1:40-41; Rashi, *Chagigah* 12b *s.v. Ruchoth U'Neshamoth; Shaar HaGilgulim* 1; *Derekh HaShem* 3:1:4; *Maamar HaChokhmah, BeHaNeshamah,* in *Yalkut Yedioth HaEmeth,* p. 266; Kaplan, *The Way of God,* pp. 347 (note 6); *Innerspace,* Chapter 2.

9.   *Nefesh HaChaim* 1:14.

10. *Niddah* 13b; *Chagigah* 12b; *Gilyon Maharsha ad. loc.; Akedath Yitzchak, Bereshith* 6:14; *Etz Chaim* 26:2. But see Rav Saadiah Gaon, *Emunoth VeDeyoth* 6:3, who maintains that the soul is created only when the body is formed, from Zechariah 12:1. But see Radak *ad. loc.* It appears that Rav Saadiah is referring to the level of *Nefesh,* while *Neshamah* is pre-created. Cf. Malbim, *Shirey HaNefesh (Melitzah)* on Song of Songs 8:8, *s.v. Achoth Lanu Ketana.*

11. *Sanhedrin* 91b. See *Etz Chaim* 5:5.

12. At the moment of death, the soul sees the *Shekhinah* (Divine Presence); *Pirkey Rabbi Eliezer* 34 (79b). Depending on its state of purity, this can either be a painful or a joyous experience. It is for this reason that when great saints knew their time was nearing, they would meditate so deeply that they would become one with God. They would essentially let their soul be drawn out of their bodies and die in a state of ecstacy. This is known as *Mithath Neshikah,* "death by the Kiss of God"; *Moreh Nevukhim* 3:51. This "kiss" is mentioned in the Talmud; *Berakhoth* 8a; *Moed Katan* 28a; *Bava Bathra* 17a; *Devarim Rabbah* 11:10. See commentaries on Psalms 91:14; Recanti, *VaYechi* (37b), on *Zohar* 3:120b; Rabbi Abraham Abulafia, *Sefer HaTzeruf* (4b), *Chayay Olam HaBa* (5b).

13. This is because its main focus of attention is the body. Most people identify themselves with their bodies. It is difficult for a soul to break this habit, and therefore, for the

23:13 The disembodied soul is intensely aware of the physical surroundings of its body. This is especially true before the body is buried.[15] The soul then literally mourns for its body for seven days.[16] This is alluded to in the verse, "His soul mourns for him" (Job 14:22).[17]

23:14 For the first 12 months after death,[18] until the body decomposes, the soul has no permanent resting place and thus experiences acute disorientation.[19] It therefore hovers over the body.[20] During this time, the soul is aware of and identifies with the decomposition of the body. The Talmud thus teaches us that "Worms are as painful to the dead as needles in the flesh of the living, as it is written (Job 14:22), 'His flesh grieves for him.'"[21] Most commentaries

first few days, the soul is literally obsessed with its previous habitation; Kaplan, *On Immortality and the Soul* in *The Aryeh Kaplan Reader* (Artscrolls, 1983), p. 181.

14. *Turey Zahav, Yoreh Deah* 339:3; *Kitzur Shulchan Arukh* 194:4. *Cf. Avodah Zarah* 20b; *Emunoth VeDeyoth* 6:4; *Pirkey Rabbi Eliezer* 34 (80a); *Radal ad. loc.* 34:36.

15. *Shabbath* 152b; *Sefer Mitzvoth Gadol, Assin DeRabbanan* 2 (Vinitzia, 5307) p. 246a.

16. After seven days, the body begins to decompose; *Pirkey Rabbi Eliezer* 34 (80b).

17. *Shabbath* 152a (end); *Midrash Ne'elam, Zohar* 1:122b; *Pirkey Rabbi Eliezer* 34; *Radal ad. loc.* 34:52.

18. For a discussion of whether the soul is aware of what is happening in the world of the living following this initial 12 month period, see *Berakhoth* 18b; *Tosafoth, Shabbath* 153a *s.v. VeNishmatho, Sotah* 34b *s.v. Avothai; Maavar Yavok* 2:25; *Nishmath Chaim* 2:22. See also *Sefer Chasidim* 9; *Makor Chesed ad. loc.* 9:14.

19. The disembodied soul spends much of its time learning how to focus. It is now seeing without physical eyes, using some process which we do not even have the vocabulary to describe. The Kabbalists call this frightening process *Kaf HaKela* ("hollow of a sling"), for it is like being "thrown with a sling from one end of the world to another"; *Shabbath ibid.;* Maharsha *ad. loc. s.v. VeHaitha; Zohar* 1:217b, 3:318b, 3:222b; *Nitzotzey Or, Zohar* 3:222b no. 1; *Migdal Oz, Teshuvah* 8:2. It also includes the concept of reincarnation; *Zohar* 2:99; *Reshith Chokhmah, Shaar HaYirah* 13 (40a). This state of total confusion and disorientation is reserved for the wicked. The righteous, on the other hand, are able to bypass this disorientation. In order to do so they must pass through a River of Fire *(Nahar DiNor)*, until they attain the highest level of communion with God, in the Garden of Eden under the Throne of Glory; *Likutey Torah (HaAri); Shaar Maamarey Chazal* on *Avoth* 6:1 (Jerusalem, 5748) p. 16b. Both of these are alluded to in the verse, "The soul of my master shall be bound up in the bundle of life with God your Lord, while He shall sling out the souls of your enemies as from the hollow of a sling" (1 Samuel 25:29); *Radak ad. loc.* The souls of those who are neither completely righteous nor completely wicked are placed in the care of an angel named *Dumah* ("Silence") to await the final judgment; *Shabbath* 152b; Maharsha *ad. loc. s.v. Nimsarim;* Rashi, *Berakhoth* 18b *s.v. Duma;* Rabbi Yochanan, *Sanhedrin* 94a, from Isaiah 21:11 ("the Burden of Dumah"); *Zohar* 1:124a, 2:263a; *Midrash Ne'elam, Zohar* 1:134b; *cf. Chagigah* 5a.

20. *Shabbath ibid.* One of the few things that the soul has little difficulty focusing on is its own body. It is a familiar pattern and some tie seems to remain. To some extent, it is a refuge from its disorientation; *On Immortality ad. loc.*

21. *Berakhoth* 18b; *Shabbath* 152a.

write that this refers to the psychological anguish of the soul in seeing its earthly habitation in a state of decay.[22] The Kabbalists call this *Chibut HaKever,* "punishment of the grave."[23] We are taught that what happens to the body in the grave can be even more painful than *Gehinam.*[24] This experience is not nearly as difficult for the righteous, however, since they never consider their worldy body overly important.[25]

23:15 This is part of the judgment of the soul which occurs during the first year after death. Aside from this, the souls of the wicked are judged for 12 months after death, while others are judged for a lesser time.[26]

23:16 It is for this reason that the *Kaddish* prayer is said during the first year after the death of a parent.[27] Unless one knows his parent to be wicked, however, he only says the *Kaddish* for the first eleven months in order not to depict him as an evildoer.[28] For this same reason, when mentioning a parent's name during the first year after death, one should say, "May I be an atonement for his/her resting place" *(Hareni Kaparath Mishkavo/a).*[29]

23:17 The main judgment after death is in *Gehinam,* where the soul

---

22. *Emunoth VeDeyoth* 6:7; *Teshuvoth Rashba* 369; *Sefer Chasidim* 1163; *Tosefoth Yom Tov* on *Avoth* 2:7; *Teshuvoth Shevuth Yaakov* 2:97; Maharatz Chajas, *Shabbath* 13a. *Cf. Tanchuma, VaYikra* 8.

23. *Emunoth VeDeyoth ibid.; Nishmath Chaim* 2:24 (end); *Maavar Yavok* 2:7; *Taamey HaMinhagim* 424 (note), 437.

24. *Midrash Chibut HaKever* 3 in *Reshith Chokhmah, Shaar HaYirah* 12 (35a-b). This varies among individuals. The more one is obsessed with one's body and the material world in general during one's lifetime, the more one will be obsessed with it after death. For the person to whom the material was everything, this deterioration is most painful. On the other hand, the person who was immersed in the spiritual finds himself very much at home in the spiritual realm and might quickly forget about his body entirely; *On Immortality ad. loc.* (p. 182).

25. *Emunoth VeDeyoth ibid. Cf. Midrash Ne'elam, Zohar* 1:123a. Nevertheless, as long as the body is in the grave, the soul is judged. Even the righteous are judged until the flesh decomposes, after which they are allowed to enter the Garden of Eden; *cf. Zohar* 2:151, 3:169; *Sefer Chasidim* 1143; *Reshith Chokhmah loc. cit.* 35d.

26. *Eduyyoth* 2:10; *Zohar* 1:68b; *Tana DeBei Elihau Rabbah* 3 (28b).

27. *Yoreh Deah* 376:5 in *Hagah; Kitzur Shulchan Arukh* 26:1. *Cf. Moed Katan* 22b. Prayers, Torah learning and charity of children may help to ease the judgment for parents, even after the initial 12 months; *Sefer Chasidim* 170, 241, 365, 611, 705, 1171.

28. *Yoreh Deah ibid.; Kitzur Shulchan Arukh* 26:17. See *Turey Zahav, Yoreh Deah* 240:12; *Pith'chey Teshuvah* 376:9.

29. *Kiddushin* 31b; Rashi *ad. loc. s.v. Hereni; Yoreh Deah* 240:9.

is cleansed in a spiritual fire,[30] and purified so that it can receive its eternal reward.[31]

23:18 The souls of the righteous are able to progress higher and higher in the spiritual dimension. Regarding this, the prophet was told, "If you go in My ways... then I will give you a place to move among [the angels] standing here" (Zechariah 3:7). God was showing the prophet a vision of stationary angels, and telling him that he would be able to move among them. While angels are bound to their particular plane, man can move and progress from level to level.[32] This is also alluded to in the verse, "The dust returns to the dust as it was, but the spirit returns to God who gave it" (Ecclesiastes 12:7).[33]

23:19 Some authorities maintain that what the sages called *Olam HaBa* (the "Future World" or the "World to Come") refers to the spiritual dimension that the soul enters after leaving the body.[34] The majority, however, consider *Olam HaBa* as a completely new stage of earth life which will be ushered in only after the Messianic Age and the Resurrection of the Dead.[35] According to these authorities, all souls pass into an intermediate dimension called *Olam HaNeshamoth* ("World of Souls") after death. It is there that they are judged and then abide[36] until the resurrection and final judgment.

---

30. The fire of *Gehinam* is actually the burning shame and agony that the naked soul experiences because of its sins; Ramban, *Torath HaAdam, Shaar HaGamul* 77a; *Ikkarim* 4:33; *Nishmath Chaim* 1:13.
31. Ramban, *Torath HaAdam, Shaar HaGamul* 78a (quoted in *Perush* to *Yad, Teshuvah* 8:1), 80a. *Cf. Shabbath* 152b; *Midrash Ne'elam, Zohar* 1:98a.
32. *Nefesh HaChaim* 1:10; Rabbi Shneur Zalman of Liadi, *Likutey Torah, Shelach* (38d). *Cf. Yeffeh Sha'ah* on *Etz Chaim* 39:4. See also Radak *ad. loc.* and on Zechariah 3:4; *Chovoth HaLevavoth* 4:4:6 (143a, 145a).
33. Sforno *ad. loc.; Koheleth Rabbah* 12:7; *VaYikra Rabbah* 18:1.
34. *Yad, Teshuvah* 8:8; *Kuzari* 1:109. See *Tanchuma, VaYikra* 8.
35. *Tosafoth, Rosh HaShanah* 16b *s.v. LeYom Din; Emunoth VeDeyoth* 6:4 (end); Raavad, *Teshuvah* 8:8; *Kesef Mishneh, Teshuvah* 8:2; *Derekh HaShem* 1:3:11; *Derekh Mitzvotekha* 14b.
36. This does not rule out reincarnation; *Reshith Chokhmah, Shaar HaYirah* 13 (39d).

TWENTY FOUR

THE PRE-MESSIANIC ERA

24:1   The coming of the Messiah and the subsequent redemption of Israel is a basic belief of Judaism.[1]

24:2   God will bring the redemption in His own time. If all Israel were to return to God, the Messiah would appear and the final redemption would be ushered in immediately.[2] Otherwise, the redemption will not occur until the final time decreed by God. This is the meaning of the verse, "I, God, will accelerate it in its due time" (Isaiah 60:22). That is, if Israel is worthy, God will *hasten* the redemption; if they are not, it will come, but only *in its due time.*[3]

24:3   Thus, we find two contradictory concepts regarding the advent of the Messianic Era in the Bible. There are many passages which indicate that the Messianic Era will be ushered in with miracles, such as, "In visions of the night, I beheld the likes of a human being who came with the clouds of heaven... and he was given... an everlasting dominion which will never pass away" (Daniel 7:13-14).[4] On the other hand, numerous passages indicate that the Messiah will come in a more prosaic manner, such as, "Behold, your king comes to you... humble and riding upon a donkey" (Zechariah 9:9).[5] Here again, we are taught that there are two

1.   Thirteen Principles of Faith 12; *Ikkarim* 4:42.
2.   *Zohar* 2:189a; *Zohar Chadash* 74. Thus, if all Israel would observe two consecutive Sabbaths completely, the final redemption would come; *Shabbath* 118b; *Tosafoth, Niddah* 13b *s.v. Ad SheYikhlu.*
3.   Rabbi Yehoshua ben Levi, *Sanhedrin* 98a; *cf. Pesachim* 54b; *Emunoth VeDeyoth* 8:2.
4.   *Cf.* Rashi, Rav Saadiah Gaon, *ad. loc.*
5.   *Cf. Targum,* Rashi, Radak, *ad. loc.* Ibn Ezra cites an opinion that this verse refers to *Mashiach ben Yoseph;* see below, note 56.

basic ways in which the Messianic Era can commence. If Israel is worthy, it will indeed be accompanied by heavenly miracles. If not, the Messianic Era will arrive through an apparently natural unfolding of historical events.[6] In either case, God Himself will guide the forces of history to eventually bring about the Messianic Era.[7]

24:4 Many of our sages maintained that there would be very little difference between now and the onset of the Messianic Era except with respect to Israel's subjugation by other governments.[8] Similarly, we are taught that the redemption will not come all at once, but gradually, in a natural manner.[9]

24:5 Nevertheless, the Messiah can come at any time, totally without warning.[10] The reason for this is that many of the traditions regarding events which will precede the Messianic Era are contingent upon factors known only to God. Not all are necessary conditions for the redemption.[11] It is for this reason that one should not attempt to calculate the date of the coming of the

6. *Ibid.; Emunoth VeDeyoth* 8:2; *Or HaChaim* on Numbers 24:17.
7. *Pesachim* 54b; *Emunoth VeDeyoth ibid.* The difference is that in the former case this guidance will be revealed in history, whereas in the latter case it will be very hidden. Likewise, in the former case, the historical process that moves inevitably towards the End of History will be miraculously jumped ahead. In the latter case, the End will come, but slowly and painfully. The degree of suffering that Israel and the world will endure during this final period will depend on just how revealed or hidden God's guidance will be.
8. Sh'muel, *Sanhedrin* 91b, 99a; *Berakhoth* 34b; *Pesachim* 68a; *Shabbath* 63a, Maharsha, Rashash, *ad. loc.;* Rambam on *Sanhedrin* 10:1; *Yad, Teshuvah* 9:2, *Melakhim* 12:2. See *Kesef Mishneh, Lechem Mishneh, Teshuvah* 8:7. Also see Abarbanel, *Yeshuoth Meshicho* (Koenigsberg, 5621) 3:7 (56b); Maharal, *Netzach Yisrael* 50. See *Avodath HaKodesh* 2:38; *Sh'nei Luchoth HaB'rith, Beth David* 1:32a, that even according to Sh'muel miracles will become the rule during the Messianic Age.
9. *Yerushalmi, Berakhoth* 1:1; *Yerushalmi, Yoma* 3:2; *Shir HaShirim Rabbah* on Song of Songs 6:10; *Etz Yosef ad. loc.; Midrash Tehillim* 22; *Zohar* 1:170a *s.v. VaYomer.* See also *Sh'nei Luchoth HaB'rith, Beth David* 1:37b; Rabbi Tzvi Hirsch Kalisher, *Derishath Tzion* (Jerusalem, 5724) 1:1 (p. 88).
10. Rav Zera, *Sanhedrin* 97a; Rabbi Yehoshua ben Levi, *Sanhedrin* 98a; *Eruvin* 43a (end). *Cf. Tosafoth, Eruvin* 43b *s.v. VeAssur; Emunoth VeDeyoth* 8:6. For a possible resolution to these seemingly contradictory traditions, see below, note 56.
11. "Do not think that the Messiah will have to perform signs and miracles. He will not necessarily change the course of nature, bring the dead back to life, or anything else like that"; *Yad, Melakhim* 11:3. "In all cases, no man knows what will happen until the time comes. These things were left purposefully ambiguous by the prophets... It is for this reason that we find so many opinions regarding these matters"; *ibid.* 12:2. See Kaplan, *Maimonides' Principles,* pp. 77, 79.

Messiah. Our sages thus taught, "May the soul of those who calculate the end rot."[12]

24:6 Many of our traditions predict that there will be an extremely advanced technology in the Messianic Era. All disease will be eliminated, as the prophet foretold, "Then the eyes of the blind will be opened, and the ears of the deaf will be unstopped. Then the lame man will leap as a hart, and the tongue of the dumb will sing" (Isaiah 35:5-6).[13]

24:7 In order that man devote himself totally to achieving spiritual perfection, many forms of labor will become obsolete.[14] A number of miracles are predicted, such as grapes as large as hen's eggs and grains of wheat as big as a fist.[15] As we now know, all this can become possible with a technology not too far removed from that of today. Indeed, when Rabbi Gamliel spoke of these predicted miracles, he stated that they would not involve any change in the laws of nature, but are allusions to a highly advanced technology.

12. *Yad, Melakhim* 12:2 (end). The entire passage reads thus: Rabbi Nathan taught: This verse penetrates and descends to the depths [Rashi: it describes something which defies human understanding], "For there is still a vision for the appointed time. It speaks concerning the end, and does not lie. Though it tarry, wait for it, for it will surely come; it will not delay" (Habakkuk 2:3; Rashi *ad. loc.*).... What is "it speaks *(vayipach)* concerning the end, and does not lie"? Rabbi Sh'muel bar Nachmani said in the name of Rabbi Yonathan, "May the soul of those who calculate the end rot *(tipach),* for once the date they have set has come and gone, they [cause people to] declare that he [the Messiah] will no longer come. Rather, anticipate his coming daily, as it is written, 'though he tarry, wait for him'"; *Sanhedrin* 97b; Maharal, *Chidushey Aggadoth ad. loc.* (p. 211*f.*), *Netzach Yisrael* 31. *Cf. Kol HaTor* (in Kasher, *HaTekufah HaGedolah*) 4:3 (p. 521*f.*).

13. *Bereshith Rabbah* 95:1. The Midrash applies this verse to the resurrection of the dead and states that God will first bring the dead back to life with the particular ailments they suffered while alive, and only then heal them. This seems to indicate that these ailments will be eliminated in a miraculous manner as opposed to through any advanced medical techonology. See below, 24:7, however, regarding Rabbi Gamliel that the "miracles" of the Messianic Age will not necessarily involve any change in the laws of nature. In addition, Rambam states a principle that a miracle can never produce more than a temporary result. Since the majority of our sages maintain that the resurrected dead will live forever, we are forced to consider the possibility that the resurrection — and by extension the healing from all sickness which will follow it — will not involve the alteration of any of the laws of nature. Accordingly, the complete elimination of disease may involve some form of advanced human intervention; see *Iggereth Techiyath HaMethim,* p. 19; *Sichoth HaRan* 141; Kaplan, *On the Resurrection* (to be published), note 39.

14. *Sifri* (315) on Deuteronomy 32:12.

15. *Kethuvoth* 111b. In *Shabbath* 30b, Rabbi Gamliel maintains that women will be able to give birth every day. When challenged as to how such a thing could be possible, he

Thus, so little labor will be needed to process agricultural products that clothing and loaves of bread will seem to grow on trees. Similarly, as we learn the secrets of all life processes, it will become possible to make trees bear fruit continually.[16]

24:8 When we think of the miracles of the Messianic Age as being technological rather than manifest, then we have no trouble understanding traditions that predict such things as space flight[17] and interstellar colonization[18] in the Messianic Age, even according to those who believe that it will not be a time of manifest miracles.

24:9 All of this would be mere conjecture and even forced interpretation if it were not for the fact that our present technological revolution has also been predicted, with an approximate date as to its inception. Almost 2000 years ago, the Zohar[19] predicted, "In the 600th year of the 6th millennium, the gates of wisdom on high and the wellsprings of lower wisdom will be opened. This will prepare the world to enter the 7th millennium, just as a man prepares himself toward sunset on Friday for the Sabbath. It is the same here. And the mnemonic for this is (Genesis 7:11), 'In the 600th year... all the foundations of the great deep were split.'" Here we see a clear prediction that in the Jewish year 5600 (1840 c.e.), the wellsprings of lower wisdom would be opened and there would be a sudden expansion of secular knowledge. Although the year 1840 did not yield any major scientific breakthrough, the date corresponds with almost uncanny accuracy to the onset of the present scientific revolution.

24:10 The tradition may have even anticipated the tremendous destructive powers of our modern technology. Thus, we are taught

used the hen as an example. Just as the embryo of a chick develops in the egg outside of the hen's body, so will we be able to make a human embryo develop from a fertilized ovum outside of the mother's body, allowing her to give birth every day. This would also indicate the elimination of Eve's curse, "In pain you will give birth to children" (Genesis 3:16).

16. *Shabbath* 30b, according to the interpretation of Rambam on *Sanhedrin* 10:1. *Cf. Yerushalmi, Shekalim* 6:2.
17. *Zohar* 1:12b on Isaiah 40:31. *Cf. Sanhedrin* 92b.
18. *Ibid.; Tikuney Zohar* 14b, on Song of Songs 6:8. See Kaplan, *On Extraterrestrial Life* (in *The Aryeh Kaplan Reader*), p. 173.
19. *Zohar* 1:117a. See Kaplan, *The Real Messiah*, p. 67.

that the Messianic Era will begin in a generation with the power to destroy itself.[20]

24:11 The rapid changes on both a technological and sociological level will result in great social upheaval. The cataclysmic changes will result in considerable suffering, often referred to as the *Chevley Mashiach* or Birthpangs of the Messiah.[21] If the Messiah comes with miracles, these may be avoided, but the great changes involved in his coming in a natural manner may make these birthpangs inevitable.[22]

24:12 There is a tradition that the Jewish people will begin to despise the values of their religion in the generations preceding the coming of the Messiah. Since in a period of such accelerated change parents and children will grow up in literally different worlds, traditions handed down from father to son will be among the major casualties. Our sages thus teach us that neither parents nor the aged will be respected, the old will have to seek favors from the young, and a man's household will become his enemies. Insolence will increase, people will no longer have respect, and none will offer correction. Religious studies will be despised and used by nonbelievers to strengthen their own claims; the government will become godless, academies places of immorality, and the pious denigrated.[23]

24:13 Judaism will suffer greatly because of these upheavals. There is a tradition that the Jewish people will split up into various groups, each laying claim to the truth, making it almost impossible to discern true Judaism from the false. This is the meaning of the prophecy, "Truth will fail" (Isaiah 59:15).[24]

24:14 It has also been predicted that a great wave of atheism would sweep the world. As a result, many would leave the fold of Judaism completely. This is how our sages interpret the prophecy, "Many

20. "Rabbi Eleazar says: The King Messiah will come in a generation which is *Ra'uiy K'lia* ('worthy of' or 'capable of bringing about its own' total destruction)"; *Pesikta Rabathai* 1 (end) p. 4b; *Shir HaShirim Rabbah* on Song of Songs 2:13 (end).
21. Maharal, *Netzach Yisrael* 36. *Cf. Sanhedrin* 98b.
22. *Emunoth VeDeyoth* 8:6.
23. *Sotah* 49b; *Sanhedrin* 97a; *Derekh Eretz Zuta* 10; *Shir HaShirim Rabbah* on Song of Songs 2:13 (end); *Etz Yosef ad. loc.; Zohar* 3:67b; *Raya Mehemna, Zohar* 3:125b.
24. Or, "Truth will be divided into flocks"; *Sanhedrin* 97a.

will purify themselves... and be refined. But the wicked will do evil; not one of them will understand. Only the wise will understand" (Daniel 12:10).[25] That is, only the wise will understand that this is a test from heaven and that they must stand firm in their faith.[26]

24:15 Of course, there will be some Jews who remain loyal to their traditions. Still others will return to the true values of Judaism after having been estranged.[27] They will realize that they are witnessing the death throes of a degenerate old order and will not be drawn into it. But they will suffer all the more for this, and be dubbed fools for not conforming to the debased ways of the pre-Messianic period. This is the meaning of the prophecy, "He who departs from evil will be considered a fool" (Isaiah 59:15).[28]

24:16 There is an apparent tradition that there will be a population explosion prior to the coming of the Messiah.[29]

24:17 There is a tradition that if Israel does not repent, God will raise up a king like Haman who will want to annihilate the entire Jewish people.[30] This may be the reason for Hitler's almost incomprehensible career.[31]

24:18 One of the most important traditions regarding the Messianic Era concerns the ingathering of the diaspora and the resettlement of the Land of Israel. There are numerous traditions that the Jewish people will begin to return to the Land of Israel as a prelude to the Messiah.[32] The ingathering will begin with a measure of political independence,[33] and according to some, with the permission of the other nations.[34] As the holiest spot in the

25. Rambam, *Iggereth Teiman* (Jerusalem, 5721), p. 5.
26. *Sichoth HaRan* 35, 220. Cf. *Zohar* 3:124b, 3:153a.
27. Cf. Deuteronomy 4:29-30, 30:1-2; Amos 8:11-12; Hosea 3:4-5; Isaiah 59:20; *Yad, Teshuvah* 7:5.
28. *Sanhedrin* 97a; Rashi *ad. loc. s.v. Mishtollel Al HaBerioth.*
29. *Tosafoth, Niddah* 13b *s.v. Ad SheYikhlu.* But see *Tosafoth, Avodah Zarah* 5a *s.v. Ein,* that this must also apply to the Jewish people; cf. *VaYikra Rabbah* 15:1.
30. Rabbi Yehoshua, *Sanhedrin* 97b. Cf. *Pirkey Rabbi Eliezer* 43 (104a); *Radal ad. loc.* 43:84.
31. See *Emunoth VeDeyoth* 8:2.
32. See Midrash quoted in *Sheveiley Emunah* 10:1 (124a).
33. Rabbi Chama, *Sanhedrin* 98a; Maharsha *ad. loc. s.v. Ad SheYikhlu;* Rabbi Moshe Cordevero (Ramak) on *Zohar* 1:119a.
34. Ramban on Song of Songs 8:13; Radak on Psalms 146:3; Abarbanel on Psalms 147:2,

Land of Israel, Jerusalem is the most important city that must be rebuilt there.[35] There is a tradition that the ingathering of the exile and the rebuilding of Jerusalem will go hand in hand as the two most important preludes to the coming of the Messiah. According to this tradition, first a small percentage of the exile will return to the Holy Land, and then Jerusalem will come under Jewish control and be rebuilt. Only then will the majority of Jews in the world return to their homeland. It is thus written, "God is rebuilding Jerusalem; [then] He will gather the dispersed of Israel" (Psalms 147:2).[36]

24:19 There is a tradition that the Land of Israel will be cultivated at that time, after a long period of desolation.[37] This is based on the prophecy, "O mountains of Israel, let your branches sprout forth; yield your fruit to My people Israel, for they are at hand to come" (Ezekiel 36:8).[38]

24:20 There is another important reason why the ingathering of the exile must precede the coming of the Messiah. One of our traditions regarding the advent of the Messianic Era is that it will mark the return of prophecy among the Jewish people.[39] Furthermore, according to the final words ever spoken by a prophet, Elijah will return as a prophet and announce the coming of the Messiah, as it is written, "Behold I will send you Elijah the Prophet before the coming of the great and awesome day of God" (Malachi 3:23).[40] This is necessary because the Messiah will be a king,

and *Mashmiyah Yeshuah,* p. 25; Malbim on Micah 4:8; *Derishath Tzion* 1:2 (p. 90). See also *Yerushalmi, Maaser Sheni* 5:2 (21b); *Tosefoth Yom Tov, Maaser Sheni, s.v. U'Tenai;* Bachya on Leviticus 11:4-7; *Yerioth Shlomo* on *Siddur Beth Yaakov, s.v. Benei Bethkha,* p. 256b. For an alternate interpretation, see Rabbi Yoel Moshe Teitelbaum, *VaYoel Moshe* 1:68.

35. *Teshuvoth Chatham Sofer, Yoreh Deah* 234; *Petach HaDevir* 3:319d; *Din Emeth* (Responsa at end of volume) 2; *Matteh Aaron* 2:274c; *Pith'chey Teshuvah, Yoreh Deah* 251:4. Also see *Teshuvoth Chatam Sofer, Orach Chaim* 203.

36. *Berakhoth* 49a; Rashi *ad. loc. s.v. VeRav Nachman; Midrash Ne'elam, Zohar* 1:139a; *Tanchuma, Noah* 11; Midrash quoted in *Sheveiley Emunah* 10:1 (124a); Abarbanel on Psalms 147:2.

37. *Cf.* Isaiah 41:18-20, 49:18-22; Jeremiah 33:10- 11.

38. Rabbi Abba, *Sanhedrin* 98a; Rashi, Maharsha, *ad. loc.* See *VaYoel Moshe* 1:66 for another interpretation.

39. Rambam, *Iggereth Teiman,* p. 30. See Joel 3:1, 3:5.

40. Radak *ad. loc.; Eruvin* 43b; *Eduyyoth* 8:7; *Targum Yonathan* on Deuteronomy 30:4;

and a king can be anointed only by a prophet.[41] Besides this, the Messiah himself will be a prophet, the greatest of them all, second only to Moses.[42]

24:21 Thus, the restoration of prophecy is very important in the unfolding of the Messianic drama. This, however, requires a number of conditions. First of all, prophecy can usually take place only in the Land of Israel, and not in any other land.[43] The Land of Israel, however, is not conducive to prophecy at all times. Before prophecy can exist in the Land of Israel, it must be inhabited by the majority of Jews in the world.[44] Thus, unless we assume that this rule is to be broken, more than half of the Jewish people will have to live in the Land of Israel before the Messianic Era commences.

24:22 One of the most important events in the Messianic Era will be the rebuilding of the Holy Temple *(Beth HaMikdash)*. Indeed, according to Rambam (Maimonides), it is the act of building the Temple which will establish the identity of the Messiah beyond any shadow of a doubt.[45] There are, however, many things involving

Pirkey Rabbi Eliezer 43 (104a). See *Yad, Melakhim* 10:2; *Kereithi U'Pelethi, Beth HaSafek* (end); *VaYoel Moshe* 1:52.

41. *Tosefta, Sanhedrin* 3:2; *Sifri,* Ramban, on Deuteronomy 17:5; *Yad, Sanhedrin* 5:1, *Melakhim* 1:3.

42. *Yad, Teshuvah* 9:2. See *Targum,* Abarbanel, on Isaiah 11:2; *Mahari Kara, Kli Paz,* on Isaiah 52:13; *Tanchuma, Toldoth* 14; *Aggadath Bereshith* 45. The expression *Biyath HaMashiach,* "Coming of the Messiah," refers to the moment when the Messiah receives this spirit of prophecy and realizes his mission; *Arba Meoth Shekel Kesef* (Cracow, 5646), p. 68c.

43. *Mekhilta* on Exodus 12:1; *Tanchuma, Bo* 5; Rashi, Radak, on Jonah 1:3; *Zohar* 1:85a, 1:121a, 2:170b; *Emunoth VeDeyoth* 3:5 (end); *Kuzari* 2:14; Ibn Ezra on Joel 3:1; *Teshuvoth Radbaz* 2:842. See Volume 1, 6:44, note 130.

44. *Yoma* 9b; *Kuzari* 2:24 (40a); *Avodath HaKodesh* 4:25. See Volume 1, 6:44, on the verse, "God your Lord will raise up a prophet *in your midst*" (Deuteronomy 18:15), that the Land of Israel is only called "your midst" when it is populated by all, or at least the majority, of the Jewish people. It is through the concentrated spiritual energy of the entire Jewish people that prophecy exists, and such concentration is only effective in the Land of Israel. Thus, if the generation is not worthy of prophecy, it cannot exist, even though there might be worthy individuals. See *Sanhedrin* 11a; *Berakhoth* 57a; *Sukkah* 28a; *Bava Bathra* 134a; *Tosefta, Sotah* 13:4; *Pirkey Rabbi Eliezer* 8 (20b); *Avoth DeRabbi Nathan* 14:1. Also see *Taanith* 30b; *Bava Bathra* 121a (end); *Tosafoth ad. loc. s.v. Yom; Sifra* on Leviticus 1:1; *Yerushalmi, Taanith* 3:4 (15a); *Shir HaShirim Rabbah* 2:27; Rashi on Deuteronomy 2:16.

45. *Yad, Melakhim* 11:4. See below, Chapter 25, notes 18, 24. See also *Yerushalmi, Maaser Sheni* 5:2 (29b); *Tosefoth Yom Tov,* Rash, *Melekheth Shlomo, ad. loc.; Sh'nei Luchoth HaB'rith, Beth David* 1:37b; *Pethil Tekheleth* (in *Shlosheth Sifrey Tekheleth,* Jerusalem,

the Temple which can only be ascertained prophetically, such as, for example, the precise location of the Altar. When Ezra rebuilt the Temple after the Babylonian exile, the place of the Altar had to be revealed prophetically,[46] and the same will apparently be true when the Temple is rebuilt in the Messianic Age.

24:23   Regarding the conquest of the Land of Israel, the Torah states, "Clear out the land and live in it" (Numbers 33:53). Many authorities maintain that this commandment remains in full force today.[47]

24:24   There is a tradition that the Land of Israel will only be regained through great suffering.[48] This has been fulfilled to obtain that part of the Land which we possess today.

24:25   Although some measure of political independence has been obtained in Israel, the complete ingathering of the exile will only be accomplished by the Messiah.[49] Regarding this, the prophet foretold, "On that day, God will stretch forth His hand a *second time* to bring back the remnant of His people... He will hold up a banner for the nations, assemble the outcasts of Israel, and gather the dispersed of Judah from the four corners of the earth" (Isaiah 11:11-12).[50]

24:26   There is a tradition that there will be great suffering before the advent of the Messiah. We are thus taught, "One third of the world's woes will come in the generation preceding the Messiah."[51]

24:27   There are prophecies that there will be a "War of Gog and

5723) 8:2 (p. 160). *Cf. Megillah* 17b (end). In *Pesikta Rabathai* 36 (162a end), *Yalkut Shimoni* 2:499, we find that the Messiah will reveal himself on the Temple roof. See also *VaYoel Moshe* 55f.; Rabbi Yehudah Gershoni, *Mishpat HaMelukhah* 11:1.

46.   *Zevachim* 62a. See Kaplan, *Jerusalem — The Eye of the Universe* 7 (p. 68, note 52), 8 (p. 74).

47.   Ramban on Numbers 33:53, and on *Sefer HaMitzvoth,* Additional Positive Commandment 4. *Megillath Esther ad. loc.* disagrees, but see *Minchath Chinukh,* "Positive Commandments according to Ramban" 4, citing *Peyath HaShulchan, Hilkhoth Yeshivath Eretz Yisrael.* See Ramban on Leviticus 18:25; Maharatz Chajas, *Berakhoth* 24b.

48.   Rabbi Shimon bar Yochai, *Berakhoth* 5a (end).

49.   *Targum Yonathan* on Deuteronomy 30:4, Jeremiah 33:13.

50.   Because the "first" redemption from the Babylonion exile was not complete, the final and complete redemption from the present exile is called the "second time"; Rashi, Radak, Ibn Ezra, *ad. loc. Cf.* Ramban on Leviticus 26:16.

51.   *Midrash Tehillim* 22:9.

Magog"[52] around Jerusalem.[53] According to this tradition, when the nations hear of the successes of the Jewish people in rebuilding their Land, they will gather to do battle against them near Jerusalem, led by "Gog, the king of Magog." The battle will symbolize the final war between good and evil. In Jerusalem, all evil will ultimately be vanquished.[54]

24:28 The Messiah of whom we have been speaking will be a direct descendant of King David, from the tribe of Judah.[55] He is therefore known as *Mashiach ben David* or Messiah the son of David. There is also a tradition that there will be another Messiah, from the tribe of Ephraim, the son of Joseph, who will precede *Mashiach ben David.*[56] He is therefore known as *Mashiach ben Yoseph* or *Mashiach ben Ephraim.*[57]

24:29 There is a tradition that Israel's enemies will only succumb to a descendant of Joseph. Thus, *Mashiach ben Yoseph* will be the one who will lead Israel to victory in the war of Gog and Magog. This is the meaning of the verse, "The house of Jacob will be a fire,

52. Ezekiel 38, 39; *Sanhedrin* 17a; *Shabbath* 118a (end); *Midrash Tehillim* 10:12; Sh'muel, *Megillah* 11a, on Leviticus 26:44. See especially *Targum Yonathan, Targum Yerushalmi,* on Numbers 11:26; *Targum Yonathan* on Numbers 24:17, Exodus 40:10, Deuteronomy 32:39; *Eduyyoth* 2:10; Rabbi Yochanan, *Berakhoth* 7b, on Psalms 2; *Yad, Melakhim* 12:2; Radak on Zechariah 14:1; *Tana DeBei Eliahu Rabbah* 1 (8a).
53. *Zohar* 2:32a.
54. Zechariah 12:2, 14:2; Radak *ad. loc.; Yalkut Shimoni* 2:578.
55. See below, 25:3.
56. *Sukkah* 52b; *Emunoth VeDeyoth* 8:2; Ramban on Exodus 17:10, Song of Songs 8:12; Maharal, *Netzach Yisrael* 36; *Pri Etz Chaim, Shaar HaAmidah, Birkhath Tishkhon; Or HaChaim* on Numbers 24:17, Leviticus 14:9. *Cf. Tosafoth, Eruvin* 43b *s.v. VeAssur,* that *Mashiach ben Yoseph* must come before *Mashiach ben David.* Rashi *ad. loc.* disagrees. See Maharsha *loc. cit.* There is an opinion that the apparent contradiction brought out in *Sanhedrin* 97a (see above, 24:3) between a "gradual, natural" as opposed to an "accelerated, miraculous" advent of the Messianic Age, is resolved by the concept of the *Trein Meshichin* (Two Messiahs); *Sh'nei Luchoth HaB'rith, Beth David* 1:37a, citing the Ari. According to this distinction, the period of *Mashiach ben David* will be characterized by revealed miracles, as per the verse, "he came with the clouds of heaven," while the period of *Mashiach ben Yoseph* will be characterized by divine concealment, as per the verse, "humble and riding on a donkey." This also explains Sh'muel's statement in *Sanhedrin* 99a that "there is no difference between this world and the Messianic Age except with respect to our subjugation by other governments" (see above, note 8), which would refer specifically to the period of *Mashiach ben Yoseph.* Thus, besides the Two Messiahs being two great individuals, they are two periods, or more correctly, two aspects of one process.
57. *Sukkah* 52b; Rashi *ad. loc. s.v. VeSafda; Targum Yonathan* on Exodus 40:11, Song of Songs 7:4; *Zohar* 1:25a, 2:120b, 3:194b, 3:243b, 3:246b, 3:252b, 3:276b; *BaMidbar Rabbah* 14:2; *Yalkut Shimoni* 2:499 (p. 808); Radak on Zechariah 2:3.

and the house of Joseph a flame, and the house of Esau stubble. They will set them ablaze, and consume them; there will be no survivor of the house of Esau, for God has spoken" (Obadiah 1:18).[58]

24:30 Concerning the relationship between the two Messiahs — the initial Messiah, *Mashiach ben Yoseph,* and the final Messiah, *Mashiach ben David* — the prophet declared, "Ephraim's envy will depart and Judah's adversaries will be cut off. Ephraim will not envy Judah, and Judah will not harass Ephraim" (Isaiah 11:13). That is, each Messiah will perform his appointed task, without jealousy.[59] It is likewise written, "Son of man, take a stick, and write upon it, 'For Judah, and the children of Israel, his companions.' Then take another stick, and write upon it, 'For Joseph, the stick of Ephraim, and all the house of Israel, his companions.' Join them together into one stick, so that they are one in your hand" (Ezekiel 37:16-17).[60]

24:31 According to ancient tradition, the initial Messiah will fight and be killed in the war of Gog and Magog.[61] He will be mourned by all Israel,[62] as it is written, "They shall look to Me because they have thrust him through, and they shall mourn for him, as one mourns his first born son" (Zechariah 12:10).[63]

24:32 Before the appearance of the final Messiah, a prophet will arise to announce his coming and to draw the Jewish people back to God. This prophet is referred to as *Eliahu HaNavi* (Elijah the Prophet). It is thus written, "Behold, I will send you Elijah the

58. Rashi, Radak, Ibn Ezra, *ad. loc.; Bereshith Rabbah* 99:2 (end), 73:5, 75:6; *Pesikta Rabathai* 12; *Bava Bathra* 123b. *Cf. Zohar* 2:120a-b, 3:194b, 3:246b.
59. Rashi *ad. loc.* See Ramban on Exodus 17:9 (end).
60. Whether the Two Messiahs are great individuals or distinct periods or processes, or all the above, this verse teaches us that they are essentially two aspects of one all-encompassing unity. According to the Gaon of Vilna, one result of this unity is that the seemingly natural and gradual aspect of the *Mashiach ben Yoseph* period is accelerated as it approaches and overlaps with the miraculous aspect of the *Mashiach ben David* period; see *Kol HaTor* 4:3 (p. 521), 5:3 (pp. 526*f.*).
61. See sources cited in note 56. See also *Zohar* 3:153b, 3:203b, 3:279b; *Targum Yonathan* on Exodus 40:10; Ibn Ezra on Zechariah 12:10, 13:7. But see Ramchal, *Kinath HaShem Tzevoath* (Bnei Brak, 1980) pp. 104-105, based on *Zohar* 3:276b; *Kol HaTor* 1:6, 1:8, that the decree of *Mashiach ben Yoseph's* death has been nullified.
62. *Sukkah* 52b; *Maharsha ad. loc.; Emunoth VeDeyoth* 8:2.
63. Rashi, Radak, Ibn Ezra, *ad. loc.*

Prophet before the coming of the great and awesome day of God" (Malachi 3:23).[64] His primary task will be to bring peace to the world by leading all people back to God. The prophecy thus concludes, "He will turn the hearts of the fathers to their children, and the hearts of the children to their fathers, lest I [God] come and strike the world with destruction" (*ibid.* 3:24).[65]

24:33 There is a tradition that Elijah will reveal himself sometime after the war of Gog and Magog,[66] immediately before *Mashiach ben David* appears.[67]

24:34 Some maintain that Elijah is a *Cohen* (hereditary priest),[68] who will serve as the *Cohen Gadol* (High Priest) in the days of the Messiah, in the Third Temple.[69]

---

64. *Eruvin* 43b; *Eduyyoth* 8:7; *Pirkey Rabbi Eliezer* 43 (104a); Radal *ad. loc.* 43:85; *Targum Yonathan* on Deuteronomy 30:4; *Tana DeBei Eliahu Rabbah* 18 (86b); *Yeshuoth Yaakov ad. loc.* 51.
65. *Targum*, Rashi, Ibn Ezra, *Metzudoth David, ad. loc.; Eduyyoth* 8:7; *Yad, Melakhim* 12:2; *Pirkey Rabbi Eliezer* 43 (104a).
66. *Emunoth VeDeyoth* 8:2.
67. *Eruvin* 43b; *Tosafoth ad. loc. s.v. DeLo;* Rash on *Eduyyoth* 8:7; *Yad, Neziruth* 4:11. See also *Chokhmath Shlomo* on *Orach Chaim* 404:1. According to *Yalkut Shimoni* 2:475 (end), Elijah will appear three days before the Messiah. There is a tradition that Elijah will not reveal himself on the eve of a Sabbath or Festival; *Eruvin* 43b; *Pesachim* 13a, in order not to interfere with their preparation; Rashi, *Pesachim* 13a s.v. *Mipeney HaTorach; Tosafoth, Eruvin* 43b s.v. *Hai.*
68. *Pirkey Rabbi Eliezer* 47 (113a); *Targum Yonathan*, Sforno, on Numbers 25:12; *Bava Metzia* 114b (top); Rashi *ad. loc. s.v. Lav; Targum* on Numbers 25:12; Ralbag on Judges 6:21. For an alternate view, see *Bereshith Rabbah* 71:12; *Yalkut Shimoni* 2:208 on 1 Kings 17, 2:209 from *Pesikta Rabathai;* Radak on 1 Kings 17:1; Mahari Kara on 1 Samuel 2:30.
69. *Targum Yonathan* on Exodus 40:10; *Zohar* 3:27b (end).

TWENTY FIVE

THE MESSIANIC ERA

25:1   The final Messiah will be a normal human being, born of human parents.[1] It is thus possible that he is already born.[2]

25:2   Similarly, the Messiah will be mortal. He will eventually die and bequeath his kingdom to his son or his successor.[3]

25:3   Tradition states that he will be a direct descendant of King David, son of Jesse, as it is written, "A shoot will come forth from the stock of Jesse, and a branch will grow from his roots" (Isaiah 11:1).[4] Likewise, in our prayers, we ask, "May the shoot of David flourish,"[5] and "May the memory of *Mashiach ben David* rise up... before You."[6] There are numerous Jewish families today that can trace their ancestry directly back to King David.[7]

25:4   The final Messiah will be the greatest leader and political genius that the world has ever seen. He will likewise be the wisest man

1.   *Yad, Melakhim* 11:3; *Yeshuoth Meshicho* 3 (45*ff.*). Even if we interpret the passage, "Behold, a young woman *(Alma)* shall conceive and bear a son, and shall call his name Immanuel" (Isaiah 7:14) to refer to the Messiah, the correct translation of *Alma* is "young woman" and not "virgin"; see Radak, *Metzudoth David, ad. loc.* The proper Hebrew word for "virgin" is *Bethulah,* and *Alma* is never translated as "virgin." Thus, there is no Jewish tradition that the Messiah will be born of a virgin.

2.   See *Likutey Teshuvoth Chatham Sofer* 98 (p. 233), that, like Moses, he might not reveal himself until later in life; *cf.* Rashi, *Sanhedrin* 98b *s.v. Iy Min.*

3.   Rambam on *Sanhedrin* 10:1 (p. 124a). See Rabbenu Bachya on Genesis 11:11 that the Messiah will not die. However, even Rambam himself continues, "His kingdom will last for a very long time. This is because man's lifetime will be vastly extended... the Messiah's kingdom will last for thousands of years"; *cf. Sanhedrin* 99a.

4.   Ibn Ezra, Radak, *ad. loc.; Sanhedrin* 98b; *Eikhah Rabbah* 1:51.

5.   *Amidah* ("Standing Prayer"), 15th blessing.

6.   *Yaaleh VeYavo,* added to the *Amidah* and *Birkath HaMazon* ("Blessing after Meal") on Festivals and New Moons.

7.   Thus, for example, the Maharal of Prague (1512-1609) was able to trace his lineage to the Gaonic line of Rav Hai (939-1038) the son of Rav Sherira, who in turn traditionally were descendants of King David. There are numerous families that still trace their lineage to the Maharal.

ever to have lived. He will put these extraordinary talents to use to precipitate a worldwide revolution which will bring perfect social justice to humanity, and influence all men to serve God with a pure heart.[8]

25:5 The Messiah will also achieve prophecy and become the greatest prophet in history, second only to Moses.[9]

25:6 The prophet Isaiah described six qualities with which the Messiah will be blessed: "God's spirit will rest upon him, the spirit of wisdom (1) and understanding (2), the spirit of counsel (3) and might (4), the spirit of knowledge (5) and fear (6) of God" (Isaiah 11:2).[10] In all these qualities, the Messiah will excel all other human beings.[11]

25:7 The Messiah will see through the sham and hypocrisy of this world. He will have the power to sense a person's spirit, thereby knowing his entire spiritual record, and judging whether he is guilty or not. Regarding this power, it is further written, "He will be filled with the spirit of the fear of God; he will not judge by what his eyes see, or decide by what his ears hear" (*ibid.* 11:3).[12] This is one sign by which the Messiah will be recognized.[13] However, similar to the gift of prophecy, this power will only develop gradually.[14]

25:8 The Messiah will use this power to determine to which tribe every Jew belongs. He will then divide the Land of Israel into land inheritances with each tribe receiving its portion. He will begin with the tribe of Levi, determining the legitimacy of each Cohen and Levite. Regarding this the prophet said, "He will purify the

---

8. Rambam on *Sanhedrin* 10:1; *Yad, Teshuvah* 9:2.
9. *Ibid.* See 24:20, note 42.
10. Rashi *ad. loc., Sanhedrin* 93b, *s.v. VeNachah.* In the Book of Ruth it is written, "[Boaz] weighed six measures of barley and placed it on [Ruth's] scarf" (Ruth 3:15). The Talmud teaches us that Boaz gave Ruth "six barleycorns" to symbolize six of her descendants (David, Daniel, Chananiah, Mishael, Azariah, and *Mashiach ben David*), each of whom would be blessed with six gifts; *Sanhedrin* 93b.
11. See *Ruth Rabbah* 7:2; *BaMidbar Rabbah* 13:11.
12. Radak *ad. loc.;* Raba, *Sanhedrin* 93b; Maharsha *ad. loc.*
13. *Sanhedrin* 93b, from the test of Bar Koziba.
14. Since Rabbi Akiba did believe that Bar Koziba was the Messiah before this test. See *Yad, Melakhim* 11:3; Radbaz, *Kesef Mishneh, Lechem Mishneh, Migdal Oz, ad. loc.*

children of Levi, and refine them like gold and silver, to become bearers of an offering to God in righteousness" (Malachi 3:3).[15]

25:9   The mission of the Messiah is sixfold. His primary task is to cause all the world to return to God and His teachings.[16]

25:10   He will also restore the royal dynasty to the descendants of David.[17]

25:11   He will oversee the rebuilding of Jerusalem, including the Third Temple.[18]

25:12   He will gather the Jewish people to the Land of Israel.[19]

25:13   He will reestablish the Sanhedrin, the religious supreme court and legislature of the Jewish people.[20] This is a necessary condition for the rebuilding of the Third Temple, as it is written, "I will restore your judges as at first, and your counselors as in the beginning; afterward, you will be called the city of righteousness, the faithful city. Zion shall be redeemed with justice, and those who return to her, with righteousness" (Isaiah 1:26-27).[21] Such a Sanhedrin would also be able to formally recognize the Messiah as the king of Israel.[22]

25:14   He will restore the sacrificial system as well as the practices of the Sabbatical Year *(Shemittah)* and the Jubilee Year *(Yovel).*[23]

25:15   Therefore, as Rambam (Maimonides) states, "If there arises a ruler from the family of David, immersed in the Torah and its commandments like David his ancestor, following both the Written and Oral Torah, who leads Israel back to the Torah, strengthening the observance of its laws and fighting God's

---

15. *Yad, Melakhim* 12:3, from *Kiddushin* 71a; *cf. Evven HaEzer* 2:5 in *Hagah.*
16. *Yad, Teshuvah* 9:2, *Melakhim* 11:4.
17. *Yad, Melakhim* 11:1.
18. *Yad, Melakhim* 11:1, 11:4. See above, 24:22.
19. *Ibid. Cf. Tanchuma, Noah* 11 (end); *Berakhoth* 49a; *Midrash Ne'elam, Zohar* 1:139a.
20. *Sanhedrin* 4:4 (37a); *Yad, Melakhim* 11:1; Ramban on Deuteronomy 16:16; *Chinukh* 491. The chain of Mosaic ordination was broken in the year 358 c.e. when the Romans killed the last ordained judges; *Bereshith Rabbah* 31:12. The *Sanhedrin* cannot be established until this ordination is reinstituted; see Volume 1, 10:39. For a discussion whether the *Sanhedrin* must be reestablished before the coming of the Messiah or by the Messiah himself, see Kaplan, *Jerusalem — Eye of the Universe* 8 (p. 74, notes 16, 17).
21. Rambam on *Sanhedrin* 1:3. See Volume 1, 10:44.
22. See Volume 1, 8:54, 10:45.
23. *Yad, Melakhim* 11:1. See *Arakhin* 32b; *Yad, Shemittah VeYovel* 12:16. See below, 25:27.

battles, then we may assume that he is the Messiah. If he is further successful in rebuilding the Temple on its original site and gathering the dispersed of Israel, then his identity as Messiah is a certainty."[24]

25:16 As the Messiah's powers develop, so will his fame. The world will begin to recognize his profound wisdom and come to seek his advice. He will then teach all mankind to live in peace and follow God's teachings. The prophets thus foretold, "It shall come to pass in the end of days, that the mountain of God's house shall be set over all other mountains and lifted high above the hills; and all nations shall come streaming to it. Many people shall come and say, 'Come, let us go up to God's mountain, to the house of Israel's God. He (the Messiah)[25] will teach us His ways, and we will walk in His paths.' For Torah shall go forth out of Zion, and God's word from Jerusalem. And he (the Messiah) will judge between nations and decide between peoples. And they shall beat their swords into plowshares and their spears into pruning hooks. Nation shall not lift up sword against nation, neither will they practice war any more" (Isaiah 2:2-4, Micah 4:1-3).[26]

25:17 In the Messianic Era, many gentiles will feel compelled to convert to Judaism, as the prophet foretold, "I will then give all peoples a pure tongue, that they may call in the Name of God, and all serve Him in one manner" (Zephaniah 3:9).[27] Once the Messiah has revealed himself, however, proselytes will no longer be accepted.[28]

25:18 Still, Jerusalem will become the center of worship and instruction for all mankind. God thus told His prophet, "I will return to Zion,

24. *Yad, Melakhim* 11:4. It is important to note that these accomplishments are a minimum for our acceptance of an individual as the Messiah. There have been numerous people who have claimed to be the Messiah, but the fact that they did not achieve these minimal goals proved them to be false; *cf.* Rambam, *Iggereth Teiman; Sefer Chasidim* 206.

25. These verses refer either to the Messiah or to Israel. In either case, the enlightenment of all peoples will be through Israel.

26. See Rambam on *Sanhedrin* 10:1; *Yad, Teshuvah* 9:2.

27. Rabbi Eliezer, *Avodah Zarah* 24a; Rashi *ad. loc. s.v. Gerim Gerurim;* Rabbi Shimon ben Eliezer, *Berakhoth* 57b; *Kesef Mishneh, Berakhoth* 10:9; HaGra, *Orach Chaim* 224:2.

28. *Avodah Zarah* 3b; Maharal, *Chidushey Aggadoth ad. loc.;* Yevamoth 24b.

and I will dwell in the midst of Jerusalem, and Jerusalem will be called the City of Truth and the Mountain of the God of Hosts, the Holy Mountain" (Zechariah 8:3). This will begin the period when the teachings of God will be supreme over all mankind, as it is written, "For the Lord of Hosts will be King in Mount Zion and in Jerusalem. [He will reveal His] Glory in the presence of His wise elders" (Isaiah 24:23). All peoples will then come to Jerusalem to seek God. The prophet Zechariah describes this graphically when he says, "Many people and mighty nations will come and seek the God of Hosts in Jerusalem... In those days, ten men out of all the nations shall take hold of the corner of the garment of every Jew and say, 'We will go with you, for we have heard that God is with you'" (Zechariah 8:22-23). In Jerusalem, the Jewish people will thus be established as the spiritual and moral teachers of all mankind. At that time, Jerusalem will become the spiritual capital of the world.[29]

25:19   In the Messianic Era, all people will believe in God and proclaim His Unity. The prophet thus foretold, "God will be King over all the earth; on that day God will be One and His Name One" (Zechariah 14:9).[30]

25:20   In the Messianic Era, jealousy and competition will cease to exist, for all good things will be most plentiful and all sorts of delicacies will be as common as dust. Men will no longer wage or prepare for war, as the prophet foretold, "Nation shall not lift up sword against nation, neither will they practice war any more" (Isaiah 2:4).[31]

25:21   In the Messianic Era, all nations will live peacefully together. Similarly, people of all dispositions will live together in harmony. The prophet spoke of this allegorically when he said, "The wolf will dwell with the lamb; the leopard will lie down with the kid; the calf, the young lion, and the fatling together, will be led by a young child. The cow will graze with the bear; their

29.   Jeremiah 3:17; *Shemoth Rabbah* 23:11; *Avoth DeRabbi Nathan* 35:9; *Malbim on Isaiah* 24:23.
30.   See Radak on Zechariah 14:1 that this refers to the Messianic Era.
31.   Rambam on *Sanhedrin* 10:1; *Yad, Melakhim* 12:5; *Emunoth VeDeyoth* 8:3.

young will lie down together; the lion will eat straw like the ox" (Isaiah 11:6-7).[32]

25:22 Although the Messiah will influence and teach all mankind, his main mission will be to bring the Jewish people back to God. The prophet thus said, "For the children of Israel will remain for many days with no king and no prince... Afterward, the children of Israel will return and seek God their Lord and David their king; they will come in awe to God and His goodness, in the end of days" (Hosea 3:4-5). Similarly, "My servant David will be king over them; they will all have one shepherd; they will also follow My ordinances and observe My laws" (Ezekiel 37:24).[33]

25:23 As society reaches toward perfection and the world becomes increasingly Godly, humanity's main occupation will only be to know God. The truth will be revealed and the entire world will acknowledge that the Torah is God's true teaching. This is what the prophet meant when he foretold, "The earth will be full of the knowledge of God, as the waters cover the sea" (Isaiah 11:9).[34] Similarly, all mankind will attain the highest levels of Divine Inspiration without any difficulty whatsoever. God thus promised through His prophet, "It shall come to pass afterward that I will pour out My spirit upon all flesh, and your sons and your daughters shall prophesy" (Joel 3:1).[35]

25:24 Although man will still have free will in the Messianic Age, he will have every inducement to do good and follow God's teachings. It will be as if the power of evil were totally annihilated.[36] This is what the prophet predicted, "I will place My Torah inside of them, and inscribe it upon their hearts... A man will no longer teach his friend and his brother saying, 'Know God!' For all of them will know Me, great and small alike" (Jeremiah 31:32-33). The prophet likewise said in God's name, "I will remove the

---

32. Radak *ad. loc.* (second comment); *Yad, Melakhim* 12:1.
33: See *Metzudoth David ad. loc.,* Rashi on Ezekiel 34:24, that "David" refers to a king descended from King David.
34. *Yad, Melakhim* 12:5.
35. Radak, *Metzudoth David, ad. loc.; BaMidbar Rabbah* 15:19 (end); Ramchal, *Maamar HaIkkarim, BeGeulah,* in Kaplan, *The Way of God,* p. 394.
36. *Sukkah* 52a; *Zohar* 1:109a, 1:128b, 1:137a, 2:41a, 2:136a, 3:54a.

heart of stone from your flesh and give you a heart of flesh" (Ezekiel 36:26).[37] That is, the inclination toward good will be strengthened in man to such an extent that he will not be drawn after the physical at all. Rather, he will constantly strengthen himself spiritually and incline toward serving God and following His Torah.[38] This is the meaning of the Torah's promise that, "God will circumcise the foreskins of your hearts and the hearts of your descendants, so that you will love God your Lord with all your heart and soul" (Deuteronomy 30:6).[39]

25:25   The Messiah will not change our religion in any way. All the commandments will be binding in the Messianic Era. Nothing will be added to or subtracted from the Torah.[40]

25:26   There is an opinion that the only books of the Bible which will be regularly studied in the Messianic Era will be the Five Books of the Torah and the Scroll of Esther.[41] The reason for this is that all the other teachings of the prophets can be derived from the Torah,[42] and since the Messiah will reveal all the meanings of the

---

37. Rambam on *Sanhedrin* 10:1.
38. Ramchal, *Maamar HaIkkarim ibid.,* p. 393.
39. That is, "God will remove the barriers keeping you from the truth"; Ibn Ezra, Ramban, *ad. loc.* Or, "remove the evil urge"; *Sukkah* 52a. See Kaplan, *The Living Torah,* on Deuteronomy 10:16.
40. *Yerushalmi, Megillah* 1:5 (7a); Thirteen Principles of Faith 9; *Yad, Megillah* 2:18; *Melakhim* 11:3; *Teshuvoth Rashba* 1:93; *Teshuvoth Radbaz* 2:666, 2:828; Abarbanel, *Yeshuoth Meshicho* 4:1 (67b); *cf.* Volume 1, 5:20, 8:41. See Maharatz Chajas, *Shabbath* 116a, *Niddah* 61b; Rabbi Yaakov Emdin (Maharibatz) on *Rosh HaShanah* 30a; *Levush, Orach Chaim* 158:1; *Mishneh Berurah* 158:1. See also *Berakhoth* 12b; *Mekhilta, Bo* 16; *Tosefta, Berakhoth* 1:12-13; *Yerushalmi, Berakhoth* 1:6 (11b); *Yalkut Shimoni* 2:295; Rashi on Jeremiah 16:14; *Ikkarim* 3:19-20. However, since many unusual circumstances will arise in the Messianic Era, some laws may be temporarily suspended. Here, the Messiah will merely be using the prerogative of every other prophet to temporarily abrogate a law of the Torah by an expressed prophetic command from God; *cf.* Volume 1, 8:44-45. See also Rashba, *Kiddushin* 72b *s.v. Mamzerim; Anaf Yosef* on *VaYikra Rabbah* 13:3; *Yad, Maaseh HaKorbanoth* 2:15; Radak on Ezekiel 45:18.
41. *Yerushalmi, Megillah* 1:5 (7a); *Yad, Megillah* 2:18; *Lechem Mishneh ad. loc.* This is disputed by Raavad *loc. cit.* who maintains that the prophetic writings will never lose their instructive value. See *Sefer Chasidim* 369; *Pirkey Rabbi Eliezer* 46 (111a); Radal *ad. loc.* 46:48; Maharatz Chajas, *Megillah* 10b, concerning *Purim* and *Yom Kippur.*
42. *Shemoth Rabbah* 28:4, 42:7; Rabbi Yochanan, *Taanith* 9a.

Torah to perfection,[43] the prophetic writings will no longer be needed.[44]

25:27 The sacrificial system will be restored in the Messianic Era. However, the only private sacrifices which will be accepted will be the thanksgiving offering.[45] Since man's heart will have been circumcised, the desire to sin will no longer exist,[46] and the private sacrifices which are brought to atone for sins will no longer be needed.[47] Similarly, the only prayers which will be necessary will be prayers of thanksgiving.[48]

25:28 Our prophets and sages did not long for the Messianic Era in order that they might rule the world and dominate the gentiles. They did not desire that the nations should honor them, or that they should be able to eat, drink and be merry. They only wanted one thing, and that was to be free to involve themselves in the Torah and its wisdom. They wanted nothing to disturb or distract them, in order that they should be able to strive to become worthy of the life in the World to Come.[49]

43. See *Targum* on Isaiah 12:3; Rashi *ad. loc.; Koheleth Rabbah* 2:1. *Cf.* Rashi on Song of Songs 1:2 *s.v. Ki Tovim.*
44. Alshekh, quoted in *Marah Panim, Yerushalmi, Megillah* 1:5 (7a).
45. *VaYikra Rabbah* 9:7; *Etz Yosef ad. loc.; Pesikta* 9 (79a); *VaYikra Rabbah* 27:12; *Tanchuma, Emor* 14; *Midrash Tehillim* 56, 100; Ramban on Leviticus 23:17 (end); Radak on Jeremiah 33:11.
46. See above, note 39.
47. *Etz Yosef, VaYikra Rabbah* 9:17; Abarbanel, *Yeshuoth Meshicho* 4:1 (68b), quoted in note 98 to Pesikta 9 (79a); *Avodath HaKodesh* 2:43; *Sh'nei Luchoth HaB'rith, Beth David* 1:37a.
48. *Ibid.* See *Tolaath Yaakov, Sod Chag Shavuoth* (33a-b); *Sh'nei Luchoth HaB'rith, Beth David* 1:37a (top).
49. *Yad, Teshuvah* 9:2, *Melakhim* 12:4.

Index

A
Abimelekh 145
Abortion 31, 44
  see Feticide
Abraham 16, 123, 145, 244
  and king of Sodom 16
  and Lot 315, 326
  pleads for Sodom 315, 326
Acausality 286
Acceptance 195, 242
Accomplishment 194, 263, 276
  see Pleasure, Reward
Adam 289, 305, 310, 329, 335, 355
Adar 128, 339
Adultery 21, 188-190, 249, 307
Advice 227
  of physician 41
  of rabbi 226, 256
Altar 75, 368
Altruism 278
Amen 75, 130
Ancestry 284
  of Messiah 372
Angels 72, 326
  stationary 359
Anger 146, 217
  divine 248, 275, 280, 337, 340
  like idolatry 55
  provoking 139
Animal, sacrifice 168
  soul 354
Animals, clean and unclean 266, 288,
  289, 308, 354
Anointing oil 188
Apparent injustice 312, 318
Asa, king of Judah 38
Ashurith script 92
Assailant, informer 32-35
Astrology 9
  see *Mazal*
Atheism 8, 163, 268, 364
Atonement 166, 170, 171, 215, 241*ff.*
  for parents 358

  must fit sin 249-255, 321-322
  none after death 221, 240
  requires confession 234
  through sacrifices 170
  through suffering 177, 223,
    245-247, 321, 322, 327
  see *Yom Kippur*
Attribute of Mercy 278
Attributes, Thirteen 279, 280
Authority, moral 158, 204
  religious 24
  usurping God's 18
Av (month) 338, 339
Awe of God 61, 62

B
Babylonian Exile 72, 368
Bar Mitzvah 126-128
Barriers, between God and man 353
  to repentance 224, 330
Bastard 200, 223, 308
  see *Mamzer*
Bath Mitzvah 127
Belief in God 1, 5, 6, 163, 193, 233,
  312
Beth HaMikdash 367
  see Holy Temple
Bible (Five Books) 75, 91, 378
Blasphemy 74, 268
Bleeding, on Sabbath 42
Blemish, spiritual 166, 226
Blessing 55, 342
  priestly 69-70, 105, 112
  reciting 55, 68, 74, 136
  spiritual 10, 144, 299, 303, 311
  to sanctify God 25
  see *Birkath HaMazon*
Blessings, on commandments 96
  noun form 97, 116-121
  verbal form 97, 112-116
  voluntary 123
  see *Amen*

Biblical Quotations